CAREER PLANNING RESOURCES

CAREER PLANNING RESOURCES
A Comprehensive Guide

Editor
Stephen Touthang

GenNext Publication

ISBN : 978-93-8022-241-7

Price : ₹ 650

First Published, 2015

Published by

genNext Publication
23, Main Ansari Road, Darya Ganj
New Delhi-110002
Ph. : 23242060, 23261060
Fax : 011-23285914
E-mail: gennext@hotmail.com
Website : www.gyanbooks.com

Laser Typesetting: Quick Media, Delhi
Printed at: Isha Print.

Cataloging in Publication Data—DK

Courtesy: D.K. Agencies (P) Ltd. <docinfo@dkagencies.com>

Career planning resources : a comprehensive guide / editor, Stephen Touthang.

pages cm

Includes bibliographical references (pages).

ISBN 9789380222417

1. Vocational guidance. 2. Career development. I. Touthang, Stephen, editor.

DDC 331.702 23

Contents

GOVERNMENT OF MANIPUR

D. M. COLLEGE OF TEACHER EDUCATION: IMPHAL

(Recognized by NCTE)

IMPHAL – 795 001, MANIPUR, INDIA

Dr. H. Ibomcha Sharma, M.A.,B.Ed., Ph.D.
PRINCIPAL

20th Feb. 2014

Foreword

We live in an age of constant flux that is unparalleled in history. If one does not update just for a moment one becomes out-dated. This is true in the case of careers too. We see traditional occupations declining and professions once unheard of are constantly emerging. Today's young people are laced with a host of choices which sometimes puts them in a dilemma. Many, including well educated persons, often fail to choose suitable professions because they lack knowledge and insight into the career search process. It is not the most qualified person who gets the most suitable job or profession but the person who knows best how to get it. The goal of career planning is to provide young people with the essential career search techniques and knowledge which will give them a competitive edge in the search for a suitable careers. Career Planning Competencies are designed to alleviate the frustrations young people face while deciding on their careers.

This book "CAREER PLANNING RESOURCES" by Stephen Touthang is a timely and relevant response to many students who are at the crossroads of life. This book gives in a succinct manner the kernel of every career touching at the same time all the pertinent details. I appreciate Stephen Touthang for the painstaking labour he has put in to bring out this book. It is a well-researched work and it is a proof of his love and concern for the student community. This book will certainly be a pathfinder for every student peering through the murk of career confusion.

Choosing the right career is the most important choice for a student. It one chooses the right career that corresponds with one's interests and aptitudes, it will give one satisfaction, fulfillment and happiness. A wrong career choice will result in negativity, frustration and passivity. It is always best to choose a career which really attracts and motivates one. Some choose their careers according to the benefits and facilities that are on offer. Such a choice of career can never be self-fulfilling. The author of this book has laid out so well what one should do as one chooses a career.

Before you read about any particular career, be sure to read carefully the section "PRELIMINARIES TO CAREER CHOICE and FACTORS THAT NEED TO BE CONSIDERED BEFORE CHOOSINI G A CAREER". It will truly enlighten you and give you an insight into WHICH career you should choose and WHY you should choose that career.

I recommend this book to be read not only by the students but also by the parents, teachers, educators, career counselors and all who are concerned about the future of our young people.

(Dr. H. Ibomcha Sharma)
Principal,
D. M. College of Teacher Education,
Imphal

Principal,
D. M. College of Teacher Education
Imphal

Preface

This book on career planning gives you the much needed direction and makes it clear there where you see yourself in the future. It makes you aware of your strength and weakness and the skills and knowledge that are required to achieve your goals in the future. A large proportion of our life is spent in achieving our career goals, thus it is very important to make sure that right steps were taken and correct planning was done in the early years of one's life. There are very few lucky ones who are born with clear mind and who knows what they want to do and where they see themselves in life ahead. But majority of the people are not sure what they want from life and so it is very important to plan out things. This is career planning is what gives wide range and insight to your young mind ... purpose.

[illegible]

Preface

This book on career planning gives you the much needed direction and makes it clear there where you see yourself in the future. It makes you aware of your strength and weakness and the skills and knowledge that are required to achieve your goals in the future. A large proportion of our life is spent in achieving our career goals, thus it is very important to make sure that right steps were taken and correct planning was done in the early years of one's life. There are very few lucky ones who are born with clear mind and who knows what they want to do and where they see themselves in life ahead. But majority of the people are not sure what they want from life and so it is very important to plan out things. Thus, career planning is what gives your career and in some way your life, true meaning and purpose.

In my interaction with many young people, I have come to realize that the majority of them are not sure of what they want to become in life. In other words, they do not have 'career clarity'. This is the reason why I have written this book so that it helps them to see the various careers and choose them according to their interests and aptitudes. Before choosing a career one has to create a solid plan, then stick to that plan or adjust it as needed, making informed choices, taking advantage of available resources and adapting with changing circumstances in order to keep things moving. By taking on this responsibility for important career development, challenging situations become learning experiences and reaching objectives are moments for wholehearted rejoicing rather than putting an entire livelihood in the hands of someone who is probably less interested in one individual's overall success.

This book is therefore designed for students, parents and teachers who are looking for up-to-date career information. It is a compendium of traditional and non-traditional careers. There are so many books already available in the market on career. Moreover, with the advancement of Information Technology and Internet, most of the information are available at the click of a mouse. In such a circumstance, one can ask a question: Is there a need for another book on career? The answer is positive "yes" because most of the books on career available in the market are just giving only the barely necessary information and nothing more. The unique features that set this book apart from other career books are:

- It is logically and systematically presented.
- It is user-friendly.
- It is comprehensive - covering almost all the careers.
- It contains all the relevant information about every career.
- It gives the various colleges, institutes and universities which one can choose to study.
- It contains answers to the Frequently Asked Career Questions (FACQ).

This book is meant to alleviate and mitigate the stress that students encounter while choosing their future careers. This book also will be a valuable help for teachers and parents who are the proto-guides for students and children. I hope this book will prove a useful guide to students and help them in choosing their future programme of studies judiciously.

Stephen Touthang

Acknowledgements

My life is hallowed by a band of magnanimous hands that have braced me to complete this book. Without them, it would be impossible for me to transform my thoughts and ideas into a concrete form. I am profoundly grateful to Dr. H. Ibomcha Sharma, Principal, D.M, College of Teacher Education, Imphal, Manipur for having gone through my manuscript and writing the foreword. I would like to recognise the great sacrifice of those who proofread my manuscript. They include: Rev. Fr. Tony Pellissery SDB, Anthony Avince, Hijam Rajesh, Editor, The Sangai Express (Imphal), Satyajit Usham, Editor, **Hueiyen Lanpao** (Imphal), Shri Th. Chittaranjan Singh, IAS. I humbly acknowledge their valuable corrections and scholarly suggestions.

My deepest gratitude goes to Rev. Fr. Mark Mangkhanpao and Rev. Fr. Joy Kurian for their brotherly love, support and encouragement. I would like to express my sincere thanks to my parents, my brother and sister. My heartfelt gratitude goes to Mr. Joseph Khamba Khoibu and family, Rev. Fr. Jacob Pamei, Mr. John Guite, Kh- Sanjit Singh and Mr. Kothyeldawn Khaling. I am immensely grateful to the priests of the Archdiocese of Imphal (Manipur) for their fraternal support and encouragement. I would like to thank all the teachers of St. Joseph's High School, Sugnu and the Sisters of St. Alphonsa Convent, Sugnu (Manipur).

I am greatly indebted to the team of Gyan Publishing House for readily accepting my manuscript and publishing it. Last of all, I would like to acknowledge the various authors of many books, magazines and articles which are my primary: source of gleaning ideas and information for the birth of this book into a tangible and substantial form.

Stephen Touthang

Comments on the Book

"I am charmed by the enthusiasm of Stephen Touthang in putting such a great effort to come out with such a valuable book. It is indeed comprehensive as its canvas covers a wide spectrum of academic streams and associated career options. It is an undeniable fact that the students often find themselves at the crossroads as to the subjects to be opted in the college and the career opportunities ahead. Even the colleges and the institutions where the courses are on offer have been listed. These are areas where the students need guidance for taking up the right course, and career based on aptitude and interest. The students will surely find this book handy and useful, and may not require looking beyond this reference book as it is exhaustive and a treasure trove of information. I am hopeful that the author will come out with more of such books useful to the student community in times to come."

Th. Chittaranjan Singh, IAS
Deputy Commissioner

"As books on Career Planning go, this is it and something more the author in his unique and inimitable style is able to strike up some sort of a conversation with not only the students but parents and guardians. This is what sets this book apart from the rest. A Catholic priest with Master's degrees in English, Sociology and Education coupled with NET (UGC), Stephen Touthang has written this book not only as a mere writer but also as an educationist. It is certainly a voluminous work that covers the whole gamut of career choices ranging from the conventional ones such as engineering, medicine, civil services, architecture etc., to the newly-emerging careers such as Company Secretary, Floriculture, Foreign Language, Photonics, Ethical Hacking and the like. A special feature of this book on career guide is the inclusion of institutions in India offering the courses plus the perks and remunerations of the career one chooses to take up. The flow of language is smooth and is not littered with academic words or expressions which will go down well with the students and the parents as well. My appeal to all parents and students is that when this book hits the market, grab it and read it and keep it for good".

Hijam Rajesh
Editor, ***The Sangai Express*** (English edition)

"In a society where choice of career for students is normally dependent either on the wishes and unfulfilled dreams of their parents or the influences of their peers with least consideration about the important issues related to the interest, ability and aptitude of the students concerned, this book is going to be of immense help not only to the students in understanding what they want in life and how to achieve that goal through proper planning of their career but also to the parents in understanding what kind of support they need to give to their children in arriving at a right decision on choosing their career which they would never regret in life later on".

Satyajit Usham
Editor, ***Hueiyen Lanpao*** (English edition)

Introduction

Many students today, find themselves trapped in a quandary when it comes to choosing a right career after completing their 10, 10+2 and graduation. Many students do not know how to choose their career – Where to start? How to choose? How to succeed? Some feel that they are good in many fields, while some others feel that they have zero talent. Those who feel that they are multi-talented will find a problem of choice. And those who feel they have no aptitude for any particular field will agonise overwhich career path they should venture into. These are some of the queries that are gyrating in the minds of many students. Choosing a right career is one of the most fundamental options in a student's life. Today, it is very sad to see many people becoming victims of wrong career choices. Mere survival considerations often force many to take up professions for which they have absolutely no aptitude. Such choices may provide one sustenance, but not true happiness and fulfillment and create adverse repercussions on society. Abdul Kalam, the Missile man of India and former president says, *"If you salute your duty, you don't need to salute anybody. But if you pollute your duty, you have to salute everybody."*

A career is not merely a sustenance provider or a means for minting money. Many government offices are dysfunctional or semi-functional because wrong people are put there. Therefore, read carefully the sections PRELIMINARIES TO CAREER CHOICE and FACTORS THAT NEED TO BE CONSIDERED BEFORE CHOOSING A CAREER. These sections will enlighten you on which path you should tread in your life.

There are myriad career options available today - more than at any other time in history. There is a rich menu of choices before you. You have only to choose the field that corresponds to your interests and aptitudes. Apart from the top-paying and popular career options such as Medicine, Engineering, Management, Chartered Accountancy etc., numerous other options are available in the field of Health Care, Travel and Tourism, Media, Retail and so on. The choice you make of a career should hinge on the job prospects in that field or but more importantly on your interests and aptitudes.

I am laying down in a succinct manner, some information on diverse careers so that you can make an informed choice of a particular career field for yourself.

Preliminaries to Career Choice

What is Career?

Etymologically the term 'Career' comes from the French word *'carriere'* meaning *'road'* or *'race course'* which in turn is derived from the Latin word '(*via) cararia*' (track for wheeled vehicles) which originated from the Latin word '*carrus*' which means '*wagon*'. Career, therefore, refers to a defined path or course that an individual has chosen to tread all through his life or for a limited period of time. It can be a long-term as well as short-term undertaking. It is choosing a particular field of work or profession that one thinks one will enjoy doing and which ultimately gives one satisfaction and fulfillment in life.

The Notion of 'Career'

According to Oxford Advanced Learner's Dictionary 'career' means 'occupation' or 'profession' with opportunities for progress and promotion. While occupation means employment for earning a livelihood, profession means a paid occupation especially one that requires advanced education and training. A career, therefore, is not simply being employed to earn a livelihood. A job, profession, or employment can be called a career only when it has an element of opportunity for progress and advancement.

Career is Different from Acquiring a Degree

Many people think that acquiring a professional degree is all it takes to have a career. Acquiring a degree, in fact, is only a stepping stone, or the first step into the field of one's career. Obtaining a degree is not a career. Today, one can see hundreds of young people with many degrees gallivanting around without any job because they have earned a degree but not the skills that make them employable. To build a career, one must have an inclination towards that occupation/field, possess the aptitude for it, and acquire the necessary knowledge and the skills that the particular profession calls for.

Career as a Service Rendered to Society

Different careers are different ways of serving society. They are meant for the common good and progress of society. Society is the heart and the cradle of humanity. To be successful and fulfilled in a career, one has to be society-oriented; otherwise, one will end-up serving and feeding only oneself. Today, in our country, many have chosen their careers in order to serve and feed themselves. When the self takes precedence, the non-self (others or society) becomes a non-entity. This selfishness will metamorphose into corruption, bribery, and the like.

Career is not about Earning Money Alone

Some people equate a career with the money attached to that particular career. For them earning money for livelihood is a career. Money is important and essential for our legitimate and comfortable living but a career is not all about money. If money alone is what you look for in a career, then you may not find true peace and happiness. Ancient sages have always detached themselves from wealth and money as these are opposed to the inner search for happiness. Ultimately, what every human being looks for in life is happiness. Money is essential but it is not "the ultimate-everything".

Career as a Vocation and Mission

The term 'vocation' comes from the Latin word *'vocatio'* which means *'a call'* or *'a summon'*. This term originated from Biblical usage. In the Bible, whenever God wanted to do something for human beings He would 'CALL' some people like the 'patriarchs' or 'prophets' or 'messengers' to carry out His work. The called were chosen from among many. Abraham, Moses, Elijah, Isaiah, Jeremiah, Peter, James, John and many others were all called in this way. They were called for a particular or specific work. The works that they performed were God's work entrusted to them; and therefore, the work was 'holy' and had to be carried out with utmost responsibility.

Careers must be also seen from this angle. A career is a vocation (God's call) to do God's work in a particular field in particular time and place. Since it is God's work, it is to be done with great responsibility and sincerity. God's work is always people-oriented and different careers are intended for the good of the people.

The term *'mission'* is derived from the Latin word *"missio"* meaning *'act of sending'* from the verb form *'mittere'* meaning *'to send'*. The word was used in the light of its Biblical usage where Christ used the word when sending out the disciples to preach the good news, to heal and to help the sick and the downtrodden in his name. First, they are called (vocation) and then they are SENT (mission) to perform the work. In this mission of the disciples, there is an element of urgency and necessity because the need of the people was and is so great. Therefore, this work cannot be procrastinated. It has to be performed *hic et nunc* without any excuse. Here, one needs to be faithful and possess a strong sense of helping people. In like manner, a career should be considered as a mission to be fulfilled in the fullest manner and not half-heartedly. One must feel the necessity of occupying a particular career field that one's occupation of a particular career will lead to a positive change in society and positively affect people. Every day, one should feel responsible for one's work and perform it faithfully.

SOME FACTORS THAT NEED TO BE CONSIDERED BEFORE CHOOSING A CAREER

There are some factors that need to be taken into account before one chooses a career. They are :

Self Assessment : The first and foremost step in planning your career is to assess and know yourself. You must analyse your interests, abilities, aptitudes, personality traits, desired lifestyle and then study the relationships between these and the career opted for.

Know your Personality : There are many personality types according to different psychologists. But we can broadly divide them into types namely, Introvert and Extrovert. You may be either introvert (prefers doing things in isolation from others) or extrovert (prefers doing things in the company of others). If you are an introvert, you should not choose a career that needs people with extrovert nature. You may be too gregarious, or you prefer lonesomeness to do creative work.

Know your Interest : You must choose the career where your interest lies. There are some people who have interest in more than one field. Even in this situation, you can choose the field in which you feel that you can succeed or perform better. Some people do not know in which field their interest lies. This indicates that they have not tried out anything yet, or perhaps have not sufficient information. Such persons can check out fields where they notice little sparks of interest for unless one tries out something, one may never know one's interests.

Know your Abilities : Ability refers to the capacity to do something. It is an act of being able to perform certain tasks or acts. Any act that you can actually do means you have the ability to do the act. Abilities include physical, intellectual, social, emotional and even financial capacities that one already possesses. You need to identify and take stock of your abilities before you opt for a particular career.

Know your Aptitudes : An aptitude is a natural propensity to do certain kinds of activities and refers to a natural ability an individual possesses, or has acquired through life experiences. Aptitudes can also be considered 'talents'. Aptitudes may be physical or mental. How can Sachin Tendulkar take up a career as an engineer when his aptitudes clearly demonstrate his excellence in cricket? If he does it would be a wrong choice.

Identify your Desired Lifestyle : You must identify what kind of lifestyle you want to live. Choose a career that will give you a space to live your desired lifestyle. But one should not be a slave to that lifestyle.

Know your Intelligence : Intelligence includes your intelligence quotient, social intelligence and emotional intelligence. Total intelligence is more important in order to be successful in life than simply having a high intelligence quotient. There are many cases where an academically brilliant executive considered a genius in his field, had failed miserably in his career only because he did not have required social intelligence and emotional intelligence. Therefore, know your various intelligences and balance them accurately.

Know your Physical Health : All careers make varying degree of physical demands and the choice should be made after carefully considering all the relevant facts associated with it. Choose a career that will be within the capacity of your physical health. For example, a person with a heart problem should not take up a career in mountaineering.

Know when to make a Timely Entry : Some careers need early entry to be successful. Belated entry may lead to frustration due to thwarted ambition and the mental agony of working under people much younger in age.

Goal Setting : Set your goals according to your academic qualification, work experience, priorities and expectations in life. Once your goal is identified, then you determine the feasible ways and objectives how to realise it.

Academic/Career Options : Narrow down your general occupational direction to a particular one by an informed decision-making process. Analyse the career option by keeping in mind your present educational qualification and further academic degrees you need to acquire.

Plan of Action : Recognise those companies, industries and sectors which you want to get into. Make a detailed plan so that you can determine how many years you will work in a company in order to achieve maximum success and switch to another if required. Decide where you would like to see yourself within 10 years time and in which position.

Grab Opportunities : Opportunity comes but once. So, whenever you get any opportunity to prove yourself and get into your desired career, try to convert it in every way to suit your purpose. Remember, a successful professional is also quite opportunistic in his moves, examining every opening to turn it to his favour.

A Few Important Tips to Keep in Mind

- Don't wait too long to plan your career. Do not say, "I will decide which career to take up after my 10+2 or graduation". Do not delay. Decide early. Decide today; keep the flame of your desired career burning. This will give you a sense of direction and strong motivation to work harder and harder everyday. Know that each day you are moving a step closer to your goal.
- Don't judge and analyse yourself – your likes and dislikes, your abilities and strengths – based only on what people around you say. Hear what people say but don't be swayed by their mere opinions. You know best your strengths, abilities and aptitudes. But this does not mean you are your best judge on the matter. There are areas where you need to seek the help of experts. Career planning is a very important step that needs careful consideration. If need be, you should not be hesitant to take the help of professional guides to help you find the career that is best suited for you.
- Be open to constructive criticism.

1

ACCOUNTANCY/FINANCE/INSURANCE

1.1 Accountancy

What is Accountancy?

Accounting or Accountancy is one of the most important fields of finance and is considered as the pedestal of all other fields in the finance sector. It is a branch of commerce that deals with aspects such as summarising, reporting and analysing financial transactions to keep financial records. It is the study of how business track their income and assets over a period of time. Accountancy is related to dealing and maintaining records of all daily financial transactions happening in business to estimate the success or failure of a business.

Importance of Accounting

The growing economic and commercial activities have made accounting an integral part of our everyday life. Any business requires an accountant who would be responsible for maintaining books of accounts. Hence, career opportunities in accounting exist almost everywhere and accountants are in high demand whether it is a new business, big or small, home-based business, corporations and government organisations. The services of accountants are required by all organisations as they must maintain systematic records of all transactions for the purpose of planning activities, managing and furnishing tax returns. Without this department, recording financial transactions, proper maintenance of staff salary and books of account, balance sheets preparations, calculation of various taxes etc. are not possible in a firm. Most decisions related to present and future projects are based on the financial records of a concern. Accounting is an important field not only in business but also in everyday life of common man. People use accounting skills while making decisions related to finance and investment options.

The Role of Computer in Accounting

With IT boom, computer has occupied almost every field and in this scenario even accounting is not possible without computers. This has increased the importance of computerised accounting. Specially designed accounting software like *Tally* is used by firms to ensure speedy and accurate accounting.

The Role of Accountants

Accountants assess the present and future economic activities of individuals, business, non-profit organisations and governmental bodies. Accountants manage many tasks besides preparing financial statements and recording business transactions. Key areas of accountant's work are audit, budget analysis, taxation, management accounting, financial accounting etc. Auditing, an important feature of each and every business, involves checking of books of accounts. Budget analysis is developing and managing the financial plans of an organisation. Taxation involves preparing tax statements for particular individual as well as business concern. Management accounting involves preparing an analysis of the assets. Financial accounting means analysing and recording the transactions and financial statements.

Forensic Accounting

Within the field of accounting, there is another option called Forensic accounting. Forensic accounting is the practice of utilising accounting, auditing and investigative skills to assist in legal matters. Forensic accounting involves Investigative accounting, i.e., legal investigation and analysis of financial documents of any firm or client, who is involved in a legal dispute of a criminal nature such as insurance fraud, employee theft, etc., and litigation support which deals with the calculation of economic damages or loss resulting from a breach of contract.

Career Areas

Career areas are like Chartered Accountancy, Company Secretary, Banking Actuary, Cost and Works Accountants. They are related to accountancy. These are advanced fields in accounting which require specific qualifications. However, to enter a career in accountancy which is an important field of finance, the basic qualification needed is only bachelor's degree in commerce.

Eligibility

The basic educational qualification for pursuing a career in Accounting is taking 10+2 with Commerce as the main subject, followed by a bachelor degree in Commerce. For Post graduate courses such as M. Com., one needs to have B.Com. at graduate level. Along with subject specialisation computer literacy is also essential. One must take a course in computer accounting software such as Tally or some other related diplomas. One can further take up more advanced positions by doing ICWA, CA, Company Secretary-ship or an MBA in Finance. After bachelor's degree in accounting, one can also go for diploma or certificate course in Forensic accounting. Some institutes offer Forensic Accounting as part of the Law degree.

Personal Attributes

Accountants should have an aptitude for mathematics and be able to analyse, compare and interpret facts and figures quickly. They must be able to communicate well and have an eye for detail. Familiarity with computerised accounting is essential. They must be able to work as a team and must have high standards of integrity and accuracy as major decisions are made based on financial statements given by them.

Job Prospects

As the economy grows and the numbers of business increases, more accountants are required to set up account books, prepare tax returns and provide management advice regarding financial matters. Accountants are always on demand and a diverse range of exciting careers are available for accounting graduates to choose from. People can start their career as a junior accountant and can reach various top level positions such as senior accountant, Chief financial officer, Auditor, Budget analyst, Finance manager, Tax consultant etc. An accountant's work can range from auditing which is the formal analysis of an organisation's financial statements to the daily book keeping that ensures the accounts are maintained correctly. Places where they can find work include public accounting firm, government departments, non-profit organisations, private firms etc. They could also start their own accounting or auditing firm.

Areas of Accounting

There are four major fields of accounting. They are :

- **Public Accountants :** Public accountants work with different clients to assist their accounting needs. They provide accounting services to individuals, businesses and governments. As public accountants, they'll focus primarily on tax functions and auditing.They advice on the most effective use of financial resources.
- **Management Accountants :** Management accountants are also called industrial, corporate private accountants. Their main responsibilities involve cost management, budgeting, asset management and performance evaluation. Management

accountants analyse and interpret financial information and assist to make sound business decision.

- **Government Accountants :** Government accountants may work at the local/state level or the central level, administer and formulate budgets, track costs and analyse programmes. With this position, you will work in a variety of government departments such as the Internal Revenue Service, Department of Defense etc.
- **Internal Auditors :** They conduct audits to ensure compliance with accounting laws and working to make sure that accounting information system are up to the standard. They verify the accuracy of financial reports and guard against waste or fraud in company operations. Specifically, they examine and evaluate their firm's financial and information systems, management procedures and internal controls to ensure that records are accurate and controls are adequate to protect against fraud and waste.

Career Options available in this field

- **Auditors :** The job of the auditor is to ensure the credibility of the financial accounting data and financial statements in private sector companies as well as public sector companies. Work in audit involves checking accounting ledgers and financial statements.
- **Budget and Credit Analysts :** Budget analysts are responsible for developing and managing an organisation's financial plans. They forecast expenditure incurred, analyse records of present and past operations. There are many opportunities for a budget analyst accountant in private as well as government agencies.
- **Financial Accountants :** Financial accountants draw information from the general ledgers to prepare financial statements. The core function of a Financial Accountant involves analysing and recording business transactions, financial statements with information from the ledgers by preparing general ledger accounts, trial balances etc.
- **Tax Accountants :** They prepare corporate and personal income tax statements and formulate tax strategies. Based on their statement financial choices are made as how to best treat a merger or acquisition, deferral of taxes, when to expense items and the like. They clarify current tax laws to clients, advise on ways to

avoid tax by smart investments and assists business in calculating annual tax returns. They need to have a thorough understanding of economics and up-to-date information on the tax code and laws of the country.

- **Management Accountants :** Management accountants work in companies and contribute to decisions about capital budgeting and business analysis. Major functions include cost analysis, analysis of new contracts and participation in efforts to control expenses efficiently. They work along with marketing and financial managers to take business decisions.
- **Teachers/Lecturers :** Teaching is another noble profession. If you have a knack for teaching and the required qualification, you can work as professors or as researchers in universities or colleges. Pursuing B. Ed., M. Ed., M. Phil., or passing the NET Exam can give an edge for those interested in teaching.
- **Forensic Accountants :** Forensic accountants frequently work for public accounting firms, banks, the IRS (Indian Revenue Service), insurance companies and law firms.

Remuneration

At the entry level an Accountant's remuneration may start between ₹ 20,000 – 40,000 per month. One can command a higher salary as the experienced are being offered handsome salary packages.

Courses

- B. Com.
- B. Com. Taxation
- M. Com.
- M. Com. Cost Accounting
- M. Com. Computer Application
- M. Com. Taxation
- M. Phil. Commerce
- Ph. D. Commerce
- Certificate in Financial Accounting
- Certified Advance Business Accountant (CABA)
- Certified Public Accountant (CPA)
- Certified Management Accountant (CMA)
- Diploma in Financial Accounting

Institutes

- **D.P. Bhosale College, Satara, Maharashtra**
  Bachelor of Commerce (Accounting)
  Affiliated to Shivaji University
  Duration: 36 months
- **St. Claret College, Bangalore, Karnataka**
  Diploma in Business Accounting
  Affiliated to Bangalore University
  Duration: 12 months
- **St. Xavier's College, Kolkata, West Bengal**
  Bachelor of Commerce (Honors)
  Accounting and Finance
  Affiliated to University of Calcutta
  Duration: 36 months
- **Indian Institute of Business Management and Studies**
  BTM 1st Stage, Bangalore
  Chartered Certified Accountant (CCA)
  Two years, Correspondence, Certification.
- **NIIT Noida, Noida (UP)**
  Banking and Accounting
  Part Time, Diploma
- **Indraprastha Institute of Finance and Accounts (IIFA), Delhi**
  Certified Accounts and Taxation
  Assistant (CATA/Graduate)
  Nine months, Part Time, Certification

1.2 Actuarial Science

What is Actuarial Science about?

You must have seen, heard and read about companies which provide insurance cover to policy holders in case of any eventuality like accidents, hospitalisation, household hazards, thefts or death and still others who look after investment schemes, employee benefits, retirement benefits and pension schemes. The policy holders are required to pay a fixed amount as installments at regular intervals and they get this money back in the event of any untoward incident or upon the maturity of the policy. Have you ever wondered who decides as to what amount of money a policy holder should pay as premium or what sum should be given as pension amount or returns by the company. Well, this exactly is what an actuary does. He calculates insurance risks and premiums. Technically speaking, the job of an actuary is to assess the financial impact of an uncertain future event. Roughly speaking, they look at the financial aspect of disaster; sarcastically speaking, they are financial astrologers.

The Work of an Actuary

An actuary has to combine the skills of a statistician, economist and financier and employ techniques of probability, compound interest, law, marketing, management, etc., to predict the outcome of future contingencies and design solutions to lessen the financial severity of such events.

How to Become an Actuary

To become an actuary one must be a Fellow of a recognised professional examining body like the Actuarial Society of India (ASI), Mumbai or the Institute of Actuaries, London. The work of an actuary is quite tedious, nevertheless it offers rewards in terms of intellectual challenge, status, job satisfaction and earnings. As their judgement is the basis of decision making for many business activities, their career paths often lead to upper management and executive positions.

Eligibility

The Actuarial Society of India and Institute of Actuaries, UK are professional examining bodies which conduct certificate, associate-ship level and fellowship level examinations and on passing these examinations, candidates become eligible to be admitted as an Associate Member of the society and can use *ASI* against their name as a registered actuary. On passing all the subjects up to and including 400 series and upon satisfying the other criteria specified for the purpose, candidates become eligible to be admitted as fellow member of the Society and can use *FASI* against his/her name as a recognised fellow.

A number of universities are offering graduate and post-graduate courses in actuarial science. Mere completion of such courses does not make one eligible to practise as an actuary but such courses give students better conceptual clarity and training by experts in a classroom environment which makes them better equipped than if they directly write papers of ASI through self study. To qualify as an Actuary, a candidate has to pass all examinations in the prescribed subjects conducted by the professional examining body such as the Actuarial Society of India and the Institute of Actuaries, UK.

Any person with minimum 18 years of age and having a high degree of aptitude for Mathematics and Statistics can take up the course and become an Actuary. Courses available include Post-graduate diploma in Actuarial Science, M.Sc. in Actuarial Science etc. A person is eligible to be considered for admission as a student member if he/she satisfies one of the following criteria :

- Should have passed 10+2 or equivalent with at least 85 per cent in Mathematics/Statistics,
- Graduate or post graduate with not less than 55 per cent marks in mathematical subjects (i.e., Mathematics or any of its branches; Statistics or any of its sub, classifications such as Mathematical Statistics and Applied Statistics, Econometrics, Computer Sciences, any discipline of Engineering, subject in science such as Physics or its branches),
- Candidates with CA/CS/CWA/MBA (Finance)/PGDMBA,
- Fully qualified members of professional bodies such as the Institute of Chartered Accountants of India (ICAI), The Institute of Cost and Works Accountants of India (ICWAI) and Certified Institute of Financial Analysts of India (IFAI) and Fellow of Insurance Institute of India (III) – passing with the subjects of Mathematical Basis of Insurance and Statistics,
- A student member of actuarial bodies such as Institute of Actuaries, London; Faculty of Actuaries in Scotland and Institute of Actuaries, Australia,
- Students from Society of Actuaries, USA and Casualty Actuarial Society, USA provided that they must have passed at least one subject from these bodies.

Course Areas

Students must take 15 subjects (14+1 optional) in preparing for the actuarial examinations. These subjects are grouped into 100 Series (CT), 200 Series (CA), 300 Series (ST) and 400 Series (SA). The subjects in CT Series cover mathematical, statistical, economic and financial techniques which are applicable internationally. The CA series contains a question of general actuarial interest and aims to test communication skills of the students with regard to application of actuarial technique learnt in the CT Series subject. The ST Series cover investment, Life Insurance,

General Insurance and Pensions and other Employee benefits. The SA Series subjects focus on the practical application of the Principles covered in the corresponding ST Series subjects and earlier subjects.

There are nine subjects in CT Series, three subjects in CA Series, six subjects in ST Series out of which the student will choose two subjects and 6 subjects in SA series out of which the students will choose one subject.

CT Series (Core Technical Stage)

CT-1 – Financial Mathematics

CT-2 – Finance and Financial Reporting

CT-3 – Probability and Mathematical Statistics

CT-4 – Models

CT-5 – General Insurance, Life and Health Contingencies

CT-6 – Statistical Methods

CT-7 – Economics

CT-8 – Financial Economics

CT-9 – Business Awareness Module

CA Series (Core Applications Concepts)

CA-1 – Core Applications concepts consisting of assets and liabilities

CA-2 – Modelling

CA-3 – Communications

ST Series (Special Technical Stage)

ST-1 – Health and Care Insurance

ST-2 – Life Insurance

ST-3 – General Insurance

ST-4 – Pension and other employee benefit

ST-5 – Finance and Investment A

ST-6 – Finance and Investment B

SA Series (Specialist Application Stage)

SA-1 – Health and Care

SA-2 – Life Insurance

SA-3 – General Insurance

SA-4 – Pension and other employee benefit

SA-5 – Finance

SA-6 –Investment

Certificates in Actuarial Techniques

A student member becomes eligible to get the Certificate in Actuarial Techniques (CAT) on passing all the CT Series subjects.

- **Associate-ship :** A student on passing all the subjects up to and including ST Series become eligible to be admitted as an Associate Member of the society and can use AASI against his/her name as a registered actuary.
- **Fellowship :** A student on passing all the subjects up to and including SA Series and upon satisfying the other criteria specified for the purpose becomes eligible to be admitted as fellow member of the Society and can use FASI against his/her name as a recognised fellow.
- **Examination Centers :** The examinations are held every year in the month of May/June and October/November at the following centers: Mumbai, Kolkata, Delhi, Hyderabad, Kanpur, Chennai, Bhopal, Bangalore, Lucknow, Coimbatore and Cuttack. Examinations are held at centers outside India if there are candidates desiring to appear at such centers. Below mentioned centers are those where examinations have been conducted in recent past but they are not permanent centers. Candidates who wish to appear from overseas centers should make a formal request to IAI. Centers outside India are Dhaka (Bangladesh), Colombo (Sri Lanka) and Port Louis (Mauritius).

Duration

There is no fixed duration to complete the course. The aspirant has to clear the Entrance Examination and the 15 subjects prescribed. A student can attempt any number of subjects at a time and in any order. However, it is better option to take the subjects in the numerical sequence in which these are numbered and not more than two or three at a time.

Personal Skills

A person with a high degree of aptitude for Mathematics and Statistics can become an actuary. The other necessary skills include good communication skills, ability to use computers and related technology, business sense, a practical outlook, a curious bent of mind, the ability to work on one's own and also be a team player as the situation demands and to be self-motivated. However, an aspirant should have single-minded devotion, total dedication and a systematic approach towards problems in order to successfully complete the various stages of the course and be registered as a fellow.

Job Prospects and Career Options

Traditionally, actuaries have been associated with insurance sector but in the present scenario with the economy opening up, actuaries are needed in sectors like non-life insurance, employee benefits, health insurance, asset-management, re-insurance, insurance broker houses and consulting companies.

The job of an actuary involves formulating policies and calculating the premium to be charged. For this, they assemble and analyse data to estimate the probability of such eventualities as death, sickness, injury, disability and property loss and formulate a sum which is advantageous to the customer as well as the company. In areas where employee benefits and retirement/pension schemes are dealt, the actuaries have to calculate the amount of money to be paid as contribution to pension fund in order to generate a certain income level post-retirement. Actuaries in administrative positions have to explain technical matters to executives, government officials, shareholders, policy-holders. Actuaries working in tandem with government/government agencies are responsible for designing social security and medicare plans. Many of these professionals work as independent consultants providing actuarial advice to clients for a fee. Some also provide investment advice. Actuaries have scope for career growth not only in India but also in countries like USA, UK, Canada and Australia where they already have the necessary infrastructure and support system available.

Some of the potential employers are :

Life Insurance

- AMP Sanmar Life Insurance Co. Ltd.
- Allianz Bajaj Life Insurance Co. Ltd.
- Birla Sun Life (Distributor Co. Ltd.)
- Aviva Life Insurance Co. Ltd.
- HDFC Standard Life Insurance Co. Ltd.
- ICICI Prudential Life Insurance Co. Ltd.
- ING Vysya Life Insurance Co. Ltd.
- Om Kotak Mahindra Life Insurance Co. Ltd.
- Max New York Life Insurance Co. Ltd.
- Met Life Insurance Co. Ltd.
- SBI Life Insurance Co. Ltd.
- TATA-AIG Life Insurance Co. Ltd.
- Life Insurance Corporation of India

Non-Life Insurance

- Bajaj Allianz
- HDFC Chhub GIC Ltd.
- ICICI Lombard General Insurance Co. Ltd.
- IFFCO-TOKIO General Insurance Co. Ltd.
- Reliance GIF
- Royal Sundaram
- Cholamandalam GIC
- TATA AIG
- Oriental Insurance
- United India Insurance
- National Insurance Co.
- General Insurance Corporation
- New India Assurance Company

Actuarial Apprentices with LIC : The Life Insurance Corporation of India takes in candidates who are graduates/ postgraduates with Mathematics and Statistics as main subjects with 60 per cent or more marks in aggregate and coming in the age-group of 18-25 years. The selection is based on a written test conducted by LIC which consists of two papers. Paper-I includes Essay Writing (Hindi or English) and Paper-II comprising Mathematics or Statistics or Actuarial Science. Candidates who have passed one or more examination of the ASI or Institute of Actuaries (London) or those having PG Diploma in Actuarial Science with more than 50 per cent marks in aggregate are exempted from appearing for the exams.

Remuneration

If one survives the grilling tests, there is a great payoff – the *median* annual salary for an actuary is handsome. Actuaries are globally in demand and can command hefty pay packets, salaries and perks. No wonder then that this profession has been rated among the best jobs in the US. In India, the trend is slowly picking up. Stipend for an actuarial trainee per month in India is around ₹ 25,000 per month. Insurance companies and consulting firms give merit to experience and qualifications with salary packets ranging from eight lakh per annum for beginners to around 40 lakh per annum for those in senior positions. In UK, a qualified actuary can earn 20 lakh per annum.

Few Institutes

- **Actual Society of India,**

  9 Jeevan Udyog, 278

  Dr D.N. Road, Fort, Mumbai-400001

  Website: www.actuariesindia.org

- **Amity School of Insurance and Actuarial Science**

  Amity Campus, Sector 44, Noida-201303

  Phone: 0120-4392304

  Fax: 0120-2431856

  Website: www.amity.edu/asias/

- **Birla Institute of Management and Technology**

  Pushpa Vihar, Sector-IV, New Delhi-110017

  Website: www.bimtech.ac.in

- **Insurance Institute of India, Gresham Assurance House**

  IVth Floor, Sir P.M Road, Fort, Mumbai-400 001

  Website: www.insuranceinstituteofindia.com

- **International Institute for Insurance and Finance**

  Platinum Jubilee Building

  Osmania University Campus PGRRCDE,

  Hyderabad-500007

  Website: www.iiifindia.com

1.3 Auditing

What is an Auditing?

Auditing is a systematic process of objectively obtaining and evaluating the accounts or financial records of a government undertaking, department, private business, or other entity based on an established criteria. In other words, Auditing involves the review, analysis and evaluation of processes, products, services, systems, organisations and employees; it is a specialised form of accounting for an organisation's financial information, which includes systems, policies and records. While auditing focusses largely on financial information, the process also may involve examination of non-financial documents that reveal information about a business's conduct.

The Role of an Auditor

An Auditor is a person from the accounts department who is trained in auditing. The main job of an auditor is verification of a company's financial records. Auditor determines the efficiency, adequacy and effectiveness of the organisation. They also review the reliability and integrity of management and ensure compliance with policies, procedures and laws. They are primarily responsible for maintaining accurate records and helping organisations operate efficiently. In addition to monitoring companies' finances, they often make recommendations for greater compliance and better management policies. Auditors may have many different roles within organisations from tax law specialists to internal resources auditing professionals. Regardless of their respective areas, all auditors are vital to the financial health of organisations.

Major Types of Audits

The major types of audits conducted by auditors include financial audit, operational, or management audit and compliance audit. A financial statement audit or attest audit examines financial statements, records and related operations to ascertain adherence to generally accepted accounting principles. An operational audit examines an organisation's activities in order to assess performances and develop recommendations for improved use of business determination of whether an organisation is following established procedures or rules.

Eligibility

To become an auditor one must have at least a bachelor's degree in Accounting. Some employers may prefer those with Master's degree in Accounting. MBA with specialisation in Finance can also be a right subject choice. Courses in Economics, Business studies and Humanities are also helpful. Some universities conduct specialised courses in Auditing. Along with subject specialisation, computer literacy is also essential. One must take a course in Computer Accounting softwares such as Tally or some other related diplomas. One can further take up more advanced courses like ICWA, CA, Company Secretary-ship or CPA (Certified Public Accountant in the US) etc. There are certain auditor certifications provided by international audit associations such as Institute of Internal Auditors (IIA), Information Systems Audit and Control Association (ISACA), etc., which are globally accepted. The Institute of Internal Auditors gives Certified Internal Auditor (CIA). Designation and ISACA provides certified Information Systems Auditor (CISA) certification respectively. CISA qualified auditors have been recognised as qualified to conduct systems audit, Reserve Bank of India (RBI), Ministry of Information Technology (MIT), National Stock Exchange, Comptroller and Auditor General of India (C&AG).

Job Prospects and Career Options

In the beginning most of the auditors work under the supervision of an established auditor. After gaining experience they can work independently. A qualified auditor has the option of joining government service, public sector undertakings or taking up a lucrative assignment in the private sector. Some auditors work as teaching staff in colleges or universities. Auditing professionals are required in virtually every company, non-profit organisation and government agency. Those employed in large firms are in part responsible for an organisation's financial health. Non-profit organisations are also very much reliant on auditors for continued solvency.

Different Types of Auditors

- **Internal Auditors :** They are employed by individual corporations, government bodies or other entities. Internal auditors work for the organisation they audit. Their job is to make sure the organisation runs efficiently and effectively. They perform financial, internal control and compliance audits for the employer. Internal auditors verify the effectiveness of their organisations' internal controls and check for mismanagement, waste or fraud. Sometimes they also help the external auditors with the financial statement audit.
- **External Auditors :** They are also known as Independent Auditors or Professional Accountants in public practice. An External Auditor audits financial statements for companies and other organisations. They also give advice in preparing income tax returns and provide guidance in matters concerning compensation and health-care benefits for employees. They are usually self-employed.
- **Government Auditors :** They work in the public sector, and are employed by local and state governments. Government auditors maintain and examine the records of government agencies and audit private businesses and individuals whose activities are subject to government regulations or taxation. Government auditor's main task is to act as assurance on compliance audit and operational audit.
- **Forensic Auditors :** Auditors could specialise in Forensic Accounting. Forensic auditors often discover information that's used as litigation support. Forensic auditors, mission is to detect, investigate and detect fraud and white-collar crimes. Forensic auditors are often employees of corporations, audit firms, government agencies and investigative and consulting services firms.

Remuneration

An auditor earns an average salary ₹ 3,74,890 per annum. Once you are established in the field and gained good experience, salary may not be a constraint. External auditors can earn more compared to internal auditors as external auditors handle more than one organisation. In the case of internal and government auditors salary is fixed to certain extent.

Courses

- B. Com.
- B. Com. Taxation
- M. Com.
- M.Com. Cost Accounting
- M. Com. Computer Application
- M. Com. Taxation
- M. Phil. Commerce
- Ph.D. Commerce
- Certificate in Financial Accounting
- Certified Advance Business Accountant (C.A.B.A.)
- Certified Public Accountant (C.P.A.)
- Certified Management Accountant (C.M.A.)
- Diploma in Financial Accounting

Useful Contacts :

Institute of Internal Auditors (IIA) Chapters in India

Institute of Internal Auditors, India

Website: www.iiaindia.org/

Chapter details :

- **Institute of Internal Auditors, India**

  Bangalore Chapter

  Stock Exchange Towers

  #51, I St Cross, J.C. Road

  Bangalore-560 027

  Phone: +91-80-22214723

- **The Institute of Internal Auditors, India**
  Mumbai Chapter
  209, Sagar Avenue, 2nd Floor
  Above ICICI Bank Ltd.
  SV Road, Andheri (W)
  Mumbai-400 058
  Phone: +91-22-67103351
- **The Institute of Internal Auditors, India**
  Calcutta Chapter
  7B, Elgin Road (Ground Floor)
  Kolkata-700 020
  Phone: +91-33-22832459
- **The Institute of Internal Auditors, India**
  Delhi Chapter
  306, Mansarovar Building
  90 Nehru Place, New Delhi-110019
  Phone: 011-46538628
- **The Institute of Internal Auditors, India**
  Madras Chapter
  C/o Mountbatten and Co,
  Kailash Apartments, 3rd Floor
  Flat No: 7. No: 9, Tiruvengadam Street
  West Mambalam, Chennai-600 033
  Phone: +919840437699
- **Information Systems Audit and Control Association (ISACA)**
  Website: www.isaca.org/

1.4 Chartered Accountancy (CA)

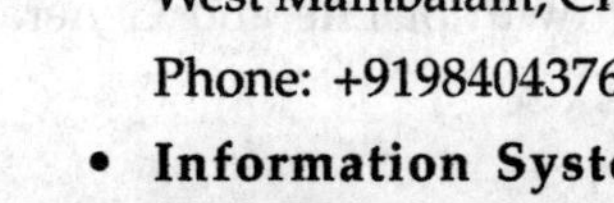

What is Chartered Accountancy?

Chartered Accountancy Course is a professional course in Accounting introduced in our country in 1949, with the enactment of the Chartered Accountants Act. The Institute of Chartered Accountants of India (ICAI) was formed the same year. This institute is both an examining and licensing body. It is the responsibility of the institute to conduct the Chartered Accountancy (CA) course. The course involves a blend of theoretical education and practical training which run concurrently for a period of three years and equips a student with knowledge, ability, skills and other qualities required of a professional accountant.

Who is a Chartered Accountant?

A Chartered Accountant(CA) is a certified number cruncher or a person who analyses numbers. He is one who is specialised in accounting, auditing and taxation. CA is employed by an organisation to audit the company's accounts as per regulations laid out by the Companies Act and the Income Tax Act. Only a person accepted as a member of the Institute of Chartered Accountants of India (ICAI) is considered a qualified chartered accountant and according to the Company's Act, only chartered accountants in professional practice are entitled to be appointed as auditors of companies in India.

Multinational Companies and Chartered Accountancy

Many multi-national companies have come forward in the Chartered Accountancy field. ICICI Prudential, Om Kotak Mahindra, Birla Sun-Life, Tata AIF Life, Reliance, HDFC Standard Life-Chartered Accountancy Co., Max New York Life, SBI Life Chartered Accountancy, ING Vysya Life etc., are the top companies in the private sector. In non-life Chartered Accountancy segment, major private players are ICICI Lombard, Royal Sundaram, Cholamandalam, IFFCO Tokyo, Tata AIG etc. All Chartered Accountancy companies come under the Chartered Accountancy Regulatory and Development Authority (IRDA) which is established to regulate, promote and ensure orderly growth of Life and General Chartered Accountancy industry in India.

Eligibility

The foundation course in chartered accountancy can be taken up along with graduation or post graduation. Commerce graduates with 50 per cent marks, non-commerce graduates with 55 per cent marks and non-commerce graduates without mathematics as a subject but with 60 per cent marks are exempted from the foundation exam and are permitted to register as articled clerks for practical training.

Job Prospects and Career Options

A qualified Chartered Accountant has the options of joining the government service, public sector undertakings or taking up a lucrative assignment in the private sector. The duty of the chartered accountant is to ensure that the financial transactions of an organisation are maintained according to the law. They keep track of the cost of management of the company and manage tax matters. Chartered Accountants work as Finance Managers, Finance Controllers, Financial Advisors or Directors (Finance) and watch over the finances in day to day management of companies. Their main areas of work include Accountancy, Auditing, Cost accountancy, Taxation, Investigation and Consultancy.

- **Accounting Department :** The accounting department prepares, analyses financial reports and documents of an organisation.
- **Auditing :** Auditing involves checking the accuracy of the financial statements, ensuring that the accounts presented are drawn up on correct accounting principles.
- **Cost Accountancy :** Cost Accountancy involves maintaining cost auditing records, compiling cost information, installing cost control and performing cost audits.
- **Taxation :** Taxation involves dealing with direct taxes like income tax and wealth tax, assessment of taxes, filing returns and providing advice on indirect taxes.
- **Investigation :** Investigation includes expert examination of specific aspects of businesses for the information of interested parties on new issues of share capital, the purchase, sale or financing or a business and for reconstruction.
- **Consultancy :** The various areas of consulting include management accounting and internal audit, corporate law advice, project planning and finance, business advice, system design and information consultancy.

Chartered accountants also act as directors, arbitrators for settling disputes, handling work related to insolvency, bankruptcy, etc., and also as executors under a will or trust in order to carry out the administration of an estate or settlements. They are also engaged in activities like market research, budget planning, working capital management, inventory control, policy planning, securities consultancy, registrar of issues of securities etc.

Some of the opportunities available for Chartered accountants are in capital markets, business houses and industry. They can also have their own consultancy or private practice which could be more lucrative and satisfying. They are also well-placed in government sector as director of finance, chief executive or the Head of the Department of the accounts, information technology etc. They help the government for proper implementation of accounting system.

Prospects Abroad

Institute of CA of India is well, recognised by Institute of England, Wales and Australia. The members of ICAI can practise, or they can go for employment in these countries. ICAI is not approved by several countries like United States of America. Since ICAI is a member of the International Federation of Accountants Committee and also International Federation of Accounting Standard board, one can do their services in these countries. But for practising, they should undergo a particular examination conducted by the respective countries. The examination conducted by the USA is called CPA (Certified Public Accountant) Examination.

How can one become a Chartered Accountant?

CA programme is of two years apart from the training period. It has three sections, Competency Professional Test (CPT) that was earlier known as Professional Education Exam PEE, Professional Competency Examination (PCE) and Final examination. The registration for CPT and PCE is open throughout the year. A student may register at any time during the year. However, as the examinations will be held twice a year in May and November, it is necessary that a student must register at least ten months before the examinations. After passing the Professional Competency Examination (PCE) candidates are eligible for registration as articled clerks/audit clerks for practical training. Computer Training Programme, i.e., 100 hours Information Technology is compulsory for the candidates who wish to register themselves as auditor clerk. Students can undergo this programme while pursuing CPT or PCE.

Articled clerk is a trainee attached to a practising accountant under a Deed of Articles for the duration of three years. During this period the articled clerk will also need to continue studies for the CA exams. An audit clerk is a person who has served as a salaried employee for a minimum period of one year under a practising chartered accountant. During the training period, candidates would be required to work in different areas learning the basics of auditing and taxation. This training enables them to learn the technical details of the job as well as to get an idea of the working environment of the profession.

Remuneration

Chartered Accountancy is a well-paid profession, be it in government sector or private firms or own consultancy. Most multi-national firms provide numerous perks besides the salary such as medical benefits, house allowance and so on. Some of the average monthly earnings range between Pre-qualification ₹ 5,000 – 10,000, Fresh CA's ₹ 20,000 – 30,000, Accounts Managers ₹ 50,000, Financial Controllers ₹ 75,000, Directors ₹ 1, 00,000 and an experienced CA may get monthly earnings more than ₹ 50,000 in India and according to the company they work for or depending upon the cities they are working in. This depends upon the involvement, commitment, hard work and dedication to the job.

Useful Contacts

- **Joint Director of Studies, The Institute of Chartered Accountants of India**

  Indraprastha Marg, New Delhi-110002
- **Joint Director of Studies, The Institute of Chartered Accountants of India**

  Anveshak-27, Cuffe Parade, Mumbai-400005
- **Joint Director of Studies, The Institute of Chartered Accountants of India**

  122, Utthamar Gandhi Salai, P.B. No. 3314, Nungambakkam, Chennai-600043
- **Joint Director of Studies, The Institute of Chartered Accountants of India**

  7, Russel Street, Kolkata-700071
- **Joint Director of Studies, The Institute of Chartered Accountants of India**

  66/77, Civil Lines, Kanpur-208001

1.5 Banking

The Important Role of Banks

Banks – 'the reservoir of wealth' play an important role in our day-to-day life as they are the organisations that take care of the money of individuals and corporate. These government authorised financial establishments are the best place to get the capital requirements or save money by different means like opening savings, current and fixed deposit accounts. Banks pay interest on the deposited money, provide loans to people for all their needs such as vehicle, home, business, education and offer services like foreign currency exchange, ATM etc.

The word bank was derived from the Italian word *'Banco'* which means *desk* or *bench* over which the transactions had happened in the earlier days.With the liberalisation of banking system, banking has become a wonderful profession that offers numerous career options. The responsibilities of the banking professions vary according to the position.

Progress in the field of Banking

With the boom in the IT field, a new dimension has been added to the face of banking. Earlier people have to wait for hours to make transactions like depositing, withdrawal, collection of drafts, etc. But now all the operations in the banks have been computerised to provide more efficient service to customers. Facilities and services like net banking, phone banking, credit cards, Automated Teller Machines (ATM) services, online information on the internet, home banking, etc., offer the customers to make their life easier and simpler. Emergence of these technologies and the entry of financial institutions into short-term lending business provide an ample scope in this field and have created the requirement of more professionals.

Eligibility

Banking is a profession not only meant for Commerce/Economics students but is open for all graduates with any academic background. Candidates after 10+2 of any stream can take up banking as their career, but graduates specialised in Commerce, Mathematics, or Economics; post-graduates like MBA holders, Chartered Accountants and Chartered Financial Analysts get more preference in the field. Many of the universities and B-schools like Indian Institute of Banking and Finance provide specialised courses in Banking and Finance and the eligibility criteria will vary depending on the courses. Diploma courses offer practical insights into the subjects of Banking and Finance and give candidates an exposure to the operational processes of the modern banking environment.

Job Prospects and Career Options

International trade and industrial liberalisation has brought a lot of changes in the banking sector and several branches of public sector banks as well as private and foreign banks are coming up at each and every corner of the country. All these factors have created an increase in job opportunities and the requirement for people with marketing and technological skills apart from financial background. The candidates can look for jobs in many establishments such as RBI, Regional reserve banks, the State Bank of India and its associate banks, nationalised banks and private banks.

MBAs and Chartered Accountants are directly recruited by private banks while nationalised banks recruit candidates through competitive examinations. Candidates with pleasing personality can find job as marketing executives, personal banking executives and home banking executives. Foreign banks usually go for experienced candidates for managerial posts. In nationalised banks, one can join as a clerk, grade. I officer, grade-II officer, or as a manager. Those joining in a clerical cadre can retire as a senior officer and those who join as probationary officer (grade I and II) can become General Manager and even Managing Director, or Chairman of the organisation. The bank manager should be aware of the marketing strategy; the area and customers of the bank; be supportive to his staff and make sure the best service is offered to his customers. The main tasks of the manager involves organising, controlling and supervising banking activities, or holding overall charge of one or more departments or branches. The clerical post has got the responsibility to keep the records of accounts, loans etc., and they also perform the services like payrolls and inventory accounting for the customers. Those who are appointed as probationary officers has to undergo a probation period of two years and during that time, services may be terminated at any time, if their work proves unsatisfactory. On completion of the probation period, the officers go through various grades like scale-I, scale-II to scale-VI, scale-VII and scale-IX.

Investment Banking, Corporate Finance Banking, Personal, Retail and Rural Banking, Treasury Management, etc., are some of the major banking activities. Let us see some of the career areas:

- **Investment Banking :** Investment Banking supports the corporate and government by raising money through issuing and selling securities in the capital market and also advise them on strategies and helps them in implementing their plans.
- **Corporate Finance Banking :** Corporate Finance Banking deals with the financial management of an organisation by raising the capital or fund for that organisation. It is through this corporate banking, the organisations are doing their transactions, deposits, fund transferring etc. It is a part of Investment Banking.
- **Personal, Retail and Rural Banking :** Individual customers belong to personal banking, and this sector provides a range of financial advice to the customers. Retail banking also deals with direct customers, their money transactions and transfers. The rural banking is for promoting loans to farmers for agriculture.

- **Treasury Management :** The sector deals with managing foreign currency and its collection. The treasury managers should be aware of the fluctuations of different currencies. They should manage the portfolio to avoid downgrading of the currency value.

Examination and Selection for Officers

Public sector banks recruit graduates at the entry level (as probationary officers) on the basis of an all India level examination. They also conduct an all India test for professionals (for senior post), who wish to enter the banking profession. Private sector/Foreign banks prefer graduates with MBA, Chartered Accountants etc., at junior positions and they are selected through campus recruitment and interviews. For the senior positions, they opt for experienced bankers.

- **The Reserve Bank of India :** The topmost financial institution in India conducts tests for three types of entry level positions i.e., for clerical grade; for Grade-I officers and for Grade-II officers. The entry point for clerical staff is in cash departments as examiners of coins and notes and they are promoted to the next grade when they successfully clear grading examinations after 5-10 years of service. RBI also conducts an All India Examination for graduates, post-graduates, professional graduates for the recruitment of Class-I officers. The maximum age limit for this examination is 26 years and the candidates are tested in logical reasoning, mental ability, numerical aptitude and general English. Selected candidates are shortlisted for an interview for the final selection.

  Selection of Probationary Officer : The selection of probationary officer in the public sector commercial banks is done by Banking Service Recruitment Board (BSRB) on the basis of a written test which consists of test of reasoning, quantitative aptitude, general awareness, English language and descriptive test. Each region has its own BSRB which carries out the recruitment. Graduates between the age group of 21-28 years are eligible for the test which is followed by an interview. Private banks recruit Officer Trainees from amongst first class graduates, Management Trainees from amongst MBAs and also recruit experienced personnel from the banking sector for middle and higher management positions. The advertisements for the recruitment in various banks appear in newspapers as well as in the Employment News from time to time, according to their vacancies.

All applicants are required to take the written test conducted by the respective Bank Recruitment Board. As the competition in the banking sector is very tough, only hard work, studies and practice can make one successful in the test. Number of books and magazines are available for the bank preparatory exam.

Bank Clerical Examination

These days, each individual bank invites, as per its requirement, the applications for the various posts in its nationwide/regional branches. The eligibility conditions and selection procedure in all cases are nearly the same. Following are the details about these exams :

Categories	*Other Posts Covered*
I. Clerk	Godownkeeper, Cashier, Clerk-cum-Godownkeeper, Clerk-cum-Cashier and other allied clerical posts.
II. Typist	Clerk-cum-typist and other clerical posts requiring typing skill in English or Hindi.
III. Steno	Stenographers, Steno-Typists (English-Hindi)
IV. Data Entry/Key Punch Operators	
V. Telephone Operators	
VI. Hindi Asstt./Translator	
VII. Telex Operator	
VIII. Agricultural Clerks	

Age Limit

Not below 18 years and not above 28 years on the date prescribed in the advertisement (upper age limits relaxable for SC/ST and other specified categories).

Eligibility:

For Clerks and Typists

Fifty per cent marks in Higher Secondary (10+2)/Intermediate/ Pre-University of a recognised University/Board or its equivalent, OR 50 per cent marks aggregate in Diploma in Banking recognised by Central/State government or U.T. administration, or 60 per cent marks in Matriculation/SSC/SSLC/10th of (10+2) of a recognised Board or Degree of recognised University in any discipline.

For Stenos, Data Entry/Key Punch Operators, Telephone Operators and Telex Operators

Matriculation/SSC/SSLC/10th of 10+2+3 pattern or equivalent.

For Hindi Translators

Minimum 50 per cent marks in the aggregate in higher secondary examination of 10+2+3 pattern/11th standard of 11+3 pattern/pre-degree or intermediate or any equivalent examination with Hindi and English as subjects. For all candidates except SC/ST candidates in whose case the eligibility is a mere pass in these examinations. OR Degree in any discipline with Hindi or English as main subjects and Hindi and English as subjects in higher secondary level.

For Agricultural Clerks

Twelfth standard of 10+2+3 pattern or Intermediate or higher secondary with agriculture as a optional subjects and 50 per cent marks, OR degree or diploma in agriculture (including Agricultural Engineering), OR matriculation/SSC (10th standard) certificate in case of village level worker with minimum of three years experience under a government.

Additional Qualification for certain posts

Typist : Speed in Typing: English 30 wpm, Hindi 25 wpm; **Stenographers :** Speed in Shorthand (besides typing speed as mentioned above) : English 80 wpm, Hindi 60 wpm; **Data Entry/Key Punch Operators :** Punching Speed 10,000 productive key depressions per hour; **Telephone Operators :** Proficiency in operation of PABX/PBX Board; **Telex Operators :** Proficiency in operation of Telex. Candidates applying for the above posts will be required to qualify in a proficiency test before the Interview if they qualify in the written examination.

Relaxation in Educational Qualifications

This is given for certain categories of students and is applicable as per prevailing rules.

Selection Procedure

All candidates who remit the requisite fee in the prescribed manner may be called for a written examination (objective as well as descriptive). The objective type test will comprise Test of reasoning, clerical aptitude, numerical ability and English language. The descriptive type test will comprise short essays or expositions on the given propositions, situations etc., in English/Hindi. The candidate has to pass in each of the objective tests and the descriptive test separately. For the post of Stenos, Typists, Data Entry Operators and Telephone Operators, candidates will be required to qualify in a proficiency test. Only the candidates who apply for the post of agricultural Clerks have to appear for objective type test in agricultural knowledge. For the post of Hindi Translator there will be a proficiency test at the time of written test.

Remuneration

Banking is a lucrative and satisfying career that offers good remuneration and benefits. The salary scale varies depending on the position. The initial salary scale for clerical grade post in the public sector banks may vary between ₹ 7,000 to ₹ 10,000 per month. The pay scale of probationary officers ranges between ₹ 14,500 to ₹ 27,078 per month. The salary package of the private banks and foreign banks are much higher when compared to the public sector and the officers can get around Rs. 3.5 lakh or more as annual income depending on their performance. The job security in these banks depend on various external factors like the economy of the parent country, performance of the bank worldwide, change in expatriate management etc.

Institutes

A few institutes offering Specialised Banking Courses for 10+2 pass facilitating easy entry into this field of employment are :

- **Bharathidasan University,**

  Palkalai Perum

  Tiruchirapalli-620024

  Tamil Nadu

  Course : BA (Bank Management)
- **Manipur University, Canchipur**

  Imphal-795003, Manipur

  Course : BA (Banking)
- **Marathwada University,**

  Aurangabad-431604

  Maharashtra

  Course : Certificate Course in Management of Bank Funds
- **Chennai University, Institute of Correspondence Education**

Chepauk, Chennai-5

Course : BBM (Bachelor of Bank Management)

1.6 Company Secretary (CS)

What is Company Secretary (CS)?

Company Secretary is a professional course administered by the Institute of Company Secretaries of India (ICSI) under the Company Secretary Act, 1980 to develop and regulate the profession of Company Secretaries in India. According to the Companies Act, companies with a paid up capital of ₹ 50 lakh are required to appoint a Company Secretary. A Company Secretary course gives knowledge and understanding of the modern practice in corporate financial and legal affair.

Who is a Company Secretary (CS)?

A company Secretary (CS) is :

- An in-house legal expert; a compliance officer of the Company;
- An expert in corporate laws, securities laws and capital market and corporate governance;
- Chief advisor to the board of directors and best practises in corporate governance;
- Responsible for all regulatory compliances of company corporate planner and strategic manager.

The Work of a Company Secretary

A Company Secretary's service is of enormous importance for a company's management. The work of a Company Secretary covers a wide variety of functions. He acts as a vital link between the company, the board of directors, shareholders, governmental and regulatory agencies. He is a compliance officer of the company as well as Corporate Planner and Strategic Manager. Apart from carrying out these functions he also looks after finance, accounts, legal, personnel and administrative functions. Company Secretary is required to handle matters related to central/state sales tax, excise laws, labour laws and corporate law.

How to become a Company Secretary?

The students who would like to join the Course of a Company Secretary after 10+2 have to undergo three stages to pursue the Company Secretaries' course. They are:

- Foundation Programme,
- Executive Programme, and
- Professional Programme.

In addition to this, the student has to undergo Practical Training for about 15 months which a student may opt after passing the Executive Programme. The student who would like to join the course after passing graduation has to undergo two stages of the Company Secretaryship i.e.,

- Executive Programme,
- Professional Programme.

Besides, the student has to undergo Practical Training for about 15 months. Foundation Programme which is of eight months duration can be pursued by 10+2 passed students of Arts, Science, or Commerce stream. Executive Programme can be pursued by a graduate of all streams except Fine Arts. Professional Programme can be pursued only after clearing the Executive Programme of CS course.

Training: A student has to undergo 15 months Management Training in companies sponsored by the institute after passing the Executive or Professional Programme, or under the guidance of a Company Secretary in Practice. After qualifying the professional examination and successful completion of training, a candidate is admitted as an Associate Member of the ICSI, and can use the letters ACS after his/her name *i.e.,* Associate Company Secretary.

Course on Company Secretaryship

Company Secretaryship course is divided into three stages – Foundation Programme, Executive Programme and Professional Programme. This course is a mixture of postal tuition, optional coaching classes and regular examinations at specified centers. Candidates who have passed senior secondary (10+2) can apply for the Foundation Programme. Graduates, post graduates (excluding Fine Arts), and those who have passed final examination of ICWAI or ICAI or of any other accountancy Institution in India or abroad recognised by the Council of the Institute can directly enroll to the Executive Programme without doing the Foundation course. Candidates who have passed the Executive Programme can apply for the final course. Registration for each examination should be done at least nine months before the month in which the examination is held. The examinations are usually held in June and December every year. Study material is provided to the students at the time of admission. In recent times, the rapid corporatisation has increased the demand for Company Secretaries in corporate functions.

Eligibility

The Company Secretary Course conducted by the Institute of Company Secretaries of India (ICSI) has three sections – Foundation, Executive and Professional. The minimum eligibility required for the Foundation course for Company Secretary is 10+2 or an equivalent examination. Candidates who have enrolled for the 10+2 examination can apply with the proof of passing the examination within six months. Candidates who have passed the Foundation Course and are not less than 17 years of age can apply for the Executive programme. Graduates, post-graduates (excluding Fine Arts) and those who have passed final examination of ICWAI or ICAI or of any other accountancy Institution of India or abroad recognised by the Council of the Institute can directly enroll to the executive programme without passing the Foundation Examination. A registered student is required to complete the Intermediate and the Final examination within the registered candidate can apply for the Professional Programme.

In essence, excellent command over English both written and oral is important for a Company Secretary. At the same time, ability to understand, analyse complex and technical issues and exercise accordingly with tact and intelligence and other essentials. It is the moral responsibility of the Company Secretary to be loyal to his organisation on knowing their top level plans and important secrets.

Job Prospects and Work Areas

Company Secretary has a great scope of employment in private companies, consulting firms, financial institutions, banks, department of company affairs and other regulatory bodies. A qualified company secretary is competent enough to take up wide range of responsibilities in legal, secretarial, finance, accounts, personnel and administrative departments of companies and is involved in major decisions, such as formulating long and short term corporate policies and programmes. Their other responsibilities include incorporation, managing public issues, act as internal legal advisor and representative, process inter-corporate loans and investments, maintain company's tax planning, tax management, tax returns, explore expansion opportunities, arrange collaborations, amalgamations, joint ventures within and outside India.

They are required to understand relevant aspects of law, update themselves with the changes to ensure proper compliance of legislations. The job also involves arranging company meetings, collecting and compiling information and recording the decisions. Nowadays, they are even foraying in capital markets and financial services industry. Their assistance in administration, management, planning and general running of the company makes them the company's chief administrator.

Remuneration

Company Secretaries command high salaries as compared to other managerial staff. The remuneration and conditions of service depend on the qualification and experience. A fresher could start with a salary of ₹ 20,000 to ₹ 30,000 per month. Salary packages, however, vary, depending on the individual's capabilities and the sector one is employed in.

Institutes

Head Office:

The Institute of Company Secretaries of India,
ICSI House, 22, Institutional Area,
Lodi Road, New Delhi 110003
Phone – (011) 51504444, 24617321-24, 24644431-32

The institute has four regional councils and several chapters under their jurisdiction.

Eastern Region

ICSI-EIRC House
3-A, Ahiripukur, Ist Lane,
Near Beck Nursing Home,
Kolkata – 700019
Phone: 033-22816541, 22816542, 22832973

Northern Region

ICSI-NIRC Building
Plot No. 4, Prasad Nagar Institutional Area Rajendra Palace,
New Delhi – 110005
Ph. 011-25763090, 25767190, 25816593

Southern Region

ICSI-SIRC House
Old No. 4, New No. 9,
Wheat Crofts Road, Nungambakkan,
Chennai - 600034
Ph. (044) -28279898, 28268685

Western Region

ICSI-WIRC House
13 Jolly Makers Chambers,
No. II (Ist Floor), Nariman Point,
Mumbai – 400021
Ph. 022-22021826, 22844073, 22047569, 22047580, 22047604

1.7 Forensic Accounting

What is Forensic Accounting?

Forensic accounting is the practice of utilising accounting, auditing and investigative skills to assist in legal matters. Forensic accounting involves legal investigation and analysis of financial documents of any firm or client, who is involved in a legal dispute. It encompasses three main areas :

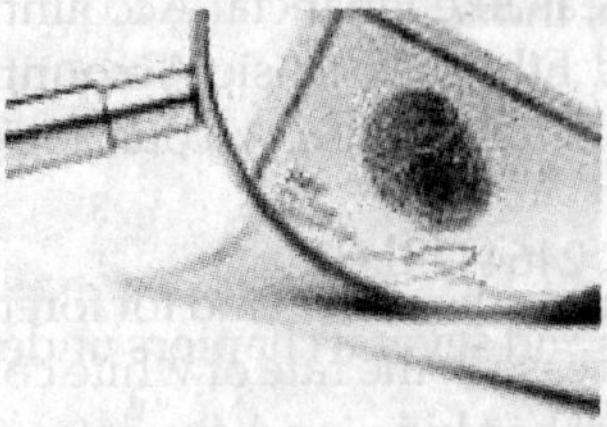

- Litigation (law suit) support,
- Investigation, and
- Dispute resolution

Litigation support represents the factual presentation of economic issues related to existing or pending litigation. In this capacity, the forensic accounting professional quantifies damages sustained by parties involved in legal disputes, and can assist in resolving disputes even before they reach the court room. If a dispute reaches the court room, the forensic accountant may testify as an expert witness. Investigation is the act of determining whether criminal matters, such as employee theft, securities fraud (including falsification of financial statements), identity theft and insurance fraud have occurred. Forensic accountant may recommend actions that can be taken to minimise future risk of loss.

Who is a Forensic Accountant?

A person who is professional in forensic accounting is known as 'forensic accountant', or 'investigative accountant'. Forensic accountant is a person who is a part accountant, a part detective and a part legal expert. He combines his knowledge of accounting and finance with law and investigative techniques to determine whether an activity is illegal. A forensic accountant is an experienced auditor, who acts as a watch-dog of accounts of a company, in order to keep a check on the frauds. These experts are responsible for using technology and implementing investigative techniques to disclose fraudulence and illegal practices in the fields of accounting, banking, financial laundering etc. They carry out elaborated audits, verify records, gather proof of finance malpractice and question people related to the misconduct.

Eligibility

Most forensic accountants have a bachelor's degree in accounting and many have additional academic preparation in fields like criminal justice or law enforcement. After bachelors degree in accounting one can go for diploma or certificate course in Forensic accounting. As part of Law, in some institutes forensic accounting is also taught as a separate paper. To work as a forensic accountant abroad, one needs a bachelor's degree in Forensic Accounting and CPA certification to begin a forensic accounting career. It is also advantageous to become a CFE (Certified Fraud Examiner), or a CFA (Certified Forensic Accountant).

Course Areas

Course in forensic accounting covers areas like Financial Accounting and Financial Frauds, Criminology and Ethics, Forensic Accounting and Fraud Investigation, Legal Framework for Forensic Accounting etc.

Job Prospects and Career Options

In India, in the wake of the Satyam scam and others, demand for forensic accountants has gone up. There is an increase in the rate of white collar crimes, such as securities fraud, and banking and investments embezzlement. As a result, the demand for professionals, who are experts in financial procedures and have strong analytical as well as investigative skills, is on the rise. Forensic accountants work in most major accounting firms and are needed for investigating mergers and acquisitions and in tax investigations, economic crime investigations, all kinds of civil litigation support, specialised audits and even in terrorist investigations. A majority of cases which these professionals deal in are divorce disputes, business carelessness investigation claims and personal injury claims.

In the World of Business

Forensic accountants work throughout the business world, ranging from private corporations or firms that help specific companies deal with suspected (or known) fraud and embezzlement to government organisations like police departments, the CBI (Central Bureau of Investigation), FBI or the CIA (Central Intelligence Agency), the Internal Revenue Service and the Bureau of Alcohol, Tobacco and Firearms. Forensic accountants also frequently work for public accounting firms, banks, the IRS (Indian Revenue Service), insurance companies and law firms.

In the Areas of Law Firms

In the areas of Law firms, forensic accountants help divorcees uncover their hidden assets. In public accounting firms forensic accountants investigate and interpret crimes, such as securities fraud and embezzlement, bankruptcies and contract disputes and other complex and possibly criminal financial transactions including money laundering by organised criminals. Corporations hire forensic accountants to investigate allegations of fraud on the part of their employees, suppliers, or customers.

In the Field of Criminal Investigation

In the field of criminal investigations, forensic accountants analyse complex financial transactions, such as those stock market manipulations and price fixing schemes. They also help government achieve compliance with various forms of regulation. The job of a forensic accountant demands reporting, where the accountability to the fraud is established and the report is considered as evidence in the court of law, or in the administrative proceeding. Forensic accountants help uncover those companies cooking the books to falsely inflate company profits, minimise losses, or divert large amounts of money to company leaders. They also provide litigation support to attorneys, and law enforcement agencies investigating financial wrongdoing.

Remuneration

Forensic accounting is one of the highly paid jobs in India. A beginner can earn a salary between ₹ 25,000 – 30,000 per month, while an experienced person can earn a lot more than that, probably in six figures. Most forensic accountants abroad begin their career-making between $30,000 and $ 60,000 and often work their way up to salaries often between $ 125,000 and $ 150,000, or more.

Courses

In the current scenario, career in forensic accounting has emerged as a lucrative option in India. Keeping in view of the increasing demand for forensic accountants, many institutes in India are offering courses to build a career in the same. The different courses available in this field are :

- Certificate Course in Forensic Accounting and Fraud Detection
- Post Graduate Diploma in Forensic Accounting

Institutes

- **The Institute of Chartered Accountants of India, New Delhi**

  ICAI Bhavan, Indraprastha Marg,

  Post Box No. 7100, New Delhi-110002

- **Institute of Chartered Financial Analysis of India University (ICFAI), Tripura**

  Kamalghat, Sadar, West Tripura Distt.-799210

1.8 ICWAI (ICAI)

What is ICWAI (ICAI)?

The Institute of Cost Accountants of India (ICAI), formerly known as Institute of Cost and Works Accountants of India (ICWAI), is the only professional body specialised in the field of Cost and Management Accountancy in India and aims at imparting coaching and training in the subject of Cost and Management Accountancy. It was established by an Act of Parliament in the year 1959, though the same was in existence as a company since 1944. The Institute has four Regional Councils in the metro cities.

Eligibility

Candidates with 10+2 qualification can join the Institute's Intermediate course after qualifying the Foundation Course examination of the Institute. Students awaiting result of 10+2 examination may be permitted to appear in the Foundation Course Examination. Similarly, students awaiting result of graduation examination may also avail the facility of provisional registration. Direct registration without appearing for the foundation course is open to graduates of any discipline. CMA certification of IMA in America and CIMA of UK is considered as a qualification which can be obtained by writing some of the papers of ICWAI (ICAI).

Job Prospects and Career Options

ICWAI (ICAI) passed candidates can hold top management position, viz., Managing Director, Finance Director, Financial Controller, Accountant, Cost Controller, Finance Manager, Chief Internal Auditor etc. in public and private sector organisations. Fellow members of the Institute would be treated at par with the persons holding Ph.D. degree as far as appointment in the posts of Professor, Associate Professor, Reader, Asstt. Professor and Lecturer in Professional/Management Institutes are concerned. They can also find self-employment in the following areas :

- Mandatory Cost Audit under Section 233 (B) of the Companies Act, 1956.
- Certification under Export and Import Policy.
- Excise Audit under Section 14-A of the Central Excise Act and Special Audit of Modvat Credit availed of under Section 14-AA of the Central Excise Act.

- Certification of manufacturing account as per Customs Act.
- Consultancy assignments.

Course Structure

In order to be a qualified Cost Accountant, a candidate has to take the examination conducted by the Institute of Cost and Works Accounts (ICWAI). The examination comprises three stages: preliminary, intermediate and final. To sit for the preliminary examination, an individual should have passed the 10+2 examination. Gazetted officers, post-graduates/engineers and other graduates with 50 per cent marks are eligible for direct registration. It is compulsory for registered students of ICWA to undergo either postal or oral tuition before appearing for the intermediate and final stages. There are four papers in the intermediate stage namely financial accounts, cost accounts, corporate laws, secretarial practice and direct taxation. In order to clear the final stage papers of cost and management accounts, the candidate has to clear auditing, indirect taxation and quantitative methods in the preliminary stage.

Foundation Course

Eligibility : One can become a student of Institute by passing foundation course examination, if he has completed seventeen years of age on the date of his application and has passed the senior secondary school examination under the 10+2 scheme of a recognised Board or an equivalent examination recognised by the central government thereto or has passed the National Diploma in Commerce Examination held by the All India Council of Technical Education or any State Board of Technical Education.

Syllabus : The subjects for Foundation Course Examination are :

- Business Fundamentals and Economics,
- Management and Organisation,
- Basic Mathematics and Statistics,
- Commercial Laws.

Qualifying Marks : A candidate shall be declared to have passed the foundation course examination if he obtains at one sitting a minimum of 40 per cent of the total marks in each paper or an aggregate of 50 per cent of the total marks of all papers in that examination. No certificate of pass except mark-sheet is issued to a candidate passing the foundation course examination.

Foundation Course Examination : It is held in the month of June and December every year.

Mode of Payment : Fee for the examination can be deposited in selected branches of State Bank of India by filling the special quadruplicate challan. The names of the branches are printed on the reverse of the challan.

Direct Registration : A person can become registered student directly without passing Foundation Course Examination if he has been confered a degree from any university or equivalent with a minimum of 50 per cent in aggregate.

Examination Papers

- Intermediate Examination – Stages : I and II

Stage-I : Paper-1 : Financial Accounting
Paper-2 : Cost Accounting
Paper-3 : Corporate Laws and Secretarial Practice
Paper-4 : Direct Taxation

Stage-II : Paper-5 : Cost and Management Accounting
Paper-6 : Auditing
Paper-7 : Indirect Taxation
Paper-8 : Quantitative Methods

- Final Examination Stages : III and IV

Stage-III : Paper-9 : Advanced Financial Accounting
Paper-10 : Information Technology and Computer Applications
Paper-11 : Operations Management and Control
Paper-12 : Project Management and Control

Stage-IV : Paper-13 : Advanced Management Accounting Techniques and Applications
Paper-14 : Advanced Financial Management
Paper-15 : Advanced Management Accounting Strategic Management
Paper-16 : Cost Audit

After passing the intermediate examination, the student is admitted to the final examination of the institute.

Examination Centres

Agartala, Ahmedabad, Allahabad, Asansol (Burnpur), Aurangabad, Bangalore, Baroda, Bhilai, Bakaro, Mumbai, Kolkata, Chandigarh,

Coimbatore, Cuttack, Chennai, Dehradun, Delhi, Dhanbad, Durgapur, Ernakulum, Guwahati, Howrah, Hyderabad, Indore, Jaipur, Jamshedpur, Jodhpur, Kanpur, Kota, Lucknow, Madurai, Mysore, Nagpur, Nasik, Netveli, Panaji, Patna, Pune, Ranchi, Rourkela, Salem, Srinagar, Tiruchirapalli, Trivandrum, Udaipur, Vijayawada and Waltair. There are some overseas centres also.

Coaching

The ICWA has made it obligatory for registered students to undergo and complete satisfactorily a course of tuition either postal or oral before they are permitted to appear at the intermediate or final exam. Postal tuition is conducted by the Coaching Directorate of the Institute through its Regional Council. Oral Tuition is imparted by the colleges, institutions and organisations recognised by the Director of Studies of the Institute for the purpose. Students are eligible to undergo coaching (Postal or Oral) for final examination. No provisional admission to coaching for final examination is allowed. The normal period for completion of total tuition for intermediate or final examination is 18 months. This period may be extended by three months for each group at the discretion of the Director of studies.

Remuneration

The initial minimum salary you can draw is around ₹ 20,000 per month. After 8–10 years of experience you can draw a salary of around ₹ 70,000 per month. It will depend on your academic records and work experience. Whilst pursuing this course it is important to gain relevant work experience.

Regional Centers of ICWA

- **Western India Regional Council of the ICWAI, Rohit Chambers,** 4th Floor, Janmabhoomi, Fort, Mumbai-400001

  (Comprising Gujarat, M.P., Maharashtra, Goa, Daman, Diu and Dadra and Nagar Haveli).
- **Southern India Regional Council of the ICWAI, ICWAI Bhawan** 65, Montieth Lane, Egmore, Chennai-600008

  (Comprising of AP, Karnataka, Kerala, T.N., Pondicherry and Lakshadweep).
- **Eastern India Regional Council of the ICWAI, ICWAI Bhawan**

  84, Harish Mukherjee Road, Kolkata-700025

(Comprising Assam, Bihar, Manipur, Meghalaya, Nagaland, Orissa, Tripura, West Bengal, Arunachal Pradesh, Mizoram, and the Andaman and Nicobar Islands).

- **Northern India Regional Council of the ICWAI, ICWAI Bhawan**

  3, Institutional Area, Lodhi Road, New Delhi-110003

  (Comprising Delhi, Haryana, H.P., J&K, Punjab, Rajasthan, U.P. and Chandigarh).

1.9 Indian Economic and Statistical Services

What is Indian Economic/Statistical Service?

The Indian Economic Service (IES) constituted in 1961 was the brainchild of Pandit Jawahar Lal Nehru for formulating and implementing economic policies and programmes of the country. The Indian Economic Service (IES) is an organised Group A central service.

Indian Economic/Statistical Service offers a very attractive opening to graduates in economic and statistics. ISS and IES are Central government services which are involved in economic planning and analysis through state boards, planning commission and other government owned bodies as its cadre posts are spread across different ministries/departments of the central government numbering around 55.

Selection

Selection to this service is through Indian Economic/Statistical Services Examination conducted by the Union Public Service Commission. Indian Economic/Statistical Service Examination is generally conducted in the month of November.

The Role of IES

The role of IES can be broadly categorised in terms of economic advice, economic administration and implementation of development programmes, besides dealing with other areas such as economic reforms, regulation, price fixation, monitoring and evaluation.

Eligibility

A candidate for Indian Economic Service must obtained a degree with economics or statistics as a subject and a candidate for the Indian Statistical Service must have a degree with statistics or mathematics or economics as a subject from any of the universities incorporated by an

Act of the central or state legislature in India or other educational institutions established by an Act of Parliament or declared to be deemed as universities under Section 3 of the Universities Grant Commission Act, 1956 or possess an equivalent qualification.

Age

A candidate should have attained the age of 21 years and must not have attained the age of 30 years on the 1st January of the year of examination. The upper age limit may be relaxed in respect of the scheduled caste, scheduled tribes, other backward classes and such other categories of persons as may from time to time be notified in this behalf by the Government of India to the extent and subject to the conditions notified in respect of each category.

Job Prospects and Career Options

The IES is the gateway to the central service as Group-A officers. Aspirants who successfully pass IES/ISS examination are placed in various cadre posts in the planning commission, planning board, ministry of economic affairs, national sample survey and other allied offices where specialists in economics and statistics are required.

The posts are primarily located in ministries/departments dealing with economic and social sectors. Besides cadre posts, IES officers go on deputation to serve in various domestic and international organisations such as UN bodies, foreign governments, state governments and regulatory bodies. Officers from the service are also appointed on deputation to posts in the central ministries/departments under the central staffing scheme.

The places of posting are usually in the State capitals or New Delhi. A candidate selected at a favourable age can expect to rise quite high in the career and touch the level of even Secretary to the Government of India in any Ministry concerned with economic affairs.

Hierarchy in Service

Grade/Designation	*Pay Structure*
Higher Administrative Grade +(HAG+)/Principal or Chief Economic Advisor	₹ 80,000 (fixed)
Higher Administrative Grade (HAG+)/ Senior Economic Advisor/Senior Advisor	₹ 67,000 (annual increment of three per cent) ₹ 79,000
Senior Administrative Grade (SAG)/	Pay Band-4: ₹ 37,400-67,000 plus

Economic Advisor / Advisor	Grade Pay: ₹ 7,600
{Including Non-functional Selection Grade (NFSG) / Director / Additional Economic Advisor}	{Pay Band-4: ₹ 37,400 . 67,000 plus Grade Pay: ₹ 6,600
Senior Time Scale (STS) / Deputy Director / Assistant Economic Advisor / Senior Research Officer	Pay Band-3: ₹ 15,600-39,100 plus Grade Pay: ₹ 6,600
Junior Time Scale (JTS) / Assistant Director / Research Officer	Pay Band-3: ₹ 15,600-39,100 plus Grade Pay: ₹ 5,400

Examination

The examination consists of :

- Written Examination
- *Viva-Voce* test of such candidates as may be called by the commission carrying a maximum of 200 marks.

Written Examination : The subjects of written examination for Indian Economic Service (IES) consists of general english, general studies, general economics-I, general economics-II, general economics-III and Indian economics.

While for Indian Statistical Service (ISS) the subjects consists of general english, general studies, statistics-I, statistics -II, statistics -III and statistics-IV.

Each paper is of three hours duration.

Standard of Papers

The standard of papers in general english and general studies will be that of a graduate of an Indian university. The standard of papers of other subjects will be that of the masters degree examination.

Application Procedure

Admission notification is published by UPSC in leading newspapers and *Employment News* generally in the month of June. One can apply online through www.upsconline.nic.in. Last date for submission of applications is generally in the month of July.

Candidates are required to apply online only by using the website www.upsconline.nic.in. Detailed instructions for filling up online applications are available on the above-mentioned website. However, candidates residing in certain remote areas specified may also apply through offline mode by using the New Common Application Form (Form-E) being used for examinations conducted by the Commission.

This form can be purchased from the designated head post offices/post offices (specified in Appendix-III of the Notice) throughout the country against cash payment of ₹ 30 (Rupees Thirty only). Each such Form can be used only once and only for one examination. In case of any difficulty in obtaining application forms from the designated HPOs/Pos, the candidates should immediately contact the concerned post master or UPSC's Forms Supply Monitoring Cell over Telephone No. 011-23389366/Fax No. 011-23387310. It may be noted that all offline applications, if any, received from candidates residing in normal areas/ abroad, shall be summarily rejected by the Commission. The option of offline application is available only to candidates residing in specified remote areas. Candidates are advised to read carefully the instructions for filling up the online application form given in Appendix-II (A) and instruction for offline applications given in Appendix-II (B) of the Notice.

Useful Contacts

- **Deputy Director**

  Room No. 251, IES Division

  Department of Economic Affairs

  Ministry of Finance

  New Delhi

  Phone: 23092491/23093570

  Fax: 23093570

  Website: www.ies.gov.in/

- **Controller of Examinations**

  Union Public Service Commission

  Dholpur House, Shahjahan Road

  New Delhi-110069

  Website: http:/upsc.gov.in/

1.10 Insurance

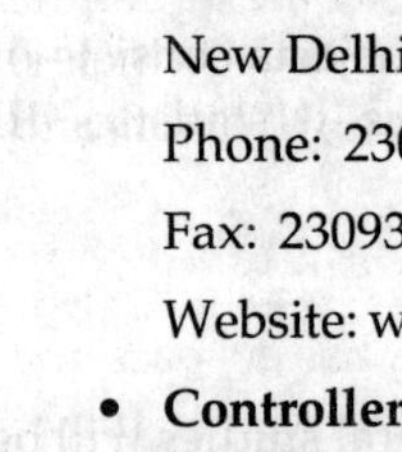

What is Insurance?

Insurance means being covered or protected against any hazards of life. It is a financial agreement that binds two people to certain obligations which is known as Policy. One who buys insurance or gets insurance coverage is the policy holder or insured and the one who sells the policy is the insurer. From time to time, the insured signs the policy he/she has an obligation to pay a certain amount of money known as premium in return for which the insurer will pay compensation in certain eventualities e.g., fire, theft, motor accident, etc.

Major Government Companies

There are about 30 insurance companies in India. The major government companies are Life Insurance Corporation of India (LIC), General Insurance Corporation (GIC) and Postal Life Insurance. While, LIC deals with insurance of life, GIC and its subsidiaries are concerned with non-life aspects of insurance such as car, marine, accident, medical and fire insurance.

Multinational Companies

Some of the multinational companies that have come forward in the insurance field are ICICI Prudential, OM Kotak Mahindra, Birla Sun-Life, Tata AIF Life, Reliance, HDFC Standard Life-Insurance Co., Max New York Life, SBI Life Insurance, ING Vysya Life etc., are the top companies in the private sector. In non-life insurance segment, major private players are ICICI Lombard, Royal Sundaram, Cholamandalam, IFFCO Tokyo, Tata AIG etc. All Insurance companies come under the Insurance Regulatory and Development Authority (IRDA) which is established to regulate, promote and ensure orderly growth of Life and General insurance industry in India.

Eligibility

To pursue a career in the insurance industry, one has to pass the entrance examination conducted by the Actuarial Society of India, Mumbai. Students who have passed 10+2 or equivalent examination are eligible. Licence is needed to work in this field which can be obtained through a training programme.

The eligible criteria for the varied posts in the Insurance industry are:

- **Administrative Officer (AO) and Assistant Administrative Officer (AAO)** : Graduate/postgraduate degree holders in any subject with minimum of 50 per cent marks from a recognised university and age between 21 and 28 years can apply for these posts. Recruitment is through a written examination and interview.
- **Development Officer** : Graduates in any discipline between 21 and 26 years of age can apply for the post of Development Officer. Selection is based on written tests in English and

Mathematics and an interview. Selected candidates have to serve as apprentice for a period of one year.

- **Insurance Agents :** The minimum educational qualification for an insurance agent is 10+2. Before joining as insurance agents, one needs to undergo 100 hours of classroom training by the respective insurance company-based on the syllabus laid down by IRDA. After completion of training, they have to appear for the examination conducted by the Insurance Regulatory Development Authority (IRDA).
- **Composite Agents :** They are the one who sell both life and general insurance policies. Eligibility criteria are the same as that of insurance agents but they have to appear for one more test, also conducted by IRDA.
- **Insurance Surveyor :** Licensed by the Controller of Insurance, the surveyor can be engineers, accountants, medical graduates etc. To hold a license of surveyor, one has to possess any one of the following :
  - (i) Fellowship or Associateship of the Institute of Insurance Surveyors and Adjustors (IISA), Mumbai.
  - (ii) Fellowship or Associateship of the Institute of Chartered Accountants or Cost and Works Accountants.
  - (iii) A degree or diploma in architecture from a recognised university or institute.
  - (iv) A degree or diploma from a recognised institute of engineering.
  - (v) A degree or diploma in Naval Architecture.
- **Actuaries :** Graduates with 55 per cent marks in mathematics/ statistics/econometrics/computer science or MBA in finance, CA, CWA, MCA are eligible to join for actuary training. Training in this field can be pursued from the Actuarial Society of India (ASI), Mumbai or The Institute and Faculty of Actuaries, London, UK. To work as an Actuary, one has to pass an entrance exam conducted by these Institutes twice a year, in May-June and October-November.

The post of Assistants, Typists, Machine Operators, Stenographers, Telephone Operators, Clerks etc., are open to graduates and school-leavers, and the age limit is between 18 – 25 years. The candidates applying have to go through a written test and interview.

The eligibility criterion for recruitment to both the LIC and GIC is the same. Those who have passed the Licentiate Examination of the

Insurance Institute of India, will get preference in LIC and GIC recruitments.

Job Prospects and Career Options

Each department of the insurance industry has their own set of responsibilities and performs various tasks. The main works are :

- **Administrative Officer (AO) and Assistant Administrative Officer (AAO) : Development Officer :** These 1st class officer group in LIC and GIC begins their job with probation-cum-training period for six months where the candidate is placed anywhere in the country. AAOs can choose any of the areas from Administration, Development and Accounts. Administration AAOs handle policy-making, policy claims up to certain limit, checking clauses and details, filing official returns and statements to higher regional offices etc. The Development AAOs deal with marketing and procurement of business, meeting prospective clients, promoting the policies and getting contracts. The Accounts AAOs manage the funds including incomes and expenses of the corporation. AAOs can be promoted to AOs after three years of working experience.
- **Development Officers :** They are 2nd class officer group, who are in charge of the development of the insurance policies. The work profile of the development officer includes recruitment of agents, training them for procurement of new business and servicing of the existing policies.
- **Insurance/Composite Agents :** Insurance agents help individuals, families and business select insurance policies that provide the best protection for their lives, health and property. They are the people who have taken up an agency from the insurance company to sell their policy on a commission basis. They work with the development officer in the insurance company and the credit for the policy of the insurance agents goes to the development officers within the organisation. Smart and efficient insurance agents working hard can become development officer over a period of time.
- **Insurance Surveyor :** Surveyors are independent professionals who are hired by the insurance companies to work as consultants, their main task is to assess the actual loss and avoid false claims filed by the insured. Their work involves a lot of fieldwork, communications, travelling, PR etc.

- **Actuaries :** This is the most important position in the insurance business which deals with a wide range of financial problems related with insurance investments, financial planning and management. They apply mathematical and statistical methods to evaluate the risk for their companies to use for strategic management decisions and determine premium rates, studies mortality trends, construct mortality tables etc., and areas related to benefits and investment.
- **Insurance Underwriter :** Underwriters assess the risk in the business and takes care of risk management. It is the underwriter who reviews the insurance applications and decides whether they should be accepted or rejected. They explain policies and quotes rates to medical personnel, other insurance companies or field representatives. Candidates with medical or life science background are preferred for this job.
- **Investment Professionals :** The funds collected from the investors have to deploy in various investment options for maximising the returns. For this investment professionals are required and this is a promising field for those with a degree in finance.

Remuneration

The pay scale in the government sector is as per government rules depending on each position. For each grade, along with their basic pay other allowances are also granted. In the private sector the salary is more lucrative. They take in management graduates to work mainly in the areas of marketing and sales with an initial salary ranging from ₹ 15,000 – 25,000 per month.

Commissions are the most common form of compensation for insurance agents and the amount depends on the type and amount of insurance sold and whether the transaction is a new policy or a renewal. On the 1st year of policy, they may get about 25-32 per cent of the premium amount, followed by 7.5 per cent in the 2nd and 3rd and 5 per cent in the 4th and 5th year. When they meet their sales goals bonuses are also awarded. Actuaries are one of the most highly paid people in the insurance sector and the entry level salary is expected to be somewhere around ₹ eight lakh per annum and with a few years experience they could earn a seven figure salary per annum especially in the private sector. For underwriters it is around ₹ six lakh per annum.

Courses

- BBA Insurance
- Diploma in Capital Marketing and Insurance Management (DCMIM)

- Diploma in Insurance
- Diploma in Insurance and Risk Management (DIRM)
- International Post-graduate Diploma in General Insurance
- International Post-graduate Diploma in Life Insurance
- MBA Insurance
- MBA Risk and Insurance
- M. Com. Banking and Insurance
- Master of Insurance Business
- Post-graduate Diploma in Banking, Insurance and Financial Services Management
- Post-graduate Diploma in Insurance and Risk Management
- Post-graduate Diploma in Insurance Business Management
- Post-graduate Diploma in Insurance Law
- Post-graduate Diploma in Insurance Management

Useful Contacts

- **Insurance Institute of India, Mumbai**

  Gresham Assurance House, 4th Floor, Sir Pherozshah Mehta, Mumbai-400 001

  Phone: 022-2266 0095

  Fax: 022-2269 3419

  Website: www.insuranceinstituteofindia.com/

- **Actuarial Society of India, Mumbai**

  302, Indian Globe Chambers, 142, Fort Street, Off D N Road, Mumbai-400 001

  Phone: +91-022 2262 6886, 2269 1051

  Fax: +91-022 2269 1052

  Website: www.actuariesindia.org/

- **Insurance Regulatory and Development Authority (IRDA), Hyderabad**

  3rd Floor, Parisrama Bhavanam, Basheerbagh,

  Hyderabad 500 004

  Phone: +91-040-66820964, 66789768

  Fax: 91-040-66823334

- **Institute of Insurance and Risk Management (IIRM), Hyderabad**

Plot no. 1149, Road No-57, Jubilee Hills, Hyderabad-500033, Andhra Pradesh
(Off: Road No. 36 Adjacent to Trinethra Super Market)
Phone: +91-40 23556470, 23600578
Fax: +91 40 23556471
Website: www.iirmworld.org.in/

1.11 Taxation

What is Taxation?

Tax is the sum total of money which is mandatory for an individual to pay to a state or anybody having an equivalency to a state. The individual/entity is termed as 'Tax payer' and the entire process is called Taxation. Taxation is a process of imposing financial charge (tax) on the citizens who earn 'taxable' income. It involves dealing with direct taxes, assessment of taxes, filing returns and providing advice on indirect taxes.

Direct Tax and Indirect Tax

Direct tax is the tax collected directly from the people in the way of income tax, property tax, wealth tax etc. While Indirect tax is the tax collected from the customers on the goods purchased or for the service provided for, e.g., VAT, sales tax, excise duty, customs duty etc.

The Indian Tax System

The tax system in India is mainly a three-tier system which is based between the central, state government and an authority of a state such as municipality, corporation or the local council. The main taxes/duties that the central government is empowered to levy are Income Tax (except tax on agricultural income, which levied by the State governments), customs duties, central excise and sales tax and service tax. The principal taxes levied by the state governments are Value Added Tax (VAT or Sales tax in states where VAT is not yet in force), Sales Tax (tax on intra-State sale of goods), Stamp Duty (duty on transfer of property), State Excise (duty on manufacture of certain goods), Land Revenue (levy on land used for agricultural/non-agricultural purposes), Duty on Entertainment and Tax on Professions and Callings. The local bodies are empowered to levy tax on properties (building houses), Octroi (tax on entry of goods for use/consumption within areas of the local bodies), tax on markets and tax/user charges for utilities like water supply, drainage etc.

Utilisation of the Tax Money

The tax paid by the citizens is the main source of income for the government. The money collected through tax is used in financing projects for developing the infrastructure and other development projects of the country. Whatever tax is being charged it has to be backed by the law passed by the legislature or the Parliament. In India, Tax is regulated and administered by the Ministry of Finance under the Government of India. The main body which is responsible for the collection of taxes is the Central Board of Direct Taxes (CBDT) which is a part of the Department of Revenue.

Some of the taxes levied in India by the government

- **Income Tax (Personal) :** The Income Tax Act of 1961 stipulates that any person who qualifies as an assessee and whose gross income is more than the exemption limit is required to pay Income Tax in accordance with the rates indicated by the Finance Act. Individuals whose income is below a specified mark need not pay any tax and such individuals are exempted.
- **Corporate Tax :** India Corporate Tax is the tax charged on the profits earned by association and companies by several jurisdictions. The rate of Corporate Tax depends on whether the profits have been passed on to the shareholders or not.
- **Property Tax :** Tax charged on property owned by individuals or corporate.
- **Sales Tax :** Tax on sale of goods.
- **Value Added Tax :** This is the tax that a manufacturer needs to pay while purchasing raw materials and a trader needs to pay while purchasing goods. VAT is eventually expected to replace Sales Tax. All goods and services provided by business individuals and companies come under the ambit of VAT.
- **Capital Gains Tax :** A Capital Gain can be defined as any income generated by pay selling a capital investment (business stocks, paintings, houses, family business, farmhouse etc.). The 'gain' here is the difference between the price originally paid for the investment and money received upon selling it and is taxable.
- **Service Tax :** As per the Finance Act of 1994, all service providers in India, except those in the state of Jammu and Kashmir are required to pay a Service Tax in India.
- **Fringe Benefit Tax :** As per Section 115 WB of the Finance Bill, expenses incurred for employees by an employer (individual/

company/local authority/trader) for purposes of entertainment, gifts, telephone, clubbing, festivals etc., will be treated as Fringe Benefits and will be taxed.

Eligibility and Course Areas

Graduates and post-graduates in commerce are generally hired for jobs in the field of taxation. To pursue graduate level courses, the aspirants must have passed higher secondary certificate examination or 10+2 from any recognised state/national Board. To be eligible for the PG courses, one has to complete graduation in the relevant stream. Many institutes in India are conducting courses in the field to produce competent professionals who can work in the field of taxation.

Job Prospects and Career Options

Jobs in taxation are very lucrative for those applicants interested in the subject of taxes. Depending on one's academic background along with working experience in taxation, jobs can be found in all corners of the globe. As you gain expertise performing complex tax audits, opportunities increase for career advancement in the organisation. From the more aggressive taxation, jobs such as lawyers and criminal defence attorneys to the more laid back jobs such as filing tax returns for corporations, the range is wide in this field. Aspirants can join any organisation as Tax Accountant, Employment Tax Specialists, State Local Tax Attorney specialists, Tax Policy Analyst, Tax Recruiter, Tax Advisor, Tax Manager, Collectors, Revenue Agents etc. One can also work independently as a consultant. Another aspect to consider when searching for a job in taxation is what type of tax most interests you. Within tax consultation you can further specialise in fields like:

- **Property Tax Consultants :** Property Tax Consultants are basically professionals who have good knowledge of the various property tax rules and regulations and cater to a set of clients who are seeking such information or advice on property taxes which may deal with landed property, commercial, residential as well as other kinds of property.
- **Income Tax Consultants :** An Income Tax Consultant or an income tax advisor is nothing but a person who helps you in filing your income tax returns every year. Income tax consultants thus are aware of the various income tax rules and provide service to clients who are individuals as well as corporate.
- **Business Tax Consultants :** Business Tax Consultant's area of knowledge deals with various issues relating to taxes that a business man must handle properly for his business to work

efficiently and effectively. Thus, a business tax consultant gives advice to business houses regarding the various business tax issues that are plaguing them.

- **Sales Tax Consultant :** A Sales Tax Consultant is a person who give advice to his or her clients regarding the various sales tax as well as value added tax related issues for which they may be seeking clarification, information or advice.

A tax consultant's or tax practitioner's primary role is to advice to his clients how to go about filing their taxes to the government. Their job also includes helping and providing complete assistance to their clients in their fundamental tax planning. Thus, tax consultants have to be aware of the various tax laws which are present in the country and which will have an impact on their clients. They should be aware of the various income tax rules and regulations and the changes which are made from time to time.

Remuneration

As a profession tax consultancy offers great rewards. Remuneration in the field of taxation varies from one organisation to the other. However, beginners can earn a salary of ₹ 2, 00,000 – 5, 00,000 per annum.

Courses

- B. Com. Taxation
- Certificate Course in International Taxation
- Diploma in Taxation
- Diploma in Taxation Laws (DTL)
- M.Com. Taxation
- Post-graduate Diploma in Taxation
- Post-graduate Diploma in Taxation Laws

Institutes

Many colleges and universities in India are conducting courses in the field of taxation, at diploma and certificate levels. Some of the prominent institutions are :

- **Annamalai University, Annamalainagar**

  Chidambaram-608002, Tamil Nadu

- **Nagpur College of Taxation, Nagpur, Maharashtra**

  Narsimha Bhavan (II Floor, Near Titan Show Room, 7 Mount Road Extension, Sardar, Nagpur-440001

- **Institute of Chartered Accountants of India, New Delhi**
- **Indian Institute of Taxation, Pattom,**
  Thiruvananthapuram-695004, Kerala
- **IGSS (Indian Global Software Solutions), Bangalore, Karnataka**
  Vijayanagar, Bangalore-560040
- **Institute of International Trade, Kolkata, West Bengal**
  Advantage Tower EN 27, Salt Lake Sector-V
  Kolkata-700091
- **University of Pune: Faculty of Commerce, Pune**
  Ganeshkhind, Pune-411007
- **Guru Nanak Dev University: Faculty of Economics and Business, Amritsar Punjab**
- **Rashtrasant Tukadoji Maharaj Nagpur University, Nagpur, Maharashtra**
  Chhatrapati Shivaji Maharaj Administrative Premises, Rabindranath Tagore Marg, Nagpur-440001

2

AGRICULTURE AND RELATED SCIENCE

2.1 Agricultural Economics

What is Agricultural Economics?

Study of economic principles, with emphasis on their application to the solution of farm, agribusiness and agricultural industry problems in relationship to other sectors is known as agricultural economics. Agricultural economics deals with the business side of agriculture. The field of agricultural economics looks at all elements of food production and applies rational thought and planning as a whole. From crops, livestock, land usage and soil content, all aspects of farm life are examined, including how its relation to one another can be strengthened.

The Role of Agricultural economists

Those who work in this business field of agriculture are known by the name Agricultural economists. Agricultural economists manage farm and other agricultural industries by applying business concepts and problem-solving techniques. Agricultural economists also predict trends in markets for farm products. They closely observe and explain changes in the market. An agricultural economist would monitor crops, prices, animal health, equipment, imports and exports, weather cycles, buying patterns and new methods of production.

A career in agricultural economics is ideal for those who enjoy agricultural business and also have a knack for calculation and economical theory. Agricultural economics combines the technical aspects of agriculture with the business aspects of management, marketing and finance thus providing range of careers in field like marketing of commodities, farms and ranches.

Eligibility and Course Areas

Students who wish to pursue a career in agricultural economics should possess a strong base in botany, physics, chemistry and mathematics. Various agricultural universities and colleges in India offer under-graduate, post-graduate, diploma and doctorate courses in agricultural economics. To be an Agricultural Economist at least a master's degree is required.

The basic eligibility criteria for a bachelor's programme in Agriculture is 10+2 or equivalent in science subjects (with physics, chemistry, biology or mathematics) with a minimum of 50 per cent marks. Minimum duration is four years. Most of the universities/institutes offer agricultural economics as a subject or specialisation of B. Sc. Agricultural Science courses. Applicants must possess a Bachelor's degree in agriculture or an equivalent qualification for studying M.Sc. in Agricultural Economics which is of two years duration. Ph.D Degree programme in Agricultural Economics requires a master's degree.

Agricultural Economics imparts with the knowledge about agricultural production, finance, marketing and policy. The study focuses on crops, animal health, prices, buying pattern, weather cycles, imports and exports, agricultural equipment and techniques of production. For a career as an agricultural scientist, a master's degree is necessary and Ph.D. in agriculture is needed for the post of a senior researcher and teaching profession. Those with post-graduate, diploma and degree in agriculture are related subjects can become agriculture technologists.Those with master's degree in agricultural economics can apply for Agricultural Research Service and National Eligibility Test conducted by Agricultural Scientists in the Indian Council of Agricultural Research (ICAR).

Job Prospects

Agriculture like other businesses has its producers, distributors and consumers – all interdependent in the market system. Globalisation and liberalisation has increased the need for well-trained personnel with knowledge of agricultural production, marketing, finance and policy. Here comes the role of agricultural economists, who have managerial skills and decision-making ability. Agricultural economists may fine opportunities in administration, management and financial advising. Other jobs include market price forecaster, agricultural statistician, farm credit analyst, managers of farm supply and commodity analyst.

After the completion of the course, students can start their own business or work in different areas like agribusiness, management, marketing of agriculture products, farm management and veterinary management. In addition, many agricultural economists pursue successful careers in government service, economic development, commodity promotion and agricultural policy analysis. Agricultural economists graduate are employed in a wide range of settings, including banks, educational institutes and research organisation, consulting farms, government departments of agriculture and environment, agrifood companies and international aid agencies. You can also opt to do research in the area. Most lucrative career in government service is the position of a scientist in Indian Council of Agricultural Research.

Career areas in this field are as follows :

- **Entrepreneurship and Small Business Management :** You can be your own boss by managing your own farm. Working in family enterprises and managing small businesses are the focus of opportunities in this area.
- **Agribusiness Management :** You may work in sales, management, appraisal, research or public relations for business that produce, buy, sell, process and distribute agricultural products.
- **Public Service :** Public service careers are available at the central, state and local levels. Careers are in such areas as agricultural production, marketing, finance, conservation and others. State and local agencies offer wide variety of careers in this area.
- **Finance and Appraisal :** Students work for lending institutions such as commercial and agricultural banks. You would have the opportunity to make loans, evaluate investment opportunities and appraise property for agricultural purposes.
- **Farm Business Management :** You would manage farm operations, work for integrated agricultural firms or own and manage your own farm.
- **International Agriculture and Development :** Job opportunities in international agriculture have multiplied in recent years mostly because of the growth of multinational firms and the efforts of businesses.

Remuneration

Salary in this sector depends on various factors such as experience, position acquired, expertise in particular field and area of employment. In government sector one get a starting pay of ₹ 12,000 – 15,000. However, a senior fellow in agricultural economic research field can expect about ₹ 35,000 – 55,000 per month as per revised scale. Financial sector like banks also offer good pay packages.

Courses

- M. Sc. Agricultural Economics
- Ph.D. Agricultural Economics

Institutes

There are several institutes / universities offering Agricultural Economics at post-graduate level and Doctoral level. Some of them are: Allahabad University, Indian Agricultural Research Institute, Tamil Nadu Agricultural University etc.

2.2 Agricultural Science

What is Agricultural Science?

The study of agriculture is termed as agricultural science. It is a multi-disciplinary field which consists of a variety of scientific, technical and business subjects that promote the efficient production of quality food on the farm and in the agricultural-food industry linked to farming. Closely related to biological science, it uses the principles of biology, chemistry, physics and mathematics to solve the problems related to agriculture. Agricultural science include research and development on production techniques; improving agricultural productivity in terms of quantity and quality; transformation of primary products into end consumer products and prevention and correction of adversities. Major areas of specialisation within agricultural science are food, plant science, soil science and animal science.

The Role of Agricultural Science Professionals

Agricultural science professionals specialise in agricultural production and livestock. They play an important role in maintaining the nation's food supply. Some of the major tasks performed by them involve improving the quality and quantity of farming; improving crop yield with less labour; conservation of soil and water; controlling pests and weeds more safely and effectively etc. In short, Agricultural scientists engage in research to discover and promote effective, practical pathways to sustainable land use, food and fiber production and food harvesting.

Eligibility and Course Areas

Students who wish to pursue a career in Agricultural Science should possess a strong foundation in botany, physics, chemistry and mathematics. Various universities and colleges in India offer under-graduate, post-graduate, diploma and doctorate courses in agriculture science, a bachelor's degree in development or applied research in agriculture. For a career as an agricultural scientist, a master's degree is necessary and Ph.D. in agriculture is needed for the post of a senior researcher and teaching profession. Those with post-graduate diploma and degree in agriculture and related subjects can become agriculture technologists

The basic eligibility criterion for B.Sc. Agriculture Science is 10+2 or equivalent with science subjects with a minimum 50 per cent mark. Duration of the course is four years and the admission to most of the institutions is based on merit or performance in the entrance examination conducted by the concerned institute/university or on the basis of marks obtained in the ICAR Examination.

B.Sc. or B.Tech degree in relevant subject is needed for the two years Master's degree programmes. In M.Sc Agriculture Science several specialisations are offered in the branches like agronomy, plant physiology, nematology, seed technology, soil science and soil conservation, sericulture, animal husbandry and dairy, horticulture, water conservation, farming system management, agricultural botany, agricultural biotechnology, agricultural economics, agricultural chemistry, agricultural marketing and so on.

For the three years Ph.D., one needs to have post-graduate degree like M.Sc. or M.Tech in related field. Almost all the agricultural universities provide Ph.D. degree in different disciplines. Several institutes offer P.G. Diploma courses in agriculture and those having a bachelor's degree with an extensive knowledge base in agricultural science can opt for these courses.

Selection

Admission to all the courses in Agricultural Science is made through entrance examination. These exams are conducted by the concerned institute/university. Indian Council of Agricultural Research (ICAR), New Delhi conducts an entrance examination separately for graduate and post-graduate courses. Eligibility requirement for the exam is 12th pass in Science/Agriculture with 50 per cent marks for graduate level courses and 60 per cent marks in B.Sc./B.Sc. (Agriculture) for post-graduate level courses. Certain institutes admit students on the basis of the marks obtained in ICAR examination. ICAR also provides fellowship for all the students of postgraduate's courses and for those students, who have got Junior Research Fellowship during the entrance exam at the post-graduate level. Indian Agricultural Research Institute (IARI), Delhi; Indian Veterinary Research Institute, Izatnagar; National Dairy Research Institute, Karnal and Central Institute on Fisheries Education, Mumbai are some of the major institutes that conduct their own entrance examination.

Job Prospects

Agricultural Science professionals/scientists are concerned with methods of converting agricultural commodities into healthy food products for consumers. They combine wide variety of scientific disciplines such as biology, chemistry, physics and mathematics to improve agricultural production methods and food quality. The tasks carried out by them depend on the type of specialisation. Among the various specialisations within agricultural science, the major broad areas are food science, plant science, soil science and animal science.

- **Food Science :** In this field, researches and works are being done for developing new and improved ways of preserving, processing, packaging, storing and delivering foods. Food science professionals/scientists analyse food content to determine levels of vitamins, fat, sugar or protein or search for substitutes for harmful or undesirable additives and preservatives.
- **Plant Science Horticulture :** This field comprises agronomy, environmental science, plant breeding and entomology. Agronomy is the scientific management of soil and the production of crops. Entomology is the study of insects and their relationship to plants. Plant breeding includes Forestry, Floriculture, etc.
- **Soil Science :** Soil Science is the study of the physical, chemical and biological composition of soils; its impact on plant growth and how various types of soils respond to things such as fertilizers, crop rotation etc.
- **Animal Science :** It is the field which conducts research and development to improve the production and processing of meats, fish and dairy products. Dairy scientists, animal breeders, poultry and fishery scientists are related scientists who specialise in nutrition, genetics, reproduction and growth of domestic farm animals. Animal scientists examine and grade livestock food products, purchase livestock or work in technical sales or marketing.

Other fields of Agricultural Science are agricultural economics, waste management, environmental science, ecology, agricultural engineering, bio-systems engineering, biotechnology, genetic engineering, microbiology etc. As an enormous and expanding field, agriculture industry offers numerous career options to agricultural professional. Most careers in these fields are either business or science related. Entrepreneurship in this field can generate handsome profits while salaried jobs with various government and private concerns provide a regular income. Agriculture professionals can seek employment in Central and state government ministries and departments; agricultural finance corporation research institutions; nationalised banks and rural banks; Krishi Vigyan Kendras; agro-industry sector; agricultural universities and various agricultural service organisations. Their work profile involves pest control, fieldwork control plant disease, food science and nutrition, conducting surveys and reports etc. Horticulture, floriculture, dairy and poultry farming, fishery, agricultural journalism etc. are some of the areas offering good career potential.

Graduates in Agricultural Science are employed as agricultural manager/inspectors in farm-related organisations, agro-industries, food processing unit, dairy fields, NGO's and breeding centers. Many of these positions can be in areas that support the marketing and distribution sector of agribusiness operations. They can also set their own business in primary economic sector such as farming, plantations, fisheries, mining, cattle rearing, poultry farming etc.

Union Public Service Commission (UPSC) and State Public Service Commission recruit post-graduates to the post of agricultural extension officer, rural development officer, field officer, agricultural credit officers, agricultural probationary officer, plant protection officer, soil conservation officer, seed production officers, agricultural assistants, farm superintendents or technical assistants. Depending on the areas of specialisations, post-graduates with doctoral degree are employed in the agricultural universities as plant pathologist, research engineer, associate professor etc. Reserve Bank of India, State Bank of India and nationalised banks offer openings for post-graduates in agriculture and allied areas as Field Officers, Rural Development Officers and Agricultural Officers and Agricultural and Probationary Officers.

Research areas of agricultural science have become more prospective with the new advances in the study of genetics and biotechnology. Scientists work with biologists and chemists to develop efficient processes for turning crops into energy sources. One can work in the private sector on applied research and product development or engage in basic research and product development or engage in basic research, mainly in universities or government agencies. Agricultural scientists can also work as consultants to business firms, private clients or to government. They can join in the Indian Agricultural Research Institute (IARI), Delhi as junior fellow researcher. Vacancies for scientists in the Agricultural Research Service (ARS) Institute are through a combined entrance test conducted by the Agricultural Scientists Recruitment Board or ASRB. Aspiring candidates can also take ARS NET (Agricultural Research Service/National Eligibility Test) examination to work as lecturers in various agricultural universities and their affiliated colleges.

The Department of Agriculture in every state recruits gazetted officers like District Agricultural Officer, Assistant Director of Agriculture through the State Service Commission (SSC). The recruitment to the post of Agricultural Development Officer (ADO)/Block Development Officer (BDO) is also through entrance examination conducted by Public Service Commission/concerned department. International Crops Research Institute for the Semi-Arid-Tropics (ICRISAT) with its headquarters at Andhra Pradesh is a non-profit, non-political organisation for research related job of agriculture field.

Remuneration

Pay scale in the field of agriculture science depends mainly upon the academic qualification, institute or university from which the degree is attained, work experience and the skill of the employee. In the government sector, a fresh graduate can earn a monthly remuneration of ₹ 9,000. Within few years of service it can increase up to ₹ 20,000. Candidates employed in private sector can get handsome salary apart from other benefits as fixed by the respective firm/company. Agricultural scientists can receive a monthly salary ranges between ₹ 18,000 and 30,000 and a lecturer will be paid according to the UGC pay scale.

Institutes

Some of the colleges offering agricultural science courses are :

- **College of Agriculture**
  Faculty of Agriculture
  Jorhat-785013, Assam
- **College of Agriculture**
  Agriculture Faculty
  Rajendranagar, Hyderabad-500030
  Andhra Pradesh
- **College of Agriculture,**
  Hebbal, Bangalore-560024
  Karnataka
- **College of Agriculture,**
  Vellayani-695522
  Trivandrum, Kerala

- **College of Agriculture,**
  Indore-452001
  Madhya Pradesh
- **College of Agriculture,**
  Pune-411005
  Maharashtra
- **Manipur Agriculture College,**
  Iroisemba, Imphal-795001
  Manipur
- **Doon College of Agriculture Science and Technology**
  28, Chakrata Road, Dehradun
  Uttaranchal
- **Institute of Agricultural Sciences**
  Banaras Hindu University
  Varanasi-221005, UP

2.3 Aqua Culture

What is an Aqua Science?

Aqua Science is the multi-disciplinary study of the earth's oceanic and fresh water environments. About three-quarter of the earth's surface is covered with water, so aqua science has emerged as an important subject area. Also known as Aquatic Science, the subject encompasses a range of disciplines concerned with the oceans, rivers, lakes, streams, ponds, wetlands, their geology and composition and the life forms that live in them. It tries to predict the quality of life for future generations, the impact of greenhouse gas emissions, ozone depletion and changes in currents and ocean temperature. In a broad sense it studies the earth's interrelated elements such as atmosphere, oceans and land mass, the changes in their processes and their relationship to the changes happening to the earth.

Subject Areas under Aquatic Science

Important subject areas under Aquatic Science include Aquaculture which refers to the cultivation of aquatic organisms such as fish, crustaceans, molluscs and aquatic plants under controlled conditions. Oceanography explores oceans and estuaries by integrating the principles of biology, chemistry, geology, meteorology and physics. Limnology studies rivers, lakes, streams, ponds using the same principles of basic science, marine geology, etc.

What is an Aquaculture?

Aquaculture involves cultivating freshwater and saltwater populations under controlled conditions and can be contrasted with commercial fishing which is the harvesting of wild fish. It further covers an important subject area called Mari-culture which refers to aquaculture practiced in marine environments. Particular kinds of aquaculture include alga-culture (the production of kelp/seaweed and other algae); fish farming, shrimp farming, shellfish farming and the growing of cultured pearls. Thus, Aquaculture is nothing but the commercial breeding and farming of various species of fish and aquatic species under controlled conditions.

The Main Aspect of Aquaculture

The main aspect of aquaculture is fish cultivation which is aimed at human consumption and for industrial and medicinal purposes. Aquaculture is perhaps one of the oldest industries in the world. One of the first known countries to adopt aquaculture is China in 2500 BC. Aquaculture however expanded and became a full-fledged industry only in the 20th century.

Difference between Aquaculture and Fisheries

Aquaculture and fisheries are related to one another and one can hardly make out any difference between the two. Though Aquaculture and fisheries have more similarities between them, there is a significant difference between aquaculture and fisheries. Fisheries are concerned with fish or shellfish. It mainly deals with catching, processing and selling of fish. On the other hand, Aquaculture is related to the cultivation of both aquatic animals and aquatic plants. Aquaculture is also called 'fish farming' and it involves the natural or controlled cultivation of shellfish, fish and seaweed in fresh water and marine environments. Fisheries are solely related to catching wild fish or raising and harvesting fish through aquaculture or fish farming. On the other hand, Aquaculture is not pertained to cultivating and harvesting fishes alone. While fishery professionals focus on commercial aspects of sea food production, processing and marketing, aquaculturists focus on the production and breeding of all varieties of commercial species. Aquaculture is a science that involves all aspects of marine life. Some examples of aquaculture include raising catfish and tilapia in fresh water ponds, growing cultured pearls and farming salmon in net-pens set out in a bay.

The Role of Aquaculturists

Farmers who breed and grow shellfish, crustaceans, finfish or aquatic plants for profit in controlled or semi-controlled settings are called aquaculturists. In general, aquaculturists may work on ocean pens off the coast growing marine finfish or on inland farms where freshwater species can be cultivated in ponds. Aquaculturists are responsible for designing and construction of fish farming ponds and fish hatchery units as well as aquarium management for the production of ornamental fish species which has great export value. Aquaculturists may be concerned with the raising of aquatic animals and plants for reasons such as production of food, stocking of public water bodies and for public or home aquaria.

Eligibility and Course Areas

The eligibilityformost of these courses is 10+2 Science preferably with physics, chemistry, biology or geology. Most institutes make it mandatory to have background knowledge in biology. It basically depends on the individual institutions. For undergraduate programmes like B.Sc. in Aqua Science, minimum requirement is generally 10+2 passed or its equivalent with biology / mathematics, physics and Chemistry. Similarly, for post graduate qualification like M.Sc. in Aqua Science, a graduate degree in science or higher degrees in related fields are preferred. One can also opt for Mariculture. Aspirants can go for Ph.D. after getting a master's degree. Diploma courses are also offered in this field by several institutes. These diploma courses can be of one to three years. Small certificate courses are also offered by some academic institutions.

These courses enable the career aspirants to learn various aspects of the marine and fishery industry such as inland and freshwater aquaculture, commercial fish production technology, fish cultivation as well as the preservation, sophisticated fish processing and post harvest and processed seafood etc. The students are also taught about water pollution and the ways of preventing the same. Marketing of the products form an important part of the course syllabus.

Job Prospects

India being surrounded by water bodies on multiple sides, the fishing industry is growing rapidly as an important industry and aquaculture is a viable career option. Fishery and aquaculture is an integrated part of marine industry. Marine industry which comprises several sea-food import-export companies, fish preservation units and seafood processing plants, agricultural universities, research organisation and state fishery departments offer plenty of employment opportunities for fisheries and aquaculture graduates.

The Central Food Technological Research Institute's (CFTRI) Biology department, Indian Council of Agricultural Research (ICAR) and the Marine Products Export Development Authority (MPEDA) encourage and boost the aquaculture industry in India.

Those who want to go into research and development can specialise in studying the life pattern, habits and breeding patterns of fishes. They can specialise in either fresh water aquaculture or coastal aquaculture. Aspirants can also study about the preservation of marine life. With water pollution is increasing rapidly. This can be prevented by disposing toxic industrial wastes safely without destroying the ecological system. A ban on the extensive fishing of some breeds is one of the new fields that is being incorporated into aquaculture studies in India and other countries as well. One can also specialise in fish processing. Processing as well as harvesting is an important part of studies in aquaculture.

Career Options

Major careers available in this field are as Aquaculturists, fish farm or aqua farm managers, hatchery unit managers, sea food exporters, sea food traders, fish breeding professionals and so on. One can find employment in the various fish farms or interested students can get into research where there is a huge need. In farm management, one performs supervisory tasks like site selection, designing and construction of ponds and other water bodies, feeding fishes, performing selective stocking, managing water quality and monitoring the fishes and preventing toxication or infection till they are harvested and also protecting the water body in general. In hatchery management, one can be engaged in brood stock collection, breeding fishes in artificial conditions, managing water quality, oxygen packing and transportation to the farms. Aquaculturists are also needed in the pharmaceutical industry for the preparation of various medicines.

Fresher in this field can start off as fishery inspectoror deep sea fishery workers. Fishery inspector's duty is to transport fish seed safely to different fishery stations. Deep sea fishery workers work as crew members in fishing vessels. For research and development, one can be involved either with the research and development sections of fishing companies or pharmaceutical companies. Teaching posts are available at all the institutes offering courses in aquaculture. One can also find jobs in equipments for cleaning, salting and freezing fishes. Self-employment is a good career option in this field.

Remuneration

Aquaculture is a viable career option. With large paths of development laying ahead the job returns are unlimited. Fresher can expect a pay package ranging between ₹ 10,000 – 25, 000 per month. Farming supervisors can get a salary between ₹ 15,000 – 25,000. For teachers, the remuneration is as per the UGC guidelines. Even while one is a research fellow, he / she can get a stipend of more than ₹ 15,000 per month. For entrepreneurs, the returns are not defined but the scope is tremendous.

Courses

There are several institutes which offer various courses in aquaculture. Most of the state agricultural universities offer bachelor', master' and doctorate programmes in aquaculture. The courses are :

- B. Sc. Aqua Culture
- M. Sc. Applied Fisheries and Aquaculture
- M. Sc. Aqua Culture and Fish Processing
- M. Sc. Aqua Culture
- M. Sc. Mariculture
- M. Sc. Coastal Aquaculture and Marine Biotechnology
- M.F.Sc. Freshwater Aqua Culture
- Ph.D. Aqua Culture
- Bachelor of Fishery Science
- M. Sc. Industrial Fisheries
- Master of Fishery Science
- Ph.D. in Fishery Science

Institutes

- **Acharya Nagarjuna University**

  Nagarjunanagar, Guntur, Andhra Pradesh

  Phone: 0863-2293001, 2293189

  Mobile: 8632346114

  Fax: 0863-2293378

- **Government Arts College for Men**

  Nandanam, Chennai, Tamil Nadu

  Phone: 044-24351048

  Fax: 044-24351048

- **Patna University**
  Ashok Rajpath
  Patna, Bihar
  Phone: 0612-2300320
  Mobile: 9431078883
  Fax: 0612-2670877
- **Sacred Heart College**
  Thevara
  Kochi, Kerala
  Phone: 0484-2663380
  Fax: 0484-2663813
- **Vidyasagar University**
  Paschim Medinipur
  Midnapore, West Bengal
  Phone: 03222-275297, 275441
  Fax: 03222-275297
- **Central Institute of Fisheries Education**
  PB No. 7392, Kakori Camp, Jaiprakash Road, Versova, Mumbai
  Maharashtra
  Phone: 022-26361446
  Fax: 022-26361573, 26348223
- **Kerala Agricultural University (KAU)**
  KAU P.O., Trissur, Kerala
  Phone: 0487-2438011, 2370432
  Fax: 0487-2370019

2.4 Fisheries Science

What is Fisheries Science?

Fisheries Science is an academic discipline of managing and understanding fisheries. This is a multi-disciplinary subject that includes the biological study of life, habits and breeding of various species of fish. It involves farming and husbandry of important fishes and aquatic organisms in fresh water, brackish water and any marine environment.

The Purpose of Fisheries

Fisheries aim at developing and maintaining sea's wealth. Fisheries are estimated to provide 16 per cent of the world population's protein and India holds the seventh position in the world with regard to the value of fish exports. Around eight million people developing fishery industry provides employment not only to the traditional fishermen, but also to the highly skilled personnel engaged in the scientific breeding and management of fisheries. The scope in the field of fishery science is increasing with the development of brackish water and fresh water aquaculture. Because of the country's expansive natural resources and dynamic entrepreneurial skills, this profession is advantageous to the Indian economy as well.

Career in Fisheries

A career in fisheries science can create a sense of fulfillment in aqua culturists, farm managers, exporters, traders, breeders and modern fishermen. The main objective of fisheries science is to make available the much needed technically competent extension personnel for transfer of technology. It helps a person to assist the research and development; to develop and execute fisheries development plan.

Eligibility and Course Areas

Fisheries Science can be studied at the graduate and post-graduate level. To become a fisheries graduate one has to pass a four years degree course, i.e., B.F.Sc. (Bachelor of Fisheries Science) from fisheries colleges of state agricultural universities. The basic eligibility criterion for B.F.Sc. is 10+2 with biological science as one of the subjects. The B.F.Sc. course enables a candidate with basic knowledge in all the three categories of fisheries science, i.e., capture, culture and post harvest technology.

Admission

For admission into various Central Institute of Fisheries Education in the country, the candidates have to appear an all India level common entrance test conducted by ICAR (Indian Council of Agricultural Research), New Delhi. Special quota for outside state candidates is allowed to the candidates who have passed entrance examination of ICAR and are getting-fellowship too.

After completing B.F.Sc., one can take M.F.Sc. (Master of Fisheries Science) which is of two years duration. After getting a professional degree in Fisheries Science, one can go into research-oriented activities.

Course Areas

B.F.Sc. students are trained in a wide variety of subjects such as aquaculture (inland and freshwater), mariculture, industrial fisheries, fish processing and post harvest technology, fish nutrition, pathology, environment, ecology and extension. Sustainable fish production practices and scientific breeding and management of fishes are major areas of specialisation. The course also contains practical experience in sea cruise, in fishing vessels for data collection and fishing, in processing plants and in aqua farms.

Personal Skills

Those who have taken fishery science as a career must possess a genuine interest in marine life and should be free from sea sickness. The field requires a lot of research work and one should have research-oriented mentality. Dedication to work, devotion, hard working, patients, curiosity and inquisitive mind are essential. Quick thinking and the ability to come up with new ideas are advantageous. A good Managerial skill is also required, as fishery science is a field which is directly or indirectly related to business. Apart from the B.F.Sc. and M.F.Sc. various fisheries institutes offerseveral vocational training courses related to fisheries and allied disciplines.

Job Prospects and Career Options

Fisheries Science offers numerous career avenues. Fisheries graduates can find employment in the public sector organisations such as the fisheries department and the nationalised banks. Opportunities lie in government agencies, state departments of agriculture and organisations such as the Central Marine Fisheries Research Institute (CMFRI). Recruitment to these institutions is through the State Public Service Commission. For those having good research skills, can find employment in organisations such as the Central Institute of Fisheries Technology (CIFT) and the National Fisheries Development Board as research assistant, biochemist, biologist, technicians, etc.

In the state government sector, a fisheries graduate can apply for the post of Assistant Fisheries Development Officer (AFDO)/Fisheries Extension Officer (FEO) and District Fisheries Development Officer. Various opportunities in central government agencies are in Marine Products Export Development Authority (MPEDA), Fisheries Survey of India (FSI), NIO, WHO, etc. They can also be employed as field bank officers, managers in agriculture loan section in nationalised as well as private banks. Job prospects are also available in private sectors in aquaculture farms, hatcheries and processing plants. Commercial fish farming, seed production and export of marine products and ornamental dishes are potential areas of self-employment and entrepreneurship development in fisheries.

M.F Sc. degree holders can be appointed as assistant professors in the faculty of fisheries and those with doctoral degree can be recruited as scientists in various agricultural and fisheries institutions. Recruitment to these positions is by the Agricultural Scientists Recruitment Board (ASRB) through a nation-wide competitive examination followed by a personal interview.

Remuneration

Remuneration in this field varies widely, depending on the area of chosen specialisation. In the private sector one may start with an initial salary ranging between ₹ 6,000 – 8,000 per month. But in the government sector, the salary range may be different but it offers stable salary. In this field, research positions are more lucrative but these are usually reserved for doctorate holders with experience.

Courses

- Bachelor of Fishery Science
- Bachelor of Science in Industrial Fish and Fisheries
- M.Sc. Applied Fisheries and Aquaculture
- M.Sc. Industrial Fisheries
- Master of Fishery Science
- Ph. D. Fishery Science

Useful contacts

- **Indian Council of Agricultural Research (ICAR),**

  New Delhi, Krishi Bhavan, D. Rajendra Prasad Road, New Delhi-110 002

- **Central Institute of Fisheries Education (CIFE),**

  Mumbai, Fisheries University Road, Seven Bungalows, Andheri (W), Mumbai – 400061

  Branches : Kolkata, Lucknow, Haryana and Kakinada

  Phone: +91 22 2636 1446/7/8

  Fax: +91 22 2636 1573

Best Colleges for Fishery Science

- **Veer Kunwar Singh University, Ara, Bihar**

  Courses : Bachelor of Science (Hons.)-Industrial Fish and Fishery

  Master of Science (Environmental Science)

- **Cochin University of Science and Technology, Kochi, Kerala**

  Courses : Master of Science in Industrial Fisheries
  Doctor of Philosophy in Industrial Fisheries

- **Andhra University, Visakhapatnam, Andhra Pradesh**

  Courses : Master of Science in Industrial Fisheries
  Doctor of Philosophy in Industrial Fisheries

- **Periyar University, Salem, Tamil Nadu**

  Courses : Bachelor of Science – Zoology (Vocational Industrial Fish and Fisheries)
  Bachelor of Science – Home Science

- **Pondicherry University, Pondicherry (Mahe), Kerala**

  Course : Master of Science-Marine Biology

- **College of Fishery Science-Pantnagar, Uttaranchal**

  Courses : Master in Fishery Science-Fishery Biology
  Bachelor of Fishery Science

- **Maharashtra Animal and Fishery Sciences University, Nagpur, Maharashtra**

  Courses : Bachelor of Fishery Sciences
  Doctor of Philosophy-Veterinary Science

- **College of Fisheries, Kochi, Kerala**

  Courses : Master of Science-Fishery Science
  Bachelor of Science-Fishery Science

2.5 Forestry/Wildlife

What is Forestry?

Forestry involves protection of forests and farming of trees to ensure timber supply and ecological balance. Forester takes care of forest resources by protecting them from fire, pests, disease, encroachment and indiscriminate felling of trees. From time immemorial forest resources have been a source of human sustenance. They are home to the most amazing herbs, medicinal compounds, natural cosmetics, etc. Forestry and wildlife go together since forests serve as home for wildlife.

Forest wealth also contributes significantly to the economy of the country. Specially trained personnel are, therefore, needed to maintain and regenerate the forest cover, forest wealth and resources. This replenishment involves the services of forestry specialists, forestry management experts and forest officers.

Eligibility and Course Areas

Various courses in forestry are available at diploma, graduate, post-graduate and Ph.D. levels. Those with physics, chemistry and biology at the intermediate level can go for B.Sc. Forestry course. Further the master level offers specialisation in subjects like Forest Management, Commercial Forestry, Forest Economics, Wood Science and Technology, Wildlife Science, Veterinary Science, etc. The Indian Institute of Forest Management (IIFM), Nehru Nagar, and Bhopal offers a study programme in Forest Management. There are also opportunities for doing Ph. D. in Forestry at the recognised centers. Those with bachelors degree in related subjects can appear for Indian Forest Service exam conducted by Union Public Service Commission.

Job Prospects and Career Options

Foresters can take-up work either in offices, laboratories or outdoors depending on their field of specialisation. Employment opportunities exists with:

- Governmental, non-governmental organisations interested in preservation of forest resources.
- Corporate having own plantations for timbering.
- Industries that utilise forest resources employ industrial and agricultural consultants.
- Indian Council of Forestry Research and Education (ICFRE) and its affiliated Forestry research institutes such as Forest Research Institute, Dehradun, Institute of Social Forestry and Eco-rehabilitation, Allahabad etc.
- Wildlife Research Institutes in Dehradun, Coimbatore etc.
- Zoological Parks.
- Wildlife ranges.
- Educational sector as tutors.

Career Options

There are various people who work in forest and wildlife conservation. They are :

- **Forester :** The forester is responsible for protecting and regenerating forests, protecting wildlife habitats, checking for and fighting wild fires, landscape management and so on. With experience foresters can graduate to managing public relations, preparing reports and managing budgets.
- **Dendrologists :** Dendrologists specialise in the scientific study of trees and woody plants. Their work involves research on the history, life span, measuring, grading, classifying the varieties of trees and studying ways and means of tree improvement through afforestation.
- **Enthologists :** Ethology is the scientific study of animal behaviour in its natural environment. An ethologist studies and analyses the evolution, behaviour and biological functions of an organism in its natural environment. Enthologists design healthy habitats for animals in zoos, aquariums and laboratories. They also study animal behaviour to enhance our knowledge of human physiology and psychology.
- **Entomologists :** Entomologists specialise in the study and control of diseases caused by insects and pests.
- **Silviculturists :** Silviculture is an aspect of Forestry that refers to the growth of plantations that yield periodic harvests.
- **Forest Range Officers :** Forest ranger officers take care of public forests, sanctuaries, botanical gardens etc. They have conservators, loggers and other junior personnel working with them. Entry into this post through the Indian Forest Service (IFS) examination conducted by the Union Public Service Commission.
- **Zoo curators :** They are responsible for animal welfare in the zoos and also undertake conservation programmes. Zoo curator plays a role in the administration of zoo functions and captive breeding programmes. They review reports made by zookeepers, calculate the budgetary requirements for the zoo and encourage research activity.

Courses

- Certificate Course in Forest Management
- B.Sc. Forestry

- B.Sc. Wildlife
- M.Sc. Forestry
- M.Sc. Wildlife Biology
- M.Sc. Wildlife
- M.Sc. Wood Science and Technology
- Post-graduate Diploma in Forest Management (PGDFM).

Institutes

- Gujarat Agricultural University, Gujarat
- Ch. Charan Singh Haryana Agricultural University Hisar-125004, Haryana
- College of Horticulture Forestry Oachghat, Solan-173230, Himachal Pradesh
- Bisra Agricultural University, Kanke Ranchi, Jharkhand
- University of Agricultural Sciences, Bangalore-560065
- College of Agriculture, Herbal, Bangalore-560024
- Kerala Agricultural University, Vellanikkara Trissur-680654, Kerala
- College of Agriculture Murtizapur Road, Akola-444104, Maharashtra
- Orissa University of Agriculture and Technology Bhubaneshwar-751003
- Punjab Agricultural University, Ludhiana-141004
- Tamil Nadu Agricultural University, Coimbatore-641003 (TN)
- Dolphin Institute of Bio-Medical and Natural Sciences (Affiliated to HNB Garhwal Univ.) Manduwala, Chakarrata Road, Dehra Dun, Uttarakhand
- Bhim Rao Ambedkar University, Agra (Uttar Pradesh)
- N.D. University of Agriculture and Technology, Kumargani, Faizabad-224229 (Uttar Pradesh)
- Manipur University, (Imphal) Manipur
- Wildlife Institute of India, Chandrabani, Dehradun (Uttrakhand)

2.6 Floriculture

What is Floriculture?

Floriculture or flower farming as it is popularly called is a discipline of Horticulture and is the study of growing and marketing flowers and foliage plants. Floriculture includes cultivation of flowering and ornamental plants for sales or for use as raw materials in cosmetic and perfume industry and the pharmaceutical sector. The persons associated with this field are called floriculturists.

The employment opportunities in this field are as varied as the nature of work itself. One can join the field of floriculture as farm/estate managers, plantation experts and supervisors, project co-ordinators, etc. Research and teaching are some other avenues of employment in the field. Marketing of floricultural products for different ventures is emerging as a potential segment of this field. Besides, one can work as a consultant or landscape architect with proper training. One can also work as entrepreneur and offer employment to others. In addition to these careers which involve research and actual growing of crops, floriculture also provides service career opportunities which include such jobs as floral designers, groundskeepers, landscape designers, architects and horticultural therapists. Such jobs require practitioners to deal directly with clients.

Eligibility

Floriculture is not available as a subject at the undergraduate/degree level. Those who wish to join the floriculture stream should enroll for an undergraduate course in Agriculture (i.e., B.Sc. Agriculture degree) after which they can opt for M.Sc. in Horticulture at the post-graduate level. M.Sc. in Horticulture offers specialisations in floriculture, pomology (cultivation of fruits) and olericulture (cultivation of vegetables).

Students graduating in these subjects find jobs with companies as supervisors, farm or estate managers, handling large-scale production of certain varieties of flowers. A combined knowledge of floriculture with management enables one to get managerial or marketing positions with organisations involved in the processing and marketing of flowers and flowering plants. Those with Ph.D. in floriculture, horticulture and related fields can get placed with reputed Research and Development cells of companies and corporate houses.

Course Areas

Courses in floriculture are available as specialisations at the post-graduate and doctoral levels. Besides there are Certificate courses and diploma courses offered by some universities. Most colleges do not conduct a separate course for floriculture or horticulture at the undergraduate level but treat it as part of the academic curriculum of agriculture. The basic eligibility criterion for B.Sc. in Agriculture is 10+2 with sciences including physics and biology. For M.Sc. in Horticulture, one must have B.Sc. degree in Agriculture or a related subject. For Ph. D. the basic eligibility criteria is a Master's degree in Horticulture/ Agriculture or allied sciences and the other qualifications required may vary from one university to another for e.g., some universities require that the candidate must be qualified in Junior Research Fellowship (JRF) conducted by UGC.

Duration

An undergraduate course in agriculture may take anything from three-four years for completion. M.Sc. course is usually a two years course. The duration of Diploma and Certificate courses varies according to the schedule of the universities and institutes offering such courses.

Selection

In most of the states, selection to the graduate course in Agricultural colleges is on the basis of an All India Entrance Examination in biology, physics, chemistry and mathematics of plus-2 levels or on the basis of the entrance examination conducted by the Indian Council for Agricultural Research (ICAR). Besides ICAR, other universities like Jawaharlal Nehru University, Delhi also conduct entrance examinations for the vacancies in their respective institutes.

Job Prospects and Career Options

Qualified floriculture specialists can be employed at various levels both in the government sector as well as the corporate sector. Some of the potential employers are :

- *Floriculture units* – Floriculturists are involved in the propagation and growing of cut flowers, flowering potted plants, foliage plants and bedding plants. They plant, prune, water, fertilise, harvest and ship these plants as well as monitor and manipulate the environment under which they are grown both indoors in green houses and outdoors in field production where the climate is favourable.
- *Outdoor design consultancy firms* – Companies engaged in horticulture landscaping maintenance of gardens.

- City planners and builders and those who carry out maintenance at various sites employ floriculturists and horticulturists.
- *Educational institutions offering related courses* – Floriculturists may teach at the college and university level. Floriculturists in college teaching follow the typical career path from instructor to assistant professor to associate professor to full professor.
- *Cosmetics and perfume industry* – Value addition in the form of extraction of pigments, essential oils, pharmaceutical and nutraceuticals compounds has emerged as one of the frontline avenues in floriculture and it is in this connection that floriculturists are employed in perfume industry.
- *Self-employment* – You can set up your own venture, growing flowers for the domestic or export market, growing ornamental plants, running nurseries or providing gardening and landscaping advisory services.

Remuneration

Salaries depend on the nature of work one is involved in while gardeners and labourers may get paid anything between ₹ 4,000 to 8,000 per month. Freelance workers, designers and consultants may negotiate their pay packets depending on the place, nature of work and hours of work. As this industry depends on lifestyle and purchasing power of the public in general and on the availability of raw materials and finished products remunerations and profits may vary. Researchers and academicians are paid as per the government norms.

Courses

- Certificate Course in Floriculture
- Diploma in Commercial Floriculture
- M.Sc. Floriculture and Landscaping

Useful Contacts

- Agricultural and Processed Food Products Export Development Authority (APEDA),

  Ministry of Commerce, Government of India

  NCUI Building, 3, Siri Institutional Area, August Kranti Marg, New Delhi – 110 016

  Phone: 91-11-26513204, 26514572, 26534186

  Fax: 91-11-26526187

  Website: www.apeda.com

- Indian Council of Agricultural Research (ICAR)
  Krishi Bhavan, Dr Rajendra Prasad Road, New Delhi – 110 001
  Website: www.icar.org.in

2.7 Horticulture

What is Horticulture?

Horticulture is a miniature version of agriculture. While agriculture deals with cultivation on a large scale, Horticulture is gardening done on a smaller scale. The name 'horticulture' is derived from the Latin terms *'hortus'* (garden) and *'cultura'* (cultivation) which means 'garden cultivation'. Horticulture is the science and art of gardening which is associated with the cultivation of fruits, vegetables, flowers, spices, ornamental plants. Horticulture deals with plant propagation and cultivation, crop production, preparation of soil, plant breeding and genetic engineering, plant biochemistry and plant physiology. This branch of agriculture supplies food products to man, feed to animals and many raw materials of plant origin to numerous industries.

Horticulture involves five major branches of study;

- **Floriculture :** It is the study of growing and marketing flowers and foliage plants, persons working in this field are called floriculturists.
- **Landscaping :** This includes design, construction and maintenance of landscapes.
- **Olericulture :** This is the study of the production and marketing of vegetables. Those who work in this field are called olericulturists.
- **Pomology :** The study of the production and marketing of fruits is called pomology and those who work in this field are called pomologists.
- **Post-harvest Physiology :** Post-harvest physiology includes areas of maintaining quality and preventing spoilage of horticultural crops.

Eligibility

Entry to this field starts from undergraduate level. Candidates who have passed 10+2 in Science stream (Class XII) with physics, chemistry and mathematics/biology/agriculture as the subjects can opt for Bachelor's degree in Horticulture as a separate discipline or as a subject of B.Sc. Agriculture Science. The same basic qualification is required for doing diploma programme. After doing B.Sc. in Horticulture one can continue his/her further study in the field by doing M.Sc. in Horticulture. Post-graduates in Horticulture are eligible for M.Phil.

For admission to Ph.D. programme different agricultural universities exercise different modes of admission. Most of the State Agriculture Universities and ICAR Institutes conduct entrance examinations for Ph.D. admissions.

Course Areas

Horticulture courses include subject areas of plant propagation, plant materials, tissue culture, crop production, post-harvest handling, plant breeding, pollination management, crop nutrition, entomology, plant pathology, economics and business.

Job Prospects

Horticulturists can enter into various fields in industry, government or educational institutions or private concerns. They can work in a wide range of areas in agribusiness, arboriculture (planting and care of woody plants), botanical gardens, conservation, crop management, floral design, food chemistry, food and vegetable production, garden centers, greenhouses, ground management, landscape construction and management, nurseries, management and sales, marketing/public relations, research and development, teaching/instruction, technical writing and publishing. Horticulture institutes and colleges, vegetable farms, fruit orchards etc., always look for skilled horticulturists. Those in government sector are responsible for the maintenance of parks, public gardens and official lawns.

Career Options

Both public and private sectors offer employment to qualified and trained horticulturists with attractive remuneration. In government sector, one can work as Horticulture Inspector, Fruit and Vegetable Inspector, Training Assistant in Krishi Vigyan Kendra (KVK), District Horticulture Officer/District Agriculture Officer, Marketing Inspector, Farm Supervisor, Section Officer and Agriculture Inspector. Option of a career as Lecturer and Assistant Professor, Associate Professor in Agriculture Universities and colleges or Technical Assistant/Technical Officer in Agriculture Universities can also be accessed. One can also work as Agriculture Development Officer or can become Scientist. Self-employment option is available as Horticulture Consultant or

Horticulture Therapist, Floral decorator/florist shop, Fruit/Vegetable/Flower grower etc. One can choose to be a horticulture entrepreneur also by setting up a horticulture farm for growing fruits, vegetables or flowers or a horticulture nursery for nursery production of horticultural plants. Horticultural professionals can get in Civil Services sector, too, through competitive examinations.

Horticultural Therapy is an exciting and challenging field. Horticultural therapists often work in conjunction or liaison with other professionals like psychologists, occupational therapists, physicians and social workers. Horticultural therapists treat those who have physical disabilities, mental health problems and learning difficulties, those recovering from major injuries or illness and elderly people. Programmes can also be developed for the rehabilitation of offenders or those suffering from drug or alcohol abuse. With more and more people opting for naturopathic treatment of diseases, growing of medicinal plants has become significant which provide attractive business opportunity to horticultural nursery/gardens.

Remuneration

Salaries for horticulturists depend on the individual's level of education/area of specialisation, the geographic location of employment and whether one is employed in private or public sector. The salary of horticulture professionals in private sector is more as compared to public sector. At the fresher level, the salary in horticulture may range from ₹ 8,000 to ₹ 10,000 per month. After two to three years of experience in the field, one can earn up to ₹ 20,000 per month. The monthly remuneration of an Assistant Horticulture Inspector (appointed by respective state or Central government) starts from ₹ 7,000 and goes up to ₹ 17,000 depending upon experience and total years of service. District Horticulture Officers get monthly salary more than ₹ 25,000. The salary of Horticulturists and scientists varies between ₹ 18,000 and 40,000. There are more benefits to a career in horticulture than salary.

Courses

- B.Sc. Horticulture
- M.Sc. Horticulture
- Post-graduate Diploma in Horticulture
- Ph. D. Horticulture

Top Colleges in Horticulture in India

- **Yashwantrao Chavan Maharashtra Open University, Nashik, Maharashtra**

  Course : Bachelor of Science (Horticulture)

- **Visva-Santiniketan, West Bengal**

  Course : Master of Science (Agriculture)-Horticulture
- **Sikkim University, Gangtok, Sikkim**

  Course : Bachelor of Science and Master of Science in Floriculture and Horticulture Management (Integrated)
- **Swami Keshwanand Rajasthan Agriculture University, Bikaner, Rajasthan**

  Course : Doctor of Philosophy (Agriculture) - Horticulture
- **Sam Higinbotom Institute of Agriculture, Allahabad, Uttar Pradesh**

  Courses : Master of Science-Horticulture (Fruit Production and Post Harvest Technology)

  Master of Science –Horticulture (Floriculture and Land Scaping)

Other Institutes of Horticulture

- College of Horticulture, Chickmagalur, Karnataka
- Carey Institute of Horticulture, Kolkata, West Bengal
- College of Agriculture, Faculty of Agriculture, Rajendranagar, Hyderabad-500030 (AP)
- Gujarat Agricultural University, Gujarat
- Dr. Yashwant Singh Parmar University of Horticulture and Forestry, Solan-Nauni-173230
- College of Agriculture, Hebbal, Bangalore-560024
- College of Agriculture, Murtizapur Road, Krishnagar, Akola-444104
- Faculty of Horticulture, Tamil Nadu Agricultural University, Coimbatore-640003
- Bhim Rao Ambedkar University, Agra
- College of Agriculture, Pune-411005

2.8 Sericulture

Meaning of the word 'Sericulture'

The word 'Sericulture' is derived from the Greek word '*Sericos*' meaning 'Silk' and the English word '*Culture*' meaning 'Rearing'. Sericulture is

the art and technology of raising silk worms for production of raw silk yarn. This agro-based industry playing an eminent role in the rural economy of India is not limited to just worms but includes all activities related to them like mulberry cultivation and even post-cocoon technology. It requires both technical know-how as well as specialisation.

What is Sericulture?

Sericulture refers to the conscious mass-scale rearing of silk producing organisms to obtain silk. Mulberry Sericulture involves the cultivation of mulberry to produce leaf rearing of silkworm to convert to the cocoon, reeling of the cocoon to obtain silk yarn and weaving to convert the yarn to Fabric. The industry comprises reeling, silk preparatory and weaving, silk knitting, silk wet and processing consisting of degumming, dyeing, printing and finishing besides garment manufacturing.

Eligibility

To become sericulture graduate one has to pass four years degree from Sericulture college of state agricultural universities or Silk institutes of various Universities. There are two types of degree, B.Sc. (Sericulture) and B.Sc. Silk Technology (Sericulture). For a course leading to a degree in Sericulture, the basic qualification required for admission is HSC (10+2) with biology and chemistry. There are post-graduate courses too for which a basic degree in sericulture is essential. The course duration for thedegree course is four years while that for post graduation is two years.

Job Prospects and Career Options

Sericulture in recent times has begun to offer a wide variety of employment and entrepreneurship options. Most importantly, every state in India has a sericulture department to focus on rearing of silk worms, production of fiber and marketing. Sericulture offers career opportunity in government research centers, silk boards, academic fields, sericulture units, agriculture sector banks, etc. One can get jobs in central government agencies like Central Silk Board/Silk Export Promotion Council/FAO/NABARD, Krishi Vigyan Kendra, etc. Candidates with M.Sc. sericulture can apply for the post of lecturer, professor and lab assistant. Sericulturists can find employment as officers, managers in the agricultural loan sector of nationalised as well as private banks.They can work as a manager in Sericulture Farm, Grainage, Silk Reeling (Filature), Silk weaving mill, Dyeing, Printing and Spinning mill and in various Central government sponsored schemes like SGSY, Welfare Department Scheme run by NGOs like Pradan, Vikash Bharati, etc. Sericulturists alsocan start an enterprise of their own.

Remuneration

Professionals who undergo proper training can earn starting salaries as high as ₹ 15,000 per month in public sector and even higher in private sector and NGOs. This grows in accordance with the experience gained. Entrepreneurs, especially those who set up business as exporters of silk products can look forward to excellent gains.

Courses

- B.Sc. Sericulture
- Diploma in Sericulture Technology and Management (DSTM)
- M.Sc. Sericulture
- Ph.D. Sericulture

Useful Contacts

- **Central Silk Board**

  CSB Complex, BTM Layout, Madivala,

  Hosur Road, Bangalore-560 068

  Karnataka

  Phone: +91-80-26282699

  Fax: +91-80-26681511
- **Central Sericultural Research and Training Institute**

  Central Silk Board, Manandawadi Road,

  Srirampura, Mysore-570 008
- **Commissioner of Sericulture**

  Government of Andhra Pradesh

  Road No. 72, Prashasan Nagar

  Adjacent to water Tank,

  Jubilee Hills

  Hyderabad-500 033, Andhra Pradesh

  Phone: 040-23541547

  Fax: 040-23541543

- **Director of Sericulture and Weaving**

  Govt. of Meghalaya, 3rd Sectt. (Nongkrak Buillding)

  2nd Phase, 2nd Floor

  Lower Lachumiere, Shillong-793 001

  Phone: 0364-2223279

  Fax: 0364-22535759

- **Director of Sericulture**

  Govt. of Assam, Near Research Gate

  P.O. Khanapara, Guwahati-781 022

  Assam

  Fax: 0361 2262922

3

ARTS/SCIENCE/COMMERCE

3.1 Anthropology

The Meaning of the term 'Anthropology'

The term 'anthropology' has been derived from two Greeks words namely *'anthropos'* which means human and *'logos'* means study. Thus, anthropology is the study of human beings in its absoluteness. Anthropology is a science which studies the origin and physical, social and cultural development and behaviour of mankind especially various human cultures, human civilisations, their traditions and customs. It not only studies the biological evolution of human beings and the socio-cultural linguistic development of humans but also their physical and cultural diversity at different ages, places and environments. Anthropology is about people, their relationships and how they live together as members of society. It contributes to the understanding and explanation of socio-cultural behaviour.

The Role of Anthropologists

Anthropologists study human societies worldwide with reference to kinship, political organisation, religion, legal system, economy, language, education, healthcare and art. In other words, they study the people's lifestyle or culture. Thus, social problems like birth control, labor unrest, juvenile delinquency, mortality rate can be dealt with the help of information gathered from anthropological study of human relics to know the biological and cultural history of the human species over the last four million years.

To know the origin and physical, cultural and social development of human beings, anthropologists as social scientists study the language, traditions, beliefs, possessions and values of people in various parts of the world and formulate hypotheses to explain their research and findings. They examine, analyse, report on and compare different cultures and how they grow, develop and interact. Anthropology is best suited for candidates who have deep interest in history and who love to travel to various places of historic importance.

The Different Branches of Anthropology

There are several branches of anthropology that deals with various aspects of human development. These include the following :

- **Physical or Biological Anthropology :** This branch deals with the biological evolution of human beings and linkage of humans with their primate ancestors. Differences between various races, human genetics and adaptations to various climatic conditions also come under this branch. Researchers in this field can study human evolution, physical variations between modern human populations, forensic anthropology, osteology and a variety of related topics.
- **Socio-cultural Anthropology :** This branch deals with the socio-cultural developments of human race from their origin. It involves the study of human cultures and societies and it encompasses topics like linguistics, studies of minority populations, studies of social norms and studies of specific types of social groups. Different methods of forming communities, difference in culture of various clans, cross-cultural communication and such other topics form the subject of study under this branch. Cultural anthropologists are particularly well-suited to work in professions involving people such as teaching, law, medicine, social work and journalism.
- **Pre-historic Anthropology :** This branch can also be called archaeology as it deals with bones, relics and artifacts dug-up and tries to reconstruct the chronological sequence of history on the basis of these findings. It focusses on the reconstruction of early history and pre-historic social customs. Anthropologists with specialisation in pre-historic anthropology are the most sought after people by museums, art houses, archaeological organisations and archives where they work as historians , museum curators etc.
- **Applied Anthropology :** Social problems like birth control, labour unrest, juvenile delinquency, mortality rate are dealt with the help of information gathered from other fields. This is the main job of anthropology that studies human through the languages that they use. Linguistic anthropology deals with subjects such as socio-linguistics. The origin and evolution of

all written as well as unwritten languages and dialects are dealt with under this branch of anthropology. Linguistic anthropologists work as linguists.

Eligibility and Course Areas

To be a professional anthropologist, one has to qualify B.Sc. in Anthropology. The minimum qualification for B.Sc. in Anthropology is 10+2 passed with Science subjects. For better career prospects one can pursue M.Sc in Anthropology for which the minimum qualification is B.Sc. in the concerned subject and further one can take up M.Phil and Ph.D. in anthropology. Some universities or colleges also offer B.A. and M.A. courses in Anthropology respectively into which, a 10+2 passed student with social science can be enrolled. B.A./B.Sc. and M.A./M.Sc. courses in Anthropology are offered by almost all major universities in India. These include Universities of Kolkata, Delhi, Allahabad, Vidyasagar, Utkal, Dibrugarh, Punjab etc.

Personal Attributes

An anthropologist needs to be prepared for physical hard work (travelling, excavating, etc.). He or she should also be open-minded and unbiased. This quality is of utmost importance as a biased person will not be able to derive the right conclusions from his or her research study. An anthropologist will be required to write down his or her findings; so some skill in the written language is also necessary. Anthropologists should be able to communicate well, develop and maintain good interpersonal relations with the people from all communities and be patient and tactful especially when interviewing people and gathering primary information.

Job prospects

Being the study of mankind as a whole, Anthropology is a very interesting subject. It opens many doors of knowledge to the biological, socio-cultural, pre-historic and every other aspect of human development. The job prospects for students of Anthropology are vast within India as well as abroad. Anthropology as a subject has far better scope in countries in the west, where they are hired in the field of medicine, law, business and other professional institutions. They are absorbed in community development programmes and public service programmes as well.

Anthropology as a subject offers great career prospects for those students who want to pursue it at a higher level. There are many fields where anthropologists can find development. The three main areas of employment are in teaching, research and working in museums. If one is planning on an academic career, then one can either find academic jobs at various universities and institutes or do research work. The scope for being a research scholar always remains open. Research students of anthropology can easily find jobs in various international development and non-governmental organisations. Anthropological Survey of India is foremost among such organisations which employ anthropologists for research jobs. Anthropologists are involved extensively with field work and research. The field work can be both physically and mentally exhaustive and involve working in locations with low comfort levels.

The demand for curators by museums gives another opening for anthropologists. They are employed by museums, art galleries, libraries and archives. Other than these jobs one can opt for jobs with NGOs working in underdeveloped areas. Anthropologists can be hired by organisations like the UNESCO, UNICEF and WHO. Many organisations like the ICMR (Indian Council of Medical Research) and the Police Department also offer employment to anthropologists for the purpose of crime detection. Other than such jobs, one can also find employment in the Human Resource Development sector of corporate houses, as anthropologists can balance the relation between society and industry. The scope for employment is varied. One can find employment as archaeologists, curators, linguists, social workers, tour guides as well as in publishing houses, social service organisations, forensic science and criminal investigations departments.

Remuneration

Since the nature of job prospects is very diverse, the salary can vary tremendously. Those employed in public sector research institutions and departments have pay packages as per the terms and conditions of the government. For non-research based jobs, the pay is generally good. Museums and libraries pay a high salary for curators. Even NGOs pay quite well. The focus for most anthropologists is more on their work rather than money. Those in international development agencies have even higher remuneration, perks and other benefits. Corporate houses and industries offer various fringe benefits other than salaries and allowances. Professors and teachers in academic institutions also have good pay packages.

Though, initially pay package in this field is not as lucrative as other hot professions, there is a tremendous amount of satisfaction associated with this profession. One can expect a starting salary somewhere around ₹ 8,000 – 12,000 per month. There also exists a stiff competition among researchers working in this field of anthropology for grant of money from national and international funding agencies. Hence, aspirants who wish to carry out research in anthropology must be well prepared. Many foreign institutions support anthropological research in India as well.

Institutes

- **Amity Institute of Anthropology**
  Noida, Uttar Pradesh
- **Andhra University College of Arts and Commerce**
  Visakhapatnam, Andhra Pradesh
- **Bangabasi College, Kolkata**
  West Bengal
- **D.M. College of Science**
  Imphal, Manipur
- **Dharnidhar Autonomous College**
  Keonjhar, Orissa
- **Dibrugarh Hanumanbux Surajmal Kanoi College (DHSK)**
  Dibrugarh, Assam
- **Dibrugarh University**
  Dibrugarh, Assam
- **Guwahati University (GU)**
  Guwahati, Assam
- **Kannur University**
  Kannur, Kerala
- **Manipur University**
  Imphal, Manipur
- **North Eastern Hill University**
  Shillong, Meghalaya

3.2 Botany

What is Botany?

Botany is a branch of biological science which deals with the study of plants. Scientific disciplines such as agricultural sciences and forestry are based on the basic science of botany. Botany studies the structure, growth, reproduction, metabolism, development, diseases and chemical properties and evolutionary relationships between different groups of plants. It encompasses the study of more than three hundred thousand

species ranging from ground-hugging mosses to giant redwood trees.

Traditionally, the concept 'plant' includes a whole range of living organisms from bacteria, algae, fungi, mosses, ferns, gymnosperms and flowering plants. In other words, plants include a large group ranging from the smallest bacteria to the largest sequoia tree. Plants play a prominent role in our day to day life, providing us with the basic necessities such as food, clothing and shelter, medicine, fibers and building materials; improving environmental condition by synthesising carbon dioxide and giving out oxygen and create aesthetic environment.

The Role of Botanists

A person qualified in botany is called a Botanist. Botanists play an important role in modern science and industry. Their work affects agriculture, agronomy (soil and crop science), conservation, forestry and horticulture. In general, botanists study the development and life processes of plants. In a broader sense, botanist is one who study and research on various aspects of the plant kingdom such as origin and development of various plant species, taxonomic classification, plant physiology, plant pathology, plant fossils, mycology (study of fungi) and so on. Overall, botanists study the behaviour of plants from the chromosome level to the reproduction process. Botanical studies have helped in the development of many medicines and drugs which are extracted from plants and are really helpful to fight many diseases. It also help in the production of plants which provide natural raw materials like cotton, rubber, paper, silk, vegetable oils etc.

Eligibility

Botany is one of the preferred choices of study among the science students. But it is necessary that the student who learns botany has interest in plants and enjoy working with them. Minimum requirement for a career as botanist is a bachelor's degree. However, for higher degrees you require to specialise in one of the many areas of botany.

Courses

Courses are offered at bachelor level, master level and doctoral level. For bachelor course, the basic requirement is 10+2 science. After graduation, one can go for post-graduation and doctoral degree. Bachelor degree is of three years and post-graduate degree is of two years duration. You need to study for an additional two to three years to obtain a doctoral degree. After doctoral degree, one can work at the administrative level or teach in institutes or do research work. In this field, a botany student can choose from many specialisations according to the area of interest. Each area of specialisation concentrates on a particular subject necessary to know about the plant.

Personal Attributes

Main attribute required is a love for outdoors. Botanists must have clear and concise verbal and written communication skills, a high-level of curiosity about the world around them, be creative in solving problems and yet have a good understanding of the scientific methods and the rigors of scientific research. They should be detail-oriented in their work. Botanists must have good interpersonal skills, mental stamina to work long hours. The ability to work with microscopes is important as most of their work is in laboratory. Computer skills are also essential to be in this scientific world. To keep up with new findings in plant science, botanists must continue to study throughout their careers.

Job Prospects

Career in Botany can be highly rewarding for those, who are allured with the aesthetic beauty of nature and flora. Botany as a field of plant science offers various specialties as well as career openings from which you can choose from, for both male and female. Various career fields in botany are that of Plant Taxonomists, Ethnobotanists, Pathologists, Paleobotanists, Palynologists, Plant Cytologists, Plant Geneticists, Plant Ecologists, Plant Scientists and Weed Scientists.

Job prospects for botanists are generally good. Challenging positions will be available for well-trained botanists. Options are not only confined to India; numerous opportunities are also available abroad. Careers in botany offer individual freedom varied work, pleasant surroundings, inspiring co-workers and travel opportunities. If you like nature and being outdoors, you might enjoy a career as botanist. Job opportunities usually depend on educational training and experience. Candidates with advanced qualifications can pursue either an academic career in institutions as lecturers and professors or a scientific career in various scientific positions such as Plant Scientists, Weed Scientists, etc.

Major Employers

The major employers of plant biologists are educational institutions, central and state agencies and industries. Almost all colleges and universities offer courses in plant science and there are faculty positions for botanists who have different specialties. In addition, educational institutions employ botanists as researchers and as administrators. Plant scientists also work in the state departments, Botanical Survey of India, and environmental protection agency, drug companies, oil industry, chemical industry, lumber and paper companies, genetic research industry, botanical gardens, nurseries, fruit growers, food companies, archaeological museums and fermentation industries hire men and women trained in botany. The demand for botanists is increasing in areas such as medical plant research, plant diseases, plant breeding and plant genetics. Some botanists work in administration and marketing for biological supply houses, seed companies, biotechnology firms and pharmaceutical manufacturers. There are few others who work as scientific writers, illustrators and photographers.

Entry to Botanical Survey of India, and other government departments is through UPSC exams. The notification of various posts is known through the leading newspapers and employments news.

Areas of Specialisations

Various specialisation as botanists are that of :

- **Plant taxonomists :** Plant taxonomy involves the identification and classification of plants. Plant taxonomists are botanists who work to identify, describe, classify and name plant species. Plant taxonomists identify new plant species previously unknown to the field. They also produce new source of plant genes. Most taxonomists are engaged in field work, which involves arduous physical activity as well as environments usually work in herbariums, botanical gardens and research institutes.
- **Plant ecologists :** Plant ecologists are botanists who work to understand the relationship between plant and the world in which they live. In other words, ecologists study the connection between plant and the world in which they live. In other words, ecologists study the connection between plants, animals and their physical environment. They examine the environmental factors such as rainfall, population, pollutants, temperature and altitude that regulate plant growth. In some cases, ecologists may be exposed to unsafe or unhealthy working conditions. For example, when plant materials have to be studied after an environmental disaster, the condition in which they have to work may not be safe or healthy. Plant ecologists are employed by government regulatory agencies and departments as well as by colleges and universities. Some may also find work with non-profit environmental organisations.
- **Plant morphologists :** Plant morphologists study the manner in which cells are arranged to give each plant its form. To determine the cellular arrangement of plant they study how different plants

transport and conduct food and water. They work generally in research laboratories.

- **Plant cytologists :** Botanists who study plant cells are known as cytologists. They study the structure, function and life history of plant cells. Cytologists study minute particles of plant tissue with the help of microscopes. They are concerned with the physical arrangement of DNA in particular species of plants. They also study the cells concerned with reproduction as well as the means by which chromosomes divide or unite. Cytologists can find employment in research laboratories and pharmaceutical industry.
- **Plant physiologists :** A plant physiologists study the internal functions and processes of plants. Plant processes include growth, respiration, cultivation, excretion, reproduction and various other functions. They develop an understanding of the biological, chemical and physical processes that are basic to plant life, so that they can regulate and control plant growth. Plant physiologists play an important role in agriculture where drought-resistance, crop production, nutritional value, quality of food crops, germination as well as the storage of seed and the production of fruit are studied. Physiologists are mainly engaged in field work as well as laboratory work.
- **Ethnobotanists :** Ethnobotany is the study of the relationship between plants and people. 'Ethno' is the study of people and 'botany' is the study of plants. Ethnobotanists study relationships between plants and human culture in a search for better medicines and more efficient food production. Ethnobotanists study the different ways in which people make use of plants and their applications for potential economic, medicinal or other benefits to humanity. Ethnobotanists develop new products for food, herbal and pharmaceutical companies and sometimes assist in managing biological resources. Ethnobotanists mainly hold research positions for companies in the pharmaceutical, cosmetic and alternative health product industries as well as universities and government health agencies.
- **Mycologists :** Mycologists study fungi and apply their findings to medicine, agriculture and industry. Fungi often live in symbiosis with plants and play an important role in the ecology of the environment. They cause decay in food and other natural products and they are also important in the chemical and pharmaceutical industries. Mycologists may spend a lot of time

out in the field collecting specimens and performing research in laboratories.

- **Plant geneticists :** Plant geneticists are botanists who study plant heredity and plant variation. Plant geneticists study the origin and development of inherited traits. Plant geneticists are employed by both government and private forestry organisations to work on programs for the improvement of trees for cultivation.
- **Palynologists :** Palynology is a highly specialised branch of systematic science and it involves the identification of plant species through analysing the pollen with light and electron microscopes. Palynology is the study of fossil and living-pollen, spores, similar plant structures etc. A palynologist's service is also used in forensic medicine and criminology because it is possible to identify pollen on clothes, shoes and the body.

Remuneration

A career in botany is very rewarding. Botanist's salary varies depending on the field one chooses, the level of education and experience, the responsibilities of the position and the geographical location. Teachers, researchers can expect a starting salary of ₹ 12,000 to 18,000 per month. In the government service the pay scale ranges from ₹ 15,000 to 30,000.

Institutes

- **MJRP Ambassy College for Girls, Jaipur**
  Ram Nagar Ext., New Sanganer Road
  Sodala, Jaipur-302019
- **Karim City College, Jamshedpur**
  Sakchi, Jamshedpur-831001
- **Kirori Mal College, New Delhi**
  University of Delhi, North Campus, New Delhi-110007
- **Agra College, Agra**
  M.G. Road, Agra, UP
- **DAV College, Ambala**
  Ambala City, Ambala-134003, Haryana
- **Ayya Nadar Janaki Ammal College, Sivakasi**
  Sivakasi-626124, Tamil Nadu
- **St. Mary's College, Wayanad**
  Sulthan Bathery, Wayanad-673592, Kerala

- **Banaras Hindu University: Faculty of Science,**
  Varanasi-221005
- **Manipal University Jaipur, Jaipur**
  Vatika Infotech City, Jaipur-Ajmer Expressway
  Post Thikaria, Jaipur-320026
- **Mumtaz Degree and PG College, Hyderabad**
  Malakpet, B. Block, Hyderabad-500036

3.3 Chemistry

What is Chemistry?

Chemistry is the study of the nature, properties and composition of matter and how these undergo changes; it is referred to as the Central Science. Chemistry is the science about basic structure of substances, i.e., what they are made of, how they interact and what role they play in living things. Those working in this field are usually called chemists. These people study the numerous compositions of matter and its related properties. Chemists search for new information about matter and the ways this information can be applied.

Importance of Chemistry

It is vital to every aspect of one's life. Everything you hear, see, smell, taste and touch involves chemistry and chemicals (matter). Chemistry plays a great role even in the air you breathe, the food you eat and the clothes you wear. Chemistry is all round us. There is a saying that:

the better we know chemistry, the better we know the world'.

Various Specialisations

There are various branches or specialisations in chemistry. Usually, most of the chemists specialise in more than one area depending on the specialisation they have chosen. Some of the specialisations are Agrochemistry, Analytical chemistry, Astrochemistry, Biochemistry, Chemical engineering, Environmental chemistry, Food chemistry, Inorganic chemistry, Organic chemistry, Nuclear chemistry, and Physical chemistry. Agrochemistry or agricultural chemistry deals with the application of chemistry for agricultural production of chemistry for agricultural production, food processing and environmental remediation as a result of agriculture. Analytical chemistry is the branch of chemistry involved with studying the properties of materials or developing tools to analyse materials. Astrochemistry is the study of the composition and reactions of the chemical elements and molecules found in the stars and in space. Biochemistry is the branch of chemistry concerned with the chemical reactions that occur inside living organisms. Chemical engineering involves the practical application of chemistry to solve problems. Environmental chemistry is the chemistry associated with soil, air and water and of human impact on natural systems. Inorganic chemistry is the branch of chemistry that deals with the structure and interactions between inorganic compounds, i.e., compounds that aren't based in carbon-hydrogen bonds. Organic chemistry is a branch of chemistry that deals with the chemistry of carbon and living things. Nuclear chemistry is the branch of chemistry associated with nuclear reactions and isotopes. Physical chemistry is the branch of chemistry that applies physics to the study of chemistry. Examples of physical chemistry are Quantum mechanics and thermodynamics.

Eligibility

A bachelor's degree in chemistry is the primary requirement for any career in this field. Bachelor's degree is of three years. For bachelor's degree, one must have completed 10+2 with science stream. After bachelor's course in Chemistry or chemical engineering one can opt for master's program. In this one can choose specialisations. Master's degree is of two years duration. There is option for further advancement in the subject field, i.e., to go for Ph.D. degree is required for teaching positions in universities and to do research in related areas.

Personal Attributes

Aspirants must have logical thinking capacity, creativity, observation skills, computing and most essentially, analytical and numerical skills. As they are required to communicate their ideas, interpersonal skills and communication skills along with team management skills is essential. Accuracy, eye for detail and time management skills are other requisites.

Job Prospects and Career Options

There are a wide variety of Chemistry careers to choose from – teaching to research and development. The field of chemistry is wide and diverse. However, your employment options depend on how far you have taken your education. With undergraduate degree one can enter into roles such as Product Testing or Analysis, Research Assistant and Laboratory Co-ordinator. Those with advanced degree, post-graduation and Ph. D. enter into research fields, managerial level and teaching posts.

Some of the options available for chemistry graduates are that of Chemist, Research Scientist, Analytical Chemist, Technical Officer, Product Development Chemist, Process Development Scientist, Quality Control Scientist, Materials Analytical Chemist, Patent Agent, Laboratory Technician/Chemist, Pharmaceutical Development and/ or Sales, Product Testing and Analysis.

Chemistry graduates are employed by those in industrial sector, government departments, health sector, research institutes, laboratories and academia. Chemists can get jobs in pharmaceutical companies, petroleum companies, chemical industries, perfume industries, research organisations like ISRO, DRDO, Bhabha Atomic ResearchCentre, etc.

After clearing NET examination they can opt for teaching positions in top universities and colleges. In forensic science field, chemists work in law enforcement organisations in the analysis of crime scene evidence.

Material chemists are employed by companies involved in polymers/plastics, semiconductors, ceramics, glasses, alloys and new generation composite materials. Newspapers and magazines employ science/technical writers to present scientific topics at an understandable level for the general public. Many chemists are employed in government civilian and military research laboratories. Pharmaceutical companies employ chemists for development of products as well as in sales department to explain their products to pharmacies and physicians. Yet, another option for chemistry graduates is that of patent lawyers or agents, those professionals who have grounding in science and are trained in specialist areas of law can act in this position.

Remuneration

In this field, salary is according to the job title, skills, education and the employer. The average starting salary fora chemist is around ₹ 7,000.A research chemist can earn between ₹ 10,000 – 40,000 per month.That of lecturers is much more lucrative.

Courses

- B. Sc. Biochemistry
- B. Sc. Chemistry
- B. Sc. Chemistry (Hons)
- B. Sc. Industrial Chemistry
- M.Sc. Applied Biochemistry
- M.Sc. Biochemistry
- M.Sc. Biochemistry (Integrated)
- M.Sc. Chemistry
- M.Sc. Chemistry (Hons)

- M.Sc. Medical Biochemistry
- M.Sc. Organic Chemistry
- M.Sc. Pharmaceutical Chemistry
- M.Sc. Soil Science and Agricultural Biochemistry
- B. Tech. Textile Chemistry
- M. Tech. Textile Chemistry
- M.D. Biochemistry
- M.Phil. Biochemistry
- Ph.D. Biochemistry
- Ph.D. Chemistry
- Advance Diploma in Technical and Analytical Chemistry (ADTAC)
- Post-graduate Diploma in Applied Biochemistry
- Post-graduate Diploma in Biochemistry

Institutes

- **Dr. Ambedkar University (Agra University)**
  Agra, Uttar Pradesh
  Course : B.Sc (Hons) Chemistry
- **Deen Dayal Upadhayaya College**
  New Delhi
  Course : B.Sc. (Hons.) Chemistry
- **Sam Higginbotom Institute of Agriculture**
  Allahabad, Uttar Pradesh
  Course : B.Sc. (Hons.) Biochemistry and Biochemical Technology
  B.Sc. (Hons.) Biotechnology
- **Deen Dayal Upadhayaya Gorakhpur University**
  Uttar Pradesh
  Course : B.Sc. (Hons.) Chemistry
- **Sathaye College, Mumbai, Maharashtra**
  Course : Bachelor of Science in Chemistry
- **Shree M.S. Chauhan Mahavidyalaya,**
  Mainpuri, Uttar Pradesh
  Bachelor of Science (Chemistry)
- **Shivpati P.G. College**
  Navgarh, Uttar Pradesh
  Course : Bachelor of Science (Chemistry)

- **Dr Hari Singh Gaur University**
  Sagar, Madhya Pradesh
  Course : M.Sc. Chemistry
- **Bangalore University, Bangalore, Karnataka**
  Course : M.Sc. Chemistry
  M.Sc. Biochemistry
- **Bharathidasan University, Tiruchchirappalli, Tamil Nadu**
  Course : M.Sc. Chemistry
  M.Sc. Biochemistry
- **Allahabad University, Allahabad, Uttar Pradesh**
  Course : M.Sc. Chemistry
  M.Sc. Biochemistry
- **Sam Higginbotom Institute of Agriculture**
  Allahabad, Uttar Pradesh
  Course : M.Sc. Clothing and Textiles
  M.Sc. Soil Science and Agricultural Chemistry
- **AVK Institute of Higher Learning, Bangalore, Karnataka**
  Course : M.Sc. Chemistry

3.4 Economics

What is an Economics?

An Economics is the branch of social science that deals with the study of production, distribution and consumption of goods and services. In other words, it is the study of how the forces of supply and demand allocate scarce resources. The term economics comes from the Greek words ***'oikos'*** (house) and ***'nomos'*** (custom or law), hence rules of the house (hold). Economics play an important role in all aspects of our life whether it is social, political or economic. It is based on this pillar that the progress of a country stands.

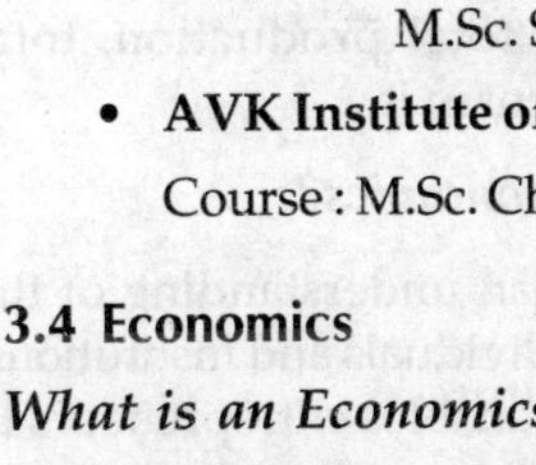

Economics is an integral part of a well-rounded liberal arts education. It occupies a strategic place among various disciplines of social sciences and is considered as a field that often overlaps with the fields of political science, sociology, geography, history and psychology. As the economic way of thinking is so useful in making sense of the world around us, economics has sometimes been called the 'queen of social science'. Economic analysis is applied throughout society, in business, finance and government, crime, education, the family, health, law, politics, religion, social institutions, war and science.

What does Economics Study about?

Economics is the study of how individuals and societies choose to employ scarce resources. It deals with what goods and services will be produced, how they will be produced and how they will be distributed among the members of the society. Economics has two branches: micro-economics and macro-economics. Micro-economics studies the behavior of specific sectors of the economy such as companies, industries or households. Micro-economics explains how 'demand' and 'supply' affect prices, wages, rentals and interest rates. Its primary concern is to help consumers and investors to make their lives better by increasing their earnings and satisfying their needs despite limited resources. Macro-economics studies a nation or the world's economy as a whole, using data about inflation, unemployment and industrial production to understand the past and predict the future. In macro-economics, we study the economic behaviour of the large aggregates such as the overall conditions of the economy in relation to total production, total consumption, total saving and total investment in it.

What is the Usefulness of the Study of Economics?

The study of economics helps to formulate an understanding of the effects of financial actions and reactions by individuals and institutions. Knowledge of economic laws and principles enables entrepreneurs to have an ideal combination of the different factors of production. An economy exists because of two basic facts.

Firstly, human wants for goods and services are unlimited and secondly, productive resources with which to produce goods and services are scarce. Therefore, an economy has to decide how to use its scarce resources to obtain the maximum possible satisfaction of the members of the society. Economics guides consumers to distribute their income in purchasing of different commodities in such a way that they can satisfy their maximum number of wants within the given resources.

What are the works of Economists?

Those who specialise in this subject field are known as Economists. They study and analyse the relationship between supply and demand of goods and services and how they are produced, distributed and consumed. They provide information to management that affects decisions on marketing and pricing of products, economic forecasts and the effect of government policies on business. Economists also help in solving problems like unfair wages, rapid population growth, and migration of people to city centers, high crime incidence and loss of human resources due to overseas migration.

Eligibility and Course Areas

Economics very often forms a part of the curriculum in many Indian schools right from class IX itself. However, minimum requirement to start a career as economists is graduation. After graduation you can go for post-graduation. Further you can do M.Phil./Ph.D. in Development studies with major emphasis on Economics. Alternatively, you can specialize in a branch like Business or Agricultural Economics, Financial Economics, Labour Economics, Industrial Economics, Banking Economics, International Economics, etc., which are offered only by a few universities. Besides, departments of economics of some universities have also introduced courses in International Business and Financial Control and Analysis.

Another option is to do Master in Business Economics (MBE). Delhi University is the most reputed one in this subject. Business Economics deals with the analysis of the behaviour of firms in markets and industries and with determination of costs and prices. Courses are at present offered by about 13 universities in India leading to Master of Business Economics or MA in business Economics.

If you are interested you can go for Econometrics which is another specialisation in this field. Econometrics combines economic theory expressed in mathematical form with statistical methods. At present the subject is available only in University of Madras; Rani Durgavati Vishwavidyalaya, Jabalpur; Sri Venkateshwara University, Tirupati and the Indian Statistical Institutes.

Most of the colleges and Universities in India offer Bachelor and Master's degrees in Economics. Universities offer honours courses leading to the award of B.A. (Hons.). It is only in three Universities *viz.*, Anna University, Birla Institute of Technology and Science and Chhatrapati Sahu Ji Maharaj University that the nomenclature of the award is M.Sc. (Economics). M.Phil. and Ph.D. courses are also offered by many Universities and specific Economics school within the country. Prominent among them are Delhi School of Economics, Jawaharlal Nehru University and Banaras Hindu University. There are two deemed Universities in Economics viz., Gokhale Institute of Politics and Economics, Pune and Gandhi Institute of Development Research,

Mumbai. Gokhale Institute of Politics and Economics offers only M.A. and Ph.D. courses and Indira Gandhi Institute of Development Research, Mumbai (IGIDR offers M.Phil. (2 years) and Ph. D. (4 years) program in Development Studies. Post-graduate diploma courses are available in Annamalai University, Gujarat University, Ahmedabad, Guru Nanak Dev University Amritsar.

Personal Attributes

Economists must have a logical and analytical bent of mind, numerical ability, an interest in current social and political activities, sincerity, commitment and devotion, an interest in problem solving, a high-level of patience with a positive and optimistic attitude, knowledge of mathematics including statistics, decision-making ability, good oral and written communication skills, good time and project management skills.

Job Prospects and Career Options

Globalisation and economic liberalisation has widened the job prospects of economists in business, education, government and non-profit sector. Well-trained economists are in huge demand across industries, not only at the national level but at the international level as well. Opportunities for economic academicians are available in finance sector, urban and rural development, foreign trade, colleges, universities, and government service. Planning commissions, management consultants and organisations associated with data collection and interpretations recruit economics graduates at lucrative terms. Economics professionals are employed as economic analyst, finance economist, econometrician, economic advisor and economist.

- **The Indian Economic Service and Reserve Bank of India :** The Indian Economic Service and Reserve Bank of India are excellent options open to those who want to join government services. Those who have specialised in economics can appear for Indian Economic Service (IES) exam conducted by UPSC which is the gateway to challenging career in which selected candidates can join the service as Group-A officers. They are placed in the Planning Commission, Planning Board, Ministry of Economic Affairs, National Sample Survey and other departments that need specialists in economics. Reserve Bank of India also conducts various tests to recruit economists in the banking sector. Post-graduates in the age group 21-28 are eligible for the examination.

- **Economic consulting :** Economic consulting is another option available for students from economics background. However, the foremost growth potential for economists lies in the private sector and most notably in scientific research and consulting firms. Research institutes like National Council of Applied Economics Research, New Delhi, Indian Council of Social Science Research and Institute of Economic Growth, New Delhi offer ample job opportunities to economists.
- **Banking and Insurance sector :** Banking and insurance sector is also a lucrative option in this field. Financial institutions like various nationalised banks, private and foreign banks and insurance companies offer good openings to post-graduate degree holders in economics. In banks, they can find jobs like branch managers, clerks, economic advisors, development officers, etc. In the Insurance sector they are generally employed as insurance consultants, insurance agents, development officers, insurance policy-makers and can even work as managers, assistant managers of the insurance company. Besides, merging of world economy gives ample career opportunities in international financial institutions and research activities. Various international organisation offer ample job opportunities to well-known economists. Some professionals may choose to enter non-profit institutions like NGOs and GOs (government organisations).
- **Taxation :** Tax, taxation, filling process of indirect and direct taxes is part of public economics. Those who have interest regarding tax matters can go for some special courses available to tax consultants like Diploma in taxation, certificate course in tax consultant and later work as tax consultants. Investment consultant is another area available for the students of economics. If you have good knowledge of capital market, money market and commodity market you can become investment consultant. Mutual fund is a growing service industry in India where knowledge of economic analysis is required for effective investment decision-making and therefore professionals from economics and finance background can find prospects in this area.
- **Teaching and Research :** Those who have keen interest in higher studies and research can opt for M.Phil. and Ph. D. and thereby aspire to take higher position in public and private sectors. Post-graduates in this field can write UGC examinations like NET

and take up teaching as a career in various colleges, universities and professional institutions.

- **Forest sector :** Forest sector is also one of the important sectors for students of economics and agricultural economics. Candidates who have completed their degree or diploma with resource economics, agricultural economics, and environmental economics can take this opportunity in India and abroad. They are employed for conservation and scientific management of forests and the utilisation of their resources. Agricultural Scientist Recruitment Board recruits scientist from economics background who have passed Master's degree in economics with specialisation in Agricultural Economics.
- **Journalism and Mass Communication :** Those with degree in economics followed by a degree in Journalism and Mass Communication have lots of opportunities in print media as well as in television. Economics academicians can work as economic journalist in business journals, newspapers, television and web channels. Newspapers and journals provide economic and business events.

Remuneration

Both the government sector as well as the corporate sector, offer arrays of employment opportunities with good pay package to economic students. In most of the government services Economists are getting between ₹ 10,000 to ₹ 12,000 as assistants, while experienced and seniors have average monthly salary of about ₹ 25,000. In colleges and universities economists are getting the UGC pay scale which is very handsome. Banks are now offering good salary packages. Economic consultants are also earning good returns depending upon the number of their clients.

Top Institutes for Studying Economics

- **Tolani Maritime Institute (TMI)**

  Course : Post Graduate Diploma in Maritime Economics and Operations
- **Lady Shri Ram College for Women (LSRC)**

  Course : B.A. Economics
- **Ramjas College**

  Course : B.A. (Hons.) Economics
- **H.R College of Commerce and Economics**
- **Ethiraj College**

Courses : B.A. (Economics)

M.A. (Business Economics)

- **Sri Guru Gobind Singh College of Commerce**

  Course : B.A. (Hons.) Economics

- **St. Albert's College**

  Course : B.A. (Hons.) Economics

- **Lala Lajpat Rai College of Commerce and Economics (LLCC)**

- **IIT Kharagpur – Indian Institute of Technology**

  Course : Integrated M.Sc. in Economics

- **Lovely Professional University**

  Courses : M.Phil. Economics (Full Time)

  M.Phil. Economics (Part Time)

  Ph. D. Economics (Part Time)

  Ph. D. Economics (Full Time)

3.5 Foreign Language

Introduction

Career in foreign language is an attractive proposition for those who have a flair and knack for languages. Our trade links are expanding overseas so the requirement for people skills in language is increasing.

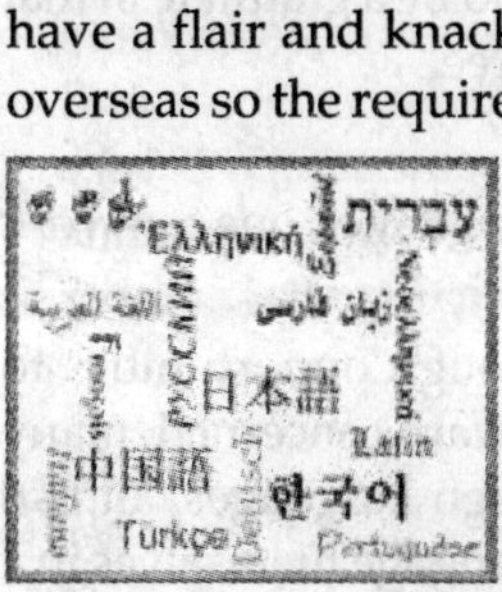

Skills in foreign languages like French, German, Russian, Chinese and more recently Japanese, Spanish and Korean are in great demand. Opportunities start from tour operators, online content writers, technical translators or decoders, interpreters and translators. Interpreters need to be au courant with the language because they have to transfer spoken statements from one language to another, whereas translators have to translate written documents which need excellent writing skills in languages.

Academic qualifications in foreign languages helps in pursuing careers in the areas of tourism, entertainment, public relations and mass communication, international organizations, embassies, diplomatic service, publishing houses, and BPOs. More and more avenues are opening up in tourism and call centers.

Eligibility and Course Areas

There are three types of courses to pursue for a career in foreign languages, i.e., Certificate Course, Diploma Course and Degree Courses. Some institutes offer both basic and advanced level courses such as post-graduate and Ph. D, some of them extending up to five-six years.

The eligibility for certificate and degree courses is 10+2. In most of the places eligibility for the diploma course is the certificate course in that language. JNU is a major institute conducting language courses. For Japanese, there is a language proficiency test conducted by the Mombusho Scholars Association. Alliance Francaise is the center for conducting various French tests like the TEF (required by the Canadian High Commission), the TCF, DELF/DALF tests and diplomas delivered by the French Ministry of Education.

Job Prospects and Career Options

Job prospects vary from secretarial, executive and public relation assignments as well as for translation and interpretation jobs. Translators are employed with industries, publishing houses, research and government organisations such as the Ministry of External Affairs (MEA) and embassies. Companies such as HP, Oracle, Samsung, Hyundai, LG, Thomson, GE, Aventis, and Moulinex are employing language experts. Other job opportunities for a language specialist are travel and tourism sector, hotel industry, exhibitions and fairs, airline offices, export agencies, radio stations, trade organisations and teaching. For pursuing a career in teaching, a teacher should be a graduate in that foreign language and must have a teaching degree.

Nature of Work

Attaining professional qualification in foreign languages, one can work in the following areas:

- **Teaching:** As teacher, a person gets enough opportunities to increase the skills. As far as teaching jobs are concerned, many institutions are offering courses in foreign languages, and so jobs exist at all levels. Those reluctant to engage themselves in a full-time profession can take private tuition as well.
- **Interpreters and translators:** Interpreters and translators both need to have a good command over two or more languages. Interpreters' job relates to interpreting spoken words of one language to another, therefore, needs to have not only good command over the language but have excellent verbal and non-verbal communication skills. The job of an interpreter can be of different types. Sometimes they are engaged in simultaneous

interpretation which is used for meetings, conferences, speeches, etc. Here the interpreter sits in a sound proof room and listens to speeches and almost spontaneously interprets it in the target language into a microphone. The other types of interpreting are consecutive interpreting and liaison interpreting. Consecutive interpreting goes on during formal speeches where the speaker halts for a while when the interpreter interprets the spoken statements to the audience. Interpreters accompany business groups and official delegations on overseas trips and are in great demand for technical translation. Translation work can be related to a variety of fields like technical, scientific literary or business. Translators work on books, scripts, articles and translate them into specified languages. Apart from having linguistic skills, a translator must possess adequate knowledge in the area of the work so as to maintain the style and essence of the original text.

- **Free-lancing :** Often, after pursuing courses in foreign languages, people like to work as freelancers. These people get work in translation bureaus, research organisations, international organisations like UNO, FAO, foreign companies, Reserve Bank of India, publishing houses etc. Expertise in foreign language coupled with other additional qualifications in areas like management, tourism, hospitality industry, airlines can be even fruitful and better the chances for employment opportunities.

Remuneration

If one opts for teaching, emoluments are according to fixed scales. A translator can earn between ₹ 100 to 400 per page. If document is of technical nature, a translator gets more. An interpreter gets paid by the hours and the current market rate is anywhere between ₹ 300 to 500 per hour. A good interpreter can earn up to ₹ 4,000 per hour. After four – five years, an interpreter can expect ₹ 15,000 to ₹ 20,000. International organisations pay better. When working for embassies, a specialist can get between ₹ 8,000 to 10,000 per month.

Courses

- Advance Course in Translation
- B.A. French
- Certificate Course in French
- Certificate Course in German
- Certificate Course in Translation
- Diploma in French

- Foreign Language and BPO Training
- Introductory Course in Translation

Institutes

- **School of Languages Jawaharlal Nehru University, New Delhi**

  Course offered : B.A. French, German, Arabic, Korean, Japanese, Chinese, Russian, Persian and English

  Duration: three years

  Eligibility: 10+2 and 45 per cent

  Selection on the basis of entrance examination

- **School of Languages Jawaharlal Nehru University, New Delhi**

  Course offered : M.A. French, German, Arabic, Korean, Japanese, Chinese, Russian, Persian and English

  Duration: three years

  Eligibility: 10+2 +3

  Direct entry for those who have done B.A. in the same university itself. Others have to take an entrance examination.

- **Delhi University, Delhi**

  Course offered : B.A. in Foreign Languages

  Duration: three years

  Eligibility: Entrance examination and Interview

- **Delhi University, Delhi**

  Course offered : M.A. in Foreign Languages

  Duration: two years

  Eligibility: B.A. in any discipline.

  Selection on the basis of entrance examination and Interview

- **Max Mueller Bhavan**

  Course offered : Diploma Certificate in German Language

  Duration: three years

- **Alliance Francaise**

  Course offered : Diploma Certificate in French Language

  Duration: three years

- **Japanese Culture and Information Centre**

  Course offered : Diploma Certificate in Japanese Language

  Duration: three years

3.6 Linguistics

What is Linguistics?

Linguistics – the science of language is the study of social, historical, political, biological, psychological and economic aspects of a language. It focusses on the sounds, words and grammar of specific languages; the relationship between languages; or the universal characteristics of all languages. The word 'linguistics' has been derived from the Latin words *'lingua'* (tongue) and *'istics'* (knowledge). Linguistics study, explore all aspects of ancient and modern languages as well as human language in general.

Major Branches of Linguistics

The major branches of study associated with linguistics are phonetics, phonology, morphology, syntax and semantics. Phonetics studies the physical aspects of language and the sounds of language, while those who focus on phonology study the function of sound in specific languages or dialects. Morphology involves the study of the units of language or 'morphemes'. Syntax studies sentence structure or how words combine to form sentences. Those who focus on semantics study the meaning involved in language. Through Linguistic courses, you will learn about organisation and use of languages as well as develop skills in critical reading, argumentation and analysis.

Eligibility and Course Areas

Linguistics, the science of language focusses on the discovery of the universal aspects of languages. Linguistics curriculums involve the description and explanation of language as well as its origin and evolution. Several under-graduate and post-graduate degree and diploma programs are conducted in the field of linguistics by various universities/institutes all over India.

The minimum requirement for admission to undergraduate programis 10+2 examination pass. To pursue education at post-graduate level, one should possess a graduation degree in linguistics or degree in any stream. Preference is given to arts scholars or those with linguistic educational background. One can also go for M.Phil. and Ph.D. in linguistics after master's degree.

Job and Career Options

A career as a linguist is an attractive proposition for those who have a flair for languages. Language skills prove to be an essential attribute in many professions. The demand for those trained in linguistics is increasing with the expanding of overseas trade links. There are several areas in which a linguist can work. He can work as an audiologist, communication disorder specialist, broadcaster/news reader, copy writer, editor, technical writer, translator, publisher, interpreter, language planner, lexicographer, teacher, psycholinguist, tour operator, and researcher. They can find employment in both public and private sectors. Major employers include government departments and agencies, education and health sectors, travel and tourism sector, journalism and mass communication related organisations, software and computational companies, interpreting and translation services, libraries, business and information management services, media and advertising, publishing houses, international organisations, market research and public relation companies.

Job opportunities for linguists are available in the Central Institute of Indian Languages, Mysore; Institute of Hindi Language, New Delhi; Anthropological Survey of India; Ministry of External Affairs (MEA) and embassies. Publishers abroad often recruit linguists for online dictionaries. Linguists may work with computer scientists to create new computer languages that are more like human languages. Linguists are also in high demand by technology companies to develop websites and voice recognition software. Linguists could also explore job possibilities in hospitals as speech therapists, with call centers as speech trainers or as dubbing and voice experts. They may go for medical transcription job as well. Often after pursuing courses in linguistics, people like to work as freelancers. Many international organisations like WHO, UN, NATO, etc., also need language experts to function effectively in various parts of the world.

Career fields which a linguist can opt for are umpteen. Some of them are :

- **Teaching :** Teaching is one of the best options for linguists. They can opt for a career as lecturer in various institutions that impart education in Indian languages. Several government agencies hire linguists to supervise language training programmes. Linguists are also hired to carry out research in various languages, or to work in specialised fields such as the determination of geogra-phical names for mapping and other purposes. Freelancing also offer very good prospects.

- **Hospitals :** People having done post-graduation in linguistics are recruited in hospitals as speech therapists or Neuro linguists, who treat speech problems in children and adults.
- **Banking :** A new upcoming field for linguists is banking and financial services sector, where more and more multi-national companies are hiring linguists for providing effective phonetics, language input, culture and customer service training to delegates.
- **Investigation :** Linguists play a major role in solving certain criminal cases. Even CBI has to take the help of a linguist in cases which involve speaker's identification. Acoustic phonetics is one of the significant courses of linguistics.
- **Publishing :** Publishers are frequently looking for graduates with knowledge of principles of textual organisation, discourse structure, grammar and semantics. In publishing, linguists are involved with producing foreign language text books, editing, consulting and planning elementary and secondary programmes of curriculum design. They can also become Lexicographers who are involved in the publishing of dictionaries.
- **Media :** Areas of the media such as television, magazine or newspapers could have similar translating, editing or lexicographic needs.
- **Public Relations :** Public relations require a good knowledge of language for communication.
- **Travel and Tourism :** There is a wide scope for the students of languages in the travel and tourism industry where proficiency in at least one language means surety of job. Employers in this field include airline offices, hotels, foreign embassies, etc.
- **Software Careers :** The software industry also offers opportunities for linguistic majors, asking linguists to develop search software, voice recognition software, dictionaries and translation software.
- **Translator/Interpreter :** Accurate translation and interpretation require linguistic knowledge. Translators are generally employed by industries, publishing houses, government and research organisations. An interpreter translates the language orally. They can find employment in judicial services, health-care and social work. There are also employment opportunities for translators and interpreters in the military, intelligence, Foreign Service and diplomatic corps.

Remuneration

Pay package varies with the kind and the place of work. A career in teaching can earn anything from ₹ 10,000 – 20,000 per month. A lecturer's pay scale is between ₹ 10,000 – 13,000 per month and professors can expect over ₹ 18,000 per month. Those working as translators get paid between ₹ 50 – 100 per page. An interpreter is paid on an hourly basis and the rate varies from ₹ 300 – 500 per hour. For those working with embassies can get between ₹ 10,000 – 12,000.

Courses

- M.A. Linguistics
- M.A. Applied Linguistics
- M. Phil. Applied Linguistics
- M. Phil. Linguistics and Phonetics
- Ph.D. Applied Linguistics
- Ph.D. Linguistics and Phonetics

Top Institutes in India that offer Linguistics

- **Karnataka University-Hubli Dharwad, Karnataka**
  Courses : Master of Arts – Linguistics
  Post-graduate Diploma in Linguistics
- **Guwahati University-Guwahati, Assam**
  Course : Master of Arts – Linguistics
- **Shreemati Nathibai Damodar Thackersey University—Mumbai, Maharashtra**
  Courses : Master of Arts – Applied Linguistics
  Post-graduate Diploma in Applied Linguistics
- **Sadar Patel University-Vidyanagar, Gujarat**
  Course : Post-graduate Diploma in Linguistics
- **Shreemati Nathibai Damodar Thackersey Women's University-Mumbai, Maharashtra**
  Courses : Master of Arts – Applied Linguistics
  Post-graduate Diploma in Applied Linguistics
- **Institute of Professional Studies-Dehradun, Uttaranchal**
  Course : Master of Philosophy (Linguistics)

- **Deccan College Post-graduate and Research Institute-Pune, Maharashtra**

  Courses : Ph.D. in Linguistics
  Master of Arts – Linguistics

- **Behrampur University-Behrampur, Orissa**

  Course : Master of Arts in Linguistics

3.7 Mathematics

What is Mathematics?

Mathematics, one of the oldest and most fundamental sciences is the study of the measurement, properties and relationships of quantities and sets using numbers and symbols. In simple words, Mathematics deals with the study of numbers and their various calculations. It is used throughout the world by all individuals in everyday life. Mathematics is an essential tool in many fields including natural science, engineering, medicine and the social sciences. Mathematicians who deal in this subject field use mathematical theory, computational techniques, algorithms and the latest computer technology to solve economic, scientific, engineering, physics and business problems.

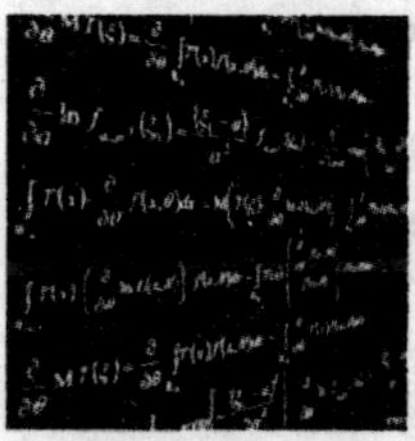

The Two Divisions of Mathematics

Mathematics is divided into two areas : Theoretical or Pure Mathematics and Applied Mathematics. Theoretical or Pure Mathematics is the study of the basic concepts and structures that underlie Mathematics. Its purpose is to search for a deeper understanding and an expanded knowledge of Mathematics itself. It is concerned with expanding and clarifying mathematical theories and laws. Applied Mathematics is a branch of Mathematics that concerns itself with mathematical methods that are typically used in science, engineering, business and industry. Thus, Applied Mathematics is a mathematical science with specialised knowledge.

Mathematics is used extensively in physics, actuarial science, statistics, engineering and operations research. Computer science, business and industrial management, economics, finance, chemistry, geology, life sciences and behavioural sciences are likewise dependent on applied mathematics.

Eligibility

For entry into the field of Mathematics, you need to have a degree in Mathematics or a B.Sc. in Pure Science with a strong aptitude for Mathematics. A bachelor's degree in mathematics is offered by most colleges and universities. Those with bachelor degree can take courses in a field that is closely related to mathematics such as computer science, engineering, Life science, physical science or economics. They can otherwise go for master level courses in pure or applied mathematics and even do Ph.D. which is required for research and academic jobs.

Personal Attributes

Prospective mathematicians must have above average intelligence and a natural feeling for numbers, spatial figures and problem solving skills. They require a keen eye for detail and a love for study and experimentation. Logical thoughts, reasoning skill and the ability to work systematically and accurately are essential. Self-discipline and a wide general knowledge are also important qualities. They must have the patience to spend long periods of time concentrating on complex problems. They must be able to work independently. They must also be able to present their own ideas clearly for which good communication skill is required. Mathematicians also should have substantial knowledge of computer programming because today most complex mathematical computation and much mathematical modelling are done on a computer.

Job Prospects

With advancement in technology mathematical applications are used in diverse areas and this necessitates more workers with knowledge of mathematics. The most common fields in which mathematicians study and find work are academics, computer science and software development, physics, engineering and operations research. Mathematical applications are also becoming involved in financial analysis, medical research, biotechnology, weather and commodity forecasting. Many of the job titles of mathematicians reflect their occupation rather than knowing them by the title of being a mathematician.

Career Options

Some of the Mathematics related careers are listed below. Among them mathematician, statistician and actuary are the careers offering great opportunity to Mathematics candidates.

- **Mathematician :** A mathematician is a person whose primary area of study or research is Mathematics. They solve problems;

make predictions related to natural changes like weather, ocean and soil erosion, financial risk analysis, market research, etc.

- **Statistician :** Statisticians apply mathematical principles to the collection, analysis and presentation of numerical data. They analyse survey results, prepare and present statements of analysis on graphs, scales or other measuring devices. They forecast future possibilities through these analyses.
- **Financial Analyst :** Financial analyst or investment analyst predicts the behavior of financial markets. They analyse financial information and advice on the monetary use of resources taking into account the risk factor.
- **Actuarial Science :** Actuarial science uses mathematics and statistics to assess risk. It applies in finance and insurance fields. The job of an actuary involves analysing data to predict and calculate long-term risks regarding financial decision and planning. They help to choose the investments based on the risk involved in it i.e., investments with more return and less risk. Actuary formulates various insurance policies and calculates the premium to be charged.
- **Operation Research :** Operations research is an interdisciplinary branch of applied mathematics and formal science that uses advanced analytical methods such as mathematical modelling, statistical analysis and mathematical optimisation to arrive at optimal or near-optimal solutions to complex decision-making problems. It applies mathematics to draw a conclusion about the problems related with costs or profits. Operation research analyst assists management in policy formulation, establishing a finance plan, and price fixation.
- **Auditor :** They provide external, independent assessment of an organisation's finances and accounting systems.
- **Accounting :** Accountant prepares financial documents, review financial performance and plan the future.
- **Teaching :** Teaching is a noble job. After B.Ed, B.Sc Mathematics or passing NET you can teach at school level or college level. A Ph.D is normally required for research and academic jobs. There is also option to start coaching center or tuition classes.
- **Bio-mathematics :** It is a combination of biology and mathematics. It uses mathematical techniques and tools in natural and biological processes.

- **Cryptography :** Cryptography is used as a branch in both Mathematics and Computer Science. Cryptography applications are used in matters related to the security of ATM cards and computer passwords.
- **Banking :** Banking sector deals with money matters for which knowledge of mathematics is required. In fields of lending loan, accepting deposits and transactions need numerical ability.
- **Computer System Analyst :** They help management decide whether implementing the proposed technology would be financially feasible. Mathematicians are highly in demand in this field for their logical and precise thought process.
- **Software Engineers :** They apply the theories and principles of computer science and mathematical analysis to create, test, analyse and evaluate the software applications and systems that make computers work.

Courses

- B.Sc. Mathematics
- B.Sc. Mathematics (Computer Applications)
- M.Phil. Mathematics
- M.Sc. Applied Mathematics
- M.Sc. Mathematics
- M.Sc. Mathematics (Hons.)
- Ph.D. Mathematics
- BS-MS Dual Degree

Institutes

- **North Gujarat University**

  PB No. 21, Rajmahal Road,

  Patan-384265, Gujarat

  Course : BA (Statistical Methods)
- **B.Sc. (Honours) School Punjab University**

  Sector-14, Chandigarh-160012

  Course : B.Sc. (Mathematics)
- **University of Poona Ganeshkhind,**

  Pune-411007, Maharashtra

  Courses : B.A. (Mathematical Statistics)

B.A. (Industrial Mathematics)

B.A. (Applied Maths)

B.A. (Applied Statistics)

- **Mohanlal Sukhadia University, Pratap Nagar**
  Udaipur-388120, Gujarat
  Course : B.A. (Mathematical Statistics)
- **Banaras Hindu University, Varanasi-221005 (UP)**
  Course : B.Sc. (Hons.) Mathematics
- **Bundelkhand University, Jhansi**
  Courses : B.Sc. (Hons.) Statistics
  B.Sc. Maths Group

3.8 Political Science

What is Political Science?

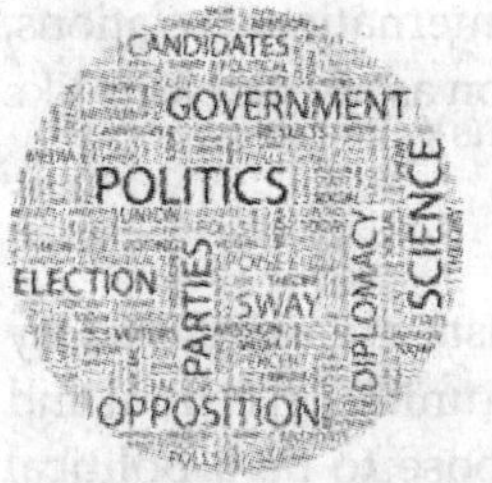

Political Science is a field of social science which deals with the theory and practice of everything related to politics. Political science involves the study of the political behaviour, system and the political structure of the country or an organisation. Political science plays a very significant role in our daily lives. Our education, jobs, lifestyle, remittances and taxes are all influenced by political decisions of the policy makers. Political science also plays an important role in the development of future leaders. It is an excellent humanities, subject best suited for students interested in learning how groups of people govern themselves, how policies are made and how we can improve our government policies at the local, state, national and international levels.

Political Scientists

Those who study political science are known as political scientists. They solve the nation's and world's problem by using tools both humanistic and scientific and a variety of methodological approaches to examine the process, systems and political dynamics of all countries and regions of the world. Political scientists may focus on political behaviour, decision-making processes, organisations and public policies. They conduct research on a wide range of subjects such as political scenario in different nations, major cities and towns, major court decisions on political affairs, relations between India and other countries, etc. They analyse the structure and operation of government, election results and conduct public opinion survey on political matters.

Eligibility

After 10+2, one can take bachelor's degree in political science and go further to take up master's degree. After that there is also an option for Ph.D. If you need to become political science/social science teacher, you need graduation degree in political science plus B.Ed. To become a Lecturer or Assistant Professor in a college of university you need to complete post graduation in political science and clear NET/SET examination conducted by (University Grants Commission (UGC). Those with graduation in this field can attempt SSC, UPSC and other competitive exams and enter into government services.

Course Areas

The course of political science covers subjects like forms of democracy, concept of nationhood, powers and functions of the executive and judiciary, the evolution of Indian Constitution, political thought and theories, foreign policy, contemporary issues in international relations, public administration and public policy formation as also subjects like economics and sociology.

Job Prospects

Approximately, 75 per cent of political scientists are employed by educational institutions. There are a lot of opportunities in central and state government services also. You could choose to be a political analyst, join the civil service, serve in the Indian Foreign Service and even teach at the college or university level. They can also opt for political journalism as a career choice.

Career Options

- **Law:** People who fully understand the nature and meaning of constitutions, rulings and regulations often pursue political science and law through law schools and become attorneys because of their deep desire for justice and making positive changes in the world.

- **Teaching:** Teaching is another popular profession for political science students. A substantial majority of the political scientists teach in intermediate colleges, degree college, or at university graduate departments and management institutes. Depending on the institution for which they work, political scientists have the choice between teaching and researching.

- **Research :** Research is the next main career option within political science related to teaching. Many teaching positions not only in the universities but also in colleges, information technology institutes, management institutions also require research activities. In addition to teaching and researching, political scientists write books and articles-based on their studies.
- **Political Journalism :** Being a political journalist is also an attractive option. Political science graduates get involve in print, television or radio journalism where they apply their expert understanding, of political system to create reports about current events. Political scientists might cover elections, conduct interviews, or attend press conferences where they often have the opportunity to ask questions. Political science graduates can also join the media as political analyst/correspondent/ researcher. However, students entering into this field must also have a degree in journalism.
- **Civil Service :** This is possibly the most popular choice of many political science students. The study of political science enables you to understand governance and how it functions as well as a detailed knowledge of public administration, political theory and philosophy that can help you in a career in government. After passing IAS examination one can enter into a career in civil service sector.
- **Administrative Service :** At central and state government level there are various options in administrative services. After taking competitive examinations one can join IAS, IPS, IFS, IRS and allied fields in central level. The state administrative jobs include BDO, Tehsildar and many other important positions. Many of them are engaged in urban planning, health planning and criminal justice systems.
- **Political Advisors :** Political advisors are political science experts who work alongside politicians and government officials helping them make important decisions in a number of different situations.
- **International Relations :** With a background in law, public administration and communications, political science graduates are best for such a career.

Remuneration

The earnings of political scientists depend on their education and experience as well as on the location and kind of position. Those with master's degree can expect a better position and salary compared to bachelor degree holders. However, main constraint is the performance rather than education. In the government sector pay is quite good. One can expect a starting pay around ₹ 10,000 – 12,000. In colleges/ universities the remuneration is according to the UGC scale which is a huge sum.

Courses

- B.A. Politics
- B.A. Politics and International Relations
- M.Phil. Political Science
- Ph. D. Political Science

Top Colleges/Universities that offer Political Science in India are:

- **Veer Kunwar Singh University, Ara, Bihar**
  Course : Master of Arts-Political Science
- **Shivaji University, Kolhapur, Maharashtra**
  Course : Master of Arts-Political Science
- **Pandit Ravishankar Shukla University, Raipur, Chhattishgarh**
  Course : Master of Arts-Political Science
- **Andhra Mahila Sabha Arts and Science College for Women, Hyderabad, Andhra Pradesh**
  Course : Bachelor of Arts in Political Science
- **Shreemati Nathibai Damodar Thackerey University, Mumbai, Maharashtra**
  Courses : Master of Arts-Political Science
  Bachelor of Arts-Political Science
- **H.J. Thim College of Arts and Science, Jalgaon, Maharashtra**
  Course : Bachelor of Arts in Political Science
- **Payyanur College, Kannur, Kerala**
  Course : Bachelor of Social Sciences-Political Science
- **St. George College, Kottayam, Kerala**
  Course : Bachelor of Science-Political Science

3.9 Social Work

What is Social Work?

Social work is all about improving the lives of people by helping them to deal with their problems such as personal issues, social issues, family issues, unforeseen outbreak of certain diseases, unemployment, etc. It is exciting, demanding and immensely rewarding profession which requires exceptional dedication to strive for social reform. Social work is a profession for those with a strong desire to improve society and people's lives.

The Role of a Social Worker

Social workers are the helping hands for needy people who are suffering from homelessness, poverty, violence, abuses and diseases like cancer, AIDS, etc. They work towards the solutions of people's social, economic and emotional problems through counselling, arranging conferences, increasing resources, spreading public awareness and starting social programmes and health services. They deal with persons, families, organisations and groups. They try to mitigate and prevent social problems caused by factors such as poverty, unemployment, alcoholism, lack of health services, family maladjustments, physical, mental and emotional handicaps, anti-social behaviour and poor housing. They work for rights of the people when violated.

The Bailiwick of the Service of a Social Worker

The area of service for a social worker is wide which can range from working in various developmental projects of the government to working for NGOs. The work of a social worker can be related to an educational programme, health, environment, or forest and water management. It is the duty of the social worker to answer their client's specific needs and to do the follow up for providing apt service to them. As a practical-oriented course, Social Work deals with the study of methods and techniques used in development activities. Emerging in the Nineteenth century, it has now become a major career choice with the increasing number of social organisations. Professional social work education began in India in 1936 with the establishment of TATA Institute of Social Sciences.

Eligibility

The minimum requirement for a professional position in this field is a bachelor's degree in Social Work (B.S.W./B.A.). It is a three year course for all those who have passed Plus 2 examination or its equivalent. A graduate in any discipline can join for the master's degree course in Social Work (M.S.W./M.A.) which is of two years duration. But students with a background in social work, psychology, social science, sociology or any other related fields will get preference.

Course Areas

Specialisation in MSW includes Human Resource Management, Criminology and Correctional Administration, Medical and Psychiatric Social Work, Family and Child Welfare, Mental Health, Rural and Urban Community Development and Law (IPC/CRPC). A master's degree in Social Work is necessary for positions in the mental health field and general supervisory positions. For higher studies in this field, one could do the doctoral and research programs like M.Phil and Ph.D. These higher degrees are usually required for teaching research and administrative jobs. Apart from these, several diploma and certificate courses are also available in the field of Social Work.

Some universities conduct entrance examination for entry to their courses in Social Work but some institutes offer admission on the basis of marks obtained in the last qualifying exam. Community organisation, social policy and planning, ecology and social work, political science, health, social problems and women's studies, childcare and family services, labour welfare and industrial relations, problems of marginalised groups, rural studies, medical and psychiatric social work, etc., are some of the subjects taught in the courses of Social Work.

Job Prospects and Career Options

Professionally social workers may be classified as three types namely Macro, Masco and Micro. Macro social workers deal with Social Work nationally and internationally by making policies and sponsorships; while Masco social workers handle social work with small organisations, agencies and groups. Micro social workers work with individuals and families.

Employment opportunities are available for social workers in private as well as public sector companies. Career opportunities in this field would depend on an individual's area of specialisation. Social workers who specialise in the areas of Human Resource Management can get jobs in the Personnel, HRM, Welfare departments of factories and commercial organisations as executive officers, trainee officers, welfare officers and social security officers. Trained professionals can get executive card jobs in government, semi-government undertakings, private organisations as labour welfare officers, welfare officers, social workers etc. Social workers can also take up teaching assignments. After a few years of experience, one can even become a consultant with various organisations and can also start freelance work.

Social workers can pursue a career as a counsellor in health-care, adoption, environmental protection, community policing etc. They can specialise in child welfare and family services, mental health services, public assistance, medical social work, community organisation, social work, planning and policy development or social welfare administration. Some of the work areas of Social workers may include :

- **Clinical Social Work :** Clinical social workers take care of the mental and physical healths care of needy people. They do psychotherapy and counselling for such people in health clinics, hospitals and agencies. Some of them do private practices.
- **School Social Work :** School social workers deal with children and teenagers as the link between students, families and the school. They understand the problems of children and try to solve them and give counselling if necessary. They also tender advice to teachers on how to cope with children in difficulties. Sometimes they form associations and groups to deal with children's problems at school.
- **Psychiatric Social Work :** The psychiatric social workers deal with mentally disturbed people. It is also referred to as clinical social work as these workers also mostly work with hospitals and clinics.
- **Criminology and Correctional Social Work:** Criminology and correctional social workers deal with the study of crimes, its causes and prevention. They work among the people in jails and juveniles in observation homes and correctional homes. They also work in juvenile courts. They network with juvenile police.
- **Medical Social Work:** Medical and public health social worker in other words known as hospital social worker, works for hospitals, nursing and personal care facilities, individual and family services agencies or local-governments. They provide support and counselling to the patients, advise family members, help plan for patient's needs after discharge.
- **Community Organisation:** Community organisers bring together people with common self-interest. They negotiate and influence the government authority and other civil organisations.
- **Research:** They do research on problems, find out solutions and help the government and other authority to help the needy people.
- **Industrial Social Work:** The industrial social workers work among the labourers and find solution to their issues and ensure the welfare of the employees.

Opportunities Abroad

Vast opportunities are available for social workers abroad. Globalisation has widened the scope of employment for students opting for social work as their career. They may choose to join international NGOs like Amnesty International, Oxfam, USAID, IGSSS, Green Peace, etc. In many countries like UK, Northern Ireland and Scotland, one should register with the governing body (GSCC in UK) to take up the career of a social worker.

Remuneration

Both governmental and non-governmental organisations appoint social workers as their employees. The remuneration in this field will depend upon the organisation in which one works, one's experience and the areas of work. Even though there is no fixed pay scale for this profession, one could get an initial pay of ₹ 5,000–10,000 per month depending on the organization. This is for grassroots community social workers. The pay package of corporate houses is more than that of government agencies. Those in the field of teaching profession can have a pay scale of ₹ 8,000–20,000 per month. Those who are working with NGOs and government projects can earn a monthly salary of ₹ 8,000 – 40,000 per month. Salaries and perks are higher in International NGOs. The social workers who are running their own NGOs also get handsome earnings.

Courses

- Bachelor of Social Work (BSW)
- Certificate Course in Social Work (CSW)
- Ph.D. Social Work
- M.Phil. Social Work
- Master of Social Work (MSW)

Best Institutes for Social Work

- Tata Institute of Social Sciences, Mumbai
- Delhi School of Social Work, Delhi
- Madras School of Social Work, Chennai
- College of Social Work, Nirmala Niketan, Mumbai
- Loyola College of Social Sciences, Thiruvananthapuram
- Department of Social Work, Pune University, Pune
- Department of Sociology, Banaras Hindu University, Varanasi
- Department of Sociology, Mumbai University, Mumbai

- School of Social Work, Mangalore University, Mangalore
- Department of Social Work, Lucknow University, Lucknow

3.10 Sociology

What is Sociology?

Sociology is the scientific study of human society and its origin, development, organisations and institutions. It encompasses the study of human behaviour, its causes and consequences; and social interaction of people in groups to understand how societies organise, develop and change. Almost any aspect of how human beings gather together in groups, how they organise and form societies can be studied within sociology.

The Role of Sociologists

Sociologists study human behaviour, which is greatly influenced and governed by social, religious and legal guidelines within the guidelines of an organisational structure. In brief, sociologists study people's behaviour in groups and provide insight into what it means to be human in today's world. This includes developing a keen understanding of human activities, interactions, political and economic tendencies. The study involves all aspects of human experience and activity. Sociologists also study the role that social institutions have on human's perspective and identity.

Eligibility

To become a professional in sociology one should have a graduate degree (B.A./M.A.) in sociology or its related fields. Degree and post-graduate degree courses are offered by private and government colleges and universities in India. A candidate should have 10+2 preferably in social sciences for pursuing sociology at graduation level. Similarly, a good percentage in sociology is needed to pursue sociology at post graduation level. Most sociologist jobs require a master's degree to work in government, research and educational settings, while working as a sociology professor or faculty member would require that the applicant holds a Ph.D.

Course Duration

- B.A. (Sociology) – three years
- M.A. (Sociology) – two years

Job Prospects

A sociology degree can open up many doors in the professional arena from government to corporate jobs. Sociologists are employed by research institutes, the criminal justice system, public health and welfare organisations, private businesses, law firms, international agencies, medical centers, educational institutions, advertising firms, survey and polling organisations. Sociologists also work in business, human resources and journalism sector. In some sectors, sociologists work closely with economists, political scientists, anthropologists, psychologists and social workers.

The most common jobs held by sociologists are that of educators or teachers, researchers, administrators, consultants and counsellors. Other careers in which those with a bachelor's degree in sociology often secure employment are as case workers, paralegals, public relations workers, urban planners, community organisers, public policy researchers and data analysts. People with sociology degree most often choose teaching as profession, teaching in a college level needs master's degree with NET and may even further advance their level with M.Phil. and Ph.D. Sociologists enter the corporate, non-profit and government world as policy analyst, directors of research, consultants, human resource managers, public information officers and programme managers.

Remuneration

Earning of sociologists depend on the education and experience of an individual, as well as on the location and kind of job. The salary can be from ₹ 6,000 – 10,000 for beginners and increases with experience and knowledge. Those employed under government sector earn between ₹ 8,000 – 30,000 per month. For assistant professors in colleges and universities salary will be as per UGC norms. A higher salary can be expected for those who are working in industries and corporate companies.

Courses

- B.A. Sociology
- M.A. Sociology
- M. Phil. Sociology
- Ph. D. Sociology

Some Institutes for Studying Sociology in India

- **A.K.L.R. Government Andhra Oriental College, Nallakunta, Hyderabad, Andhra Pradesh**

  Course : B.A. (Hons.) Sociology

- **Aligarh Muslim University, University Road, Aligarh, Uttar Pradesh**
  Courses : B.A. (Hons.) Sociology
  M.A. Sociology.
- **Arambag Girls College, Hooghly, West Bengal**
  Course : B.A. (Hons.) Sociology
- **B.J.B. Autonomous College, Bhubaneshwar, Orissa.**
  Course : B.A. (Hons.) Sociology
- **Banki College (Autonomous), Banki, Cuttack, Orissa**
  Course : B.A. (Hons.) Sociology
- **Bharat Ratna Dr. B.R. Ambedkar University, Delhi**
  Course : B.A. (Hons.) Sociology
- **Chhattisgarh University (CGU), Raipur, Chhattisgarh**
  Courses : B.A. (Hons.) Sociology
  M.A. Sociology
- **D.M. College of Arts, Imphal**
  Course : B.A. (Hons.) Sociology
- **Damber Singh College, Tadong Gangtok, Sikkim**
  Course : B.A. (Hons.) Sociology
- **Dayalbagh Educational Institute, Dayal Bagh Road, Agra, Uttar Pradesh**
  Courses : B.A. (Hons.) Sociology
  M.A. Sociology
- **Dibrugarh University, Dibrugarh, Assam**
  Courses : B.A. (Hons.) Sociology
  M.A. Sociology
  M.Phil. Sociology
  Ph.D. Sociology
- **Acharya Nagarjuna University, Nagarjuna Nagar Guntur, Andhra Pradesh**
  Course : M.A. Sociology
- **Dibrugarh University, Dibrugarh, Assam**
  Courses : B.A. (Hons.) Sociology
  B.A. Sociology
  M.A. Sociology
  M.Phil. Sociology
  Ph.D. Sociology

- **Central University of Bihar (CUB), Patna, Bihar**
  Course : M.A. Sociology
- **Assam University, Silchar, Assam**
  Courses : M.A. Sociology
  M.Phil. Sociology
  Ph.D. Sociology
- **Banasthali University, P.O. Banasthali Vidyapeeth Tonk, Rajasthan**
  Courses : B.A. Sociology
  M.A. Sociology
  Ph.D. Sociology
- **Christ University, Bangalore, Karnataka**
  Courses : B.A. Sociology
  M.A. Sociology
  M.Phil. Sociology
  Ph.D. Sociology
- **Dr. B.R. Ambedkar Open University (BRAOU), Hyderabad, Andhra Pradesh**
  Courses : M.A. Sociology
  M.Phil. Sociology
  Ph.D. Sociology
- **Guwahati University, Guwahati, Assam**
  Courses : M.A. Sociology
  Ph.D. Sociology
- **Goa University, North Goa**
  Courses : B.A. Sociology
  M.A. Sociology
  Ph.D. Sociology
- **Himachal Pradesh University,**
  Courses : M.A. Sociology
  M.Phil. Sociology
  Ph.D. Sociology
- **IGNOU-Indira Gandhi National Open University, Maidan Garhi, Delhi**
  Courses : M.A. Sociology
  Ph.D. Sociology

4

BIOLOGICAL SCIENCE AND TECHNOLOGY

4.1 Biochemistry

What is Biochemistry?

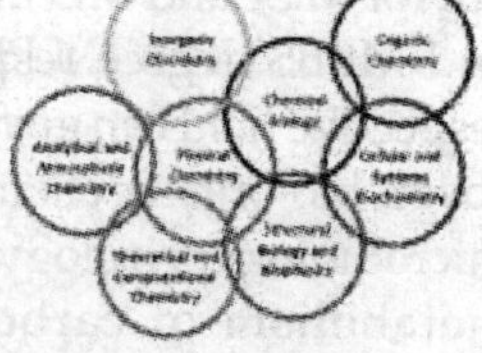

Biochemistry is the study of structure, composition and chemical reactions of substances in living organisms. It is an interdisciplinary programme in which the principles of Chemistry, Biology, Genetics, Mathematics and Physics are applied to the study or investigations of biomolecules, atoms, organelles, cells, tissues and organisms. Biochemistry is often defined as the 'chemistry of life' because it aims to explore and understand aspects of life. It is a branch of chemistry, which is concerned with the biological processes taking place in cells and organisms. Hence, the study of biochemistry deals with the chemical combinations and reactions which take place in biological processes such as growth, metabolism, reproduction, heredity as well as the effect of environment on living organisms.

The Work of Biochemists

Those who study the chemistry of living beings are called biochemists. Biochemists study the elements, compounds and chemical reactions that are controlled by enzymes in living organisms. Biochemists get into the minutest characteristics of living organisms. They delve deep into the structures and functions of biomolecules such as enzymes, proteins, carbohydrates, fats and other numerous processes related to metabolism of mankind. They are involved in production of biochemical products by experimenting, analysing and researching. They may be identifying the way in which DNA, which carries the genetic information, is transferred between cells and can be manipulated.

The Contribution of Biochemistry in Different Fields

Biochemistry contributes to progress in a wide variety of areas including health, agriculture and environment. Biochemistry finds application in clinical and forensic science and in food and pharmacological industries. Biochemistry is the key player in modern biomedical research as biochemists contribute to the design of new drugs. Biochemists working in medicine are sometimes called Molecular biologists. They study bacteria, viruses and other organisms to understand the chemical basis of life. They also determine the effects of chemicals on medical problems such as cancer, aging or obesity.

Eligibility and Course Areas

There are several courses in biochemistry. Minimum requirement to take a course in this field is 10+2 Science. Students having background in science at 10+2 level can take up B.Sc. Biochemistry. Further, one can opt for M.Sc and MD in Biochemistry whose eligibility is a B.Sc. degree and MBBS degree respectively. Those with a master's degree in the respective field can go for Ph.D. and M.Phil. in Biochemistry. The course covers bio-organic chemistry, biophysical chemistry, human physiology, microbiology, virology, basic immunology, enzymology, intermediary metabolism of carbohydrates, structural biology, biogenetics, biomembranes, computer applications in biology, nutritional and clinical biochemistry and molecular biology.

Job Prospects and Career Options

Biochemistry being an interdisciplinary subject, graduates in this field enjoy a wide range of career opportunities. They can find work in many walks of life in industry, hospitals, agriculture, research and educational institutions. Biochemistry finds application in clinical and forensic science laboratories, pharmaceutical industry, agrochemical companies and in food/beverages industries.

Both private and public sector offer employment for biochemists. The Department of Agriculture, the National Institutes of Health and the Environmental Protection Agency are some of the government agencies that employ biochemists. Industries that produce pharmaceuticals, agricultural chemicals, foods, feeds and consumer products employ biochemists in research. Some of them get employment in marketing, management, science information, technical writing and editing. Biotechnology companies employ biochemists in quality control, clinical research, manufacturing and information systems with applications to the environment, energy, human healthcare, agriculture and animal health. Colleges and universities employ the majority of biochemists as teachers or researchers in schools of arts and sciences, medicine, engineering, pharmacy, dentistry, veterinary medicine and agriculture.

Career areas in this field include:

- **Agriculture :** A biochemist engaged in this field develops and innovates new improved techniques for crop cultivation, pest control management and crop storage management. Contributions made in this field by biochemists have helped to better the output and quality of agricultural produce. Employers include seed companies, agricultural universities/colleges, chemical manufacturing companies and agricultural departments.
- **Medicine :** Biochemists working in medicine are sometimes called molecular biologists. Here biochemists perform diagnostic tests and investigations for finding out causes of various diseases confronting mankind. Their major concern is to study the role of genetic transmission of diseases from one generation to another. They study bacteria, viruses and other organisms to better understand the chemical changes that take place in the cells of the body parts which signal the onset of various diseases such as tuberculosis, cancer, diabetes and mental disorders like epilepsy. They do researches related to identification and analysis of chemical processes like muscular contraction, reproduction and metabolism. They provide diagnostic services; carry out tests on blood, urine and other body fluid. Hospitals, public health laboratories, medical research institutes and the pharmaceutical industry employ biochemists.
- **Research :** Biochemistry is a field of intense research. Biochemists are employed to carry out research in various fields like development of new crops, pest control methods, quality improvement, drug manufacturing, and identifying causes of various diseases in living organisms. Employment opportunities exist in research labs, biotechnology companies, pharmaceutical companies, private industry, non-profit research institutes, forensic labs and government laboratories. They can also work as researchers at colleges and universities in the areas of biochemistry.
- **Food and Nutrition :** Biochemists in nutrition analyse food products to measure their vitamins, proteins, carbohydrates and minerals. Nutritional biochemists improve the health of both humankind and animals. A nutritional biochemist that

specialises in animals usually works in the agriculture industry developing new feed and conducting animal science research. A nutritional biochemist (for humankind) tries to improve public health, either by reducing malnourishment or analysing the nutritional components of certain diseases like diabetes and obesity. In this field biochemists have researched and studied the effects of certain food stuffs, minerals, proteins, carbohydrates, fats, vitamins, when consumed in excess or in deficient quantities on the human body. They also work on developing new crops or making crops that improve human health. There are also positions for nutritional biochemists in the Nutraceuticals' industry examining or developing foods that can provide medicinal benefits.

- **Drug Development :** Drug companies employ biochemists to research the causes of diseases and to develop drugs to combat these diseases. Biochemists diagnose diseases and develop new drug compounds and vaccines.
- **Education :** There are opportunities as educators, as high school teachers, professors and curriculum developers. To become a professor you need to fulfill the norms set by University Grants Commission. Curriculum developers work with publishing companies, online education providers and state boards of education to develop educational standards for high school or post-secondary students. The minimum education requirement for curriculum development is an undergraduate degree, though most employers will prefer to hire curriculum developers with some teaching or technical writing experience.
- **Writer :** Science writer is also a career for biochemistry majors. science writers work for publishing companies, writing textbooks, manuals and non-fiction works about science usually on a freelance basis. They also work for newspapers, magazines and trade publications.
- **Military Careers :** The military medical service corps also hires biochemists, with a minimum of a master's degree to provide clinical service to soldiers and their families. In the military, biochemist will work in research and development, blood banks, health services or in toxicological research.
- **Toxicology :** Toxicologists examine the effect of chemicals on humans, animals and the environment. Toxicologists work in laboratories for the government, private or non-profit firms and

their research is used in policy development, law enforcement and forensic investigation.

- **Administrative positions:** The increasing reliance on biochemical technology in medicine, agriculture and biotechnology industries requires administrators, consultants and legislative aides who have a thorough understanding of modern biochemistry.
- **Self-employment:** Some biochemists are self-employed consultants who advise government or industry.

Remuneration

Pay scale varies based on employer, position, qualification and experience. In private sector a biochemist can earn a starting salary of about ₹ 15,000 – 20, 000 per month. Those employed as researchers in government sector can have a starting salary of ₹ 9,000/- per month along with government perks/allowances. One can command higher salary as one gains experience; generally MNCs and private companies pay higher.

Institutes

- **Sriram College of Arts and Science, Chennai**
  Perumalpattu, Chennai-602024
- **Amrita Institute of Medical Sciences (AIMS)**
  Schools and Research Centers
  Amrita Health Sciences Campus, AIMS Ponekkara Post, Elamakkara, Kochi-682041, Kerala
- **Acharya's Institute of Medical Sciences, Bangalore Rural, Karnataka**
  No. 51, Cholanagar, R.T. Nagar Post, Bangalore Rural-560002
- **Christian Medical College, Vellore**
  Thorapadi P.O., Bagayam, Vellore-632002
- **Sai Institute of Paramedical and Allied Sciences, Dehradun**
  Woodland House, Subash Nagar Chowk, Mohbewala, Dehradun-248001
- **Sri Ramachandra Medical College and Research Institute (Sri Ramachandra University)**
  Chennai 1, Ramachandra Nagar, Porur, Chennai-600116
- **Banaras Hindu University: Faculty of Science**
  Varanasi, UP-221005

- **Post-graduate Institute of Medical Education and Research**
  Chandigarh, Sector-12 (Chandigarh)-160012

4.2 Bioinformatics

What is Bioinformatics or Computational Biology?

Bioinformatics or computational biology is the use of information technology in the field of molecular biology or the application of computer technology to the management and analysis of biological data. Here, computers are used to gather, store, analyse and merge biological data. It is an emerging inter disciplinary research area and is increasingly being used to improve the quality of life. The ultimate goal of bioinformatics is to uncover the wealth of biological information hidden in the mass of sequence, structure, literature and other biological data and to obtain a clearer insight into the fundamental biology of organisms and to use this information to enhance the standard of life for mankind.

Importance of Bioinformatics

The importance of Bioinformatics is unlimited in the genomic era (genome is the complex molecular chains that constitute each organism's unique genetic heritage). The hereditary information of an organism is encoded in the DNA. Genomics, the study of an organism's entire genome, is developed to understand the basic molecule of life which is known as the code of life. DNA directly controls the biological make-up of humans or any living organism. Studying the structure of DNA has made amazing success over many genetically transferring diseases. It is variations and errors in the genomic DNA which ultimately define the likelihood of developing diseases or resistance to the same disorders.

Bioinformatics could have profound impact in fields as varied as human health, agriculture, the environment, energy and biotechnology to advance biomedical research and development. It is being used now in the areas of molecular medicine to help produce better and more customised medicines to prevent or cure diseases. It has environmental benefits in identifying waste cleanup bacteria and in agriculture it can be used for producing high yield low maintenance crops. These are just few of the many benefits bioinformatics can offer.

Eligibility

A course in bioinformatics is suitable for those with a graduation or post-graduation in molecular biology, genetics, microbiology, chemistry, pharmacy, veterinary sciences, physics, mathematics, engineers, IT professionals, Ph.Ds and medicos. Programmes at different levels are available in the field such as B. Tech, Master Degree, Advanced Diploma and M.Tech. Study of Bioinformatics begins at the undergraduate level. The basic educational qualification to enter a programme in Bioinformatics is 10+2 completed with science as the subject. The details of the educational qualification for different courses in this field are listed below:

Job Prospects and Career Options

The career prospects in the field have been steadily increasing with more and more use of information technology in the field of molecular biology. Job prospects are in all sectors of biotechnology, pharmaceutical and biomedical sciences, in research institutions, hospital and industry. Some of the specific career areas that fall within the scope of bioinformatics include Sequence assembly, Database design and maintenance, Sequence analysis, Proteomics (the study of protein, particularly their structures and functions), Pharmacogenomics, Pharmacology, Clinical pharmacologist, Informatics developer, Computational chemist, Bio-analytics and Analytics.

Work in Bioinformatics

The work involved in the specific career areas are Drug design utilising 3-D structure modelling and computational chemistry (Chemin-formatics), comparing genetic data between species and within species (Genomics), Genomic analysis in an attempt to find drug targets (Pharmacogenomics), characterisation of proteins and their interactions (Proteonomics), prediction of the function of genes and proteins based on sequence and structural data.

One can work in pharmaceutical and biotech companies where bioinformatics technologies are applied throughout the drug discovery process. One can also take up teaching jobs in public institutions if one has the skill in teaching. Indian companies like Satyam, Wipro, TCS, Reliance, Silicon Genetics, Accelrys and IBM Life Sciences Pubgene, and Tessella are recruiting bioinformatics candidates because it has made a substantial new market for IT infrastructure.

Selection

Generally, admission to the courses in Bioinformatics is through entrance tests. Admission to B. Tech. Bioinformatics programme is based on an objective type test with questions to evaluate class 11-12 level of knowledge of physics, chemistry and biology.

M.Sc. Bioinformatics entrance tests typically assesses knowledge of physics, chemistry, botany, zoology and mathematics of the 10+2 level, and to evaluate knowledge of life sciences, physical and mathematical sciences through short answer questions of the bachelor's degree level. In the short answer questions, the applicant may choose questions from the various science related to the subjects of his/her background.

For an advance diploma course in Bioinformatics, one may expect a section of paper with objective type questions of the 10+2 and bachelor's degree level in the biological, physical and mathematical sciences and another section/paper with a mix of questions from the subject matter of physics, chemistry, mathematics, biology, biochemistry, biotechnology, computer science and related disciplines of the bachelor's and master's degree level.

Since applications are invited from graduates and post-graduates of diverse disciplines for the master's and advance diploma programmes respectively, the question in the entrance examination would not have a bias in favour of any student.

Remuneration

The median salary of a senior research scientist in bioinformatics is around ₹ 15, 24,590 per annum, while assistant professor gets around ₹ 4,68,000 per year and research associate gets around Rs. 2,40,000.

Courses and Educational Qualifications:

- **B. Tech in Bioinformatics**

  Candidate should complete 10+2 with physics, chemistry, Biology and English.

- **Master's Degree in Bioinformatics**

  Candidate should complete their graduation in any of the following subjects such as B.Sc./B.Sc. (Agriculture)/ BCS/BE/ B.Tech./MBBS/B. Pharm./BAMS/BHMS/B.V.Sc.

- **Advanced Diploma in Bioinformatics**

  Candidates having a post-graduation in any of the following subjects such as M.Sc. in life sciences, physics, chemistry, mathematics, biotechnology, biophysics, botany, zoology, biochemistry, microbiology, pharmacology, computer science or equivalent), M.Sc. (Agriculture) or M. Tech. or MBBS are eligible for the advanced diploma course.

- **M.Tech. in Bioinformatics (Engineering)**

  Pharmacy graduate, medical, dental and veterinary science graduates as well as post graduates in science are eligible for the admission to M. Tech. other than this eligibility for the courses in Bioinformatics in different colleges varies with the universities.

- Advanced Bioinformatics (ABI)
- B. Sc. Bioinformatics
- B. Sc. Biotechnology and Bioinformatics
- B. Tech. Bioinformatics
- Certificate Course in Bioinformatics
- Diploma in Bioinformatics
- M. Sc. Bioinformatics
- M. Sc. Biotechnology and Bioinformatics
- M. Tech. Bioinformatics
- Post-graduate Diploma in Bioinformatics

Institutes

- **Indian Institute of Information Technology**
  Bioinformatics Division, Allahabad (Uttar Pradesh)
- **Madurai Kamaraj University**
  Madurai, Tamil Nadu
- **SRM University**
  Chennai, Tamil Nadu
- **University of Pune**
  Bioinformatics Centre
  Pune, Maharashtra
- **Institute of Bioinformatics and Applied Biotechnology**
  Bangalore, Karnataka
- **Pondicherry University: Bioinformatics Centre**
  Puducherry (Puducherry)
- **University of Calcutta**
  Kolkata, West Bengal
- **Jamia Millia Islamia (A Central University)**
  New Delhi
- **University of Hyderabad**
  Hyderabad, Andhra Pradesh

- **Institute of Bioinformatics and Biotechnology**
  Pune, Maharashtra
- **Mar Athanasios College for Advanced Studies**
  (MACFAST), Thiruvalla, Kerala
- **Amity Institute of Biotechnology, RBEF, E-27,**
  Defence Colony, New Delhi
- **Bharthiyar University, Muruthamalai Road**
  Coimbatore, Tamil Nadu

4.3 Biophysics

What is Biophysics?

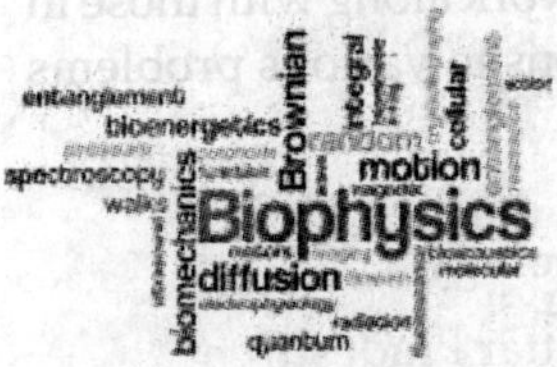

Biophysics is an interdependent science discipline that employs unique methods of physics and physical chemistry to acquire knowledge on the biological systems present in our world. Biophysics is a bridge between biology and physics. It applies the principles of Physics and Chemistry. It also uses the methods of Mathematical Analysis and Computer Modelling in order to understand how biological systems work. It explains biological function in terms of the molecular structures and their properties.

What does Biophysics deal with?

Biophysics is one of the most fascinating and intellectually challenging fields of scientific study as it deals with humans. Biophysics shares a strong bond with other advanced biological fields such as biochemistry, bioengineering, systems biology, nanotechnology and agro physics. It can be said that biological systems is the very root of all our existence. Biophysics incorporates the study of all levels of biological organisation from molecules to ecosystems. The main aspect of biophysics and chemistry is to study and explain the structures of living organism and the mechanisms of life processes.

The Usefulness of Biophysics

The applications of Biophysics depend on society's needs. One of the first major findings in biophysics was the discovery of the double helix structure of the DNA molecule in 1953. Biophysics helped create powerful vaccines against infectious diseases. Biophysical methods are increasingly used to serve everyday needs from forensic science to bioremediation. Medical imaging technologies including MRI (Magnetic

Resonance Imaging), CAT (Computed Axial Tomography) scans, etc. are the inventions of Biophysics.

The Role of Biophysicists

One who studies biophysics is known as Biophysicist. They study life at every level from atoms and molecules to cells, organisms and environments. Biophysicists attempt to explain why our biophysical environment behaves as it does. Biophysicists study how organisms develop, see, hear, think and live. They investigate the brain processing and storing information, the heart pumping blood, muscles contraction, plants using light in photosynthesis, genes switched on and off and the like. Biophysicists usually work with groups or with teams of other scientists and professionals of other backgrounds collaboratively in solving common problems. For example, they work along with those in medical and criminology fields to find solutions to various problems they come across.

The Major Areas of Biophysics

The major areas of biophysics are the following:

- **Molecular biophysics** – It is the study of large molecules and particles of comparable size which play important roles in biology.
- **Radiation biophysics** – It consists of the study of the response of organisms to ionising radiations such as alpha, beta, gamma and X-rays and to ultraviolet light.
- **Physiological biophysics** – It is called by some as classical biophysics and is concerned with the use of physical mechanisms to explain the behaviour and the functioning of living organisms or parts of living organisms and with the response of living organisms to physical forces.
- **Mathematical and theoretical biophysics** – It deals primarily with the attempt to explain the behaviour of living organisms on the basis of mathematics and physical theory.
- **Medical biophysics** – It deals with the study that uses physics to describe or affect biological process largely for the purpose of medical application. The areas of research combining physics and physiology include medical imaging such as MRI, Computed Tomography and PET (Positron emission tomography), oncology and cancer diagnosis using radio-labeling and molecular imaging and vasculature and circulatory system function.

Eligibility

Eligibility for those who intend to pursue biophysics career is that they must basically have an undergraduate degree in physics, biology and chemistry. Some institutes also offer undergraduate programmes with special attention given to biophysics. In India, however, there are only few universities that offer courses in biophysics at the undergraduate level.

Duration of Study

Most biophysicists begin their career with a four-year Bachelor of Science degree in Biophysics and then go on to earn a master's degree and a Ph.D. in physics or a sub-discipline of physics. Biophysicists who wish to do research generally need to obtain a Ph.D. and spend one to five years in post-doctoral research in a university or government laboratory. In medical biophysics, one to two years of post-degree clinical (residential) training is required.

Course Areas

Course areas of Biophysics include molecular biophysics, membrane biophysics, neurobiophysics, biophysical techniques, bioenergetics and medical biophysics.

Personal Attributes

Biophysicists must have an aptitude for physics, biology and mathematics and be able to pay close attention to detail. Interest in scientific phenomena, patience, perseverance, precision and tremendous inclination to search for real solutions is the strength of all biophysicists. Personal qualities of being able to think creatively and work independently as part of a professional and interdisciplinary team will be helpful. They should have excellent writing and computer skills, should possess patience and curiosity about the physical world. The motivation for scientific work should be intense as often a sustained effort to pursue research is required.

Job Prospects and Career Options

The field of Biophysics is the perfect choice for those who are fascinated by physics and biology. There is wide range of careers open for biophysicists. Those with Ph.D. have much scope for employment than those with graduates and post graduates.

Career avenues include the following

Biophysicists can find employment as a biophysics researcher or scientist with research institutes or government organisations in various academic grades for research-oriented programmes. A biophysicist can also find employment in a biophysics related industry. Biologically-oriented high-tech companies, pharmaceutical companies and the like will hire the services of a qualified and experienced biophysicist. A biophysicist can even find employment as a professor or member of faculty in a university, medical or dental college offering a programme in biophysics. Forensics laboratories, chemical companies, food processing plants, drug manufacturers, cosmetic industry and manufacturers of agricultural chemicals (fertilisers, pesticides, weedicides, etc.) also employ biophysicists. There is a wide range of opportunities abroad in Biophysics, to carry on higher studies and to work.

A few world class organisations for employment

Some of the world class organisations that hire biophysicists are :

- National Institute for Research in Reproductive Health (NIRRH), Mumbai,
- All India Institute of Medical Sciences, New Delhi
- Institute of Microbial Technology, Chandigarh,
- Indian Institute of Science (IISC), Bangalore and
- National Institute of Virology (ICMR), Pune.

Remuneration

The pay scale varies tremendously based on your skill level and experience. However, even at the entry level biophysics jobs offer good pay. Fresher can expect a pay scale of ₹ 15, 000 to 20,000. With experience and performance the salary increases. For those in the research sector in universities, the pay scale is much lucrative with allowance.

Institutes

Many prestigious institutions in India and abroad offer bachelor course and master course in Biophysics. Only few universities in India offer Biophysics course in undergraduate level. But, after the formal twelve year secondary school education, candidates can do graduation in science stream. There is option available to study Biophysics at the master's degree and Ph.D. degree. List of colleges offering biophysics courses are :

- Aligarh Muslim University, Aligarh (Uttar Pradesh)
- Dr Babasheb Ambedkar Marathwada University

  Faculty of Science and Faculty of Life Sciences

  Aurangabad (Maharashtra)
- Mahatma Gandhi University: Faculty of Applied Sciences

  Kottayam (Kerala)

- Manipur University, Imphal (Manipur)
- Punjab University, Patiala (Punjab)
- University of Madras, Chennai (Tamil Nadu)
- All India Institute of Medical Sciences (AIIMS) New Delhi
- Guru Nanak Dev University, Amritsar (Punjab)
- Mangalore University : Faculty of Science Mangalagangothri (Karnataka)
- Punjab University, Chandigarh
- University of Kalyani: Faculty of Science, Nadia (West Bengal)
- University of Mumbai, Mumbai (Maharashtra)
- University of Delhi, Delhi
- University of Madras, Chennai (Tamil Nadu)

Courses

- B.Sc. Biophysics
- M.Sc. Biophysics
- M.D. Biophysics
- M.Sc. Bioscience
- Ph. D. Bioscience

4.4 Biotechnology

What is Biotechnology?

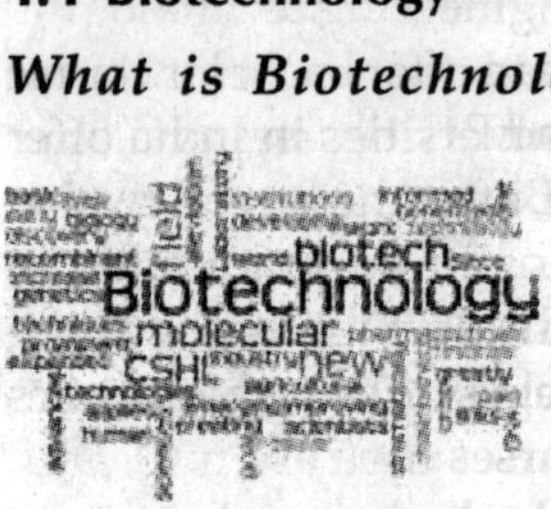

Biotechnology is a research-oriented science, a combination of Biology and Technology. It covers a wide variety of subjects like Genetics, Biochemistry, Microbiology, Immunology, Virology, Chemistry and Engineering and is also concerned with many other subjects like Health and Medicine, Agriculture and Animal Husbandry, Cropping system and Crop Management, Ecology, Cell Biology, Soil Science and Soil Conservation, Bio-statistics, Plant Physiology, Seed Technology etc. Bio-technology is the use of living things especially cells and bacteria in industrial process. There is a great scope in this field as the demand for biotechnologist is growing in India as well as abroad.

Applications of Biotechnology

There are many applications of biotechnology such as developing various medicines, vaccines and diagnostics, increasing productivity, improving energy production and conservation. Biotechnology's intervention in the area of animal husbandry has improved animal breeding. It also helps to improve the quality of seeds, insecticides and fertilisers. Environment biotechnology helps for pollution control and waste management.

Most of the information that has led to the emergence of biotechnology in the present form has been generated during the last five decades. The setting up of a separate Department of Biotechnology (DBT) under the Ministry of Science and Technology in 1986 gave a new impetus to the development of the field of modern biology and biotechnology in India. More than 6000 biotechnologists of higher skill are required in India as per the report from the Ministry of Human Resource Development. To overcome this vast requirement the Department of Biotechnology (DBT) has highlighted the need to set up a regulatory body for the maintenance of standard education under the name of 'All-India Board of Biotechnology Education and Training' under the AICTE.

Eligibility

If you want to join a course in biotechnology you must have a background in science that is Physics or agriculture, chemistry and biology at the intermediate level and then you can join for B. Tech. In India, some universities offer the B. Sc. biotechnology which one can join after class 12 or equivalent examination with physics, chemistry and mathematics. Graduates in all sciences/engineering technology/medicine are eligible for the post-graduate (M.Sc.) course in biotechnology. Programmes in Biotechnology and P.G. courses available are M.Sc. Biotechnology, M.Sc. (Agriculture) Biotechnology, M.V.Sc. (Animal) Biotechnology, M.Tech. Biotechnology, M.Sc./M.V.Sc. in Veterinary, M.Sc. (Marine) Biotechnology, Medical Biotechnology and M. Tech in Biomedical Engineering /Biotechnology. Depending upon the aptitude and necessity, more advanced courses such as Ph. D. and Post-Doctoral Research in Biotechnology can also be pursued.

Integrated M.Tech programme offered at IIT Delhi and Kharagpur is through a Joint Entrance Examination (JEE), which is held for students who have successfully completed the 10+2 or equivalent examination with Physics, Chemistry and Mathematics. For admission to IIT, a pass in the IIT-JEE is required. The Jawaharlal Nehru University, New Delhi, AIIMS, Jadavpur University, Kolkata and Anna University also offer integrated M.Tech course. Selection to the graduate courses (B.E./B.Tech.)

is based on merit, i.e., the marks secured in the final examinations of 10+2 and through entrance examinations. Entrance to the IITs is through JEE and for other institutions through their own separate entrance exams and other state level and national level exams. Apart from the IITs, some other famous institutes also recognise JEE scores for selection. Selection to the post-graduate courses (M.Sc./M.Tech.) in different universities is through an All India Combined Entrance examination conducted by JNU, New Delhi and to IITs through GATE in two years/ four semesters M.Tech courses and through JEE in five years integrated M.Tech courses in Biochemical engineering and Biotechnology.

Personal Qualities Required

A prospective biotechnologist should have a scientific aptitude and a keen interest in the biological sciences. He should be methodical and patient by nature, able to work neatly and accurately and have a flair for laboratory work. The ability to work independently is another important aspect. Ability to use computers in work is very important. Biotechnology needs certain skills of problem solving, information technology skill, analysing and interpreting skills.

Duration

B.Sc. course is of three years duration and M.Sc. course is of two years. B.Tech course is of four years duration and five year for integrated M. Tech programme offered at IIT Delhi and Kharagpur. The Department of Biotechnology has therefore, launched an integrated Manpower Development Programme which includes training of scientists/ technologists for the expanding biotechnological R&D activities and for filling critical gaps in internal competence. The programme includes:

- Short-term Training Courses
- M.Sc./M. Tech./Post Doctoral Programmes
- National and Overseas Associateship
- Visiting Scientists from Abroad Programme
- Short-term Training Course for Industrial personnel
- Technician Training
- Biotechnology teaching/training programme for school
- Biotechnology Publications
- Popular Lectures
- Biotechnology films, etc.

Job Prospects

Biotechnology as a subject has grown rapidly. And as far as employment is concerned, it has become one of the fast growing sectors. Employment record shows that biotechnology has a great scope in future. Biotechnologists can find careers with pharmaceutical companies, chemical, agriculture and allied industries. They can be employed in the areas of planning, production and management of bio-processing industries. There is a large scale employment in research laboratories run by the government as well as the corporate sector. Biotechnology students in India may find work in government-based entity such as universities, research institutes or at private centers as research scientists/assistants. Alternatively, they may find employment in specialised biotechnology companies or biotech-related companies such as pharmaceutical firms, food manufacturers, aquaculture and agricultural companies. Companies that are engaged in business related to life sciences (ranging from equipment, chemicals, pharmaceuticals, diagnostics, etc.) also consider a biotech degree relevant to their field. The work scope can range from research, sales, marketing, administration, quality control, breeders, and technical support. Armed with this powerful combination of fundamental cell, molecular biology and applied science, graduates are well-placed to take up careers in plant, animal or microbial biotechnology laboratories or in horticulture, food science, commerce and teaching.

Some major organisations employing biotechnologists in India include Hindustan Lever Ltd, Thapar Group, Indo-American Hybrid seeds, Bincon India Ltd, Bivcol, IDPL, India Vaccines Corporation, Hindustan Antibiotics, National Botanical Institute, National Chemical Laboratories, and Tata Engineering Research Institute.

Career Options

There is increasing popularity, explosive growth and a lot of opportunity available in the field of Biotechnology. You can be a Research Scientist, Teacher, Marketing Manager, Science Writer, Bioinformatist, Quality Control Officer or Production in-charge in Food, Chemical and Pharmaceutical Industry, Analyst (Venture-Capitalist) Environmental/ Safety Specialist. Biotechnology companies require Corporate Executives with business /management Degrees. A graduate in Biotechnology can get job in government sectors such as Universities and Colleges, Research institutes or at Private Centers as Research scientists/assistants.

- **Lab Technician :** This includes cleaning and maintaining equipment used by scientists and working on the various pieces of lab equipment as instructed.

- **Research Associate :** If you are interested in Research and Development, then becoming a Research Associate can be an interesting career as it allows you to carry out experiments under the instruction of established Scientists.
- **Research Scientist :** If you wish to enter the field at a high-level, you may choose to become a Research Scientist to design, carry out experiments, and write reports for future publication.
- **Engineer (Chemical, Electrical, Environment and Industrial) :** This position would involve engaging in a range of projects from building robots to assisting with Research and Development.
- **Sales Representative :** As a sales representative, you would work with hospitals, doctors and a wide range of medical institutions to keep them aware of biotechnology's latest offerings, as well as trying to encourage their approval for your products over rival products in the market.
- **Marketing :** In biotechnology marketing, you will manage and devise campaigns aimed at particular customer areas, through such methods as working with advertising agencies and maintaining a visible presence at medical conventions and trade shows.
- **Business Development Manager :** This position involves working with colleagues to introduce products and to negotiate agreements with strategic partners.

Remuneration

The amount of remuneration depends upon academic qualification, institute or university from which the degree is attained and the level of work experience gained. In the corporate sector, fresh IIT pass outs may get anything in the range of ₹ 70,000 to 85,000 as annual income and fresh B.Sc./B.Tech graduates from other universities may get anything in the range of ₹ 50,000 to 70,000 as annual income. There are not much jobs if you are a mere graduate in biotechnology. In fact biotechnology is a field of research which demands at least master's degree or biological sciences. After graduation you may get more opportunity in marketing job but if you really want good package in this field you should look forward to Ph.D. then you will get ₹ three-eight lakhs per annum. A research scientist earns an average of ₹ 4, 82,843 per year.

Institutes

- Indian Institute of Information Technology :

  Bioinformatics Division, Allahabad (Uttar Pradesh)

- Madurai Kamaraj University, Madurai (Tamil Nadu)
- SRM University, Chennai (Tamil Nadu)
- University of Pune : Bioinformatics Centre, Pune (Maharashtra)
- Institute of Bioinformatics and Applied Biotechnology Bangalore (Karnataka)
- Pondicherry University : Bioinformatics Centre Puducherry (Puducherry)
- University of Calcutta, Kolkata (West Bengal)
- Jamia Millia Islamia (A Central University), New Delhi
- University of Hyderabad, Hyderabad (Andhra Pradesh)
- Institute of Bioinformatics and Biotechnology, Pune (Maharashtra)
- Mar Athnasios College for Advanced Studies (MACFAST), Thiruvalla (Kerala)
- Amity Institute of Biotechnology, RBEF, E-27 Defence Colony, New Delhi

Useful Contacts

- Department of Biotechnology, Ministry of Science and Technology, Block 2, 7th Floor, CGO Complex, Lodhi Road, New Delhi-110 003.
- Centre for DNA Fingerprinting And Diagnostics (CDFD), Nacharam, Hyderabad-500 076.
- The Institute of Life Sciences, Nalco Square, Chandrasekharpur, Bhubaneshwar-751 023.
- National Institute of Immunology, Aruna Asaf Ali Marg, New Delhi-110 067.
- National Centre For Cell Sciences, CCS Complex, University of Pune Campus, Ganeshkhind, Pune-411 007, Maharashtra.
- National Brain Research Centre, Manesar, Gurgaon Distt. Haryana-122 050.
- National Centre For Plant Genome Research (NCPGR), JNU, New Delhi.

4.5 Nanotechnology

What is Nanotechnology?

The word *'Nano'* in Greek means 'dwarf'. Nanometer (nm) is a unit of measurement used to measure very small particles like atoms and molecules. One nanometer is equal to one-billionth (10-9) of a meter. Entirely different from bulk material, nano-materials are 5,000 to 50,000 times smaller than the diameter of a human hair. These light but strong transparent materials are very active and aggressive in any chemical reaction. Nano-materials can be mixed with strong or weak materials to make them thousand times stronger and more efficient. Carbon and diamond are super examples of nano-materials.

Nanotechnology, therefore, can be defined as 'the science of miniature'. It is a promising technology of the future as it is currently one of the most exciting and wide areas of research which may lead to greatest technological advances in our times. It is a global phenomenon and an emerging field that finds its way into a myriad of industrial applications spanning across all areas of science and technology. It is a form of molecular engineering and technology to develop novel materials and devices in different fields in the nano-range.

Two Major Categories of Nanotechnology

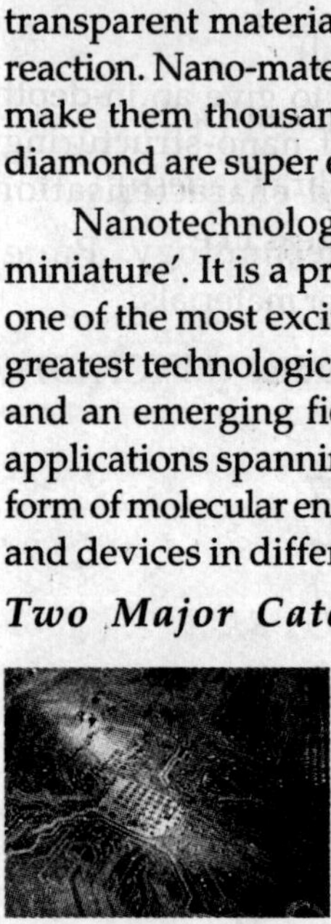

The two major categories of Nanotechnology are Nanoscale technology and Molecular manufacturing. Nanoscale technology covers small structures and can be used for introducing stronger materials, better medicines and faster computers and so on. Molecular manufacturing is an attempt made at building mechanical manufacturing systems that join molecules together.

Eligibility and Course Areas

For pursuing a career in the field of Nanotechnology, the aspirant must have a post-graduate qualification in the subject i.e., they must have an M.Tech or M.Sc. degree in Nanotechnology. At present, no reputed institute in India is offering courses in Nanotechnology at the graduation level. Eligibility criteria for doing post-graduation in Nanotechnology is Bachelor's degree with minimum of 50 per cent marks in Physics, Chemistry, Mathematics and Life Sciences and with PCM (Physics, Chemistry, Mathematics) as subsidiary subjects. The M. Tech course in Nanotechnology is of great benefit because students who come from different streams enrich each other to intensify their knowledge. The candidates, who wish to pursue higher studies in Nanotechnology, can apply for M. Tech in Nanotechnology after completing their B. Tech degree in any one of the following subjects, i.e., in Material Science, Mechanical, Biomedical, Chemical, Biotechnology, Electronics and Computer Science. Those who have completed M.Sc. in Physics, Chemistry, Material Science, Biotechnology and Computer Science can also join for the M. Tech Course. The admission to the five-years integrated M. Tech Course in Nanotechnology is through entrance test.

Course Areas

The curriculum of Nanotechnology is designed to give an in-depth understanding on the underlying concepts of nano-structuring, fabrication techniques for nano-devices and characterisation techniques. The courses are mainly focussed on areas like :

- Designing of durable, resistant and cheaper materials.
- Designing of electronic components with special emphasis on dimension and power.
- Techniques for tapping solar energy and increase in its power.
- Convergence of genetic medicine, nanotechnology and development of unique drug delivery system.
- Relation between environmental science and nanotechnology.

These courses help students to understand the various methods to synthesise and pattern on a nanoscale on various substrates. These are supported by project work undertaken on both group and individual basis and conducted in close collaboration with the related industries.

Job Prospects and Career Options

A professional in the field of Nanotechnology can easily find lucrative career opportunities in various sectors. They can work in the field of nano-medicine, bio-informatics, stem cell development, pharmaceutical companies, nano toxicology and nano power generating sectors. Other work fields include – Health Industry, Agriculture, Environment Industry, Food and Beverages, Space Research, product development and advising, Academic and Teaching, R&D in government sector, universities and private research institutes, Genetics, Biotechnology, Communication and Media, Forensic Science and many other new industries emerging as a result of advances in nanotechnology.The CSIR (Council of Scientific and Industrial Research) has set up 38 laboratories across the country to carry out research and development work in the field of Nanotechnology. Those with Ph.D. in Nanotechnology will have vibrant opportunities in the Research and Development sectors. Some of the companies in India that provides job prospects are Cranes Software International Limited, Bangalore; Innovations Unified Technology, Mumbai, etc.

Remuneration

This field is expected to boom in future and throw up a large number of job opportunities with handsome pay packages. The initial pay scale depends upon the industry. In government sector, a person with an M.Tech degree can expect a salary of around ₹ 20,000 – 30,000 per month. This is a field that has a manifold scope for perks and other benefits. Depending on the qualification, experience and nature of work, the pay package may vary from ₹ 6, 00,000 – 12, 00,000 per annum.

Courses

- Certificate Course in Nanotechnology
- Diploma in Nanotechnology
- Integrated Dual Degree (B.Tech./M.Tech.) in Nanotechnology
- M.Sc. Nanoscience
- M.Tech. Health Care Nanotechnology (Integrated)
- M.Tech. Nanomedical Sciences
- M.Tech. Nanotechnology
- M.Tech. Nanotechnology (Integrated)
- Ph. D. Nanoscience and Technology
- Ph. D. Nanotechnology

Nanotechnology: Research Centres

- **Nano Mission, Department of Science and Technology, New Delhi**

  Technology Bhavan, New Mehrauli Road, New Delhi-110016

  Phone: 011-26963695

  Website: www.nanomission.gov.in

- **National Physical Laboratory, New Delhi**

  Dr. K.S. Krishnan Marg, New Delhi

  Phone: 91-11-25742610, 91-11-25742611

  Fax: 91-11-25726938, 91-11-25726952

  Website: www.nplindia.org

- **National Chemical Laboratory (NCL), Pune**

  Dr. Homi Bhabha Road, Pune-411008

  Phone: 020-2590 2013

  Fax: 020-2590 2636

  Website: www.ncl-india.org

- **Central Scientific Instruments Organisation, Chandigarh**

  Sector 30-C, Chandigarh-160030

  Phone: 0172-2651722, 2652728

  Fax: 0172-2657267

  Website: www.csio.nic.in

Top Ten Nanotechnology Colleges in India

- **Amity Institute of Nanotechnology (AINT)**

  Amity University, Uttar Pradesh

  E-2 Block, 3rd Floor, Sector-125, Noida-201303

- **Jawaharlal Nehru Center for Advanced Scientific Research (JNCASR)**

  Jakur, Bangalore-560064

- **School of Nana Science and Technology**

  National Institute of Technology Calicut (NITC)

  Pin-673601

- **Amrita Centre for Nanosciences**

  Amrita Institute of Medical Sciences

  Amrita Vishwa Vidyapeetham

  AIMS Ponnekkara PO

  Kochi – 682041

- **Centre for Nanotechnology and Advanced Biomaterials (CeNTAB)**

  Sastra University, Thirumalaisamudram, Thanjavur

  Tamil Nadu-613042

- **Department of Physics**

  Indian Institute of Science

  Bangalore 560012

- **Centre for Research in Nanotechnology and Science (CRNTS)**

  IIT Bombay, Powai, Mumbai-400076
- **Department of Mechanical Engineering and Material Science Programme**

  Indian Institute of Technology, Kanpur-208016, UP
- **Indian Institute of Technology, Delhi**

  Hauz Khas, New Delhi-110016
- **National Institute of Technology,**

  Kurukshetra-136119, Haryana

4.6 Photonics

What is Photonics?

Photonics is a hi-tech subject that evolved as a result of the fusion of optical technology with electronics. It is the use of light to obtain, convey or process information. It is the science of mastering the techniques involved in the emission, detection, transmission and modulation of light. This sub-discipline of physics deals with the study of photons and the elementary particle of light. It deals with the instruments required for laser guns, optical fibers, optometric instruments, etc.

Importance of Photonics to Human life

What can light particles – photons do in our daily lives? Can you imagine about such light that can carry the equal of 300,000,000 simultaneous telephone calls? All these are made possible through Photonics, the technology of light energy. In photonic system, information signals are conveyed as pulses of light and these optical signals are transmitted through optical fibers. Optical fibers are strands of special glass around 10 micron (100 um) in diameter (i.e. about the thickness of a human hair) which can carry thousands of times more information than electrical wires. Photonic devices that are used to convert electrical signals into optical signal and back again where necessary can be made up from a variety of materials including semi-conductors and even optical fibers. These devices are also used to manipulate and process optical signals directly without the need for conversion.

Advantages of Photonics

The technology of Photonics is used for imaging, health-care, medicine, defence, optics and electronics. It has strong reputation of solving research problems through advanced spectroscopy, lasers, microscopy, and fibre optic imaging. Photonics is also put to use in biotechnology, microbiology, medicinal sciences, surgery and life sciences. It is even applicable for industrial manufacturing, entertainment, metrology which is the science of measurement that deals with weights and measures and Photonic computing. Photonic computing uses photons of laser light to perform the logic that makes computing work. Apart from these industries, the technology has steadily penetrated into military applications.

Eligibility

Those who have completed 10+2 in Science stream (Physics, Chemistry and Mathematics) with a minimum mark of 50 per cent are eligible for graduation courses in Photonics and Opto-electronics. A candidate having a Bachelor's degree in Physics and Mathematics, Applied Physics or Electronics can pursue M.Sc. in Photonics or Optoelectronics. One can obtain M.Tech, M.Phil. and Ph.D. in the field of Photonics and the eligibility is a Master's degree in Physics or Photonics. There are some diploma courses also that would help one to become a Photonics technician. Two-year technician programme help one to become a photonics technician. Apart from the educational qualifications, some personal skills are required in order to be an expert in Photonics.

Job Prospects and Career Options

Photonics specialists can work as engineers, technicians or technologists, and research officers in government offices. Manufacturing, design, research, development, systems and applications are some of the fields they work in. The range of application of Photonics extends from energy generation and detection to communication and information processing.

The scientists have to do more research work on Photonics, while the engineers design Photonic equipments. The photonics technician helps the engineers often start their career as assistant to experienced engineers. Based on qualifications they can either become research directors or principal engineers. Graduates can find work in the telecommunication companies. They could find key positions in a variety of other industries and R&D organisations involved in the area of networks, semi-conductor technology, fibre and integrated optics, opto-electronics and software.

In the industrial manufacturing, a career in photonics is helpful since laser is used for cutting, drilling and welding. In automobile manufacture, photonics testing offers advantages over mechanical methods of testing interior and brake noise. Some of the major companies in Photonics are Eagle Photonics (Bangalore and Chennai), Kwality Photonics Pvt. Ltd, Sphere Optics, J-2 Optronics, Sahajanand Technologies Pvt. Ltd, Optiwave Photonics Limited (Hyderabad), John F. Welch Technology Centre (Bangalore), Advanced Photonics, Sterlite Optical Technologies Ltd., etc.

This is one of the highly paid careers among the science-oriented careers. Remuneration varies on the basis of experience and education. One can earn 20,000 – 35,000 per month at the beginning of their career.

Institutes

- **The International School of Photonics, CUSAT**

  Cochin University of Science and Technology, Cochin-22, Kerala

  Phone: +91-484-2575396, 2577550

  Fax: +91-484-2577595

  Website: www.photonics.cusat.edu, www.cusat.ac.in
- **Indian Institute of Technology, Madras**

  Department of Physics, Chennai-600036

  Phone: +91-4422574851

  Fax: +91-4422574852

  Website: www.physics.iitm.ac.in
- **Indian Institute of Technology, Delhi**

  Department of Physics, Delhi-110 016

  Phone: +91 (11) 26591361

  Fax: 0280-2571982

  Website: www.web.iitd.ac.in/~optoelectronics/index.htm
- **Manipal Academy of Higher Education – MAHE**

  A Deemed University under UGC Act, Manipal – 576 104 Karnataka

  Phone: 0920-2571978

  Fax: 0820-2571982

  Website: www.admissions.minipal.edu
- **Periyar EVR College (Affiliated to Bharathidasan University)**

  Khaja Malai Tiruchiapalli, Tiruchiapalli (Tricy) – 23, Tamil Nadu

  Phone: 0431-2420079

Fax: 0431-2423478

Website: www.periyarevrcollege.com

- **Rajarshi Shahu Mahavidyalaya, Department of Photonics, Latur, Maharashtra**

  Opp. Central Bus Stand, Chandra Nagar, Latur – 413512, Maharashtra

  Phone: 02382-245933

  Fax: 02382-2536645

Institute Abroad

- **The Department of Physics, Australian National University**

  The Australian National University, Canberra ACT 0200, Australia

  Local T: 6125 5111, Interstate T: 02 6125 5111, International T: +61 261255111

  Website: www.photonics.anu.edu

- **Department of Physics, University of Strathclyde**

  John Anderson Building, 107 Rottenrow

  Phone: 0141 548 3366, Outside UK: +44 141 548 3366

  Fax: 0141 552 2891, Outside UK: +44 141 552 2891

  Website: www.phys.strath.ac.uk/postgraduate/courses

Useful Contact

- **Photonics Lab**

  Prof. Vinod Krishan (Dean Academic)

  Indian Institute of Astrophysics, 2nd Block, Koramangala, Bangalore-560034

  Phone: 080-25530672 Ext: 270

  Website: www.iiap.res.in

5

COMPUTER SCIENCE AND INFORMATION TECHNOLOGY

5.1 Call Centers

What is a Call Center?

A call centre is a service centre with adequate telecom facilities, access to internet and wide database, which provide voice-based or web-based information and support to customers in the country or abroad through trained personnel. Call centers exist in all sectors of business including banking, utilities, manufacturing, security, market research, pharmaceuticals, catalogue sales, order desk, customer service, technical queries (help desk), emergency dispatch, credit collections, food service, airline/hotel reservations and the like. The wide area of services provided by the call centers makes it a lucrative career with a range of opportunities.

Inbound and Outbound Calls

Traditionally, call centers meant only voiced-based customer support. But now most call centers are more of a contact centre, offering e-CRM services that include voiced-based customer support as well as e-mail response, web-based text-chat services and other customer interaction channels. The call centre services can be ***'inbound'*** where in calls are received from customers enquiring about a service or product that an organisation provides. The call centre services can be ***'outbound'*** where in calls are made to customers to sell products or collect information/ money, etc. Call centre services can also 'specialised' in business processing where in-calls are made from one company to another company.

Some call centers stick to only domestic businesses dealing with customers within the country and they are called domestic call centers; while others such as an International call centers mainly deal with clients from abroad say from US, Europe, Australia, UK, etc. There is a great scope for call centers in India with a large population of educated English speaking group. The wide range of opportunities, comparatively well paid jobs for the minimum qualification it requires, and the facilities the companies provide like to and fro transport, subsidised meals and medical facilities makes Call centers a good option.

Eligibility and Course Area

There are no specific educational qualifications required to become a CSE (Customer Service Executive/Operator or call centre adviser/ representative, customer service representative) in a call centre. It is a good option for plus two or fresh college graduates, housewives and retired people.

Personal Skills and Attributes

The skills required vary depending on the project and the type of business that is being handled. A very good command over English language is the main skill required for International Call Centers. Domestic Call Centers insist on fluency in Hindi. Computer literacy, typing speed, knowledge of customer behaviour, marketing skills (a certificate or Diploma in Marketing in case of 'outbound' tele-marketing is preferable), the ability to enter and retrieve information quickly from databases and an ability to analyse problems are other useful skills that come in handy.

Good communication and listening skills are important. CSE (Customer Service Executive) should have the patience to listen to and comprehend the need, be unfailingly polite, good natured and reasonably intelligent to choose between options and remedy problems effectively to the satisfaction of the customer. Persuasive skill (aggressiveness) is needed in an 'outbound' contact centre where you either collect money from defaulting customers or try to promote sales and encourage customers to use your company's products. They may be required to work at odd hours especially in International Call Centers where the customers may be calling from places where the timing may be several hours behind IST.

Training

A fresher has to undergo intense training to make themselves suited for the job. The training include accent training, listening skills, 'slang' training, accent neutralisation, telephone etiquette, telesales etiquette and cyber grammar, interaction skills, customer relation, management skills and call centre terminology. They are also given a thorough knowledge on the product of the company, even how it could malfunction and breakdown and fail to arrive at its objectives and how to deal with complaints of customers. Continuous training at regular intervals including updating on the latest references and slang the callers are likely to use, updating on the new products, developing faster ways of accessing information is a must for growth in this field.

There is no standardised training period. It can be between two weeks to twelve weeks depending on the project. There will be an initiation programme which includes familiarising the company's work culture, and the international environment they deal with and the nature of their clients abroad. Then, the actual training begins which includes both theoretical and on job training.

In India, the training is usually done by the company itself. There are many institutes that give training in this field abroad and recently the trend is picking up in India also. International certifications from STI knowledge, a leading provider of call centre training in the US have recently been introduced in India. STI offers international certifications following a Web-based examination after completion of the course. The certifications are Help Desk 2000, Call Centre 2000, and Knowledge 2000 for the entire three-tier that is the operators, managers and director.

Job Prospects

There is a great scope for call centers in India. The large population of educated English speaking people, and the comparative low-cost are encouraging more and more companies from abroad/inland to base or outsource their call centers to India. GE capital, American Express, Wipro Spectra mind, Infowavz International (Mumbai), Daksh, Reliance InfoTech are some of the call centers which are on a recruitment spree.

- **Call centre operators/Customer care executives:** This is the entry level in call centers. Your general duties include answering telephone calls, taking down details of the caller's query and logging this information on a computer, providing the caller with appropriate information or advice in some cases, selling a caller products or services. In outbound call centre services such as tele-marketing, an operator will also need to identify potential customers and make outgoing calls marketing their organisation's product, occasionally following-up calls by sending letters, faxes or e-mail, deal with customer complaints, etc. A call centre operator's duties will depend on the type of product or service that the organisation provides, and the type of client he/she is servicing. Customer service executives can move on to the technical, financial or the insurance sector.

- **Call centre Supervisors and Managers** : After working as an operator for three or four years, you will be promoted to a supervisory level-based on your ability and performance. As vacancies occur it will be published in house, an interview will be conducted and promotions are made. As a supervisor, you will be in charge of the various operators working under you. You can be promoted to the managerial level depending on your experience, ability and skills acquired.

Performance is measured (performance appraisal) based on targets achieved in the particular business. In ***outbound call centres***, (like tele-marketing) your performance is calculated on sales per hour or in collection department of a bank, performance is measured on contacts made and money collected. In ***inbound call centres***, performance is measured on the basis of average talktime, that is, the time you take to satisfy the customer, analysis made, understanding of the problem and the courtesy extended to the customers.

All call centre experience is regarded as worthwhile experience for customer relations, sales jobs or insurance sector. One has a better chance of moving on to other industries with experience in call centers for example, insurance sector if you have had experience dealing with insurance clients.

Remuneration

As a fresher, one could start his/her career in an International Call Centre as a Call Center Executive and earn attractive pay packages ranging from ₹ 8,500 to ₹ 12,000 (under graduate and graduate respectively) approximately per month other than bonuses for outstanding performances.

Institutes

- Akiko Sherman InfoTech, 13/9, Padam Singh Chowk, Ajmal Khan Road, New Delhi-110005.
- North Star Call Centre College, B-109, Sector-5, Noida-201301 (UP), India.
- Ian Stern, A-62 DDA Complex (Ring Road), Defence Colony, New Delhi-110024.
- ProEdge Solutions (P) Limited, Above UTI Bank, Srinagar Colony Main Road, Srinagar Colony, Hyderabad-500073.
- Trans-India Management Systems, 305, University Plaza, Vijay Cross Roads, Navrtangpura, Ahmedabad-380009.
- EduTech India, 7/2 Brunton Road, Bangalore-560025.

- EduTech India, No. 8 (old no. 39), Khader Nawaz Khan Road, Nungambakkam, Chennai-600006.
- EduTech India, 402, Fourth Floor, Kant Chambers (Near RK Studios), SION-TROMBAY Road, Chembur, Mumbai-400071.
- EduTech India 62, Second Floor, Lakshmi Market, New Delhi-110067.
- JTS Institutes #35, Infantry Road, Bangalore-560001.

5.2 Ethical Hacking

What is an Ethical Hacking?

Ethical Hacking is a white hat technique, wherein the hacker breaches the security of a computer system or the network to expose the security system's vulnerability. Security is one of the major concerns of our present cyber era. Security is not merely a concern in physical space any longer but also in cyber space. Breaking into computer systems which once was a pastime for geeks, now has become a full-fledged career option. In recent years, there has been alarming increase in the number of cyber crime cases on the Internet like hacking e-mail accounts, stealing and intercepting sensitive data, password attacks, abusive e-mails, etc. This has increased the demand for ethical hackers who are our saviours.

Although hacking is an offence, it is considered ethical only when it is done under a contract between the hacker and the organisation. When we hear the word 'hacker' it engenders a feeling of fear. But 'ethical hackers' also known as a 'white hat' is our friend. An ethical hacker is someone, who hacks with legal permission to strengthen systems and makes them penetration-proof. Ethical hacker is a network or computer experts who help in finding loopholes in an IT-system and break into it.

Who are Ethical Hackers?

Ethical Hackers are technically skilled IT professionals with a strong desire to solve problems and prevent malicious hackers from causing damage to network systems. Ethical hackers are *au fait* with computer and networking algorithms. They report the loopholes in the security system to the owners and provide solutions to protect the network. In other words, ethical hackers try to penetrate networks, detect the vulnerabilities in the security systems and fix them before any troubleshooter can take advantage of it. An ethical hacker is generally appointed by huge corporate companies to ensure the safety and privacy of their data. Computer security is a global issue and it's the job of an ethical hacker to make the cyber safe, now and forever.

Eligibility

Those who have an educational background in computer science or IT or computer engineering can enter the field of ethical hacking. They must know programming languages like C, C++, Python, Ruby, etc. The understanding of widely used operating systems like the various versions of Windows, Linux and Firefox is also an important part of your knowledge base. Some of the known certifications in Ethical Hacking are CEH (Certified Ethical Hacker) and CHFI (Computer Hacking Forensic Investigator) offered by EC Council, CCNA Security (Cisco Certified Network Professional), SCP's SCNS (Security Certified Network Specialist) and SCNP (Security Certified Network Professional), CISSP (Certified Information Systems Security Professional) offered by Intl. Information System Security Certification Consortium and many more. Certification from SANS institute in the US though expensive is another valuable certifications offered by Cisco, Microsoft, Novell, etc. Ethical hacking course trains a student to find loopholes in a network or a programme using similar methods as that of hacking. The intense certifications mentioned above provide critical network security fundamentals for all network administrators. Skills covered include design and implementation of firewalls, IDS, wireless security, Cryptography, Linux security and Windows security among others.

Personal Attributes

Being computer savvy and gadget-friendly are the pre-requisites to become an ethical hacker. To be a professional ethical hacker you also require motivation, dedication, analytical thinking, and initiative, problem solving ability, investigative nature and formal training in ethical hacking. Honesty, integrity and trustworthiness are also highly essential in this field. Ethical hackers must have adaptability and resourcefulness to troubleshoot any unforeseeable snags during testing software and systems. They must also have good computer hardware and software knowledge. Above all, he must be a certified ethical hacker.

Job Prospects

With internet use mounting worldwide and cyber crimes burgeoning day by day, ethical hackers have become an integral workforce of any IT security industry today. However, currently there is a huge gap between the demand and supply as far as ethical hackers are concerned. Hence, scope for a fresher is lucrative not only in India but globally.

Internet security and Networking are the two fastest-growing industries where ethical hackers can find employment in ethical hacking and information security. Ethical hackers are hired to find out any vulnerability that might exist in their network and to find out ways to fix them. They can join the government as well as private organisations as cyber security experts. IT firms are the main recruiters of ethical hackers. However, it is not limited only to IT companies but such experts are also required by financial service providers, airlines, retail chains, hotels and several government agencies.

Government agencies such as military and law enforcement agencies, defence organisations, forensic laboratories, detective companies, investigative services offer challenging roles to ethical hackers. Some skilled hackers work for investigation agencies like the Central Bureau of Investigation, the National Security Agency, and the Federal Bureau of Information.

Some large organisations employ security testers; while others use contractors to audit their systems. Graduates can set-up their own companies offering ethical hacking services. Graduates can set-up their own companies to audit their systems. Companies such as Wipro, Infosys, IBM, TCS, Tech Mahindra, HCL, Airtel, Reliance and many more are also looking for good ethical hackers.

The kind of jobs available is that of Network Security Systems Manager, Network Security Administrator, Systems/Applications, Security Executive, Web Security Administrator, Web Security Manager, etc.

Remuneration

A fresher in the field can earn a minimum of ₹ 2.5 lakh per annum. Initially, one has to work as an assistant or trainee for security system till he can be experienced enough to be an ethical hacker on his own. After becoming a penetration tester or ethical hacker, one can make ₹ 20,000 to ₹ 25,000. With experience, one can expect up to ₹ 4.5 lakh per annum. However, those with work experience of five years or more can get from ₹ 10 to ₹ 12 lakh per annum.

Courses

- Certificate Course in Cyber Laws
- M.Sc. Cyber Forensics and Information Security
- Post-graduate Diploma in Cyber Laws
- Post-graduate Diploma in Digital and Cyber Forensics and Related Laws

- Advance Diploma in Ethical Hacking
- Certificate in Information Security and Ethical Hacking
- Certified Information System Security Professional (CISSP)
- CCNA Certification
- Certified Ethical Hacker (CEH)
- Post-graduate Diploma in IT Security

Institutes

Many institutes in India offer certificate and diploma courses in Ethical Hacking and related fields like Cyber Forensics, Information security and the like. Getting International certifications like CEH (Certified Ethical Hacker) and CHFI (Computer Hacking Forensic Investigator) offered by EC Council, CCNA Security (Cisco Certified Network Professional), SCNS (Security Certified Network Specialist) and SCNP (Security Certified Network Professional) from SCP, CISSP (Certified Information Systems Security Professional) offered by Intl. Information System Security Certification Consortium and many more. Certification from SANS institute in the US is well-known and valuable.

- **Koenig Solutions (Indian Centers of EC-Council's Certified Ethical Hacker)**

  Website: www.eccouncil.org/ceh.htm and www.konigsolutions.com.
- **Innobuzz Knowledge Solutions**

  Website: www.innobuzz.in.
- **IMT Ghaziabad**

  Website: www.imt.edu/cum.

5.3 Information Technology

What is Information Technology?

IT, an acronym for Information Technology is a buzz phrase we have heard *ad nausem* in our contemporary daily parlance. It is a branch of engineering that deals with the use of computers and telecommunications to store, retrieve, transmit and manipulate data, often in the context of a business or other enterprise. The term is used as a synonym for computers and computer networks but it also encompasses other information distribution technologies such as television and telephones. Several industries are associated with information technology such as computer hardware, software, electronics, semi-conductors, internet, telecom equipment, e-commerce and computer services.

The Scope of IT

IT is the area of managing technology and spans wide variety of areas that include computer software, information systems, computer hardware, programming languages but are not limited to things such as processes and data constructs. In short, anything that renders data, information or perceived knowledge in any visual format whatsoever, via any multimedia distribution mechanism is considered part of the IT domain.

The Functions of IT Professionals

IT professionals are highly specialised in their field which is probably why they are called "IT nerds." They perform a variety of functions (IT Disciplines/Competencies) ranging from installing applications to designing complex computer networks and information databases. A few of the duties that IT professionals perform may include data management, networking, engineering computer hardware, database and software design as well as management and administration of entire systems. Information technology is beginning to spread further than the conventional personal computer and network technologies and more into integrations of other technologies such as the use of cell phones, televisions, automobiles and more which is increasing the demand for such jobs.

The Two Main Sectors in the Field of IT

- **Hardware :** This includes the physical elements of the computer system and deals with the designing, manufacturing and maintenance of computers. This area also includes the assembling of the manufactured components of the computers.
- **Software :** This includes the set of instructions by which a computer is programmed for working and performing the specified tasks. This realm includes the work of designing the programmes for various purposes. Programmes may be for controlling the functioning of the computers or they may also be some user-friendly programmes for specific needs. The programs may also come in the form of packages, which are designed for meeting the different kinds of requirements for large number of people.

Functional Areas in Hardware

- **Manufacturing :** This involves the work of production and assembly of components of computer systems.

- **Maintenance :** People in maintenance look after the smooth functioning of the machine and help in rectifying and detecting the breakdown in them. They also help in taking preventive measures so that least amount of damage could be caused to the computer systems and peripherals.
- **Research and Development :** It involves designing of chips and circuits, computer architecture and integration of peripherals. It also includes improvement and upgrading of the existing systems.
- **Management :** Managers ensure that the development and production work goes smoothly. They look after the allocation of resources and planning.

Functional Areas in Software

- **Manufacturing :** This involves the preparing the set of instructions or programmes to let the computer work. This further needs combining of application of computer science and telecommunications principles and creativity.
- **Software Development :** This involves updating and development of existing operations as well as their refining and improvement. All this is carried out in various stages like analysis, designing, construction, implementation etc.
- **Data Entry :** The data for the programmes which are made have to be fed in computers. So this work is done at data entry level.
- **Programmers/Coders :** They prepare programmes either for general purpose or user-friendly programmes or some specific programmes for individual use along with testing and integrating them.
- **Support Services :** They vary in nature and can range from helping customers in the purchase of the software, suggesting its right kind of application and providing them with the required training at the initial stage of its use.

Technical Areas for Career

- **Computer Operations :** It requires handling of computer peripherals along with other accessories like CD-ROMs, disk drives, printers, etc.
- **Database Administration :** It involves management and main tenancy of data.
- **Sales and Marketing :** The work here involves selling of the computer system and its marketing to different companies or individuals.

- **Data Centre Management :** It involves management of the dedicated facilities, which houses the critical servers and other networking and back-up equipments. Data centers typically house those equipments which have to be kept operational 24 × 7 × 30.

Career Options for IT Professionals

- **Software Engineers :** They designed programmes and specialised packages for the required purposes. Their work even involves research and development.
- **Web Developers :** They are electronics and computer engineers who are engaged in developing websites for the Internet.
- **System Analysts :** They look after the work of final testing of the software and advising the clients on the purchase and installation of the computer systems. They also are responsible for researching the organisational procedures and planning their computerisation.
- **Consultants :** They provide expert guidance to the companies during the purchase of the computer system. System analyst or designers with considerable amount of experience can work as consultants.
- **Technical Writers :** They are involved in writing manuals for computers.
- **E-commerce :** They are adept in the net-com business, e-commerce fundamentals and its security issues and assist in developing websites for commercial purposes.
- **Knowledge Engineers :** They are expert in designing of the computer systems, which are associated with a human expert, like medical diagnosis or safety systems for industry.
- **Webmasters :** They handle the task of configuration and setting up of the websites and its development. They have to take care of the security of the websites and create firewalls against the hackers and stalkers.
- **Networking :** Their work involves designing of networks, implementation of support servicing and management.
- **Computer Education :** This job involves giving training to the end users, students or computer professionals in advanced technologies.

Important IT Companies in India

Some of the well-known software companies include:

- Accenture
- ADP
- Apps Associates
- Birla soft
- Broad ridge
- Cap Gemini
- Capital IQ
- Curator
- CMC Ltd.
- Cognizant Technology Solutions
- Computer Associates
- Cordys
- CSC
- Cybage Software
- Dell
- DST Global Solutions
- Google
- HCL
- HP
- IBM
- IGATE Global Solutions
- Infosys
- Larsen and Toubro Ltd.
- NUT Ltd
- Microsoft
- Oracle
- Patni Computer Systems (P) Ltd.
- Polaris
- Tata Consultancy Services
- Verizon
- Virtusa Technologies
- Wipro Technologies Ltd.
- Yahoo etc.

Although the software engineering sector is currency dependant, highly competitive and hectic, it is a lucrative career option. It surely offers a bright future for the IT professionals. Average salaries for freshers vary between Rs. 3.5 lakhs to Rs. 4.5 lakhs per annum depending on the recruiting company.

5.4 What is Business Process Outsourcing (BPO)?

Business Process Outsourcing (BPO) is a sub-set of outsourcing that involves the contracting of the operations and responsibilities of specific business functions or processes to a third-party service provider. Originally, this was associated with manufacturing with firms such as Coca Cola that outsourced large segments of its supply chain. In the contemporary context, it is primarily used to refer to the outsourcing of business processing services to an outside firm, replacing in-house services with labour from an outside firm.

BPO is typically categorised into back office outsourcing which includes internal business functions such as human resources or finance and accounting and front office outsourcing which includes customer-related services such as contact center services. BPO that is contracted outside a company's country is called 'offshore outsourcing'. BPO that is contracted outside a company's neighbouring (or nearby) country is called 'near shore outsourcing'.

BPO is a distinct form of information technology (IT) outsourcing, which focusses on hiring a third-party company or service provider to do IT-related activities such as application management and application development, data center operations or testing and quality assurance. In the early days, BPO usually consisted of outsourcing processes such as payroll. Then, it grew to include employee benefits management. Now, it encompasses a number of functions that are considered non-core to the primary business strategy. Now, it is common for organisations to outsource financial and administration (F&A) processes, human resources (HR) functions, call center and customer service activities and accounting and payroll. These outsourcing deals frequently involve multi-year contracts that can run into hundreds of millions of dollars. Often, the people performing the work internally for the client firm are transferred and become employees for the service provider. Dominant outsourcing service providers in the BPO fields (some of which also dominate the IT outsourcing business) include US companies IBM, Accenture and Hewitt Associates as well as European and Asian companies Capgemini, TCS, Wipro and Infosys.

Many of these BPO efforts involve location for BPO activities. Frequently, BPO is also referred to as ITES – Information Technology-Enabled Services. Since most business processes include some form of automation, IT 'enables' these services to be performed.

An offshoot of BPO is KPO – Knowledge Process Outsourcing. It was considered by some to be a sub-set of BPO. KPO includes those activities that require greater skill, knowledge, education and expertise to handle. For example, an insurance company might outsource data entry of its claims that forms as part of a BPO initiative. It may also choose to use a KPO service provider to evaluate new insurance applications-based on a set of criteria or business rules; this work would require efforts of more knowledgeable set of workers than the data entry would. The current definition of KPO encompasses R&D, product development and legal e-discovery as well as a number of other business functions. Also coming into use is the term BTO – Business Transformation Outsourcing. This refers to the idea of having service providers contribute to the effort of transforming a business into a learner, more dynamic, agile and flexible operation.

5.5 What is Computer Science?

Computer Science is the science of using computers to solve problems. Mostly, this involves designing ***software*** (computer programmes) and addressing fundamental scientific questions about the nature of computation, but also involves many aspects of ***hardware*** and architecting the large computer systems that form the infrastructure of commercial and government enterprises.

Computers have become an indispensable adjunct of almost every person. They are utilised in industries, business houses, sciences, research organisations, educational institutions, etc. There is a wide scope of employment as Operators, Programmers, Analysts, Engineers, Sales Persons and many more in the management services and consultancies, data processing departments of industries, steel plants, aeronautics and space. Persons working with computers must have the knowledge of the computer language depending on the type of work.

6
COSTUME AND FASHION INDUSTRY

6.1 Beauty Care

"Beauty lies in the eyes of the beholder," a famous Shakespearean phrase discusses about the external and internal beauty of a human being. Who doesn't want to look beautiful or handsome in the other's eyes? When you talk about external beauty be it your face, skin, hair or even nails – everyone, no matter men or women are beauty conscious and wants to look perfect. This has led to the flourishing of the field of Cosmetology, generally known as 'Beauty Care'.

The Meaning of Cosmetology

Derived from the Greek word *'kosmetikos'*, which means 'skilled in adornment', Cosmetology is the study and application of beauty handling. 'Beauty care' that helps people look their best is a field for those who have an eye for beauty and enjoy interaction with others. With the work environment getting increasingly competitive and professional and the growing awareness of health and beauty among men and women, the need to appear well-groomed and attractive has assumed greater importance in today's world. This has resulted in the growth of beauty products and beauty treatments, turning beauty care into a fast growing and lucrative career. Broadly, cosmetology includes everything from beauty therapy to health care. Work in this field involves the knowledge and use of a range of treatments and equipments to enhance the appearance of the face, body and hair.

The Role of a Beautician

The main task of a beautician is to give an attractive appearance to their clients. In this field, success has no relationship to the age of the practitioner. Although tastes and trends in beauty keep on changing the basic job of a beautician, beauty professionals remain the same.

Hairstyling, skin care, cosmetics, manicures, pedicures and electrology are the specialisations or various fields of cosmetology. This is a field where one can easily get into and be successful. Since, the working medium of this field is a live person, it is one of the most rewarding of all art works.

Eligibility

Cosmetology takes care of our beauty professionally. They may be medical professionals and non-medical cosmetologists. Even though both of them in the broad sense do the same job basically, they possess completely different qualifications and methods of application. To be a Medical Cosmetologist one needs to have a post-graduate degree in Dermatology (MD or diploma/DNB) after MBBS, but a Non-medical Cosmetologist doesn't need any professional qualifications as such, besides good hands on experience. Those who have a keen interest and inclination in beauty care can enter the field after completing schooling at a minimum age of sixteen years.

Rather than high academic inputs, a beautician requires practical skills, which can be gained not only by professional training but also with a great deal of hands-on practice. This can be acquired either by working at a good saloon or by enrolling for a course at a reputed beauty school. There are short-term diploma and certificate courses in beauty and hair care available which if taken will be an advantage for budding beauticians in their career growth. The duration of the courses depends upon the specialisation and varies according to the institution. In the USA and Europe, Cosmetologists need to be licensed to practice in their field.

Job Prospects and Career Options

Cosmetology has a variety of fields such as hairstyling, aesthetics, manicure, pedicure and electrolysis which one can specialise in. This is a profession, possible to practice in more than one specialisation concurrently. To achieve professionalism and a good reputation in this field, a beauty specialist must blend his/her technical skills with a dash of creativity and imagination.

- **Hairstyling :** A specialised area of cosmetology, hair styling deals not only with cutting but also with other services such as shampooing, colouring, texturising, perming, straightening, bonding and also restorative treatment. In hairstyling alone, one can specialise in cuts, colour or perms and even choose to be a wig stylist. Hair specialists use a wide range of technique to make hair look healthy and attractive. They advice clients on suitable hair styles and teach them how to care for their hair. They are required to know about the care and application of hair pieces, wigs and other accessories.

- **Aesthetics :** Aestheticians deal with the skin care treatments such as facial treatment, massage, waxing, peeling, etc. The aestheticians also do aromatherapy, spa treatments, make ups, body wraps and also laser treatments. They should be aware of skin types, and also knowledgeable to recommend skin care products for their clients apt for their skins. Qualified aestheticians can even work in hospitals by training patients how to take care of their skin after surgery.
- **Manicure and pedicure :** Derived from the Latin words *'manus'* (hands) and *'cura'* (care) a manicurist takes care of hands and nails. They beautify the hands and nails by cleaning and shaping the nails. Besides, putting nail polishes some manicurist may decorate nails with paintings or designs or even with imitation jewels. The same treatment done on feet is called pedicure. One could even specialise in *mehandi* designing which is used to decorate hands and legs.
- **Electrolysis :** An electrologist removes unwanted hair permanently using a method called electrolysis that uses an electric probe. Laser treatment is an advanced form of hair removal by radiation of light.

Medical Cosmetology is a scientific field of medicine and medical cosmetologist or cosmetic dermatologist can start his own practice or work in any hospital as cosmetic surgeons, dermatologist and surgical aides. They are physicians first who care for the external aspects of the living body. They treat diseases and prescribe treatments taking the health of the patient into consideration. They do surgical procedures such as liposuction, lifting of body parts, correcting deformities and thus reshaping and correcting abnormalities as well as non-surgical procedures like chemical peeling of skin, administering Botox, thread lift, etc for rejuvenation.

Cosmetologists can get jobs in cosmetic companies or industries. Cosmetic companies like Revion and Lakme offer a number of opportunities as beauty executives, cosmetologists and even beauty advisors or consultants. Another opportunity in cosmetic firms is a sales job as a salesperson. Besides a detailed knowledge of the products they promote; they must possess excellent knowledge of grooming, skin, hair and nail care.

The specialised fields of cosmetology such as hair styling, skin care, cosmetics, manicure / pedicure and electrology offers a variety of job opportunities in the respective areas. Beauty salons, spas, resorts and star hotels are some other areas one could get a job after becoming a cosmetologist. Experienced cosmetologists, especially make-up artists and hair stylists are in great demand in the fashion, advertising, film, television and theatre industry. In this field, make-up artists require specialised knowledge of make-up applications that will hold out under powerful studio lighting.

Beauty care specialists can work with beauty parlours ranging from luxurious salons at five star hotels to commercial establishments and small, intimate owner-run parlours. A beginner in this field can work under an experienced beautician, which helps to gain a tremendous amount of experience and to keep in touch with new developments. After gaining the requisite experience, one could set-up their own beauty salons or clinics. To open their own parlour, one needs thorough professional knowledge of beauty culture, sufficient funds, an accessible location, quality equipment and materials and dollops of business sense. One can be appointed as instructor in health clubs and allied fields or teach in cosmetology schools. They can work as a Consultant Cosmetology expert in newspaper, magazines and web publishers.

Remuneration

The remuneration depends upon the size and reputation of the business one works for. One starting out with beauty parlours can take home anything from ₹ 3000 to ₹ 10,000 per month. But they can demand your price as far as you practice all the aspects of the job and become successful and popular. A make-up artist charges anywhere from ₹ 500 to ₹ 4000 to do a bridal or photographic make-up. During season the pay scale may increase two-fold. For make-up and hair dressing in advertising campaigns one can earn around ₹ 1500 to ₹ 2500 for a day's work. In modelling assignments, the pay scale is much higher and it would be around ₹ 3500 or more per day depending on the top-line professionals.

Courses

- Certificate Course in Beauty Therapy
- Certificate Course in Hair Dressing
- Certificate Course in Trichology
- Diploma in Beauty Therapy
- Diploma in Hair Dressing
- Foundation Course in Beauty Management
- Intensive Course on Hair Styling and Beauty

- Post-graduate Diploma in Beauty Technology and Cosmetology
- Special Course on Chemical Hair processes.

Institutes

In India some institutes such as Annamalai University offer Post Graduate Diploma in Health Science for medical cosmetology. The nation also has a number of institutes offering certified courses in beauty care and hair styling. There are several training schools for beauty and hair care courses and most of them require no particular academic qualification. The duration of the courses depends upon the specialisation and varies according to the institution.

6.2 Fashion Designing

What is Fashion Design?

Fashion Design is the art of the application of design and aesthetics or natural beauty to clothing and accessories. Fashion design is influenced by cultural and social latitudes and has varied over time and place. Fashion designers work in a number of ways in designing clothing and accessories and because of the time required to bring a garment into the market, must at times anticipate changing consumer tastes.

The Work of Fashion Designers

Fashion designers attempt to design clothes which are functional as well as aesthetically pleasing. They must consider who is likely to wear a garment and the situations in which it will be worn. They have a wide range and combinations of materials to work with and a wide range of colours, patterns and styles to choose from. Though most clothing worn for everyday wear falls within a narrow range of conventional styles, unusual garments are usually sought for special occasions such as evening wear or party dresses. Some clothes are made specifically for an individual as in the case of *haute couture* or bespoke tailoring. Today, most clothing is designed for the mass market especially casual and everyday wear.

Different Types of Fashion

The garments produced by clothing manufacturers fall into three main categories, although these may be split up into additional, more specific categories:

- ***Haute Couture:*** Until the 1950s, fashion clothing was predominantly designed and manufactured on a made-to-measure or *haute couture* basis (French for high-fashion), with each garment being created for a specific client. A couture garment is made to order for an individual customer and is usually made from high-quality, expensive fabric, sewn with extreme attention to detail and finish often using time-consuming, hand-executed techniques. Look and fit take priority over the cost of materials and the time it takes to make.
- ***Ready-to-wear:*** Ready-to-wear clothes are a cross between *haute couture* and mass market. They are not made for individual customers, but great care is taken in the choice and cut of the fabric. Clothes are made in small quantities to guarantee exclusively, so they are rather expensive. Ready-to-wear collections are usually presented by fashion houses each season during a period known as Fashion Week. This takes place on a city-wide basis and occurs twice a year. The main seasons of Fashion Week include spring, summer, fall/winter, resort, swim and bridal.
- ***Mass Market:*** Currently the fashion industry relies more on mass market sales. The mass market caters for a wide range of customers, producing ready set by the famous names in fashion. They often wait around a season to make sure a style is going to catch on before producing their own versions of the original look. In order to save money and time, they use cheaper fabrics and simpler production techniques which can easily be done by machine. The end product can therefore be sold much cheaper.

Career Options Available in Fashion Industry

Some of the jobs available in the fashion industry are :

- **Fashion Designer :** He conceives garment combinations of line, proportion, colour and texture. While sewing and pattern-making skills are beneficial, they are a pre-requisite of successful fashion design. Most fashion designers are formally trained or apprenticed.
- **Technical Designer :** He works with the design team and the factories overseas to ensure correct garment construction, appropriate fabric choices and a good fit. The technical designer fits the garment samples on a fit model and decides which fit and construction changes to make before mass producing the garment.

- **Pattern-Maker (or Pattern Cutter) :** The pattern-maker drafts the shapes and sizes of a garment's pieces. This may be done manually with paper and measuring tools or by using a CAD computer software programme. Another method is to drape fabric directly onto a dress form. The resulting pattern pieces can be constructed to produce the intended design of the garment and required size. Formal training is usually required for working as a pattern-maker.
- **Tailor :** The tailor makes custom designed garments made to the client's measure especially suits (coat and trousers, jacket and skirt). Tailors usually undergo an apprenticeship or other formal training.
- **Textile Designer :** He designs fabric weaves and prints for clothiers and furnishings. Most textile designers are formally trained as apprentices and in school.
- **Stylist :** He co-ordinates the clothes, jewelry and accessories used in fashion photography and catwalk presentations. A stylist may also work with an individual client to design a co-ordinated wardrobe of garments. Many stylists are trained in fashion design, the history of fashion and historical costume and have a high-level of expertise in the current fashion market and future market trends. However, some simply have a strong aesthetic sense for pulling great looks together.
- **Fashion Buyer :** Buys the mix of clothing available in retail shop, department stores and chain stores. Most fashion buyers are trained in business and/or fashion studies.
- **Seamstress :** Sews ready-to-wear or mass produced clothing by hand or with a sewing machine either in a garment shop or as a sewing machine operator in a factory. She or he may not have the skills to make (design and cut) the garments or to fit them on a model.
- **Teacher of Fashion Design :** Teachers of fashion design teaches the art and craft of fashion design in art or fashion school.
- **Custom Clothier :** He makes custom-made women's clothes: day, cocktail and evening dresses, business clothes and suits, trousseaus, sports clothes and lingerie.
- **Illustrator :** He draws and paints clothing designs for commercial use.

- **Fashion Forecaster :** He predicts what colours, styles and shapes will be popular ('on-trend') before the garments are on sale in stores.
- **Model :** Model wears and displays clothes at fashion shows and in photographs.
- **Fit Model :** Fit model aids the fashion designer by wearing and commenting on the fit of clothes during their design and pre-manufacture. Fit models need to be a particular size for this purpose.
- **Fashion Journalist :** Fashion journalist writes fashion articles describing the garments presented or fashion trends for magazines or newspapers.
- **Alterations Specialist (Alterationist) :** Alteration specialist adjusts the fit of completed garments, usually ready-to-wear and sometimes re-styles them.

  Note: Despite tailors altering garments to fit the client, not all alterationists are tailors.
- **Image Consultant, Wardrobe Consultant or Fashion Advisor :** He recommends styles and colours that are flattering to the client.

What is National Institute of Fashion Technology (NIFT)?

National Institute of Fashion Technology (NIFT) was set up in 1986 under the aegis of the Ministry of Textiles, Government of India. It has emerged as the premier Institute of Design, Management and Technology, developing professionals for taking up leadership positions in fashion business in the emerging global scenario. NIFT has been granted statutory status under the act of Parliament of India in 2006, empowering the Institute to award degrees and other academic distinctions. The Institute is a pioneer in envisioning and evolving fashion business education in the country through a network of twelve professionally managed domestic centers at New Delhi, Bangalore, Chennai, Gandhinagar, Hyderabad, Kolkata, Mumbai, Raebareli, Bhopal, Kannur, Patna and Shillong. NIFT has further spread its wings globally with the opening of an international centre at Mauritius. NIFT has set academic standards and excelled in thought-leadership by providing a pool of creative genius and technically competent professionals. The Institute provides a common platform for fashion education, research and training. The curriculum at NIFT allows students to easily blend into a global network as well as acquire a greater appreciation of local industry trends. The multi-disciplinary and broad-based structure aims at an all-round development of students. Deriving from the changing paradigms of industry and commerce, its content as well as the methodology is constantly reviewed by academia and industry experts.

Programmes Offered by NIFT

Undergraduate Courses

- B. Des. (Fashion Design)
- B. Des. (Leather Design)
- B. Des. (Accessory Design)
- B. Des. (Textile Design)
- B. Des. (Knitwear Design)
- B. Des. (Fashion Communication)

Post-graduate Course

- M. Des. (Master of Design)

NIFT offers B.F.Tech. (Apparel Production) in the technology discipline at undergraduate level and M.F.Tech. (Master of Fashion Technology) at the master level. NIFT also offers M.F.M. (Master of Fashion Management) in the management discipline at master level.

NIFT Centers

NIFT has 13 centers at present in India and one international center. They are located in Bangaluru, Kolkata, Bhopal, Mumbai, Chennai, New Delhi, Gandhinagar, Patna, Hyderabad, Raebareli, Kangra, Shillong and Kannur.

The General Calendar of Admission Process in NIFT	***Tentative Months***
• Announcement of Admission	November
• Application Form Available	November to December
• Written Entrance Examination	First week of February
• Declaration of Written Examination Result	Mid March
• Situation Test/GD/Interviews	April-May
• Declaration of Final Results	End of May

Admission Pattern

Bachelor Programmes	**Test**	**Weightage**
• Design	GAT (General Ability Test)	40 percentage
	CAT (Creative Ability Test)	40 percentage
	Situation Test	20 percentage

	Test	Weightage
• Apparel Production	GAT (General Ability Test)	60 percentage
	MAT (Managerial Ability Test	40 percentage
Master Programmes	***Test***	***Weightage***
• Design	GAT (General Ability Test)	40 percentage
	CAT (Creative Ability Test)	40 percentage
	GD (Group Discussion)	10 percentage
	Interview	10 percentage
• Management	GAT (General Ability Test)	40 percentage
	MAT (Management Ability Test)	40 percentage
	GD (Group Discussion)	10 percentage
	Interview	10 percentage
• Technology	GAT (General Ability Test)	40 percentage
	MAT (Management Ability Test)	40 percentage
	GD (Group Discussion)	10 percentage
	Interview	10 percentage

Eligibility Criteria for Various Programmes in NIFT

Eligibility for Bachelor's Programme – Design

B.Des. (Fashion Design/Leather Design/Accessory Design/Textile Design/Knitwear Design/Fashion Communication)

- The plus two levels examination in the 10+2 pattern of examination of any recognised central/state board of secondary Examination such as Central Board of Secondary Education, New Delhi and Council for Indian School of Certificate Examination, New Delhi.

OR

- General Certificate Education (GCE) Examination (London/Cambridge/Sri Lanka) at Advanced (A) level.

OR

- Any public school/board/university examination in India or in foreign countries recognised by the Association of Indian Universities as equivalent to 10+2 system.

OR

- A pass grade in the senior secondary school examination conducted by the National Open School with a minimum of five subjects.

OR

- Three or Four-year Diploma recognised by AICTE or a State Board of Technical Education.

Eligibility for Bachelor's Programme – Technology

B.F.Tech. (Apparel Production)

- The +2 level examination in the 10+2 pattern of examination of any recognised central/state board of secondary examination such as Central Board of Secondary Education, New Delhi and Council for Indian School of Certificate Examination, New Delhi with physics, chemistry and mathematics.

OR

- General Certificate Education (GCE) Examination (London/Cambridge/Sri Lanka) at Advanced (A) level with physics, chemistry and mathematics.

OR

- Any public school/board/university examination in India or in Foreign countries recognised by the Association of Indian Universities as equivalent to 10+2 system with physics, chemistry and mathematics.

OR

- A pass grade in the senior secondary school examination conducted by the National Open School with a minimum of five subjects with physics, chemistry and mathematics.

OR

- Three or Four-year Diploma recognised by AICTE or a State Board of Technical Education (Engineering Background). Candidate must pass in with physics, chemistry and mathematics.

Note : The upper age limit for applying in bachelor's programme is restricted to 23 years as on 1st November.

Eligibility for Master's Programme – Design

M.Des. (Master of Design)

- A graduation degree from a recognised University in any discipline.

OR

- Bachelor's degree in Applied Arts (Fashion Design/Visual Communication/Graphic Design/ Industrial Design/ Multimedia Design/Product Design/Textiles and Accessories.

OR

- B.A. (Fine Arts) or B.Sc. (Textiles and Clothing)

OR

- B. Arch.

OR

- Design Diploma/Degree from NIFT/NID only.

Candidates having relevant industry experience in areas of Fashion/Textile/Communication Design would be preferred.

If a candidate possessing graduation degree in any discipline applies for the course, then he or she has to compulsorily undergo two months of (i.e. eight weeks) training programme to develop the desired skills before taking on the course itself.

Eligibility for Master's Programme – Management

M.F.M. (Master of Fashion Management)

A three-year bachelor's degree or equivalent in any discipline recognised by the Association of Indian Universities or Diploma in Accessory/Fashion Design/Fit from NIFT only. For foreign bachelor's degree, not recognised by the Association of Indian Universities, proper certification by a national body constituted in the country concerned for granting equivalence will have to be produced.

Eligibility for Master's Programme – Technology

M.F.Tech. (Master of Fashion Technology)

B.E./B.Tech.(Textiles/Apparel/Mechanical/Industrial/Production/Electronics/Computer/Information Technology).

Note : NIFT degree is recognised worldwide. NIFT has been granted statutory status under the act of Parliament of India in 2006, empowering the Institute to award degrees and other academic distinctions.

Few other good Institutions offering courses in Fashion Education are :

- National Institute of Design, Ahmedabad
- Central Leather Research Institute, Chennai
- National Institute of Fashion Design, Chandigarh
- Srishti School of Design, Bangalore
- Symbiosis Centre of Design, Pune
- Pearl Academy, Delhi and Jaipur
- Arch Academy of Fashion, Art and Design, Jaipur
- Wigan and Leigh College, Delhi, Mumbai, Bangalore, Kolkata, Hyderabad, Pune, Indore, Lucknow, Ahmedabad, Chennai
- Apeejay Institute of Design, New Delhi
- Sophia Polytechnic, Mumbai
- Raffles Design International, Mumbai
- North-east Institute of Fashion Technology, Guwahati

- Army Institute of Fashion Design, Bangalore
- IILM School of Design, Gurgaon
- Bangalore Institute of Fashion Technology (BIFT), Bangalore
- Arch Academy, Jaipur, Rajasthan
- International Institute of Fashion Technology, Delhi
- Gandhi Institute of Fashion and Textile Design, Ahmedabad

6.3 National Institute of Design (NID)

What is National Institute of Design (NID)?

The National Institute of Design (NID) is internationally acclaimed as one of the foremost multi-disciplinary institutions in the field of design education, applied research, training, design consultancy services and outreach programmes. It has been the recipient of significant national and international awards since it was established in 1961 as an autonomous institution under the Ministry of Industry, now known as Ministry of Commerce and Industry, Government of India. NID's graduates have made a mark in key sectors of commerce, industry and social develop-ment by taking the role of catalysts and through leadership. NID has been recognised as a Science and Industrial Research Organisation by the Department of Science and Technology, Government of India.

Courses

Graduate Diploma Programme in Design (GDPD) commences with a two-semester Foundation Programme is geared to assist in developing attitudes and sensorial skills, necessary for further specialisation in specific areas of design. The purpose is to create an awareness of the environment and to arouse the students' creative faculties. The primary concern of the foundation programme is to introduce the students to the fundamentals of design, to inculcate in them the practice of design as a problem solving process and to develop a highly evolved aesthetic sensitivity and 'design' attitude.

In the foundation programme, basic design courses are augmented by related studies of science and liberal arts, to help and develop an understanding of the Indian milieu and the relevance of design. The foundation programme is geared to inculcate the development of values, attitudes and sensorial skills necessary for any design specialisation. It aspires to create an awareness of the changing environment by constantly relating the students' learning to real life situations. The programme provides the necessary direction, stimuli, facilities and experience to foster creativity and thereby help each individual discover their own identity, ability and potentiality.

The foundation programme is the basis on which the remaining design curriculum is built. It also makes students appreciate the multi-disciplinary nature of design. This four-year intensive professional UG programme is offered in the following three faculty streams (possible areas of design specialisation through projects are given in brackets):

- **Industrial Design :** Product Design, Furniture and Interior Design, Ceramic and Glass Design
- **Communication Design :** Graphic Design, Animation Film Design, Film and Video Communication, Exhibition Design.
- **Textile and Apparel Design :** Textile Design.

Eligibility

Admission is open to students who have passed or who will appear for the qualifying examinations under the higher secondary (10+2) or equivalents like AISSCE/IB/ICSE, etc. It is understood that individual students, who have passed the Institute's admission tests/interviews will be admitted provisionally to the education programme subject to passing their qualifying examinations before they join the Institute.

Competence in technical and related subjects will normally be considered an advantage. The medium of instruction at NID is English. Upper age limit for candidates is 20 years (relaxable by three years for SC/ST candidates) as on 1st June of the year of admission.

Admission Procedure

Admission announcements are issued in the leading national dailies in the last week of September every year. Application forms along with the prospectus for admission is available on request from the second week of October on payment of requisite fees by Demand Draft of any scheduled bank drawn in favour of the National Institute of Design payable at Ahmedabad. Forms are also available at selected branches of Bank of India across the country. Forms downloaded from NID's website<www.nid.edu> along with required amount of DD drawn in favour of National Institute of Design payable at Ahmedabad are also accepted.

Admission is on the basis of NID's method of selection which extends beyond the students' previous academic qualifications. The NID Admission Committee systematically seeks evidence of the perception, attitudes, achievement and motivation essential for a challenging and satisfying design career. The objectives of the tests and the interviews are to ascertain thes ecriteria. The tests at the various centers consist of design aptitude tests. Based on scores obtained from these tests, shortlisted candidates are called for second phase of admission procedure.

The second phase of the admission procedure includes studio tests followed by interviews at Ahmedabad. All those called for the second phase are required to attend the studio tests and interview which completes the process of selection. The procedures, grades and weightage for each year will be decided by the Admission Committee for the year.

Norms for the Selection

The norms for the selection are the sole prerogative of the Admission Committee and the decision of the Admission Committee and the Management in any of the matters concerning the admission process and selection will be final. Any direct or indirect attempt to influence the admission committee or its members, academic office bearers or management will lead to automatic disqualification of the candidate.

The graduate diploma programme students are admitted only into the foundation programme and their entry into different design domains is not automatic. On successful completion of the Foundation Programme, the final decision on the specific design domain will be recommended by the Semester Jury. All students are required to be present for the Orientation programme may mean an automatic withdrawal by NID of its admission offer. Students who leave the Institute after joining will forfeit the entire tuition fees and other charges and will get only the refundable deposit.

As per the Government of India requirement fifteen per cent and seven and a half per cent seats are reserved for Scheduled Caste and Scheduled Tribe candidates. Three per cent of seats are reserved for differently-abled persons as per the Persons with Disability Act, 1995. The qualifying candidates need to meet the eligibility and admission requirements of NID.

Number of Seats

Intake into the Graduate Diploma Programme is 60 and for the post-graduate Diploma Programme are 165. The number of seats available for PGDPD in different discipline is as under:

- Product Design 15
- Furniture and Interior Design 10
- Ceramic and Glass Design 10
- Toy Design and Development 10
- Apparel Design and Merchandising 15

- Lifestyle Accessory Design 10
- Textile Design 15
- Animation Film Design 10
- Film and Video Communication 10
- Graphic Design 10
- New Media Design 10
- Software and User Interface Design 10
- Information and Digital Design 10
- Strategic Design Management 20

Important Dates

- Issuing of forms starts from – October
- Issuing of form by post from NID – November
- Obtaining forms from BOI – November
- Receiving completed forms at NID – December
- Test for PGDPD – January
- Test for GDPD – January

6.4 Footwear Technology

Introduction

Footwear has been a necessity for humans for centuries. It protects our feet from dirt and cold as well as sharp piercing through by sharp sticks, thorns, nails and stones. The first shoes were basically nothing more than bags that were secured over the feet. Typically, these bags were made from very thick durable material such as animal's hide. Over time the type of shoes a person wore began to become something of a status symbol. Royalty and other higher class individuals for instance, could afford to have several pairs of fitted and attractive shoes made. These were often made from luxurious materials and adorned with items like gems and ribbons. Today, footwear plays a very significant role in enhancing the overall appearance and as such it has great impact in the field of fashion. It symbolises not only one's passionate statement but also personal taste and a sense of comfort. India ranks second among the footwear producing nations. Besides being a fashion statement, footwear has also become a matter of health and comfort. Huge research is going on in the orthopaedic footwear segment due to the increase in various foot related ailments. As a result, the scope for a career in this field has increased rapidly.

Designing

Footwear requires a blend of artistic talent and creativity. Footwear technology has come a long way from traditional shoemakers cutting and stitching leather to specialised professionals utilising modern technology, working at high-tech laboratories, on sophisticated machines, experimenting with a varied range of materials from leather, plastic, canvas, jute to rubber and even cloth.

Footwear designers create new styles of footwear, keeping in mind the popular demand in the markets. They also design footwear collections for leading footwear companies. Patterns are made and graded by them, according to which companies produce samples. Computer Aided Design (CAD) systems have now made the entire process mechanised.

Eligibility and Course Areas

There are different courses in the field, i.e., certificate, diploma, graduate and post-graduate diploma. Eligibility for undergraduate/diploma courses in footwear manufacturing technology, shoemaking or design is a pass in 10+2 level. Advanced diploma course in footwear technology require the candidate to be a graduate in any stream or diploma holder in leather, engineering or footwear technology. However, footwear technology courses offered as B.Tech./M.Tech. programmes are open to science/engineering students only.

Admission to most of these courses is made through entrance examinations. Duration of graduate courses such as B.Tech is generally four years and for post-graduate or M.Tech programme it is two years. Several certificate and diploma courses are also offered by private institutes in this field and the programme duration varies from six months to one year depending upon the type of the course.

Personal Attributes

Candidates should possess a good manual dexterity as well as a flair for fashion and foresight regarding upcoming trends in the industry. The ability to draw or sketch ideas on paper is important as that's usually the chosen medium for communicating these ideas of those in charge of production. Creativity, imagination and good communication skills are also vital for success in this career. They should be innovative and must have the knowledge of foot anatomy, a flair for colour selection and application, tailoring and sewing, knowledge about footwear components, dyes and production processes. Besides, they must be aware of Computer Aided Design (CAD) as present day world of fashion require latest technological background.

Job Prospects and Career Options

Footwear designing technology is a lucrative career option and it is an important area of fashion. Career opportunities are growing for qualified footwear designers and leather technologists, major reason being the high growth of the consumption level of the latest leather products and footwear over the years. This surge in demand is mainly because of the high fashion consciousness of the customers as well as the wide media exposure in this field. The profession has become challenging as it blends the sensitivity of a designer and the artistic capabilities of a cobbler.

The footwear industry has a range of jobs in areas comprising research and development, design, manufacturing operations, sales and marketing – retail and wholesale, quality control and management. Career opportunities are available for qualified professionals with multinationals that are active in the field of leather production, product development, posses, processing and designing as well as with leather research centers, footwear designing institutes, footwear production units, sports shoe manufacturers, in the orthopaedic market – designing specialist shoes for private clients, fashion houses and other similar industries. They could work as Footwear Designers – as seniors or assistants, Footwear Buyers, Fashion Trend Analysts, Footwear Technicians, Footwear Line Builders, Production Co-ordinators and Managers, Marketing Managers and so on.

Most graduates enter the industry as design assistants before progressing to become designers. On-the-job learning is a crucial part of developing skills. Once you establish yourself as a reliable designer you could freelance and earn handsomely or you can join any leading brands and go up in the ladder and reach top position in the company. Major Employers in this field are Bata, Action shoes, Flex, Liberty Group, Woodland, Lee Cooper etc.

This profession is not only lucrative but also demanding and it's highly competitive. Designers are needed to design the products according to latest trends. As designers one could specialise in one area such as women's, children's or sports' footwear. Experienced technicians are required to operate the machines for manufacturing the product and marketing involves retail buying and selling. Marketing managers have to decide on marketing policies such as organising shoe fairs and exhibitions.

Remuneration

Since, employment opportunities are diverse, earnings can vary tremendously. Initially one can expect a starting salary somewhere around ₹ 10,000 – 12,000 per month. International players offer even more high pay packages which may be between ₹ 15,000 – 20,000 per month. Earnings of independent footwear designers depend upon the nature of their assignment. Entrepreneurs in this field can earn a lot per annum depending upon the size of their business. High end designing firms pay extremely well.

Courses

- Certificate Course in Footwear Design and Production.
- Certificate Course in Footwear Technology.
- Certificate Course in Shoe Designing and Pattern Cutting.
- Computer Aided Shoe Designing.
- Bachelor of Design (B.DES.) Leather Design.
- Diploma in Footwear Designing and Production.
- Diploma in Footwear Technology (DFT).
- Diploma in Leather Goods and Accessories Design (DLGAD).
- Post Graduate Diploma in Footwear Technology.
- Shoe Production.

Institutes

Some of the premier institutes that offer courses in this field are :

- The Footwear Design and Development Institute (FDDI), Noida.
- The Central Leather Research Institute (CLRI).
- Chennai Footwear Training Centre (CFTC), Chennai.
- National Institute of Fashion Technology, New Delhi and Gandhinagar.
- AVI School of Fashion and Shoe Technology, Chandigarh.

7

DEFENCE AND INTELLIGENCE SERVICE

The Indian defence system consists of three professional uniformed services: Air Force, Navy and Army.

7.1 Indian Air Force (IAF)

Introduction

The Indian Air Force (IAF) of India was commissioned on 8 October, 1932 with Wapiti aircraft. Air Marshal Subroto Mukherjee, one of the founding members of the Air Force took over on 1st April, 1954 as the first Indian Chief of Air Staff. Today, the IAF is the fourth largest Air Force in the world with its forty-five squadrons and the most sophisticated fighter aircrafts like Mirage 2000, MIG-29, MIG-27, Jaguar, MIG-25, MIG-23 and MIG-21. The transport wing has the huge IL-76 (Gajraj), AN-32 and other smaller aircrafts.

The Main Task of the Air Force

The major activity of the Air Force is that of flying combat aircrafts and helicopter. Other activities include ... such as aeronautical engineering, electronics and computer engineering as well as administrative, financial and planning duties.

7
DEFENCE AND INTELLIGENCE SERVICE

The Indian defence system consists of three professional uniformed services. Air Force, Navy and Army.

7.1 Indian Air Force (IAF)

Introduction

The Indian Air Force (IAF), the youngest of the three defence services was commissioned on October 8, 1932, with four single-propeller engine Wapiti aircrafts, six pilot officers, two airmen and 19 Hawaii Sepoys. Air Marshal Subroto Mukherjee, one of the founding members of the Air Force took over on 1st April, 1954 as the first Indian Chief of Air Staff. Today, the IAF is the fourth largest Air Force in the world with its forty-five squadron strength and some of the most sophisticated fighter aircrafts like Mirage 2000, MIG- 29, MIG-27, Jaguar, MIG-25, MIG-23 and MIG-21. The transport wing has the huge IL-76 (Gajral), AN-32 and other smaller aircrafts.

The Main Task of the Air Force

The major activity of the Air Force is that of flying combat aircrafts and helicopters. Other activities include technical work such as aeronautical engineering, electronics and computer engineering as well as administrative, financial and planning duties.

Two Streams of Joining the Air Force

One can join the Air Force either as an Officer or Airman. The officer cadre provides opportunities for men having 10+2 (Intermediate), graduate, engineering and post-graduate degrees in their three different branches. Women who are graduates, engineers and post-graduates can join as an Officer in the Air Force. The officers will be posted either as a Pilot or a Navigator or a Technical or a Ground Duty officer in any one of the Air Force bases. Women have opportunities only in the Officer cadre of the Air Force.

In the Airmen cadre, there are opportunities even for class X pass (matriculate) and below candidates, 10+2 (Intermediate), diploma, graduates, post-graduates, etc., in their technical and non-technical trade fields.

7.1.1 As an IAF Air Man

Young men can join as an Airman in either the Technical or Non-Technical trades of the Air Force. The airman cadre provides opportunities for men (only men) with matriculate or below, 10+2/ intermediate, graduates, diploma holders and post-graduates in either of the three combatant groups, i.e., 'X', 'Y' or 'Z' of the technical and non-technical trades. Candidates shortlisted after the initial selection procedure are allotted a suitable trade and go through a rigorous training regimen at one of the training institutes. Thereafter, they are inducted and posted as airmen at any of the air force stations.

Each trade offers opportunities to grow and enhance your skills. Depending on your inclination and talent/suitability you can move from one trade to another and grow in ranking. One can even get commissioned as an officer in the air force.

As an airman under the Technical Trades, the type of work involves the maintenance and testing of aircraft and flying related equipment. One will also be directly or indirectly involved in the maintenance and overhaul of ground equipment and armament. As an airman in the Non-Technical trades, the work involves assistance and support to the various functions from weather forecasting to maintenance of records and files of the Indian Air Force in all its branches.

As an airman, apart from your basic pay, you are also entitled to a number of perks and benefits. Even during the training period you get a monthly stipend of ₹ 2850 if you join Combatant Z. The basic pay of the lowest ranking 'Aircraftsmen' (AC) to the highest ranking 'Master Warrant Officer' (MWO) in the three combatant groups ranges from

₹ 4500 – 10,700 per month. Along with the pays there are benefits such as free accommodation, free ration, medical facilities, children's schooling, insurance cover, retirement benefits, etc.

The Technical Trades and Non-Technical Trades grouped under three combatant groups – Combatant 'X', Combatant 'Y' and Combatant 'Z'. The various trades in each group areas given:

Groups Combatant 'X' Combatant 'Y' Combatant 'Z'

Technical Trade

- Radio Fitter — * Photo Technician
- Radar Fitter — * Safety Equipment Worker
- Missile Fitter (E) — * Machinist
- Missile Fitter (L) — * Mechanical Transport Technician
- Missile Fitter (M) — * Air Defence System Operator
- Workshop Fitter (B) — * Radio Technician
- Workshop Fitter (C)
- Instrument Fitter
- Electrical Fitter
- Airframe Fitter
- Plant Maintenance Fitter (E)
- Plant Maintenance Fitter (M)
- Engine Fitter
- Weapon Fitter

Non- Technical Trade

- Education Instructor — * Ground Training Instructor — * Musicians

* Meteorological Assistants
* Air Field Safety Operator
* Radio/Telephone Operator
* Clerk General Duties
* Equipment Assistant
* Clerk Pay Accounting
* Medical Assistants
* Mechanical Transport Drivers
* Aircraft Hands General Duties
* Catering Assistant

As an airman in the Indian Air Force, you get the opportunity to move ahead in your ranking by moving on to specialised trades or also become an officer. Enterprising airmen are nominated at regular intervals for the post of officers.

Eligibility

The required eligibility criterion is Matriculate and below/Intermediate (10+2)/Graduate/Post Graduate/Diploma in Engineering.

The airman cadre provides opportunities for men with matriculate or below, 10+2/intermediate, graduates, diploma holders and post graduates in either of the three combatant groups, i.e., 'X', 'Y' or 'Z' of the Technical and the Non-Technical trades. Candidates shortlisted after the initial selection procedure are allotted a suitable trade and go through a rigorous training regimen at one of the training institutes. Thereafter, they are inducted and posted as airmen at any of the Air Force Stations.

Career Options

The career options and eligibility for the candidates having different educational qualifications for the Airmen Cadre in the different trades of the Air Force are given in the following links.

- Matriculate and Below
- Intermediate (10+2)
- Graduate
- Post-graduate
- Diploma in Engineering

Physical Standards

Physical fitness is one of the most important prerequisites for joining the Air Force. Irrespective of the trade you are applying for, you must fulfill the basic physical standards.

Basic Requirement for all Candidates

Height : To join Air Force as an airman, you should be at least 152.5 cm tall. There are, however, some trades that have different requirements.

Mechanical Transport Driver and Certain Technical Trade: Minimum height of 165 cm and Minimum leg length – 99 cm.

IAF Police : Minimum height – 175 cm.

Ground Training Instructor and Musician : Minimum height – 167 cm.

Clear Medical Record : You should have a clear medical record with history clear of any or all of the following

- Mental Sickness/Fits
- Diseases/Skin Ailments
- Surgical Deformity

Chest : Minimum Expanded Chest (75 cm) and Minimum Range of Expansion (5 cm).

Vision : You must fulfill some minimum visual standards in order to qualify. You should have a minimum corrected vision of at least 6/12 in each eye. You could also have 6/6 in the healthier eye and 6/18 in weaker eye with spectacles with power not more than +/-5.50 Dioptres, inclusive of astigmatism in any meridian with full field of vision and Minimum CP-IV unsafe colour vision.

There are, however, other detailed visual and colour standards that are specific to different trades.

Hearing : You should have normal hearing, i.e., you should be able to hear forced whisper from a distance of six meters in each ear individually.

Dental : You should have healthy gums and a good set of teeth. It is advisable that candidates reporting for medical exam must ensure a high-level of personal hygiene and bring the latest prescription and spectacles for corrected vision to avoid delay.

Height and Weight Standards for Men

Height in cm (without shoes)	15-17 yrs	18-22 yrs	23-27 yrs	28-32 yrs	33-37 yrs	38-42 yrs	43-47 yrs	48 yrs and above
152	46.0	47.0	49.0	50.0	51.0	52.0	52.5	53.0
154	47.0	48.0	50.0	51.5	52.5	53.0	54.5	54.0
156	48.0	49.0	51.0	52.5	53.5	54.0	54.5	56.0
158	49.0	50.0	52.0	54.0	55.0	55.5	56.0	56.5
160	50.0	51.0	53.0	55.0	56.0	56.5	57.0	57.5
162	52.0	52.5	54.5	56.0	57.5	58.0	58.5	59.0
164	52.5	53.5	55.5	57.5	59.0	59.5	60.0	60.5
166	53.5	55.0	57.0	59.0	60.5	61.0	61.5	62.0
168	55.5	56.5	58.5	60.5	62.0	63.0	63.5	64.0
170	56.5	58.0	60.0	62.0	64.0	64.5	65.0	65.5
172	58.5	60.0	61.5	63.5	65.5	66.0	66.5	67.5
174	59.5	61.0	63.5	65.5	67.5	68.0	68.5	69.0
176	61.0	62.5	65.0	67.0	69.0	69.5	70.0	71.0
178	62.5	64.0	66.5	68.5	70.5	71.5	72.0	72.5
180	64.4	65.5	68.0	70.5	72.5	73.0	74.0	74.5
182	66.0	67.5	69.5	72.0	74.0	75.0	75.5	76.5
184	67.0	70.0	71.5	74.0	76.0	76.5	77.5	78.0
186	69.0	70.5	73.0	75.5	78.0	78.5	79.0	80.0
188	70.5	72.0	75.0	77.5	79.5	80.0	81.0	82.0
190	72.0	73.5	76.0	78.5	80.5	81.0	82.0	83.0
192	73.5	75.0	78.0	80.5	82.0	82.5	83.5	84.5
194	75.0	76.5	79.0	81.5	83.0	83.5	84.5	85.5
196	76.5	78.0	81.0	83.5	85.0	85.5	86.5	86.5

Becoming an Officer

As an airman in the Indian Air Force, you get the opportunity to move ahead in your ranking by moving on to specialised trades or also become an officer. Enterprising airmen are nominated at regular intervals for the post of officers and will be granted one of the following Commissions:

Permanent Commission

An airman, between 19 and 20 years of age with the right educational qualifications, can volunteer or apply to the Flying Branch for a Permanent Commission. After you clear the selection procedure, you can look forward to a career as a pilot in the Indian Air Force. If you are already serving as an airman, you can apply for selection as an officer in the Ground Duty Branches (other than the Medical Branch).

Branch Commission

You can also be nominated for the post of officer during the course of your career. In recognition of your hard work and competence, the Air Force station where you operate can recommend you for a Branch Commission. On approval, you can join the Ground Duty Branches (other than medical branch) in the rank of Flying Officer. You can then look forward to a promotion upto the rank of Squadron Leader. (Only Master Warrant Officers/Warrant Officers/Junior Warrant Officers and Sergeants of the Technical and Non-Technical Trades can be nominated for the Branch commission).

Honourary Commission

The Indian Air Force also grants Honourary Commission to deserving airmen during their last year of service. This is granted on the recommendation of your Air Force Station. Better pay and enhanced allowances also accompany this Commission that is granted on special occasions like 26th January or 15th August. (Only Master Warrant Officers and Warrant Officers can be nominated for Honourary Commission).

Application Procedure

The advertisement inviting applications for vacancies for Airman Cadre will appear in the leading newspapers across India. The advertisements are also published in the Employment News or the *Rozgar Samachar*. The application should be sent in the required format mentioned in the advertisement, before the last date. The selection procedure for picking the candidates is quite strict and elaborate. The five steps involved are:

- Processing of Application
- Testing the Abilities
- Conducting Medical Examination
- Preparing Merit List
- Undertaking Enrollment

Process of Application

After checking all eligibility wise application forms, one will receive an Admit Card that will contain all the relevant details like the date, time and venue of your examination. The subjects tested on will depend on the trade you have applied for. The following are the subjects for examination.

- **Technical Streams :** You will be tested in four papers – English, Mathematics, Science and Intelligence and General Awareness.
- **Non-Technical/MTD Streams :** You will be tested for English and Intelligence and General Awareness. (The examination is based on the CBSE (X/XII) curriculum/syllabus).
- **Education Instructors :** The pattern of the paper is in keeping with the basic minimum educational qualification required. Here, you will also be interviewed after the examination.

Testing of Abilities

The selection tests will be held at any of the Airmen Selection Centers across India. One should take the admit card and all the original certificates to the venue, at the time of the examination. These will be verified before you proceed for the examination.

Conducting Medical Examination

After you have successfully cleared the examinations, you will be sent for a medical examination, which shall be conducted by a medical officer of the Armed Forces. After the medical examination, you are either declared 'Fit' or 'Unfit' or 'Temporarily Medically Unfit' (TMU).

Preparing Merit List

If you have successfully cleared the examination and are declared medically fit/TMU, your name will feature in the All India Merit List. This list will be displayed at the Airmen Selection Centers, where the tests were conducted. A call letter will be sent to you, requesting you to report to the Airmen Selection Centre for enrollment.

Undertaking Enrollment

Apart from the enrollment formalities, the candidates should take a Trade Aptitude Test, to determine the right trade for him. Depending upon the score as well as the position in the Merit List, candidates will be assigned to one of the streams in the Technical or Non-Technical Trades.

After the candidate has completed enrollment formalities, he will be sent to the Administrative Training Institute for 26 weeks for Basic Combatant Training. Thereafter, the candidate would be sent to one of the Training Institutes for specialisation in the trade that he is assigned.

Selection

The selection tests will be held at any of the following Airmen Selection Centres across India.

- **Andaman and Nicobar :** Eight Airmen Selection Centre, C/o AF Station Tambaram, Chennai-600 046, Telephone No. 237 5556-Extension 3383.
- **Andhra Pradesh :** 12 Airmen Selection Centre, AF Station Bowenpally, Secunderabad-500 011-Telephone No. 775 3551 Extension 267.
- **Arunachal Pradesh :** 11 Airmen Selection Centre, Borjhar, Guwahati-781 015, Telephone No. 840976-Extension 333.
- **Assam :** 11 Airmen Selection Centre, Borjhar, Guwahati-781 015, Telephone No. 840976, Extension 333.
- **Bihar :** 11 Airmen Selection Centre, Borjhar, Guwahati-781 015, Telephone No. 840976-Extension 333.
- **Chandigarh :** 1 Airmen Selection Centre, 48, Mansfield Road, Ambala Cantt.-133 001, Telephone No. 640 270, 624 410 Extension 4410.
- **Chhattisgarh :** 12 Airmen Selection Centre, AF Station Bowenpally, Secunderabad-500 011, Telephone No. 775 3551-Extension 267.

  UP: 3 Airmen Selection Centre, AF Station Chakeri, Kanpur – 208 008, Telephone No. 451 730-Extension 460.
- **Dadra and Nagar Haveli :** 6 Airmen Selection Centre, AF Station, Cotton Green, Mumbai-400 033, Telephone No. 371 4982-Extension 251.
- **Daman and Diu :** Six Airmen Selection Centre, AF Station, Cotton Green, Mumbai-400 033, Telephone No. 371 4982-Extension 251.
- **Goa :** Six Airmen Selection Centre, AF Station, Cotton Green, Mumbai-400 033, Telephone No. 371 4982-Extension 251.
- **Gujarat :** Six Airmen Selection Centre, AF Station, Cotton Green, Mumbai-400 033, Telephone No. 371 4982-Extension 251.
- **Himachal Pradesh :** One Airmen Selection Centre, 48, Mansfield Road, Ambala Cantt.-133 001, Telephone No. 640 270, 624 410-Extension 4410.
- **Haryana :** One Airmen Selection Centre, 48, Mansfield Road, Ambala Cantt.-133 001, Telephone No. 640 270, 624 410-Extension-4410.

New Delhi 2 Airmen Selection Centre, Race Course Camp, New Delhi – 110 003, Telephone No. 3377652, 3010231-Extension 7652.

- **Jammu and Kashmir** : 1 Airmen Selection Centre, 48, Mansfield Road, Ambala Cantt.-133 001, Telephone No. 640 270, 624 410- Extension 4410.
- **Jharkhand** : 10 Airmen Selection Centre, AF Station Bihta, Patna – 801 103, Telephone No. 235 502-Extension 440.
- **Karaikal** : Eight Airmen Selection Centre, C/o AF Station Tambaram, Chennai-600 046, Telephone No. 237 5556-Extension 3383.
- **Karnataka** : Seven Airmen Selection Centre, No. 1 Cubbon Road, Bangalore- 560 001, Telephone No. 559 2199.
- **Kerala** : 14 Airmen Selection Centre, VII/302-b, Vayu Sena Road, Kakkanad, Kochi -682 030, Telephone No. 427 010.
- **Lakshadweep and Minicoy Islands** : 14 Airmen Selection Centre, VII/302-b, Vayu Sena Road Kakkanad, Kochi-682 030, Telephone No. 427 010.
- **Maharashtra** : 6 Airmen Selection Centre, AF Station, Cotton Green, Mumbai-400 033, Telephone No. 371 4982 Extension 251.
- **Mahe** : 14 Airmen Selection Centre, VII/302-b, Vayu Sena Road, Kakkanad, Kochi-682 030, Telephone No. 427 010.
- **West Bengal** : Four Airmen Selection Centre, (Near Plata Gate) AF Station, Barrackpore-743122, Telephone No. 560 1251-Extension 350.
- **Yanam** : 12 Airmen Selection Centre, AF Station Bowenpally, Secunderabad-500 011, Telephone No. 775 3551-Extension 267.

Remuneration

As an airman in the Indian Air Force, you are assured of a stable and professionally satisfying career. Apart from your basic emoluments, you will also be entitled to a number of perks and benefits. And as you grow in rank and stature, you also get many growth opportunities on your way, including the possibility to become an Officer.

Even before you are appointed as an Aircraftsman, you start earning. During your training period, you get a monthly stipend of ₹ 2850 if you join Combatant Group X or Y and ₹ 2650 if you join Combatant Group Z. After you complete your training, you are entitled to the full basic pay and allowances.

Perks and Benefits

As an airman, you and your family are entitled to a large number of perks and benefits. The benefits include, free accommodation for you and your family, medical facilities including specialist service, free ration and clothing, attractive life insurance cover up to ₹ five lakh, on normal subscription which also includes easy loans, children's education and also includes a variety of recreational activities, which can be used by all airmen and their families.

Eligible airmen can apply for selection as Officers Flying (Pilot) Branch within the age group of 19 to 20 years. Opportunities are also available for serving airmen for selection to the officer's rank in the Ground Duty Branches (other than Medical Branch) as per the rules. After retirement, the airman is entitled to pension, medical insurance cover and gratuity, apart from canteen facilities. In addition, the air force allows relaxation in age and reservation in government services as an ex-serviceman.

Your pay and perks are divided according to your rank and the Combatant Group you are selected for. The following table displays the emoluments that each rank is entitled to.

Rank

Gross Pay at the Minimum of the Scale

	Combatant Group X	*Combatant Group Y*	*Combatant Group Z*
Master Warrant Officer	10,768	9,839	9,624
Warrant Officer	9,839	9,624	9,009
Junior Warrant Officer	8,437	8,223	7,622
Sergeant	7,336	6,364	5,584
Corporal	6,121	5,763	4,762
Leading Aircraftsman	5,942	5,406	4,590
Aircraftsman	5,441	4,834	4,548

7.1.2 As an IAF Officer

One can join the Air Force as an Officer in either one of the three branches, the Flying, Technical or the Ground branch. The officer cadre provides opportunities for men with 10+2/Intermediate (only in the flying branch), graduates (all three branches), engineers (all three branches) and post-graduates (all branches except the Flying branch). Women who are graduates, engineers and post-graduates can join as an Officer in the Air Force. Candidates short-listed after the initial selection procedure, go through a rigorous training regimen at one of the Air Force training establishments. Thereafter, they are commissioned as officers and posted either as a Pilot or a Navigator or a Technical or a Ground Duty officer at any of the Air Force Stations.

Only the officer cadre of the Air Force provides opportunities for women. But they will be appointed only on 'Short Service Commission' i.e., for a term of 10 years which you can extend up to 10 more years depending on your conduct or retire at the age of 40 whichever comes first. Only men will be granted 'Permanent Commission' from the Indian Air Force, i.e., will be accepted in service for life. They can also opt for 'Short Service Commission'.

- **The Flying Branch:** This includes Fighter pilots who fly combat or fighter planes carrying ammunition and missiles; Transport pilots who fly planes which carry men and materials and Helicopter pilots who provide air support to a moving army or are used for Para-dropping men and supplies. This branch also includes navigators who fly along with the pilot and guide the aircraft by using the latest avionic equipment.
- **The Technical Branch:** This consists of all the engineering sections which are responsible for the engineering equipment and weapons systems of the air force. Aeronautical engineers in the mechanical department ensure the proper maintenance of all aircrafts; while those in the electronics department handle the electronic and communication equipment in aircraft.
- **The Ground Duties Branch:** It includes all the departments that provide logistical, meteorological, educational and administrative support to the flying and technical branches. This includes the Air Traffic Control Officer, who provides control and advisory services to enable the pilot to conduct flights in total safety. The Fighter Controller monitors the skies for any potential threat and selects the appropriate air defence system using modern electronic equipment to intercept these threats. The Logistics Officer is responsible for provisioning the aircraft with spares, fuel, armaments and so on; while the meteorological

branch officers are engaged in conducting scientific conditions. There are also other branches such as administration, education and accounts.

Eligibility and Physical Standards

Intermediate (10+2)/Graduate/Post-Graduate/Engineer

The three branches of the Air Force are Flying, Ground duty and Technical branch. The Officer cadre provides opportunities for men with 10+2/intermediate (only in the Flying branch), graduates (all three branches), engineers (all three branches) and post-graduates (all branches except the Flying branch) in the various positions. Women with graduate (all three branches), engineering (all three branches) and post-graduate degrees (all branches except the Flying branch) have openings as an Officer in the Air Force. The career options and eligibility for the candidates having different educational qualifications for the Officer Cadre in the different branches of the Air Force are given in the following links.

- Intermediate (10+2)
- Graduate
- Post-graduate
- Engineers

Physical Standards

Physical fitness is one of the most important prerequisites for joining the Air Force. Irrespective of the branch you are applying for, you must fulfill some basic physical standards.

General Physical Requirements Common for all Candidates

- You must be in good physical and mental health and free from any disease/disability which is likely to interfere with efficient performance of duties. There should be no evidence of weak constitution, bodily defects or overweight.
- The height and weight standards for men and women differ.
- Your chest should be well-developed. The minimum range of expansion after full inspiration should be five cm.
- There should be no disease of bones and joints of the body.
- You should be free of any past history of mental breakdown or fits.

- Your hearing should be normal without any evidence of present or past disease of the ear, nose and throat.
- There should be no sign of functional or organic disease of the heart and blood vessels. Your blood pressure should also be normal.
- The muscle of the abdomen should be well, developed without any enlargement of the liver or spleen. Any evidence of disease of internal organs of the abdomen can be a cause for rejection.
- An un-operated hernia can make you unfit for selection. If operated, this should have been done at least six months prior to the present examination and healing should be complete without any potential for recurrence.
- There should be no hydromel, varicocele or piles. If operated for hydrocele, varicocele, this should have been done at least six months prior to the present examination and healing should be complete without any recurrence.
- Urine examination will be done and any abnormality if detected can be a cause for rejection.
- Any disease of the skin which is likely to cause disability or disfigurement will also be a cause for rejection.
- Vision will be tested. You must have good binocular vision. In case you have undergone or are detected to have undergone Radial Keratotomy or any other procedure to improve the visual acuity, you will be permanently rejected.
- You should have sufficient number of natural and sound teeth. A minimum of 14 dental points will be acceptable. When 32 teeth are present, the total dental points are 22. You should not be suffering from severe pyorrhoea.

Conditions pertaining to women that will entail rejection for all Air Force Duties :

- Acute or chronic pelvic infection
- Severe menorrhagia
- Severe dysmenorrhea
- Complete prolapsed of uterus
- Pregnancy/Amenorrhea
- Any other gynaecological condition, if so considered by the specialist

Height and Weight Standards for Men

Height in cm.	*Average weight in kg.*		
(Without shoes)	*18 yrs*	*20 yrs*	*22 yrs*
152	44	46	47
155	46	48	49
157	47	49	50
160	48	50	51
162	50	52	53
165	52	53	55
168	53	55	57
170	55	57	58
173	57	59	60
175	59	61	62
178	61	62	63
180	63	64	65
183	65	67	67
185	67	69	70
188	70	71	72
190	72	73	74
193	74	76	77
195	77	78	79

Height and Weight Standard for Women

Height in cm.	*Average weight in kg.*		
(Without shoes)	*18 yrs*	*20 yrs*	*22 yrs*
143	36.8	40	41
145	37	41	42
146	38	42	43
148	39	42	43
150	40	42.5	44
152	42	43	45
154	43	44	45.5
156	43	44.5	46
158	45	46	46.5
160	46	47	47.5

Height in cm.	*Average weight in kg.*		
(Without shoes)	*18 yrs*	*20 yrs*	*22 yrs*
162	46	47.5	48.5
163	47	48	49
165	49	50.5	51.5
168	50	51.5	52.5
170	51	52.5	53.5
173	53	55	56
175	55	56.5	57.5

* If you belong to North Eastern regions of India, Garwahal or Kumaon or are a Gurkha then the height is relaxed by five cm.

Application Procedure

You can begin your Air Force joining process by sending your application to the relevant branch. IAF will scan your application and based on merit, will call you to one of their selection boards. Candidates shortlisted after the initial selection procedure will go through a rigorous training regimen at one of the Air Force training establishments. After which they are given a short service commission as officers and posted at any of the Air Force Stations. The procedure for sending your application to the Indian Air Force is fairly simple. The first stage is to watch out for the advertisement inviting applications in the leading newspapers and the Employment News. After you spot the relevant *ad*, you should send your application in the format mentioned in the advertisement, before the last date of receiving of application.

Eligibility Criteria for Joining the Indian Air Force as an Officer

Flying Branch : You surely are propelled to newer heights in the flying branch of the Indian Air Force. You are trained either as a Fighter pilot or a Helicopter pilot or a Transport pilot and are a part of various peace and wartime missions. As an engineer, you enter the Flying branch through the Air Force Academy.

Air Force Academy : The Air Force Academy is one of the most prestigious training establishments of the Indian Air Force. Here, you are trained and prepared for your responsibilities as a pilot.

The following are the three modes of entry for engineers to join the Flying branch:

- **Combined Defence Service Examination (CDSE) :** You can take the Combined Defence Service Examination (CDSE) (written test conducted by UPSC) to join the Flying branch of the

Indian Air Force. Men can join the Air Force through this mode of entry and will be given a Permanent Commission. For applying through any of the entry points mentioned above, you must fulfill the following eligibility criteria:

Age : 19 to 23 years; Marital Status: Single; Nationality: Indian; Gender: for men only.

Educational Qualifications : Graduate (Three-year degree course) in any discipline from a recognised university (with physics and mathematics at 10+2 level)/B.E./B.Tech. (Four-year course). Final year students can also apply, provided they do not have any backlog. No percentage bar for CDSE entry.

- **National Cadet Corps Special Entry (Through CO NCC/DG NCC) :** As Air Wing Division 'C' Certificate holder of the National Cadet Corps, you can apply to the Flying branch of the Indian Air Force. Men can join the Air Force through this mode of entry and will be given a Permanent Commission.

  For applying through any of the entry points mentioned above, you must fulfill the following eligibility criteria:

  Age : 19 to 23 years; Marital Status: Single; Nationality: Indian; Gender: for men only.

  Educational Qualifications : Graduate (Three-year degree course) in any discipline from a recognised university who have attained 60 per cent marks in aggregate in all papers put together and have Physics and Mathematics at 10+2 level or B.E/B.Tech (Four-year course) from a recognised university with minimum 60 per cent marks in aggregate in all papers put together. Final year students can also apply, provided they do not have any backlog and should have minimum 60 per cent marks in aggregate up to the previous year/semester.

  NCC Air Wing Senior Division 'C' certificate.

- **Flying (Pilot) Short Service Commission (For men and women) with term of engagement of 14 years with no further extension.**

  Both men and women are eligible to apply for short service commission in the flying branch. Short Service Commission in Flying branch is for 14 years with no further extension. For applying through any of the entry points mentioned above, you must fulfill the following eligibility criteria:

  Age : 19 to 23 years, 19 to 25 years for CPL Holders (Issued by DGCA, India); Marital Status: Single; Nationality: Indian; Gender: applicable for both men and women.

Educational Qualifications : Graduate (Three-year degree course) in any discipline from a recognised university who have attained 60 per cent marks in aggregate in all papers put together with physics and mathematics at 10+2 level OR B.E/B.Tech (Four-year course) from a recognised university with minimum 60 per cent marks in aggregate in all papers put together. Final year students can also apply, provided they do not have any backlog and should have minimum 60 per cent marks in aggregate upto the previous year/semester. Upper age limit for candidates holding valid and current Commercial Pilot Licence issued by DGCA (India) is relaxed up to 25 years.

Ground Duty

Meteorological Branch

Permanent or Short Service Commission : You can look forward to a fulfilling career as an officer in the Meteorological Branch. Handling the latest satellite imagery and state-of-the-art monitoring equipment, you would render specific advice to the operators on all aspects of weather. To join as an officer in the Meteorological Branch you need to fulfill the following requirements:

Age : 20 to 25 years; Marital Status: Single; Nationality: Indian; Gender: Applicable for both men and women.

Educational Qualifications : Post-graduate in any science stream/ mathematics/statistics/geography/computer applications/ environmental science/applied physics/oceanography/meteorology/ agricultural meteorology/ecology and environment/geophysics/ environmental biology. All candidates should have scored a minimum of 50 per cent marks in aggregate in all papers of Post-graduation put together and should have studied Mathematics and physics in Graduation with minimum of 50 per cent marks in both subjects.

Technical Branches

As an officer in the Technical Branch, you would be in-charge of some of the most sophisticated equipment in the world. You can apply for the Technical branch via any of the two schemes listed below:

Direct Entry Scheme: After you have completed your engineering, you can join the Technical Branch through the Direct Entry Scheme. Both men and women can use this mode of entry to apply to the Indian Air Force.

University Entry Scheme (UES)

Eligibility Criteria: Aeronautical Engineering (Electronics) and Aeronautical Engineering (Mechanical) Permanent Commission (for men)/Short Service Commission (for men and women).

Aeronautical Engineering (Electronics) : As an Aeronautical Engineer in the Electronics stream, you will be responsible for the communication and signals required on the Air Force station. You will also be in-charge of the execution of preventive maintenance and servicing of aircraft. With further in-service training, you could also move to the repair and overhaul divisions of the Indian Air Force. To join as the Aeronautical Engineering (Electronics) stream you must fulfill the following eligibility criteria:

Age : 18 to 28 years; Marital Status : Candidates below the age of 25 should be unmarried; Nationality : Indian; Gender : Applicable for both men and women.

Educational Qualifications (Aeronautical Engineer-Electronics)

Candidates applying for Aeronautical Engineer (Electronics) branch would be eligible if they have undergone any one of the following educational qualifications. A four-year degree and a minimum of 60 per cent marks in aggregate in all papers put together from a recognised university, OR cleared section A and B examination of Associate Membership of Institution of Engineers (India), OR cleared section A and B examination of Aeronautical Society of India, OR graduate membership examination of the Institute of Electronics and Telecommunication Engineers by actual studies. All the candidates should have studied at least eight subjects out of the list of eighteen subjects mentioned below while pursuing any one of the above mentioned qualifications:

1. Physics/Engineering Physics
2. Mathematics/Engineering Mathematics
3. Engineering Graphics/Engineering Drawing
4. Electrical Engineering/Electrical Technology
5. Control Engineering
6. Microprocessors
7. Digital Electronics/Basic Electronics
8. Computer Networks
9. Information Technology
10. Network Theory Design
11. Telecommunication Systems
12. Electronic Circuit Design
13. Radar Theory
14. Switching Theory

15. Instrumentation
16. Microwave Engineering
17. Antenna and Wave Propagation
18. Electronic Devices

- **Aeronautical Engineering (Mechanical)**

  After you join the Indian Air Force as an Aeronautical Engineer in the Mechanical stream, you could be placed at a position that requires you to be involved with preventive maintenance and servicing of aircraft or of common user and specialist application vehicles. You could also be involved in the safety and maintenance of firearms and ammunition at an Air Force Base.

  To join the Aeronautical Engineering (Mechanical) stream, you must fulfill the following conditions:

  Age : 18 to 28 years; Marital Status : Candidates below the age of 25 should be unmarried; Nationality : Indian; Gender : Applicable for both men and women.

Educational Qualifications (Aeronautical Engineer-Electronics)

Candidates applying for Aeronautical Engineer (Mechanical) branch would be eligible if they have undergone any one of the following educational qualifications:

A four-year degree qualification and must have secured a minimum of 60 per cent marks in aggregate in all papers put together from a recognised university, OR cleared section A and B examination of Associate Membership of Institution of Engineers (India), OR cleared section A and B examination of Aeronautical Society of India.

All the candidates should have studied at least eight subjects out of the list of eighteen subjects mentioned below while pursuing any one of the above mentioned qualifications:

1. Physics/Engineering Physics
2. Mathematics/Engineering Mathematics
3. Engineering Graphics/Engineering Drawing
4. Automotive Engineering/Plant Engineering/Industrial Engineering
5. Engineering Mechanics/Strength of Material
6. Aerodynamics
7. Thermodynamics and Applications/Heat Power Engineering
8. Heat and Mass Transfer

9. Theory of Machines (Kinematics and Dynamics of Machinery)
10. Fluid Mechanics/Turbo Machines
11. Flight Mechanics
12. Machine Drawing/Machine Design
13. Mechatronics
14. Material Science/Metallurgy
15. Vibrations
16. Workshop Technology/Manufacturing Technology/ Production Engineering
17. Hydraulics and Pneumatics
18. Aircraft Structures

University Entry Scheme (UES)

Permanent Commission (For men only)

Educational Qualifications: The candidate must be currently studying in pre-final year of B.E./B.Tech. degree course in the relevant streams of engineering as mentioned above and must have secured minimum of 60 per cent marks in aggregate up to the last semester for which results have been declared, at the time of applying/AFSB testing. There must be no backlog/arrears of papers of previous semesters. On completion of degree, minimum 60 per cent of marks in aggregate in all papers put together are mandatory.

Age: 18 to 28 years; Marital Status: Candidates below the age of 25 should be unmarried; Nationality: Indian; Gender: Applicable only for men.

The time of release of advertisements varies for the different modes of entry for the Flying Branch.

Mode of Entry: Month of Release of Advertisement:	
NDA	April/November
CDSE	April/November
NCC	June/December
SCC (Women)	January/July

How to Join the Indian Air Force

Ground Duty Branch

The time of release of advertisement varies for the Air Traffic Controller/Fighter Controller and other Ground Duty Branches are as below:

Branch	*Month of Release of Advertisement*	*Send Applications to*
		Post Bag No. 001, DHQ Post Office, New Delhi-110011
Administrative	January/July	
Logistics		
Accounts		
Education		
Meteorology		
Air Traffic Controller/ Fighter Controller (Administrative)	April	Post Bag No. 001, DHQ Post Office, New Delhi – 110011

Technical Branch

You can apply to the Technical Branch through the University Entry Scheme or the Direct Entry Scheme. The time of release of the advertisements varies for the two schemes:

- Direct Entry Scheme
- University Entry Scheme

Direct Entry Scheme

State	*Month of Release of Advertisement*	*Send Applications to*
Haryana,HimachalPradesh, Jammu and Officer Kashmir, Punjab, Chandigarh and Delhi	January/July	Command Education Headquarters Western Air Command, IAF, Subroto Park, New Delhi-110010
Assam, Arunachal Pradesh, Manipur, Meghalaya, Mizoram, Nagaland, Orissa, Sikkim, Tripura, West Bengal,	January/July	Command Education Officer Headquarters Eastern Air Command, IAF, Nong Lyer, Shillong, Meghalaya
Uttar Pradesh, Bihar	January/July	Command Education Officer Headquarters Central Air Command, IAF, Bamrauli, Allahabad - 211012, Uttar Pradesh
Gujarat, Rajasthan, Dadra and Nager Haveli, Daman and Diu	October	Command Education Officer Headquarters South Western Air Command, IAF, Sector 9, Gandhinagar-382009, Gujarat

Kerala, Andaman and Nicobar Islands, Lakshwadeep and Pondicherry	October	Command Education Officer Headquarters Southern Air Command, IAF, Aakulam, Thiruvananthapuram-695031, Kerala
Madhya Pradesh and Maharashtra	January/July	Command Education Officer Headquarters Maintenance Command, IAF, Vay Sena Nagar, Nagpur – 440007, Maharashtra
Andhra Pradesh, Goa, Karnataka, Tamil Nadu	January/July	Command Education Officer Headquarters Training Command, IAF, Munni Reddy Palaya P.O. Bangalore-560006, Karnataka.

University Entry Scheme

State	*Month of Release of Advertisement*	*Send Applications to*
Haryana,Himachal Pradesh, Jammu and Kashmir, Punjab, Chandigarh and Delhi	October	Command Education Officer Headquarters Western Air Command, IAF, Subroto Park, New Delhi-110010
Assam, Arunachal Pradesh, Manipur, Meghalaya, Mizoram, Nagaland, Orissa, Sikkim, Tripura, West Bengal	October	Command Education Officer Headquarters Eastern Air Command, IAF, Nong Lyer, Shillong, Meghalaya
Uttar Pradesh, Bihar	October	Command Education Officer Headquarters Central Air Command, IAF, Bamrauli, Allahabad - 211012, Uttar Pradesh
Gujarat, Rajasthan, Dadra and Nager Haveli, Daman and Diu	October	Command Education Officer Headquarters South Western Air Command, IAF, Sector 9, Gandhinagar-382009, Gujarat
Kerala, Andaman and Nicobar Islands, Lakshwadeep and Pondicherry	October	Command Education Officer Headquarters Southern Air Command, IAF, Aakulam, Thiruvananthapuram-695031, Kerala

Madhya Pradesh and Maharashtra	October	Command Education Officer Headquarters Maintenance Command, IAF, Vay Sena Nagar, Nagpur – 440007, Maharashtra
Andhra Pradesh, Goa, Karnataka, Tamil Nadu	October	Command Education Officer Headquarters Training Command, IAF, Munni Reddy Palaya P.O. Bangalore-560006, Karnataka.

IAF Officer College

- **Indian Air Force**
  Air Headquarters (Vayu Bhavan), Motilal Nehru Marg, New Delhi-110106
- **Defence Public School**
  Chilla, P.O. Shamti, Solan – 173212
- **Supper Brilliant Point Coaching Institute**
  J1/1 DDA Flats Kalkaji, New Delhi – 110019

Selection

The selection procedure for picking the candidates is quite strict and elaborate. The four steps involved are :

- Scanning of Application
- Testing Officer like Qualities
- Conducting Medical Examinations
- Preparing All India Merit List

Scanning of Application

After checking all eligibility-wise application forms for the three branches, you will receive a call letter with further instructions. If you have applied to the Flying Branch through NDA or CDSE, your applications will be sent for processing to UPSC. Thereafter, you will receive a call letter for writing the UPSC exam. Men after clearing the UPSC Examinations take the Pilot Aptitude Battery Test (PABT). If you are a woman applying for the Short Service Commission or applying as an NCC Senior Division 'C' Certificate holder, you skip the UPSC exams and move to the next step, i.e., PABT, after your application has been processed. PABT comprises a written test in which a candidate's perception and grasp of the subject is gauged. This is followed by two machine tests for checking the basic co-ordination and psychomotor skills.

If you have applied to the Ground Duty Branch, your application will be sent to the Air Headquarters for short-listing. Then, the candidates need to undergo an officer intelligence-rating test. If you have applied to the Technical Branch, you will be required to take the Engineering Knowledge Test (EKT). If you pass the EKT, you move to the next step.

Testing Officer like Qualities

After you have successfully cleared Step one, you will receive a call letter to report to any one of the Air Force Selection Boards (AFSB) located at Dehradun, Varanasi and Mysore. At the Air Force Selection Boards, you undergo a number of psychological tests, an interview and group activities which are collectively called the Officer Like Qualities (QLQ) Tests.

The Psychological Tests are written tests that are conducted by a Psychologist. The Group Tests are interactive indoor and outdoor tests. We expect active physical participation from you. The Interview involves a personal conversation with our Interviewing Officer.

All of the above are screening tests. If you do not make the passing grades, you are routed back home the same day. If you have applied through NDA/CDSE (for Flying Branch) there is no screening; you are tested for your second/third choice of Army and Navy.

All the conference held on the last day, all the assessors, i.e., the Psychologist, Ground Testing Officer and Interviewing Officer, discuss your performance. Based on your performance, you will be selected for the next step.

Conducting Medical Examinations

If you have applied for the Flying Branch and are found suitable by the Selection Board, you would be sent to the Air Force Central Medical Establishment, New Delhi or Institute of Aviation Medicine, Bangalore for a thorough medical examination. If you have applied for the Technical or Ground Duty Branches and are found suitable, you would be asked to return home and await a call for a medical examination depending upon your position in the merit list.

Preparing All India Merit List

An All India Merit List is compiled on the basis of your performance at the group tests as well as the medical examination. If you qualify the merit list, depending upon vacancies, you are instructed to go to the training academy.

Remuneration

Air Force not only offers you an adventurous and challenging career, but also takes care of your needs including basic accommodation, health care, recreational areas and education facilities for your children. Even before you are commissioned as an Air Force officer you start earning a monthly stipend of ₹ 8000 during your training period at any of the Air Force Training Establishments. And on successful completion of your training you receive the retrospective D.A. for the complete training period. Once you are commissioned as a Flying Officer, besides getting an attractive pay package, you and your family enjoy an excellent way of life. Depending on your branch, you start your career with the following emoluments on the grant of Permanent Commission.

Post	*Monthly Income*
Flying Branch (Pilots/Navigators)	₹ 16,900 (approx)
Technical Branch (Electronics/Mechanical)	₹ 13,400 (approx)
Ground Duty Branches	₹ 12,400 (approx)

The other benefits include living accommodation with 2-3 bed rooms (depending upon the rank). Insurance cover of ₹ 10 lakh at low premium rates, an annual leave of 60 days and 20 days casual leave, liberal Leave Travel Concessions to you and your family, Liberal loans for purchase of cars, computer or a house from the Air Force Group Insurance Society, Medical Facilities including specialist services to you and your family, Ration, Schooling facilities and opportunities for higher learning and facilities for recreational as well as competitive sports and other adventural activities.

After retirement, you are offered a large number of benefits like pension, medical facilities, use of the canteen and so on. The following is the pay you get according to your rank and branch chosen:

Rank	*Flying Branch*	*Technical Branch*	*Ground Duty Branches*
Flight Lieutenant	₹ 2.43 lakh	₹ 1.88 lakh	₹ 1.77 lakh
Squadron Leader	₹ 3.04 lakh	₹ 2.33 lakh	₹ 2.21 lakh
Wing Commander	₹ 3.42 lakh	₹ 2.70 lakh	₹ 2.58 lakh
Group Captain	₹ 3.75 lakh	₹3.02 lakh	₹ 2.90 lakh
Air Commodore	₹ 3.85 lakh	₹ 3.34 lakh	₹ 3.23 lakh

The Prospect of Career Growth as an Officer in the Air Force

As an officer in the Indian Air Force, the sky is the limit for you. You start your career as a Flying Officer and can rise up to the rank of Air Marshal. The chosen one from the Flying Branch becomes the head of the family, i.e., the Chief of Air Staff. The exact rank structure for commissioned officers is given below:

Junior Level Officers

- **Flying Officer (Fg Offr):** Taking off a career in Air Force, this is the first rank an officer wears after successful completion of the training. The officer is posted as a Squadron Pilot or an Adjutant or a Security Officer or a Welfare Officer in any of the small Air Force stations and given charge of men and affairs.
- **Flight Lieutenant (Flt Lt):** Beginning the climb to the top, Flight Lieutenant is the next rank in the Indian Air Force hierarchy. Equivalent to a Captain in Army and Lieutenant in Navy, a Flight Lieutenant takes on junior level supervisory responsibilities and is posted as a Pilot or an Adjutant or a Security Officer in any of the medium level Air Force Stations.

Executive Level Officers

- **Squadron Leader (Sqn Ldr):** Taking on bigger responsibilities under his wings, the Squadron Leader undertakes many tasks. Equivalent to a Major in Army and Lt. Commander in Navy, the Squadron Leader is the operational in-charge of a squadron's role. He is a senior level supervisor and takes responsibilities as a Flight Commander or a senior Administrative Officer in medium level Air Force Stations or an Asst. Provost Marshal or a Commanding Officer of Airmen Selection Centers.
- **Wing Commander (Wg Cdr):** Gearing up for the higher grounds, the Wing Commander takes on additional responsibilities. He is equivalent to Lt. Col in Army and Commander in Navy and is posted as a Commanding Officer of Flying Squadrons, or Chief Administrative Officer of medium to large Air Force stations or Commanding Officer of Liaison Units or Staff Appointment at Air HQs/Command HQs.
- **Group Captain:** Taking charge of men and management, the Group Captain heads large Air Force Stations. Equivalent to Colonel in Army and Captain in Navy, he may command a medium-sized Air Force Station or be Chief Operations Officers or a Chief Engineering Officer of a large Air Force Station or hold key Staff Appointments at the Air HQs/Command HQs.

- **Air Commodore:** The chosen few make it to this position. An Air Commodore is equivalent to Brigadier and Commodore in Navy and is posted as an Air Officer commanding large AF Stations or Staff Appointments (senior level) at Air HQs/ Command HQs.
- **Air Vice Marshal:** Only the daring few can climb this high in the Air Force hierarchy. An Air Vice Marshal is equivalent to Major General in Army and Rear Admiral in Navy. He is responsible for taking strategic decisions and is posted as the Principal Staff Officer (PSO) at Command HQs or as Assistant Chief of Air Staff at Air HQ.
- **Air Marshal:** Just one step below the top of the ladder, the Air Marshal Commands a lot of power. He is equivalent to Lt. Gen. in Army and Vice Admiral in Navy. He is posted as the Commander-in-Chief (C-in-C) at Command HQs or as the PSO at Air HQs or Command HQs.
- **Air Chief Marshal:** The top of the rank is for the best of the best from the flying branch. The Air Chief Marshal heads the Air Force family and is responsible for all strategic and tactical decisions, regarding the Indian Air Force in the times of peace and war.

7.2 The Indian Army

The Genesis of the Indian Army

The Indian Army is one of the largest in the world with a history going back several hundred years. It was during the British era that a Military Department very similar to the present Ministry of Defence was set up but with most of the senior positions occupied by the British. It was after Independence, on 14th January, 1949, the Army had its first Indian Commander-in-Chief (later Field Marshal) KM Cariappa. The Army headquarters is located in Sena Bhavan and portions of the south block of the Red Fort in Delhi.

Career Opportunities

Armed Forces offer excellent career opportunities to the adventurous young candidates. It is a career that offers immense facilities, a privileged life style and of course, honour in serving the country. The Armed Forces characterise the ideals of service, sacrifice, patriotism and our country's composite culture. The basic responsibility of the Army is to safeguard the territorial integrity of the nation against external aggression. In addition, the Army is often required to assist the civil administration during internal security disturbances, and in the maintenance of law and order, in organising relief operations during natural calamities like floods, earthquakes and cyclones and in the maintenance of essential services.

The Two Categories of the Armed Forces

The two main lines of work in the armed forces are categorised under the Fighting Forces and the Support Services. The Fighting Forces comprise the armoured corps, artillery, signals, engineering and the infantry (and similar divisions in the navy and air force); while the Support Services include electronic and mechanical engineering, ordinance corps, medical corps, intelligence and education.

The Functioning of the Indian Army

The Indian Army functions under the Chief of Army Staff (COAS), formerly designated as Commander-in-Chief. COAS is assisted by Vice-Chief of the army staff and seven other Principal Staff Officers (PSOs) namely, the two Deputy Chiefs of the Army Staff, Adjutant General, Quarter Master General, Master General of Ordnance, Military Secretary and Engineer-in-Chief.

Divisions of the Army

The Army is divided into six operational commands (Field armies) and one training command. Each command is under a General Officer Commanding in chief, who has an equal status to the Vice-Chief of Army Staff (VCOAS) and working under the control of Army HQ in New Delhi. The major field formations are Corps, Division and Brigade which are commanded by a Lieutenant General, Major General and Brigadier respectively.

The Indian Army is organised into five regional commands:

- HQ Central Command, Lucknow
- HQ Eastern Command, Kolkata
- HQ Northern Command, Udhampur

- HQ Southern Command, Chandimandir, and
- HQ Southern Command, Pune.

In addition, there is an Army Training Command at Shimla for the purpose of laying down the training policies for the Army. The Indian Armed Forces employ more than a million young men and women each year. One can join the Army as an officer or as an Army Man. The recruitment to the Armed Forces is voluntary and every citizen of India, irrespective of his caste, class, religion and community is eligible for recruitment provided he meets the laid down physical, medical and educational criteria. Recruitment into the Army is carried out according to Recruitable Male Population (RMP) of each state.

7.2.1 Indian Army Officer

As an officer in the Indian Army, you will be part of one of the world's finest Armies. A career in the Army will teach you to face the toughest of situations in life with panache you have never known before. Two broad ways are available for those wishing to join the army as commissioned officers. They are permanent Commission and Short Service Commission. A permanent Commission is for those who want to make a career in the army until retirement; while a short-service commission allows you to join on a five-year contractual basis, after which you can exercise the option to continue or not.

Recruitment (Army Officer)

Recruitment of Commissioned Officers in the Armed Forces is mainly through the Union Public Service Commission (UPSC) under permanent Commission. For Technical Branches, Women special entry scheme and NCC special entry scheme and service, recruitment is made directly through the respective Recruiting Directorates for the Army under Short Service Commission.

The permanent commission provides opportunities for men with 10+2/Intermediate, graduates and engineering graduates as officers.

10+2 (Through NDA)

One has to take an entry level exam conducted by Union Public Service Commission (UPSC) to join NDA (National Defense Academy). This exam is conducted twice a year in all major cities throughout India. It is restricted to boys between the ages of 16½ and 19. The months of commencement of the course each year is January and July. Applications are to be sent in response to the advertisement which will be published in leading newspapers during March/April. NDA exam conducted by UPSC is based on the CBSE syllabus. The subjects of the written examination consists of Mathematics (300 marks) and General Ability (600 marks). Those who clear the written exam go through a five-day interview process with the State Selection Board. On completion of the NDA course, candidates are sent to the respective service academies for their pre-commission training. The IMA (Indian Military Academy) trains Gentlemen Cadets (GCs) for commission into the Army.

Graduates (Direct Entry)

The UPSC holds an All-India Competitive Examination known as the Combined Defence Services Examination (CDSE), twice a year for University graduates or equivalent. Successful candidates can join Indian Military Academy for their pre-commission training after the interview conducted by the Service Selection Board and if finally selected, depending on their merit list ranking, are sent to Indian Military Academy. Candidate should be in the age of 19-24. The course commences each year in the month of January and July. Interested candidates can apply in response to advertisement in March/April and October/November.

Engineering Graduates (Direct Entry)

An Engineering graduate can join the Indian Military Academy directly. They only need to attend the Service Selection Board interview. Age at the time of joining should be between 20-27 years. The course commences every year in the month of January and July. One can apply directly to Additional Directorate General of Recruiting (TGC) in response to advertisement published in March/April and October /November.

University Entry Scheme

Students who are in final and pre-final years of engineering degree course can also apply to Indian army as an officer. They are eligible for induction into technical branches/services of the army as commissioned officers under the University Entry Scheme. Age should be between 19-25 years for final year engineering students and 18-24 for pre-final year engineering students. Month of commencement of course in each year is July. Selection is based on campus interview and Service Selection Board (SSB) interview. Applications should be sent in response to the advertisement published in July.

10+2 PCM (Tech)

There is another option for 10+2 PCM (Tech) candidates through which one can enter directly to Indian Military Academy. Age limit falls between 16½ to 19 ½ years. Month of commencement of course in each year is January and July. One has to apply directly to the Recruitment Directorate in May and November.

Other Recruitments

Government has approved the creation of a 6,000 strong Support Cadre of Special Commissioned Officers. These posts will be filled up by eligible Junior Commissioned Officers (JCO) and OR. Under this entry, serving JCOs/NCOs/OR in age group of 30-35 years, with an Army Senior School Certificate Pass (Class XI CBSE Pattern) Qualification will be eligible for commission after screening/selection through Service Selection Board and Medical Board. They will undergo a pre-commission training of one year duration. The officers so commissioned will earn promotion up to the rank of Colonel. The rules for substantive promotion and acting promotion will be the same as for regular officers. These officers will be employed in units as sub-unit Cadres/QM/Job/ERE appointment up to the rank of Major. They will retire at the age of 57 years serving about 20-25 years as officers.

Medical graduates from the Armed Forces Medical College, Pune are directly inducted as permanent Commissioned Medical officers in the Armed Forces. For recruitment of Regular Commissioned/Short Service Commissioned Medical officers from the graduates/post-graduates of Civil Medical Colleges, the Director General of the Armed forces Medical services conducts an all India competitive exam.

Short Service Commission

Indian Army has an alternative career, called short service commission which gives an option of joining in the Indian Army and serving as a commissioned officer for five years. The short-service commission is for those who are not certain about committing to a permanent position in the forces. At the end of the period, you are allowed to opt for a permanent commission. Alternatively you can also choose for another five years and also can choose to resign from your post at any time during this period. The short-service commission is also open to women.

Officers Training Academy

Short Service Commission facilitates recruitment of qualified technical graduates through the SSBs, to attend the Officers Training Academy (OTA), Chennai, after medical tests, for a ten month course. Candidates should be in the age group of 19-24. The course commences each year in the month of May and October/November. Interested candidates should apply in response to advertisement published in March/April and October/November On completion of training, the successful candidates are inducted as Short Service Commissioned Officers in the technical branches of the army.

Women's Special Entry Scheme

Women recruits are usually taken into the support services with a large number serving as medical officers and nurses. The WSES for officers offers non-technical, technical and specialist entry for unmarried females or issueless widow or divorcee candidates not below 19 years and above 27 years and having B.A., B. Com., B.C.A., B. Sc. in physics, chemistry and mathematicsa person should have a minimum aggregate of 60 per cent and above marks. Moreover, students with 50 per cent marks and holders of NCC 'C' candidates with 'B' or higher grade can also apply in this category.

For Technical Entry B.E., B.Tech. or equivalent or a higher qualification in civil or electrical or mechanical or electronics engineering and architecture is needed. Specialist entry is for those with 50 per cent marks in:

- Graduate B.Sc. with a minimum one-year diploma in computer science.
- Graduate with a minimum one-year diploma in communication or journalism or public relations or psychology.
- B.E. in remote sensing.
- P.G. degree in earth science/computer science/English/ geography/mathematics/physics/computer applications/ botany/zoology/biochemistry/organic chemistry or statistics.

Month of commencement of course in each year is March and September. Selection is based on written exam and SSB Interview and medical examination. Candidates should apply directly in response to advertisement in June/December. Women officers receive training at Officers Training Academy, Chennai.

In women special entry scheme, the initial contractual period is five years but in case any candidate is found unfit or unsuitable within first six months, her commission can be terminated any time before the expiry of the five years period. The scheme further provides that the entire lady Officers granted commission under this scheme would serve the Indian Army for a period of five years from the date of grant of Commission subject to fulfillment of other conditions. In addition, the lady officers carry reserve liability to serve the Indian Army for a period of five years plus two years on voluntary basis or up to 37 years of age, whichever is earlier. It means that after their release, the lady Officers remain on reserve for five years and can be recalled for duty during this period in case of emergencies. This period could be extended by two more years if the Officer so desires or up to 37 years of age, whichever is earlier. WSES (O), however, does not have any provision for permanent commission, although this matter is said to be under consideration of the Government of India. Lady Officers in the two entries other than WSES (O), like AMC, ADC, etc., however, have the provision for permanent commission.

The advertisement for recruitment of lady Officers under the WSES (O) appears from time to time as per requirement, normally twice every year in most of the national and important regional newspapers. The candidates are required to apply to the Additional Directorate General of Recruiting (Women Entry Section), West Block-III, R.K. Puram, New Delhi – 110066. Short-listing of eligible candidates is done at the Additional Directorate level and the short-listed candidates are then required to appear before the Service Selection Board (SSB). The selected candidates are then required to undergo a medical examination which is usually done by a special Medical Board at the nearest Military Hospital. The broad indications of medical standards are that the height and weight should not be less than 36 kgs and 142 cms respectively for women candidates. Corrected distance vision should be at least 6/6 for better eye 6/18 for the worse eye and Myopia of not more than minus 5.5 D including.

NCC Special Entry Scheme

Unmarried male graduates from a recognised university with a total of 50 per cent marks and above and between 19 and 25 years of age who have obtained a minimum of 'B' Grade in NCC 'C' Certificate may apply for Short Service Commission. These graduates are exempted from appearing in the CDSE conducted by the UPSC and are selected through the Service Selection Boards in Allahabad, Bhopal and Bangalore. The courses commences in May each year. Candidate should be in 19 – 25 years. Apply directly and the initial short listing of applications will be done at Additional directorate general recruiting Army Headquarters. Candidates short listed will be called for SSB interview by Additional directorate General of Recruiting. Candidates recommended by the Service Selection Board will undergo medical examination by a board of service medical Board.

Short Service Commission Technical

Short Service Commission (Technical) gives opportunities to unmarried male engineering graduates. Educational qualification of the candidate should be a degree in Engineering or equivalent degree from a recognised University in civil/electrical/mechanical/telecommunication/electrical and electronics/computer science/engineering/technology/architect/industrial/production. Candidates who are yet to pass the technical degree examination can also apply but they will be required to submit proof of passing the degree/provisional degree certificate to Recruiting Directorate (TGC Entry), West Block-III, RK Puram, New Delhi–110 066. Age limit is 20 – 27 years.

The selection process includes initial screening and the short-listing of applicants will be done at the Recruiting Directorate of the Army headquarters. Those short-listed will be required to appear before the Service Selection Board (SSB) where they will have to undergo group test, psychological test and interview. Candidates who qualify at the SSB and are found medically fit by a Medical Board will be placed in the order of merit. The final selection will be made in that order up to the number of vacancies available at that time. Selected candidates for Short Service Commission (Technical) will be sent to the Officers' Training Academy, Chennai. The training lasts for 49 weeks at the expense of the government.

Officers will be required to serve five years and may be considered for grant of permanent commission thereafter as per existing rules.

Pay and Ranking

₹ 8000 per month to IMA (Indian Military Academy) and OTA Gentlemen Cadets.

Rank	*Basic Pay Start*	*Yearly Increment*	*Maximum*
Lieutenant	8,250	300	10,050
Captain	9,600	300	11,400
Major	11,600	325	14,850
Lt. Colonel	13,500	400	17,100
Colonel	15,100	450	17,350
Brigadier	16,700	450	18,050
Major General	18,400	500	22,400
Lt. General	22,400	525	24,500
Vice Chief of Army and Army Commanders			26,000 Fixed
Chief of Army Staff			30,000 Fixed

Allowances

- Dearness Allowance (DA) : As declared from time to time by Government of India.
- Counter Insurgency/Field/High Altitude allowance as applicable
- Kit Maintenance Allowance
- City Compensatory Allowance

- Transportation Allowance
- Aviation Allowance to those eligible
- Specialist/Technical Pay to those eligible
- Subsidised Accommodation
- Free Rations
- Free Medical Treatment
- Insurance worth Rs. 8 lakh through Army Group Insurance Fund (AGIF)
- Conveyance Allowance
- House Building Allowance
- Canteen Stores Department (CSD) facilities
- Membership of Clubs and Institutes at subsidised rates
- Leave
- 60 days Annual Leave
- 20 days Casual Leave

Travel

- Free Railway Warrant for self and family during Annual Leave (up to 1500 km)
- Leave Travel Concession (LTC)
- Six Form D (Concession vouchers, 40 per cent concession) during a calendar year
- Rail Reservations through the Movement Control Office (MCO)

Education

- B.A./B.Sc./B.C.A. degree to NDA Cadets
- Career Courses as applicable to all
- Study leave with full pay to entitled officers
- Specialist courses for Technical Officers
- Staff/Technical Courses for selected officers
- Management courses for senior officers

Recreation

Indoor and Outdoor Sports Facilities Golf, Tennis, Squash, Aquatics, Hockey, Football, Basketball, Athletics

Adventure Activities

Mountaineering, Skiing, River rafting, Gliding, Hot Air Ballooning, Trekking and many more.

7.2.2 Lower Ranks in Indian Army

Recruitments in Army for lower ranks are broad, based. Every male citizen, irrespective of caste, class, religion and domicile is eligible for recruitment in Army provided the person meets the laid down age, educational, physical and medical standards. It is carried out according to the Recruitable Male Population (RMP) of each state. RMP of a state is reckoned to be 10 per cent of male population of the state. A new system of recruitment has been introduced with effect from 1st April 1988. Under the revised system, recruitment of *jawans* in the Army is carried out through Open recruitment rallies planned well in advance, keeping in view the geographical, demographical and topographical considerations. At least one such rally is held each month, combining districts, areas and regions, depending upon the response anticipated. Advance publicity is made of a rally in particular area/district.

Territorial Army: Territorial Army is organisations of units formed by ordinary citizens from all walks of life who generally, while continuing to pursue their normal vocations also volunteer for military service. These citizens on joining the Territorial Army undergo a short period of rigorous training which makes them reasonably competent soldiers. They join their units for two months every year for refresher training to keep in touch with the art of soldering. Whenever a need arises, personnel of the Territorial Army are called up for active service and join their units within a specified time frame. Territorial Army has participated in wars along with the regular Indian Army. They have been raised to maintain essential services like Railways, Oil sector and Medical (Departmental Units) during emergencies. Some units formed for national development tasks lay re-forestation and reclamation of wasteland have rendered commendable services.

Eligibility

Category	*Education*	*Age*
Soldier General Category	SSLC/Metric	16-21
Soldier Technical	SSLC/Metric (Moths, English and Science) 45 per cent aggregate marks in Class The	16-23
Soldier Clerk/Store keeper Technical	SSLC/Metric (English and Moths) 45 per cent aggregate marks in Class The	16-23
Soldier Nursing Assistant	SSLC/Metric (Moths, English and Science) 45 per cent aggregate marks in Class The	16-23

Soldier Tradesman		
(i) General Duties	Non-metric	16-20
(ii) Specified Duties	Non-metric	16-25
Havildar Education		
(i) Group 'X'	Post-graduate/Trained Graduate	20-25
(ii) Group 'Y'	B.A./B.Sc. (Metric with English and Maths)	16-25
Religious Teacher (JCO's)	Graduate in any discipline In addition, qualification in his denomination	27-34
JCO (Catering)	10+2 with science and one Year cookery diploma/Certificate from a recognised Food Craft Institute.	21-27
Surveyor Automated Cartographer	B.A. /B.Sc. with Maths having passed Metric and 12th (10+2) with Maths and Science	20-25

Note : Dispensation in education for enrollment as soldier (GD) is permissible to some selected states/region/class and communities by the government. Details may be obtained from nearest BRO/ZRO physical standards. The minimum physical standards have been laid down region-wise and are as follows.

Region	*States*	*Height (in cms.)*	*Weight (in cms.)*	*Chest (in cms.)*
Western Himalayan Region	J&K, HP, Punjab Hills (Area South and West of the Inter State Border between HP and Punjab and North and east of road of Mukerian, Hoshiarpur, Garhshankar, Ropar and Chandigarh), Garhwal and Kumaon regions of UP.	163	48	77
Eastern Himalayan Region	Nagaland, Manipur, Tripura, Mizoram, Meghalaya, Assam, Arunachal Pradesh, Sikkim and Hill Region of West Bengal.	157	48	77
Western Plains Region	Punjab, Haryana, Chandigarh, Delhi Rajasthan and Western (UP) (Meerut and Agra Division).	170	50	77
Eastern Plains Region	Eastern UP, Bihar, West Bengal and Orissa	169	50	77
Central Region	Madhya Pradesh, Gujarat, Maharashtra, Dadar, Nagar-Haveli, Daman and Diu.	167	50	77
Southern Region	Andhra Pradesh, Karnataka, Tamil Nadu, Kerala, Goa and Pondicherry	165	50	77

Special Physical Standards

Region-States-Category

Ladakhi

Gurkha both Nepalese and Indians

Andaman, Nicobar Islands, Lakshadweep Group including Minicoy: - Settlers

Locals

Tribals of recognised tribal areas

Brigade of the Guards

Med Arty

Corps of Military Police

Clerks GD/SKT

Soldier Tradesmen – normal physical standards given above minus two CMS in height, one cm in Chest and two kgs inweight. The following are eligible for relaxations in physical standards.

Candidate Profile	*Height (in cms.)*	*Weight (in cms.)*	*Chest (in cms.)*
(a) Candidates between 16 to 18 years of age	1	2	1
(b) Sons of Servicemen/Ex-Servicemen/ War Widows/Widows of Ex-Servicemen	2	2	1
(c) Adopted son/son-in-law of a War Widow, if she has no son	2	2	1
(d) Outstanding sportsmen (National/State level sportsmen and those who have represented District/College/School in State/University/Board Championship and earned 1st/2nd Position.)	2	5	3

Recruitment: How to Apply

All recruitments are done only through rallies. Please contact your nearest Branch Recruiting Office/Zonal Recruiting Office for details. Rally schedule is also published in leading vernacular newspapers/ *Employment News*. Report to rally site on the dates announced on Notice Board along with your educational certificate, character certificate and six passport size photographs.

Physical Fitness

To determine the physical Fitness, the following tests carrying 100 marks are held :

(a) One Mile Run

(b) Pull Ups

(c) Balance

(d) Nine Feet Ditch

Marking system is as follows:

(a) One Mile Run

(i) 5.40 Mins and below – 60 Mks

(ii) 5.41 Mins to 5.50 – 48 Mks

(iii) 5.51 Mins to 6.00 – 36 Mks

(iv) 6.01 Mins to 6.20 – 24 Mks

(b) Pull Ups

(i) 10 and above – 40 Mks

(ii) 9 – 32 Mks

(iii) 8 – 28 Mks

(iv) 7 – 21 Mks

(v) 6 – 16 Mks

(c) Balance and Nine Feet Ditch

(i) These are qualifying tests, hence no marks are awarded.

Written Examination

Common Entrance Examination (CEE) is conducted on last Sundays of each month for recruitment of soldiers. It comprises the following two papers:

(a) Paper I – Compulsory for all soldier categories

(b) Paper II – For soldier Technical, Soldier CIK (GD/SKT) and Soldier Nursing Assistant.

Paper I – It generally comprises questions on IQ/numerical ability, general knowledge and current affairs. Duration of papers is 60 minutes. Total marks-100, Pass Marks-32.

Paper II (Sol. Tech) – 50 marks. It generally comprises Physics, Chemistry and Mathematics. Duration – 30 minutes, Pass marks – 16.

Paper II (Sol CIK/SKT) – 50 marks. It generally comprises Mathematics and English (Language).

7.3 The Indian Navy

The Indian Navy (IN)

The Indian Navy (IN) also known as *Bharatiya Nau Sena* is the naval branch of the armed forces of India whose history can be traced back to 1612. It is the world's fifth largest and reliable three dimensional forces, capable of operating above, on and under surfaces of the oceans. Navy is responsible for the defence and security of India's maritime interests. A fleet of submarines, destroyers, freights and other support vessels operate under the Indian Navy.

The Division of Indian Navy

The Indian Navy operates three commands each under the control of a Flag Officer Commanding-in-Chief in the rank of Vice Admiral. The three Commands are:

- The Western Naval Command (Headquarters at Mumbai)
- The Eastern Naval Command (Headquarters at Visakhapatnam)
- The Southern Naval Command (Headquarters at Kochi).

The Western and the Eastern Naval Commands are operational commands and exercise control over operations in the Arabian Sea and the Bay of Bengal respectively. The Southern Command is designed as the Training Command, operating on the Arabian Sea. Besides these, the Navy has important bases in Kolkata and Goa. Women were inducted into the Indian Navy for the first time in 1992 when twenty-two women were trained for education, logistics and law cadres. Service conditions are same for men and women officers.

Advantages of Serving in the Navy

A career in Indian Navy is always in high demand as it is a profession which offers personal, financial, emotional security and status in the society. Officers and Sailor Cadres are the major lines of work in the Indian Navy. One has to serve Indian Navy for a minimum period of 15 years as general sailor or 20 years as Artificer or 20 years as Officer. After that, they are qualified for a generous pension. Those who join Navy at 20 years of age could choose to retire from service with an assured monthly pay check for the rest of your life by the age of 35 to 40. And even after retirement, one could enjoy the canteen and medical facilities as you did while in service.

Indian Navy Officers

The Indian Navy Officers are broadly classified as:

Executive Officers: They seek for the command of a naval ship, submarines and aircraft, can specialise in any of the fields like,

- Gunnery and Missiles

- Navigation and Direction
- Anti-Submarine Warfare
- Communications
- **Aviation (Pilot):** Most Navy Pilot fly ship-borne helicopters and shore-based maritime reconnaissance aircraft, fighter aircraft such as Sea Harrier or Mig-29K etc.
- **Observer:** Observer officer operates various state of the art equipment including sonics, sonars, radars and communication equipment.
- Submarine
- **Hydrography:** Hydrographic Officers are responsible for collecting information required for making the nautical charts used by the Indian Navy and other Navies around the world.
- **Diving:** Diving Officer's job range from under water inspection and repair of ships to defence of Indian Navy maritime assets. Alternatively one may opt to become a Diving Cadre Officer wherein one would be required to undertake a Clearance Diving Officers' course and/or a maritime Commando course.
- **Law:** Law Officers deals with the legal needs of the Navy.
- Air Traffic Control
- **Naval Armament Inspection:** Naval Armament Inspection Officers ensure the quality, safety and reliability of naval armament supplied to the Navy by various agencies.
- Logistics
- **Provost:** Provost Officer deals with policing, regulatory and security and vigilance needs of the Navy.

Engineering

Engineering Officers, who work in gigantic naval dockyards and indigenous production units, are responsible for keeping all the hi-tech machinery and propulsion systems of the navy serviceable. One can join in the Naval Architecture Cadre of the Engineering Branch that involves in the designing, construction, quality controlling, repairing and new construction works of naval vessels.

Electrical

Electrical Officers are those who are in charge of managing and maintaining the ship's integral power generation and distribution system like propulsion, radar, radio, underwater weapons, missile, computer etc.

Education

Education Officers play a major role in the training of naval officers and sailors by giving scientific and methodical instructions, including theoretical aspects of technical subjects of all branches of the Navy. An Educational Officer can specialise in like Meteorology or Oceanography and in almost all specialisations of the Executive Branch.

The basic training for all the officers inducted into the Indian Navy under various schemes is given at Naval Academy Ezhimala (NAVAC), located in Kannur (Cannanore) of Kerala.

7.3.1 Recruitment of Officers in the Navy

Recruitment as an Officer in the Navy is carried out on the basis of All India Merit and is advertised through the *Employment News* and all important national and regional newspapers/dailies. The Commission in the Indian Navy is open to young men and women of the country. They have the option to join the Executive, Technical and Education Branches of the Indian Navy.

There are two modes of Entry in the Indian Navy namely, UPSC Entry and Non-UPSC Entry:

Entry through Union Public Service Commission (UPSC)

UPSC holds a competitive examination for the entry into the National Defence Academy (NDA)/Naval Academy (10+2) and Combined Defence Services Examination (CDSE), twice a year. The UPSC entries are Permanent Commission (PC) entries in which the UPSC conducts a written examination which is followed by an interview by the Service Selection Board (SSB). Result of qualified candidates is forwarded to UPSC for making the final merit. Medically fit candidates who are in the merit are appointed by ADG (Rtg)/IHQ of MoD (Navy).

Educational Qualifications

(I) UPSC Entries

- **National Defence Academy (NDA) and Naval Academy Examination:**

  Candidates who have completed 10+2 (PCM) examination or in the 12th standard are eligible to appear in NDA examination. Successful candidates can join in the NDA or Naval Academy as Naval cadets.

- **Combined Defence Services Examination (CDSE)**

  Graduates in any discipline are eligible to appear in the Combined Defence Services Examination. The degree should be recognised by the University Grants Commission (UGC). Successful candidates join the Naval Academy for the Naval Orientation Course (NOC).

(II) Non-UPSC Entries

The Non-UPSC entries are both for Permanent Commission (PC) and Short Service Commission (SSC). The duration of the Short Service Commission is 10 years, extendable to 14 years. There is no written examination for the Non-UPSC entries. In this case, the applications are invited and shortlisted at Integrated Headquarters of the Ministry of Defence (Navy) [IHQ of MoD (Navy)] on the basis of marks secured in the qualifying educational examinations i.e., 10+2, graduate or post-graduate. The shortlisted candidates are sent for SSB interviews. Thereafter, a merit list, comprising qualified candidates, is prepared as per the availability of vacancies.

The Non-UPSC entry schemes are:

- **10+2 (B. Tech Entry):** Under this scheme, candidates with 10+2 (PCM) qualifications after selection through the Services Selection Board are sent to Naval Academy for the NOC. Thereafter, they undergo a four years Engineering course at INS Shivaji/Cochin University of Science and Technology (CUSAT) for Naval Architecture. On successful completion of the course they are granted permanent commission in the Executive/Marine/Electrical/Electronic Engineering/Naval Architecture branch of Indian Navy.
- **University Entry Scheme (UES):** Final year engineering students are eligible for induction into the technical Branches/Cadres of the Navy. Naval selection teams from the IHQ of MoD (Navy) and Command Headquarters visit AICTE approved Engineering colleges across the country to shortlist the candidates. The shortlisted candidates based on all India Merit are called for interview at the Services Selection Board. The successful candidates, thereafter, are put through the medical tests. Final selection is based on all India Merit on the basis of marks obtained in the SSB interviews.
- **Special Naval Architects Entry Scheme (SNAES):** Government has recently approved the induction of 45 Naval Architect officers into the Naval Architecture Cadre of the Engineering Branch of

the Indian Navy, as Short Service Commission Officers, under a Special scheme of 'Special Naval Architects Entry Scheme' (SNAES). An empowered Naval team visits IIT Kharagpur, IIT Chennai, Cochin University of Science and Technology (CUSAT) and Andhra University, where B. Tech (Naval Architecture) course is conducted to select the candidates through campus interviews. The selected candidates undergo medical examination at the nearest Military Hospital and if found fit are selected for training.

Interview and Selection

Stage-I (Day-1) – Stage-I selection system includes

- **Officer Intelligence Rating Test (OIRT).**

  Picture Perception and Description Test (PDPT): Picture is flashed for 30 seconds. The candidate has to broadly note down seven basic parameters viz., number of characters, age, sex, mood, action relating to past, present and future for each character in one minute.

- **Discussion of the picture – 30 minutes**

  In this phase, batch is divided into different groups. Strength of group is around 15 candidates. Each candidate narrates his individual written story verbatim. Subsequently, in Part-II all the candidates have to come to discuss among themselves and achieve a common consensus about the characters and theme of the story. Once all candidates have undergone this stage the results for stage one testing are declared. Successful candidates are retained for stage-II testing and the balance is asked to leave after a short brief on general shortcomings.

Stage-II (Day-2)-In the second Stage, Psychological Tests are performed that includes

- **Thematic Apperception Test (TAT)**

  Twelve pictures including one blank are shown for 30 seconds each. Candidates are asked to write a story around what led to the situation. What is going on and what would be the outcome? Picture is shown for 30 seconds and they are asked to write it in four minutes. In the blank slide, they have to think a picture of their own choice and to write a story around that.

- **Word Association Test (WAT)**

  In this test, a series of 60 words are shown to the candidates one after another for 15 seconds each. The candidate is required to write down the first thought or idea comes to his mind.

- **Situation Reaction Test (SRT)**

  This test consists of 60 routine life situations regarding day to day activities. The situations are printed in a booklet and the candidate is asked to write his reactions by completing the sentences, as to how they would feel, think and act up these situations.

Self-description – 15 minutes

Candidate is asked to write separate paragraphs on each context about the opinion of his parents/guardian, friends, teachers/superiors.

Stage-III (Day-3) – Stage-III selection process includes

- **Group Discussion**

  Two topics of common interest (social issues and current events) are discussed. It is an informal discussion and not a debate. Each topic is allotted 20 minutes each. No definite conclusion is required to be deduced.

- **Group Planning Exercise (GPE)**

  It comprises five stages namely, explanation of the model, reading of the narrative by GTO, five minutes for self-reading by candidates, 10 minutes for individual written solutions and 20 minutes for group discussion. Narration of the group solution and definite conclusion is required.

- **Progressive Group Tasks (PGT)**

  It is the first outdoor task. A set of four obstacles with progressively increasing level of difficulties are to be completed in 40 to 50 minutes. Structures helping material and load are provided to the group.

- **Group Obstacle Race (GOR)**

  It has one obstacle similar to progressive group task with helping material and load to be carried. Group is divided into two Sub-Groups and assigned the same obstacle in turn in such a way that one group is working; the other is not allowed to watch it. Time allotted to each sub group is 15 minutes.

Lecturette

It is an individual task and the candidate is required to give a short talk to the group. Three minutes are allowed to prepare any chosen topic from the four given in the Lecturette Cards for the talk.

Stage-IV (Day-4) – Stage-IV Selection Process Includes

- **Individual Obstacles**

  A set of 10 obstacles is set to be tackled individually. Obstacles are numbered from one to ten, denoting the points each one carries. Each individual will be given three minutes.

- **Command Task**

  Each individual is nominated as commander for one task consisting of one obstacle similar to the Progressive Group Task. Time given is 15 minutes.

- **Final Group Task**

  Task consists of one obstacle similar to the progressive group task. Time given to complete this task is 15-20 minutes.

Personal interviews are conducted by Interviewing Officer (IO) from Day-2 to Day-4.

Stage-V (Day-5) – Stage-V includes

Closing address by Deputy President of the Board,

Conference,

Announcement of Results, and

Dispersal.

The candidates recommended by Service Selection Board (SSB) have to undergo a medical examination at the nearest Service Hospitals. The medical examination procedure for candidates is as follows:

- **Special Medical Board (SMB):** Special Medical Board (SMB) of officer candidates will be held at designated hospitals over duration of five to six days. Candidates will be declared Fit/ Temporarily Unfit or Permanently Unfit. Candidates declared Temporarily Unfit are to report back to the hospital for examination after the specified time. Candidates who still do not qualify will be declared Permanently Unfit.

- **Appeal Medical Board (AMB) :** Candidates who are declared permanently unfit by Special Medical Board are eligible for Appeal Medical Board after depositing a sum of a requisite amount in the government treasury. No fees will be charged from temporarily unfit candidates. Unfit candidates get a maximum of 42 days to report for AMB at designated command hospital. Candidates declared unfit by Appeal Medical Board are eligible to appeal for Review Medical Board.

- **Review Medical Board:** The president of Appeal Medical Board will intimate the candidate, the reason of his/her being unfit through a leaflet and guide him/her for Review Medical Board. However, he will explain to the candidate that holding of the Review Medical Board is at the discretion of DGMS (Navy) and DGAFMS based on the merits of the case and it is not his/her right. RMBs are conducted at Army Research and Referral Hospital, Delhi and Armed Force Medical College, Pune. The selected Officer candidates, inducted into the Indian Navy under various schemes are given basic training at Naval Academy, *Ezhimala* (NAVAC). The period of initial training for cadet entry and direct entry graduate candidates is four years and 22 weeks respectively. Branch specific training is subsequently imparted at other naval establishments.

Medical Standards

All candidates intending to join the Indian Navy must be physically and medically fit as per laid down standards. Proficiency in sport, swimming and extra-curricular activities is desirable.

- **Height :** The preferable height for a candidate of 18 years of age is 157 cms for males and 152 cms for females.
- **Weight :** The weight should not vary from average by more than 10 per cent.

Anthropometric Measurement

The acceptable anthropometric standard for aviation i.e., Short Service Commission (Aviation and Observer) entry for both male and female are as follows :

- Minimum Height – 162.5 cm
- Sitting Height – minimum-81.5 cms, maximum – 96.0 cms
- Leg length – minimum – 99.0 cms, maximum – 120.0 cms
- Thigh Length – Maximum – 64.0

Pay Scales of Officers

Rank	*Pay Bands/Scale*	*Grade Pay*	*MSP*
Sub-lieutenant	PB-3/ 15,600-39,100	5,400	6,000
Lieutenant	PB-3/ 15,600-39,100	6,100	6,000
Lieutenant Commander	PB-3/ 15,600-39,100	6,600	6,000
Commander	PB-4/ 37,400-67,000	8,000	6,000

Captain	PB-4/ 37,400-67,000	8,700	6,000
Commodore	PB-4/ 37,400-67,000	8,900	6,000
Rear Admiral	PB-4/ 37,400-67,000	10,000	Nil
Vice Admiral Vice Admiral (C-in-C/VCNS)	PB-4/ 37,400-67,000	12,000	Nil
Vice Admiral (Fixed C-in-C/VCNS)	Apex Scale 80,000	Nil	Nil
Admiral	90,000/Fixed	Nil	Nil

Allowances

- Flying (for qualified Aircrew – 9,000-14,000/-PM)
- Submarine (for qualified Submariner – 9,000-14,000/- PM)
- Marcos (for qualified as Marcos – 9,000-14,000/- PM)
- Diving (for Clearance/Ship Diver – 8,000-14,000/-PM)
- Sea Going (for all Officers Serving onboard Ships (sailing only) – 4,200-5,200/- pm on basis of rank
- Technical (for Technical Officer – 2,000-5,000/- pm)
- Hydrographic (for qualified Hydrography – 400-1,200/- pm)
- Uniform (for all Officers – 16,000 (initial) and 5,000 (every 3 years)

Perks

- Free medical facilities for self and family
- Canteen facilities
- Free Ration
- Mess/club/sports facilities
- Group insurance
- Furnished government accommodation at best location
- Pension with all benefits
- Leave – 60 days annual leave and 20 days casual leave
- Leave encashment (up to 300 days)

Indian Navy Sailor

Sailors are the sepoys of the Indian Navy who are responsible for operating and maintaining propulsion machinery, weapons, sensors etc. Sailors in the navy are imparted with requisite training at various intervals during their service. They are liable to serve anywhere in India, on board ships and Sub-marines or abroad as deemed necessary by the service.

The initial training for the sailors is given at INS Chilka, located at Khurda, District of Orissa. This is followed by further training at various naval establishments all over the country. Prior to release from service sailors are also given pre-release courses to enable them to settle down in civil life.

Eligibility

Artificer Apprentices (AA)

- **Educational Qualification :** Applicant should have passed class 12th or equivalent with subjects of Physics, Chemistry and Mathematics with 55 per cent marks
- **Age :** 17 – 20 years
- **Training :** The training for Artificer Apprentice will generally be for nine weeks Basic Training at INS Chilka followed by eight weeks sea training. Thereafter, four years training in technical training establishments of the Navy. On completion, candidates will have qualification equivalent to Diploma in electrical/ mechanical/aeronautical engineering which is recognised by the Government of India for purposes of employment in central/ state government.

Senior Secondary Recruit

- **Educational Qualification :** Applicant should have passed Class 12th (Intermediate) with science stream with compulsory subjects of physics and mathematics and optional subjects of chemistry or biology or computers.
- **Age :** 17 – 21 years
- **Training :** The training of for Senior Secondary Recruit will generally be 24 weeks Basic Training at INS Chilka followed by 24 weeks professional training in the allotted trade in Naval Establishments all over the country. Branch/Trade will be allocated as per requirement of service.

Matric Entry Recruits (MR)

Steward and cooks are the two branches recruited through Matric Entry.

Educational Qualification : Applicant should have passed 10th class examination.

Age : 17 – 21 years

Non-matric Entry Recruits (NMR)

To pass are recruited through Non-matric Entry.

Educational Qualification : Applicant should have passed 6th class examination.

Age : 17 – 21 years

Training : The training for Matric Recruit and Non-matric Recruit will generally be 15 weeks basic training at INS Chilka followed by professional training at respective naval establishments as per trade. The beginning of engagement of sailor with the Indian Navy is subject to successful completion of training. The period of the initial engagement for Metric Recruit and Non-Matric Recruit sailor is 15 years. However, engagement (i.e., service) period is extendable with maximum limit being till the attainment of 57 years of age, which in turn, depends on the rank attained and satisfactory performance by the sailor while in the service.

Musician (MUS)

Educational Qualification : Applicant should have passed 10th class examination and should be able to exhibit an aptitude for music.

Musical Ability : Candidates applying should have proficiency in western notation, aural aptitude, knowledge of theory of music and actual practical skill on any musical instrument. The candidates applying should have proficiency in playing String, Keyboard, Woodwind, Brass and Percussion Instruments both of Western and Indian origin.

Age : 17 – 21 years

Recruitment Process

AA/SSR/MR/NMR/Musicians

Recruitment of sailors in Indian Navy is application-based and is carried out on the All India Merit on the basis of written examination, physical fitness test and medical examination. Recruitment publicity is carried out on all India basis through advertisements in all leading national and regional newspapers and *Employment News* in December/January and June/July every year. Publicity material is also dispatched to a large number of schools/colleges and all Zillah Sanik Boards. The local administration carries out the publicity drive in rural/backward areas through local media.

How to Apply

The application form in the prescribed format may be typed on plain paper or downloaded from the website of Indian Navy. The forms will be published in important newspapers. Candidates applying for more than one type of entry are required to submit separate applications. However, only one application form is to be filled for a particular entry.

Choice of entry is to be clearly indicated on the application form. You can apply only for one entry between Mr Cook/Mr Steward/NMR Topass in a batch. All applications for AA and SSR, MR, MUS, NMR are to be addressed to the authority promulgated and should reach the authority only through ordinary post.

Indian Navy conducts recruitment for enrolling sailor recruits at 34 examination centers across the country. Candidates are permitted to appear for examination at one centre for recruitment in accordance with the domicile certificate issued by the district level government authorities.

The various Entries for recruitment of sailors are:

Type of Entry	*Commission*	*Gender*	*Age*	*Eligibility Criteria*
Artificer Apprentice	Non Commission	Male	17-20	10+2 with Physics, (AA) Chemistry and Mathematics with 55 per cent marks
Direct Entry Petty Officer (Sports) DEPO (Sports)	Non-commission	Male	17-22	10+2 (any stream)
Senior Secondary Recruit (SSR)	Non-commission	Male	17-21	10+2 with Physics and Maths
Senior Secondary Recruit (Sports) SSR (Sports)	Non-commission	Male	17-21	10+2 (any discipline)
Matric Recruit (MR) Entry	Non-commission	Male	17-21	10th
Matric Recruit (Sports) – MR Sports	Non-commission	Male	17-21	10th
Musicians	Non-commission	Male	17-21	10th
Non-matric Recruit (NMR) Entry	Non-commission	Male	17-21	6th
Non-matric Recruit (Sports) – NMR (Sports)	Non-commission	Male	17-21	6th

AA/SSR/MR/NMR

Written Examination

Written examination will be conducted at the designated centre on the promulgated date and time. The objective type 60 minutes duration question paper will be bilingual (Hindi and English) and comprises of four sections, i.e., English, Science, Mathematics and General Knowledge.

The Non-metric entry question paper will be of 40 minutes duration and it comprises of two sections i.e., Mathematics and General Knowledge.

Physical Fitness Test (PFT)

Candidates who qualify the written test are permitted to undergo PFT which consists of 1.6 Km run to be completed in Seven minutes, 25 squad ups (*Utah Baithak*) and 10 Push-ups. Candidates undergoing PFT will do so at their own risk. Those who qualify PFT are taken for medical examination.

Medical Test

Entry level medical standards are different entries. Medical examination will be conducted by authorised military doctors as per medical standard prescribed in current regulations applicable to sailors on entry. Candidates declared 'temporary unfit' during medical examination can avail specialist review from the specified military hospital within a maximum period of 21 days. Those who are declared 'permanent unfit' can appeal for specialist opinion in a military hospital on payment of requisite amount by Military Receivable Order (MRO) in the government treasury within 21 days. Medical fitness certificate from other than that of the specialist opinion in the designated military hospital will NOT be considered. All the selected candidates, prior to enrollment, have to undergo a Final Enrollment Medical examination at INS Chilka (Orissa).

Musicians

The Director of Music (DOM) at INS Kunjali will be responsible for conduct of recruitment for Musician sailors as per schedule promulgated by IHQ MOD (Navy). All applications for MR (Musician) entry has to be addressed to the Commanding Officer, (for Director of Music), INS Kunjali, Colaba, Mumbai – 400 005.

Service Benefits

Allowances

- Accommodation and house rent allowances
- Leave : 60 days annual leave and 30 days casual leave
- Insurance cover worth ₹ 20,00,000 given by IHQ MOD (Navy)
- Gratuity and accumulated leave encashment
- Pension after completion of requisite service
- Children education fee
- Leave travel concession

- Free railway warrant during annual leave
- Free medical treatment
- Kit maintenance allowance
- Free ration

Pay Scale

All the sailors have been divided into two groups namely, 'X' and 'Y'. Artificer Apprentices fall under 'X' group and rest of the sailors in group 'Y'.

All recruits shall receive a stipend during their training at the rate of ₹ 5700 per month. On successful completion of training Grade Pay, Military Service Pay, Group 'X' pay (if applicable), Dearness Allowance and allowances of the trade to which they stand allotted less the stipend already paid. The rate of stipend will be increased by 50 per cent every time the DA payable on revised pay band goes up by 50 per cent.

Pay scales of sailors are as follows:

Rank (₹)	*Pay Band (₹)*	*Pay in Pay Band (₹)*	*Grade Pay*	*MSP (₹)*	*'X' Group Pay*
('X' Group (Artificer Apprentices Sailors)					
Apprentice	PB-1	5,200-20,200	2,000	2,000	1,400
Artificer V	PB-1	5,200-20,200	2,400	2,000	1,400
Artificer IV	PB-1	5,200-20,200	2,800	2,000	1,400
Art III-I	PB-2	9,300-34,800	3,400	2,000	1,400
Chief/Art	PB-2	9,300-34,800	4,200	2,000	1,400
MCPO II	PB-2	9,300-34,800	4,600	2,000	1,400
MCPO I	PB-2	9,300-34,800	4,800	2,000	1,400
'Y' Group (SSR/MR/NMR)					
Seaman II	PB-1	5,200-20,200	2,000	2,000	1,400
Seaman I	PB-1	5,200-20,200	2,400	2,000	1,400
Leading Seaman	PB-1	5,200-20,200	2,800	2,000	1,400
Petty Officer	PB-1	5,200-20,200	2,800	2,000	1,400
Chief Petty Officer	PB-2	9,300-34,200	4,200	2,000	1,400
MCPO II	PB-2	9,300-34,800	4,600	2,000	1,400
MCPO I	PB-2	9,300-34,800	4,800	2,000	1,400
Honourary Commissioned Officer					
Hon Sub-Lieutenant	PB-3	15,600-39,100	5,400	6,000	
Hon Lieutenant	PB-3	15,600-39,100	6,100	6,000	

Medical Officers

The Armed Forces Medical Services is amongst one of the best options available to a medical graduate in our country. As an officer in the Army Medical Corps, a candidate is liable to be employed in the Indian Army, Navy or Air Force in any part of the country or world. The armed forces offer a prestigious and professionally satisfying career for doctors as commissioned officers with high status associated with Group-A gazetted posts of Central Government.

There are ample avenues to specialise in basic specialties and super specialties fields like Physiotherapy, Advance Nursing, Radiography, Lab Assistant, Dental Operation Room Assistant and Blood Transfusion etc. Most of the post-graduate courses are conducted at Armed Forces Medical College (AFMC), Pune and various other teaching hospitals of the armed forces. However, the service also offers opportunities to avail study leave at government expense for the super-specialty courses at reputed civil institutions in India and abroad.

Selection Procedure

Recruitment to the medical posts is through Permanent Commission (PC) and Short Service Commission (SSC). 50 per cent graduates passing out from the Armed Forces Medical College, Pune are taken directly into permanent commission and the rest are offered short service commission. Doctors from civil medical colleges are offered only SSC entry. SSC officers are required to serve for a minimum period of five years. The SSC may be extended by another two terms of five years and then four years up to a maximum of 14 years. AFMC graduates offered SSC are required to serve for a minimum period of seven years extendable by another seven years.

Short Service Commission

Notification for the post of doctors (male and female) in Indian Navy through SCC is published in leading newspapers twice a year. Eligible candidates are called for interview at New Delhi to assess their merit and suitability for grant of Short Service Commission in the Army Medical Corps and subsequent secondment to the Navy. Based on the results of the interview, candidates who have been short listed are subjected to medical examination at designated Armed Forces hospitals in New Delhi. Medically fit candidates are granted commission subject to verification procedures as deemed necessary and required for commissioning.

Permanent Commission

SSC officers are allowed three chances to appear in departmental interviews for grant of permanent commission at any time after completion of two years SSC service, i.e., two chances in first tenure of five years and one chance in second tenure of five years but before completion of nine years and six months of service. Also, there should be no break in service and they should fulfill the conditions of eligibility laid down. The age limits for granting PC for different professional educational qualification are :

- MBBS (Max. 31 years)
- Post-graduate Diploma (Max. 31 years)
- Post-graduate Diploma MD/MS (Max. 35 years)

The ranks granted on first appointment in the AMC are:

- **Captain/Surgeon Lieutenant/Flight Lieutenant:** Applicable to doctors commissioned from civil who have acquired their Permanent Medical Registration Certificate.
- **Lieutenant/Surgeon Sub-Lieutenant/Flying Officer:** Applicable to Medical cadets passing out from AFMC Pune, till completion of their internship in Service hospitals.

Promotion

Promotion till the rank of Lieutenant Colonel/Surgeon Commander/ Wing Commander is by time subject to satisfactory service and fitness for higher rank. Further, promotion to higher ranks is by selection-based on vacancies. If an officer does not get promoted to the rank of Colonel/ Surgeon Captain/Group Captain by selection grade, then he/she is granted time scale promotion to the rank of Colonel/Surgeon Captain/ Group Captain (Time Scale) on completion of 24 years of reckonable commissioned service.

Few Training Centres

- **INS Dronacharya (Gunnery School)**

  Fort Kochi, Kochi 682001, Kerala

  Phone: 0484-228341-45

  Fax: 0484-226108

- **INS Garuda (Aviation Establishment)**

  INS Venduruthy, Naval Base, Kochi-682004, Kerala

  Phone: 0484-22662394, 2667361 (SO)

  Fax: 0484-2662394

The following schools are located in this establishment:

-Observer School

- School for Naval Airman (SFNA)

- Naval Institute of Aeronautical Technology (NIAT)

- School for Naval Oceanography and Meteorology (SNOM)

- **INS Agrani (Leadership Training Establishment)**

  Red Fields, Coimbatore-641018

  Phone: 0422-2315531/35/36/37/38

  Fax: 0422-2315538

- **INS Hamla (Logistics Training Establishment)**

  Marve, Malad (West), Mumbai-400064

  Phone: 022-28824864

- **INM (Institute of Naval Medicine)**

  Institute of Naval Medicine

  C/o INHS Asvini, Colaba, Mumbai-400005

  Phone: 022-8822570

- **INS Kunjali (Musician Training School)**

  Near US Club, Colaba, Mumbai-400005

  Phone: 022-2215219

- **Naval Academy Ezhimala (NAVAC)**

  Naval Academy Ezhimala (NAVAC), located in Kannur (Cannanore) of Kerala,

  NAVAC will conduct the basic training for all officers being inducted into the...

  Base depot ship for administrative and logistic support for NAVAC

Contact

- **The Commandant (for Training Captain)**

  Indian Naval Academy

  Naval Academy PO, Ezhimala, Kannur

  Kerala-670310

  Phone – Commander Training Team: 04985-223700

Adjutant: 04985-224164

Flotilla Duty Officer: 04985-222786

Fax: 04985-224164/65

- **INS Chilka**

  INS Chilka is a premier basic training establishment for sailor of the Indian Navy demanding and comprehensive training regimen as can be expected in a Boat. P.O. Chilka, Distt: Khurda, Orissa-752 037

  Phone: 06756-220466

  Fax: 06756-227087

- **INS Venduruthy (Seamen Training School)**

  Naval Base, Kochi-682004

  Phone: 0484-2662750

  Fax: 0484-2668868

- **INSMandovi (Provost)**

  Verem, Goa-403109

  Phone: 0832-2402010/11

  Fax: 022-22152194, 22150550

- **INS Shivaji (Engineering Training Establishment)**

  Lonavla-410402, District-Pune,

  Maharashtra

  Phone: 02114-284861-67

  Fax: 02114-284701

- **Shipwright School**

  Poth Nirmatha Avenue, Vishakhapatnam

  Phone: 0891-2558386

  Fax: 0891-2558389

Useful Contacts

- **For Officer Entry**

  JDMPR (OI & R)

  Room No. 205, C-Wing, Sena Bhavan, New Delhi-110011

  Phone: 011-23011282/23010097

  Fax: 011-23011282

- **For Sailor Entry**

  JDMPR (NRO)

  Room No. 232, C-Wing, Sena Bhavan, New Delhi-110011

  Phone: 011-23793067

  Fax: 011-23010759

- **For Medical Entry**
  Director AFMS (P)
  Office of DGAFMS, PO-DHQ, M-Block, New Delhi-110001
  Phone: 011-23093253
  Fax: 011-23093093
- **Service Selection Board (SSB)**
  12 SSB, Bangalore
  The President
  12 Services Selection Board, Selection Centre South
  Cubban Road, Bangalore-560042
  Phone: 080-25327671
  Fax: 080-25594954
- **33 SSB, Bhopal**
  The President
  33 Services Selection Board, Selection Centre Central
  Sultania Infantry Line, Bhopal-462018
  Phone: 0755-2702223
  Fax: 0755-2735980

- **NSB, Agrani**
  The President
  Naval Selection Board, INS Agrani,
  Red Fields, Coimbatore-6410
  Toll free-1800-425-4599
  Fax: 0422-2325957

7.4 The Indian Coast Guard (ICG)

What is Indian Coast Guard (ICG)?

Indian Coast Guard (ICG) alias *Bharatiya Thatrakshak* is a branch of the Indian Armed Forces operating under the Department of Defence of the Union Ministry of Defense. It was established on 19th August, 1978 and it is the fourth service created to guard India's vast coastline and for enforcing the maritime laws of the country. The coast guards are responsible for the security of the Indian territorial waters and the Indian Exclusive Economic Zone to prevent poaching, smuggling and other illegal activities. Besides conducting search and rescue operations, they also protect and preserve the marine environment of the country.

Indian Coast Guards are not part of the Indian paramilitary forces. Coast guards works in close co-operation with the Indian Navy,

Fisheries Department, Revenue Department and the central and state police forces.

Divisions of Indian Coast Guard (ICG)

The Indian Coast Guard force is led by a Director General and a Deputy Director General. The central headquarter of ICG is located at New Delhi. The Operations of Indian Coast Guard are split into four regions:

- **Western Region** (*with the Regional Headquarter at Mumbai*) **:** The entire coast line from Daman to Kanyakumari including the Union Territory to Lakshadweep comes under the operational and administrative control of the Commander, Coast Guard Region (West). There are five coast guard district headquarters (Porbandar, Mumbai, Mangalore, Kochi and Goa), seven coast guard stations, one air station and two air enclaves on the western seaboard of India.
- **Eastern Region** (*with the Regional Headquarter at Chennai*)**:** The entire coastline from Kanyakumari to Kolkata comes under the jurisdiction of the Commander, Coast Guard Region (East). There are four coast guard district headquarters (Chennai, Vizag, Paradip, Haldia and Kolkata), four coast guard stations, one air station and one air enclave on the eastern seaboard of India.
- **Andaman and Nicobar Region** (*with the Regional Headquarter at Port Blair*) : Port Blair District HQs are located at Diglipur and Campbell Bay. The region has a force level of one OVP, two FPVs, two FPVs (Jet), one IPV, two IB, two Hovercrafts, eight IB, two Dornier aircraft and two ALH helicopters in this region.

Educational Qualifications and Physical Standards

One can enroll in Indian Coast Guard as Officers or *Yantriks* (technicians) or *Naviks* (sailors). The educational qualifications and physical standards for these posts are given below:

Officers

Name of Post	Branch	Educational Qualification	Age as on 1st July of The year of Recruitment	Physical Standard
Assistant Commandant (GD) Male/Female	General Duty	Bachelor's degree with 60% marks in aggregate of a university recognized by Central/State Govt. / UGC and minimum 60% in class XII Std of 10+2+3 Scheme with Mathematics & Physics	21-25 yrs of age (5 yrs relaxation for SC/ST and 3 yrs for OBC)	Height 157 cms (M) & 152 cms (F) proportionate to Height, Eyesight 6/6 & 6/9 without glasses

Assistant Commandant (GD)-SSA (Only Female)	General Duty (Short Service) appointment for a period of 8 yrs which may be extended to 10 yrs and further Extendable Up to 14 yrs	Bachelor's degree with 60% marks in aggregate of a university recognized by Central/State Govt. /UGC and minimum 60% in class XII Std. of 10+2+3 scheme with Mathematics & Physics.	21-25 yrs of age (5 yrs relaxation for SC/ST and 3 yrs for OBC)	Height 152 cms (F) proportionate to Height, Eyesight 6/6 & 6/9 without glasses
Assistant Commandant (GD-P/N) (Male/Female)	General Duty (Pilot Navigator)	B.Sc. with Physics and Mathematics and 55% marks in aggregate and minimum 60% in class XII Std. of 10+2+3	19-27 yrs of age (5 yrs relaxation for SC/ST and 3 yrs for OBC)	Height 152.5 cms Max. 197cm Leg length Min. 99cms Weight proportionate to Height, Eyesight 6/6 & 6/9 without Glasses
Assistant Commandant (GD-P-CPL) SSA (Male/Female)	General Duty Branch (Pilot-License-) Short service appointment for a period of 8 yrs which may be extended to 10 yrs and further extendable up to 14 yrs)	12th class passed or equivalent with 60% marks in 10+2+3 or equivalent and should possess current Commercial Pilot License on the date of selection	19-27 yrs of age (5 yrs relaxation for SC/ST and 3 yrs for OBC)	Height Min 162.5 cms Max 197 cm, Leg Length Min. 99 cms, weight proportionate to Height, Eyesight 6/6 without glasses
Assistant Commandant (Tech) (Only Male	Technical Branch	Degree with 60% marks in aggregate in Naval Architecture/Mechanical/ Marine/Electrical/ Electronics & Telecommunications/ Design/Production Aeronautical/Metallurgy/ Aerospace/Control Engineering or equivalent and minimum 60% in class XII Std. of 10+2+3 scheme of Education. OR Should have passed section A & B of institution of Engineers (India) Examination in any of the Discipline listed above With 55% marks	21-25 yrs of age (5 yrs relaxation for SC/ST and 3 yrs for OBC)	Height 157 cm Weight proportionate to Height, Eyesight 6/12 & 6/36
Deputy Commandant (Law) (Male/Female)	Law Branch	(i) a degree in Law with 8 yrs experiences in legal matters. (ii) Should be qualified for enrolment as an advocate in a High Court. Desirable: a)A post graduate degree in Law b) Knowledge/ Experience, assignment Connected with International Law/Maritime Law	below 45 yrs (5 yrs relaxation for SC/ST and 3 yrs for OBC)	Height 157 cms (M)/152 cms (F), Weight proportionate to Height, Eyesight 6/6 & 6/12 (with glass) 6/60 (without glass)

Yantriks and Naviks

Yantriks and *Naviks* are the normal posts of Indian Coast Guard. Only male can apply for these posts.

Name of the Post	Education Qualification	Age as on 1st of the month of scheduled basic training	Physical Standard
Yantriks	Matriculate and Diploma in Mechanical/Electrical/ Electronics/Aeronautical Engineering	18-22 yrs (5 yrs relaxation for SC/ST and 3 yrs for OBC	Height 157cms, Weight proportionate to Height, Eyesight 6/12 and 6/24
Naviks (General Duty)	12th class in 10+2+3 scheme with Maths & Physics	18-22 yrs (5 yrs relaxation for SC/ST and 3 yrs for OBC	Height 157 cms Weight Proportionate to Height, Eyesight 6/6 and 6/9 withoutglasses
Naviks (Domestic Branch)	10th Standard pass	18-22 yrs (5 yrs relaxation for SC/STand 3yrs for OBC)	Height 157 cms Weight Proportionate to Height, Eyesight 6/18 and 6/36 without glasses

Job Prospects and Career Options

The Coast Guard has a dedicated and professional team of officers who operate ships and aircrafts for safeguarding the country's maritime interests. Indian Coast Guard offers various job opportunities to the young and educated youth of the country. One can enroll in Indian coast guard as Officers or *Yantriks* (technicians) or *Naviks* (sailors).

Officers are appointed in the Coast Guard in one of the three branches as General Duty Officer/General Duty (Pilot/Navigation) or Pilot officer, Technical officer and Law officers.

- **General Duty Officer Branch:** General Duty Officers Branch is the operational branch of the Indian Coast Guard. Command of ships at sea can only be exercised by officer of the general duty branch. The general duty branch officer operates weapons, sensors and performs the command function which demands a wide sphere of knowledge of equipment. The safety of the ship and men, manoeuvering of the ship in war and in peace time operations are the major responsibilities of the general duty officer.
- **Pilot/Navigator Officer Branch:** Indian Coast Guard operates fixed wing aircraft from shore air stations for surveillance of the Exclusive Economic Zone. In addition, helicopters are embarked on Coast Guard Offshore Patrol Vessels to provide local surveillance and perform search and rescue mission at sea. Operating these aircrafts at sea is challenging task and will bring

your special skills to the fore. As an officer of the pilot branch, one will have the opportunity to serve both in the shore air stations along the coasts of India as well as embark ships.

- **Technical Officer Branch:** Modern ships and aircrafts are abounding with advance technology and machinery. The technical branch officer is responsible to keep all these equipment serviceable. They will get the opportunities to work in shore jobs in coast guard repair organisations. Technical officers are usually required to have an Engineering background.
- **Law Officer Branch:** Law officers act as legal advisers to their respective commanders. They also prosecute and defend cases filed by or against the Indian Coast Guard. Presently, there is one law officer posted in each of the four regions. The law officers in Indian Coast Guard have strength of 10 at present including two lady officers. The legal branch in the Indian Coast Guard is headed by a Deputy Inspector General (DIG), who is designated as the Chief Law Officer (CLO).
- **Women in Coast Guard:** Women are appointed in Coast Guard only as officers in general duty, general duty (pilot/navigator) and general duty (CPL holders, short service entry) branches. Women officers are posted in non-sea going appointments. Unlike the other armed forces, women officers in coast guard have the option to serve till superannuation, except for CPL holders and general duty branch – short service appointment. The selection process for women is similar to that of male candidates.
- **Yantriks :** The *Yantriks* are the backbone of coast guard and are responsible for operating and maintaining the machinery and equipment fitted on Indian Coast Guard ships and aircrafts. Diploma holders in Mechanical, Electrical, Electronic and Aeronautical branches of engineering can join in coast guard as *yantriks*.
- **Naviks:** Young dynamic male candidates with 10+2 qualification can join in *Naviks* (general duty) branch and can specialise in various streams namely, (a) seaman (b) communication (c) mechanical engineer (d) electrical (e) aviation. Candidates with 10th qualification can join in domestic branch of *Naviks* as cooks and stewards.

Recruitment and Selection Procedure

Officers

The recruitment of Assistant Commandants is conducted twice a year in the month of January/February and August/September. The advertisement for the recruitment will be given in all leading national newspapers in both Hindi as well as in English. The shortlisted candidates are called for Preliminary Selection Board (PSB) as per their choice of centers from Mumbai, Chennai, Kolkata, Delhi, Kochi, Vizag and Port Blair. The PSB consists of Mental Ability Test, Group Discussion and Picture Perception and Discussion Test (PPDT). The candidates who qualify PSB are called for Final Selection Board (FSB) at Mumbai/Chennai/Delhi. The candidates, subject to their medical fitness are selected as per merit list.

Training Pattern

The selected candidates have to undergo:

- 20 weeks basic training in the Naval Academy at INS Mandovi, Goa
- 36 weeks afloat training onboard Coast Guard Ships
- 48 weeks technical courses at various Naval Schools
- 24 weeks watch-keeping onboard Coast Guard Ships

Yantriks and Naviks

The recruitment for the normal posts *(Yantriks* and *Naviks)* in Indian Coast Guard is conducted bi-annually in the month of April and October. The advertisement for the recruitment will be given in *Employment News* all over India, both in Hindi as well as in English in the month of January and November. Interested candidates who fulfill the eligibility criteria must forward their application in prescribed format given in the advertisement with one additional recent coloured passport size photograph alongwith attested Xerox copies of all necessary certificates to the respective address of zonal recruitment centre by ordinary post only.

The recruitment of *Yantrik* will be conducted in ten centers all over India viz., New Delhi, Mumbai, Chennai, Kolkata, Vizag, Kochi, Paradip, Tuticorin, Gandhinagar and Nagpur. The shortlisted candidates are called for selection tests at centre of their choice. These candidates are subjected to a written test and the qualifying candidates have to undergo interview and medical examination. If qualified they are selected as per merit list.

The recruitment of *Naviks* will be conducted in six zones viz., Western Zone, Eastern Zone, North Eastern Zone, A&N Zone, North West Zone and North Zone. Selection of candidates is based on the order of merit depending on their performance in Written Test, Physical Fitness Test (PFT) and Fitness in the Medical Examinations. The shortlisted candidates are called for selection tests (written test) at convenient center at various zones. These candidates are subjected to mental ability test (verbal and non-verbal), (only non-verbal in case of DB), entrance test and interview. During the written test and interview the candidates have the option of answering in Hindi/English. The qualified candidates are to undergo medical examination and those who clear the medical examination are selected as per merit list.

Written Test: The objective type question paper will be bilingual (Hindi and English) and consists of English, Science, Mathematics and General Knowledge. Duration of the Test (Total 1½ hours): Mental Ability Test – 30 minutes, Written Test – one hour (Candidates are required to pass in both the tests).

Physical Fitness Test (PFT): All those who pass the written test will be subjected to the PFT. PFT will consist of 1.6 km run to be completed in six minutes 30 seconds; 20 squad ups (*Uthak Baithak*); 10 pushups. Candidates undergoing PFT will do so at their own risk.

Interview: Candidates clearing the above tests will appear for interview.

Training Pattern: The selected candidates have to undergo :

- 20 weeks basic training with Navy at INS Chilka, Orissa
- eight weeks basic training onboard Coast Guard Ships
- 30 weeks professional training at various Naval Schools.

Service Benefits: Given below is the detailed pay scale and service benefits of Officers, *Yantriks* and *Naviks*.

Officers

Director General	₹ 37,400 – 67,000 with Grade pay ₹ 12,000
Inspector General	₹ 37,400 – 67,000 with Grade pay ₹ 10,000
Deputy Inspector General	₹ 37,400 – 67,000 with Grade pay ₹ 8,900
Commandant	₹ 37,400 – 67,000 with Grade pay ₹ 8,700
Commandant (Junior Grade)	₹ 15,600 – 39,100 with Grade pay ₹ 7,600
Deputy Commandant	₹ 15,600 – 39,100 with Grade pay ₹ 6,600
Assistant Commandant	₹ 15,600 – 39,100 with Grade pay ₹ 5,400

They pay would include Dearness allowance, Kit Maintenance allowance and Transport allowance. In addition, other allowances will be admissible based on nature of duty/place of posting such as flying allowance, sea duty allowance and Island special duty allowance.

Yantriks

Pradhan Sahayak Engineer	₹ 9,300 – 34,800 with Grade pay ₹ 4,800
Uttam Sahayak Engineer	₹ 9,300 – 34,800 with Grade pay ₹ 4,600
Sahayak Engineer	₹ 9,300 – 34,800 with Grade pay ₹ 4,200
Pradhan Yantrik	₹ 9,300 – 34,800 with Grade pay ₹ 4,200
Uttam Yantrik	₹ 5,200 – 20,200 with Grade pay ₹ 2,800
Yantrik	₹ 5,200 – 20,200 with Grade pay ₹ 2,400

Naviks

Naviks (General Duty)

Pradhan Andhikari	₹ 9,300 – 34,800 with Grade Pay ₹ 4,800
Uttam Andhikari	₹ 9,300 – 34,800 with Grade Pay ₹ 4,600
Andhikari	₹ 9,300 – 34,800 with Grade Pay ₹ 4,200
Pradhan Navik	₹ 5,200 – 20,200 with Grade pay ₹ 2,800
Uttam Navik	₹ 5,200 – 20,200 with Grade pay ₹ 2,400
Navik	₹ 5,200 – 20,200 with Grade pay ₹ 2,000

Naviks (Domestic Branch)

Pradhan Andhikari	₹ 9,300 – 34,800 with Grade Pay ₹ 4,600
Uttam Andhikari	₹ 9,300 – 34,800 with Grade Pay ₹ 4,200
Andhikari	₹ 9,300 – 34,800 with Grade Pay ₹ 4,200
Pradhan Navik	₹ 5,200 – 20,200 with Grade pay ₹ 2,400
Uttam Navik	₹ 5,200 – 20,200 with Grade pay ₹ 2,000
Navik	₹ 5,200 – 20,200 with Grade pay ₹ 1,900

Other Benefits

- Entitled rations, free clothing, free medical treatment for self and family including dependent parents.
- Government accommodation for self and family on nominal license fee.
- 45 days Earned leave and 8 days Casual leave every year with leave travel concession for self, family and dependent parents as per government rules.

- Contributory Pension Scheme, Provident Fund and Gratuity on retirement.
- Canteen and various loan facilities.
- Sports and adventure activities such as river rafting, mountaineering, hot air ballooning, hang gliding and wind surfing etc.
- Insurance cover of ₹ 40 lakh at a premium of ₹ 4,000 per month as Group insurance (for Officers).
- Insurance cover of ₹ 20 lakh at a premium of ₹ 2,000 per month as group insurance (for *Yantriks* and *Naviks*).

Training Centres

- **INS Chilka**

  P.O. Chilka, Distt.-Khurda,

  Orissa – 752 037

  Phone: 06756 220466

  Fax: 06756-227087

- **INS Mandovi**

  Verem, Goa-403109

  Phone: 0832 – 2402010/11, 2402761/62

  Fax: 0832-2402763

Useful Contacts

- **Chief Public Information Officer/Principal Director (HRD)**

  Coast Guard Headquarters, National Stadium Complex,

  New Delhi-110001

  Phone: 011-23386766 (Chief Public Information Officer)/ 23387412 (Principal Director)

- **Coast Guard West Region**

  Worli Sea Face PO, Worli Colony, Mmbai-400030

  Phone: 022-24301028

- **Coast Guard East Region**

  Coovum River Mouth, Near Napier Bridge, Chennai-600009

  Phone: 044-24301028

- **Coast Guard North West Region**

  Coast Guard Region (NW)

Post Box No. 09, Sector-11, Gandhinagar-382010

Phone: 079-23243136

- **Coast Guard Andaman and Nicobar Region**

  Post Box-716, Haddon

  Port Blair-744102

  Phone: 03192 235613

7.5 The Paramilitary Forces (PMF)

The Paramilitary Forces

The Paramilitary Forces are the protective services that have been constituted to maintain internal security and support Defence services of the country. They are responsible for guarding our national boundaries from external aggression. They are the agencies of the Ministry of Defence or the Ministry of Home Affairs which act as armed forces auxiliaries.

Organisations under the Paramilitary Forces

The organisations that serve as the Paramilitary Forces of India are:

- Border Security Force (BSF)
- Central Reserve Police Force (CRPF)
- Indo-Tibetan Border Police Force (ITBPF)
- Central Industrial Security Force (CISF)
- National Security Guard (NSG)
- Railway Protection Force (RPF)
- Special Frontier Force (SFF)
- Assam Rifles
- Vigilance Organisations
- Fire Services
- State Police Forces and
- Coast Guards

Each of these units plays a well-defined role besides coming to the nation's rescue in times of natural calamities and emergencies. All the branches of PMF excluding the Indian Coast Guard are under the Ministry of Home Affairs. The largest force of the PMF is the Central Reserve Police Force (CRPF) which assists the Indian Police in maintaining law and order. The CRPF, BSF and ITBP together constitute the Central Police Organisation (CPO).

How to Join in the Paramilitary Forces

One can enter any service of the Paramilitary Forces of India (PMF) after completing their Class X, XII or Graduation. Women are also allowed to join the paramilitary forces' services.

Graduates in any stream, who are 20-25 years of age, may apply for recruitment to the posts of sub-inspectors in BSF, CISF, CRPF, ITBP and SSB. Female candidates are eligible for recruitment to CISF and CRPF only. Differently abledcandidates are not eligible to these posts.

7.5.1 Border Security Force (BSF)

A Brief Genesis of BSF

The Border Security Force alias BSF is a paramilitary force. It is the border guarding force of India which was established on 1st December 1965 and entrusted with the responsibility of guarding India's land border during peace time and to prevent transnational crime. It currently stands as the world's largest border guarding force with strength of 240,000 personnel in 186 battalions, including women personnel. 'Duty Unto Death' is the motto of BSF.

The Three Operational Branches

The BSF has three operational branches namely,

- General Branch
- Technical Branch
- Medical Branch

The General Duty Branch covers all the general duties of BSF. The vigilance charge is also dependent on them. The Technical Branch deals with all the technical work required from time to time for the smooth functioning of the force. This branch looks after the maintenance and repair of equipments for telecommunication and construction purposes. The Medical Branch provides all the facilities regarding medical purposes and they undertake all the responsibility for the fitness and well-being of personnel.

The Important Role of the Technical Arms Wing

The troops of BSF are supported by the technical arms wing which is in charge of the construction and maintenance of buildings required by the forces as well as the maintenance of arms and other combat equipments. Personnel of technical arms are engineers qualified in civil or electronic/electrical engineering. The Signals arm of the BSF is a very important constituent of this force. It is the duty of the signal officers to keep the line of communication working and to pass on information to senior officers at all times and seeks the necessary advice on matters relating to internal security.

The Major Tasks of BSF are:

- **Peace time:** They are to promote a sense of security among the people living in the border areas, prevent transformer crimes, unauthorised entry into or exit from the territory of India, prevent smuggling and any other illegal activity. In addition to their duties, BSF has been deployed for counter-insurgency and internal security duties.
- **War time:** They are to hold ground in less threatened sectors, protection of vital installations, assistance in control of refugees, anti-infiltration duties in specified areas.

The BSF men are trained in patrolling the borders be it on camels' back or horses' back, on foot, on speed boats or on helicopters. The work is daunting and requires deep commitment. The BSF has assumed a strategic role in vital activities concerning security and defence. It is a prestigious and a dignified profession and being qualified for BSF, is a big dream for most aspiring Indian candidates.

BSF Rank Structure

The Border Security Force (BSF) has officers of different grades and the rank structure of BSF is as follows:

1. Director General
2. Special Director General
3. Additional Director General
4. Inspector General
5. Deputy Inspector General
6. Commandant
7. Second-in-Command
8. Deputy Commandant
9. Assistant Commandant
10. Subedar Major

11. Inspector
12. Sub-Inspector
13. Assistant Sub-Inspector
14. Head Constable
15. Constable
16. Constable (Tradesmen)

Eligibility and Recruitment

How to Join BSF

The Border Security Force (BSF) has officers of different grades and each hierarchy has different eligibility criteria. The recruitment in Border Security Force (BSF) is being made in the following ranks:

General Duty Cadre

- Constable: The major component of Border Security Force.
- Sub-Inspector: One-third of the posts are filled up by direct recruitment and two-third by promotion.

Communication Set-up

- **Assistant Commandant:** 50 per cent posts of assistant commandant are filled by direct recruitment (including 10 per cent from SSCO) and balance 50 per cent by promotion from inspector to assistant commandant, assistant sub inspector (radio mechanic), head constable (radio operator).

HC (Head Constable)

- *Head Constable (Fitter):* Vacancies are advertised from time to time in all leading newspapers and *Employment News*. Selection to non-gazetted posts (constables, sub inspectors) is made by the Staff Selection Commission of BSF. These recruitments are made on the basis of written test, physical and medical test in the respective categories by the Ministry of Home Affairs, Government of India. Selection to gazetted posts (assistant commandants) are made by the Special Selection Board of Central Police Organisation. Selection to senior position is based on time scale as well as service records. In service training is provided to aspiring personnel.

Constable Recruitment

Constables form the major component of BSF. The working of the force mainly depend on the capability and effectiveness of the personnel.

Candidates having the right aptitude, capability and fitness in all respect are appointed as constables in BSF. For appointment of the post of constable (general duty) in BSF, male candidate must meet the following eligibility condition.

Eligibility : Matriculation or 10th Class Pass.

Age Limit : Age should be 18 to 23 years on 1st August of the year of the examination. Age relaxation is available for SC/ST/OBC/Ex-servicemen and other categories as per the instructions issued by the government.

Physical Standards

Category	*Height*	*Chest*	*Weight*
General	170 cms	80-85 cms	Proportionate to Height and age As per medical Standards
Men belonging to hill area of Garhwal, Kumoan, Himachal Pradesh, Gurkha, Dogras, Marathas, Sikkim, Leh and Ladakh, Kashmir Valley and Northeast.	78-83 cms	80-85 cms	do
For ST of all the state and UTs including Nagas/Mizos.	162.5 cms	76-81 cms	do

Medical Standards

Eye Sight : The minimum distant vision should be 6/6 and 6/9 of both eyes without correction i.e., without wearing of glass.

The candidates must not have knock knee, flat foot, varicose vein or squint in eyes and they should possess high colour vision. They must be in good mental health and bodily health and free from any physical defect likely to interfere with the efficient performance of the duties.

Method of Selection

The selection procedure for the post of constable (GD) completes in seven steps.

- Preliminary screening/physical measurement
- Document checking
- Physical efficiency test (PET): One mile Run, High Jump, Long Jump.
- Written test (Literacy and Intelligence test)
- Interview
- Medical examination

- Merit List

There are extra 10 marks for NCC/sports/cultural/technical qualification.

Final selection of the candidates will be made in order of merit in each category.

Reservation : There will be reservations for SC/ST/OBC, Ex-servicemen and other categories of personnel in accordance with the instructions issued by the Government from time to time. The reserved vacancies will be calculated and recruitment made with reference to the allocations made to the states/UTs under item-III above. Quota for SC/ST for various States/UTs will be fixed having regard to the number of SC/ST population in such states/UTs. The unfilled reserved vacancies may also be filled through special recruitments.

Sub Inspector

One-third of the sub inspector posts are filled up by direct recruitment and two-third by promotion.

Eligibility : Degree of a recognised University or equivalent.

Age Limit : Age should be 20-25 years on 1st August of the year of the examination. Relaxable for SC/ST/OBC in accordance with the instructions issued by the Government from time to time.

Physical Standards

Height	*Chest*	*Weight*
170 cms	80-85 cms	Weight must be proportionate to Height
Relaxable : By five cms for candidates belonging to hill area of Garhwal, Kumoan, Himachal Pradesh, Leh and Ladakh Gurkha, Dogras, Marathas, Sikkim, Kashmir Valley and North-east.	77-82 cms for STs	do

Medical Standards

Eye Sight : The minimum distant vision should be 6/6 and 6/9 of both eyes without correction i.e., without wearing of glass.

The candidates must not have knock knee, flat foot, varicose vein or squint in eyes and they should possess high colour vision. They must be in good mental health and bodily health and free from any physical defect likely to interfere with the efficient performance of the duties.

BSF Sub-inspector Examination

Candidates who are selected in Physical Efficiency Test are eligible for the written test. The written test for BSF sub-inspectors consists of two papers :

- Paper-I – two hours
  General Intelligence and reasoning
  Numerical Ability
  General Awareness
  Professional Test
- Paper-II – two hours
  Language Comprehension like essay writing etc.

Final selection of the candidates will be made in order of merit in each category.

Assistant Commandant

Fifty per cent posts of assistant commandant are filled by direct recruitment (including 10 per cent from SSCO) and balance 50 per cent by promotion from Inspector to AC. The criteria for direct recruitment are as under :

Eligibility

General : Degree from recognised university/institution or equivalent; possession of NCC 'B' or 'C' Certificate or outstanding achievements in sports or athletics will be an added qualification.

Technical : With B.Sc. (Physical, Chemistry and Mathematics) and above educational qualification with the Electronics stream are deputed for appointment in the rank of assistant commandant (technical) form the executive posts, after they undergo Battalion Signal Officers course. These officers later on work in higher posts in communication hierarchy in BSF, apart from performing general duties in various ranks, since communication officers are also part of general cadre of officers.

Age Limit : Age should be 19 – 25 years on 1st August of the year of the examination. Relaxable in the case of SC/ST/OBC candidates in accordance with the instructions/orders of government from time to time.

Physical Standards

	Male	*Female*
Height	165 cms	157 cms
Chest	81-86 cms	N/A
Weight	50 kgs	According to height But not less than 46 kgs

Medical Standards

Eye Sight or without Glasses

With Glass	*Without Glass*
Distant Vision	Distant Vision
6/6 or 6/9	6/12 or 6/9
Near Vision	Near Vision
J-I	J-II

Colour vision : Must possess high colour vision.

The candidates must not have knock knee, flat foot, varicose vein or squint in eyes and they should possess high colour vision. They must be in good mental health and bodily health and free from any physical defect likely to interfere with the efficient performance of the duties.

BSF Assistant Commandant Examination

Candidates who are selected in Physical Efficiency Test are eligible for the written test.

The written test consists of multiple objective type questions in general knowledge, elementary mathematics and analytical aptitude. Final selection of the candidates will be made in order of merit in written test, physical efficiency test and interview as prescribed by the government.

Assistant Sub-Inspector

Eligibility

Matriculation with Three year Diploma in radio and TV technology/ electronics/tele-communications/computer/electrical/ mechanical/ engineering domestic appliance from an institution recognised by state/ Central Government or 10+2 or Intermediate or equivalent with Physics, chemistry and mathematics, having 50 per cent marks in physics, chemistry and mathematics from a recognised Board.

Age Limit : Age should be 18-25 years on 1st August of the year of the examination. Relaxable for SC/ST/OBC in accordance with the instructions issued by the central government from time to time.

Physical Standards

	Height	*Chest-Un Expanded*	*Expanded*	*Weight*
General Category	170 cms	81 cms	86 cms	proportionate to Height
Tribals/Adivasis having 162.5 shall be	162.5 Cms	77 cms	82 cms	do

Relaxable: by five cms for candidates belonging to hill area of Garhwal, Kumoan, Himachal Pradesh, Leh and Ladakh Gurkha, Dogras, Marathas, Sikkim, Kashmir Valley and Northeast.

Medical Standards

Vision : Eye sight near vision better eye J-I, J-II,6/6 and 6/9 high grade. Must pass high-grade color vision test.

The candidates must not have knock knee, flat foot, varicose vein or squint in eyes and they should possess high color vision. They must be in good mental health and bodily health and free from any physical defect likely to interfere with the efficient performance of the duties.

BSF Assistant Sub-Inspector Examination

Candidates who are selected in physical efficiency test are eligible for the written test. The written test for BSF Assistant Sub Inspector Radio Mechanic consists of multiple objective type questions in general knowledge, elementary mathematics and analytical aptitude. Final selection of the candidates will be made in order of merit in written test, Physical efficiency test and interview as prescribed by the government.

BSF Pay Scales and Promotions

The pay scales vary from ₹ 6,000 for constables to ₹ 80,000 for the Director General. Each rank has its own range of pay. For instance the pay band for a head constable is from ₹ 5,200 – 20,200 and for a Subedar Major it is from ₹ 9,300 – 34,800.

Promotion Avenues (Gazetted Officer)

- **Inspector to Assistant Commandant:** Inspector with five years regular service in the grade, having medical category SHAPE (S-Psychological, H-Hearing, A-Appendages, P-Physical Capacity, E-Eye Sight)-I with educational qualification as Matriculation and having undergone Basic Trg, PL Weapon course and Coy Comdr. Course are considered for promotion. Two years service in a service coy for all Inspector/Sub (GD) or two years service in a duty Bn for Sub (Comn) is pre-requisite.
- **Assistant Commandant to Deputy Commandant:** Assistant Commandant of BSF with six years regular service in the grade, medical category SHAPE-I and having qualified carrier courses like (i) Commando and Weapon training (ii) YOC by AC (DE), Re-orientation course by promoters and having two years command experience as Coy Comdr in a service coy is considered for promotion.

- **Deputy Commandant to Second in-Command :** Deputy Commandant of BSF with five years regular service in the grade, possessing two years service as deputy commandant in a duty Bn and having medical category SHAPE-I are considered for promotion to 2IC. Must have qualified one of the following courses. BSW/MMG/MOR/FE and qualified CC course.
- **2nd-in-Command to Commandant :** Second-in-Command with fouryears, regular service as 2IC with two years service as 2IC in Duty Bn and medical category SHAPE-I is considered for promotion to the rank of commandant. Should have qualified senior command course.
- **Commandant to Additional DIG :** Commandant of BSF with three years regular service as commandant with total 18 years group A service and possessing two years command as commandant in a duty Bn and having medical category SHAPE-I is considered for promotion to the rank of Addl. DIG. Should also have undergone Higher Command course.
- **Additional DIG to DIG :** Additional DIG with two years regular service in the grade with 20 years group A service and having medical category SHAPE-I is considered for promotion to the rank of DIG. Should have undergone courses/Trg as prescribed by DG BSF from time to time.
- **DIG to IG :** DIG of BSF with four years' service as DIG and having 24 years group-A service with medical category SHAPE-I is considered for promotion to the rank of IG. Should have undergone courses/Trg as prescribed by DG BSF from time to time.

Promotion Avenues (Non-Gazetted Officer)

The rank structure of non-gazetted cadre of BSF is as:

- Constable
- Head Constable
- Sub Inspector
- Subedar

The promotion of the members of the force shall be based on merit and suitability in all respects, with due regards to seniority and service in the medical category. Every member of the force shall, before any promotion be required to pass pre-promotion course. These promotion examinations which are of a qualifying nature permit a constable to be promoted to the next higher rank of head constable upon being first brought on list-A. Similarly, promotion from the rank of head constable to sub inspector would require such a person to be first brought on the promotion qualifying list-B. In the case of promotion from the rank of sub inspector to subedar, the same is dependent on a sub inspector qualifying C.

The candidate appearing in list A, B and C test (i.e., DPC tests) must fulfill the following eligibility conditions :

Promotion Test	*Minimum Service Require*	*Minimum Educational Standard*
Constable to Head Constable (List-A)	Eight years as Constable of which five years service coy of duty Bn with Medical Cat Shape-I	Matric/10th Class pass or equivalent, Basic Trg and MR-II SLC/JSLC/GLC or pre-promotion Course prescribed for technical posts
Head Constable to Sub-Inspector (List-B)	Five years service as HC together with 18 years of service with Med Cat Shape-I And two years service in Service Coy	Matric/10th Class pass or equivalent, Basic course, MR-I Pre-promotion Course Prescribed for the posts
Sub Inspector to Subedar (List B)	Three years service as Sub Inspector, Med Cat Shape-I and two years command of an Platoon in a Service Coy	Matric/10th Class pass or equivalent, Basic Trg. prescribed at entry level, MR-I, JLC PW or W&T Course PC (Tac)

Training Institutes

The main training institutions are :

- **BSF Academy**

  PO. Tekanpur, Dist Gwalior (MP)

  India-475005

  Website: www.acy.bsf.gov.in

- **BSF Training Centre and School**

  (School of Excellence for Counter Insurgency and Commando Type Specialised Training)

  PO. Meru Camp, Distt. Hazaribag (Jharkhand)

  Website: www.tcs.bsf.gov.in

- **Central School of Weapons and Tactics (CSWT), Indore**

  Bijasan Road, Near Aerodrome, Indore (MP)

  Website: www.csw.bsf.gov.in

Training Schools for Special Training

- **Central School of Motor Transport (CSMT)**

  BSF Academy, Tekanpur

  Gwalior, MP

- **The National Training Centre for Dogs (NTCD)**

  Border Security Force Academy

  Post- Tekanpur

  Distt. Gwalior, MP

- **BSF Signal Training School-I, Tigri Camp, New Delhi**
- **BSF Signal Training School-II, Yelahanka, Bangalore**
- **BSF 'G' Training School, New Delhi**

Subsidiary Training Centres (STCs)

STCs covering border states

- STC BSF Hamhama (Kashmir)
- STC BSF Udhampur (Jammu)
- STC BSF Kharka (Punjab)
- STC BSF Jodhpur (Rajasthan)
- STC BSF Baikunthpur, Siliguri (Bengal)
- STC BSF Churachandpur, Manipur (Assam, Manipur, Meghalaya and Nagaland)

STCs/BTCs covering inter land

- STC BSF Tekanpur (Gwalior)
- STC BSF Yelahanka (Bangalore)
- STC BSF Hazaribagh (Jharkhand)
- STC BSF Indore (MP)

7.5.2 Central Reserve Police Force (CRPF)

A Brief Genesis of CRPF

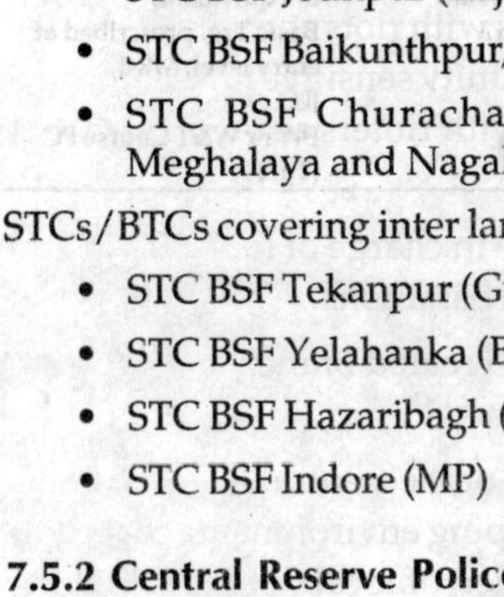

The Central Reserve Police Force popularly known as CRPF is one of the oldest, largest and most experienced armed police forces of the country. It is a paramilitary force that came into existence as the then Crown Representative's Police on 27th July, 1939. It became the Central Reserve Police Force on enactment of the CRPF Act on 28th December, 1949, after Independence. The primary responsibility of the Force is to help states in management of internal security and riot control. Rapid Action Force (RAP) is a specialised wing of CRPF, which was especially raised for countering terrorism and insurgency in 1992. The force has the distinction of having two exclusive *'Mahila'*, i.e., women battalions.

The Organisational Units of CRPF

- **119 Executive Battalions:** These battalions form the bulk of the Central Reserve Police Force. Its basic role is that of a striking reserve force to be placed at the disposal of states and union territories for operations of short duration and return to the barracks once the task is accomplished.
- **Two Mahila Battalions:** It's one of its kinds in the Indian paramilitary as they consist solely of women. Their role is similar to that of the executive battalions with special emphasis on law and order problems in which women may be involved in large numbers.
- **Seven Rapid Action Force Battalions:** This elite branch of the Central Reserve Police Force deals with riots and related unrest. They are usually placed in community sensitive areas and have been very successful in dealing with rioters as well as gaining confidence of the minorities.
- **Five Signals Battalions:** They are in charge of maintaining the lines of communications between battalions.
- **Special Duty Group:** This newly-created branch specialises in countering terrorism and insurgency.
- **Green Force:** A specialised outfit of the Central Reserve Police Force. This is responsible for stopping environmental degradation and sustaining the regeneration of local flora and fauna.

The headquarters of the Central Reserve Police Force is located at Block No. 1, CGO Complex, Lodhi Road, New Delhi. It is headed by Director General, who is assisted by three Addl. Directors General, five Inspectors General of Police, a Financial Advisor and Director (Medical).

The Organisational Structure

The different branches in the force head quarters are:

- **Administration:** The administration directorate is functioning under the overall supervision of IG (Adm). He is assisted by DIG

(Adm), DIG (Welfare), DIG (Works), Asstt. Director (Adm/Accts) and Asstt. Director (Legal) and PRO.

- **Personnel :** The personnel directorate is functioning under the overall supervision of IG (Pers). He is assisted by DIG (Pers), DIG (CR and Vig), DIG (Org), DIG (Estt) and DIG (Rectt).
- **Training :** The training directorate is functioning under the overall supervision of IG (Training). He is assisted by DIG (Training-I) and DIG (Training-II).
- **Operations :** The operations directorate is functioning under the overall supervision of IG (OPS). He is assisted by DIG (OPS-I) and DIG (OPS-II).
- **Provisioning :** The provisioning directorate is functioning under overall supervision of IG (Prov and Commn). He is assisted by DIG (Prov) and DIG (MT/Ord) and Asstt. Director (Prov).
- **Communication :** The communication directorate is functioning under the overall supervision of IG (Prov and Commn). He is assisted by DIG (Comn), DIG (Eqpt), DIG (Tech) and DIG (IT).
- **Finance and Accounts :** The finance branch and pay and accounts office are functioning under the direct supervision of FA. He is assisted by Dy. FA and DD (Accounts).
- **Medical :** The medical branch is functioning under the overall supervision of IG/Director (Medical). He is assisted by two CMO level officers.

The CRPF Rank Structure

Group 'A' (Gazetted Officers)

1. Director General (Apex Scale of the Indian Police Service)
2. Additional Director General (Higher Administrative Grade of the IPS cadre, also available to BSF cadre)
3. Inspector General (IG/DIR.ISA)
4. Deputy Inspector General (DIGP)
5. Additional Deputy Inspector General (Addl. DIGP)
6. Commandant
7. Second-in-Command (21C)
8. Deputy Commandant
9. Assistant Commandant

Executive (Non-Gazetted)/Combative Staff

1. Subedar Major
2. Inspector
3. Sub Inspector
4. Asstt. Sub Inspector
5. Head Constable
6. Constable

Ministerial/Hosp Staff (Non-Combative)

1. Office Supdt.
2. PA to IGP/Dir.
3. Head Clerk/Steno Gr. II
4. Hindi Translator Gr. II
5. UDC/Steno Gr. III
6. LDC
7. Asstt. Matron
8. Sister-In-Charge
9. Ward Sister
10. Staff Nurse
11. Pharmacist (SG)
12. Pharmacist/Radiographer
13. Laboratory Technician
14. Electrician
15. Lab. Asstt/X-ray Asstt.
16. Telephone Operator
17. Asstt. Operator Room

Group 'C' (Executive/Ministerial/Hospital)

1. HC (Senior Gestetner Operator)
2. CT (Daftry)/Plumber

Group 'D'

1. Dresser/Nursing Asstt./Ayah/Cook/Barber/Dhobi/Water Carrier (SG)
2. Cook/Barber/Dhobi (NSG)

3. Peon/SK/Farrash/Safai Karmachari/Water Carrier/ Follower/Steward/Ward boy/Mali/Chowkidar/ Masalchi/ Kahar/Table Boy/Carpenter/Staff for Sister Mess.

Eligibility

How to Join CRPF

The CRPF gives opportunity to those who have passed VIII standard up to graduates. Women can also get entries in some categories of CRPF. The Selection Board of Central Police Organisations (CPO) selected the officers of CRPF through competitive examination, physical test, medical test and interview.

One can join the CRPF at these levels :

- **Assistant Commandant (Group-A Gazetted Officer) :** Fifty per cent posts are meant for local promotion and 50 per cent through direct recruitment by conducting competitive examination through SSB (CPOs) in rotation by the paramilitary forces.
- **Sub Inspector :** Twenty five per cent of the vacancies occurring in a year are being filled by direct recruitment through Staff Selection Commission.
- **Constable (GD) :** Hundred per cent vacancies are filled by direct recruitment from open market.
- **Constable (Tech/Trade) :** Recruitment of tradesmen and technical staff is decentralised and the vacancies of these categories are filled by unit commandant under the directions of Sectors IsGP after observing all due formalities.
- **Followers :** (Cook/Water Carrier/Barber/Washerman/*Safai Karamchari* are the members of the CRPF that comes under followers category): By respective unit commandant under the directions of Sectors IsGP after observing due formalities.
- **Head Constable**
- **Assistant Sub Inspector (ASI)**

Categories		Educational Qualification	Age	Physical Standards		
				Height	Weight	Chest
Assistant Commandant	Men	Graduation	19-25	165 cms	According to	81-86 cms
	Women	do	do	157 cms	Height but not less than 50 kg	
Sub-Inspector	Men	Graduation Possession of NCC 'B' or 'C' certificate Or outstanding Sports certificate is Considered desirable Qualification	20-25	170 cms		
	Women	do	do	157 cms	43 kg for Minimum height Of 157 cms	
Assistant Sub Inspector (ASI)	Men	+2 types, Shorthand	18-25	165 cms	do	77-82 cms
	Women	do	do	do	do	
Constable	men	SSLC/Matriculation	8-23	170 cms	proportionate To height and age	80-85 cms
	Women	do	do	157 cms		

Recruitment and Selection

Assistant Commandant

Assistant Commandant is recruited on the basis of written test, physical efficiency test (PET) and interview. The written test consists of two papers totaling 300 marks.

- Paper-I : General Awareness, General Intelligence and Reasoning, Numerical Ability (200 marks).
- Paper-II : Essay in Hindi or English, Précis Writing (English) and Comprehension of given passage in English (100 marks).

After qualifying the written test, the candidate has to undergo the Physical Efficiency Test (PET) comprising:

1. 100 m. race to be completed in 16 seconds (Men) and four min. (Women)
2. 800 m. race to be completed in three minutes (Men) and four minutes (Women)
3. Long jump: 3.5 m for men and 3 m for women
4. High Jump: 1.05 m for men and 0.90 m for women
5. Short Putt (7.26 kg): 4.50 m. for men only

The candidate will be given three chances to qualify the minimum requirement in long jump, high jump and short putt. Failure in any of these events leads to disqualification. On clearing PET, you will be called in for an Interview. Here your psyche and aptitude will be assessed along with your general awareness and general intelligence. Preference in selection is given to outstanding sports men and NCC cadets who have good record. Finally, you have to clear a medical examination and then make it into the merit list.

Engineering and medical professionals can also enter the medical and technical wings of the CRPF at the level of assistant commandant or above through the same selection procedure.

Medical Officers

The post of medical officers are filled up by direct recruitment, failing which, by transfer on deputation or transfer of suitable persons holding equivalent or analogous posts under the central or state governments or public sector undertaking or autonomous bodies or transfer on deputation or re-employment or medical officers of army medical corps, possessing the qualifications prescribed for direct recruits.

Age Limit

Between 23 and 30 years (relaxable for government servants and released army medical corps officers upto five years in accordance with the instructions or orders issued by the government).

Educational Qualifications

- A recognised medical qualifications included in the First Schedule or the Second Schedule to the Indian Medical Council Act, 1956 (102 of 1956) and enrollment in any State Medical Register maintained under that act.
- Compulsory rotator internship.

Physical Standard

Height: 157 cms. Relaxable by two cms for *Gurkha, Garhwali, Kumaonees, Dograsm Marathas* and three cms in respect of *Adivasis* and female candidates.

Chest: 77cms. Unexpanded and 82 cms expanded.

Weight: Proportionate to the height and age.

Sub Inspector

Sub Inspectors are recruited on the basis of physical efficiency test (PET), written test and interview. The candidates who on screening are found medically fit are allowed to appear in physical efficiency test. The test consists of:

- one mile run in 6.5 minutes
- 12 feet long jump in three chances

Those who clear physical efficiency test are allowed to appear in a written examination carrying 300 marks. It consists of:

- Paper-I : General Intelligence and Reasoning, General Awareness and Numerical Ability.
- Paper-II : Language Comprehension and communication writing skills.

Written test is followed by an interview, which carries 100 marks. Final selection is subject to passing the medical examination.

	Direct Recruitment
Sub Inspector (Cryptographers)	-A degree from a recognised university with English and Mathematics and also Matric with English, Maths and Physics. -Pass the selection Aptitude test -Must confirm to the CRPF physical standard *Note :* The percentage of direct recruitment and promotion from feeder posts have been fixed as 10 per cent and 90 per cent respectively.
Sub Inspector (Radio Operator)	-A degree from a recognised university with Maths, Physics, Statistics or Computer science as one of the main subject -Pass the selection Aptitude test -Must confirm to the CRPF physical standard *Note :* As long as suitable department candidates are available no direct recruitment will be carried out except in a very exceptional cases. The percentage of direct recruitment and promotion from feeder posts has been fixed as 10 per cent and 90 per cent respectively.
Sub Inspector (Technical)	-Graduate in Engg. Telecommunication/ Electronics/Computer Science Or Qualified AMIE or Grade IETE -Must pass the selection Aptitude test -Must confirm to the CRPF physical standard *Note :* As long as suitable department candidates are available no direct recruitment will be carried out except in a very exceptional cases. The percentage of direct recruitment and promotion from feeder posts has been fixed as 10 per cent and 90 per cent respectively.

Assistant Sub Inspector (Ministerial Staff)

	Direct Recruitment	*Departmental Candidates*
Assistant Sub Inspector (Technical)	-Matric with English, Physics, Maths	Head constable (Radio Fitters) will be eligible for conversion

	With three-yrs diploma in Radio Engineering/ Electronics/Computer. -Preference will be given to those trained in software/hardware of computer. -Must pass the selection Aptitude test -conform to the CRPF physical standard	if in possession of the following qualifications: - 2-yrs as Radio fitter - A clear record of service -Pass the selection Aptitude test -candidates with above qualification will be re-mustered as ASI (Tech) on successful completion of Basic Radio *Mechanic course.*
	Note: The percentage of direct recruitment and remustering of departmental candidates has been fixed as 70 per cent and 30 per cent respectively.	
Assistant Sub Inspector (Draftsman)	-Matric with English, Science and Maths and 2-yrs Draftsman Course from a recognised ITI. -Pass the selection Aptitude test -confirm to the CRPF physical standard ***Note :*** The vacancies will be filled through direct recruitment only.	

Constable

A constable is recruited on the basis of physical efficiency test (PET), written test and interview. The candidates who on screening are found medically fit are allowed to appear in physical efficiency test. The test consists of :

- one mile run in 6.5 minutes.
- 12 feet long jump in three chances.

Those who clear physical efficiency test are allowed to appear in a written examination consisting of questions on various subjects like general awareness, elementary mathematics and basic knowledge of English/Hindi. It is followed by an interview. Final selection is subjected to passing the medical examination.

Followers: (Cook, Water carrier, Barber, Washerman, *Safai Karamchari)*

Candidates who are found fit in eligibility and PET will be put through respective trade test. Test is prescribed as per recruitment of the job. The candidate will be medically examined after the trade test, to assess their physical and medical fitness as prescribed in the eligibility conditions. Those who fail in the medical examination will not be considered for the post of followers. A merit list will be prepared on the basis of the marks obtained in the VIII class from a recognised central/ state school and the marks obtained in the trade test of a particular job.

The Promotional Avenues of Gazetted Officers

After joining service as assistant commandant, the following promotional avenues are available to cadre officers :

Rank	*Qualifying service for Promotion*
Deputy Commandant	six years as Assistant Commandant
Second-in-Command	five years as Dy. Commandant (with total 11 years Group 'A' service)
Commandant	five years as Second-in-Command (with 16 years Group 'A' Service)
DIGP	three years as Commandant (with 20 years Group 'A' Service)
IGP	three years as DIG (with 24 years Group 'A' Service)

CRPF Training Centers

- **Internal Security Academy**

  ISA, CRPF, Mount Abu

  Rajasthan-307501.
- **CRPF Academy, Gurgaon**

  CRPF, Kadarpur, Gurgaon

  Haryana-122101.
- **Central Training College (CTC)-I, Neemuch**

  CTC, CRPF, Neemuch

  Madhya Pradesh-458445.
- **Central Training College (CTC)-II, Coimbatore**

  CTC, CRPF, Coimbatore

  Tamil Nadu-641017.
- **Central Training College (CTC)-III, Mudkhed**

  CTC, CRPF, Mudkhed

  Maharashtra-431806.
- **Central Training College (CTC), Gwalior**

  CTC, CRPF, Gwalior

  Madhya Pradesh-474001.

- **Counter Interagency and Anti Terrorist School-Silchar (CIAT-I)**

  CIAT, School CRPF, Udharband

  Silchar, Assam-780030.
- **Counter Interagency and Anti Terrorist School-Shivpuri (CIAT-II)**

  CIAT, School CRPF, Shivpuri

  Madhya Pradesh-473551.

Recruit Training Centres

There are four recruits' training centres in the force for training the newly recruited constables.

- Recruits Training Centre (RTC-I),

  Neemuch, Madhya Pradesh.
- Recruits Training Centre (RTC-II),

  Avadi, Chennai-Tamil Nadu.
- Recruit Training Centre (RTC-III), Peringome

  RTC, CRPF, Srinagar, (J&K)-190063.

Useful Contacts

- Directorate General

  Central Reserve Police Force

  Block No.1, CGO Complex, Lodhi Road

  New Delhi-110 003.

  Website: www.crpf.gov.in
- CRPF Recruitment

  DIG Recruitment

  Block No. 1, CGO Complex, Lodhi Road

  New Delhi-110003.

  Website: www.crpfrecruitment.org

7.5.3 Indo-Tibetan Border Police Force (ITBPF)

What is ITBPF?

The Indo Tibetan Border Police Force (ITBPF) is one of the Indian paramilitary forces, deployed on the border guarding suites from Karakoram Pass in Laddakh to Jachep La in Arunachal Pradesh covering

3,488 km of Indo-China border. It is a specialised mountain force and most of the officers and men are professionally trained mountaineers and skiers. ITBPF personnel are affectionately called *'Himveers'*. The motto of the ITBPF is *"Shaurya-Dridata-Karm Nishtha"* (i.e., valour-determination-devotion to duty). The ITBPF's motto has always inspired its men in accepting challenges to bring glory to the nation and honour to the force. ITBPF conducts long range and short range patrols to keep an effective vigil on inaccessible areas on the border.

The Indo-Tibetan Border Police is a force synonym to adventure. Serving in such a force is dare-devilish as well as challenging. Some of the attractive features of the force are – skiing, mountaineering, trekking, river rafting and the thrill of proximity to the mountains.

ITBPF Rank Structure

- Director General
- Addl. Director General
- Inspector General
- Deputy Inspector General
- Commandant
- Second-in-Command
- Deputy Commandant
- Assistant Commandant
- Subedar Major
- Inspector
- Sub-Inspector
- Assistant Sub Inspector
- Head Constable
- Constable

How to join in ITBPF

Indo-Tibetan Border Police Force recruits young candidates at the four levels :

- Assistant Commandant
- Sub-Inspector
- Head Constable
- Constable

Vacancies are advertised from time to time in all leading newspapers and the *Employment News*. Like other official jobs, there is a reservation of 15 per cent for members of the Scheduled Caste, 7.5 per cent for

Scheduled Tribes and 27 per cent for other Backward Class candidates. The candidates are required to undergo written tests followed by a physical efficiency test, a medical examination and finally an interview.

The recruitment process for various posts in ITBP is as follows :

Assistant Commandant (General Duty)

Assistant commandant (general duty) is Group 'A' service (Basic pay, ₹ 15,000 – 39,100). Assistant commandants are recruited by the Combined Special Selection Board constituted by the Ministry of Home Affairs through UPSC.

Eligibility : Graduate

Age Limit : 19 – 25. Relaxation in age for member of Scheduled Castes and Scheduled Tribes – five years. Ex-servicemen and demobilised personnel of armed forces with not less than sixth months in the armed forces – service rendered in Army, Navy and Air Force plus three years. Meritorious sports persons – up to five years. (10 years for SCs/STs and eight years for OBCs).

Physical Standards

Category	Height	Weight	Chest	Eyesight
General	165 cm. & above	50 kgs (min)	80-85 cms	6/6 – 6/12
Candidates belonging to Garhwal, Kumoaon, Himachal Pradesh, Leh and Laddakh, Kashmir Valley, Gurkha, Marathas, Dogras, Sikkimese and Northeastern States shall be 165 cms.	165 cms	—	77-82 cms	—
For Tribals/Adivasis including Mizos and Nagas	162.5 cms	—	do	—

Method of Selection

Written examination for assistant Commandant is conducted in two papers viz.,

- Intelligence Test, and
- General Knowledge and Essay Writing.

Thereafter, the Special Selection Board conducts a physical efficiency test, medical examination and an interview for selecting the candidates.

Sub-Inspector (Technical Cadre)

Category	*Gender*	*Age*	*Qualification*
Sub-Inspector (Stenographer)	(for Male and Female	20-25 yrs	B.A. English (100WPM in Shorthand and 40 WPM in typing). Hindi (80 WPM in Shorthand typing 25 WPM. Candidates)
Sub-Inspector (Telecommunication)	(for Male candidates)	20-25 yrs	(i) Bachelor's degree in Science with Physics, Chemistry and Maths or Information Technology, or Computer Science or Electronics and Instrumentation from a recognised University or Institution, (ii) Bachelor in Computer Application from a recognised University or Institution, (iii) B.E. in Electronics and Communication or Instrumentation or Computer Science or Electrical or Information Technology from a recognised University or Institution, (iv) Associate Member of Institution of Electronics and Communication or Instrumentation or Computer Science or Electrical or Information Technology Engineers or equivalent from a recognised University or institution.
Sub-Inspector (Education)	(for Male and Female	20-25 yrs	Degree from a recognised University or equivalent with Psychology as a subject or degree from a candidates) recognised University with Bachelor of Education/Bachelor of Teaching or equivalent.
Sub-Inspector (Pharmacist)		18-25 yrs	Matric with Diploma in Pharmacy
Sub-Inspector (Lab Technician)		18-25 yrs	Matric with Diploma in Medical Lab. Technology
Sub-Inspector (Radiographer)		18-25 yrs	Matric with two yrs Diploma in Radio Diagnosis
Sub-Inspector (Overseer)	(for Male only)	18-25 yrs	Matriculation equivalent with Diploma in Civil Engineering from an Institute recognised by the Central Government.

Physical Standards

Category	Height	Weight	Chest	Eyesight
General	170 cms & Above	50 kgs (min)	80-85 cms	6/6 – 6/9
Candidates belonging to Garhwal, Kumoaon, Himachal Pradesh, Leh and Laddakh, Kashmir Valley, Gurkha, Marathas, Dogras, Sikkimese and Northeastern States shall be 165 cms.	165 cms	—	77-82 cms	—
For Tribals/Adivasis including Mizos and Nagas	162.5 cms	—	do	—

Method of Selection

Selection of Sub-Inspectors in ITBP is conducted in two parts :

1. Part-I

   Consists of a written test in general intelligence, reasoning, general awareness, numerical ability and English language.

2. Part-II

   Has the physical efficiency test, medical examination and interview.

Constable

Constable (General Duty) : Indo-Tibetan Border Police conducts recruitment-rallies in different parts of the country for enlisting constables. It is the Group 'C' service of ITBPF. (Basic pay ₹ 6,460 – 20,200). The recruitment of constable (general duty) is done by the Staff Selection Commission.

Eligibility : Matriculation or 10th class pass from a recognised Board/University.

Age Limit : 18 – 23.

Relaxation in Age

- For members of the Scheduled Castes and Scheduled Tribes – five years.
- Ex-servicemen and demobilised personnel of Armed Forces with not less than six months in the Armed Forces.
- Service rendered in Army, Navy and Air Force plus three years.
- Meritorious Sports Persons – up to five years; (10 years for SCs/STs and eight years for OBCs).

Constable (Technical Cadre)

Category	Gender Age	Qualification
Constable (Motor Mechanic)	(for Male only) 18-25 yrs	(i) Matric/10th class pass from a recognised Board. (ii) Certificate from a recognised institution/ ITI in automobile/motor mechanic trade.
Constable (Animal Transport)	(for Male only) 18-25 yrs	Matriculation or equivalent from a recognised Board.
Constable (Driver)	(for Male only) 20-25 yrs	(i) Matric/10th class pass from a recognised Board. (ii) Valid driving license for light/medium/ heavy vehicles with minimum two years experience in driving.
Constable (Tailor/ Gardener/Cobbler)	(for Male only) 18-23 yrs	(i) 10th class pass from a recognised Board. (ii) two years work experience in respective trade or one year certificate from industrial training institute/vocational institute with at least one year experience in respective trade or two years diploma from industrial training institute in the trade.
Constable (Water Carrier/Safai Karamchari/Cook Washerman/Barber)	(for Male only) 18-25 yrs	10th class pass from a recognised Board.
Constable (Pioneer/ Mason/Carpenter	(for Male only) 18-23 yrs	Matriculation or equivalent from a recognised Board with one year's experience in the trade of Mason or carpenter or plumberor electrician or welder or painter.

Physical Standards

Category	Height	Weight	Chest	Eyesight
General	170 cms and above	50 kgs (min)	80-85 cms	6/6 – 6/9
Candidates belonging to Garhwal, Kumoaon, Himachal Pradesh, Leh and Laddakh, Kashmir Valley, Gurkha, Marathas, Dogras, Sikkimese and Northeastern States shall be 165 cms.	165 cms	—	77-82 cms	—
For Tribals/Adivasis including Mizos and Nagas	162.5 cms	—	do	—

Method of Selection

Selection process of the constables in ITBPF consists of :

- **High Bar Test :** Candidates will be put through the height bar test and qualified candidates will be sent for five km race.

- **Race (PET) :** After height bar test, the candidates will be subjected to five kms race to be completed within 24 minutes.
- **Documentation :** The candidates who qualify in the physical standard test will be required to produce all relevant documents in original only.
- **Biometric verification :** Finger impression in respect of registered candidates will be captured immediately and will be verified on subsequent recruitment tests to avoid impersonation.
- **Written Test (100 marks) :** (i) The candidates who qualify the documentation stage will be required to appear in a written test. (ii) NON-OMR, based multiple choice question paper will be set (Bilingual, i.e., in Hindi and English) to assess the general awareness/general knowledge, knowledge of candidate in English/Hindi. The question paper will carry 100 objective types multiple choice questions and would carry 100 marks. (iii) Minimum qualifying marks for general and ex-servicemen – 35 per cent and for SC/ST and OBC category candidates is 33 per cent.

Other Cadres

There are a number of technical cadres viz., medical, telecommunication, paramedical, engineering, veterinary, motor transport, education, clerical, stenography, hindi translator and tailor etc. Pay scales and perks of various ranks in these cadres are identical to that of general duty cadre.

Post	*Gender*	*Age*	*Qualification*
Assistant Commandant (Medical Officer)	(for male and female candidates)	23-30 yrs	recognised medical qualifications included in the First Schedule to the Indian Medical Council Act-1956 (102 of 1956) and enrollment in any state Medical Register Maintained under this Act. Compulsory Rotatory Internship.
Assistant Commandant (Engineer)	(for male and female candidates)	30 yrs	Degree in civil engineering.
Assistant Commandant (Veterinary Assistant Surgeon)	(for male and female candidates)	30 yrs	Degree in Telecommunication Engineering or Electrical Communication Engineering or equivalent.
Inspector (Hindi Translator)	(for male and female candidates)	20-30 yrs	Master's degree from a recognised university in Hindi or English with Hindi and English as

			compulsory or elective subjects or as the medium of examination at the degree level.
			Master's Degree from a recognised university in any subject other than Hindi and English with Hindi and English as compulsory or elective subjects or either of the two as the medium of examination and the otheras a compulsory or elective subject at the degree level.
			Master's Degree from a recognised university in any subject other than Hindi and English with Hindi or English as the medium of examination at the degree level.
			Bachelor's degree from a recognised university with Hindi and English as compulsory or elective subjects or either of the two as the medium of examination and the other as compulsory orelective subject plus a recognised Diploma or Certificate course in translation from Hindi to English and vice versa or two years experience of translation work from Hindi to English and vice versa in Central or State Government department including Government of India undertakings and working knowledge of computer application or equivalent.
Inspector (Staff Nurse)	(for male and female candidates)	18-25 yrs	Matric with Registration under Nursing Council
Head Constable (Combatant Ministerial)	(for male and female candidates)	18-25 yrs	Inter-mediate or Senior Secondary School certificate (10+2) examination from a recognised Board or University or equivalent. Typing speed of

			35 words per minute in English or 30 words per minute in Hindi only on computer. Preference will given to candidates possessing higher qualifications and having knowledge of basic operation of computer.
Head Constable (Telecommunication)	(for male and female candidates)	18-25 yrs	10+2 pass with physics, chemistry and mathematics having aggregate of 45 per cent marks in physics, chemistry & maths from a recognised board or university.
			10th class pass from a recognised board with two years Industrial Training Institute certificate in electronics or electrical or computer from a recognised Institute.
			10th Class pass from a recognised board with Science (PCM) and with three years Diploma in electronics or communication or instrumentation or computer science or information technology or electrical froma recognised institute.
Head Constable (Radio Operator)		18-23 yrs	Matric with science.
Head Constable (Education)	(for male & female candidates)	20-25 yrs	Degree from a recognised university or equivalent with psychology as a subject or Degree from a recognised university with Bachelor of education/Bachelor of teaching or equivalent.
Head Constable (Radio-Technician)	(for male only)	20-25 yrs	Matric with science
Head Constable (Motor Mechanic)	(for male only)	19-25 yrs	(i) Matric/10th class pass from a recognised Board. (ii) Certificate in motor mechanic from a recognised institution/ITI with three years practical experience in the trade in a reputed workshop or three yrs diploma in automobile engineering.

Head Constable (Veterinary)	(for male only)	18-25 yrs	(i) Matriculation or equivalent from a recognised board. (ii) Must have passed Veterinary Stock Assistant course from a recognised institution.
Head Constable (Telecommunication)	(for male only)	18-25 yrs	(i) Matriculation or equivalent from a recognised Board. (ii) Diploma or Certificate course from an industrial training institute or any other recognised institution.

ITBP Training Centres

- ITBP Basic Training Centres, Bhanu.
- National Institute for Training in Search, Rescue and Disaster Response (NITSRDR), Bhanu.
- ITBP Academy, Mussourie.
- Mountaineering and Skiing Institute, Auli.

ITBP Contact Details

- **Indo-Tibetan Border Police Force**

  Block No.-2, C.GO. Complex, Lodhi Road, New Delhi-110 003

  Fax No. 011-24360427.

  Website: www.itbpolicw.nic.in

Promotional Avenues

Gazetted Officers

The promotional prospects are bright and officers can reach up to the level of Deputy Inspector and Inspector General.

- An Inspector in ITBP with five years of regular service becomes eligible for promotion to the rank of assistant commandant.
- After 6 years of service as an assistant commandant, he becomes eligible to the position of deputy commandant.
- After 11 years in Group-A (Class-I) service including five year service as deputy commandant, the officer can get promotion to the rank of second-in-command.
- With 15 year Group-A (Class-I) service including four years as second-in-command the officer becomes eligible to get promoted to the rank of commandant.

Non-Gazetted Officers

The promotion prospects are bright and a person can reach up to the level of assistant commandant and deputy commandant.

- A person joining as sub-inspector becomes eligible for promotion to the rank of Inspector after putting three years of service.
- After putting three years as Inspector, he is eligible to the subedar major.
- On completion of five years of service as inspector/subedar major, he is considered for promotion as assistant commandant.
- On completion of six years Group 'A' (Class-I), he becomes eligible for promotion as deputy commandant.

Note : Promotion in each rank from constable to inspector is subject to passing departmental promotion tests.

- The person joining as constable becomes eligible for promotion to the rank of head constable after eight years of service.
- After 13 years service including eight years service as head constable, he becomes eligible to the rank of sub-inspector.
- After 16 years service including three years service as sub-inspector, he becomes eligible to the rank of inspector.
- After 19 years service including three years as inspector, he becomes eligible to the rank of subedar major.

Other Cadres

Medical Cadre

- A medical officer (Group-A) is given promotion as senior medical officer (deputy commandant) after four years of regular service.
- On completion of six year service as senior medical officer or 10 years of total service in the cadre he is promoted as chief medical officer (ordinary grade).
- After rendering six years service as chief medical officer (ordinary grade) he gets promoted as chief medical officer (selection grade).
- One post of director (medical) is available and this post is filled by promotion from amongst the chief medical officers (selection grade) with not less than three years service in the grade or 17 years of total service.

Engineering Cadre

- An assistant commandant (engineer) on completion of six years of regular service in the grade becomes eligible for promotion to the rank of deputy commandant (engineer).

- The deputy commandant (engg) with 15 years Group 'A' (Class-I) service of which 10 years should be as deputy commandant (engineer) becomes eligible for commandant (engineer).
- Commandant (Engineer) with 18 years Group 'A' (Class-I) service of which minimum 10 years of regular service should be in the rank of commandant (engineer), becomes eligible for additional deputy inspector general (engineer).

Veterinary Cadre

- An assistant commandant (veterinary assistant surgeon) on completion of six years of regular service in the grade becomes eligible for promotion to the rank of deputy commandant (veterinary surgeon).
- After five years of regular service as deputy commandant (veterinary surgeon) one is eligible to be promoted as commandant (senior veterinary surgeon).

Pay Scales

Each rank in Indo-Tibetan Border Police Force has its own pay scale. The pay scales vary from ₹ 8,000 for constables to ₹ 80,000 for the Director General.

Perks and Allowances

- Dearness Allowances (DA)
- Free ration
- Leave travel concession
- City compensatory allowance
- Leave travel concession
- Pension after completion of requisite service
- Gratuity and accumulated leave encashment
- Insurance coverage
- Washing allowance etc.

7.5.4 Central Industrial Security Force (CISF)

Assistant Sub-Inspector (Clerk/Typist) and Sub-Inspector (Steno)

Any Indian citizen both male and female who fulfils the eligibility requirement can apply for the recruitment to various posts. Details of the two categories of posts are:

(A) Assistant Sub-Inspector (Clerk/Typist);

(B) Sub-Inspector (Steno)

Age : ***For Category A :*** Minimum 18 years.

For Category B : Minimum 19 years. Maximum 25 years as on January 1 of the year of recruitment for both the categories. Five years relaxation for SC/ST candidates and upto 35 years in case of departmental candidates.

Eligibility (for both Categories): Intermediate or Senior Secondary (10+2) or equivalent examination of recognised University/Board.

Technical Qualification

For Category A : Speed of 30 wpm in English typewriting or 25 wpm in Hindi is required.

For Category B : a speed of 80 wpm is stenography and 35 wpm in typewriting in English or 30 wpm in Hindi is required.

Physical Standards (For both categories)

For Male Candidates : Height: 167 cms Chest: 81 cms (Unexpanded) and 86 cms (expanded). Relaxation in height: 160 cms for hillmen and tribesmen.

For Female Candidates : Height: 153 cms.

Visual Standard for All : With or without glasses 6/6 in one eye and 6/9 in the other eye. Near vision of 0.6 in one eye and 0.8 in the other eye. Candidates should not have knock knee or flat feet and certain other mentioned deformities.

Selection : The eligible candidates will be put through the written test consisting of one objective type paper in general knowledge. IQ, arithmetic and language (Hindi or English) in the case of Category A and general knowledge, IQ and general English in the case of Category-B. Candidates who secure the prescribed minimum marks in written test shall be allowed to appear in typewriting test or typewriting and stenography for two categories as applicable. Candidates who qualify in typewriting and stenography tests will be put through an interview by the Board. Eligible ex-servicemen are exempted from written test, stenography and typewriting tests. They will be called to appear for interview only. Candidates may appear for both the categories.

Note : Employment in CISF also involves postings in remote, rural and semi-rural areas. Female candidates are not given any special consideration in such postings if vacancies are to be filled in such areas. They are treated as equal to their male colleagues and accept to be subject to the remoteness of the place and being often the lone female member in the police office of that Unit. All applications duly filled should be in prescribed pro forma as given in the advertisement in leading newspapers/*Employment News*.

Sub Inspectors (Fire Wing) Exam

Only male candidates are invited to apply for the posts of: A. Sub-Inspector (Mech./Fire) and B. Sub-Inspector (Fire) in the CISF Fire Wing.

Age: Minimum 19 years and maximum 25 years on January 1. (five years relaxation for SC/ST/CISF departmental candidates).

Eligibility: ***For Category-A:*** Matriculation or equivalent and three years Diploma in mechanical/electrical/automobile engineering or equivalent from a recognised university or Board/Institution.

For Category-B : Degree in science with PCM/equivalent or matriculation or equivalent and three years Diploma in mechanical/civil/electrical/automobile/chemical/mining/aeronautical/telecommunication engineering or equivalent from a recognised university or Board/Institution.

For both categories : Desirable qualification is (i) having passed fire-fighting courses from a recognised institution (ii) proficiency in games, sports and athletics, membership of NCC.

Physical and Visual Standards : Same as for male candidates of CISF ASI (clerk/typist) and SI (steno) mentioned earlier. The candidates should not have knock knee, flat feet and certain other mentioned deformities.

Selection

Selection is based on written examination in GK, IQ and language (Hindi/English), physical efficiency test and interview. Qualified candidates have to undergo a medical examination. Selected candidates are liable to serve anywhere in the country.

Apply in the prescribed proforma along with other requirements as and when given I the advertisement published in *Employment News*/ leading bewspapers.

Constable (General Duty)

Only male candidates are invited to apply for filling the rank of constable (GD) in the Central Industrial Security Force.

Age : Not less than 18 years and not more than 23 years on the date of selection. Upper age limit is relaxable for SC/ST/OBC candidates.

Physical Standards : Height: 170 cms

Chest : 80 cms (unexpanded) and 85 cms (expanded)

Relaxation in height : 165 cms for *Gurkha, Garhwalis, Kumaonees, Dogras, Marathas and Adivasis* including *Mizos* and *Nagas* etc. Height: 165/162.5 cms. Chest: 78/76 cms (with expansion of

5 cms). Eye Sight: Distant vision: 6/6 in one eye and 6/9 in the other eye. Near vision: 0.6 in one eye and 0.8 in the other eye.

Candidates should not have knock knee, flat and squint eyes.

Eligibility : Matriculation or equivalent examination.

Selection : Candidates who qualify in the physical efficiency test (PET) will be put through a written test and interview. Final selection is made strictly according to merit and vacancies allotted on the basis of aggregate marks obtained by the candidates in eligibility, PET, literacy test (written test) and interview and subject to medical fitness.

Apply as and when the vacancies are advertised in leading newspapers/*Employment News.*

7.6 Border Roads Organisation (BRO)

What is the Border Roads Organisation (BRO)?

The Border Roads Organisation (BRO) is an organisation that maintains roads that serve the border areas of India. It is staffed with a combination of Border Roads Engineering Service officers from the General Reserve Engineer Force (GREF) and officers from the Corps of Engineers of the Indian Army. The organisation develops and maintains arterial roads on the borders of India. The BRO is involved in the construction of a tunnel at the Rohtang pass.

The Important Role of Border Roads Organisation (BRO)

BRO's activities have help to accelerate the economic development of the North and Northeastern Border States of India. The road construction teams have to deal with harsh climatic conditions. The BRO faces environments like the icy Himalayan mountain tops, the marshes of West Bengal and the deserts of Rajasthan. The BRO builds and maintains roads at high altitude; some of the BRO roads are built as high as 5,608 meters (18,399 ft) above sea level.

The Border Roads Organisation operates a network of over 32,885 kilometers (20,434iles) of roads and 12,200 meters (40,026 ft) of permanent bridges. BRO has operations in 22 states, including the Andaman and Nicobar Islands, a union territory.

Brief History of the Border Roads Organisation (BRO)

The Border Roads Organisation (BRO) was formed on 7th May, 1960 as the Border Roads Development Board with Indian Prime Minister Jawaharlal Nehru as its chairman. The Border Roads Organisation (BRO) is led by the Director General of Border Roads, who holds the rank of Lieutenant General.

The Structure of the Border Roads Organisation (BRO)

The Border Roads Organisation (BRO) consists of the General Reserve Engineer Force (GREF) – the execution force – under the Ministry of Surface Transport and officers from Indian Army Corps of Engineers, who are deputed on loan to this organisation. The GREF includes civil, electrical and mechanical engineers. They are selected from engineering college across India through the annual Engineering Service Examination conducted by the Union Public Service Commission. The staff also includes administrative officers, supervisors and other trades. The organisation's operations are spread across India, Bhutan, Myanmar, Tajikistan and Afghanistan.

The fundamental unit of the BRO is similar to a platoon. This functional platoon composed of civil engineer officers from the GREF and army civil engineers is in charge of activities such as formation cutting, surfacing and safety mechanisms to maintain correct rod geometry. The BRO unit also handles the construction of permanent and temporary bridges, causeways and airfields.

The Projects of the Border Roads Organisation (BRO)

The Border Roads Organisation (BRO) includes 18 projects which are divided into Task Forces, Roads Construction Companies (RCCs), Bridge Construction Companies (BCCs), Drain Maintenance Companies (DMCs) and other function platoons. The organisation also includes base workshops, store divisions, training and recruitment centers and other staff. The Border Roads Organisation (BRO) is also incharge of maintenance of its road networks. In many places landslides, avalanches and snow block the routes and have to be cleared as quickly as possible. BRO also employs more than two lakhs (200,000) local workers in the task.

The various Posts and Trades in the Border Roads Organisation (BRO)

Any male Indian citizen who fulfills the eligible criteria can apply for the following posts in General Reserve Engineer Force (GREF) (Central Government) generally in the age group 18 to 25 years.

Name of the Post/Trade

- Blacksmith
- Bootmaker
- Carpenter
- Charge Electrician
- Charge Mechanic
- Cook
- Draughtsman Grade-I (LS) (Mech)
- Draughtsman Grade-I (LS) (Civil)
- Driver Engineer Static
- Driller
- Driver Mechanic Transport
- Driver Road Roller
- Electrician
- Hindi Translator
- Hindi Typist (LDC)
- Lower Division Clerk
- Leading Hand (Nursing)
- Leading Hand (Non Tech)
- Lab Assistant (Micro)
- Lineman/Tele Mech
- Machinist
- Masalchi
- Mess Waiter
- Mason
- Nursing Assistant
- Operator Excavating Machinery
- Overseer
- Painter
- Radio Operator
- Store Supervisor Grade-II
- Storekeeper Technical
- Storeman

Name of the Trade/Post

- Steno Grade-III
- Sanitary Inspector/Supervisor (Nursing/Sanitation)
- Safaiwala
- Superintendent Building and Roads Grade-I
- Superintendent Electrical and Mechanical Grade-II

Name of the Trade/Post

- Supervisor Non-Technical Grade-I
- Supervisor Non-Technical Grade-II
- Surveyor and Draughtsman (Field and Topo)
- Tailor
- Tin and Copper Smith
- Telephone Operator
- Turner
- Upper Division Clerk
- Upholsterer
- Vehicle Mechanic
- Welder
- Washerman
- Barber
- Packer Gde I
- Radio Mechanic
- Blood Transfusion Assistant
- Lab Assistant
- Leading Hand (Sig) Line
- Moulder
- Operation Room Assistant
- Supervisor Cipher-II
- Pioneers

Trades/posts are liable to be changed or added from time to time. Vacancies are advertised in the *Employment News/Rozgar Samachar* along with the details of eligibility, selection etc. Candidates are required to apply in response to the advertisement. Applications should be submitted to Commander, GREF, Dighi Camp, Pune-411015.

Group-C Non-Gazetted Posts

Applications are invited from Indian citizens to fill up the under mentioned posts in the Special Service Bureau under Ministry of Home Affairs, Government of India.

(A) Field Assistant (Tele)

(B) Senior Field Assistant (Tele)

(C) Deputy Field Officer (Tele)

(D) Radiographer

Age : For the posts of A, B, C: 20 to 28 years on specified date. For all posts relaxation is given to SC/ST by five years and to OBC by three years.

Eligibility : For A : Matriculation or equivalent with mathematics and science. For B : Matriculation or equivalent with mathematics and science and two years ITI certificate in electronics from a technical Institute OR 10+2 OR Intermediate in science with physics and mathematics. For C : B.Sc with physics/chemistry/mathematics, OR three years diploma in telecommunication or electronics from a government recognised technical institute after having passed 10+2 standard. For D : Matriculation or equivalent from a recognised Board/ University and two year Diploma in radiography.

Apply as and when the advertisement is published in *Employment News.*

Constable (General Duty)

Applications are invited from male Indian citizens ordinarily resident of the states, as may be specified for filling up the posts in the rank of constable (GD) in the Special Service Bureau.

Age : 18 to 23 years on specified date. Age relaxable by five years in the case of SC/ST) three years for OBC and as per government orders for ex-servicemen.

Physical and Medical Standards : Height : 170 cms, Chest: 80 cms with expansion five cms. Weight: Proportionate to height and age. More details are given in the advertisement. Candidates should be fit to work within as well as outside the territory of India.

Eligibility : Matriculation or 10th pass from a recognised Board/ University.

Selection : Based on recruitment tests comprising of (i) physical measurement (ii) physical efficiency test, (iii) written test in GK/general awareness, knowledge of elementary mathematics and test of basic knowledge in English/Hindi, (iv) interview, (v) medical examination. Grace marks are awarded to candidates having creditable achievements in sports, adventure sports, NCC, scouts and guides and other extra-curricular activities. Participation should be at least at state level.

Apply as and when the notification is published in *Employment News*.

Head Constable

Male Indian citizens are invited to apply for the posts in the rank of head constable (Tele) Group-C, Non-Gazetted in Special Service Bureau under Ministry of Home Affairs, Government of India.

Age : 18 to 23 years on specified date. Relaxable by five years for SC/ST, three years for OBC and by 12 years for departmental candidates.

Physical and Medical Standards : As specified in the advertisement.

Eligibility : Matriculation or equivalent with mathematics and science and diploma in radio or electrical or mechanical subjects.

Apply as and when the advertisement is published in *Employment News*.

7.7 Intelligence Services

What is an Intelligence Agency?

An Intelligence agency is a governmental agency that is devoted to information gathering for purposes of national security and defence. Means of information gathering may include spying, communication interception, cryptanalysis, co-operation with other institutions and evaluation of public sources. The assembly and propagation of this information is known as intelligence analysis.

An intelligence officer can be referred to a modern-day Sherlock Holmes. Holmes is famous for his intellectual knack and is renowned for his enormous scope of observation, his astute logical reasoning, his ability to take almost any masquerade and his forensic science skills to solve difficult cases. The need for contemporary versions of detective or intelligence agencies has been increasingly felt in modern society with spiraling crime rate especially in cities.

Indian Intelligence Agencies

India has a number of intelligence agencies of which the best known are the Research and Analysis Wing (RAW), India's External Intelligence Agency and the Intelligence Bureau, the Internal Intelligence Agency etc. Over the last hundred years, the face of the intelligence services in the country has changed considerably. The Central Bureau of Investigation (CBI) has emerged as the most important investigative body for serious crimes from murder to match fixing.

Eligibility and Course Areas

The selection to various posts in CBI is mainly through UPSC and SSC competitive examinations. The examination tests candidates in English language and general knowledge. An interview and a compulsory medical examination follow the test. Graduates (upper age limit is 25 years) are eligible to appear for the examination. Superior posts are usually filled from State Police Service and IPS officers. Junior posts are filled on direct recruitment. Recruitment in RAW is made in two ways.

- The first way : on the campus recruitment of civil service candidates at the foundation course, and
- The second way : recruitment of university graduates.

Special appointments are made in technical or scientific field through campus interviews at such institutes. RAW prefers persons who have had some experience of working in government organisations. Interview panels include experts and selectors from UPSC. Educational qualification required in intelligence service is law with experience.

A student interested in making a career in intelligence services can opt for any of the following courses :

- LL.B.
- LL.M.
- Forensic Science, and
- Criminology.

Job Prospects and Career Options

- **Central Bureau of Investigation (CBI) :** The CBI has four officer grade posts:
  - (i) Deputy Superintendent of Police (DSP),
  - (ii) Superintendent of Police (SP),
  - (iii) Deputy Director General (DIG), and
  - (iv) Inspector General (Commissioner of Police).

For the post of Deputy Superintendent of Police (DSP) direct recruitment is done through the Union Public Service Commission (UPSC) examination. In other three posts Indian Police Service (IPS) officers are filled on deputation or promotion. Entry to the IPS is through UPSC.

Other personnel employed by the CBI include Assistant Public Prosecutor, Senior Public Prosecutor (SPP), and Sub Inspectors. Assistant Public Prosecutor and Senior Public Prosecutor (SPPs) are recruited directly through competitive examinations conducted by the Staff Selection Commission. Public Prosecutors must possess a degree in law. For the post of Assistant Public Prosecutors, the candidate must possess a minimum of five years experience in law. For the post of Senior Public Prosecutors, the candidate must possess a minimum of 10 years of experience in law. Appointment to the rank of Sub Inspector is through a competitive examination conducted by the Central Staff Selection Commission. The candidate should clear written test, interview and medical.

Physical requirements prescribed: Height: five feet six inch (minimum), Chest: 32 inches, Age between 18 – 25 years of age, educational qualification must be a graduate.

All officers who are recruited directly are trained by the CBI at the Police Academy in Ghaziabad (UP). IPS officers are trained at Hyderabad. The CBI also runs a special training centre at Lok Nayak Bhavan, New Delhi.

- **Investigation Bureau (IB) :** The investigation Bureau is primarily concerned with the collection and analysis of information; it has no legal powers to investigate.

  Job in the IB : Grade-I and II officers work with the Investigation Bureau. Grade-I includes Assistant Director, Deputy Director, Joint Director, Special Director / Special Secretary. Superior posts are usually filled from State Police Service and IPS officers. Grade-II includes Security Assistant (Constable), Junior Intelligence Officer, Assistant Central Intelligence Officer, Deputy Central Intelligence Officer, Assistant Director. There is direct recruitment for the junior posts. Deputy Central Intelligence Officers and Assistant Directors may be appointed through deputation or by direct recruitment.

- **Research and Analysis Wing (RAW) :** RAW began as an integral part of Investigation Bureau (IB). However, it later emerged as a separate organisation. RAW comprises of two main sections:

  (i) The internal intelligence section, and

  (ii) The counter intelligence section.

  The two divisions of RAW have a strong information network that helps in acquiring sensitive information about crime and counter intelligence from all parts of the country. RAW also works towards offsetting the intelligence offensives of other countries against India.

Jobs in RAW

The following personnel are mainly employed by RAW: Attaché (Undersecretary), Deputy Field Officer, Field Officers and Senior Field Officers. Other personnel working in RAW include specialists in technical and scientific fields, Foreign language specialists etc. Language specialists deal with foreign countries and is involved in the study of foreign service materials characteristics. RAW recruits interpreters who are promoted to assistant foreign language examiner and then to deputy foreign language examiner. Interpreters are directly recruited to the language cadre. There is no SC/ST quota or reservation for any of these jobs.

- **Detective Agencies**

  Jobs in private detective agencies : Private detectives handle commercial, industrial and domestic cases. The job of the private detective begins with thorough background analysis of the case. Detectives are involved in collecting relevant information, analysing them and documenting the findings. They may work in association with forensic experts, pathologists, criminologists and handwriting specialists. Training in this field is offered through private agencies run by retired CBI, army intelligence and police officers.

Remuneration

In the case of CBI, RAW, IB pay scale varies based on the posts held. Anyhow, starting salary ranges between ₹ 10,000 – 20,000. For posts in the upper step of the ladder it is more. Private detectives charge on a daily basis. Depending upon the nature of the case and the size of the detective organisation involved, they may charge between ₹ 1,000 to 5,000 per day.

Courses

- LL.B.
- LL.M.
- Diploma in Criminology
- M.A. Criminology and Criminal Justice Administration
- M.Sc. Forensic Science
- Post Graduate Diploma in Criminology and Police Science
- Post Graduate Diploma in Criminology and Penology
- Post Graduate Diploma in Criminology and Forensic Science
- Ph. D. Criminology and Criminal Justice Administration

8

DESIGNING

8.1 Animation

Introduction

Everyone knows *Mickey Mouse, Donald Duck, Tom and Jerry* and *Stuart Little* – some animated characters that always delight and entertain us. Do you know how these characters were born and how it is possible to create wonders with the art of drawing? The answer is 'animation' – one of the fastest growing and most in-demand industries in the world. Multimedia *alias* multiple media as the name suggests is an enormous field that uses more than one medium of communication. It is an art that merges text, images, graphics, animation, audio and video to create virtual magic. Animation is only a component of multimedia.

A Brief History of the Art of Animation

The art of animation started with the cavemen who used to draw pictures on the rock surfaces. Though animation was formally demonstrated in 1828 by a French man, Paul Roget, the first animated film *'Humorous phases of funny faces'* by J. Stuart Blackton was made in 1906 by drawing comical faces on a blackboard, photographing them and then erasing it to draw another stage of the facial expression. It was in 1914, that the first cartoon named *'Gertie, the Dinosaur'* by Winsor McCay, consisting of 10,000 drawings was shown as a film in the theaters. In the early twenties, traditional animation techniques were developed and more sophisticated cartoons were produced. It was during this time that Warner Bros and Walt Disney studios came to exist. Computer animation started during seventies and eighties and had greater impact and with the passage of time, more and more advanced techniques were developed.

The Meaning of the word 'Animation'

Animation which derived its name from the Latin word *'anima'* meaning *'soul'* can be defined as the art of breathing life to a character. As it is blend of entertainment industry and technology, it is concerned with design, drawing, layout and production of graphically rich and attractive multimedia clips. In other words, animation is making of movies, games, or cartoons by moving the drawings or models of animals or people with the help of computers, or other electronic means. Time and space play a critical role in animation.

The Role of Animators

Animators are the talented artists who create characters for a variety of projects like movies, television, advertisements and so on. An animator's task is to read the script carefully, study the storyboard and try to get into the character. In other words, he needs to know and understand the character. Job opportunities are on the rise for an animator and they are in great demand as it is a growing industry and has become a popular feature in movies and advertising.

Creating an idea, developing it into a story script and giving technical assistance to it are the procedures in making an animation. Besides, the most commonly used animations are: two-dimensional (2-D) and three-dimensional (3-D). There is also puppet animation, clay animation, sand animation, vegetable animation etc. Both 2-D and 3-D animation can be created digitally. Two-dimensional images are shallow in appearance, while three-dimensional images have a feel of depth to them, thus making them look more real.

- **Cel or 2-D Animation:** Also known as classical animation. It deals with more with drawing and framing and is the base of 3-D animation. 2-D animators work mostly on paper creating frames to define a sequence that are then moved at varying speeds to create the illusion of motion. The process involves creating large number of drawings and scanning them into the computer and importing them into the software that helps in setting the timing and layers for the scanned sequence of images. Toonz Harlequin, Adobe Flash, CelAction, Anime Studio, Toon Boom Animation, Animaker are some of the software used for creating 2-D animation characters.
- **Computer generated Imagery or 3-D animation :** 3-D or three-dimensional animation which has more depth and is more realistic are a series of images/objects created using computers or any other digital media. In addition to the skills in drawing,

composition and character design. 3-D animators deal with modeling, rendering, texturing and lighting. The texture, lighting and colour of the 3-D objects are modified using software programmes and virtual cameras are used to focus, resise, zoom and illuminate the figures. This digital animation has the power to create effects not possible with classical animation. Film, advertising, video and gaming are the fast growing fields for 3D animation. This technique makes extensive use of animation software programmes like 3Ds Max (Autodesk), Softimage/XSI (Avid), MAYA (Autodesk) etc. It could also find in the other areas like advertising, web graphics to create websites and all.

Eligibility

Training is the most essential and important aspect for the creation of a skilled professional in the field of animation. To become an animator, one doesn't require any specific academic qualification. Those with basic sketching skill and a passion for animation can enter this field. For getting a better job prospect, one should have a degree or diploma in animation.

Degree and Diploma courses are in abundance nowadays apart from online services. Minimum educational qualification for a degree and diploma courses in animation is plus two or equivalent. Any graduate preferably arts graduate could apply for post graduation in animation. But some institutions such as Industrial Design Center (IDC), Indian Institute of Technology (IIT) and National Institute of Design (NID) follows eligibility criterion that only graduate of architecture, technology and engineering, fine arts can apply for the PG course in these institutes.

Besides these graduate and post graduate courses, there are several professional courses that focus on various styles and techniques. These courses i.e., courses in traditional animation, stop-motion animation, rotoscoping, computer generated 3-D and 2-D animation, Clay-mation, Photoshop, Human anatomy, Drawing etc helps one to specialise in a particular area. One should also have a basic knowledge in computer.

Apart from professional training, there are several personal skills also that one must possess to be a good animator. What makes to go a long way in making a good animation is a good sense of colour, proportion, size, design etc.

Personal skill

An animator should have an artistic bent of mind with a lot of passion and imaginative skills. Creativity is the most wanted quality for this career as animation starts with developing an idea to a story. The art of sketching or drawing is another basic skill one should possess. Patience, discipline and dedication to work is a vital ability as this field involves a lot of hard work and long hours of thorough planning. He or she should have a sound understanding of anatomy of humans, animals or birds and body movements and lighting effects. Good communication skill is also needed as most of the time it will be teamwork. One good animator should be one good actor also. So that only he could express the character well through his animation.

An animator should have a good sense of colour, proportion, size, design, visualisations, knowledge of background art and layout. They must have expertise in computer design software. Knowledge of programming languages (C++, Java) will be an added benefit. It is advantageous to understand photography, lighting and movement for those planning to work in computer animation. They must be able to visualise how an object will link in three dimensions and have the know-how to make an animated object look real.

Job Prospects

A strong portfolio of work is an essential part of landing a job in computer animation and becoming an animator. Numerous job opportunities are available in India and abroad in the exciting field of animation. It opens the door to film industries such as Hollywood, which is the world of special effects and imagery for films. Specialised computer knowledge and skills are essential for various jobs in the field of animation.

It is a booming industry with wide job openings and one can work on full length animation movies or any other related fields like television, advertising industry etc. An Animated feature film which offers considerable employment prospects is a combined talented effort of a wide variety of artists. A typical animation film requires around 500 animators. Some of the jobs offered in the industry are:

Content Developer

- **Modeller :** He is the one who makes the models for animation? Modeler has a solid understanding of anatomy, form and volume.
- **Story Broad Artist :** Those with strong drawing skills could be hired as storyboard artists who can visualise a sequence of events from frame to frame.
- **Character Animator :** He or she brings characters to life and generally has knowledge of traditional animation, stop-motion animation as well as clay-mation.
- **Background Artist :** The background artist is the person who specialises to paint the background of the characters and sets the background for the project.

- **Layout artist :** Layout artist is just like a cinematographer of that animation project as they are to decide the lighting and camera angles and he is sketching the background design for the animation.
- **2-D animator :** The 2-D animator is involved in the creation of a high volume of separate drawings that define a sequence.
- **In-between animator :** In-between animator can learn all the basics of animation and it is the beginning position of an animator.
- **Scanner operator :** The scanner operator does the scanning of the clean up artist's drawings.
- **Compositing artist :** Compositing consists of layering individual frames of animation on top of one another to create final images. These images are then strung together to create complete shots or mini animated movies.
- **Special effects artist :** The special effects artist integrates live-action footage with Computer Generated Imagery (CGI) or other elements (such as model work) – Audio and Video specialist, visualisers.
- **Texture artist :** The texture artist applies a surface to the 3-D modeled character, object or environment.
- **Rigging artist :** A rigging artist takes the modeled, textured 3-D character or object and sets it up with a skeletal system or joints (if required). Without this step, the 3-D model would not be able to animate, talk or move fluidly and correctly.
- **Clean-up artist :** The clean-up artist checks the accuracy and consistency of the design and drawings. To be a good clean-up artist, he should have good draftsman skill with the knowledge of density, width, volume and mass.
- **Lighting artist :** They create variations of shade, colour intensity and shadows.
- **Digital link and paint artist :** It is the duty of a digital link and paint artist to give colours to each frame.
- **Editor.**
- **Key frame animator :** The key frame animator draws the pictures of a movement's beginning and end.
- **Rendering artist :** Rendering artist takes all the data in a scene such as models, textures, animation, lighting, etc., and output the

correct combination in the form of individual frames of animation.

- **3-D animator :** The 3-D animator takes the sculpted, textured and rigged 3-D model and breathes life into it. This is done by putting in order the key frames in such a way that they appear to be in motion.
- **Image editor :** Image editor assembles various visual and audio components of the film into a coherent and effective whole.

Website designing, CD-Rom production, graphics designing and three-dimensional product modeling are some other fields where animators can gain employment. Though entertainment through film and television is the main area of application in this profession, animation is also needed in other areas like business, sales, engineering, education and advertising. It has chances in fashion designing and interior designing and even in medical, legal and insurance companies for their presentations and models. The gaming industry that includes video and mobile games is looking forward for good animators. Some animation institutions appoint students for teaching assistance, so they can take career in teaching profession also. Animators could even find jobs at print media and publishing firms. Freelance work is another option for animators particularly those specialising in web animation.

Career Option

India has over 300 animation studios employing over 12,000 animation professionals. Besides this, Indian companies are creating as number of animated films and cartoons for US and European studios. Therefore, chances for good creative animators never end.

Nature of Work

Creating an animation consists of idea development, pre-production, production and post-production. The characters are created in idea development. In the pre-production, the ideas are converted into layouts. Scriptwriting, storyboarding, character development, backgrounds, layout designing, animatics and voice come under pre-production. The actual result of the story can be visualised in the production stage which is a blend of animation in-betweening or tweening (i.e., the creation of intermediate frames between two main images to give the appearance that the first image flows monthly into the second one), scanning, compositing, i.e., combining images from different sources to create a finished frame of animation, background preparation and colouring. Final sound recordings, color editing, testing and special sound effects are all added at the post-production stage. Post-production stage activities include editing, special effects (SFX), colour correction, compositing, voice and music editing and rendering. Rendering is the final touches to an animation scene in which the data is converted to the raster image or animation.

Remuneration

The good salary is the most attractive part of this profession. Within few years these professionals can earn six-digit salary. As a junior animator or trainee one could get between ₹ 10, 000 to 15, 000 per month. A three to five year experienced animator will get ₹ 25, 000 to 40, 000. And a well-experienced animator who has a good portfolio of excellent animation work could easily get ₹ 50,000 – 60,000 per month.

Top Institutes for Courses in Animation

- **Arena Multimedia, Delhi, Bangalore, Noida and Mumbai**

  Bachelor's course in web and graphic design, film making, audio-visual editing and advertising.

- **Global School of Animation, New Delhi and Chennai**

  Graduate course in creative animation and diploma course in animation design, game programming, game art and design.

- **Maya Academy of Advanced Cinematic (MAAC), Delhi, Mumbai, Pune and Nagpur**

  Undergraduate course in 3-D animation, multimedia, graphics & web designing and certificate course in game art.

- **Tekno Point Multimedia, Mumbai and Bangalore**

  Courses: HTML-5 for beginners, Rich internet application, action script-3.0, Flash builder-4.5, Dreamweaver CS 6, Como TIA CTT+ Classroom training.

- **Picasso Animation College, Delhi, Hyderabad, Ghaziabad, Lucknow, Bangalore, Chandigarh and Udaipur**

  Undergraduate course in multimedia with specialisation in digital film marketing and visual effects and post graduate course in multimedia, pgamma game art, web graphics, pbeta DFM and pexpert max.

- **Massco Media (MM), Noida**

  Post graduate degree course in mass communication, advertising and journalism,

  Diploma in mass communication, advertising and journalism,

Post graduate programme in television production and broadcast, journalism, advertising and event management and corporate communication.

- **Zee Institute of Creative Arts (ZICA), Mumbai**

  Undergraduate course in animation and visual effects, animation film making, film making with visual effects and visual communication.

  Diploma course in animation and visual effects, animation film making, 2-D animation, gaming and graphic designing, web designing.

- **Toonzwebel Academy (TWA), Kolkata, Kerala and Lucknow**

  Diploma courses in 2-D and 3-D animation.

- **Whistling Woods International Institute** (Affiliated to the Deakin and Griffith University, Australia, Bradford College (UK), Syracuse University (US) and New York University).

  Undergraduate course in media and communication and post graduate programmes in media and entertainment.

- **Apeejay Institute of Design, New Delhi**

  Undergraduate programmes in design, multimedia and fine arts, and

  Post Graduate courses in Designing.

Other Institutes that offer Animation

- **RLV (Radha Lakshmi Vilasam) College of Music and Fine Arts** Ernakulum (Kerala),

  Tripunithura, Ernakulum – 682301.

- **Dr. John Matthai Centre: School of Drama and Fine Arts Regional Campus , University of Calicut**

  Aranattukara, Thrissur – 680618.

- **Bhartiya Sangeet Mahavidyalaya, Govt. Hindi Huzrat School** Huzrat Road, Otwali, Gwalior – 474001, Madhya Pradesh.

- **Karnataka University, Pavate Nagar, Dharwad**

  Dharwad – 580003.

- **FLAME School of Performing Arts, Pune**

  150/7,"Jaideep" Prathamesh Park,

  Baner-Balewadi Road, Pune – 411045.

- **Kalai Kiviri College of Fine Arts, Tiruchirappalli**
  18, Benwells Road, Tiruchirappalli – 620001 Tamil Nadu.
- **Capital College of Fine Arts, New Delhi,**
  AD 22A, Power Appt. Outer Ring Road,
  Pitampura, New Delhi – 110088.
- **University of Mumbai: Department of Music, Mumbai**
  Vidyapeeth Vidyarthi Bhavan, 'B' Road,
  Church gate, Mumbai – 400020.
- **Queen Mary's College, Chennai**
  Near MRTS Railway Station, Light House, Opposite Gandhi Statue, Marina, Next to DGP Office, Chennai – 600004.
- **Kurukshetra University, Kurukshetra**
  Kurukshetra – 132119.
- **Sai Nanak College of Music and Performing Arts, Navi Mumbai**
  1st floor, Shiva Sedan, Plot-9a, Opp. Mender, New Yew ale Hosp, 2nd left rd. behind Shari, Sector -9, Vashi, Navi Mumbai – 400705).

There are many institutes in India and abroad that offer graduation and diploma courses in animation besides the online services that offer courses in animation. Several institutes offer placements for their students and institutes like IDC-IIT (Industrial Design Centre, Mumbai) offer students stipend per month for teaching assistance.

8.2 Computer Aided Design (CAD)

What is Computer Aided Design?

A few years back, planning and structural designing of complex buildings, machines etc. were done on drawing boards and paper with various tools like pencil, eraser, compass, scale etc. With the advent of computer technology especially with the software named CAD/CAM, these jobs have become easier and simpler. Computer-Aided Design and Drafting (CADD), most popularly known as Computer- Aided Design is an electronic tool

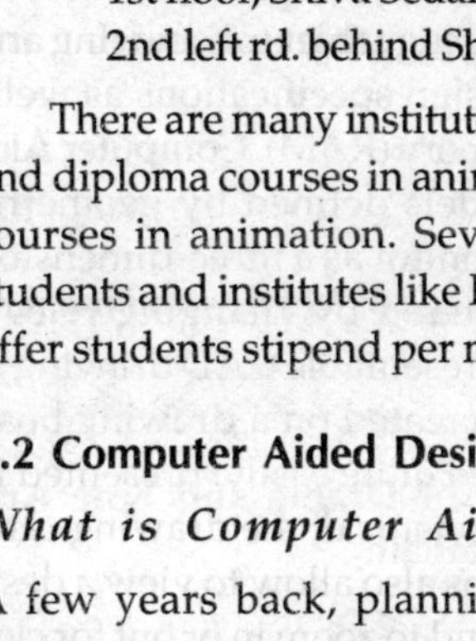

which enables quick and accurate drawing with the use of computer. CAD makes use of computer software programmes, special purpose hardware as well as graphics to generate drawings. CAD software is often referred to as CAD/CAM software. CAM (Computer Aided Manufacturing) is a system of automatically producing finished products by using computer controlled production machines.

A Brief History of Computer Aided Design

Though the world's first Computer Aided Design (CAD) software was developed in the early 1960s, CAD became popular in the beginning of 1980s. It was Ivan Sutherland who developed the first CAD software named '*Sketchpad*' in 1963. But before that in the year 1957, Dr. Patrick J. Hanratty had developed a commercial CAM software system, a numerical control programming tool called '*PRONTO*' and for that reason Dr. Hanratty is known as 'the father of CAD/CAM'.

Creativity, Science and Business are Combined

Creativity, science and business are combined in the CAD fields which are used to design curves and figures in two dimensional (2-D) space or curves, surfaces or solids in three (3-D) objects. In addition to the software, CAD systems require a high quality graphics monitor and graphics card, a mouse, light pen or digitising tablet for drawing and a special printer or plotter for printing design specifications as well as high speed CPU's and large amount of memory (RAM). Computer Aided Design involves creating computer models defined by geometrical parameters that appear on a computer monitor as a three-dimensional representation which can be readily altered by changing relevant parameters. This neat, clean and highly presentable CAD drawing has a number of advantages over drawings created on a drawing board. These electronic drawings can be modified quite easily; presented in a variety of formats and the existing components of the drawing can be rearranged to the new shape. CAD systems also allow to view a design from any angle with the push of a button and to zoom in or out for close-ups and long-distance views. With proper shading and rendering, the models made by CAD can be made to look exactly like pictures.

Usefulness of Computer Aided Design Software

Earlier Computer Aided Design software was used merely by engineers especially architectural engineers and mechanical engineers. With the passage of time, CAD has made its access in all fields where creativity and designing is required. It is widely used for product design in automotive, shipbuilding and aerospace industries, prosthetics (artificial device for replacing missing body parts), industrial and architectural design and even to produce computer animation in movies, advertisements etc. As a result, many new career avenues have been opened in the field of CAD, nowadays this technology is used not only by engineers and architects in their design process but also other design professionals as well.

Application of CAD software

The application of CAD software are mostly allied with engineering fields like architecture, civil, mechanical, automobile, electrical, interior design and related firms. All these fields involves lot of designing and most of the professionals and companies do their designing and drawing with the CAD software. CAD system enable an engineer/designer to develop and convey their ideas on screen, take a print out or save it for future editing and thus save a lot of valuable time on their drawings. It facilitates lower design costs and a shorter design time. Engineers and designers use CAD software programmed in a wide variety of industries to design and manufacture physical products ranging from buildings, bridges, roads, aircraft, ships and cars to digital cameras, mobile phones, televisions etc.

Skilled personnel with outstanding drawing skills and computer knowledge can excel in the field of Computer Aided Design. Professionals working in computer aided designing jobs are usually called CAD operators or Drafters. The major tasks performed by these professionals are evaluating, preparing and producing drawings and designing layout and sketches using computers.

Eligibility and Selection

Many institutes offer exclusive programmes in various CAD/CAE (Computer Aided Engineering) softwares such as Auto CAD, CNC, Pro/E, CATIA (Computer Aided Three dimensional Interstice Application), UG (Unigraphics), etc., as well as Diploma in CAD which covers various computer aided designing concepts and also important CAD software. Eligibility criteria for the CAD courses vary depending on the institutes. but for Diploma course it is usually a Diploma/Degree in mechanical/production/automobile/plastic/electrical engineering. For CAD programmes based on AutoCAD, the eligibility is ITI-D/Man or Diploma/Degree in mechanical/civil/architecture/interior design. Candidates with plus two also have an option for studying engineering drawing with CAD.

To become an expert CAD professional, one should possess graduation in engineering. Some reputed institutes teach CAD software as part of their curriculum along with their four years Bachelor's degree course. CAD programmes are also available as two year post graduate programmes i.e., M.E. or M.Tech in CAD/CAM which focus more specifically on the technical aspects of the discipline. The eligibility for post graduate programme is normally graduation in engineering. Apart from B.Tech./B.E./A.M.I.E., some institutes accept B.Sc. (with mathematics or statistics or computer science or physics as compulsory subject)/B.C.A./bachelor's degree holders in environmental or disaster management/B.A. or B.Sc. (with geography or geology honours) qualified candidates. After PG, one can opt for specialised CAD software, depending on their areas of interest and their profession.

Aspirants should always make sure that the courses offered are accredited programmes that offer the latest in software and equipment. Usually CAD programmes are offered for a short period ranging from three months to six months up to one year. These programmes are designed to provide the basic technical background necessary to produce mechanical drawings using both manual and computer-aided drafting techniques. However, post graduate programme in CAD are of two year duration.

Personal Attributes

Besides educational qualification, one should have thorough knowledge about the field of computers. Drawing skill is an essential attribute needed in the profession of CAD, as it mainly deals with designing layouts and sketches. It is a field which requires the combination of logical thinking, creativity and artistic skills. CAD professionals must possess strong technical, analytical, interpersonal and organisational skills. They must be able to execute all types of 2-D and 3-D design modifications and geometry analysis. In addition to these, candidates should have good mechanical and mathematical skills. As CAD is a technology based field, individuals who have taken CAD as their career has to update their knowledge on regular basis.

Job Prospects and Career Options

CAD is applicable in almost all fields but is extremely valid to the designing fields such as architecture, mechanics, civil, automobile and even interior design. High quality designs and drawings can be made in a very short period of time using the different CAD software. The job prospects of the CAD professional vary on their specialisation in the profession. The major tasks of these people are creating designs or sketches of buildings, structures, machines, cars or any other product as per the requirement of the client with regards to various possible loads and constraints. After making 2-D drawings of buildings/ products and drafting, 3-D modeling is done which helps making the model of the actual building/product. With 3-D models the client can see how the building will look after construction along with all the internal utilities and the external visuals of the building including the colours.

Areas of Specialisation in CAD

Some of the areas of specialisation in the field of Computer Aided Design are :

- **Drafters :** Drafters prepare technical drawings and plans which are used by production and construction workers to build everything from microchips to skyscrapers. They can work with architectural, engineering and related services firms. Depending on their qualifications, Drafters can be classified as;

  Structural Drafter : who support civil engineer and architects.

  Mechanical Drafter : who deals with machinery and mechanical devices.

  Electrical Drafter : who are associated with the electrical distribution system etc.

- **Design Technician :** Design Technicians are individuals who are responsible for the technical aspects of the construction. These people make creative ideas about shape, colour and texture.

- **Engineering Aids :** Engineering Aids wing assists construction engineers in developing final construction plans by preparing lands surveys, maps, sketches, drawings and blueprints. They also estimate costs, perform quality assurance tests on building materials etc.

Depending on the specialisation, job opportunities are available for CAD professionals in manufacturing industries, research and development firms etc. CAD professionals with engineering degrees can find openings in the field of aerospace industries, industrial and architectural design, shipbuilding expertise, automotive industries etc. Opportunities are also available in advertising and films industries where CAD systems are widely used for giving special effects through computer animation. Here one can work as bench animator, motion capture animator, shadier, game design animator or special effects artist. Auto CAD professionals can take up the career in three dimensional design or industrial design. Those people with advanced Auto CAD skills can find employment as a graphic artist, a 3-D modeller, a production artist, a multimedia designer, an architectural or engineering drafts person and more. Teaching is another option, as the number of

CAD/CAM training institutes are coming up. With several years of experience, one can start up their own firm or can work as an independent freelance CAD designer.

Remuneration

The pay scale of CAD degree/diploma holders vary greatly depending on the level of education and experience as well as areas of specialty. In the initial stage a CAD professional can earn not less than ₹ 30,000 per month. Depending on the organisation and candidate's skills, within a short period of time, the salary may rise to ₹ 40,000 to 45,000.

Courses

There are many CAD programmes available in the industry for designing and sketching purpose. These programmes can assist to execute 2-D drawings, 3-D drawings, renderings, shadings, engineering calculations, space planning, structural design, piping layouts, plan design, project management etc. Some among the CAD softwaresare AutoCAD (1982) and Autodesk Inventor (1999) from AutoDesk, Uni-Solid from Unigraphics, CATIA (Dassault Systems), Pro/Engineer (PTC), Mechanical Desktop, SolidEorks (1995), Ansys, Ideas, Adina etc. With advanced CAD programmes, one can create animated images. The courses available in this field are :

- AutoCAD Training,
- CATIA,
- Certificate Course in Coral Draw,
- M.E. Computer Aided Design (CAD),
- M. Tech. Computer Aided Design (CAD/CAM), and
- Unigraphics.

Institutes in India

- **Computer Aided Design Centre, Kolkata, West Bengal**

  Course : Certificate Course in AutoCAD with AutoLISP.

- **E-Mumbai, Maharashtra**

  Course : Diploma in AutoCAD Engg. and Development.

- **CADCAMGURU Institute, Pune, Maharashtra**

  Course : Certificate Course in AutoCAD.

Institutes Abroad

- **College of Electrical Training (CET), Australia**
  Course : Introduction to AutoCAD.
- **Alliance Learning, United Kingdom**
  Courses : AutoCAD Foundation Certificate.
  AutoCAD Intermediate and Advance Certificate.
- **Buckinghamshire Hew University, United Kingdom**
  Course : 3-D AutoCAD.
- **Cavendish College, United Kingdom**
  Courses : AutoCAD 2008 Beginners.
  AutoCAD 2008 Intermediate Certificate.
- **City University, United Kingdom**
  Course : Advanced AUTOCAD (Credit Bearing).

8.3 Graphic Designing

What is Graphic Design?

Graphic Design is a process of visual communication which combines words, images and ideas to present the information to the audience. Graphic Design in simple words, deals with aesthetically creating visual designs with the aid of computer to convey a message to the viewers. In other words, Graphic Design is an artistic and professional discipline that focuses on visual communication and presentation toward the goal of delivering a message or creating a product. Graphic Design is a part of marketing campaign that involves visual communication. Graphic design attempts to transmit specific messages by means of appropriate visual material. These messages may be aimed at projecting a certain image of an organisation, transmitting information or promoting a service or product.

Who are Graphic designers?

Graphic designers or graphic artists plan, analyse and create visual solution to communication problems. Graphic designer is a person in the graphic arts who puts together art, text and other visuals to produce professional printed results. Graphic designers influence how we view the world using colors, illustrations, photos and fonts. A graphic designer creates the graphics primarily for published, printed or electronic media. Graphic designers develop the layout and production design of newspaper, magazines, corporate reports, journals and other publications. They also design the logos, packaging and promotional material that give companies and their products a distinctive identity.

Eligibility

A Bachelor's degree in graphic design or fine arts is usually required for most entry-level and advanced graphic design positions Bachelor's degree programmes in fine arts or graphic design are offered to many colleges, universities and private design schools. Bachelor's degree course is of three-years duration and eligibility is 10+2 with a creative bent of mind. There is one-year Diploma in visual communication. There are also two-years and 1-year programme for the candidates who have attained 18 years and with 10+2 education.

Personal Attributes

Creativity is very important factor for a career in design. The more creative a person is, the farther he will go in this field. Graphic designers must possess a combination of skills including technical, computer and design skills and the ability to detain audience. The abilities to work independently and under pressure are equally important traits. Graphic designers must be open to new ideas and influences and quick to react to changing trends.

Job Prospects and Career Option

Graphic designing as a career is the right choice if you love to draw and sketch. Graphic design is globally universal skill. Therefore, it is possible for you to work all over the world. Due to tremendous growth of the media industry there is excellent employment options in this career area. There are a variety of graphic design jobs for those interested in this field. You have the freedom to choose which area of graphic design you'd like to pursue based on your talent. Graphic design career opportunities include: creative directors, layout artist, flash designer, web designer, multi-media designer, logo designer, brand identity designer, prepress technician etc.

- **Creative Director/Art Director :** Creative Directors are hired by different types of media outlets – particularly advertising agencies, magazines, newspapers and television networks. An Art director manages the team that consists of artists, graphic designers, photographers, copywriters and production staff. These people are the ones who do a lot of the less creative work in a design studio.

- **Layout artist :** They are in charge with the structure and layout of images and text for print media such as magazine works, flyers, posters etc. They are required to have knowledge and experience in using various computer software like Adobe Illustrator, Adobe Photoshop and Macromedia Freehand. Employment opportunities for layout can be found with advertising agencies, magazine and newspapers, public relations firms and manufacturers. There is also a strong demand for freelance layout artists or in-house layout artists.
- **Brand identity designer :** In large cities, graphic designers can find employment with a company as a brand identity designer. Brand identity designers are responsible for developing products and promotional materials that will mould how the company is viewed by the public. A company's brand identity can be represented in terms of design through a unique logo, or signage. Brand identity design is what helps consumers remember the company and often what brings them back. The right brand identity design can be one of the company's strongest marketing tools as it translates the values and strategic vision of a company into a consistent image that consumers become familiar with.
- **Logo designer :** Many graphic designers specialise in logo production. They are hired by companies to produce signage, in-office products and even marketing and promotional materials. A logo is a brand identity image, or a tag of a company or product. A logo is a tangible concept that provides a company with a visual image and that fosters recognition by consumers. Similar to the brand identity designer, a logo designer works to mould the company's public image using colour, type and graphics.
- **Flash designer :** Some graphic designers design and create web sites. They use flash animations, one of the trendiest technologies used in web design, to design unique applications for company websites. A flash designer creates interactive movies using customised effects on text, navigation, animation and video.
- **Illustrators :** Illustrators conceptualise and create illustrations that represent an idea or a story through two-dimensional or three-dimensional images. As an illustrator, you may find employment with magazines, periodicals, book and software publishers, manufacturers or working with various types of electronic media. There are also opportunities in the motion picture and video industries and computer game design industry

as well. They work as freelance illustrators and do work in several of these industries on a contract basis.

- **Web designer :** A graphic designer who specialises in coding can work as a web page or website designer. A web designer creates pages, layout and graphics for web pages. Their main task is to create an aesthetically pleasing and user friendly site. As a web designer, you will make decisions regarding what content is included on a web page, where things are placed and how the aesthetic and continuity is maintained from one screen to the next.
- **Multimedia designer :** A multimedia designer produces sketches, scale models, drawings or plans. He can explore careers in the field of television, audio or film production as well as set or production design. He can find employment with film studios, television stations, advertising agencies and video production houses. You may also be able to work with live productions such as live theater and live concerts.
- **Prepress technician :** Graphic designers are often employed as prepress technicians for magazines and newspapers. Prepress technicians are responsible for several tasks before publications go to print – such as checking for text, layout and other errors, colors and graphic placement, and more. Prepress technicians also find work in desktop publishing. Job prospects in prepress area available in several industries such as traditional printing and publishing, advertising, public relations, graphic design and business.

The career of graphic designer is an exciting one that has many different opportunities from working for a major corporation to owning your own online graphic design business. The graphic designers get a wide scope in creative media such as electronic media, packaging, film and animation, advertising agencies, marketing firms, design studios, educational institutes, printers and typesetters, exhibits and displays, audio-visual media, publishers, manufacturers and department stores. This is really a flexible career. You can work from the comfort of your own home and you can even use your skills in design to accomplish business projects.

Remuneration

Salaries for Graphic designers vary upon their level of responsibility, experience, training and the industry in which they work. Starting pay for freshers is about ₹ 7,000 to ₹ 10,000. With experience and ability, salary increases. Those with creativity, salary is not a constraint. On an average the salaries of the candidates for the job of graphic designer vary between ₹ 1,25, 000 to 3,00,000 per annum.

Best Institutes for Graphic Designing in India

- **National Institute of Computer Arts, Mumbai, Maharashtra**
  Course : Certificate Course in Graphic Designing.
- **National Institute of Design, Ahmedabad, Gujarat**
  Courses : Post Graduate Diploma Programme in Design in Graphic Design.
  Post Graduate Diploma Programme in Design-Transportation and Automobile Design.
- **The Academy of Animation and Gaming, Gurgaon, Haryana**
  Course : Graphic Design.
- **Jaspal Bhatti Film School, Mohali, Punjab**
  Course : Certificate Course in Graphic Designing.
- **Raffles Millennium International (Design), New Delhi**
  Courses : Bachelor of Design (Graphic Design),
  Bachelor of Design (Product Design).
- **Varia Design, Ahmdabad, Gujarat**
  Course : Certificate Course in Graphic Design.
- **Sumeru Academy of Digital Arts, Pune, Maharashtra**
  Course : Certificate Course in Graphic Designing.
- **International Institute of Creative Courses, Ranchi, Jharkhand**
  Course : Diploma in Graphic Design.

8.4 Web Development

What is Web Development?

Web development is a broad term for the work involved in developing a website for the Internet (World Wide Web) or an intranet (a private network). Web development covers all the people who plan, build and manage a website. The web development process includes web design, web content development, client-side/server-side scripting and network security configuration, among other tasks. However, web development more specifically refers to non-design aspect of building a website, i.e., writing mark-up and coding.

Who are the developers?

Those who are professionally qualified to develop a website are known as web developers. A web developer is a programmer who specialises in or is specifically engaged in the development of World Wide Web applications. A web developer is the architect of a website, creating the foundation upon which designers and content editors apply their work. A web developer uses software, computer languages and other tools to make a website look, act and feel the way a user needs and expects. A web developer is responsible for programming the functionality of a web site. In short, it is the web developer who plans and programmes a website.

Eligibility

As far as the skills needed, a web developer needs to gain some expertise in mark-up language, more specifically HTML, XML (extensible Markup language), XHTML and server side scripting languages such as ASP (Active Server Pages from Microsoft), PHP (Hypertext Preprocessor which is an open source language) and style sheet language which is used to style documents written in mark-up languages such as Cascading Style Sheet, simply known as CSS. Programming expertise is also important for those aiming for top developers' jobs. Understanding of some graphic packages such as Illustrator, Photoshop, Flash and Dreamweaver is important, since its application is heavy in web image processing and optimisation. As in any of the other IT professions, Web developers must also continually keep updating their skills.

Job Prospects

With the growing number of internet users and the subsequent increase in the number of websites have resulted in the high demand for qualified web development professionals in India as well as abroad. Their skills and services are in demand in all sectors. Web developers are looked for not only to create a new website, they are also associated with the maintenance and up gradation of existing websites.

Work environments for web developers vary widely, from large corporations or governments to small businesses. In larger organisations, web development team consists of more than one developer, whereas in small concerns there can be only a single web developer or web master. Web developers are employed across all industrial sectors from finance and retail to public organisations. They may be employed directly by IT consultancies, software houses, web design agencies or work in an organisation's IT department. Advertising agencies, web portals, online gaming companies, media outlets, marketing firms and in-house corporate communications departments are some other places where web developers find employment. Developers may be full-time employees, part-time consultants or work on a contract basis as freelancers.

Remuneration

Web developer salaries in India vary by experience, technical skill, job role and the company they are employed in. Web developers can get a starting pay of ₹ 30,000 – 40,000 per month. Some experience along with good creative skills can earn him a salary as high as ₹ 75,000 or even more. In the US, some of the highest paying states for Web developers are New Jersey, California, District of Columbia and New York.

Courses

- B.Tech./M.Tech. Computer Science and Engineering,
- M.E. Computer Science and Engineering,
- M. E. Computer Science and Information Technology,
- M. Tech. Computer Science and Information Technology,
- Master of Computer Application (MCA),
- Advance Diploma in Software and Web Development (ADSWD),
- Web Development Programme, and
- Master of Computer Application (MCA) (Correspondence/ Distance Education).

Best Colleges for Web Design and Development

- **Raffles Design Institute, Mumbai, Maharashtra**

  Course : Bachelor of Design (Multimedia Design).
- **Raffles Millennium International (Design), New Delhi**

  Courses : Bachelor of Design (Multimedia Design),

  Bachelor of Design (Graphic Design).
- **IMS DIA Design and Innovation Academy, Noida, Uttar Pradesh**

  Courses : B.Sc. in Multimedia and Animation,

  Diploma in Multimedia and Animation.

- **TGC Animation and Multimedia, New Delhi**

  Courses : Advanced Certification in Web Design and Interactive Multimedia,

  Advanced Certification in PHP.
- **WLC College India, New Delhi**

  Courses : Bachchor in Graphic Design,

  Post Graduate Level-Visual Communication.
- **Ramgarhia Girls College, Ludhiana, Punjab**

  Courses : Diploma in Web Designing and Multimedia.

  Certificate Course in Web Designing and Multimedia.
- **Dev Samaj College for Women, Chandigarh, Punjab**

  Course : Certificate Course in Web Design and Multimedia.
- **Apeejay College of Fine Arts, Jalandhar, Punjab**

  Course : Bachelor of Multimedia.
- **Asian Academy of Film and Television, Noida, Delhi-NCR**

  Course : Certificate Course in Internet and Web Design.
- **Digikore College of Animation and Design, Pune, Maharashtra**

  Diploma in Advertising and Design (Print, Web and Multimedia).
- **Government Polytechnic College, Ghaziabad, Delhi-NCR**

  Post Graduate Diploma in Web Designing.
- **Government Polytechnic College, Jhansi, Uttar Pradesh**

  Post Graduate Diploma in Web Designing.
- **National Trust of Education and Management (NTEM), Bhubaneshwar, Orissa**

  Course : Certificate Course in Web Designing.
- **Don Bosco IGACT, Cochin, Kerala**

  Course : Diploma in Web Design and Animation.
- **Madras Christian College, Chennai, Tamil Nadu**

  Bachelor of Science (Visual Communication).

8.5 VLSI/Chip Designing

What is VLSI/Chip Designing?

VLSI means '*Very Large Scale Integration*'. It is all about Integrated Circuit (IC) design. Usually we call it as 'Chip Design'. Integrated circuits

of IC chips are semi-conductors which contain numerous pathways, which connect thousands or even millions of transistors and other electronic components. Integrated circuit design or IC design is a subset of electrical engineering and computer engineering, encompassing the particular logic and circuit design techniques required to design integrated circuits or ICs. In IT parlance, the chip is the wafer thin slice of silicon that forms the base for an integrated circuit.

Engineering students who want something more challenging and creative than a routine software job can choose this field. Electronics students who are good at programming with strong mathematical and analytical background are well suited for this career area. Chip design is a field with continuous changing technology which envisages the need for constant technological and innovational up gradation. Hence, one must continue studying as a continuous process, to keep up with the ever changing scenario.

The Role of Chip Designers

Chip designers are basically design engineers who define the chip's architecture, create circuit designs, run simulations, supervise layout, tape out the chip to the foundry and evaluate the prototype once the chip comes back from the laboratory. Chip designers work to make faster, cheaper and more innovative chips that can automate parts or the entire function of electronic devices. A chip designer's job ranges right from the architecture, logic design, circuit design and physical design of the chip to the testing and verification for the final product. So, a chip architect visualises the product, do complete research or study about it, measure the cost against estimated markets for the chip. The two popular languages being used today for chip designing are ***Verilog*** and ***VHDL***.

The Need for Chip Design

There is a great potential for Chip Design. There is a demand for chips in every sector, be it automobiles, consumer electronics or high-end servers. In our daily life, too, the role of these chips are very significant. Chips are present in most of the electronic appliances which we use every day from mobiles, remote of TV to dishwashers and so on.

Eligibility

An entry-level engineer in IC design must possess a least a B.E. or Bachelor of Technology in electronics, telecommunications or computer science. You could either go for M.Tech. or PG in the subject or take up short-term courses. At times chip design is offered as a subject along with Electronics Engineering. Apart from IC-related knowledge, one should also have knowledge of assembly level programming and 'C' programming.

Job Prospects

At present, India has huge potential in the market. India's chip industry is growing at a rate of 20 per cent annually. There are over 160 chip design firms in India. The vast pool of talent and growing domestic market has helped the country emerge as an important centre for chip design. The increasing demand for consumer electronic items has opened up a range of career opportunities in chip design industry.

Some of the major recruiters are Texas Instruments (TI), PMC Sierra, Alliance Semiconductor, Analog Devices, Cadence, Synopsys, Cypress Semiconductor, HCL Technologies, Intel, Micron Tech, Philips Semiconductor, Qualcomm, Wipro, e-Infochips etc.

Career Options

The main job functions in this industry are :

- **Design Engineer :** He takes specifications, defines architecture, does circuit design, provides consultancy for layout, tapes out the chip to the foundry and evaluates the prototype once the chip comes back from the lab.
- **Product Engineer :** He is responsible for production release and is therefore regarded as a team leader of the project. He ensures manufacturability, develops characterisation plan, assembly guidelines, quality and reliability plan. He evaluates from the point of view (statistical analysis), the chip with the design and verification engineer, through characterisation from the reliability qualification and manufacturing yield.
- **Test Engineer :** He develops test plan for the chip based on specifications and data sheet, creates characterisation and production programme for the bench test or the ATE (Automatic Test Equipment), designs test board hardware, correlates ATE results with the bench results to validate silicon to compare with simulation results. The work of Product and Test engineers are interdependent. Test engineer work closely with product engineer to ensure smooth release to production and post release support.

- **Applications/Systems Engineer :** He defines new products from system designed or used by the customers and complies with appropriate standards.
- **Process Engineer :** This is a highly specialised function which involves new wafer process development, device modeling and lots of research and development projects.
- **Packaging Engineer :** This is another highly specialised job function generally part of system engineering team. He develops precision packaging technology; new package designs for chips, does the characterisation of new packages and does electrical modeling of the new designs.
- **CAD Engineer :** This is an engineering function that supports the design engineering function. He is responsible for acquiring, maintaining and or developing all CAD tools used by all other engineers. He is supposed to evaluate and integrate new tools in the company specific flow.

Remuneration

Salaries and remuneration paid are also one of the highest in the industry. The starting pay for a fresher is ₹ 4,00,000 upwards per annum with the variation depending on the nature of the organisation and competency level of the candidate. Salaries keep pace with experience and within three years, deserving VLSI professionals are known to earn ₹ 75,000 – 1, 00,000 per month.

Courses

- M.E. VLSI Design,
- M.E. Embedded System Technology,
- M.E. Embedded System,
- M. Tech. Embedded System Technology,
- M. Tech. Embedded System Design,
- M. Tech. Microelectronics and VLSI Design,
- M. Tech. VLSI Design,
- M. Tech. VLSI Design and Embedded System,
- Post Graduate Diploma in VLSI and Embedded System, and
- Post Graduate Diploma in VLSI Design (Correspondence/ Distance Education).

Few Embedded Systems and VLSI Design Colleges in India

- Alpha College of Engineering, Doddagubbi, Bangalore.

- Azad College of Engineering and Technology, Hyderabad.
- B.S. Abdur Rahman Engineering College, Vandular, Chennai.
- Ballari Institute of Technology and Management, Bellary.
- Bangalore Institute of Technology, Basavanagudi, Bangalore.
- BNM Institute of Technology, Banashankari IInd Stage, Bangalore.
- Chaitanya Bharathi Institute of Technology, Gandipet, Hyderabad.
- CMR Institute of Technology, Marathalhalli, Bangalore.
- Dhole Patil College of Engineering, Wagholi, Pune.
- Dr Ambedkar Institute of Technology, Vishwavidyalaya, Bangalore.
- Greater Noida Institute of Technology, Greater Noida, Delhi.
- Guru Gobind Singh Indraprastha University, Dwarka, Delhi.
- IES College of Technology, Bhopal.
- International Institute of Information Technology, Gachibowli, Hyderabad.

9

ENGINEERING

What is Engineering?

Engineering is the science of applying scientific and mathematical principles, experience, judgment and common sense to produce things that engenders comfort and benefit to people. Engineers design bridges, roads, railways, dams, harbours, etc., and life-saving medical equipments, as well as the processes for cleaning up toxic spills and systems for mass transit. In other words, engineering is the process of producing a product or system.

According to the Annual Report of ABET (Accreditation Board of Engineering and Technology) of USA in 1982 defined Engineering as, *"The profession in which a knowledge of the mathematical and natural sciences gained by study, experience and practice is applied with judgement to develop ways to utilise, economically, the materials and forces of nature for the benefit of mankind."* Engineering is therefore an art of applying scientific and mathematical principles, experience, judgement and common sense to make things that benefit people. It involves planning, designing and executing structural works. The profession deals with a wide variety of engineering tasks including designing, supervision and construction activities of public works like roads, bridges, tunnels, building, airports, dams, water works, sewage systems, ports, etc., and offers a multitude of challenging career opportunities.

Who should go for Engineering?

People who have a flair for science and have a strong proclivity for innovating new gadgets, instruments, equipments, etc., are eligible for studies in engineering. Mere acquisition of BE/B.Tech. degree is not enough. Engineering is a life-long education and engineers shall continue to keep abreast with the technology and contribute towards technological advancement.

A person must demonstrate the following characteristics in order to become a true engineer :

- An ability to apply knowledge of mathematics, science and engineering;
- An ability to design and conduct experiments, as well as to analyse and interpret data;
- An ability to design a system, component or process to meet desired needs;
- An ability to function on multi-disciplinary teams;
- An ability to identify, formulate and solve engineering problems;
- An understanding of professional and ethical responsibility;
- An ability to communicate effectively;
- The broad education necessary to understand the impact of engineering solutions in a global and societal context;
- Recognition of the need for and an ability to engage in life-long learning;
- Knowledge of contemporary issues; and
- An ability to use the techniques, skills and modern engineering tools necessary for engineering practice.

What are the different stages of Engineering Education in India?

- **Post-Matric Technical Education :** Diploma level courses are meant for the training of middle level man-power needed for a wide range of professional duties for application of knowledge in field operation, in production and construction, testing and development, etc., and such functions are offered in 291 Polytechnic institutions with an annual enrollment capacity of about 50,000 students. They offer a variety of specialisation in engineering and technology as well as in a few non-technological fields. The courses are normally of three years duration where full-time institutional instruction is offered and three and half to four years when instruction is on a sandwich or on part-time basis. Recently a number of diversified courses and facilities for evening part-time education have also been provided in some polytechnics situated in metropolitan cities where the demand for such courses exists.

About two dozen women polytechnics with courses of special interest to, and employment potential for women have also been established particularly to cater to the needs of the socially and economically inhibited classes who might be reluctant to take advantage of the facilities generally available in the regular polytechnics.

The products of the diploma courses are expected to take up supervisory positions in field and industry.

- **Degree Level:** For the professional engineers and technologists, facilities for technical education are available in 1200+ engineering colleges offering courses leading to the award of Bachelor's degree in engineering and technology. The total admission capacity annually for these courses is of the order of 200,000. Duration of most of these degree courses was initially five years and with the new pattern of secondary education of 10+2, change over completely by 1981-82 to a duration of four years (except architecture).
- **Post Graduate Courses:** For the benefit of those who have higher level academic achievements as also for undertaking research and development activities in engineering and technology, post graduate courses have been offered widely in the various selected institutions offering degree courses. The number of the institutions offering such post graduate courses is about 100 with an annual intake capacity of about 2,000 plus. These courses normally lead to the master's degree in the concerned discipline and are of two years/one and half-year duration. Facilities also exist at these centers offering part-time courses at the Post-graduate level for those who are already in service. Duration of such courses normally is three years.

Institutional Framework

Vocational Training/Craftsman courses are offered at the Industrial Training Institutes. The diploma courses are offered in the polytechnics which are widely spread over all the states and union territories and are affiliated to the respective State Boards of Technical Education who lay down in general the levels and standards of the courses and guide the system of evaluation of the students appearing at the examination. Degree and postgraduate courses are offered in colleges affiliated to the various universities, certain university departments and institutions declared as of national importance or as deemed universities.

- **Indian Institutes of Technology** : These are the apex institutions for engineering education and research. Each Institute conducts a first degree course and master's degree course in a wide range of subject fields and also offers facilities for research and doctoral works. The main emphasis at the institutes is on the post graduate studies and research with an inter-disciplinary approach. To this end each institute has developed good departments of physics, chemistry, mathematics and social sciences which interact with the departments of engineering and technology. The student enrolment at the institutes at the undergraduate level is limited to 1250 and admission at the postgraduate level is designedly kept at about the same order as in the under-graduate courses. The institutes are in various stages of consolidation and development. As part of the national plan of science and technology, five centers of advanced study and research have been set up in the Indian Institutes of Technology in Energy Studies (Delhi), Material Science (Kanpur), Cryogenic Engineering (Kharagpur), Ocean Engineering (Madras) and Resource Engineering (Bombay).
- **Indian Institute of Science, Bangalore:** The Indian Institute of Science, Bangalore is the oldest and leading post graduate and research centre in science and engineering and has facilities in special fields which include electronics and communication engineering, aeronautical engineering, heat and power engineering, high voltage engineering, power engineering, biochemistry, chemistry, physics and mathematics. A major centre in automation and control systems and another in electronics design technology are in the process of establishment.
- **The National Institutes of Technology (NITS):** The National Institutes of Technology (NITS) is an engineering, science, technology and management school system in India comprising 30 autonomous institutions located in one each major state/territory of India. Since their inception decades ago, all NITS were referred as Regional Engineering Colleges (RECs) and governed by their respective state governments. A parliamentary legislation in 2002 brought them under the direct purview of India's federal government. In 2007, through legislation, the Indian government declared these schools as Institutes of national importance at par with the indian Institutes of Technology. NITs were founded to promote regional diversity

and multi-cultural understanding in India. Therefore, in the NIT school system, half of the student population in each batch is drawn from the respective state of the NIT and the other half is drawn from the rest of India on a common merit list. This is different from the Indian Institutes of Technology or IITs. An IIT need not accept specified number of students from any region of India as the IIT admission criteria is based only on the performance of a student in an entrance examination. NITs offer degree courses at bachelor's, master's and doctorate levels in various branches of engineering and technology. Various nationwide college curves rate most of the NITs over other colleges in India, except for the IITs and a few other institutions. NITs function autonomously, similarly to IITs, sharing only entrance tests. The autonomy enables the NITs to set up their own curriculum, thereby making it easier to adapt to changing industry requirements.

- **State Colleges and University Departments :** In addition to the above institutions offering courses at degree and postgraduate level, there is a wide network of engineering colleges established and administered by the state governments, universities and private agencies; they are also affiliated to the respective universities and offer degree courses in a variety of subject fields. Some of them are more than a century old and have been pioneers in engineering education in the country. Many of these state colleges and university departments are making significant contribution in the field of technical education.

Why should you choose Engineering as a career?

Engineering is one of the most versatile professions one can opt for as a career. Engineering degree is so versatile that you can enter any area of economy whether it is banking, administrative service, tourism, defence service and many more in addition to mainstream engineering profession. Unlike other professions, knowledge of the nature of engineering and the role of engineersis concerned with the design and production of so many objects, devices and systems which are an integral part of our environment and day-to-day life. These systems are as vital to society as are our school, health care and legal system. Engineers probably have a wider choice of environment in which to work and a greater variety of jobs, than is possible in any other profession.

The purpose of engineering is to design and manufacture the hardware of life and make it comfortable. Form bicycle to aeroplane; to television to computer; all add to the quality of life we are living today. Moreover, engineering profession is rewarding – socially as well as economically. There is a record of two million engineers in the United States, making the engineering profession the second largest in the nation.

How to become an engineer in Indian?

To become an engineer, one has to acquire a qualification in engineering from any of the recognised institution. As discussed earlier there are three levels of engineering courses available at engineering institutions in the country.

- Degree (BE/B.Tech.) and postgraduate degree courses offered by engineering colleges (both in government and private sector), universities, National Institute of Technology (NIT) and Indian Institute of Technology (IIT).
- Diploma courses offered by polytechnics.
- Training in engineering skills offered by Industrial Training Institutes (ITI).

Over and above the BE/B.Tech. programmes conducted by engineering colleges/NITs/IITs and other central institutes, there are professional bodies recognised by the Government of India to award AMIE (Associate Member of Institution of Engineers) equivalent to any degree in engineering to cater mainly to working people in the private and public sectors. Students who cannot join an engineering college due to any reason can complete a diploma in engineering from any of the polytechnics and then join an engineering college through lateral entry scheme or can complete AMIE to become equivalent to a BE/ B.Tech degree holder in engineering.

To join an engineering college in our country, a student has to opt for science stream after matriculation, i.e., plus 2 Science with subjects such as physics, chemistry, mathematics, computer science, biology, biotechnology and engineering drawing etc. Though majority of the branches of engineering colleges needs mathematics, physics and chemistry as compulsory subjects at (10+2) level, some of the branches also admit students having mathematics and physics as compulsory subject and any one of chemistry/computer science/ biology/ biotechnology/ engineering drawing as the third subject.

A science student after completing B.Sc. with major in physics/ chemistry/mathematics can also join any of the three years B. Tech. programme in engineering offered by some institutions/universities. Moreover, students can also complete M.Sc. in electronics/radio physics/information technology, etc., and join the engineering profession. However, entering the engineering college after (10+2) and acquiring the B.Tech./BE to join the engineering profession is the most popular route to become an engineer.

9.1 Aeronautical Engineering

What is an Aeronautical or Aerospace Engineering?

Aeronautical or Aerospace Engineering is a challenging field that deals with the development of new technology in the area of aviation, space exploration and defense systems. It specialises in the designing, construction, development, testing, operation and maintenance of both commercial and military aircraft, spacecrafts and their components as well as satellites and missiles. As aerospace engineering involves design and manufacture of very high technology systems, the job requires manual, technical as well as mechanical aptitude.

The Role of Aeronautical Engineers

Aeronautical Engineers usually work in teams under the supervision of senior engineers, bringing together their skills and technical expertise. Though highly paid, the work is very demanding. An aeronautical engineer needs to be physically fit and fully dedicated to his work. One needs to be alert, have an eye for detail and should have a high level of mathematical precision to be successful.

Specialisation in the field

The specialisation includes areas like structural design, navigational guidance and control systems, instrumentation and communication or production methods or it can be in a particular product such as military aircrafts, passenger planes, helicopters, satellites, rockets etc. Engineers may work in areas like design, development, maintenance as well as in the managerial and teaching posts in institutes. They find a very good demand in airlines, aircrafts manufacturing units, air turbine production plants or design development programmes for the aviation industry. Aerospace environment is sophisticated with rewarding career opportunities involving leading-edge technology.

Eligibility

To be an aeronautical engineer one should have a graduate degree (BE/ B.Tech.) or at least a diploma in Aeronautics. The degree and post graduate degree courses are offered by the engineering colleges and Institutes of Technology (IITs) and the diploma courses are available at polytechnics.

The basic eligibility criteria for a BE/B.Tech. is 10+2 or equivalent examination with physics, chemistry and mathematics and must have a fairly high percentage of marks in the aggregate. One must also pass the qualifying examination-JEE (Joint Entrance Examination) conducted by the IITs.

Selection

Selection to the graduate courses (BE/B. Tech) is based on merit *i.e.* the marks secured in the final exams of 10+2 and through entrance exams. Entrance to the IITs is through 'JEE' and for other institutions through their own separate entrances examinations and other state level and national level examinations. Most of the institutes conducting engineering courses in Aeronautics consider JEE score as the qualifying grade.

There is also the Associate Membership Examination of the Institute of Engineers (AMIE), which enables working people in the private and public sector or diploma holders to acquire a bachelor's engineering degree through distance education by studying the syllabus and appearing for the Associate Membership examination of the Institute of Engineers (AMIE) conducted by ASI (The Aeronautical Society of India). This degree is equivalent to aeronautical engineering degree. Those with a degree in electronics, mathematics or physics can also find opportunities in this area.

Some institutes offer post graduate (M.Tech.) and doctoral (Ph.D.) programmes in Aeronautics. The Madras Institute of Technology offers a three years Graduate programme in aeronautical engineering for B.Sc. students, subject to their having passed mathematics and physics at the graduation stage. The Indian Institute of Science (IIS), Bangalore has M.Tech and Ph.D. programmes in Aeronautics.

Duration

The duration is four years, ending with a degree recognised by the Ministry of Education, Government of India. The diploma courses are of two-three years duration.

Personal Skills

Aeronautical engineers should have an eye for detail and be good at problem-solving. They need mathematical precision and design skills, computer skills and the ability to communicate well. They also need good planning ability and a knack for working under pressure. An aeronautical engineer needs to be physically fit and may need to often work at great speed especially in checking and maintenance of aircrafts during turnarounds. They must have a normal colour vision.

Job Prospects and Career Options

Aeronautical Engineers work with one of the most technologically advanced branches of engineering. The main thrust in this area is on design and development of aircrafts to space and satellite research. Jobs are available with the national, international, public and private airline services as well as aircraft-manufacturing units.

Job opportunities for an Aeronautical Engineer in India lies with various airlines like Air India, Indian Airlines, Helicopter Corporation of India and flying clubs, private airlines and government owned air service and aircraft manufacturers like the Hindustan Aeronautics Ltd. (HAL) with its factories at Bangalore, Nashik, Koraput, Kanpur, etc., Defence Research and Development Laboratories, National Aeronautical Lab (NAL), Aeronautical Development Establishment, Civil Aviation Department etc. The Defence services and Indian Space Research Organisation (ISRO) also happen to be two major employers.

Career Options

Initially, candidates begin to work as graduate engineer trainees or junior engineers. Keeping in view their performance, academic background and aptitude, they are placed for training in the aircraft maintenance/ overhaul or support section. On completion of training they are placed as assistant aircraft engineers or assistant technical officers. They have to clear departmental examinations for further promotions. They may advance to administrative or executive positions or become consultants. Aeronautical engineers are assisted by aircraft mechanics in maintenance of aircraft frame, engine, electrical system and other ancillary fittings.

Remuneration

Engineers in government organisations are paid official scales while those in the private sector are paid according to the scales decided by the management of the company. The approximate starting salaries in the government / public sectors such as HAL, NAL are ₹ 8,000 to ₹ 10,000 (excluding other allowances). In the private sector, the scales are decided by the management of the company and are approximately ₹ 8,000 to 15,000 per month plus perks. Engineering graduates with management degrees get a starting pay of ₹ 10,000 to 40,000 per month plus perks. Entrepreneurs get fringe benefits of free travel for self and family also, apart from numerous other perks.

Institutes

Some of the outstanding institutes that offer Aeronautical Engineering are Indian Institute of Technology in Chennai, Mumbai, Kanpur and Kharagpur and also by the Punjab Engineering College, Chandigarh. The Madras Institute of Technology offers a three years graduate programme in Aeronautical Engineering for B.Sc. students, subject to their having passed mathematics and physics at the graduation stage. The Indian Institute of Science (IIS), Bangalore has M.Tech. and Ph.D. programmes in Aeronautics. Some other institutes are :

- **Hindustan Institute of Engineering Technology**
  40 GST Road, P.B. No. 1306
  St. Thomas Mount, Chennai-600016
  Tamil Nadu.
- **Nehru College of Aeronautical and Applied Sciences,**
  Coimbatore, Tamil Nadu.
- **Indian Institute of Aeronautical Engineering**
  179, Kalidas Road, Dehradun-248001
  Uttaranchal.
- **Hindustan Electronics Academy**
  61, Cambridge Road
  P.B. No. 806, Ulsoor, Bangalore-560008
  Karnataka.
- **Institute of Aviation Technology**
  1265, Sector 6, Bahadurgarh,
  Haryana-124507.
- **Indian Institute of Aeronautics**
  Patna Airport
  Patna-800014, Bihar.

9.2 Architectural Engineering

Meaning of Architecture?

Architecture, the science of building, is the visualisation of building blocks. It is the area of study which deals with the designing and planning of buildings and structures and the spaces between them. Architecture is a highly competitive and multi-disciplinary profession which involves a variety of tasks at work. This is a field which covers various fields including spatial design, aesthetics, safety management, material management etc.

Who are Architects?

Architects are licensed professionals trained in the art and science of building. They are involved in all the phases of the building construction, i.e., the functional, safety, economical and have to satisfy the needs of its occupants. They are responsible persons for the planning, designing and supervision of construction works for houses, office buildings, skyscrapers, landscapes and even entire cities. An Architect is a combination of artist, professional and businessperson. They ideate, sketch, make blueprints of their designs and then sees them come to life as cottages, skyscrapers and even monuments. Apart from designing and construction, architects are trained in activities ranging from conceptual problem solving to project management.

One can rise to a successful position in the field through talent and hard work. Success in this competitive profession is measured by the size of responsibility entrusted to an individual, an invitation to partnership in a firm or ideally, a well-established private practice.

Eligibility and Course Areas

A Bachelor's degree in Architecture (B. Arch.) or Diploma in architecture is needed to become a qualified architect. For practical purposes there is no difference between the two qualifications. The basic eligibility criteria for B. Arch. is 10+2 (Senior Secondary) or equivalent referred to as the qualifying examination from a recognised Board/University with a minimum of 50 per cent marks in Science subjects (physics, chemistry and mathematics). Besides this, the candidate must qualify an entrance examination.

Entrance Tests

Admission to first year of five years full time undergraduate course in Architecture (Bachelor of Architecture) in various colleges of India is through national and state level entrance examinations. The CBSE conducts a national level entrance examination - All India Engineering Entrance Examination (AIEEE) on all India basis for entry to undergraduate programmes in B. Architecture and B. Planning in government and private institutes. The paper consists of mathematics, an aptitude test and a drawing test. The National Aptitude Test in Architecture (NATA), the online test with drawing examination is conducted by the National Institute of Advanced Studies and Architecture in association with the Council of Architecture (COA). NATA scores are used by admissions authorities of different unaided and government aided schools/colleges of architecture, to provide common measures for comparing the qualifications of applicants. NATA measures aesthetic sensitivity, critical thinking, perception, observation and architectural awareness.

Entrance to architecture programmes at the Indian Institute of Technology (IITs) is through the national level Joint Entrance

Examination (JEE). Private institutes conduct entrance examination of their own. Different states also hold separate entrance examinations for admission to architecture and engineering colleges in the state.

Duration and Course Content

The B. Arch. degree programme is of five years duration and includes a period of practical experience. The apprenticeship (usually for one semester) has to be done under a practising architect. The B. Arch. degree prepares the theoretical foundations and gives some practical insight on which a student later develops proficiency and functional accuracy.

Subject content of B.Arch. course includes architectural design (drawing and painting), acoustics, surveying and leveling, estimating and costing, methods of construction, material management, history of architecture, draftsmanship, environmental planning, applied mechanics, structural designing, computer applications etc. Some colleges teach architecture-related software packages such as AutoCAD and 3-D Studio Max.

Apart from the degree course in B. Arch., diploma in Architecture is also available in some institutes as full time or part time. It will take seven years to complete the part-time diploma courses. After completing B. Arch, the candidates if they wish can go for post graduation, i.e., Master of Architecture (M. Arch.) which is of two to three semester duration. At postgraduate level one can specialise in areas like construction management, town planning, interior design, naval architecture, landscape designing, building engineeringand management etc.

Doctoral programmes (Ph.D.) can be pursued after M. Arch. or with a B. Arch. plus five years experience in professional practice or teaching or research.

Personal Skills

A successful architect requires special qualifications like designing talent, business aptitude, social awareness and legal knowledge. They must have excellent communication and drawing skills, keen observation, vivid imagination, creativity, ideas and the ability to visualise. Other qualities include leadership, managerial qualities, resourcefulness and ability to work as a team. They must also possess sufficient gasp of all aspects of building technology to be able to design for various needs under different conditions. Computer literacy also is required for writing specifications, two and three dimensional drafting and financial management. Knowledge of CADD is essential.

Basic training makes an architecture graduate to design and execute any type of building or complex.

Job Prospects and Career Options

Major career paths include :

- **Landscaping :** This involves designing sites for hospitals, parks, hotels, tourists or historic landmarks.
- **Designing Layouts :** This requires designing the framework and design guidelines for urban projects, including residential projects, planning and utilisation of open space into parks and infrastructure development.
- **Town Planning :** This involves overall planning of a town from infrastructure development to road transport, parks as well as shopping and residential centers.
- **Construction Management :** This requires providing both managerial as well as technological insights and construction advice to the client. Generally, MBAs and civil engineers are offered such roles.

With the country's current growth in industrial and economic activities, there exists wide employment opportunities for architects, both in the public and private sectors. A qualified architect can work with government organisations like central and state public works departments, housing and urban development corporation, municipalities, city development authorities, state housing boards etc. They are also employed in industrial ventures, consultancy and private architectural firms. The most privileged scope in the field of architecture is private practice. With some years of experience in an organisation, the architect can set up his own business. Architectural practices or individual architects may choose to specialise in one of a number of areas such as housing, hospital or educational facilities.

A qualified architect, to work as a consultant or to set up private practice, must register with the Council of Architecture before starting their profession. The Council of Architecture constituted by the government of India is charged with the responsibility to regulate the education and practice of profession throughout India besides maintaining the register of architects. This body along with the Indian Institute of Architects – the national body of architects in the country, lays down the guidelines for working hours, work environment, fees etc.

Remuneration

A fresh architectural graduate working as a trainee with established architects, start with a salary of ₹ 15,000 per month, while a senior architect can earn ₹ 30,000 – 40,000 per month. Associate architect could earn over ₹ 50,000 a month and principal architects command over ₹ 75,000 per month. From the level of senior architect onwards, architects get a share of the profits earned on their projects and the share rises with their seniority and experience.

In this field, individuals practising through their own firm could be thousands to lakhs. Consultants charge anywhere between four and 10 per cent of the total cost of construction in case of apartments and multi-storied buildings. They also charge 15–20 per cent of the total cost of construction in the case of independent houses and bungalows.

Useful Contacts

- **Council of Architecture**

  India Habitat Centre,

  Core 6 A, Ist Floor,

  Lodhi Road, New Delhi – 110003.

  Phone: 91-11-24654172
- **Indian Institute of Architects (IIA)**

  Head Office Prospect Chambers Annexe,

  Dr. D.N. Road, Fort,

  Mumbai – 400001.

  Phone: +912222046972, 22884805
- **The Director National Institute of Advanced Studies in Architecture,**

  CDSA, Survey no. 58 & 49/4,

  Bavdhan Khurd, Paud Road, (Before Ambrosia Resort; Off Chandni Chowk),

  Pune – 411021, Maharashtra.

  Phone: 020-6573-1088

9.3 Audio/Sound Engineering

Brief History of Sound Engineering

Everyone has a predilection for music no matter it is live or recorded. During the nineteenth century, several attempts for recording sounds were made in Europe and USA. Though the mechanised reproduction of music can be traced back as far as the ninth century, it was done most successfully by Thomas Edison in 1877. He invented a machine named

Phonograph which could be termed as the first practical sound recording and reproduction device for recording and reproducing sound. Coming all the way from 1877, technically, the recording industry has advanced drastically and has become part and parcel of our lives by the twentieth century.

What is an Audio Engineering?

Audio Engineering is a branch of audio science that is concerned about capturing sound, recording, copying, editing, mixing and reproducing sound using electronic and mechanical devices. It involves both production and post production tasks. Production part may involve everything from setting-up to the actual recording. Audio engineers use a variety of devices to record even the slightest sound variations. Electronic mixing board (console board) which contains variety of switches, dials, lights and meters is a vital part in audio engineering as it can control sound input while recording or editing. In the post production section, the recorded material gets polished or 'morphed' into sound. Digital audio workstations signal processors and sequencing software are the other integral components used in audio engineering.

Who is an Audio Engineer?

An audio engineer is someone with experience and training in production and manipulation of sound through mechanical and digital means. Those who have studied any course in audiography and sound recording can become an audio engineer. They are responsible for the final sound that we hear in music, i.e., in songs, background scores in videos, films, advertisements and so on. An audio journalist should have a nose for news. They may sometimes be recording engineers and sound engineers even though the latter are the persons who develop instruments for the audio engineers.

Audio engineering is one of the most popular and promising career in the modern generation that offers immense opportunity in the field of film, video production, sound broadcasting and advertising both in India and abroad. To be good in this field, lot of commitment and interest is required.

Eligibility

To become a successful audio engineer, one should be well trained in any degree or diploma courses in audiography, sound recording, sound engineering and audio engineering. No specific educational qualification is required for training in this field. However, for the post graduate courses in audio engineering one should have a bachelor's degree. Though not necessary, a basic knowledge in physics and mathematics will be an advantage for the audio engineers, as they have to undergo many calculations such as reverberations of the room, calculating the delay time etc. Moreover, practical training will make the person good at audio engineering. Besides these courses, there are several online courses.

One who has the background in electrical engineering and fine arts can also pursue a career in this field. He should be expert in using various recording equipments such as mixing consoles and microphones. Signal processors, tape machines, digital audio work-stations, music sequencers, speakers, preamplifiers, amplifiers are some of other equipments used by the audio engineers.

Course details

A course in audio engineering involves the study of the technical and creative aspects of sound recording, editing and mixing. Most of the courses often start with the basic theory and frequencies of sound and covers a broad area in recording, post production, live-sound reinforcement and as well broadcasting. Along with the technical aspects such as sound mixing, giving special effects, etc., candidates are also well trained in the usage of the recording tool, microphones and the like. Audio wiring, advanced communication skill, MIDI (Musical Instrument Digital Interface), electronic music, sound recording, music business, multi-track production techniques are some of the other course areas in audio engineering. During their curriculum, the candidates are trained not just recording music but also recording other sounds like dubbing.

Personal Skill

Those aspiring to make a career in the field should have keen interest and love for music. Audio engineers require a combo of creativity, technical knowledge and an aptitude for working with electrical, electronic and mechanical systems and equipments. As music production is a team work, one should have good communication skill and team spirit. The working hours of an audio engineer can be long and irregular, so they should have the ability to cope with the situation. Concentration, patience, good understanding, good sense of pitch, timing and rhythm are the other flair needed for an audio engineer. They must be proficient with different types of recording media, such as analog tape, digital multi track recorders and workstations and computer knowledge. With the advent of the digital age, it is important for the audio engineer to be versed in the understanding of software and hardware integration from synchronisation to analog to digital transfers.

Job Prospects and Career Options

Holding a diploma or degree in audio engineering is the first step for pursuing a career in this field. After successful completion of a course, one could find job opportunities in the field of movies, television, advertising and broad casting, live concerts, multimedia organisations, CD production, schools and so on. But the most attracting field for an audio engineer is the music industry. One can start as an assistant to a recording engineer to set all equipments and instruments. Gradually, on the basis of experience, he can become a reputed audio engineer. Another option is in the recording studio and the major tasks performed here are the operation of microphones, mixers, and software and recording of sounds, music and speech. With experience, one could specialise in different aspects of sound, music, dialogue, special effects and become a music producer or start their own recording studio.

Besides studios, audio engineers can also work on a freelance basis. As the audio engineering field is becoming highly competitive, those who have talent and specific skills can fare well.

Some of the career options in this field are :

- **Studio Engineer :** Studio engineer is there to record sounds, music and speech in the studio and make the sounds better by controlling it. It is one of the major posts in audio engineering.
- **Sound recordist:**
- **Broadcast Engineer :** Broadcast engineer is there to set all the broadcast equipments right.
- **Sound Editor :** There are three divisions in sound editors that are dialogue editor, music editor and sound effects editor. Sound editor should be able to handle these three although the big industries will have separate editor posts.
- **Re-recording mixer.**
- **Dialogue editor :** He is the one who edits the dialogues in the movies, TV channel programmes etc.
- **Music editor :** The sound effects editor is responsible for the final version of the sound effects.

- **Mastering Engineer :** With the challenging position, mastering engineer is the link between the final mix and the CD. He is also known as post production engineer.
- **Location sound Engineer.**
- **Mix Engineer :** The mix engineer is responsible for the final product, the music. He will mix down all the tracks of recordings into one. He will get the royalty of the work that makes this position very glamourous.
- **Foley Recordist/Editor.**
- **Recording Engineer :** Recording engineer is responsible for setting the equipments right for recording including microphones, placing the instruments, mixing the headphones for musicians etc.
- **Sound Designer :** Sound Designer is a person who designs and creates the soundtrack and covers all the non-compositional elements of a film, music and performances etc. He is responsible for the audio tracks from the dialogue to the re-recording the final tracks.
- **Pro tools operator.**
- **Studio manager :** Studio manager is responsible for booking and maintaining all the recordings in the studio. With a very good organisational skill, studio manager set all the background work for the music producers, engineers, musicians and also handling the financial matters.
- **Programmer.**

Remuneration

Audio engineering is one of the careers that bring recognition along with money. Depending upon effort one puts on his work, he could get the money. Most of the companies may pay the remuneration around and above ₹ 10,000 to their audio engineers. A recognised audio engineer can get a high salary from the industry. Abroad he may get an average of $18,540 as he starts his career.

Courses

- Certificate in Audio Engineering,
- Certificate Course in Audio and Visual Education,
- Certificate Course in Sound Recording and Reproduction,

- B.A. Audio Engineering and Digital Film Making,
- Diploma in Audio and Video Production,
- Diploma in Sound Engineering,
- Diploma in Fundamental and Audio Visual Education,
- Diploma in Sound Recording and Sound Engineering,
- Diploma in Video Editing and Sound Recording,
- Post Graduate Certificate Course in Audiography and Television Engineering, and
- Post Graduate Diploma in Audiography.

A. Few Institutes

- **Digital Academy – The Film School, Mumbai**

  H.O. Centre and Studio's, Plot No. C-3, Street

  No-11, MIDC, Andheri (East)

  Mumbai-400093.

  Mobile: +91-9324069648

  Email: response@dafilmschool.com

  URL: www.dafilmschool.com
- **SoundideaZ Academy – Mumbai**

  216, Godfey Villa, Pali Market, Pali Naka

  Bandra West, Mumbai-400050.

  Phone: 022-26403906

  Email: info@soundideazacademy.com

  URL: www.soundideazacademy.com
- **SoundtechMedia Institute of Audio Techno Chennai**

  270/1, Lloyds Road, VDM Complex

  Royapettah, Chennai-600 014.

  Phone: +91-44-28131113 Mobile: +91 98846 13285

  Email: info@soundtechmedia.com
- **Ramoji Academy of Film and Television-Hyderabad**

  Ramoji Film City, Hyderabad, Andhra Pradesh.

  Phone: 08415-246555, Extn: 6705

  URL: www.raft.ramojifilmcity.com

9.4 Agricultural Engineering

What is Agriculture?

Agriculture refers to the production of food and other goods by systematic and controlled growing of plants and living organisms. It involves working on the land, harvesting the crops, rearing and management of farming as well as breeding and raising livestock. In the broad sense, Agriculture includes agronomy, animal husbandry, horticulture, floriculture, aquaculture, silviculture and the like. Agriculture plays a major role in the Indian economic scenario contributing around 23 per cent to the Gross Domestic products (GDP). Around 62 per cent of Indian population depends on agriculture for their livelihood.

What is Agricultural Engineering?

The application of the principles of engineering and biological science to agriculture is known as agricultural engineering. Agricultural engineering sometimes known as biological engineering is a diverse engineering discipline which mainly focuses on the creation and development of tools (i.e., farm machineries and other implements related to agriculture) that can improve farming techniques. It can also be defined as a field of agricultural science where engineering principles are applied for the improvement and advancement of agriculture industry. Modern agriculture is highly competitive and technology-driven with a wide variety of specialties and techniques. Hi-tech agricultural graduates are in great demand due to the global trend toward standardisation of all agricultural products and equipment.

Who are Agricultural Engineers?

Agricultural Engineers are those who design agricultural equipment and agricultural structures by means of better engineering methods, inventions and new technologies. In other words, they have to look after the agricultural functioning to bring about efficient increase in food productivity. With their engineering skills and knowledge, agricultural engineers solve problems related to agricultural equipment, water quality and water management, biological products, livestock facilities, food processing and many other agricultural areas. Agricultural engineers can either specialise in designing power and machine systems, animal or plant production, environment management or in food and bioprocess. Some of the major jobs handled by agricultural engineers involve improving agricultural farm equipments, farm structures, rural electrification, biogas, new technologies in the design and manufacture of agricultural products and conservation of soil and water.

The Four Branches of Agricultural Engineering

The four main branches of Agricultural Engineering are :

- Farm equipments,
- Rural structures,
- Soil conservation, drainage and irrigation, and
- Rural electricity.

Eligibility

Students who wish to pursue a career in Agricultural Engineering should possess a strong foundation in physics, chemistry and mathematics. To become a qualified agricultural engineer one should have a Bachelor's degree (BE/B.Tech.) or a Master's degree (ME/M. Tech.) in Agricultural Engineering or at least a diploma in Agricultural Engineering with a minimum of three to four years of experience in the field of landscaping, plantation of vegetables, fruits etc.

Educational Qualification and Selection

The basic eligibility criteria for BE/B.Tech. in Agricultural Engineering is 10+2 or equivalent with physics, chemistry, mathematics and preferably biology. Duration of bachelor's course in agricultural engineering is four years. Besides the required educational qualification, the candidates have to appear for the entrance examination conducted at the state level, national level or university level. Indian Council of Agricultural Research (ICAR), New Delhi conducts an All India Examination for admission to Agricultural colleges for B.Tech. courses all over the country. All India Engineering Entrance Examination (AIEEE), Joint Entrance Examination (JEE) conducted by IIT are the other two entrances which are accepted by various institutes. Apart from these, each state/institute may conduct their own entrance examination and some among them are state entrance examination conducted by Uttar Pradesh Technical University (SEE UPTU), EAMCET by Andhra Pradesh, KCET by Karnataka and so on.

ME./M.Tech. courses are of two years duration and most institutes admit candidates to these programmes through Graduate Aptitude Test in Engineering (GATE). BE/B. Tech. in Agriculture/Horticulture or its equivalent is the minimum qualification. Some institutes conducted their own entrance examination for the post graduate programmes. Candidates with master's degree can go for the three years Ph.D. course.

Post graduate degree and diploma courses in agriculture are also offered by various institutes which is usually of two years duration. Eligibility for diploma courses in agricultural engineering is 10+2 and these courses can be done through polytechnics. The Indian Institute of Management (Ahmedabad) offers post graduate Diploma in Agribusiness Management (earlier known as Specialisation Package in Agriculture). A number of agricultural universities have now introduced management courses in agriculture and related subjects.

Course Areas

Bachelor's course in agricultural engineering covers the areas like basic physical engineering, agriculture sciences, soil conservation, drainage method, irrigation practices, firm machinery, dairy engineering and the like. Specialisation in crop process engineering, farm machinery and power, soil and water conservation are some of the course areas at the post graduate level.

Personal Skills

The major task of an agricultural engineer is the enhancement of agricultural production and for that they should be familiar with product engineering, equipment research and designing. They should possess practicality, organising skills, communication skills, precision, understanding power and capacity to toil. Other desired attributes are logical thinking, ability to deal with people diplomatically, having patience, ability to keep calm under pressure and inevitable crises, creativity, flexibility to understand and apply new technologies. Ability to conceptualise forms or structure and draw sketches will be added advantage. Besides all these, agricultural engineers require a good intellect and must have a desire to make a difference to the future of farming.

Job Prospects

Agriculture Engineering is technologically sophisticated and ever expanding field that offers bright career prospects to agricultural graduates. Agriculture engineers can build up a career in any country around the world and in a variety of sectors, no matter whether it is private or public. Their major task is to improve farming techniques and agricultural products and for that they combine engineering and biological science principles so that farming is made easier, efficient and more profitable. Some of the specialisations in the field of agricultural engineering include :

- Agricultural equipment designing,
- Conservation of soil and water,
- Crop production,
- Dairy Management,
- Bio-renewable products,
- Processing of agricultural products etc.

Water resource management, forestry, mining and rehabilitation, urban and rural development, machine development, product planning, crop storage and processing are some of the work areas of agricultural engineers. Lucrative careers prospects are available for qualified agricultural engineers in fields like :

- Government and public sector organisations.
- Agribusiness firms,
- Food processing and retail industry,
- Research organisations and laboratories,
- Banks and Financial Corporations, and
- Sales and management.

Central and state government organisation and private firms recruit agricultural engineers as agricultural officers for the development of agriculture in a district. In farm equipment manufacturing industry, they design, develop and manage various types of agricultural related equipments. Planning and construction of warehouses or go-downs for the storage of food grains and green houses or glass houses for the intensive cultivation of horticultural crops; designing and development of food processing machinery are some of the duties perform by the agricultural engineers in food processing industry.

Those interested in research activities can become agricultural research scientists by joining in research organisations like Indian Agricultural Research Institute (IARI), Indian Council of Agricultural Research (ICAR) etc. Banks, finance and insurance companies hire agricultural graduates and in these organisations, they can work as field officers, rural development officers and agricultural and probationary officers.

Teaching is another option for those who have a good academic record and they can start as assistant/associate professors in agricultural universities and institutes. One can venture into business by setting up farms, production and marketing of food grains and other farming activities. Agricultural engineers can provide consultancy services to agricultural workers and farming and agro industries. They could also work irrigation and drainage projects, canal irrigation programmes, land reclamation and soil conservation projects. Agricultural engineers can work with NGOs in rural areas as part of their rural development programme.

Remuneration

Compare to other branches of engineering, agricultural engineers receive excellent pay package at the beginning itself. The remuneration depends on the status of the industry and experience, qualification and the ability of the employee. They can find job openings both in India and abroad.

In India, in the government organisations, a fresh graduate in agricultural engineering can expect a salary ranging between ₹ 20,000 to 25,000 per month. Within one to two years of experience, the monthly pay scale may increase to ₹ 30,000 or more depending on the efficiency, capability and seniority of the employee. Those who are working with private organisations, MNC's and NGO's can earn a good amount. A lecturer in the field of agricultural engineering can earn an initial amount of ₹ 30,000 and above per month plus other allowances.

A Few Institutes

- **College of Agricultural Engineering**
  Rajendra Agricultural University
  Pusa, Samastipur-848125, Bihar.
- **Allahabad Agricultural Institute** (Deemed University)
  Allahabad-211007, UP.
- **Institute of Agricultural Sciences**
  Banaras Hindu University
  Varanasi-221005, UP.
- **Sardar Vallabhbhai Patel University of Agriculture and Technology**
  Meerut-250110, UP.
- **College of Agricultural Engineering and Technology**
  Orissa University of Agriculture and Technology
  Bhubaneshwar, Orissa.

- **College of Agricultural Engineering**
  Tamil Nadu Agricultural University
  Coimbatore, Tamil Nadu.

9.5 Automobile Engineering

What is Automobile or Automotive Engineering?

Automobile Engineering *alias* Automotive Engineering or Vehicle Engineering is one of the most challenging careers in the field of engineering with a wide scope. This branch deals with the designing, developing, manufacturing, testing, repairing and servicing automobiles such as cars, trucks, motorcycles, scooters and the related sub-engineering systems. For the perfect blend of manufacturing and designing automobiles, Automobile Engineering uses the features of different elements of engineering such as mechanical, electrical, electronic, software and safety engineering.

Specialisation in the field

To become a proficient automobile engineer, specialised training is essential and it is a profession which requires a lot of hard work, dedication, determination and commitment. The major task of an automobile engineer is the designing, developing, manufacturing and testing of vehicles from the concept stage to the production stage. This broad field of engineering has many sub-sections and the areas of specialisation include engine systems, electronics and control systems, fluid mechanics, thermodynamics, aerodynamics, supply chain management and the like. It involves understanding the mechanism of vehicle chassis, internal combustion engine, electrical systems, motor transport affairs, workshop technology, research and design.

The Three types of Automobile Engineers

Automobile engineers are mainly classified into three streams like Product or Design Engineers, Development Engineers and Manufacturing Engineers. Product Engineers or Design Engineers are those who deal with the designing and testing of the components and systems of automobiles. They design and test each part of the visualised automobile, seeing that it meets all requirements, performs as required, that the material meets desired durability and so on.

Manufacturing engineers deal with activities like how to create and assemble the whole parts of automobiles. They have to design and lay out the equipments, machine rates and line rates, specification of automation equipment and manufacturing safety procedures. Those who deal with connecting all systems in a completed automobile are called Development Engineers. They have the responsibility for directing the delivery of the engineering elements of the complete automobile manufacturer, governmental regulations and the customer who buys the product. Development Engineers have to provide the Production Engineer details about the spring rate that he would want to utilise in the vehicle.

Eligibility and Course Areas

Students who have strong foundation in mathematics, physics, chemistry, biotechnology and computer science can find a lucrative career in the field of automobile engineering. Numerous institutes all over India conduct several undergraduate (B.E. /B.Tech.) and diploma programmes in Automobile Engineering.

The basic eligibility criteria for BE/B.Tech. in automobile engineering is 10+2 or equivalent examination with physics, chemistry and mathematics or biotechnology, bio-informatics, biomedical with a fairly high percentage of marks in the aggregate. After pursuing the bachelor's degree (B.E/B.Tech), one can go for a postgraduate degree, i.e., ME/M.Tech. and after that one can take up the Ph.D. degree.

After 10th, one can also choose the diploma programme in automobile engineering and after the diploma they can take up PG diploma or even an engineering degree as some colleges give admission to diploma holders with 50 per cent marks. In certain engineering colleges, mechanical engineering students can opt for automobile engineering as an optional subject.

Selection

Admission to the BE/B.Tech. courses is made on the basis of marks obtained in 10+2 and the merit in the entrance examination (e.g., IIT JEE, AIEEE, BITSAT, State Entrance Examinations etc.) conducted both at national and state level. In state entrance exams, selection will be based on the rank obtained in the entrance exam. Selection to the ME/ M.Tech. courses is through GATE examination (The Graduate Aptitude Test in Engineering). Diploma holders can take AMIE examination to be equivalent with the degree holder. Admissions to some of the institutions are made by their own separate entrance examinations.

Duration

BE/B.Tech. courses in Automobile Engineering are of four years (eight semesters) duration while ME/M.Tech. degree and post graduate diploma courses in Automobile Engineering are of two years. Diploma courses in Automobile Engineering are of three years and Ph.D. course is of two years.

Job Prospects

Automobile Industry has been booming in recent times due to the growing demand for vehicles and the job prospects for automobile engineers have also increased rapidly both in India and abroad. The work of automobile engineer involves planning, designing, developing, manufacturing and testing the performance and efficiency of automobiles and their component parts including the engine chassis and transmission systems. They design new models by keeping a view in their mind about the performance, capability, strength and appearance of the automobiles and also the expenditure.

The major responsibility of an automobile engineer is to maintain the high standard of vehicle by using traditional methods and state of the art technology. With the computer knowledge in CAD (Computer Aided Design), CAM (Automation), ERP, automobile engineers can find employment in computer aided industries as designers or they can design models of vehicles by joining the research and development wing of companies. Diploma holders in automobile engineering can start their own business enterprise like automobile maintenance workshop or automobile garages. Automobile maintenance engineers are offered the post of general supervision of mechanics in workshop, factory or garage. B.Tech. holders in automobile engineering with an MBA degree could reach the frontline in marketing management careers.

Candidates with master's degree and with five years experience in teaching at graduate level or industrial experience in a reputed firm can get employment as a lecturer. Ph.D. degree holders in automobile engineering can work as a researcher or scientist and can further help in the development of the field.

Some of the career prospects in the field of automobile engineering are :

- Automobile Engineering Technicians,
- Safety Engineering,
- Emissions Research,
- NVH (Noise, Vibration and Harshness) Engineers,
- Performance Engineer,

- Vehicle Dynamics Controller,
- Operations Research, and
- Designing.

Remuneration

The remuneration depends on the status of the industry and experience, qualifications, and ability of the employee. A fresh graduate in automobile engineering can earn a monthly salary of ₹ 15,000 to 20,000. The candidates from well-known technological institutions like IITs, NITs and BITs will get high pay package according to their academic excellence and skills. The remuneration will increase up to ₹ 40,000 per month after having three or four years experience. Best car manufacturing companies like Honda, Audi, and Skoda offers an awesome pay along with several perks.

Institutes

There are few institutions in India offering courses in automobile engineering. The demand is more as compared to the production. B.E/ B.Tech. course in automobile engineering is offered by elite technological universities including the IITs and NITs. Other pioneer institutes are Birla Institute of Technology, Institute of Technology (Banaras Hindu University), College of Engineering and Technology (Anna University) and several other state level engineering colleges. Some other institutes are like :

- PDA College of Engineering, Gulbarga,
- Nehru Samaraka Vidya Kendra Trust, Jayanagar, Bangalore,
- Impact Polytechnic, Hebbel, Bangalore,
- Vishwakarma Institute of Technology, Pune,
- MH Saboo Siddi K College of Engineering, Byculla, Mumbai, and
- JMM Institute of Technology, Chitradurga, Bangalore.

9.6 Biomedical Engineering

What is Biomedical Engineering?

Biomedical Engineering *alias* BME is an emerging and exciting discipline of engineering that has got tremendous potential for research, development and employment. Biomedical engineering may be defined as the study and application of engineering principles and techniques to the medical field. It is a combination of technical knowledge in biology and medicine to improve life quality. This is interdisciplinary field that bridges life science and engineering has an important role in prevention, therapy and rehabilitation as it combines the principles of two dynamic professions, medicine and engineering. It is an apt career for those who have a keen interest in medicine and health care.

What is Bio-medical Engineering Concerned about?

BME is concerned with the development and manufacture of prostheses, medical devices, diagnostic devices, drugs and other therapies. This unique field encompasses bio-instrumentation, bio-materials, bio-mechanics, medical imaging, genetic engineering, orthopedic surgery, cellular and tissue engineering. The combination of mechanical engineering, electronics engineering, and sciences with computers for communication and control led to the emergence of inter-disciplinary courses such as mechatronics, computer integrated manufacturing (CIM), geographical information system (GIS), biotechnology, bio-mechanics, bio medical instrumentation and bio medical engineering.

The Important Role of Bio-engineers

Bio-medical Engineering is getting more popular because of the increase in the growing complexity of medical technology around the world. And as a result, there is a huge demand for trained professionals to bridge the gap between clinical medicine and applied medical technology. These professionals are termed as bio-engineers or biomedical engineers. A bio-medical engineer has to be an expert in engineering sciences, biological sciences and medical sciences. They must be capable of defining a medical problem in engineering terms and find a solution that satisfies both engineering and clinical requirements. They usually design and develop devices and systems ranging from cardiac monitors to clinical computers, artificial hearts to contact lenses, wheel chairs to artificial tendons. They are also integral part in the management of technology in hospitals and health care delivery.

Eligibility and Course Areas

To become a Biomedical Engineer, one should hold a Bachelor's degree in bio-medical engineering (B.E.)/B.Tech. in BME. The basic eligibility criteria for a B.E. are higher secondary or its equivalent examination in the science stream. The course is of four years duration and the candidates have to appear for the entrance examination conducted by the respective institution.

After 10+2, one can directly do B.E. in biomedical engineering or B.E. in other branches of Engineering such as electrical engineering, mechanical engineering, computer engineering, electronics engineering or chemical engineering and then become a bio-medical professional by completing a post graduate course in Bio-medical Engineering. Otherwise, one can do B.E. in any branch of Engineering and go for a post graduate course in medical technology, which is considered equivalent to a post graduate course in Biomedical Engineering. One could also take up this career after completing an MBBS degree and then opt for a post graduate degree in bio-medical engineering/medical technology. A flair for research coupled with excellent academic records enables a candidate to obtain a doctorate degree from India or abroad.

Course Content

The main objective of bio-medical engineering is to bring an improvement in the overall quality of healthcare. A course in Bio-medical engineering includes study of biology, chemistry, physics, calculus, biotech, principles of design, materials science, bio-mechanics and life sciences. The course enables a candidate to gain technical expertise in biology and medicine simultaneously and contribute effectively in the development and improvement of healthcare solutions. Bio-medical engineers apply the concepts of biology, physics as well as chemistry to develop products and devices for diagnosis and treatment.

Personal Skills

A Bio-medical professional should be good engineer and have aptitude for life science systems as well as terminology. They must have a sound knowledge in the basic engineering field. Good communication skills both written and verbal and a keen interest in biology as well as mathematics is a must. Ability to work as part of a team, creativity, an analytical bend of mind is some of the other personal skills counted for this career. They must have exceptional skills in observation, concentration, investigation, critical thinking and record keeping. Since the medical technology is changing so fast, it is very important to keep abreast of this changing technology. So, the candidate should be dexterous and alert. Administrative skills, computer knowledge and high-level software development skills will be an added advantage.

Job Prospects and Career Options

Bio-medical engineers are proficient scientists who use the principles of engineering and life sciences and conduct research on the biological aspects of human and animal life. They may be called upon in a wide range of capacities to design instruments, devices and software, to being together knowledge from many technical sources to develop new procedures or to conduct research needed to solve clinical problems. Specialists in this field are concerned with developing imaging systems such as magnetic resonance, ultrasound and X-ray machines, techniques and devices to automate or control body functions etc.

Bio-medical Engineering has many well established areas of specialisation and some among them are :

- **Bio-instrumentation** – It specialises in the application of electronics and measurement techniques to develop devices for diagnosis and treatment of diseases.
- **Bio-mechanics** – It specialises in the application of mechanical principles on living organism and also the analysis of mechanics of organisms.
- **Bio-materials** – This area of science is about the natural or man-made material used for the medical application.
- **Molecular, cellular and Tissue Engineering** – It deals with the development of artificial materials and tissue that used for artificial blood vessels and organs, replacement of skin and bone.
- **Clinical Engineering** – It deals with the development and maintenance of computer database of medical instruments and equipment record in hospitals.
- **Orthopaedic Bio-engineering** – This science helps to understand the function of the bones, muscles and the joints. It also helps to design and develop artificial joint replacement.
- **Navigation Systems** – It is a specialised branch that use software tools and specialised imaging equipment to create a digital picture of the insides of a human patient's body.
- **Rehabilitation Engineering** – It is used to design, develop, adapt, test, evaluate, apply and distribute technological solutions to problems faced by individuals with disabilities like communications, hearing vision. The rehabilitation engineers improve the capabilities and develop the quality of life for such individuals.
- **Systems physiology** – It is the study of living systems including molecular processes, isolated tissues, organ systems and the whole organism. This study also includes the analysis of how various systems interact and function.

Bio-medical engineers and technologists can find job openings in a wide range of global industries which may include modern health care, hospitals, medical equipment manufacturing units, industrial firms, educational and medical institutions, pharmaceuticals, government regulatory agencies and so on. In hospitals, they have to work closely with other healthcare professionals like physicians, nurses, therapists and technicians. They develop customised devices and provide advice for selecting, handling and maintaining medical equipments. In industries, bio-medical engineers use their understanding of living systems and technology.

Remuneration

Decent pay can be expected for bio-medical engineering professionals. The remuneration depends upon the working area, the companies and the institutions. Those who are working in private hospitals and clinics can earn between ₹ 15,000 and 25,000 per month. In the research and teaching institutions the pay scale varies between ₹ 18,000 – 25,000 per month, while in medical equipment manufacturing companies one can earn ₹ 20,000 – 30,000. The pay scale in the government sector is slightly low as compared to the private sector. In government agencies, the pay package per month varies between ₹ 16,000 – 22,000 per month.

Courses

- B.E. Biomedical Engineering,
- B.Tech. Biological Sciences and Bio-engineering,
- B.Tech. Bio-engineering,
- M.Tech. Bio-medical Technology,
- B.Tech. Bio-medical Engineering,
- B.Tech. Bio-medical Instrumentation,
- B.Tech. Bio-engineering,
- M.Tech. Biological Sciences and Bio-engineering,
- M.Tech. Biomedical Bio-engineering, and
- M.Tech. Bio-medical Instrumentation.

(A) Few Institutes

- **Indian Institute of Technology (IIT), Kanpur**
  Kanpur-208016 Uttar Pradesh.
- **ACS College of Engineering, Bangalore**
  Kambipura, Mysore Road
  Bangalore, Karnataka-560074.
- **Sathyabama University, Chennai**

Jeppiaar Nagar, Rajiv Gandhi Road
Chennai-600119.

- **National Institute of Technology (NITRR), Raipur**
  Chhattisgarh G.E. Road
  Raipur-492010.
- **Jerusalem College of Engineering, Chennai**
  Valachery Main Road, Narayanapuram,
  Pallikaranai, Chennai-600100.
- **Saroj Institute of Technology and Management (SITM), Lucknow**
  Ahimamau, Arjunganj, Sultanpur Road
  Lucknow.
- **Karunya Deemed University, Coimbatore**
  Karunya Nagar, Coimbatore-641114.
- **Godavari Institute of Engineering and Technology (GIET), Rajahmundry**
  NH-5, Chaitanya Knowledge City
  Rajahmundry-533296.
- **Rajiv Gandhi College of Engineering (RGCE), Chennai**
  Nemili, Sriperumbudur, Chennai-602105.

9.7 Broadcast Engineering/ Broadcast Technology

What is Broadcasting?

Broadcasting is an important tool for mass communication and it is the method of distribution of audio and video content via any audio or visual communication medium, normally by using electromagnetic radiation (radio waves). The programmes which we see on TV or listen on radio involve several steps like content acquisition, production, transmission and reception before they reach the end users. For the production and delivery of these programmes several equipments namely camera, microphones, switchers, editing systems, storage systems, play-out and specialised technical facilities like studios, transmitters, etc., are required. Broadcasting is the technology that encompasses all of the above equipment and various other media production systems. Apart from the commercial TV and radio, broadcasting technology has been used for the purposes of private recreation, non-commercial exchange of messages, experimentation, self-training and so on.

The field of Broadcast Engineering

Due to the growth in the entertainment industry, Broadcast Engineering is becoming a lucrative career field across the world. India is the third largest television market in the world with over 400 registered satellite channels, 82 Mn cable homes, 60,000 cable operators and 6,000 MSOs, six DTH operators, 270 private FM stations. Digitalisation of broadcasting and new media delivery methods like IPTV and Mobile TV are expected to result in huge demand for skilled manpower in broadcast media industry.

Broadcast Engineering which is considered as a sub division of electrical engineering can be defined as regulation of equipments for signal strength, clarity and range of sounds and colors in radio and television broadcasting. Most of the engineering divisions like electrical engineering, electronics and communication engineering, computer engineering, information technology and audio engineering are integrated in broadcast engineering. Radio Frequency (RF) Engineering and Audio Engineering, the two prime areas of electrical engineering, are also related with broadcast engineering.

The work of Broadcast Engineering Technicians

Professionals involved with broadcasting are termed as broadcast engineering technicians. Broadcasting technicians are responsible for instantaneous updates and live pictures that flash across our screens from any part of the world. Broadcasting technicians in their day-to-day affairs carry out their work on transmitter technologies of radio and television stations. They work for the entire chain in broadcasting; that is, right from the studio end to the transmitter end. Broadcasting technicians maintain the fluidity of broadcast signals through the use of sound and video equipment. It is these people who ensure the quality, the volume, colour, brightness, contrast, strength and clarity of the broadcast programme material to be transmitted. They install, test, operate and repair electronic equipment that is used to transmit radio, television and cable programmes and control the input and timing of material to be signaled and the type of broadcast feed to be signaled – whether from camera, studio, local, network, live or film programming. Broadcasting technicians also produce soundtracks for motion pictures, operate sound for live events and concerts and record music in recording studios.

Personal Attributes

Broadcasting technology is a career that suits those who have an interest in controlling and supervising broadcast equipments used for transmitting content to various channels. As a broadcasting technician, one should have knowledge of the latest technologies such as DTV, NTSC and digital audio broadcasting. He must be well-informed about broadcast automation systems for the studio, automatic transmission systems for the transmitter plant, maintaining radio towers and the like. Ample job opportunities are available for these technicians with more radio and television stations coming up.

Organisations in the Field of Broadcasting

There are organisations related to the broadcasting field which works for the welfare of its members. AIR and Doordarshan Engineers Association is a body representing the India Broadcasting Engineering Services Officers (Group-A) working in All India Radio and Doordarshan. Broadcast Engineering Society (BES) India is the apex body of government for maintaining exclusive affairs of broadcast engineering as a profession in the country. The BES India aims to project interests of broadcast engineering profession in India and overseas; opens avenues for newest technologies through conferences and exhibitions; provides platform for interaction with broadcast professionals and industry across the globe and encourages broadcast professionals by offering various awards and prizes in different areas of broadcasting engineering.

Eligibility

Broadcast Engineering is not offered as a main discipline in undergraduate engineering courses. Candidates with four years bachelor's degree course in electrical engineering, electronics and communication engineering, computer engineering, information technology and audio engineering can pursue a career in broadcast engineering. After graduation, the candidates can specialise in broadcast engineering at the post graduate level or can start working right after graduation with broadcasting firms.

Diploma, post graduate and certificate level courses in broadcast technology are offered by several institutes in India. The pre-requisite for applying to these courses is 10+2 in science stream from any recognised institute with mathematics and physics as compulsory subject. The candidates are also required to pass an entrance examination for getting admission. These courses are specifically designed to prepare people to work in technical positions to broadcast stations and other electronic media. Those who complete these courses are eligible to become a licensed Broadcast Engineer.

Top Institutes

Some of the top institutes in India that offer courses in broadcasting engineering include Zee Institute of Media Arts, Mumbai; Symbiosis Institute of Media and Communication, Pune; Indian Film and Television Institute, Meerut; Broadcast Engineering Society, New Delhi etc.

Broadcasting programme will train candidates in the hard and soft skills that are required by every employer. These courses focus on understanding the technology required by every employer. These courses focus on understanding the technology required for content acquisition, production and transmission in radio and television broadcasting. Candidates are likely to learn to install, maintain and repair electronic equipment used to develop video and audio for broadcast. The course content involves troubleshooting broadcast equipment to component level, performing routine and preventative maintenance of computer systems and networks and performing maintenance on all broadcast transmission systems etc. In addition to theoretical inputs, the students are also given extensive hands on experience in real working environment at in-house facilities. They are offered internship opportunities with local radio and television stations.

On completion of the course, students will develop good understanding of broadcast technologies, issues and operational and maintenance needs of broadcasting infrastructure. They are expected to assume responsibilities as technical experts/facility managers with production houses, broadcasters, network operators, integrators, broadcast equipment manufacturers, suppliers and media institutions and in other domains of broadcast industry. Students can also peruse higher studies in related areas like media technology, science communication etc.

Personal Skills

Those who wish to pursue a career in broadcast engineering must have sound knowledge in areas of mathematics, physics and electronics. They must possess computer proficiency and networking knowledge to operate in broadcasting stations and in equipments operating in digital technology. Although requirements vary from station to station, a broadcast engineer/technologist should have knowledge in a wide array of technology from modern digital methods to traditional broadcast systems. Knowledge of electrical and electronic equipment, ability to find and repair faults, good practical and technical skills is the vital attributes needed in this profession. A broadcast engineer should always keep up to date with new technologies in the digital and multimedia systems.

Other essential skills required are patience, ability to work as a team, good communication skill, flexibility and willingness to work for long hours etc. Moreover, a broadcast engineer requires excellent problem solving skills, analytical bent of mind and passion or work so as to become successful in their career.

Job Prospects and Career Options

All communication related organisations require services of broadcast engineering technicians. Ample job opportunities are available for skilled professionals in this field with the increase in number of television channels and radio stations. Broadcast engineering positions usually require working knowledge of audio engineering, computer engineering, and radio frequency engineering or other closely related field. For entry level position in this industry, a graduate degree with specialised technical training is needed.

Broadcast engineers work with a team which includes producers, studio managers, presenters and other technical staff in the broadcasting industry. Responsibilities of broadcast engineering technicians vary according to the size of the broadcasting organisation. In smaller stations, they handle numerous responsibilities while in larger stations tasks tend to be specialised. Even though the job title varies like broadcast technician, broadcast engineer, broadcast operator etc. All entail almost the same work profile. The major tasks include operating, maintaining, updating and repairing hardware and systems used across television, radio, podcasts and other channels, ensuring that programmes are broadcast on time to the highest possible level of quality and so on. An up-to-date knowledge of and flexibility with IT skills and new technology e.g., digital and multimedia systems is very much essential to be successful in this profession.

Broadcast engineers may work in a range of locations and varied situations. They may be required to work for long hours at late night while telecasting news and other live programmes. Apart from studio and set work, there may be outside broadcasts, when sound and images are relayed live back to a studio or straight to the network. Whatever may be the location and media, the typical work profile of a broadcast engineer includes :

- Maintaining programming logs, as required by station management.
- Controlling audio equipment to regulate the volume and sound quality during radio and television broadcasts.

- Monitoring strength, clarity and reliability of incoming and outgoing signals and adjusting equipment as necessary to maintain quality broadcasts.
- Regulating the fidelity, brightness and contrast of video transmission, using video console control panels.
- Observing monitors and communicating with station personnel to determine audio and video levels and to ascertain that programmes are airing.
- Selecting sources from which programming is received or through which programming may be transmitted.

Broadcast engineers may have varying titles depending on their level of expertise and field of specialty. Some of them are :

- **Broadcast Design Engineer:** Broadcast Design Engineer manages broadcast projects or leads efforts on project subsystems. Their responsibilities include creating equipment lists, floor plans, rack and console elevations, conceptual and detailed audio, video and control diagrams, patch panel and custom I/O panel layouts for technical systems. They assist with budgets, timelines and members of his/her project engineering team in order to successfully execute the overall project plan.
- **Broadcast System Engineer:** Broadcast System Engineer alias Multimedia (MM) Software Engineer Development (BSD-SD) is responsible for developing features specific to broadcast streaming and transcode systems design on proprietary and industry standard multimedia frameworks.
- **Broadcast IT System Engineer:** Broadcast IT System Engineers provide direct technical and problem-solving support for broadcast based IT systems that includes broadcast based network, hardware, software, server environments and end-user software applications.
- **Broadcast Network/Maintenance Engineer:** Broadcast Network/Maintenance Engineers are responsible for maintaining specialist equipment for video production and broadcast; setting up and monitoring audio visual links between studios and channel in different locations; installing and testing new facilities and equipment, monitoring transmission links during channel broadcasts, repairing hardware, software and other broadcast technology systems, developing and using awareness of best practice in health and safety for workplace.

- **Outside Broadcast Engineer :** Outside Broadcast Engineers are responsible to look after the broadcast equipment and systems that are needed to televise sport, news, music concerts and other events that are not based in a TV studio.
- **Remote Broadcast Engineer :** Remote broadcasting is done from a location away from a formal television studio and is considered an electronic field production (EFP).
- **Video Broadcast Engineer.**
- **TV Studio Broadcast Engineer.**

Broadcast technicians with a wide range of skills and knowledge are more likely to find better job opportunities than those with focussed skill sets. Both government and private broadcasting organisations offer varied job opportunities for broadcast engineering technicians. Broadcasting engineers/technicians/operators are highly in demand in audio-visual media like television channels and radio stations. Small radio stations recruit only one broadcast technician whereas big radio stations hire multiple technicians with requisite specialisations and considerable experience in the particular areas. They can easily find jobs in video and recording studios, theaters, live concerts, sports stadiums, film industry and in multimedia organisations. They can also work with space and marine agencies and can assist a recording engineer to set up his equipments and instruments. Most technicians start off their careers in small broadcasting stations as an assistant in network operations. Within a short span of years, after obtaining an exposure in this field, they can take the roles as supervisory technicians, broadcast engineers, chief engineers and even rise to managerial positions.

Remuneration

Lucrative pay packages are offered to broadcast engineers in the media industry. A trainee or fresh graduate in this field can earn an initial salary between ₹ 15,000 and ₹ 20,000 per month. The initial pay scale of a fresh broadcast engineer with excellent technical skills will not be less than ₹ 25,000 per month. A well-experienced engineer can expect higher pay packages, about ₹ 50,000 to 60,000 per month depending on their employer. However, salaries may shoot up exceedingly depending on one's qualification, promotions earned performances and higher degrees. In the government sector, broadcast engineers are provided with living and medical facilities and other perks.

Television stations usually pay higher salaries than radio stations, commercial broadcasting usually pays more than public broadcasting and stations in large markets pay more than those in small markets.

Courses

- Broadcasting Animation in 3-D,
- Certificate Course in Announcing, Broadcasting, Comparing and Dubbing (ABCD),
- Certificate Course in Internet Broadcasting,
- Certificate in Satellite and Broadcast Communications,
- Diploma in Broadcast Animation,
- Diploma in Broadcast Media,
- Graduate Diploma in Print, Broadcast and Online Media Journalism,
- MFA Broadcast Journalism and Video Production,
- NDTV Broadcast Training Programme,
- Post Graduate Diploma in Broadcast Technology,
- Post Graduate Diploma in Broadcasting Journalism, and
- Post Graduate Diploma in Print, Broadcast and Online Media Journalism.

Institutes

- **Monad Educational Society, New Delhi**

  Diploma in Mass Communication and Journalism,

  Certificate Programme in Mass Communication and Journalism.
- **Amity University, Noida, Uttar Pradesh**

  Bachelor of Journalism and Mass Communication.
- **Guru Gobind Singh Indraprastha University, New Delhi**

  Bachelor of Journalism and Mass Communication.
- **Sathyabhama University, Chennai, Tamil Nadu**

  Doctor of Philosophy in Visual Communication.
- **Karunya University, Coimbatore, Tamil Nadu**

  Master of Philosophy – Journalism and Mass Media,

  Doctor of Philosophy – Journalism and Mass Media.
- **I.I.M.T Engineering College, Meerut, Uttar Pradesh**

  Bachelor of Journalism and Mass Communication.
- **East Point College of Engineering and Technology, Bangalore, Karnataka**

  Bachelor of Arts.

- **Mangalayatan University, Aligarh, Uttar Pradesh**

  Bachelor of Journalism and Mass Communication – Electronic Media,

  Diploma in Broadcast Journalism and Radio Jockeying.

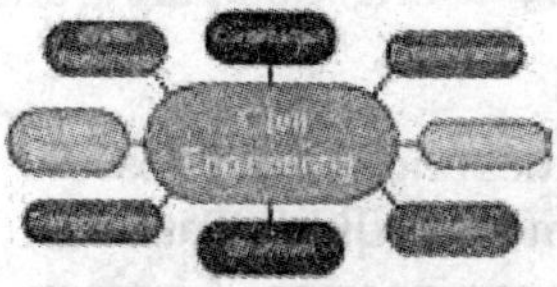

9.8 Civil Engineering

What is Civil Engineering?

Civil Engineering is the oldest branch of engineering that incorporates the design and construction of roads, airports, tunnels, bridges, water supply and sewage systems, dams, harbuors, railroad systems, docks, power supply systems, building and even nuclear power plants. Civil engineering offers areas of specialisation such as structural engineering, highway engineering and water management.

Most civil engineers today deals with roads, railways, structures, water supply, sewer, flood control and traffic. In essence, civil engineering is a profession which makes the world more habitable place to live in.

Who is a Civil Engineer?

A civil engineer is one who is responsible for planning and designing a project, constructing the project to the required scale and maintenance of the product. A civil engineer requires not only a high standard of engineering knowledge but also supervisory and administrative skills. The planning part of their work involves site investigation, feasibility studies, creating solutions to complications that may occur and the actual designing of the structures. They have to work with the guidelines of the local government authority and get plans approved by the relevant authority. They may prepare cost estimates and set construction schedules. Construction work involves dealing with clients, architects, government officials, contractors and the supervision of work according to standards. Their work also involves the maintenance and repair of the project.

Major Specialisations

The major specialisations within civil engineering are structural, water resources, environmental, construction, transportation, geo-technical engineering etc. On most projects, civil engineers work in teams or in co-ordination with many other engineers. They can find work as a superior of a construction site or a managerial position or in design, research as well as teaching in government services or private concerns. They can also work as independent consultants.

Who should go for Engineering?

Only those who excel in science and mathematics and should possess the proclivity to innovate new gadgets, instruments, equipments, etc., for the benefit of human beings should go for engineering. A person must demonstrate the following to become an engineer in a true sense :

- Ability to apply the knowledge of mathematics, science and engineering;
- Ability to design and conduct experiments as well as to analyse and interpret data;
- Ability to design a system, component or process to meet desired needs;
- Ability to function on multi-disciplinary teams;
- Ability to identify, formulate and solve engineering problems;
- An understanding of professional and ethical responsibility;
- Ability to communicate effectively;
- Ability to engage in life-long learning;
- Knowledge of contemporary issues;
- Ability to use techniques, skills and modern engineering tools necessary for engineering practice; and
- Ability to understand the impact of engineering solutions in a global and societal context.

The Different Stages of Engineering Education in India

- **Post-Matric Technical Education :** Diploma level courses are meant for the training of middle level man-power needed for a wide range of professional duties, for application of knowledge in field operation, in production and construction, testing and development, etc., and such functions are offered in 291 polytechnics with an annual enrolment capacity of about 50,000 students. They offer a variety of specialisation in engineering and technology as well as in a few non-technological fields. The courses are normally of three years duration where full-time institutional instruction is offered and three and a half to four years when instruction is on a sandwich or on part-time basis. Recently, a number of diversified courses and facilities for evening part-time education have also been provided in some polytechnics situated in metropolitan cities where such courses are in great demand. The qualified diploma holders are expected to take up supervisory positions in field and industry.

- **Degree Level :** For the professional engineers and technologists, facilities for technical education are available in 1,200 plus engineering colleges offering courses leading to the award of Bachelor's degree in engineering and technology. The total admission capacity annually for these courses is of the order of 2,00,000. The duration of most of these degree courses was initially five years and with the new pattern of secondary education of 10+2, it changed over completely by 1981-1982 to a duration of four years (except architecture).
- **Post Graduate Courses :** The number of institutions offering post graduate courses is about 100 with an annual intake capacity of about 2,000 plus. These courses normally lead to the master's degree in the concerned discipline and are of two years/ one and a half year duration. Facilities also exist at these centers offering part-time courses at the post graduate level for those who are already in service. Duration of such courses normally is three years.

Eligibility and Course Areas

A bachelor's degree in engineering is the minimum requirement to become a qualified civil engineer. A post graduate degree is required for research or teaching posts and an additional degree in business administration is desirable for management positions.

Engineering courses are available at two levels. There are the degree and postgraduate degree courses offered by the engineering colleges and Institutes of Technology (IITs) and the diploma courses available at polytechnics. There is also the Associate Membership Examination of the Institute of Engineers (AMIE), which enables working people in the private and public sector or diploma holders to acquire a bachelor's engineering degree through distance education. IIT Chennai and Institute of Post Graduate Studies and Research, Hyderabad gives MS courses in civil engineering through distance education, the basic qualification of which is BE/B. Tech. in engineering.

The basic eligibility criteria for a BE/B.Tech. in civil engineering is 10+2 or equivalent examination with high percentage of marks in science subjects (physics, chemistry and mathematics).

Selection

Selection to the graduate courses (BE/B.Tech.) is based on merit on merit, i.e., the marks secured in the final exams of 10+2 and through entrance examinations. Entrances to the IIT's are through 'JEE' (Joint Entrance Examination) and for other institutions through their own separate entrance examinations and other state level and national level examinations. Apart from the IITs, some other famous institutes also recognise JEE scores for selection. Selection to the postgraduate courses (M.Sc./M.Tech.) in different universities is through the 'All India Combined Entrance Examination' conducted by JNU, New Delhi and to IIT's through 'GATE' in two years/four semesters M.Tech. courses and through JEE in five years integrated M.Tech. courses.

Duration

BE/B.Tech. courses are of four years duration. The diploma courses are of two-three years duration.

Fee

In private colleges fees range from approx. ₹ 1 lakh to ₹ 2 lakh annually for a bachelor's degree. In IIT's it varies between ₹ 15,000 to 20,000 per year.

Remuneration

The earnings depend on the industries employing civil engineers such as central or state government departments or private concerns. In India, a bachelor's degree candidate in civil engineering can receive a starting salary of R. 15,000 up to ₹ 20,000 approximately with two-three years experience. With more experience or as an established independent consultant one could earn more. Companies abroad in Singapore, UAE etc. pay around ₹ 1, 00,000 for candidates with two-three years experience. In USA, according to a salary survey by the National Association of Colleges and Employers, a bachelor's degree candidate as an initial salary is offered an average of $30,616 a year, master's degree candidates received an average offer $44,080, and Ph.D. candidates are offered $53,280. Average salary of engineers employed by the federal government is about $60,078.

Institutes

Engineering Colleges of National Importance

- **Indian Institute of Technology (IIT), Powai.** Mumbai-400076.
- **Indian Institute of Technology, Hauz Khas** New Delhi-110016.

- **Indian Institute of Technology**
  North,
  Guwahati-781039, Assam.
- **Indian Institute of Technology**
  Kanpur-208016, Uttar Pradesh.
- **Indian Institute of Technology**
  Kharagpur-721302
  West Bengal.
- **Indian Institute of Technology**
  Chennai-600036
  Tamil Nadu
- **Indian Institute of Technology**
  Roorkee-247667, Uttarakhand.
- **Indian Institute of Technology**
  BHU, Varanasi-221005, Uttar Pradesh.
- **Institute of Technology, Allahabad**
- **Indian School of Mines,**
  Dhanbad-826004, Jharkhand.

9.9 Computer Engineering

What is Computer Engineering?

Computer Engineering involves designing and testing of computer components. It is a branch of engineering and computer science angles, combining the principle and techniques of these two for the making and development of computer and computer-based systems. Professionals who work with computer hardware and software are termed as Computer Engineers.

Who are Computer Engineers?

Computer engineers are a part of a team who apply their knowledge of mathematics and science for the design and development of computer. Those who deal with the computer equipment as such are termed as computer hardware engineers and those who deal with the computer programmes are called computer software engineers. Computer software or software is a collection of computer programmes, procedures and documentation that performs the major tasks on a computer system.

Software engineers should have strong programming skills as they are concerned with the design and development of many types of software including computer games, word processing and business applications, operating systems and network distribution and compilers which convert programmes to machine language for execution on a computer.

Hardware engineers are involved in the research, designing, testing, manufacturing and installation of computer hardware such as computer chips, circuit boards, computer systems and related equipments. Their work is similar to that of electronic engineers but their work is exclusively limited to computers and computer-related equipments. Computer engineers have the option of moving into hardware or software positions or blending the two. On projects, both these engineers usually work together as a team. It is these computer engineers who design software and hardware computer-based systems for embedded micro controllers, designing – VLSI chips, analog sensors, mixed signal circuit boards and operating systems.

Eligibility and Course Areas

Students who wish to pursue a career in computer science and engineering need a strong foundation in both mathematics and science particularly chemistry and physics. To become a computer engineer one should have a graduate degree (B.E./B. Tech.) or post graduate degree (M.E.) or at least have a diploma in computer engineering. A diploma holder in computer engineering can become a junior engineer in various public and private sector jobs. Master's degree in computer engineering is required for teaching.

The basic eligibility criterion for a B.E./B.Tech. in computer engineering is 10+2 or equivalent examination with physics, chemistry and mathematics. The eligibility for diploma in computer engineering is 10+2 with science subjects. After bachelor's degree, one can go in for a post graduate degree, i.e., M.E./M.Tech. The eligibility for M.E./ M.Tech. in computer engineering is B.E./B.Tech. in computer engineering. The Associate Membership of the Institution of Engineers (AMIE) also offers courses in computer engineering in distance mode, equivalent to B.E./B.Tech. provided by other institutes/universities. There are various universities and technological institutions in various parts of our country offering Ph.D. programmes in computer engineering.

Selection

Admission to the B.E./B.Tech. courses is highly competitive and only those with high academic performance in the board examination, i.e., in the marks secured in the final examinations of 10+2 and in the entrance test can expect admission. Selection is generally made on the basis of the marks obtained in +2 and the merit in Common Entrance Test (CET) conducted by the competent authority. Admission the IIT's (Indian Institute of Technology) is through IIT JEE (Joint Entrance Examination) and for other major institutions through AIEEE (All India Engineering/Pharmacy/Architecture Entrance Examination). OR their own separate entrance examinations and other state level and national level examinations. Admission to the B.E./B.Tech. in computer engineering in the Associate Memberships of the Institution of Engineers (AMIE) is done through the Associate Membership Examination of the Institute of Engineers.

Selection to the M.E./M.Tech. programmes in various engineering colleges and universities like the IITs and NITs is through GATE (Graduate Aptitude Test in Engineering).

Duration

B.E./B.Tech. courses in computer engineering are of four years (eight semesters). Diploma course in computer engineering is of three years. M.E./M. Tech. in computer engineering is of two years (four semesters).

Job Prospects

System study, analysis, design and programming are the main areas which provide various probabilities to the computer science and engineering graduates to shape themselves in their career. Computer engineers develop computer programmes for industries. Their work involves the design, development and maintenance of software. They are engaged in analysing problems for solutions, formulating and testing, using advanced communications or multimedia equipment or working in teams for product development.

A computer engineering graduate with a high percentage of mark and good communication skills are easily absorbed in reputed companies. Along with the degree in computer science, the candidate should be well trained in the latest software. Software and IT companies are the main employers of these graduates. They can also find job opportunities in a variety of environments in university, research, private and public industries, government departments, business organisations, commercial organisations and the manufacturing sector.

Career Options

Computer engineers can work as a software/hardware engineer which are the two main sectors in the computer industry. Software is the set of programmed instructions that enable a computer to performed specified functions and hardware covers the physical elements of a computer system and is concerned with the design, development, assembly, manufacture and maintenance. They can work as programmers, web developers and e-commerce specialists with industries that build or use computer-based systems such as telecommunications, automative, aerospace etc. National and multi-national computer manufacturing companies, computer hardware system design and development companies, computer networking companies, software development companies as well as hardware assembling and maintenance companies, data processing departments of modern industries and in areas where computer and computer-aided systems are used such as aeronautics and space science, the petroleum industry, chemical plants and power plants and management consultancy organisations are some among the probable work places.

Diploma holder in computer engineering can start their own business enterprise with very little investment. A person with good academic record *i.e.*, a master's degree in computer engineering with five years experience in teaching at graduate level or industrial experience in a reputed firm can be employed as a lecturer. Qualified candidates can find employment as a software engineer in software companies in India and abroad.

Remuneration

In India, fresh graduates in computer engineering can get a starting salary of ₹ 10,000 – 25,000 and within one or two year of experience it may gradually increase to ₹ 50,000 or more per month. A lecturer in this field can earn an amount of ₹ 8000 – 13,500 plus dearness allowances. Fresher from the best technological universities/colleges (IITs and NIITs) are offered annual pay package of up to 10 lakh.

Courses

- B.E. Computer Science and Engineering,
- B.E. Computer Technology,
- B.Sc. Software Engineering,
- B.Tech. Computer Science and Engineering,
- B.Tech. Computer Science and Information Technology,
- B.Tech. Computer Software Engineering,
- Computer Science and Engineering (DIPIETE/AMIETE),
- Diploma in Computer Science and Engineering,
- Diploma in Computer Technology,
- Diploma in Software Engineering,
- M.E. Computer Aided Design (CAD)

- M.E. Computer Science and Engineering,
- M.E. Computer Science and Information Technology,
- M.E. Computer Technology and Applications,
- M.E. Computer Software Engineering,
- M.E. Systems Engineering and Operations Research,
- M.Tech. Computer Aided Design (CAD/CAM),
- M.Tech. Computer and Communication Engineering,
- M.Tech. Computer Applications in Industrial Drives,
- M.Tech. Computer Science and Engineering,
- M.Tech. Computer System and Networking,
- M.Tech. Internet and Networking,
- M.Tech. Network and Internet Engineering,
- M.Tech. Network Engineering,
- M.Tech. Soft computing and Machine Learning,
- M.Tech. Software Engineering,
- B.Tech - M.Tech. Computer Science and Engineering, and
- Ph. D. Computer Science and Engineering.

Institutes

The important computer engineering colleges in India which offer courses in computer engineering / sciences / technology :

- Indian Institute of Technology, Mumbai (Maharashtra)
- Indian Institute of Technology, New Delhi
- Indian Institute of Technology, Guwahati (Assam)
- Indian Institute of Technology, Kanpur, (Uttar Pradesh)
- Indian Institute of Technology, Kharagpur (West Bengal)
- Indian Institute of Technology, Chennai (Tamil Nadu)
- Institute of Technology, BHU, Varanasi (Uttar Pradesh)
- Institute of Technology, Roorkee (Uttar Pradesh)
- Birla Institute of Technology, Mesra, Ranchi (Jharkhand)
- National Institute of Technology
- Institute of Technology, (Uttar Pradesh)
- College of Engineering and Technology (Anna University)

Regional Engineering Colleges of National Importance

- Motilal Nehru Regional Engineering College, Allahabad (Uttar Pradesh).
- Maula Azad College of Technology, Bhopal (Madhya Pradesh).
- Calicut Regional Engineering College, Calicut (Kerala).
- Regional Engineering College, MG Avenue, Durgapur (West Bengal).
- Regional Engineering College, Hamirpur (Himachal Pradesh).
- Malviya Regional Engineering College, Jaipur (Rajasthan).
- Dr. B.R. Ambedkar Regional Engineering College, Jalandhar (Punjab).
- Regional Institute of Technology, Jamshedpur (Jharkhand).
- Regional Engineering College, Kurukshetra (Haryana).
- Visvesvaraya Regional College of Engineering, Nagpur, Maharashtra.
- Regional Engineering College, Rourkela (Orissa).
- Regional Engineering College, Silchar (Assam).
- Karnataka Regional Engineering College, Surathkal, Srinivasnagar (Karnataka).
- Sardar Vallabhbhai Regional College of Engineering and Technology, Surat (Gujarat).
- Regional Engineering College, Tiruchirapalli (Tamil Nadu).
- Regional Engineering College, Warangal (Andhra Pradesh).

9.10 Electrical Engineering

What is Electrical Engineering?

Electrical Engineering is a branch of engineering that deals with the study of diverse utilisation of electricity and equipments that generate and distribute power. This is divided into heavy current – telecommunications, radar, computers etc. Conventional areas like generation, allocation, distribution and transmission of electricity come under the purview of electrical engineering. The broad field of electrical engineering involves working with all manners of electronic devices from pocket calculators to supercomputers. In this area, the engineer's task involves generating, distributing and using electrical power in the fields of communication, control system, electronic computer, industrial electronics and instrumentation etc.

What is the Work of an Electrical Engineer?

Electrical engineers design and develop electrical systems, research new and innovative designs and system, supervise and plan manufacturing process of high end electrical systems. This role provides a number of challenges ranging from problem identification and the selection of appropriate technical solutions, materials, test equipment and procedures, to the manufacture and production of safe, economical, high-performance products and services. Electrical engineers work to combine technology with creativity, taking ideas and turning them into reality. In fact, electrical engineers are involved in the practical application of electrical energy.

Importance of Electricity

Electricity has become the basic need for survival. From household to industrial plants, communication and satellite navigation system, electronic equipment, computers etc., all require electricity. Hence, electrical engineering which deals with study and application of electrical systems is widely applicable in each and every aspect of our daily life. Virtually every industry utilises electrical engineers, so employment opportunities are extensive.

Eligibility

A bachelor's degree in engineering is the minimum requirement to become a qualified electrical engineer. A post graduate degree is required for research or teaching posts and an additional degree in business administration is desirable for management positions.

Course Areas

Engineering courses are available at two levels. There are graduate and postgraduate degree courses offered by the engineering colleges and Institutes of Technology (IITs) and the diploma courses available at polytechnics. Associate Membership of the Institution of Engineers (AMIE) also offers courses in electrical engineering which is equivalent to B.E./B.Tech. provided by other institutes/universities.

The basic eligibility criteria for a B.E./B.Tech. in electrical engineering is 10+2 or equivalent examination with high percentage of marks in science subjects (physics, chemistry and mathematics). While for post graduate programmes, one should have done electronic engineering. One can even opt for super specialty or Ph.D. programme in electrical engineering. For the purpose, the person should have done M.E. in electrical engineering or electronic engineering.

Selection

Selection to graduate courses (B.E./B.Tech.) is based on merit, i.e., the marks secured in the final examinations of 10+2 and through entrance examinations. Entrance to the IITs is through JEE scores for selection. The national level examination AIEEE is also conducted for admissions in NITs in India and many other prestigious colleges. Selection to the post graduate courses (M.E./M.Tech.) in different universities is through an 'All India Combined Entrance Examination' conducted by JNU, New Delhi and to IITs is through 'GATE'.

Duration

B.E./B.Tech. courses are of four years duration. The diploma courses are of two-three years duration. Post Graduate course M.E./M.Tech. is of two years duration.

Personal Attributes

A successful electrical engineer possesses not only an understanding of his area of concentration but also a broad grasp of engineering in general. An electrical engineer is expected to have detailed knowledge of electrical networks, electrical energy converters and equipments that uses electromagnetic field theory, electrical energy distribution systems etc.

Job Prospects and Career Options

The scope of electrical engineering lies in the areas of generating electricity, its distribution and transmission. As everything from house to industry requires electricity to function, there are tremendous career prospects in this field in India as well as in other developed countries across the world. Globalisation has also created huge demand for technically qualified engineers to keep pace with growing industrial needs.

Different types of employers offer jobs to electrical engineers. Employers range from computer-technology corporations and chemical companies to power and telephone companies. Both small and large companies in the private sector and the government sector offer placement for electrical engineers. Electrical engineers can find employment in electrical equipment and systems manufacturing industry, public sector industries like petroleum, steel and chemical industry, research and design.

Electrical graduates are employed in Electricity Boards/Utility companies and large industries as engineers and managers, responsible for installation, maintenance, operation of power handling equipments and systems. Industries manufacturing large electrical machines and equipments employ engineers in design, production and testing. Electrical engineers also find employment in atomic power plants, hydroelectric power plants as well as thermal power plants. Many electrical engineering graduates opt for careers in the food, pulp and paper, chemical, aircraft and automobile industries.

Educational institutions and research establishments recruit electrical engineers as faculty and scientists. One can also do research work in this field by joining research labs and institutes. Teaching career is also rewarding. They can join an engineering college/university as a full time or part time lecturer /professor. They can also enter into self-employment by starting own ventures.

Entry into Government Departments

As an electrical engineer, entry for junior posts in the government departments is by direct recruitment through advertisements in newspapers. Selection to gazetted posts is through competitive examinations conducted by Union and State Public Service Commission. UPSC conducts an engineering service examination annually for vacancies in central engineering services and various state public service commissions conduct their own competitive examinations for vacancies in state engineering services. Young engineers have chances in the defense services also. For selection into the defense services – Indian Army, Indian Air Force, Indian Navy, applications are invited through national dailies and *Employment News.*

Remuneration

Pay scale of an electrical engineer depends on experience, higher qualification and capabilities. Fresh graduates from elite technological institutions like Indian Institutes of Technology (IITs), National Institutes of Technology (NITs) and Birla Institute of Technology get more remuneration as compared to others. The average starting salary of electrical engineering graduates in India ranges between ₹ 15,000 – 25,000. Whereas, those with M.Tech. degree can expect much more. Senior electrical engineers with more than five years of working experience can earn between ₹ 35,000 to 80,000 per month. The pay package in foreign countries is much higher as compare to India.

Courses

- B.E. Electrical and Electronics Engineering,
- B.E. Electrical Engineering,
- B.E. Electrical, Electronics and Power Engineering,
- B.E. Electrical and Electronics Engineering (Honours),
- B.Tech. Electrical and Instrumentation Engineering,
- B.Tech. Electrical and Electronics Engineering,
- B.Tech. Electrical Engineering,
- Diploma in Electrical and Electronics Engineering,
- Diploma in Electrical Engineering,
- M.E. Electrical Engineering,
- M.E. Power Systems Engineering,
- M.Tech. Electrical Engineering,
- M.Tech. Electrical Power System,
- Ph.D. Electrical and Electronics Engineering, and
- Ph.D. Electrical Engineering.

Institutes

- Indian Institute of Technology (IITs) in New Delhi, Mumbai, Guwahati, Kanpur, Kharagpur etc.
- Birla Institute of Technology (BITS) – Pilani and Ranchi
- Delhi College of Engineering, Delhi,
- University of Roorkee, Roorkee, Uttar Pradesh etc.
- Various Regional engineering colleges in different states.

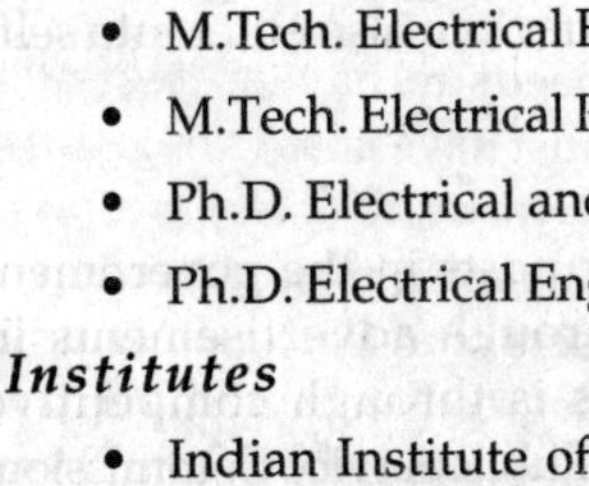

9.11 Electronics Engineering

What is Electronics Engineering?

Electronics Engineering covers a wide range of applications which make our life easier and enjoyable such as television, radio, computers, telecommunication etc. They help us to see, hear and communicate over vast distances and do things faster. Electronics has a major role in improving productivity in industries like oil, energy, agriculture and so many other important sectors of economy. In steel, petroleum and chemical industries it is the electronic devices that direct, control and test production processes.

Health care industry depends on electronic instruments to perform chemical tests and to check body functions. The safety in transportation, factories and mines and in homes relies heavily on electronics.

The Work of an Electronics Engineer

An electronics engineer must find new solutions to the practical problems affecting our daily lives. An electronics engineer will work in team with other specialists to design, fabricate, produce, test and supervise the manufacture of complex products and systems, i.e., electronic equipments and components for a number of industries including hospitals, computer industry, electronic data processing systems for communication and in defence. They supervise production and manufacturing processes and oversee installation and maintenance. Electronics engineers work with devices that use extremely small amounts of power. They work with microprocessor, fiber optics and in telecommunication, television, radio etc.

Eligibility and Course Areas

To become an electronics engineer one needs to have a degree in electronics engineering (B.E./B.Tech.) or must have passed the AMIE. (Associate Membership Examination of the Institute of Engineers) in electronics or graduate membership Examination of the Institution of Electronics and Telecommunication Engineers or at least a diploma in electronics engineering. A post graduate degree is required for most research or teaching posts and management positions. An additional degree in business administration is desirable for those seeking administrative or management positions.

The basic eligibility criterion for a B.E./B.Tech. is 10+2 or equivalent examination with physics, chemistry and mathematics. Admission to these courses is highly competitive and only those with high academic performance in the board of examination, i.e., the marks secured in the final examinations of 10+2 and in the entrance test can expect admission. Entrance to the IITs is through 'JEE' (Joint Entrance Examination) and for other major institutions through AIEEE (All India Engineering/ Pharmacy/Architecture Entrance Examination) or their own separate entrances exams and other state level and national level exams.

Duration

The duration is four years for B.E./B.Tech. courses. The diploma courses in polytechnics are of three years duration. The focus in the study programme is on understanding electronic networks and devices, electro-magnetic field theory, computer fundamentals as also their protection and communication and control systems.

Personal Attributes

A creative and inventive mind with an interest in physics and mathematics is essential to take up this challenging career. They should have good analytical skills, an eye for detail, sustained attention and the ability to work as part of a team. They should also have good communication skills.

Job Prospects

An electronics engineer can get a job in central government, state governments and their sponsored corporations in public enterprises and the private organisations like All India Radio, Indian Telephone Industries, MTNL, National Physical Laboratories, Civil Aviation Department, Post and Telegraph Department, Co-ordination Department, Bharat Electronics Limited, Development Centers in various states etc. dealing in manufacture, sales and services or electronics consumer goods and appliances. Electronics engineers are also absorbed into the entertainment transmission industry, research establishment and defence. They can also take up teaching and research in one of the many engineering colleges in India or abroad.

Career Options

As an Electronic Engineer, entry for junior posts in the Government departments is by direct recruitment through advertisement in newspapers. Selection to Gazette posts is through the competitive examinations conducted by Union and State Public Service Commission. UPSC conducts an Engineering Service Examination (Telecommunication and Electronics Engineering group) annually for vacancies in central engineering services and various state public service communications conduct their own competitive examinations for vacancies in state engineering services.

Employment in the Defence Service and other sectors

In the defense services, young engineers start as second lieutenants. For selection into the defence services – Indian Army, Indian Air Force, Indian Navy, applications are invited through national dailies and *Employment News*. Similarly, vacancies in the private and public sector are advertised through leading daily newspapers of the country and the *Employment News*. Mostly the candidates are interviewed after thorough scrutiny of their basic inputs and the selections are made on merit. Central Electronics Ltd., Indian Railways, Atomic Energy Commission, Hindustan Aeronautics Limited, Ministry of Civil Aviation, Directorate General posts and telegraphs departments are some of the prospective employers in the field.

Starting one's own business

Electronics Engineers can start their own business by manufacturing electronic parts, goods and components. He can also start a repair or assembly shop for television receivers, amplifiers and recording equipments. Since, electronic is a labor intensive and talent-oriented field, it gives high returns for a given initial investment. Loan facilities are offered by banks and small scale industries development corporations for starting a business.

Remuneration

Earnings of an electronic engineer vary with market demand and among organisations. Working experience, qualifications, ability are important factors in determining the pay level. In India, a bachelor's degree candidate in electronics engineering can receive a starting salary of ₹ 7,500 up to 15,000 approximately with one-two years experience.

Courses

- B.E. Applied Electronics and Instrumentation Engineering,
- B.E. Electronics and Communication Engineering,
- B.E. Electronics and Instrumentation Engineering,
- B.E. Electronics and Power Engineering,
- B.E. Electronics and Telecommunication Engineering,
- B.E. Electronics Engineering,
- B. Tech. Applied Electronics and Engineering,
- B. Tech. Applied Electronics and Instrumentation,
- B. Tech. Electronic Instrumentation and Control Engineering,
- B. Tech. Electronics and Biomedical Engineering,
- B. Tech. Applied Electronics and Instrumentation,
- B. Tech. Electronics and Communication Engineering,
- B. Tech. Electronics and Instrumentation Engineering,
- B. Tech. Electronics and Media Technology,
- B. Tech. Electronics and Telecommunication Engineering,
- B. Tech. Electronics Engineering,
- Diploma in Electronics and Communication Engineering,
- Diploma in Electronics and Instrumentation Engineering,
- Diploma in Electronics and Telecommunication Engineering,
- Diploma in Electronics Engineering,

- Electronics and Telecommunication Engineering (DIPIETE/AMIETE),
- M.E. Applied Electronics,
- M.E. Electronics and Communication Engineering,
- M.E. Electronics and Telecommunication Engineering,
- M.E. Electronics Engineering,
- M.E. Electronics Product Design and Technology,
- M. Tech. Applied Electronics,
- M. Tech. Digital Electronics,
- M. Tech. Electronic Instrumentation and Control Engineering,
- M. Tech. Electronics and Communication Engineering,
- M. Tech. Electronics and Instrumentation Engineering,
- M. Tech. Electronics and Telecommunication Engineering,
- M. Tech. Electronics Engineering,
- M. Tech. Power Electronics,
- Ph. D. Electronics and Communication Engineering, and
- Ph. D. Electronics Engineering.

Institutes

- Indian Institute of Technology (IITs) in New Delhi, Mumbai, Guwahati, Kanpur, Kharagpur etc.
- Birla Institute of Technology (BITS) – Pilani and Ranchi,
- Delhi College of Engineering, Delhi
  University of Roorkee, Roorkee, Uttar Pradesh etc.
- The various Regional engineering colleges in different states.

9.12 Environmental Engineering

What is Environmental Engineering?

Environmental Engineering related to environmental science is a broad field that applies the principles of science and engineering to protect and improve environmental conditions. The field focuses on design and technology for improving environmental quality. The main areas of environmental engineering include air pollution control, industrial hygiene, radiation protection, hazardous waste management, toxic materials control, recycling, waste supply, wastewater management, storm water management, solid waste disposal, public health and land management. Within each of these major categories, there are many sub categories.

Who are Environmental Engineers and what is their work?

Environmental Engineers are technical experts concerned with local and worldwide environmental issues. They combine the principles of biology and chemistry to develop solutions to environmental problems and work in a wide variety of settings with various engineering mechanisms. The major task of environmental engineers is to protect public health by preserving and enhancing the environment. They are engaged in designing various pollution control equipment and devices, construction, installation, implementation and operation of environmentally related procedures. They are also involved in the protection of wildlife, conduct research on proposed environmental projects, analyse scientific data, perform quality control checks and design municipal water supply and industrial wastewater treatment systems. Environmental engineers also attempt to prevent the production and repercussion of acid rain, global warming, ozone depletion as well as harmful automobile emissions.

Eligibility

An individual aspiring for a career in environmental engineering can join B.E./B.Tech. programme after his or her plus-two with physics, chemistry and mathematics. The B.E./B.Tech. is of four years duration. Admission to B.Tech. programme is made generally through entrance tests.

Course Areas

The course area varies depending on the institution and programme. Common core environmental engineering course include organic chemistry, hydrology, surface water quality engineering, surface water quality modeling, the quality of the air and the meteorology. All the environmental engineering programmes provide classroom instruction and hands-on laboratory experiences.

Personal Skills

Besides, basic engineering training and educator orientation, organisation, logical thinking and analytical skills are required. The ability to apply environmental engineering principles to a variety, they must have good communication skills and a knack for lucid explanation, creative and flexible mind, scientific aptitude and decision attributes.

Job Prospects and Career Options

Environmental engineers are in great demand for solving issues related to waste and air pollution and sometimes in areas concerned with hazardous waste cleanup. Management of hazardous waste is the largest area of work for environmental engineers. They would need to keep up-to-date with the new policies and laws in environmental protection. They sketch regulations to prevent damage to applications of environmental engineering include environmental impact assessment and mitigation, for *e.g.*, afforestation of a nearby area to mitigate the effects of deforestation in an area, water supply and treatment, wastewater conveyance and treatment and air pollution control or quality management.

Ample job opportunities are available for environmental engineers and their duties vary depending on the project and may include collecting and analysing data, performing quality control checks, evaluating and devising solutions for environmental hazards. These professionals are recruited in central and state pollution control boards and several NGOs in every state who are up in arms against all forms of environmental pollution. They can work with air pollution control, green house gases, ozone depletion, and side effects of pollution on human beings, animals and plants, water quality management, land conservation and report on environmental impact of proposed construction projects.

Environmental engineers may be employed in :

- Government agencies/departments as health and safety officers to monitor and regulate waste discharges;
- Laboratories – to develop pollution control systems;
- Municipal agencies – to design and take care of the water supply systems;
- Various industries/companies – to plan their air or waste water treatment systems, to treat and dispose of hazardous chemicals;
- Universities/colleges – to teach and conduct research on environmental control;
- Manufacturing and pharmaceutical companies; and
- International firms working for environmental related projects.

Environmental engineers can work as consultants helping their clients to comply with regulations and to clean up hazardous sites. Distilleries, fertilisers plants, textile mills, water treatment industries, refineries, mines, food processing industries, etc., use the service of environmental engineers. They also work with mining engineers to develop production techniques, assist civil engineers in designing water supply and waste disposal system and toil with chemical and nuclear engineers in waste disposal.

Remuneration

Candidates with B.E./B.Tech. in environmental engineering may receive an initial payment between ₹ 15,000 – 30,000 per month and those with post graduate degree may earn between ₹ 30,000 – 50,000. Ph.D. degree holders can earn an amount not less than ₹ 50,000 per month. The remuneration of a licensed engineer is supposed to be ₹ 1 lakh per month. More work experience and specialised training can make this profession a high paying career. Multinational companies operating on environment projects offer lucrative pay packages and perks to environmental engineers.

Courses

- B.E. Environmental Engineering,
- B.E. Environmental Science and Engineering,
- B. Tech. Environmental Engineering,
- M.E. Environmental Engineering, and
- M. Tech. Environmental Engineering.

Institutes that offer Environmental Engineering

- P.M. College of Engineering (PMCE), Sonipat, Haryana.
- ITM University Gurgaon, Haryana.
- Gurgaon Institute of Technology and Management, Gurgaon, Haryana.
- Manav Rachna International University (MRIU), Faridabad, Haryana
- Alagappa Chattier College of Engineering Technology, Karikudi, Tamil Nadu.
- Bengal Engineering and Science University (BESU), Shibpur, Howrah, West Bengal.
- Bharath Institute of Science and Technology (BIST), Chennai, Tamil Nadu.
- BMS College of Engineering, Bangalore, Karnataka.
- Chandigarh College of Engineering and Technology (CCET), Chandigarh, Punjab.
- American Power Conversion, Mangalore, Karnataka.
- Arulmigu Kalasalingam College of Engineering, Krishnankoil, Virudthunagar.

- Aryabhatta Knowledge University, Patna, Bihar.
- C. Abdul Hakeem College of Engineering and Technology, Melvisharam, Vellore, Tamil Nadu.
- CBP Government Engineering College, Pitampura, Delhi.
- GMR Institute of Technology, Srikakulam affiliated to the University of Kakinada.
- Hindustan College of Science and Technology, Agra, Uttar Pradesh.
- Hindustan College of Science and Technology, Mathura, UP.
- Hindustan Institute of Technology and Science, St. Thomas Mount, Chennai, Tamil Nadu.
- IILM Academy for Higher Learning, Greater Noida, Delhi.
- Institute of Engineering and Technology, Lucknow, UP.
- Institute of Technology, Banaras Hindu University, Varanasi.
- Jabalpur Engineering College, Ranchi, Jabalpur.
- MAM College of Engineering and Technology, Tiruchirapalli, Trichy.
- Manipal Institute of Technology, Manipal, Udupi.
- Punjab Engineering College, Sector-12, Chandigarh.

9.13 Fire Engineering

What is Fire Engineering?

Fire Engineering is a very dicey profession which requires a strong sense of commitment to public service. Fire Engineering is a field which explores the various possibilities of preventing fires. It can be defined as the art and science of designing building and facilities for life safety and property protection in the event of an unwanted fire. This includes the application of scientific and engineering principles, based on an understanding of the phenomena and effects of fire and of reaction and protection systems including detection, alarm and sprinkler systems.

The role of fire engineers

Fire engineers have to work in shifts in dangerous conditions and are at risk of burns, smoke inhalation and exposure to chemicals. They need to be patient and disciplined, quick and efficient, reliable, self-confident and able to work well in teams. They need to know about streets and places in their district, the handling of dangerous goods and building construction. They also need to know about fire-fighting, different types of fires and how to deal with them and about rescue methods and equipments.

The role of fire engineers span engineering design to operations and management. In India, the major fire engineering programme is the one conducted by National Fire Service College at Nagpur that offers a three and a half years programme leading to bachelors of engineering. Fire engineers' main responsibility is reducing the consequences of fire if there is an incident. They are responsible for determining causes of fire and methods of fire prevention. They find new ways to maintain and improve the present fire-fighting equipment.

Eligibility and Course Areas

Most of the occupations in fire engineering require a bachelor's degree. A degree in fire engineering can be a bachelor of engineering and post graduate qualification of either Master's or Ph.D. level. The entry requirement for the post graduate qualification is generally a bachelor of engineering, B.E. degree in chemical, civil, mechanical or electrical engineering.

The selection for B.E. in fire engineering is through entrance test and it is normally held in May/June. The eligibility for B.E in fire engineering is B.Sc. with chemistry and either physics or mathematics or both as optional subjects. The age limit for joining B.E is 19 to 24 and the duration of course is three and a half years. Apart from the educational qualification, candidate should possess some specified physical qualification. He should be physically fit and free from organic disease to undergo practical training. Minimum acceptable physical standards for the fire engineering course are Height: minimum 165 cms. Weight: 50 kgs, Chest measurement: 81 cms with five cms expansion, Vision: 6/6, preferably without any aid.

Job Prospects and Career Options

A degree in fire engineering makes one eligible for the management cadre in fire service in the government or public sector. Fire engineers have always been in great demand by corporations, educational institutions, consulting firms and government departments, in large companies and they are also recruited by the fire brigades. When there are instances of fire accidents, fire engineers are called upon to assess the extent of the damage, investigate the cause of the fire, the efficiency of equipment installed and so on.

There is a vast scope of employment chances for fire engineers in large manufacturing organisations particularly those like petroleum refineries, petrochemicals and plastic, fertilisers, textiles, LPG and LNG handling and bottling plants, chemicals and other plants where there are risks of fire. Fire engineers are also employed by fire departments of local government bodies, insurance companies, architectural and building design, project management, aircraft industry, industrial processing and any area of safety where the possibility of fire or combustion represents a hazard. Fire engineers may also work as surveyors in insurance companies.

Remuneration

In government sector, the starting gross salary of a fire engineers could be in the range of ₹ 5,000 to 7,000 per month. Opportunities for getting a job in industry, office complexes or other private sector establishments generally exist after a few years of experience. In private sector, salary on joining may gross around ₹ 8,000 – 14,000 per month.

Courses

- B.E. Fire Engineering,
- B. Tech. Fire and Safety Engineering,
- Certificate Course in Fire and Safety Engineering (CFSE),
- Diploma in Course in Fire and Industrial Safety Engineering,
- Diploma in Course in Fire and Safety Engineering Management (DFSEM),
- Diploma in Fire Engineering,
- Diploma in Course in Industrial Safety Engineering (DISE), and
- Post Graduate Diploma in Fire and Safety Engineering (PGDFSE).

Top Fire Engineering Colleges in India

- **Rashtrasant Tukdoji Maharaj Nagpur University, Nagpur, Maharashtra**

  Course : Bachelor of Engineering – Fire Engineering.
- **Yashwant Rao Chavan Maharashtra Open University, Nashik, Maharashtra**

  Courses : Diploma in Fire Safety Engineering Management, Certificate in Fire Safety Engineering Management.
- **Cochin University of Science and Technology, Kochi, Kerala**

  Course : Bachelor of Technology in Safety and Fire Engineering.

- **Indira Gandhi Open University, New Delhi**

  Courses : Advanced Diploma in Rescue, Fire Fighting and Safety Diploma in Fire Safety.

- **Fairy Land College of Fire Engineering & Safety Management, Chandrapur, Maharashtra**

  Courses : Diploma in Fire Service Engineering, Diploma in Fire Engineering and Industrial Safety Management.

- **Hyderabad Institute of Fire Engineering, Secunderabad, Andhra Pradesh**

  Courses : Post Graduate Diploma in Fire and Safety Engineering, Diploma in Fire & Safety Engineering.

- **Shiv Kumar Singh Institute of Technology and Science, Indore, Madhya Pradesh**

  Course : Bachelor of Engineering in Fire Technology.

9.14 Genetic Engineering

What is Genetic Engineering?

Genetic Engineering (GE) is a highly sophisticated and advanced branch of science which involves a wide range of techniques used in changing the genetic material in the DNA code in a living organism. Genetic engineering means the deliberate modification of the characters of an organism by the manipulation of its genetic material. Genetic engineering comes under the broad heading of Biotechnology. There is a great scope in this field as the demand for genetic engineers are growing in India as well as abroad.

What is a Cell?

A cell is the smallest living unit, the basic structural and functional unit of all living matter, whether a plant, an animal, humans or a fungus. While some organisms are single celled, others like plants, animals, humans, etc., are made up of a lot more cells, e.g., humans have approximately million cells. A cell is composed of a 'cell membrane' enclosing the whole cell, many 'organelles' equivalent to the organs in the body and a 'nucleus' which is the command centre of the cell. Inside the nucleus are the chromosomes which are the storage place for all genetic (hereditary) information which determines the nature and characteristics of an organism. This information is written along the thin thread, called DNA, a nucleic acid which constitutes the genes (units of heredity). The DNA governs cell growth and is responsible for the transmission of genetic information from one generation to the next.

Aim of Genetic Engineering

Genetic engineering aims to re-arrange the sequence of DNA in gene using artificial methods. The work of a genetic engineer involves extracting the DNA out of one organism, changing it using chemicals or radiation and subsequently putting it back into the same or different organism, e.g., genes and segments of DNA from one species is taken and put into another species. They also study how traits and characteristics are transmitted through the generations and how genetic disorders are caused. Their research involves researching the causes and discovering potential cures if any.

Specialisations in Genetic Engineering

Genetic engineering has specialisations related to plants, animals and human beings. Genetic engineering in plants and animals may be to improve certain natural characteristics of value, to increase resistance to disease or damage and to develop new characteristics. It is used to change the colour, size, texture, etc., of plants otherwise known as GM (Genetically Modified) foods. Genetic engineering in humans can be to correct severe hereditary defects by introducing normal genes into cells in place of missing or defective ones.

Eligibility

The basic eligibility criteria for a graduate degree (BE/B.Tech.) is 10+2 or equivalent examination with biology, chemistry and mathematics as well as genetics as part of the biology or a bachelor's degree in science or molecular biology. A qualified genetic engineer must have a graduate/post graduate degree in genetics or related fields such as bio-technology, molecular biology, micro-biology or bio-chemistry or a doctorate (Ph.D.) from a recognised university based on two – three years of his own research under the guidance of a professor.

Course Areas

Most institutes do not offer courses in genetic engineering as a special discipline but as a subsidiary in bio-technology, micro-biology, bio-chemistry streams. Undergraduate and post graduate courses in Bio-technology offer specialisation in genetic engineering.

Selection

Selection to the graduate courses (BE/B. Tech.) is based on merit, i.e., the marks secured in the final examinations of 10+2 and through entrance examinations. Entrance to the IITs is through JEE and for other institutions through their own separate entrance examinations and other state level and national level examinations. Apart from the IITs, some other famous institutes also recognise JEE scores for selection. Selection to the post graduate courses (M.Sc./M.Tech.) in different universities is through an All India Combined Entrance Examination conducted by JNU, New Delhi and to IITs through GATE in two year/four semesters M.Tech. courses and through JEE in five years integrated M.Tech. courses in Bio-chemical engineering and Bio-technology.

Personal Attributes

To be a successful genetic engineer, one must have sharp analytical mind, an aptitude for research, high levels of concentration, eye for details, lively imagination, abundant physical stamina to put in long hours of work, ability to work as a team, moreover, he should have a sound moral sense.

Job Prospects and Career Options

There is an increasing demand for genetic engineers in India as well as abroad. Genetic engineers are mainly absorbed in medical and pharmaceutical industries, the agricultural sector and the research and development departments of the government and private sectors. They can also take up teaching as an option.

Genetic engineering involves developing hybrid varieties of plants, making a plant disease resistant by transferring genes from a plant that already has the characteristic, introducing Genetically modified foods by changing the colour, size, texture of the produce of plants such as fruits and vegetables. Genetic engineering in humans can be to correct severe hereditary defects by introducing normal genes into cells in place of missing or defective ones.

A team headed by Ian Wilmut and his colleagues at the Roslin Institute in Edinburgh, Scotland made history when they produced a lamb named Dolly, an exact genetic copy or clone of a sheep. This landmark discovery of the regeneration of an exact replica of a whole animal by transferring nuclei from the cells of that animal to unfertilised eggs of another animal without the help of a male counterpart has given researchers a wide area open to be discovered. With this discovery, genetic engineering has become globally recognised.

Remuneration

Genetic engineers with a post graduate degree can earn between ₹ 5,000 – 8,000 per month. Whereas, those with doctoral degree can earn up to ₹ 10,000 as a starting pay.

Courses

- Certificate Course in Genetic Engineering, and
- M.Sc. Plant Breeding and Genetics.

Institutes

Institutes that offer Genetics at the undergraduate level are :

- Kakatiya University, Warangal, Andhra Pradesh.
- Osmania University, Hyderabad, Andhra Pradesh.

Some of the universities that offer genetic engineering courses at postgraduate and doctorate levels are :

- Bio-Informatics Centre of Jawaharlal Nehru University (JNU), New Delhi.
- Indian Institute of Technology (Kharagpur and Delhi).
- Delhi University, New Delhi.
- University of Calcutta, Kolkata, West Bengal.
- MKU-Coimbatore, Tamil Nadu.
- Birla Institute of Technology (Pilani, Rajasthan).
- University of Lucknow.
- Jadavpur University (Kolkata, West Bengal).

9.15 Petroleum Engineering

What is Petroleum Engineering?

Petroleum Engineering is a discipline in which the principles of geology, physics and engineering are applied for the recovery, development and processing of petroleum. It is basically mining engineering but deals only with oil and gas.

The need for Petroleum Engineering

Petroleum and petroleum products are valuable for any country. Shortage of petroleum could make industries, automobiles and households come to a standstill. They are dependent on petroleum in some way or other. There is a need to find more petroleum reservoirs to meet the growing demand. But the search for petroleum is not an easy task in complex geological locations. This has resulted in a huge demand for professionally trained personnel to meet the challenge.

Petroleum engineering covers a wide range of activities from the discovery of natural sources, examination of the natural characteristics and the development of modern machinery for the extraction and processing of petroleum.

Division of Petroleum Industry

The petroleum industry is broadly divided into two major sectors – the upstream sector and the downstream sector. Work in the upstream sector consists of the exploration, production and exploitation of oil and natural gas. The downstream sector comprises the refining, marketing and distributing functions.

Eligibility

Successful completion of 10+2 examination with physics, chemistry and mathematics as subjects, is the minimum criteria required to pursue a bachelor's degree in petroleum engineering. One must also pass the qualifying entrance examination of the particular institute or AIEEE or JEE conducted by the IITs which will be an added advantage for admission to top institutes. For pursuing master's degree, i.e., M.Tech. in petroleum engineering one must complete B.Tech. or B.E. in chemical or petroleum engineering. Those who have completed M.Sc. in chemistry are also eligible to pursue M.Tech. degree in petroleum engineering.

Job Prospects and Career Options

Petroleum Engineering degrees are not very popular in India because of fewer universities offering courses in petroleum engineering and less awareness of this engineering field among the aspirants. Employment opportunities are also not that great due to scarcity of oil in the market and low oil prices. Though job opportunities are limited in India, a qualified petroleum engineers have ample opportunities in the Middle East with very high annual income packages. Other countries and areas where much of the oil exploration and production activity is taking place include Africa, South America, Russia and the North Sea.

Major oil corporations both central and state, and innumerable small and independent oil exploration, production and service companies are the employers for this profession. They may also work for companies that produce drilling equipments, supplies and refining processes. Those with higher degrees can opt for the research field. Research and development work in petroleum technology is carried on at the Indian Institute of Petroleum (IIP) in Dehradun. They can also find jobs in educational institutions. One with professional degree in petroleum technology can find employment opportunities in government undertakings like Indian Oil, Oil India Limited, HPCL (Hindustan

Petroleum Corporation Limited), BP (British Petroleum) and ONGC (Oil and Natural Gas Corporation). Fresher may find opportunities in public undertakings as well as in corporate sector that deal with petroleum exploration and extraction.

Remuneration

Earnings for engineers vary significantly by specialty, industry and education. Petroleum engineers regularly top the list of highest starting salaries. The reason for the high remuneration is due to relatively low number of qualified workers in the industry. In India, petroleum engineers are paid monthly salary between ₹ 25,000 to 40,000 apart from other perks and benefits. The average annual starting salary of petroleum engineers in developed countries is about $ 50,000 and the mean annual salary is more than $80,000.

Courses

- B.E. Petroleum Engineering,
- B.Tech. Applied Petroleum Engineering,
- B.Tech. Petrochemical Engineering,
- B.E. Petroleum Engineering,
- B.Tech. Petroleum Engineering,
- B.Tech. Petroleum Refining and Petrochemicals Engineering,
- B.E. Petroleum Engineering,
- B.Tech. Petroleum Refining Engineering,
- B.Tech. Petroleum Reservoir and Production Engineering,
- M.E. Petroleum Engineering,
- M.Tech. Petroleum Exploration,
- M.Tech. Petroleum Refinery Engineering, and
- M.Tech. Petroleum Refining and Petrochemical Engineering.

Top ten colleges offering petroleum engineering courses in India :

- Indian Institute of Technology (IIT), Mumbai.
- Indian School of Mines University (ISM), Dhanbad.
- University of Petroleum and Energy Studies (UPES), Dehradun.
- Pandit Deendayal Petroleum University (PDPU), Gandhinagar.
- Maharashtra Institute of Technology (MIT), Pune.
- M.S. Engineering College, Bangalore.
- L.D. College of Engineering, Ahmedabad.
- G.H. Patel College of Engineering, Vallabh, Vidyanagar, Gujarat.

- Rajiv Gandhi Institute of Petroleum Technology (RGIPT), Uttar Pradesh.
- Universities of Petroleum and Energy Studies (UPES), Dehradun.

9.16 Robotics/Robotic Engineering

What is Robotics?

Robotics is a field of engineering concerned with the development and application of robots and computer systems for their control, sensory feedback and information processing. It is an exciting area of computer controlled technology.

What is Robotic Engineering?

Robotic engineering is a sub field of mechanical engineering, electrical and computer engineering and computer science. This is a rapidly growing field with advances in computing constantly opening up new possibilities for robotics application. The term 'robotics' includes research and engineering activities which involves the designing and development of robotic systems.

Who are Robotic Engineers?

The experts working in the area of robotics are called robotic engineers. Robotics engineers are basically concerned with the science of robotics that is the science of flexible automation. Robotics engineers design robots, maintain them, develop new applications for them and conduct research to expand the potential of robots. These engineers use computer-aided design and drafting and computer-aided manufacturing (CADDs/CAM) systems to perform their tasks. Their duties include analysing designs, debugging programmes, standardising and servicing the robots and combining the robots with new mechanical devices.

The Use of Robots

Robots are machines that are devised to replace human beings. They are also employed in jobs which are too dirty, dangerous or dull to be suitable for humans. Some of the robots function manually while others function on remote control. It is an artificial agent guided by computer or electronic programming. The many types of robotics systems include robotic manipulators, robotic hands, mobile robots, walking robots, aids for disabled persons, tele-robots and micro electro-mechanical systems. Today, robots are taking over most of the manipulative, hazardous and tedious jobs in factories, mines, atomic plants, space ships, deep-sea vessels, etc., from man. Robots are used in industries for speeding up the manufacturing process. They are also used in the field of nuclear science, sea-exploration, servicing of transmission of electric signals, designing of bio-medical equipments and others.

Eligibility and Course Areas

A bachelor's degree in engineering or a related field which is of four years duration is required for most entry-level positions in robotics engineering. Robotics being an interdisciplinary course invites students who have completed their graduation in mechanical engineering, electrical engineering, instrumentation engineering or computer engineering with an interest in robotics and artificial intelligence. Most colleges or universities offer robotics engineering as specialisation of other engineering degrees rather than as a stand alone programme. However, now there are universities that offer robotics engineering degrees itself.

For advancement in positions you need a master's degree or Ph.D. A Ph.D. is required to teach in this field as well as for most high level research positions. A master's degree requires two years, while a Ph.D. takes three to five years to complete.

Job Prospects

With the amazing progress of computer science and related research technologies, jobs in the field of robotics are gaining momentum. Use of robots is expected to increase in the near future from production line robots to experimental robotics for the medical, military and automotive industries. One can specialise in control or hardware design of robots.

Robotics engineering may lead to potential career opportunities in manufacturing, research and engineering, agriculture, mining, space exploration, power-plant maintenances and a variety of other areas. Besides, there is a great scope for qualified experts and researchers to associate themselves with different segments of R&D in robotics. Today's gaming industry is possibly providing the most enjoyable variation of the kind of intelligence provided by robotics. Games like X-Box, PCs and Play Station are putting this extensively to use. High precision robotic jobs such as welding and riveting also require the use of robots. They are also put to use in special situations that would be dangerous for humans like cleaning toxic wastes or exploring dreadful places like under water exploration.

Career Options

Robotics engineers can advance to management positions and become robotics managers or directors of automation. Some robotics engineers advance by moving into robot sales or by starting their own robotics consulting firms. A candidate having an M.E degree in robotics can get job opportunities in space research organisations like ISRO and also industries which manufacture microchips. Job opportunities also exist in Indian Institute of Technology for doing extensive research work in artificial intelligence. The Indian Institute of Chemical Biology offers openings for research fellowships in robotics and artificial intelligence. NASA is the ultimate job destination for those interested in applying robotics to space science. In India, organisations like BHEL, BARC, ISRO and DRDO besides other companies like Intel recruit robotics and artificial intelligence specialists from micro-chip manufacturing.

Remuneration

Earnings vary depending on the experience of the robotics engineer, the location and the kind of job. In India, one can expect a starting salary of ₹ 5-6 lakh per annum for a fresher. Benefits usually include paid holidays and vacations, health insurance and retirement plans.

Courses

- B.E. Robotics and Automation Engineering,
- Certificate in Embedded Systems and Robotics,
- Diploma in Industrial Automation and Robotics,
- M.E. Automation and Robotics,
- M.E. CAD/CAM and Robotics,
- M.E. Robotics,
- M.Tech. Industrial Automation and Robotics,
- M.Tech. Intelligent Systems and Robotics, and
- M.Tech. Robotics.

Institutes

Robotics is an inter disciplinary course in India. It is taught as a specialisation of mechanical, electrical engineering or computer programmes. Robotics engineering can be studied at the IITs and Indian Institute of Science, Bangalore. A few other institutes that offer this specialisation are the National Institute of Technology, University of Hyderabad, Jadavpur University and the Birla Institute of Technology and Science.

Top Universities for Robotics studies in India

- **West Bengal State University, North 24 Parganas, West Bengal**

  Course : Master of Engineering-Industrial Automation and Robotics.

- **Amity University, Noida, Uttar Pradesh**

  Course : M.Tech-Robotics.
- **Indian Institute of Information Technology, Allahabad, Uttar Pradesh**

  Course : Master of Technology-Robotics.
- **National Institute of Technology, Kurukshetra, Haryana**

  Course : Master of Technology-Robotics and Automation.
- **Institute of Technology and Management, Gurgaon, Haryana**

  Courses : Master of Technology-Robotics & Automation, Master of Technology-Robotics and Automation (Part Time).
- **Bhubanananda Orissa School of Engineering, Cuttack, Orissa**

  Course : Post Graduate Diploma in CAD/CAM Robotics.
- **SRM University, Kanchipuram, Tamil Nadu**

  Course : Master of Technology-Robotics.
- **University College of Engineering, Hyderabad, Andhra Pradesh**

  Course : Master of Technology-Automation and Robotics (Mechanical).

9.17 Telecommunication Engineering

What is Telecommunication Engineering?

Telecommunication Engineering is the exchange of information over a distance through electronic means and deals with communication systems such as cables, radio, satellite communications, TV, radar, navigational communication equipments and the like. Telecommunication engineering is involved with the designing, manufacturing and operation of telecommunication devices. This exciting field of engineering is gaining tremendous popularity and the wide area of services provided by the telecom sector makes it lucrative career for the youngsters with a range of opportunities.

Importance of Telecommunication Industry today

With the explosion of electronic media, telecommunication industry has become one of the fastest growing sectors in every corner of the world. This field plays an indispensable role in our day to day life and its technology has helped us to see, hear and communicate over vast distances. In this era of information and communication, more digitally enhanced communication devices like mobiles, internet and satellites are paving way to expansion for the wider reach of communication technology. As a result, there is a great demand for trained professionals in the industry and hence the importance of telecommunication engineering.

The Role of Telecommunication Engineers

Telecommunication engineering is an apt career for those who are interested in the fields of microelectronic devices, signal processing, data networking, coding, compression, encryption and transmission. Telecommunication engineers deal with the line, wireless or radio communication. Their major tasks include designing and installation of telecommunications equipment according to the client's interest. They are responsible for the network maintenance, quality control of the products and developing software in the telecom industry and troubleshooting. A telecommunication engineer should possess good knowledge of fiber optics, cellular technology, laser technology and the like.

Eligibility and Course Areas

Students who have a strong foundation in physics, chemistry and mathematics can opt for a career in Telecommunication Engineering. To become a telecommunication engineer one should have a graduate degree (BE/B.Tech.) or post graduate degree (M.E.) or at least a diploma in Telecommunication.

The basic eligibility criterion for BE/B.Tech. is higher secondary or 10+2 with physics, chemistry and mathematics with fairly high percentage of marks in aggregate. In some universities diploma holders in telecommunication engineering or those with B.Sc. degree are eligible for admission to the B.E. course. After the bachelor's degree, one can go in for a post graduate degree, i.e., M.E./M.Tech. in Telecommunication engineering. Some institutes offer MBA courses besides certificate and diploma and post graduate diploma courses. The basic eligibility for MBA and diploma courses is graduation and for post graduate diploma courses it is B. Tech./B.E.

Selection

Admission to BE/B.Tech. courses is made on the basis of the marks obtained in plus two and the merit in the entrance examinations. Entrance to the IITs is through the JEE and for other major institutions through AIEEE (All India Engineering/Pharmacy/Architecture Entrance Examination) or their own separate entrance examinations and other state level and national level examinations.

A student with B.Tech. degree in telecommunication from an AICTE (All India Council of Technical Education) approved university can get admission to ME/M.Tech. courses.

Symbiosis Institute of Telecom Management admits students to MBA course on the basis of marks obtained in Symbiosis National Aptitude Test (SNAP), group discussion and personal interview. In Amity Institute of Telecom Technology and Management, Noida, the admission is based on CAT, MAT and GMAT score. The Institute of Electronics and Telecommunication Engineers (IETE) is the national apex professional body of electronics and telecommunication, computer and IT professionals. The institute conducts both the graduate-ship and examination (AMIETE – Associate Membership of Institute of Electronics and Telecommunication Engineers) and (DIPIETE – Diploma of Institute of Electronics and Telecommunication and Computer Science and Engineering) streams. A pass in AMIETE examination is recognised by Government of India for the purposes of recruitment to superior posts and services under the Central Government while a pass in DIPIETE examination is recognised by the Ministry of HRD, Government of India for the purpose of employment to posts and services under the Central Government in the appropriate field. The institute also conducts post graduate level course ALCCS (Advanced Level Course in Computer Science) which is equivalent to M.Tech. in computer science and is recognised by the Ministry of HRD for the appointment to superior posts and services under the central government.

Duration of the Course Content

B.E/B.Tech. courses are of four years duration and the post graduate diploma, ME/M.Tech. and MBA courses are of two years. The duration of the diploma courses are one year and that of certificate course is three months. A course on telecommunication teaches students on various telecommunication devices such as mobile phones, cable TV, satellites, computer networking, radar and navigation. Particular emphasis is placed on wireless communication, mobile telephony, GSM architecture, internet protocol media system, CDMA, GPRS network, symbian operating system, voice over internet protocol, designing optical networks and understanding and designing data network.

Job Prospects

Some of the career prospects in this field of Telecommunication engineering are :

- **Research and Development :** Telecommunication engineers can work in the field of research and development which involves testing and conducting studies on new materials and chemical interactions.
- **Production :** The production engineers are engaged in developing and buildingthe materials, machinery, assembly line operations and quality standardisation.
- **Sales and Marketing :** Telecommunication engineers with the ability to understand customer needs evaluate potential applications and advice on matters regarding marketing can work in the field of sales and marketing.
- **Teaching :** People with excellent academic record, great communication skills, great interest in teaching and excellent command over the subject can work as teachers in this field. They are responsible for completing the syllabus of the students within stipulated period and should handle all type of teaching work in accordance with the task.

Career Options

Many job opportunities are available for graduates in the telephone industry. They could be employed as engineers/test engineers, software/application engineers, product managers, customer support staff, installers/repairers, power reactor operators, power distributors/dispatchers and many more. Cable and satellite networks, information and broadcasting sector, railways or police wireless organisations, aerospace industry, telecommunication service providers, mobile phone service providers are some other areas that one could get a job. They can also find employment in this field as design development, production, quality assurance, sales, servicing and software engineers.

Employment opportunities are available in the field of paramilitary force like the BSF, CRPF and defence-related organisations. Candidates with BE/B.Tech. in telecommunication with two or three years experience can work as teachers and those with ME/M.Tech. can work as lecturers or researchers etc. Those with MBA graduation can obtain managerial jobs.

Remuneration

Remuneration in this field depends upon the status of the industry, experience, qualification and ability of the employee. When compared with the government sectors, private firms offer much better salary. Depending upon the firm, fresh graduates can expect an initial monthly salary of ₹ 10,000 and above. With few years of experience it may gradually increase to ₹ 20,000 or more per month.

Courses

- B.E. Electronics and Telecommunication Engineering,
- B.E. Telecommunication Engineering,
- B.Tech. Electronics and Telecommunication Engineering,
- B.Tech. Telecommunication Engineering,
- Diploma in Electronics and Telecommunication Engineering,
- Diploma in Telecommunication Technology,
- Electronics and Telecommunication Engineering (DIPIETE/AMIETE),
- M.E. Electronics and Telecommunication Engineering,
- M.Tech. Electronics and Telecommunication Engineering,
- M.Tech. Networking and Telecommunications,
- MBA Telecommunication System Management, and
- Post Graduate Diploma in Telecommunication.

Best Institutes that Offer Telecommunication Engineering

- JB Knowledge Park, Faridabad, Haryana.
- Manav Rachna International University (MRIU), Faridabad, Haryana.
- P.M. College of Engineering (PMCE), Sonipat, Haryana.
- Lovely Professional University, Phagwara, Punjab.
- Vishwakarma Maritime Institute, Pune, Maharashtra.
- Gurgaon Institute of Technology and Management, Gurgaon, Haryana.
- Acharya Pathasala Rural College of Engineering, Bangalore, Karnataka.
- AMC College of Engineering, Bangalore, Karnataka.
- Bangalore Institute of Technology, Bangalore, Karnataka.

- College of Engineering and Information Technology, Jalgaon, Maharashtra.
- GSSS Institute of Engineering and Technology for Women, Mysore, Karnataka.
- SRM Institute of Science and Technology, Chennai, Tamil Nadu.
- Rungta College of Engineering and Technology, Bhilai, Chhattisgarh.
- Bombay Trust's College of Engineering and Technology, Bambhori, Jalgaon, Maharashtra.
- Vemana Institute of Technology, Bangalore, Karnataka.
- Vivekananda Institute of Technology, Bangalore.
- T. John Institute of Technology, Bangalore, Karnataka.
- Sri Siddhartha Institute of Technology, Tumkur, Karnataka.

9.18 What is All India Engineering Entrance Examination (AIEEE)?

The All India Engineering Entrance Examination (AIEEE) is an examination organised by the Central Board of Secondary Education (CBSE) in India. Introduced in the year 2002, this national level competitive test is for admission to various under-graduate engineering and architecture courses in institutes accepting the AIEEE score, including five Indian Institutes of Information Technology (IIITs) and thirty National Institutes of Technology (NITs). The examination is generally held on the last Sunday of April and results are announced in the last week of May or the first week of June. Candidates are ranked on all-India basis and state basis. Thus, they have an All India Rank (AIR) and a State Rank (SR).

The examination consists of two papers: Paper-I and Paper-II. Paper-I has three sections: mathematics, physics and chemistry with equal weight for each subject. Each section consists of multiple choice objective-type questions. Paper-I has a negative-marking scheme wherein an incorrect answer is negatively marked with one fourth of the maximum marks allotted to the question. Paper-II has three sections: mathematics, drawing and aptitude. Mathematics and drawing sections have multiple choice objective-type questions and the Aptitude section has drawing-based questions. The duration of each paper is three hours. Candidates are not allowed to carry any textual materials, calculators, logarithmic tables or electronic devices into the examination hall. The number of questions and their maximum marks has been variable through the years. The questions are based on a syllabus that is common to syllabi of all the state boards in India and the Central Board of Secondary Education. Candidates can opt for question papers either in English or Hindi language. For admission to B.Tech. or BE courses in the participating institutes the candidate is required to take the Paper I; for admission to B.Arch. or B.Planning courses the candidate is required to take Paper-II. Students can opt to take any one or both the papers. The examination was conducted in offline pen and paper mode till 2010.

In 2011, as per the orders of the Ministry of Human Resource Development, CBSE conducted the Paper-I in the Computer-Based-Test mode for the first one lakh candidates who opted for the same, while the remaining students took the examination in the conventional pen and paper mode. The number of attempts which a candidate can avail at the examination is limited to three in consecutive years.

9.19 What is IIT-JEE?

The Indian Institutes of Technology are institutions of national importance established through an act of Parliament. These institutes play a leading role in technological manpower development and research programmes comparable with the best in the world. Admissions to undergraduate for all Indian and foreign nationals at these institutions are made through the Joint Entrance Examination (JEE).

Institute of Technology, Benaras Hindu University, Varanasi is one of the oldest institutions devoted to education in various engineering disciplines. Indian School of Mines, Dhanbad, a deemed university, is the oldest institution of its kind in India. The admissions to the under-graduate programmes at these institutions are also made through JEE. These institutions are known for providing quality technological and scientific education and for research in frontier areas. The environment at all these institutions is highly conducive for :

- Building of solid foundation of knowledge,
- Development of personality,
- Confidence building, and
- Pursuit of excellence and self-discipline.

Enhancement of creativity through motivation and drive which helps to produce professionals well trained for the rigors of professional and social life. Today, the alumni of these institutions hold key positions in industry/academia in India and abroad.

Each institute has well-equipped modern laboratories, a state-of-the-art library and computer networks. The selected candidates live in a pleasant and intellectually stimulating environment. The teaching methods rely on direct personal contact between the teacher and the students. Living in such an environment with people having similar goals and aspirations is an exciting experience during one's academic life.

Credit-based academic programmes offer flexibility allowing students to progress at their own pace. A minimum level of performance is necessary for satisfactory progress. The medium of instruction is English. These institutes offer courses leading to bachelor's degree in a number of engineering, technology and science disciplines.

M.Sc. integrated courses in pure and applied sciences and M.Tech. (Integrated) courses in a few disciplines are also offered by some of these institutes. In addition, some IITs offer dual-degree M.Tech. programmes, wherein both B.Tech and M.Tech degrees are awarded at the end of the programme. The current pattern which has been followed since 2006 consists of two objective type papers each containing mathematics, physics and chemistry sections. The syllabus of the examination is predominantly based on topics covered by the CBSE Board Examination (AISSCE) and the ISC Board Examination. The pattern of questions, optical mark recognition answer sheets has been adopted since 2006. In previous years, there were separate mathematics, physics and chemistry papers, each of two hours duration that contained both subjective and objective questions. The current pattern is adopted so as to reduce the students' stress.

Given the importance attached to the IIT-JEE is 25 years. For candidates belonging to SC, ST and PD categories, the relaxed age limit is 30 years. From 2007, a candidate is allowed to take the JEE two times at the most. This has been done mainly to reduce stress on students and discourage the concept of 'cram schools'. Furthermore, from 2007 on, students who are selected for admission to an IIT cannot attempt the examination again in the future. From 2008 six new IITs have been opened with 120 seats each increasing the total number of seats to almost 7,000. For 2009, admissions have been made to two more IITs, namely IIT Indore and IIT Mandi (Himachal Pradesh) taking the seats count to 9,600.

Candidates applying for JEE should have either completed or appearing in any one of the following qualifying examinations :

- The final examination of the 10+2 system, conducted by any recognised Central/State Board such as Central Board of Secondary Education, New Delhi; Council of Indian School Certificate Examination, New Delhi etc.

- Intermediate or two-years pre-university examination conducted by a recognised Board/University.
- Final examination of the two-years course of the Joint Services Wing of the National Defence Academy.
- General Certificate Examination (GCE) Examination (London/Cambridge/Sri Lanka) at the advanced (A) level.
- High School Certificate Examination of the Cambridge University.
- Any Public School/Board/University examination in India or in any foreign country recognised by the Association of Indian Universities as equivalent to 10+2 system.
- H.S.C. Vocational examination.
- Senior Secondary School examination conducted by the National Open School with a minimum of five subjects.
- Three to four-years diploma recognised by AICTE or a State Board of Technical Education.

In case the relevant qualifying examination is not a public examination, the candidate must have passed at least one public (board or pre-university) examination at an earlier level. The candidates belonging to the general category must secure a minimum of 60 per cent marks in aggregate in their qualifying examination. Candidates belonging to SC/ST and PD categories must secure a minimum of 55 per cent in aggregate in the qualifying examination. If any board awards only letter grades without providing an equivalent percentage of marks on the grade sheet, the candidate should obtain a certificate from the Board specifying equivalent marks and submit it at the time of counseling. In case, such a certificate is not provided by the candidate, the decision of the Joint Implementation Committee regarding his/her eligibility shall be held final.

Physical Fitness : All qualified candidates will have to submit a physical fitness certificate from a registered medical practitioner in the prescribed format that will be made available to them at an appropriate time. They will be admitted only if they are physically fit for pursuing a course of study at the participating institutes.

10
ENVIRONMENTAL SCIENCE

10.1 Archaeology

The Meaning of the term 'Archaeology'

The word 'archaeology' is derived from two Greek words *'archaios'* which means 'ancient things' and *'logos'* means 'theory or science'. Archaeology was first put to use by the Romans in the eighteenth century but it was given more accuracy by Heinrich Schliemann who brought to light the origins of Greek civilisation.

What is Archaeology?

It is the scientific and systematic study of the past and human cultures through the recovery, analysis and documentation of material remains and environmental data like architecture, artifacts, features, landscapes and bioffacts. It is the field of conservation and protection of architectural relics, old monuments, inscriptions etc. In fact, Archaeology is the science that helps a to build up a picture of the past.

Archaeology is a multi-disciplinary science which draws help from geography, history, anthropology, chemistry, geology, art and literature. It is also regarded as one of the four branches of Anthropology, which is the study of the physical and social characteristics of humanity. The cultural and social events of the past have been relived through archaeological studies. Archaeological studies or inputs are considered important in issues such as environmental conservation, urban societies and town planning. These discoveries involve a variety of field techniques and laboratory procedures.

In India, the importance of preserving the rich and cultural heritage was initiated by General Alexander Cunningham. It was he who established the Archaeological Survey of India in 1862 for the maintenance, conservation and preservation of centrally protected monuments and archaeological sites in the country. Due to his contribution in Indian history and Archaeology, Cunningham is considered as 'the father of Indian history and Archaeology'.

The Role of Archaeologists

Those who are involved with the studies of archaeological discoveries are termed as archaeologists. The main activities of an archeologist include preliminary fieldwork, excavation of sites and periodical classification of them as well as dating and interpretation of materials so excavated. They probe into the past and define earlier civilisations. Their researches and findings are preserved and maintained for present and future learning. Modern archaeologists have enhanced the accuracy of their work with scientific techniques of carbon dating of artifacts and the use of DNA analysis.

Eligibility

Archaeology is as career for those who have an acute interest and training in culture and history. It is preferable for candidates to have background of ancient history and culture. The basic eligibility criteria or Bachelor course in History/Archaeology (B.A. level) of three-years duration is 10+2 or equivalent. After graduation one can opt for a post graduate diploma or degree course in Archaeology.

Graduates in History in any stream with an aggregate of 55 per cent marks can apply for diploma; post graduate diploma or post graduation (M.A./M.Sc.) in different fields of Archaeology. Duration of these courses may vary from one year to two years. Admission to the two years post graduate diploma course at the Institute of Archaeology, the academic wing of the Archaeological Survey of India in New Delhi is on the basis of a written examination and an interview.

At a higher level, those interested in conducting research on the various branches of Archaeology can do Ph.D. but before applying for research fellowship, they must have completed their post graduation.

Personal Skills

The essential attributes needed for an archaeologist is a perceptive and probing mind, keen observation, analytical and logical thinking. They must also possess creativity, accuracy and should be able to recognise and appreciate arts. They should be adaptable to physical stress and strain since they may have to work outdoors sometimes in uncomfortable conditions. Besides dedication, a lot of patience is required since researches in this field can take years on one project. In order to conduct archaeological research, archeologists need to be conversant with the geo-physical conditions.

Course Areas

Numismatics, epigraphy, archives and museology are the important branches of Archaeology. Applied sciences, theory and methods in Archaeology, protohistory, art, museology, chemical preservation, and antiquarian laws are some of the subjects covered in Archaeology. The course also consists of a detailed study of illustrated manuscripts, fossils, inscriptions and coins. Archaeology has a large number of sub-disciplines and specialisations. Historical Archaeology, archeometry, Computational archaeology, isotope analysis, geo-archaeology, bio-archaeology are some of the specialisations. After doing the basics of the archaeological course, one can specialise in any of these fields.

In order to become an archaeologist, the aspirant need spend several years training, taking tests and examinations, writing term papers and thesis and doing continuous research. Apart from these, there will be field work where one should observe the excavation of sites, analysing the relics and monuments, intern with a senior Archaeologist, learn new techniques of excavation and practice using GPS tools and digging and also drawing and photography.

Job Prospects and Career Options

The task of archaeologists is to study architectural relics or monuments or whatever it may be to identify the period to which they belong which might later become historical evidence. They examine the relevance of any evidence, which may range from ruins of large cities to stone flakes and thus trace the stages of development of civilisations. They analyse the data and write reports on their findings.

Artifacts, features and ecofacts are the three basic kinds of archaeological evidence that are useful to the archaeologists. Artifacts are objects like pots, beads, copper plates, etc. made by people which can be moved without altering their appearance. Study of artifacts often requires the knowledge of other languages like Urdu, Sanskrit and Persian as they may contain inscriptions. Features consist of houses, tombs, people etc. which cannot be separated from their surroundings without changing their form. Eco-facts, the natural objects like seeds, animal bones etc. found with artifacts or features, disclose how ancient people responded to their surroundings.

The profession of Archaeology offers interesting job opportunities to those who have a fascinating for the past. Specialists in the field of Archaeology can work as numismatics and epigraphists. Numismatics is the study of old coins, tokens and other related objects while Epigraphy is the study of inscriptions on ancient monuments, rocks, temples, copper plates etc.

In India, students who pass out from the Institute of Archaeology, the academic wing of the Archaeological Survey of India have brighter prospects because they are readily absorbed by the Archaeological Survey of India (ASI). Archaeologists can seek jobs in government sectors through examinations conducted by Union Public Service Commission or Staff Selection Commission and also in private environment monitoring companies or in similar organisations. They are employed in Defence services, museums, Ministry of Information and Broadcasting, cultural centers and historical division of the Ministry of External Affairs. A degree holder in archaeology can work as tourist guides, heritage managers, interpreters, resource persons of trip organisers in the tourism industry. After obtaining doctoral degree or successfully clearing SLET (State Level Eligibility Test) or NET (National Eligibility Test) one can take up teaching and research work. Archaeologists can even seek employment in other disciplines as historians, linguists and surveyors.

Archaeology graduates have great scope abroad for jobs as well as research as various colleges and universities are well furnished with research programmes. Here one can work as curator, heritage conservator, archivist or even as teacher.

Remuneration

The pay scale for an archeologist depends on their education, level of skill and who they work for. Since the nature of job prospects is very diverse, the salary can vary tremendously. The basic pay scale of an assistant archaeologist employed with the archaeological Survey of India is between ₹ 9,000–15,000 including allowances. The promotion is based upon the performance. The salary scale of the Director General varies between ₹ 25,000–30,000. The minimum pay scale of archaeologists working in colleges and universities is around ₹ 16,000 to 20,000 per month. A doctoral degree in this field entitles one to reach higher pay scale and it is a must for a rise in this career. The initial pay scale in private firms can be much higher when compared to the government sector. The remuneration with time and experience expands to the advantage of archaeologists.

Courses available

- Advance Diploma in Archaeology and Museology,
- B.A. Indian History Culture and Archaeology (IHC),
- M.A. Ancient Indian History, Culture and Archaeology,
- M.A. Archaeology,

- M.Phil. Ancient Indian History, Culture and Archaeology,
- Master in Archaeology and Heritage Management,
- Ph.D. Ancient India History, Culture and Archaeology,
- Ph.D. Archaeology, and
- Post Graduate Diploma in Archaeology,

Useful Contacts

- Archaeological Survey of India, Janpath, New Delhi – 110011, website: www.asi.nic.in.
- National Archives of India, Janpath, New Delhi – 110011, website: www.nationalarchives.nic.in.
- Regional Office, Bhopal – phone: 0755-2660173; Telefax: 0755-2660117.
- Record Centre, Jaipur – phone: 0141-2707499; Telefax:0141-2701815.
- Bhubaneshwar- Telefax: 674-2471327.
- Pondicherry – Telefax: 0413-2253104.
- Indian Council of Historical Research, 35, Ferozeshah Road, New Delhi – 110001, website: www.ichrindia.org.

10.2 Astronomy

What is Astronomy?

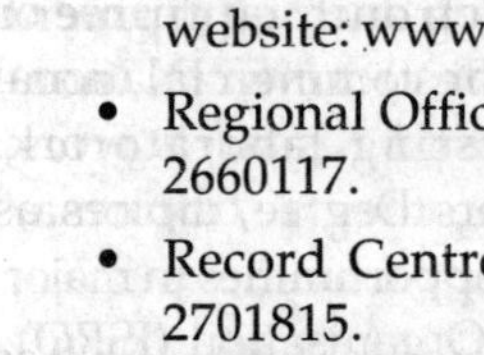

Astronomy is the oldest and the most fascinating science which deals with the celestial bodies and the material universe beyond the earth's atmosphere. It is the science of the universe which includes the study of motion, nature, law, constitution, history and possible future developments of heavenly bodies like the sun, planets, stars, comets, meteors, galaxies, satellites and the like.

Branches of Astronomy

Astronomy sometimes considered as a sub-field of Physics is further divided into several branches such as astrophysics, astrometeorology, astrobiology, astrogeology, astrometry and cosmology. All these branches together help to unravel the mysteries of the universe. It is a promising and amazing career for those who are interested in the mysteries of the universe and has a desire to unravel them. Since each country is going in for nuclear testing, the need for scientists in the field of Astronomy is increasing.

In the professional level, Astronomy is divided into observational astronomy and theoretical astrophysics. While the former deals with observing celestial bodies by using telescopes, binoculars, cameras, unaided eyes and collecting data for building and maintaining instruments; the latter is concerned with data analysis finding out the conclusions of observations of computers and explaining the observational results. Theoretical astrophysics is more analytical and astrophysicists model data.

The Work of an Astronomer

An astronomer usually works for the government, defence and space research organisations, electrical and electronic equipment manufacturers and so on. They may work for commercial/non-commercial research, development and testing laboratories, observatories, planetarium, science park and others. Degree/diploma/doctorate holder in these disciplines can find job opportunities in major establishments like the Indian Space Research Organisation (ISRO), the Vikram Sarabhai Space Centre (VSSC), Space Physics Laboratories, Space Applications Centres, etc. One can also join non-profit organisations like Bangalore Amateur Astronomers (ABAA) which is involved in telescope making, organising observation sessions for the public and popularisation of Astronomy.

The prospects of travelling to far distant lands are also open as international seminars and conventions are held regularly in different countries.

Eligibility and Course Areas

A doctoral degree is the usual educational requirement to become an astronomer, since most of the work tends to be related to research and development. Those who opt for this field should pass their plus-two examination under the science stream, especially in physics and mathematics. For pursuing a career in theoretical or observational astronomy one may go through the science stream after plus-two. Since universities offering under-graduate programma in Astronomy are rarely found, one can join for a major/honours in physics with mathematics as a subsidiary subject. Thereafter, take a master's degree in physics or astronomy. After the successful completion of M.Sc., one can do specialisation in astronomy leading to Ph.D. which enables one to become an astronomer/astronaut/astrophysicist or a scientist/research officer etc. in the field of space research.

For doing Ph.D. which is mandatory to do research, one should appear for the Joint Entrance Screening Test (JEST) examination. For pursuing a career in instrumentation/experimental Astronomy after plus-two, one can go for Bachelor of Engineering (B.E.) in electrical/ electronics/electrical communications. An engineer with a B.Tech. or B.E. degree could also enter the field as a research scholar.

Personal Skills

The essential quality to become an astronomer is curiosity and greater concentration. They should have above average intelligence, high imagination, persistence, problem-solving and analytical skills and must possess both mathematical and computer skills. Lots of patience is required in this field as the astronomers have to work long for irregular hours. Excellent oral and written communication skills are also important because most astronomers are expected to work as part of a team. They must be capable of explaining scientific phenomena and conveying the information in an easily absorbed format and language. Rather, astronomers must apply equal measures of analytic thinking and imagination, logic and intuition to answer the most fundamental questions about the cosmos.

Job Prospects and Career Options

Working on research is the main profession of an astronomer and this may usually involve travelling, working long hours including day and night. The work of an astronomer involves analysis and interpretation of enormous data gathered by observatories and satellites and making scientific papers or reports on their findings. They make observations with ground-based telescopes or any other sources and apply their knowledge to solve problems in navigation, space flight and satellite communications.

A beginner in the field of astronomy may be inducted as a researcher into an existing team which would be already working on a project. Ph.D. holders begin their careers in a post doctoral research position in which they may work with experienced physicists as they continue to learn about their specialty and develop ideas and results to be used in later work. Initial work may be under the close supervision of senior scientists. Depending on their areas of specialisation, astronomers are classified into various groups like observational astronomers, stellar astronomers and solar astronomers.

Most jobs in the basic research and development usually require a doctoral degree. The Ph.D. holders ultimately teach at the college or university level. Master's degree holders are qualified for many jobs in manufacturing and applied research and development. Some master's degree programs prepare students for a specific research skill that does not require a Ph.D. Bachelor degree holders in this field are often qualified as technicians, research assistants or other types of jobs.

Institutes

- CV Raman Institute, Bangalore.
- Madurai Kamaraj University, Tamil Nadu.
- Inter University Centre for Astronomy and Astrophysics, Maharashtra.
- Physical Research Laboratory, Ahmedabad.
- Mahatma Gandhi University, Kerala.
- Indian Institute of Astrophysics.

  Block-II, Koramangala, Bangalore.
- Tata Institute of Fundamental Research

  Pune, Maharashtra.

10.3 Disaster Management

What is a disaster?

Disaster can be defined as some dangerous situation or event that can happen unexpectedly anywhere at any time. The word 'disaster' originated from the French word *'desastre'* which is a combination of words *'des'* (bad) and *'aster'* (star) and therefore, disaster indicates bad star. Disasters that cause serious threat to normal life, property, environment as well as the process of development may be rapid or slow and can be classified as natural disaster, man-made disaster and hybrid disaster (e.g. epidemics).

What is Disaster Management?

Disaster Management also known as Emergency Management is all about dealing with all kinds of disasters. Its major objective is to reduce the shocking effects of a disaster on the affected community and to help them return to normal life within a short period. Disaster management is a multi-disciplinary area covering a wide range of issues like monitoring, evaluation, search and rescue, relief, reconstruction and rehabilitation operations. The highly responsible profession includes the plans and actions before, during and after the disasters. It is a combination of mechanisms such as timely warning, alerts, fast response and efficient coordination. Even though we cannot stop or avoid natural disaster, it is possible to resist aftermath calamities of such disasters.

Disaster Management is the method of controlling a disaster by using skillful ways. Its techniques or methods are based on the economic status of a country and hence it varies from country to country. Disasters are managed better and quicker by the developed countries than the developing countries. Developing countries are reporting high number of deaths related to disaster and India has second place in it due to its geographical position, climate and geological setting. The course is beneficial for social workers.

Disaster Management in India

In India, the state and central government take responsibilities of disaster management and the government has included disaster management as a programme to study. Many institutes offer courses in disaster Management that would help one to get into the field of emergency supervision. Many government and non-government organisations need emergency management professionals to work for the betterment of society. It is a fairly paid industry and in spite of all the risk, disaster management is one of the careers that give mental satisfaction to those who wants to serve the society.

Eligibility

Disaster Management courses are offered at the short term certificate, under-graduate, post-graduate degree and diploma levels. Basic educational qualification, i.e., higher secondary certificate examination (10+2) is needed to pursue a career in disaster management. But for masters or MBA, the student should be a graduate in any field (even from a professional field such as engineering or medicine graduate), who has a minimum average of 50 per cent marks from any recognised institute or university. Jamsetji Tata Centre for Disaster Management offers masters course in disaster management to prepare aspirants for this profession.

Course Areas

Disaster Management courses aim at enhancing knowledge, capacities and skills and perspective on disasters. The course covers different areas of disaster management which include management of the situation of emergency, response to the needs of the people and the area, evacuation process, distribution of food and medical care for the injured people. Some of the topics of the course are approaches and planning for the disaster, conflict and its analysis, data management and analysis, disaster risk reduction strategies, legislative structures for controlling disasters, development planning, Geographical

Information System (GIS- a computer-based information system which is used to digitally represent and analyse the geographic features present on the earth surface and the events that take place on it) its design and application. Basic economics, disaster financing and logistics management are other topics that are included in the study area along with psychological care and public health planning. The Government of India has included disaster management as a subject to study for the Central Board of Secondary Education (CBSE) students.

Job Prospects

Disaster management is more of a service related field, so one should enter the field fully prepared, i.e., to manage emergency situations and should respond to the needs of the people and areas affected in a quick and efficient manner. They have to be prepared and should have a plan in mind as to how to combat any disaster if it occurs. The right planning helps to decrease the intensity and impact of the disaster.

Career Options

Civil servants, civil engineers, police and defence personnel, paramilitary personnel, fire fighters and other protective service workers on their training period will undergo training and workshops on disaster management which would be very helpful for them. India being a country prone to frequent natural calamities in its diverse landscapes, the need for disaster management professionals is on the rise. In this field, employment opportunities are offered in the disaster management departments, drought management departments, law enforcement authorities, relief agencies etc. and insurance companies, industries in the high-risk fields like chemicals, mining and petroleum which have their own disaster management cells. One can work as a social worker, environment expert, rehabilitation worker etc. Engineering professionals in the field of disaster management can design buildings that help resist disasters. Graduates in disaster management can start their own consultancies as well.

NGOs and International organisations such as World Bank, Asian Development Bank (ADB), United Nations Organisations (UNO), Red Cross, and UNESCO offer various opportunities for professionally trained disaster management professionals. They are recruited for conducting training and workshops on disaster management to the general public and for other related activities.

Remuneration

Disaster management is a well-paid field but the wages depend on the organisation and your experience. The packages will be high for experienced people in the field. As this is a risky field, government and non-government organisations offer fairly good remuneration for the candidates. A fresher can get between ₹ 8,000 to 10,000 while a two-three years experienced person could earn not less than ₹ 15,000.

Courses available in disaster management are as follows :

- Certificate Course in Disaster Management,
- Diploma in Disaster Management,
- Diploma in Psychosocial Care and Support in Disaster Management,
- Disaster Mitigation and Consequence Management,
- M.A. Disaster Management,
- MBA Disaster Management,
- M.Phil. Disaster Management,
- M.Sc. Disaster Management,
- Ph. D. Disaster Management,
- Post Graduate Certificate Course in Disaster Management, and
- Post Graduate Diploma in Disaster Management.

Top Institutes that offer courses in Disaster Management

- **Jamsetji Tata Centre for Disaster Management**
- **The Indira Gandhi National Open University, New Delhi**
  Courses : Certificate in Disaster Management,
  Post Graduate Diploma in Disaster Management.
- **Annamalai University, Chidambadam, Tamil Nadu**
  Courses : Master of Arts in Disaster Management,
  Master of Engineering in Disaster,
  Management and Engineering.
- **Tata Institute of Social Sciences, Mumbai, Maharashtra**
  Courses : Master of Arts in Disaster Management,
  Master of Science in Disaster Management.
- **Mahavira Institute of Technology and Management, Gurgaon, Haryana**
  Course : Master of Business Administration – Disaster Management.
- **Pondicherry University, Pondicherry (Mahe), Kerala**
  Courses : Doctor of Philosophy-Coastal Disaster Management,
  Master of Science-Coastal Disaster Management.

- **Apex College of Management, New Delhi**
  Master of Philosophy – Disaster Management.
- **Nalanda Open University, Patna, Bihar**
  Course : Certificate in Disaster Management.
- **Vardhman Mahaveer Open University, Kota, Rajasthan**
  Course : Certificate in Disaster Management.

10.4 Environmental Science

What is Environmental Science?

Environmental Science is the branch of science dealing with the study

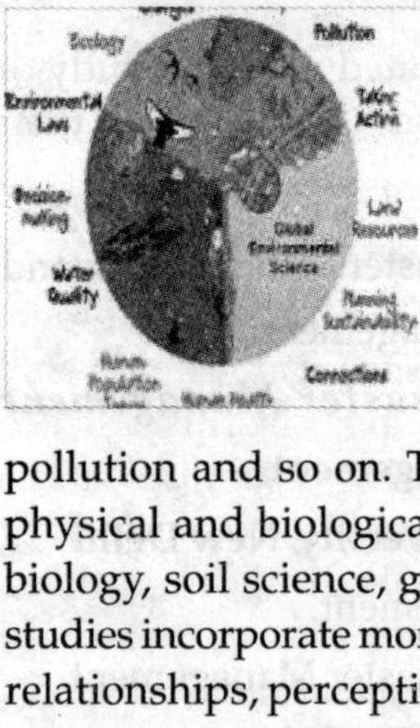

of different components of environment, the factors influencing the changes in the environment and the interdependence of living things within their environment. These include the study of climatic change, conservation of energy, biodiversity, ground water and soil contamination, technologies developed to treat air pollution, sound pollution and so on. This interdisciplinary academic field combines physical and biological science context including physics, chemistry, biology, soil science, geology and geography. Wholly, environmental studies incorporate more of the social sciences for understanding human relationships, perceptions and policies towards the environment.

Importance of Environmental Science

Environmental Science is becoming an interesting and one of the most sought after careers because of the increased awareness about the clean environment. A formal training programme in the field of environmental science is needed for those who are interested to build up a career in this field. One can work in this field as environmental scientists, environment educationist, environment engineers, environment biologists, environment modelers, environmental journalists and environment-related technologists in laboratories that engage in soil and water testing, pollution detection and control.

Field of Study

Environmental Science is a broad field of study; yet no specific separation is needed because its branches overlap with each other. However, to make things easier, environmental science has been divided as :

- **Environmental Chemistry :** It deals with the chemical changes in water, air and soil.
- **Ecology :** It is the study of interactions of various species of living organism with one another and with the physical and chemical environment.
- **Geosciences :** It is also known asearth science. It deals with the study of demographical part of the environment including oceans, biosphere, mountain, solid earth etc.
- **Atmospheric Science :** The study of the gaseous layer that covers the earth like a blanket.
- **Environmental Assessment :** It deals with the ways and methods to improve and enhance the environment.
- **Environmental Microbiology :** It is related with the study of composition and physiology of microbes (bacteria) and their communities in the environment.

Eligibility

Usually, environmental science is taught as a M.Sc. programme. Graduate courses (i.e. B.Sc.) in Environmental Science are offered only by a few institutions. In the graduate level, most institutes teach Environmental science as a specialised course. The eligibility criteria for three years B.Sc. in Environmental Science is 10+2 examination or equivalent with physics, chemistry and biology. Engineering diploma holders can also join the course. Andhra University, Gandhi Institute of Technology and Management (GITAM), Visakhapatnam and University of Madras, Chennai etc. offer Bachelor of Environmental Management (BEM) course. Eligibility criteria and duration of this course is as same as that of B.Sc. course.

The requirement for two years M.Sc. Environmental Science is B.Sc. Environmental Science or a bachelor's degree in any discipline of science namely zoology, botany, physics, chemistry, biology or agriculture science. Work experience is preferred by some institutes for the M.Sc. course and some institutes conduct entrance examinations. Candidates with master's degree in Environmental Science can opt doctoral and post doctoral courses like M.Phil. and Ph.D. and can become environmental scientists. Ph. D. courses are offered by Post Graduate Studies and Research, Hyderabad and Osmania University.

Certain institutes offer short term PG courses in environmental science and environment management. The Centre for Environmental Education and Research and Advocacy (CEERA) of the National Law School of Indian University, Bangalore offers one year post-graduate

Diploma in Environmental Law (PGDEL) to graduates in any discipline through distance learning mode. Short term courses are also offered by Sikkim Manipal University, Indira Gandhi National Open University (IGNOU), New Delhi.

Course Areas

The curriculum of the courses may vary from institute to institute. Generally, it involves observation of changes in the earth's atmosphere by pollution, global warming, forest conservation, soil erosion, pollution control, industrial hygiene, radiation protection, hazardous waste management, toxic materials control, water supply and other allied areas in this field. Graduate programmes help students to specialise their knowledge and skills in the field which is essential for an increase in job value. Post graduate programmes will help one to obtain an understanding of today's most complex environmental issues through the studies in advanced technical skills, conservation theory and waste management.

Job Prospects and Career Options

Professionals in the field of environmental science are in great demand for the preservation and protection of our environment. The major task of Environmental Science graduates/professionals is to find new ways to conserve and improve the natural resources of the environment. For that, they study the effects of various sources of pollution on nature and environment and try to control these harms as much as possible with appropriate methods. Through their work they convey hope and commitment to the public. They can work with different government departments and agencies like forest and environment, pollution control boards, urban planning, water resources and agriculture. They can also get employment in media as environmental journalists, assistant professors in universities or colleges and also with the NGOs working for environmental protection. Some of the work areas of Environmental Science professionals are :

- **Industrial Sector :** In the industrial sector, environmental professionals/scientists work for maintaining an ecological balance, bio-diversity and wasteland management and the preservation of natural resources.
- **Research and Development :** In the research and development wings of various universities and government organisations, they conduct research studies to develop theories or methods for controlling the sources of environmental pollution.

- **Environmental Consultants** : Consultants can work with central and state pollution control board and offer advice related to the environment.
- **Forest Management** : Trained professionals in environmental science are needed for management and maintenance of forest and wildlife.
- **Environmentalist** : They help to protect the environment from destruction or pollution. Cleansing of rivers and forests are some of the activities in which the environmentalist is involved.
- **Environmental Journalism** : Trained journalists in this field are required for reporting environmental issues and related comprehensive news.
- **Social Development** : To create awareness among public about various environmental issues and their responsibility to keep the natural system in a condition that it sustains life.

Remuneration

Trained professionals are offered handsome salary and benefits by the central and state pollution control boards. A graduate can expect a payment anywhere between ₹ 7,000 – 12,000. Those with postgraduate degree may start with a salary range between ₹ 10,000 – 20,000 per month which can go up to 35,000 per month. There are many firms related to environmental projects operating on an international level. Such companies offer highly lucrative compensations to Indian environmental scientists.

Courses

- B. Sc. Environmental Science,
- Bachelor of Environmental Laws,
- M. Phil. Environmental Science,
- M. Sc. Environmental Botany,
- M. Sc. Environmental Microbiology,
- M. Sc. Environmental Science,
- M. Sc. Environmental Technology,
- M. Sc. Environmental Science,
- Ph. D. Environmental Science,
- Post Graduate Diploma in Environmental Laws,
- Post Graduate Diploma in Environmental Studies, and

- Post Graduate Diploma in Industrial Safety and Environmental Management.

Institutes

- College of Engineering, Waltair Visakhapatnam, Andhra Pradesh.
- Delhi College of Engineering, Delhi.
- LD College of Engineering, Ahmedabad, Gujarat.
- Adichuachanagiri Institute of Technology, Chickmagalur, Karnataka.
- PES College of Engineering, Mandya, Karnataka.
- Sri Jayachamarajendra College of Engineering, Mysore, Karnataka.
- Vidya Vardhaka College of Engineering, Mysore, Karnataka.
- Kolhapur Institute of Technology and College of Engineering, Kolhapur, Maharashtra.
- Giani Zail Singh College of Engineering and Technology, Bhatinda, Pubjab.
- Y.C. College of Science, Karad-415110.
- School of Environmental Sciences University of Poona, Pune.
- Manipur University, Imphal, Manipur.
- University of Delhi, Delhi-110007.
- Mohanlal Sukhadia University, Udaipur-313001, Rajasthan.
- Mt. Carmel College, Bangalore, Karnataka.
- St. Joseph's Arts and Science College, Bangalore, Karnataka.
- Government Arts and Science College, Bangalore, Karnataka.
- Bharathiar University, Coimbatore-641046, Tamil Nadu.
- Indian Agricultural Research Institute (IARI), New Delhi.

10.5 Geography

What is Geography?

Geography – the 'science of the earth' is a diverse term which deals with aerial differentiation of the surface of the earth. Derived from the Greek words *'Geo'* or *'Gaea'* (Earth) and *'graphein'* (to describe or to map), Geography literally means 'to describe or write about the earth'. Hence Geography can be described as the study of earth, location and distribution of its physical and cultural features, land forms; climate,

soils, vegetation, minerals, water and human resources. Geography is not a mere academic subject but it involves finding out the facts on earth. The individuals associated with geography are called Geographers.

Who are Geographers?

Geographers are scientists who study about the physical details of the environment, its effects on human and wildlife, weather and climate patterns, economics and culture. The Greek scholar of the third century BC, Eratosthenes who had calculated the circumference of the earth for the first time is considered as the father of Geography; while Alexander Von Humboldt is regarded as the founder of modern Geography. The modern geographer's scope extends far beyond describing the earth.

Branches of Geography

Physical Geography and Human Geography are the major branches of Geography which are closely interconnected. Also known as geosystems or physiography, physical Geography is the study of physical features of earth such as rivers, landforms, climate, hazards and many more that occupies the atmosphere, bio-sphere and geo-sphere. It is further subdivided into geo-morphology, hydrology, coastal geography, oceanography, quaternary science, landscape ecology, climatology, and environmental geography. Human geo-graphy deals with the study of human, political, economic, social and cultural activities. The subdivision of human geography includes economic geography, cultural geography, political geography, health geography, urban geography, historical geography, marketing geography and social geography.

Career in Geography

Geography provides numerous options for those who have a keen interest in subjects like countries, people, economy, climate etc. Due of the latest technological developments like Remote Sensing and Geographical Information System (GIS), careers in geography are becoming more promising and challenging than ever before. Remote sensing is the science that acquires information about an object, area or anything, without direct contact with the objects. The informations are transferred with the help of electromagnetic radiation (EMR) which is a form of energy that reveals its presence by the observable effects it produces when it strikes the matter. GIS is a computer based information system which is used to digitally represent and analyse the geographic features present on the earth's surface and the events that take place on it. In GIS data collection, GPS (Global Positioning System) technology which uses satellites and computers to compute positions anywhere on earth with unequalled accuracy and flexibility has tremendous amount of applications.

Eligibility

Graduation in Geography is the basic qualification needed to get into the field of geography. But for enhanced career prospects, master's and doctoral degrees are essential. Various institutes and universities in India offer courses in various field of geography. Candidates who have passed 10+2 with high marks in social sciences including Geography or equivalent can apply for the bachelor's course in Geography which is offered in both arts and science stream (i.e., B.A. Geography and B.Sc Geography). A base in mathematics, statistics, and computer science is needed in graduate studies. On completion of bachelor's degree, an aspirant can do masters/M.Phil./Ph.D. programmes. Bachelor's degree with minimum of 50 per cent marks is required for master's degree and at the master level one can choose any specialised courses in geography like cartography, urban and town planning, regional planning physiography, climatology, oceanography, population studies environmental geography etc. Some institutes offer courses in Remote Sensing and Geographical Information Systems (GIS) like courses in Geo-informatics which are the most demanded module of this era.

A course in Geography covers almost all the subjects such as environment, people, economy, ocean, physical features of earth agriculture, natural resources and the like.

Personal Skill

Perceptive and probing mind, keen observation, analytical and logical thinking and computer skills are the much needed qualification in the field of geography. Interest in mathematics and science can help one to be good in this profession and as any other careers; communication skill plays a major role. Field work sometimes may require travel to remote and less developed areas. Geographers must be physically fit and be healthy to work in any situation and locale and must keep an updated data regarding the earth and the changes occurring. They should enjoy travelling, reading, studying and be able to work independently.

Job Prospects and Career Options

Many government and non-government institutes along with research centers offer several career options for qualified geographers with numerous specialisations. Some of the specialised areas are :

- **Economic Geography:** Economic Geography is the study of geographic location, distribution and spatial organisation of economic activities. Economic geographers analyses economic problem in terms of space, place and scale.
- **Cultural Geography:** Cultural Geography focus on analysing the cultural phenomenon which includes the study language, religion, economy and much more.
- **Political Geography:** Political Geography is about the political process in relation with spatial structures and it studies the relationship between the government and people, trades and treaties, political power, boundaries and policies etc.
- **Historical Geography:** Historical Geography deals with all the physical, fictional, theoretical geographies of the past. It also includes how the people intermingled with the environment and created the cultural features.
- **Tourism Geography:** Tourism Geography is the study of travel and how the environment and its features help in the tourism aspects of a specified area.
- **Transportation Geography:** Transportation Geography can be considered as a branch of economic geography which explores the spatial interaction or movement of goods, information and people.
- **Regional Geography:** Regional Geography examines the exclusive characteristics of both the nature and human of a region.
- **Medical Geography:** Medical Geography also known as the health geography is the research on health and spread of diseases in the world. It also looks how climate effect human's health.
- **Geomorphology:** It is the scientific study of landforms and the processes that shape them.
- **Hydrology:** Hydrology explores the water resources and water cycle. Chemical hydrology, ecohydrology, hydrogeology, hydro informatics, Isotope hydrology, hydrometeorology and Surface hydrology are the branches of hydrology.

- **Glaciology:** Glaciology is one of the major areas of polar research. It is the study of different forms of ice which also includes the history and future of glaciers.

Best Geography Colleges in India

- **Karnataka University, Hubli-Dharwad, Karnataka**
  Course : Master of Science Geography.
- **Deen Dayal Upadhyaya Gorakhpur University, Gorakhpur, Uttar Pradesh**
  Courses : Bachelor of Arts in Geography,
  Master of Arts in Geography.
- **Guwahati University, Guwahati, Assam**
  Course : Master of Science in Geography.
- **Visva Santiniketan, West Bengal**
  Courses : Bachelor of Arts in Geography,
  Master of Arts in Geography.
- **Veer Kunwar Singh University, Ara, Bihar**
  Course : Master of Arts- Geography.
- **Sharadchandra Pawar Mahavidyalaya, Satara, Maharashtra**
  Course : Bachelor of Arts - Geography.
- **Saheed Bhagat Singh Evening College, New Delhi**
  Course : Four Year Undergraduate Programme in Geography.

10.6 Geology

What is Geology?

Geology is a portmanteau word composed of '*Geo*' which means 'earth' and '*logos*' meaning 'science'. Geology is the branch of science that deals with the study of the earth, its environment, history, minerals etc. Different branches of Geology are structural geology, mineralogy, planetology, geomorphology, geological engineering and so on.

Who is a Geologist?

A Geologist is a person who studies the composition of the earth. Geologists are scientists who study the earth's crust to obtain an accurate picture of its structure, history and composition. Geologists play a vital role in exploring the mineral wealth and natural resources.

The Main Function of Geologists

The main function of the geologists is to assess the natural disasters and its effects on environment, to explore areas rich in under-water resources, oil, natural gas and minerals. They can assess whether the conditions in particular areas are suitable for laying railway lines, construction of roads, bridgesand buildings. The geologists can also explore the natural resources deep in the sea. Their services are also important for oil explorations. They determine the quality of soil by conducting geo-chemical and geo-physical tests. Construction of reservoirs, roads, bridges, underground tunnels, etc., is based on the report of the geologist about the density of the earth. Geologists work for private industries, the federal government, museums, colleges and universities.

Eligibility and Course Areas

There are a number of institutes and universities offering bachelor, master and doctorate degree in Geology. For admission to B.Sc. General or Honours, 10+2 with science either in non-medical or medical subjects with at least 50 per cent marks is required. For master's degree, a bachelor's degree with Geology as one of the subjects is required with minimum 50 per cent marks and for Ph.D. there is requirement of at least 55 per cent marks in master's degree. However, the rules for admission to bachelor's, master's and research degree vary from university to university/institutes.

To start a career in Geology, one should complete at least a master's degree in Geology such as M.A. or M.Sc. in Geology. While a bachelor's degree in Geology will secure some entry-level positions, the better qualified you are, the better position you can secure. Students interested in a professional career in the Geo-sciences should prepare to continue their education into advanced degrees. A master's degree is required for major professional entry-level positions, a Ph.D. is necessary for university teaching and to secure higher-level research positions.

Job Prospects and Career Options

Career in Geology is an exciting and interesting option as there is a plethora of job opportunities in Geology all over India. People studying Geology can work as geologists, meteorologists, geographers or oceanographers. The person having degree in Geology can pursue a career in petrology (study of rocks), paleontology, geo-physics, mining, environmental education, research and field study. Opportunities in Geology range from studying and predicting man-made and natural disasters to exploring mineral resources.

Job in the Public and Private Sectors

Geologists have a numerous avenues in both public and private sectors. The Union Public Service Commission conducts tests for placements in central government agencies like the Geological Survey of India and the Central Ground Water Board. Similarly, Coal India, Mineral Exploration Authority, Oil & Natural Gas Corporation, Hindustan Zinc and several other organisations engaged in mineral explorations utilise the services of geologists. Experienced geologists, especially those with an advanced degree in geology or business administration can advance to top positions in industry, government and education sector. These positions may be in research or administration.

Remuneration

Salaries in government sector offer a decent living style as well as prestige to a geologist. Public sector organisations such as ONGC, HPCL, IOC etc. offer very good perks as well as working conditions to geologists. Salaries in private sectors are extremely high and commensurate with qualifications and experience. A fresh geologist can expect to start with anything between ₹ 15,000 – 25,000 per month which can shoot up with right experience and talent.

Working condition

Most professional geologists spend at least part of their working career doing fieldwork, sometimes in remote areas in difficult conditions. Geologists generally begin by doing fieldwork. Hard physical labour, long hours and limited companionship are all part of field work. The geologists have to work on various sites. They may stay away from home for many days which may be depressing to a few.

In the oil, mining and quarrying industries geologists work in exploration, surveying and surface mapping in geologically promising areas of the world, looking for new prospects and working out the size of the reserves.

Courses

- B. Sc. Geology (Honours.),
- B.Sc. Applied Geology,
- B.Sc. Geology,
- M.Sc. Applied Geology,
- M.Sc. Applied Geology (Tech.),
- M.Sc. Geology,
- M.Sc. Geology (Tech.),
- M.Sc. Geology and Applied Chemistry,

- M.Sc. Marine Geology,
- M. Tech. Applied Geology,
- Ph. D. Geology, and
- M.Sc. Agrometerology.

Best Geology Colleges in India

- **Karnataka University, Hubli-Dharwad, Karnataka**

  Courses : Master of Science-Applied Geology, Post Graduate Diploma in Ground Water Geology.
- **Guwahati University, Guwahati, Assam**

  Course : Master of Science in Geological Science.
- **Saveetha University, Chennai, Tamil Nadu**

  Courses : Master of Engineering-Geological Information System, Integrated Bachelor of Engineering/Master of Engineering-Civil Engineering with specialisation in Geological Information System.
- **Ranchi university, Ranchi, Jharkhand**

  Courses : Bachelor of Science-Geology, Master of Science-Geology.
- **Rajasthan University, Jaipur, Rajasthan**

  Courses : Master of Science-Geology, Doctor of Philosophy-Geology.
- **M.G. Science Institute, Ahmedabad, Gujarat**

  Courses : Bachelor of Science-Geology Master of Science-Geology
- **Institute of Professional Studies, Dehradun, Uttaranchal**

  Course : Master of Philosophy (Geology).
- **Hiworth Education, Hyderabad, Andhra Pradesh**

  Course : Bachelor of Science (Geology).

10.7 Geophysics

What is Geophysics?

Geophysics, a major branch of the earth sciences and a sub discipline of physics is the study of the Earth by quantitative physical methods especially by seismic, electromagnetic and radioactivity methods. As the name implies, geophysics involves the application of physical theories and measurements to discover the properties

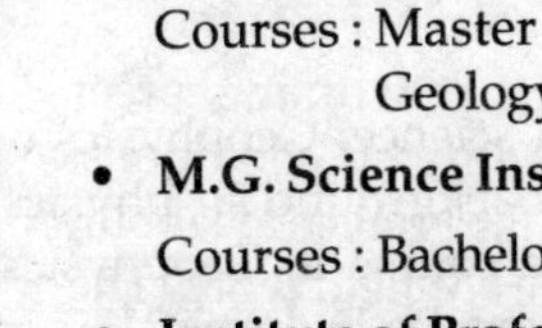

of the earth. Geophysics is the term used to describe the study of the earth's surface, core, geological levels and anything impacting the planet such as gravity, electric and magnetic forces. Geophysics is applied to societal needs such as mineral resources, mitigation or natural hazards and environmental protection. Career fields in geophysics include working in magnetic, seismology and geodesy.

The function of geophysicists

Geophysicists study the structure, composition and the physical aspects of the earth and its atmosphere and apply scientific principles in order to solve problems. These scientists use geophysical methods to study the earth and its composition including its atmosphere, internal make-up, oceans, electrical and other fields. Geophysicists involve in field investigation, measure, examine and explore the physical properties of earth from below the ground to the atmosphere or from the depths of the ocean to the top of the volcanoes. Geophysicists are also involved in environmental studies, archaeological excavations, water resource management, forensic investigations, the earth's climate and the causes and prediction of natural phenomena such as earthquakes, volcanic activity, landslides and tsunamis. Geophysicists examine the physical aspects of earth with the help of radar, dynamite, computers, magnetometers and gravimeters.

Eligibility

To become a geophysicist a degree in earth science, Geophysics or Geology is required. Those with a strong background in physics, mathematics or computer science can take a course in Geophysics. Geophysics can be studied at the master's and Ph.D. levels. IITs in India offer M.Sc. /M.Sc. - Ph.D. dual degree programme. For M.Sc. programme in geophysics candidates with minimum 50 per cent marks in B.Sc. mathematics and physics as subjects are eligible. Positions in research require master's degree.

Course Areas

Studies include a foundation in geology, geophysics, physics, mathematics and chemistry and geophysical fundamentals covering geophysical exploration, global studies, rock properties and data acquisition methods.

Job Prospects and Career Options

Some career avenues and specialisations for geophysicists are :

- **Exploration geophysics** : Exploration geophysics is the applied branch of geophysics which uses surface methods to measure the physical properties of the presence and position of ore, minerals, hydrocarbons, geothermal reservoirs, groundwater reservoirs and other geological structure in terms of mineral prospecting, mapping and acquiring a comprehensive understanding of the geosciences of specific terrain. Exploration engineers, petroleum engineers, mining engineers and other professionals and may be responsible for the supervision of a team. They may have to spend a considerable amount of time in the field, sometimes in remote locations.

- **Seismology :** It is the scientific study of earthquakes and the propagation of elastic waves through the earth or through other planet-like bodies. Earthquake effects such as tsunamis as well as diverse seismic sources such as volcanic, tectonic, oceanic, atmospheric and artificial processes such as explosions.
- **Geodesy :** Geodesy also named geodetics is a branch of earth science that deals with the study of earth as a whole planet. Geodesists study the size, shape, and gravitational field of the Earth and other planets. They also study phenomena such as crustal motion, tides and polar motion.
- **Atmospheric physics :** Atmospheric physics is the application of physics to the study of the atmosphere. In other words, it is the study of the atmosphere in terms of its physical properties and dynamics. Geophysicists investigate the earth's magnetic and electric fields and compare its outer atmosphere with those of other planet.
- **Geomagnetism :** It is the study of the earth's magnetic field including its origin, telluric currents driven by the magnetic field and the interaction of the magnetic field with solar wind. Geomagnetists work to discover the origins of the planet through the study of magnetic fields.
- **Marine Geophysics :** Marine Geophysics is a scientific discipline that is concerned with the application of geophysical methods to problems of marine geology. Marine geophysics is associated with the concepts and problems of seafloor spreading, continental drift and plate tectonics.
- **Environmental Geophysics :** It is a branch of earth science where geophysical techniques may be used to monitor environmental impact of, for example, water contaminants by creating maps of the subsurface and investigating ground movement.
- **Paleomagnetism :** It is the study of the record of the earth's

magnetic field preserved in various magnetic minerals through time.

- **Meteorology :** It is the study of earth's atmosphere as well as the atmospheric conditions. Meteorology also deals with weather forecasting by applying physical and mathematical principles to atmospheric conditions. Meteorologists can find work in meteorological departments, military, TV/radio stations, educational institutes and consulting meteorology business.
- **Oceanography :** It is the scientific study of the oceans which cover about 70 per cent of the earth's surface. It includes ocean's physical properties, oceanic mapping and exploration.

Remuneration

Salary of geophysicists varies depending on education, experience, position, employer and geographical location. In mining and oil exploration sector salary is lucrative. A fresher can expect to start with anything between ₹ 15,000 – ₹ 25,000 per month which can shoot up with experience and talent. One can go ahead and reach administrative level after gaining experience and career advancement. The salary ranges from ₹ 1 lakh to 2 lakh per month in administrative jobs depending upon the sector one has joined.

Courses

- M.Sc. Applied Geophysics,
- M.Sc. Applied Geophysics (Integrated),
- M.Sc. Applied Geophysics (Tech.),
- M.Sc Geophysics,
- M.Sc. Geophysics (Tech.),
- M.Tech. Applied Geophysics,
- Ph.D. Geophysics.

Institutes

There are only few institutes that conduct courses in Geophysics. A few among them are :

- **Indian School of Mines University : Department of Applied Geophysics**

  Dhanbad, Jharkhand.
- **Kurukshetra University : Department of Geophysics**

  Kurukshetra, Haryana.

- **Benaras Hindu University: Department of Geophysics**

  Varanasi, Uttar Pradesh.
- **Adikavi Nannaya University: School of Earth and Atmospheric Sciences**

  Andhra Pradesh.
- **Anantapur Campus: Department of Bioscience**

  Anantapur, Andhra Pradesh.
- **Cochin University of Science and Technology**

  Department of Marine Geology and Geophysics

  Cochin/Kochi, Kerala.
- **Madha Arts and Science College, Chennai, Tamil Nadu.**
- **Karavali College, Mangalore, Karnataka.**
- **Pulipati Prasad Institute of Medical Sciences (PIMTECH) College of B.Sc (MLT)**

  Andhra Pradesh.

10.8 Meteorology

What is Meteorology?

Meteorology is referred to as the science of atmosphere, which is the blanket covering the earth. The word 'Meteorology' comes from the Greek word '*meteorol*' which refers to 'something that occurs high in the sky' Meteorology is a sub-discipline of atmospheric science that mainly focusses on various aspects of the atmosphere especially that of the weather and climate. In this field, we study about weather, climate and the forces that cause change in our environment. In simple terms it is the study of weather and weather forecasting.

The main task of a Meteorologist

A meteorologist is also called climatologist or atmospheric scientist. The main task of a meteorologist is to collect and analyse information on atmospheric conditions. He is responsible for forecasting the weather by measuring temperature, humidity, pressure, wind speed, rainfall and air quality using various equipments like rain gauge, anemometer, thermometer, barometer and so on. Now there are more complex observing techniques using satellites. These observations are plotted on charts and meteorologists analyse them and forecast the weather. The field involves research, teaching, consulting and forecasting. There are three aspects of meteorology – observation, understanding and prediction of weather.

Eligibility

Career aspirants in this field must be good at mathematics and science. To begina career as a meteorologist one must have at least a bachelor's degree in meteorology or atmospheric science. Bachelor's degree is of four year duration. A master's degree in meteorology with relevant specialisation is essential for positions such as operational meteorologists, physical meteorologists, synoptic meteorologists, environmental meteorologists and hydrometeorologists. Master level programmes are of two year duration. Candidates who are aspiring to become researchers and scientists must complete a Ph.D. programme in Meteorology. Duration of a doctoral programme is normally over three years.

Job Prospects and Career Options

Meteorologists are usually employed by weather broadcasting stations, environmental agencies, and government agencies such as meteorology departments, industrial weather research facilities, military department, satellite space research centers, radio and television stations and global weather centers. Space applications centers also recruit meteorologists as the launching of satellite also depends on weather conditions.

The Indian Meteorological Department (IMD), National Centre for Medium Weather Forecasting and Indian Institute of Tropical Meteorology recruit candidates through Union Public Service Commission (UPSC). Those with master's degree can apply for the posts. Besides government entries, private enterprises can also join universities as researchers. There is great scope for research as several institutes like Indian Association for the Cultivation of Science, Indian Institute of Tropical Meteorology recruit people for various research works. Aviation is another choice in the field. Airline companies hire their own meteorologists. Another career opportunity for meteorologists is lecturing at a university or college.

Specialised career areas

Major specialised career profiles available for meteorologists are as consulting meteorologists, broadcast meteorologists, aviation meteorologists, operational meteorologists, physical meteorologists, synoptic meteorologists, environmental meteorologists and hydro-meteorologists and so on. Weather forecasting is the heart of meteorology. Atmospheric scientists who forecast the weather are known as operational meteorologists; they are the largest group of specialists. Physical meteorologists study the atmosphere's chemical and physical properties, the transmission of light, sound and radio waves and the transfer of energy in the atmosphere. Synoptic meteorologists are responsible for the development of new weather forecasting tools and technology. Hydro-meteorologists study the effects of hydrologic cycles on the atmosphere. Environmental meteorologists research the effect of specific atmospheric changes caused on the atmosphere due to problems such as pollution and shortage of food, fuel and water.

A few institutes and organisations in India where meteorologists can find jobs are Indian Institute of Tropical Meteorology, India Meteorology Department, Indian Air Force, Space Application Centre, National Remote Sensing Agency, Defence Research and Development Organisation, Indian Space Research Organisation and so on.

Remuneration of Meteorologists

Salaries depend on education, experience and place of employment. Initial salary one can earn is about ₹ 10,000 per month. With experience they can earn around ₹ 25,000 per month. In government service meteorologists belonging to grade II get ₹ 15,000 – 26,000 per month. One having outstanding knowledge and experience can also find job in abroad. There the salary is not an issue at all.

Courses

- M. Sc. Agricultural Meteorology,
- M. Sc. Meteorology,
- Ph. D. Atmospheric Science and Astrophysics,
- M.Tech. Atmospheric Science,
- M. Sc. Satellite Meteorology and Weather Informatics, and
- Ph. D. Earth and Atmospheric Science.

Best Institutes for Studying Meteorology in India are :

- **Andhra University, Visakhapatnam, Andhra Pradesh**

  Courses : Master of Science in Meteorology,
  Doctor of Philosophy-Meteorology.

- **Cochin University of Science and Technology, Kochi, Kerala**

  Course : Master of Science in Meteorology.

- **Deen Dayal Upadhyaya Gorakhpur University, Gorakhpur, Uttar Pradesh**

  Courses : Master of Science in Chemistry,

  Master of Science in Mathematics.

- **College of Horticulture, Trissur, Kerala**

  Course : Master of Science – Agricultural Meteorology.

- **College of Agriculture, Hissar, Haryana**

  Courses : Master of Science – Agricultural Meteorology,

  Doctor of Philosophy - Agricultural Meteorology.

- **College of Science and Technology, Visakhapatnam, Andhra Pradesh**

  Courses : Master of Science in Meteorology,

  Doctor of Philosophy-Meteorology and Oceanography.

11
FINE ARTS

11.1 Dance

Indian Dance

In India, dance is an age-old tradition. The vast sub-continent has given birth to varied forms of dancing, each shaped by the influences of a particular period and environment. Indian dance is an extremely intricate art requiring skill, hard work and discipline. All Indian dances portray some expression of life and almost every dance posture has a specific meaning. Dance themes are derived from mythology, folklore, legends and classical literature. Indian dance is said to have originated from *'Natya Shastra'*, which a detailed script is written on all aspects of Indian dance. The author of *'Natya Shastra'* was Bharata Muni who wrote it sometime in the second century B.C.

Divisions of Indian Dance

The two main divisions of dance are classical and folk forms. There are dance forms typical to certain parts of the country and these dance forms are based on ancient dance discipline. The various classical forms are *Bharatnatyam* of Tamil Nadu, *Kuchupudi* of Andhra Pradesh, *Odissi* of Orissa, *Kathak, Kathakali* and *Manipuri.* The uniqueness of Indian classical dances is that they are all devotional in content. Of all these dance forms, *Bharat Natyam* is believed to be the oldest and the purest Indian classical dance.

Training in dance should start as early as age six or less, much before the official professional training. Besides an inborn talent, the basic requirement for a full time professional training is matriculation or 10+2. Some institutes at the time of admission even give preference to students having a talent. Careers in this field can be that of a performer, teacher and choreographer.

Eligibility

To take up a course in this subject the basic requirement is 10+2. However, for post graduate level courses graduation in the subject is compulsory. Courses offered in this area are certificate courses, bachelor courses, diploma courses and post graduate level courses.

Duration of various courses: Certificate course is of one year, Bachelor courses is of three years, Diploma and Post Graduate courses is of two years. Training in this field is available at a number of schools and institutes all over India. The Kathak Kendra in Delhi, the Kalashetra in Chennai, Bharatiya Kala Kendra in Delhi are some of the prominent institutes conducting courses in Dance.

Courses areas included history and evolution of dance and dance forms, the characteristic features of the dance form one specialises in, covering all aspects of dance as a performing art.

Personal Attributes

Main attributes are talent, versatility, sense of rhythm, dedication, grace, an expressive facial and body language, an ability to interpret roles, attractive appearance, stage presence, creativity, physical stamina etc.

Job Prospects

Dancers can find employment in kala kendras, academies, TV channels, dance troupes. There are also many other opportunities for self-employment in the form of holding private classes or starting an institution.

Career Options

Career options available in this area are that of a performer, teacher and choreographer.

- **Teaching :** To be in this field one needs an aptitude to teach, initiative and patience. They must also have thorough knowledge of practical and theoretical aspects of dance. They should have a perfect sense of rhythm and some proficiency in music. Dancers who take up teaching as a profession can find opportunities in schools, colleges, universities, dance institutes and even open schools of their own.
- **Choreography :** The choreographer designs and composes dance sequences and co-ordinates the stage settings, music, costumes and supervises rehearsals. Choresographer must have creative or imaginative powers and an ability to interpret music and compose dance routines for solo as well as group performances.

They must be able to work along with a team. Prospects in this field are expanding with more and more stage and TV shows. Choreographers can find employment in troupes performing stage shows, TV shows and in films.

- **Performing :** To be a performing artist one must have attractive appearance, facial expression, an ability to interpret roles and stage presence. Performers have to spare time everyday for practicing. They must also have to keep in touch with the interest of the general public. They must travel a lot and give performances to be popular. Besides professional training, dedication, talent and the right contacts can only help a performer to become well established. Performing artists can form their own troupes or even work with other troupes. They also have the option of starting schools and devote time for teaching.

Courses

- B.A. Dance,
- B.F.A. Dance,
- Bachelor of Dance (B. Dance),
- Certificate course in Dance,
- Diploma in Dance,
- M.A. Dance,
- M.F.A. Dance,
- Master of Dance (M. Dance), and
- Ph.D. Dance.

Institutes

- **Benaras Hindu University: Faculty of Performing Arts, Varanasi**
  Varanasi – 221005.
- **Kurukshetra University, Kurukshetra (Haryana),**
  Kurukshetra – 132119.
- **Kinkini Dhvani Institution of Performing Arts, Noida**
  G-118 Sector 25, Noida (Uttar Pradesh).
- **Guru Nanak Dev University, Amritsar (Punjab)**
  P.R.O. Office, Amritsar - 143005.
- **Ajmer Music College, Ajmer (Rajasthan)**
  Jawaharlal Hospital Road, Ajmer – 305001.

- **Andhra University: College of Arts and Commerce, Vishakhapatnam**
  Vishakhapatnam – 530003 (Andhra Pradesh).
- **Punjab University: Faculty of Arts , Chandigarh**
  Sector 14, Chandigarh – 160014.
- **Potti Sreeramulu Telegu University, Hyderabad**
  School of Fine Arts, Lalithakala Kshetram, Saroobgh Public Gardens, Nampally, Hyderabad. – 500004 (Andhra Pradesh).
- **Tilak Maharashtra University, Pune**
  University Bhavan, Gultekadi, Pune – 411037.

11.2 Music

What is Music?

Music is one of the most profound achievements of human beings. It creates emotions and expresses feelings. Music also soothes the mind.

Talent, genuine interest, sincerity and willingness to work hard can guarantee a big success in the field of music. Having an inborn talent to sing is a wonderful gift. But making a career out of this talent demands regular devoted practice. Joining an institution and getting trained is one of the first steps towards making a career in Music but the main emphasis is a real dedication and commitment.

A person considering a career in music should have a genuine love for music, a musical sense which means a sense of timing and rhythm besides versatility, creative ability and also stage confidence. At the same time one needs to have publicity-contacts with the right people, money for training and for making demo-cassettes for commercialisation.

Variety of Opportunities in Music

Just as there is a wide variety of forms in music like classical, folk, jazz, pop, rock, fusion, etc., there are also a variety of opportunities in this field. Besides becoming a performer (vocal or instrument) or a teacher, one can be a composer/song writer, music publisher, music journalist, Disc Jockeys/Video Jockeys, Music Therapist, Artist manager/PR and so on in the Music Industry. Today, the advent of satellite television, the growing popularity of the music channels and corporate sponsorship of musical events has all made music big business. Although fame and money in this field depends a lot on luck and getting a good break but once you are established, there is an ample scope for making good money in this field.

Eligibility

There is no specific qualification required to enter into this field. However, to take up a course in this subject the basic requirement is 10+2. Courses offered in this area are certificate courses, bachelor courses, diploma courses and post graduate level courses.

Duration for these courses: Certificate course is of one year, Bachelor's course is of three years, Diploma and Post Graduate level course is of two years.

Training in this field is imparted by many schools and institutions. Most prominent among them is Kalashetra in Chennai and Bharatiya Kala Kendra in Delhi. Course areas include music theory, music interpretation, history of music, composing, voice instruction etc.

Personal Attributes

Among the attributes, one that tops the list is a good voice. Other attributes include inherent talent, dedication, determination and hard work, creativity and adaptability, team work, accept criticism in the right spirit, self confidence, ambition and others.

Job Prospects

Talented and qualified persons can find numerous employment opportunities in this field with the advent of satellite television and music channels. Various employers in this area are :

- Television channels like Doordarshan,
- AIR and private FM channel stations,
- Music channels,
- Government departments of culture and public relations,
- Production houses,
- Music troupes,
- Music research organisations as a musicologists,
- Music companies,
- Educational Institutions, Kala Kendra etc.,
- Hospitals as music therapist,
- Newspapers and magazines as music critic or correspondents,

- There are also many opportunities for self-employment in the form of holding private classes at home or opening a music school or producing and directing independent programmes.

Career Options

Today, with music getting the league of big business, there are lists of careers one can choose from in the Music Industry. Besides becoming a performer (vocal or Instrumental) or a teacher, one can be a composer/ song writer, music publisher, music journalist, disc jockeys/video jockeys, music therapist, artist manager/PR and so on in the music industry.

- **Music composer/Songwriter :** Those with flair in writing and an inborn talent in music can take up the career as a music composer. A composer creates and writes music, may combine it with lyrics to give a new song. Musicians in this field create music or lyrics alone or create both together. Composers are required to write music creatively based on their knowledge of sound, understanding of various musical styles and taste of the audience to which it has to be presented. A song writer or lyricist must understand the theme, mood and audience, the music into which one is putting words. There are separate categories known as Jingle writers who specialise in writing music for radio and television commercials. Composers/songwriters can create music for film, television/radio jingles, folk songs and for albums. Musicians who are interested in this area are often required to know about the business aspect of song writing such as copyrights, networking, publishing, contracts and performing rights. Jingle writers can get in through contacts in ad firms and production houses, contacts with directors/producers help to get in film/television companies.
- **Singers/Performers :** Performing artists may work alone or in a group with or without musical instrument. One could be a classical or pop artiste or an instrumental musician. Performance careers differ widely and depend a great deal upon the instrument played and the performance medium. A high standard of musical and technical skill is required and expected from performers in all areas. They can undertake challenging performance in concert halls, small or large ensembles, in studios as recording artists and live shows in lounge settings, pubs, night clubs and the like. They can also work for film industry as playback singers.

- **Producers :** Producers bring together the various elements of recording and works to present them as an artistic whole. They book the studio, hire musicians and engineers, oversee the production of the recorded music and control the recording budget. They have the final say on the development of their material. To be a successful producer, technical knowledge and tack is a potent combination. Sometimes ex-artists/sound engineers enter this field.
- **Artist/Music Management :** This is considered as one of the emerging options. Artist management is the planning, organising and negotiating of an artist's career. They work in the business area of music and deals with the tough, unpleasant stuff behind the scenes. The work involves meeting with radio and television producers and getting air time for their artist, negotiating with recording companies and programme sponsors. Perseverance and knowledge of music and media industries are vital. Experience and training in music as well as a business background helps to be successful in the field.They can work for a particular artist or band as well as in an artist management firm, performing organisation and touring music group.
- **Music Journalist :** They review performances and recordings, conduct interviews with performers for various publications and write music reviews. They give news and updates on new releases and performers. Some may work as music critic also. This is one of the options available in music field for freelancing. They can also work for newspapers, magazines and websites. To take up this career one must have keen interest and knowledge in music, flair for writing and good command of language.
- **Music Educator/Teacher :** Teachers can open music schools and also conduct private classes. Music teaching is often in demand at schools, colleges, universities and institutional set-ups. Their main job is to instill an interest and enthusiasm for music among the students. Main attributes required for them is classical music qualification, initiative and patience. They must have a thorough knowledge of music to impart training to their students.
- **Music Therapist:** Music therapist is a unique breed of musician-counsellor with specialised training in the use of rhythm and melody to improve psychological and emotional well being. Emotional stability and insight are essential for competent therapists. They must have the ability to explore, interpret and develop the creative use of sound. Music therapist provides

therapeutic programmes to people of all age group with psychiatric disorders, mental retardation and developmental disabilities, speech and hearing impairments, physical disabilities, and neurological impairments. A career in music therapy offers challenge, opportunity and distinctive rewards to those interested in working with people of all ages with various disabilities. Music therapists are employed in psychiatric hospitals, community mental health agencies, rehabilitation centers, nursing homes and residences for mentally disabled. They can also do private practice.

- **Musicologist :** With good knowledge of music, an aptitude for research and excellent communication skills, one can work as musicologist in research institutes.
- **Video Jockeys (VJs) and Disc Jockeys (DJs) :** With the advent of various music channels video jockeying is becoming an exciting career option for the music mad generation. Their job includes introducing a music video, conducting interviews with artists and music personalities. No specific educational background is required for VJs/DJs except some personal attributes. However, background in mass communication, visual communication or the performing arts comes in handy. Main attributes required to work in this visual medium are excellent presentation skills, clear voice, presence of mind, in-depth knowledge about various styles of music, musicians and albums, communication skills, confidence, ability to take split-second decisions, good body language and dress sense.
- **Music Librarian :** Colleges and public libraries offer opportunities for trained music specialists with knowledge of library and research technique. Some opportunities for music librarians also exist in radio, television and motion pictures. In addition to any music qualification they need to have bachelor's degree in library and information science.

Courses available in Music

- B.A. (Hons.) in Classical Vocal Music,
- B.A. (Hons.) in Rabindra Sangeet,
- B.A. (Hons.) Music,
- B.A./B.Sc. Combination of Music,
- B.A. Music,
- Bachelor of Music (B.Music),

- Certificate Course in Music,
- Diploma in Folk Music,
- Diploma in Music,
- Diploma Proficiency Course in Music,
- M.A. Music,
- M.Phil. Music,
- Master of Music (M. Music),
- Ph.D. Music, and
- Ph.D. Rabindra Sangeet.

Top Ten Music Colleges in India

- **Visva Santiniketan, West Bengal**

  Courses : Master of Music, Hindustani Classical Music-Vocal,

  Master of Music-Hindustani Classical Music Instrumental (Sitar, Esrai, Tabla, Pakhawai).

- **University of Delhi, New Delhi**

  Courses : Doctor of Philosophy in Music,

  Post Graduate Diploma in Music.

- **Karnataka University, Hubli-Dharwad, Karnataka**

  Courses : Master of Arts-Music (Vocal),

  Master of Arts-Music (Tabla).

- **Shreemati Nathibai Damodar Thackersey University, Mumbai, Maharashtra**

  Course : Bachelor of Arts-Music.

- **Shivaji University, Kolhapur, Maharashtra**

  Courses : Diploma in Classical Music,

  Diploma in Instrumental Music.

- **Padmaja Naidu College of Music, Bardhaman, West Bengal**

  Courses : Bachelor of Arts-Combination of Music,

  Bachelor of Arts (Hons.)-Classical Vocal Music.

- **Dayalbagh Educational Institute, Agra, Uttar Pradesh**

  Courses : Master of Arts-Music with specialisation in Sitar/Tabla/Vocal Music,

  Doctor of Philosophy-Music.

- **Pandit Panchakshari Gavaigalvar Music College, Gadag, Karnataka**

  Courses : Bachelor of Arts in Music.

11.3 Painting

What is Painting?

Painting is an art form in which colors and lines make a visual impression. It is the means of expressing one's ideas or feelings to others in pictorial form. Painting not only mean the traditional painting canvas but also on glass, ceramic, pot and fabric as well as it could be using different paint media such as watercolor, pastels, oil and so on. Not only brushes but knives, spatula, nibs and even twigs could be used for painting designs.

Taking up painting as a hobby is one thing but taking it up as a career is a different thing altogether. For making a living out of painting, not only talent but also an ability to market yourself, make people want to buy your products is of utmost importance. Once you decide on a career in painting, you can try out the different styles or media to work with, get trained and specialise in a particular style or develop your own unique style.

Painting is a Prospective Career Option

Comparatively, painting as an art piece is appreciated by more and more people these days as against a few art connoisseurs earlier. Moreover, paintings are in vogue these days, for decorating interiors. With more and more art galleries coming up in metro cities in India, budding painters have a platform to display their works while the lay man has an opportunity to view the paintings and buy a piece or two.

Eligibility

Artistic talent is inherent, it is God's gift and one has to polish or sharpen this talent. One could attend an art school, do a course or train under a master painter.

Even though painting is an art that requires no qualification, by taking a course a person can be trained and his inherent ability can be polished and developed under a trainer. There are many fine arts colleges and institutions offering under-graduate level degrees in drawing and painting. You can do bachelor's, master's or diploma courses to hone your skills. Minimum qualification is 10+2 to take up bachelor diploma course which is of three years and one year duration respectively. Master level course is of two years and qualification required is degree. There are also various short term courses.

Personal Attributes

In this field, creativity is more important than educational qualification. As per technicality is concerned, you should be aware of the different shades of colours and the methods that help in mixing them. To make money in this field you should have the ability to sell yourself. You must have good communication and language skills to present your work.

Job Prospects and Career Options

Indian paintings have huge demand world-wide and pieces of paintings done by Indian artists have soared in the global market. Requirement for different forms of paintings such as allegorical, religious, historical, landscape and portraiture have also churned out unexpected demand for talented professionals. These days, paintings have also become an integral part of interior decoration. Be it a commercial enterprise or a house or hotel, an elegant painting hung on the wall is a common sight. This too has increased the demand for paintings. Hence, a career in this area is a right choice for those with artistic talent.

Painters can specialise in a particular medium such as glass, ceramic, oil, or a particular style such as sketching and Indian folk painting. There are various career choices for a painter. He can opt freelancing or work under someone. A freelancer can hold his/her own painting exhibitions. They can also work for art galleries where the art work can be kept for auction and can be sold for prices depending on the work. If you join some firm, then you will have comparatively routine work to do.

Painting is a career which you can carve out of your hobby. Making a name initially in the field is not easy. As in any other fine arts field, perseverance is the name of the game. One should keep contacting art galleries, exhibit their paintings, make connections, meanwhile keep at improving one's talent. If you are apprehensive about taking a full time painting career, you could do freelance work as a painter, while continuing with a regular job.

A painter's work is not limited to canvas that is framed and sold in galleries or exhibitions. You can try your hand in doing art work or cartoons for newspapers, magazines, posters, film and TV industry. They could also diversify and be an illustrator, graphic artist, henna artist or take up website designing and animation. One can also opt for teaching as a career by joining fine arts institutes/colleges or stating own coaching classes.

Remuneration

A painter's earning is hard to be defined. If you work under a firm, salary depends on the concern you join. Income in this field is based on the skill and the popularity of your work. But, once you are established in this field, your earnings will keep on multiplying.

Courses

- B.A. Painting,
- B.A. Painting, Sculpture, Applied Arts,
- B.F.A. Painting,
- Certificate Course in Painting,
- Diploma in Painting,
- M.A. Drawing and Painting,
- M.A. Painting, Sculpture, Applied Arts,
- M.F.A. Painting,
- M.Phil. Drawing and Painting,
- Ph.D. Painting, and
- Post Graduate Diploma in Painting, Sculpture, Applied Arts.

Institutes

- Santhanu's Chitira Vidyalayam, Chennai.
- RLV (Radha Lakshmi Vilasam) College of Music and Fine Arts, Ernakulum, Kerala.
- Karnataka University, Dharwad Karnataka.
- Sri Venkateshwara College of Fine Arts, Hyderabad.
- Jawaharlal Nehru Architecture and Fine Arts University (JNAFAU), Hyderabad.
- Ooviyaas School of Design and Fine Arts, Chennai.
- Dr. Babasaheb Ambedkar Marathwada University: Department of Fine Arts, Aurangabad (Maharashtra).
- M.S. University of Baroda: Faculty of Fine Arts, Vadodara (Gujarat).
- North Maharashtra University, Jalgaon (Maharashtra).
- Allahabad University: Faculty of Arts, Allahabad (Uttar Pradesh).
- Andhra University: College of Arts and Commerce, Vishakapatnam.
- Dayalbagh Educational Institute, Agra (Uttar Pradesh).

12
HEALTHCARE AND ALLIED FIELDS

12.1 Medicine

Introduction

Medicine is one of the most sort after and rewarding career for those who have a flair for science and philodemic concern for human beings. A doctor's profession involves a lot of hard work and at the same time, it gives the satisfaction of curing patients and at times even saving lives. It is a very demanding profession which requires keen observation, analytical mind, precision, accuracy and timely decision. No error can be committed as it would risk the life and health of the patient directly. Medical profession is more of a responsibility than a privilege. It is more of what you can give to the society than what you can get from it. If you have no sincere love for people, this profession would be a wrong choice as it would turn them into economic objects. Those who take up this profession should view it as a vocation and not as a position to fill one's coffers.

Eligibility

The basic or degree level qualification for a medical profession is MBBS which is of five and a half years duration (including one year internship). Selection for MBBS is through an All India Entrance Examination. The qualification required for entrance is 10+2 or equivalent with science subjects (physics, chemistry and biology). In the case of private medical colleges entrance examinations are conducted by the institutes individually. In addition to MBBS, a candidate should complete House Surgency or internship for one year.

All India Entrance Examinations which one can Appear for Admission into MBBS Course

The following exams are the All India Entrance Examination for admission into MBBS/BDS courses. All the students who have completed 10+2 with science (physics, chemistry and biology) are eligible for this :

- Central Board of Secondary Education (CBSE), New Delhi (15 per cent Seats) — December
- All India Institute of Medical Sciences, New Delhi — January
- Manipal Academy of Higher Education, Manipal — February
- St. John's National Academy of Health Sciences, Bangalore — March
- Armed Forces Medical College (AFMC), Pune — January
- Bharati Vidyapeeth, Pune — April
- Mahatma Gandhi Institute of Medical Sciences, Warda — January
- JIPMER (Jawaharlal Nehru Institute of Post graduate Medical Education and Research) — February
- CMC, Vellore — February
- Sri Ramachandra Medical College and Research Institute, Chennai — March
- Jawaharlal Nehru Medical College, AMU, Aligarh — March
- BHU Institute of Medical Sciences, Varanasi — January
- GGS IP University (VM Medical College), Delhi — December

This is not an exhaustive list.

Course Areas

The course content includes anatomy, physiology, bio-chemistry, microbiology, pathology, pharmacology, forensic medicine, general medicine, surgery, ophthalmology, ENT (ear, nose and throat), gynaecology and obstetrics, paediatrics, orthopaedics and preventive and social medicine.

After MBBS, candidates can go for post graduate level studies (MD or MS) through another entrance. At the post graduate level, there is specialisation in Medicine and Surgery. A post graduate programme (MD or MS) is usually of three years duration. The major specialisations include general medicine, general surgery, paediatrics, obstetrics and gynaecology, dermatology, ophthalmology, orthopaedics, ENT (ear, Nose and Throat), psychiatry, anesthesiology etc.

Those with post graduation (MD or MS or M.Sc. in Medicine) can further opt for super-specialisation, i.e., they can go for Ph.D. in any specialised area of medicine. MD or MS holders can complete the doctoral programme (Ph.D.) in two years and M.Sc. Medicine holders in three years.

For practising as a physician or surgeon, one needs to have completed the MBBS course from a recognised medical college and must possess a licence from the State Medical Council to practise.

Career Options / Specialisations

Some of the common areas of specialisation in Medicine and Surgery are :

- **General Practitioner or Physician :** He diagnoses and treats the every day and sundry ailments of the human body. MBBS holders practise as physicians.
- **General Surgeon :** He is one who specialises in surgery for all organs of the body. He can further specialise in specific areas. Duties involve examining the patient to determine the extent and nature of injury, treatment through operation and giving post operative care. Surgery is of various types orthopaedic, plastic, neuro, etc.
- **Anesthetists or Anesthesiologists :** He administers anesthetics to a patient undergoing surgical operation according to the nature of operation. It is he who makes surgical procedure as painless as possible. His duties involve examining the patient to determine his capacity to withstand shock of operation and anesthesia. He or she has huge responsibility and has to be present throughout the operation.
- **Psychiatrist :** He diagnoses and treats mental disorders. Psychiatry has two major branches: The first is Psychotherapy, the application of psychological techniques to the treatment of mental illnesses. This branch uses non-drug therapies and will not use physical techniques such as drugs or surgery. The second branch is Psychiatry, where medical therapies are used. After diagnosing physical and behavioural symptoms, drugs and other means may be used for treatment.
- **Neurologist :** He diagnoses and treats diseases related to brain and nervous system. They also specialise in nenro-surgery.

- **Pediatrician :** He treats new born babies and children.
- **Ophthalmologist or Eye Specialist :** Treats diseases and disorders of eyes.
- **Pathologist :** Investigates the cause of various diseases and the possibilities for their prevention. His duties involve conducting chemical, microscopic and bacteriological test in labs and examining blood, tissues, urine, etc., to find out the cause for disease.
- **Cardiologist :** Also called heart specialist. Treats diseases related to heart and circulatory system.
- **Gynaecologist-Obstetrician :** Diagnoses and treats diseases and disorders of human female reproduction system. They care for pregnant women from conception through delivery.
- **Dermatologist :** One who specialises in the diagnosis and treatment of skin problems.
- **Orthopaedist :** One who specialises in the diseases connected to skeletal system. Orthopaedics is that branch of medicine that deals with the correction of deformities and prevention of disorders in joints, muscles, tendons, ligaments, cartilage, all bones and bony tissue.
- **Gastroenterologist :** Treats diseases related to liver, pancreas, stomach, intestine, bowels and gall bladder.
- **Radiologist :** Diagnoses diseases and disorders by studying X-ay pictures of affected parts and gives treatment such as therapeutic radiation to affected parts of the body.
- **ENT specialist :** Treats disorders of ear, nose and throat.
- **Tuberculosis Specialist :** Treats ailments due to infection by tubercular disease.
- **Venerologist :** Treats venereal or sexual diseases.
- **Bacteriologist :** Also called Microbiologist. Conducts research and laboratory experiments on occurrence, growth, development, control and utilisation of bacteria and other micro-organisms.
- **Physiologist :** Studies normal functioning of different organs and tissues of human body and investigates effects of physical environments such as variations in altitude, speed, temperature, etc., on its vital functions.

- **Nutritionist :** Gives instructions regarding food values and utilisation of foods in human body to keep it healthy and control diseases. He prescribes diet for various diseases.
- **Chiropodist :** Also called pedicurist, treats foot diseases and abnormalities. He treats corns, etc., using surgical instruments.

What is AIPMT and how can one appear in AIPMT for admission into a good Medical College?

For admission to 15 per cent of the total seats for Medical/Dental courses in all Medical/Dental colleges run by the Union of India, state governments, municipal or other local authorities in India except in the State of Jammu and Kashmir, the Central Board of Secondary Education (CBSE) conducts All India Pre-Medical/Pre-Dental Entrance Examination. As per the revised scheme of examination the AIPMT examination is conducted in two stages as per the following schedule :

- Preliminary examination, and
- Final examination.

Pattern of AIPMT

- **Preliminary Examination :** This examination consists of one paper containing 200 objective type questions (multiple choice) from physics, chemistry and biology (botany and zoology) to be answered on the specially designed machine-gradable sheet using ball point pen only.

  Duration : 3 hours.
- **Final Examination :** This examination is only for those who qualify in the preliminary examination. The final examination consists of one paper containing 120 objective type questions (multiple choice) from physics, chemistry and biology (botany and zoology) to be answered on the specially designed machine-gradable sheet using ball point pen only.

  Duration : 3 hours.
- **Eligibility :** The candidate should be at least 17 years of age at the time of admission or will complete the age on or before 31st December during the year of admission. To be eligible to appear in competitive entrance examination, candidate must have passed any of the qualifying examinations as mentioned in the *Information Bulletin*. Provided also that to be eligible for competitive entrance examination the candidate must have passed in the subjects of physics, chemistry, biology and English individually and must have obtained a minimum of 50 per cent marks taken together in physics, chemistry and biology at the

qualifying examination. In respect of candidates belonging to Schedule Caste/Schedule Tribes or Other Backward Classes the marks obtained in physics, chemistry and biology taken together in qualifying examination be 40 per cent instead of 50 per cent for general candidates. Those who are taking plus two examinations in the year can also appear for the entrance test provisionally subject to their fulfilling the condition later.

- **Information Bulletin and Application Form:** Bulletin containing the Application Form and other details is available from October or as notified and can be taken against cash payment of ₹ 800 for General Category and ₹ 450 for SC/ST category including examination fee from notified Canara Bank branches. There is provision for submission of application online also. Visit www.aipmt.nic.in. To prepare for PMT you have to study your course material well and clear your concepts in physics, chemistry and biology to answer objective type questions and application of various concepts. You can also buy some guide books for PMT from the market and study these along with your course book. Regular coaching or correspondence course will also help you in this matter.

Entry into AIIMS after completing 10+2 Science

In order to join AIIMS, you have to appear in the competitive examination after completing your plus-two science (physics, chemistry and biology). The competitive entrance examination will be of three and a half hours duration and will have one paper consisting of 200 objective type (multiple choice of reason assertion type) questions from physics, chemistry, biology and general knowledge. The details of distribution of marks are as follows :

Subject	*Total*
Physics	60
Chemistry	60
Biology (Botany and Zoology)	60
General Knowledge	20
Total	200

The general standard of the vompetitive entrance examination will be that of 12th class under the 10+2 Scheme/Pre-Medical/Intermediate science or an equivalent. No syllabus for the examination has been prescribed by AIIMS.

Every year, 50 seats are available for admission to the graduate medical course, leading to the award of the degree of MBBS of All India Institute of Medical Sciences. Out of these, seven seats are reserved for the Schedule Castes, four seats for the Scheduled Tribes and five for the Foreign Nationals nominated by the Government of India. The remaining 34 seats are occupied by the General candidates on the meritological basis in the competitive examination. If the requisite numbers of suitable candidates are not available from the above two reserved categories, the vacant seats are filled by the candidates from the general category.

Entry into Christian Medical College (CMC), Vellore after completing 10+2 Science

Christian Medical College (CMC), Vellore also conducts an all India competitive examination for admission into MBBS course. The performance in this examination is the basis called for interviews and final selection. The entrance examination is conducted on the basis of 10+2 syllabus. The test is of multiple choices and contains questions on physics, chemistry, biology and general ability. The total number of seat for MBBS course in CMC is 60.

- **Eligibility :** Candidates should have passed in English and obtained 50 per cent marks aggregate in physics, chemistry and biology taken together both at qualifying and competitive examinations. Only candidates who qualify in the written test are called for the interviews. The duration of MBBS course is of four and a half years and is followed by one year of Compulsory Rotating Residential Internship. The course is taken in three stages, following a short foundation course which provides basic principles of communication, ethics and problem Based learning. The first stage is for 12 months and covers the basic sciences of anatomy, physiology and biochemistry. The next stage is for 18 months and includes pharmacology, pathology, microbiology and forensic medicine. The last stage is for 24 months and covers ophthalmology, otorhinolaryngology, community medicine, general medicine, pediatrics, surgery, orthopaedic surgery and obstetrics and gynecology.

  For more information on the admission calendar and prospectus, etc., write to: Registrar, Christian Medical College, Vellore, 632 002, Tamil Nadu.

As both AIIMS and CMC entrance examinations are highly competitive one only few students crack it and, therefore, if anyone wants these top medical colleges, he or she needs to prepare for the initial stage for the admission test. The following books may be helpful for preparing AIIMS/CMC admission test along with your 10+2 syllabus.

- Physics by H.C. Verma.
- Chemistry by O.P. Agarwal and Physical Chemistry by R.C. Mukherjee.
- Biology by M.P. Kaushik and Ramesh Gupta.
- Tata McGraw Hill Publication in Physics, Chemistry, Biology.
- Medical entrance guide by any reputed publisher.

How to get Admission in Armed Forces Medical College (AFMC) for MBBS course

Admission to MBBS course is based on written examination. The written examination is held on 1st Sunday of May. Successful candidates are called for interview in June for the courses starting in July. Admission is subject to medical fitness.

- **Course duration :** The duration of MBBS course is four and a half years followed by internship of one year.
- **Service Liability :** Students have compulsory liability to serve as commissioned officers in the Armed Forces Medical Services. The offer of the type of commission will depend on the vacancies available. The candidates' parents/guardians are required to sign a bond agreement at the time of admission.
- **Eligibility :** A candidate should be a citizen of India or be a subject of Nepal or Bhutan or a person of Indian origin migrated from Pakistan or any other foreign country with the intention of permanently settling in India; must be unmarried. Marrying during the course is not permitted; should be medically fit as per prescribed standards by the Government of India, Ministry of Defence.

  He must have attained the age of 17 years on 31st December of the year of application, but must not have attained the age of 22 years on that date (not more than 24 years in case of candidates who have passed or are appearing in final B.Sc. examinations).

  Academic qualifications : A candidate must have passed all the subjects opted for in the first attempt of the qualifying examinations as a regular candidate with English, physics, chemistry and biology taken simultaneously and securing not less than 60 per cent of the aggregate marks in these three science subjects taken together and not less than 50 per cent marks in

English and 50 per cent marks in each of the science subjects. They must have also passed an examination in mathematics of the 10th standard.

- **Number of Seats :** A total of 130 students (105 boys and 25 girls) will be admitted.
- **Syllabus for the Examination :** The general standard of the entrance examination will be that of 11th and 12th under the 10+2 scheme/pre-medical/intermediate science or an equivalent examination of the State Education Board/Indian University.
- **Method of Selection :** Candidates who are found provisionally eligible as per the criteria of the eligibility which will be called at one of the examination centres to appear in the competitive examination on 1st Sunday of May. Issue of admit cards, however, does not necessarily mean acceptance of eligibility which will be further scrutinised at subsequent stages of selection.

  The written examination centre will be allotted to candidates depending upon the administrative arrangements for the examination and availability of adequate seating capacity.

  The roll number of the candidates who qualify for interview based on the above written examination will be published in the leading newspapers.
- **Interview of the Candidate :** On the basis of their performance in the written examination selected candidates in order of roll numbers will be called for an interview to be held in the month of June at AMFC, Pune. The exact date of the above interview will be intimidated to the selected candidates. Request for change of date of interview will not be entertained. The candidates will be required to produce originals of all certificates/mark sheets at the time of interview. All candidates will produce result or proof of having appeared in the qualifying examination held, at the time of interview (if the result of such examination has not been declared).

  On the basis of the above test and interview two merit lists namely, one for boys and one for girls will be drawn up and admissions will be offered only to candidates in accordance with their merit position. Individual letters of admission will be sent only to selected candidates who would be required to join AFMC. The remaining candidates will be on waiting list. The result will be published by the DGAFMS in the newspapers.
- **SC/ST Candidates :** Ten seats are reserved for SC/ST candidates. SC/ST candidates must qualify in the written

examination and come within the zone to be called up for the interview. They must come within the first 500 in the final combined merit list of boys and girls.

- **Medical Standards :** The candidate must be in good physical and mental health and free from disability likely to interfere with the efficient performance of duty in the Armed Forces. Medical examination will be done by a Board of Officers at AFMC, Pune, prior to admission to the college. Medical Board will categorise as fit and unfit, in accordance with the prescribed standards.

Entry into Jawaharlal Institute of Post-graduate Medical Education and Research (JIPMER)

The various courses offered by JIPMER are as follows :

Under-graduate Courses

- MBBS — 98 seats
- B.Sc. Nursing — 75 seats
- B.Sc. (Medical Laboratory Technology) — 30 seats
- B.Sc. (Medical Radiation Technology) — four seats
- B.Sc. (Operation Theatre Technology) — four seats
- B.Sc. (Perfusion Technology) — four seats
- B. Sc. (Dialysis Technology) — four seats
- B.Sc. (Nuclear Medicine Technology) — four seats

Post-graduate Courses

- MD and MS — 124 seats
- M.Sc. (Medical Bio-technology) — nine seats
- M. Sc. (MLT-Microbiology) — four seats
- M.Sc. (Medical Biometrics and Information) — five seats
- Ph.D. — 18 seats

Super Specialty Courses

- D.M. (Cardiology) — three seats
- D.M. (Neurology) — two seats
- D.M. (Neonatology) — one seat
- D.M. (Clinical Immunology) — one seat
- D.M. (Clinical Pharmacology) — one seat
- D.M. (Clinical Hematology) — one seat

- M.Ch. (Cardio Thoracic Surgery) three seats
- M.Ch. (Urology) three seats
- M.Ch. (Neurosurgery) one seat
- M.Ch. (Surgery Gastroenterology) two seats

Fellowship Courses

- Fellowship in Diabetology three seats
- Fellowship in Pediatric Critical and Emergency Care two seats
- Fellowship in Oncology two seats
- Fellowship in Tropical Parasitology one seat

Certificate Courses

- Medical Record Officer 15 seats
- Medical Record Trainee 15 seats
- P.G. Diploma in Public Health Management 20 seats
- One year certificate course in Blood Banking Technology four seats
- Nine months certificate course in Emergency Medical Trauma Technician 20 seats

Admission Procedure for MBBS, How to Apply

Admission for MBBS is carried out every year. Notification will be published every year in all major newspapers of India. Application form and prospectus will be available in State Bank of India, JIPMER Campus and can be obtained in person or by post on paying the prescribed fee in cash or by bank demand draft. Online application will be available on the website www.jipmer.edu.in.

P.G. Degree Courses

- M.D. (General Medicine),
- M.D. (Anatomy),
- M.D. (Pathology),
- M.D. (Microbiology),
- M.D. (Physiology),
- M.D. (Pharmacology),
- M.D. (Paediatrics),
- M.D. (Anesthesiology),
- M.D. (Dermatology),

- M.D. (Bio-chemistry),
- M.D. (Community Medicine),
- M.D. (Radiotherapy),
- M.D. (Radio-Diagnosis),
- M.D. (Transfusion Medicine & Immunology Hematology),
- M.D. (Forensic Medicine),
- M.D. (Psychiatry),
- M.D. (Pulmonary Medicine),
- M.D. (Obstetrics and Gynecology),
- M.D. (General Surgery),
- M.D. (Orthopaedics Surgery),
- M.D. (Ophthalmology), and
- M.D. (Oto-Rhino-Lyryngology).

How to Apply

Admission for all the courses will be carried out every year. Notification will be published in the month of December every year in all major newspapers of India. Application form and prospectus will be available in State Bank of India, JIPMER Campus and can be obtained in person or by post by paying the prescribed fee in cash or by bank demand draft. Online application will be available on the website: www.jipmer.edu.in

Ph.D. (Full Time)

Subject	**Seats**
Anatomy	two
Physiology	two
Biochemistry	two
Pathology	two
Microbiology	two
Pharmacology	four
Clinical Immunology	two
Clinical Paediatrics	two
Total	**18**

Admission for the above courses will be carried out for every year. Notification will be published in the month of May every year in all major newspapers of India.

M.Ch.

Subject	Seats
Urology	three
Cardiothoracic Surgery	three
Neurosurgery	one
Surgical Gastroenterology	two
Total	**nine**

How to Apply

Admission for the above courses will be carried out for every year. Notification will be published in the month of May every year in all Newspapers of India and application form and prospectus available in State Bank of India, JIPMER campus and can be obtained in person or by post by paying the prescribed fee in cash or by bank demand draft.

Entry into Manipal Academy of Higher Education (MAHE) to Become a Doctor

The under-graduate entrance process is based on the candidates rank in the All India MAHE Under-graduate Entrance Test (UGET).

- **Eligibility** : General Category – Indian nationals, pass in 10+2, A level, IB, American 12th grade or equivalent with physics, chemistry, biology and English and 50 per cent in PCB. Admissions are through merit in the entrance test.
- **Test Pattern** : In all there will be three question papers with multiple choice objective type questions.

  For details please visit MAHE website: www.manipal.edu.

Top 10 Medical Colleges in India

- All India Medical Institute of Medical Sciences, Delhi,
- Bangalore Medical College, Bangalore,
- Kasturba Medical College, Manipal,
- Madras Medical College, Chennai,
- Christian Medical College, Vellore,
- Armed Forces Medical College, Pune,
- St. John's Medical College, Bangalore,
- Osmania Medical College, Hyderabad,
- JIPMER, Pondicherry, and
- Maulana Azad Medical College, Delhi.

(*Source* : survey done by ***India Today***)

Job Prospects

They can find employment:

- In government or private hospitals;
- In nursing homes/clinics/health departments;
- In medical services of the army, navy and air force, under Ministry of Defence;
- In charitable institutions;
- In medical colleges and training institutes as teachers;
- In research institutes and medical colleges as researchers;
- In the industrial sector;
- In private practice/self-employment.

Remuneration

The earnings of a doctor through private practice depends on his/her popularity. The doctors who are working in government hospitals are well paid. The pay varies for those working with private hospitals. A fresh MBBS may get a pay scale ranging between ₹ 10,000 – 20,000.

Dentists beginning their careers in government hospitals can expect their salaries to be around ₹ 7,000 and those who hold postgraduate degrees can begin at salaries of ₹ 8,000. A dentist setting up a private practice can earn much more.

12.2 Different Systems of Medice

12.2.1 Ayurveda

The Meaning of the term 'Ayurveda'

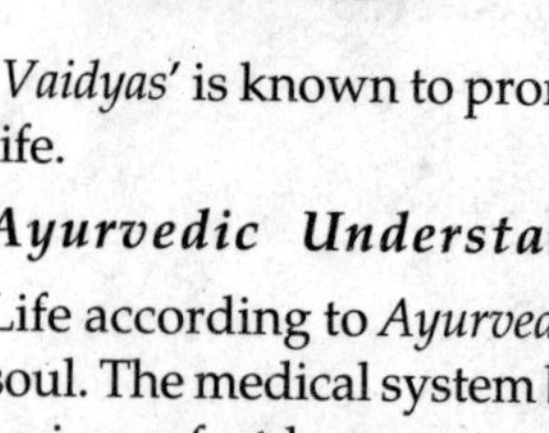

Ayurveda, the perfect science or knowledge of life, is believed to be the oldest treatment method which evolved around 600 BC in India. The word *'Ayurveda'* originated from the two words *'Ayur'* meaning 'Life' and *'Veda'* meaning 'Knowledge'. *Ayurveda* practiced by special physicians called *'Vaidyas'* is known to promote positive health, natural beauty and long life.

Ayurvedic Understanding of Life

Life according to *Ayurveda* is a combination of senses, mind, body and soul. The medical system believes that human beings and nature should be in perfect harmony and that disease occurs when the equilibrium between these two is disrupted. Restoration of this fundamental balance, through the use of nature and its products is the main goal of this medical system. The concept is not just on curing bodily ailments but also on preventing. *Ayurveda* emphasises that '*Prevention is better than cure*'. In *Ayurveda* which is basically a humoural medical system, diseases are understood as an imbalance between the body's three humours, *Vata* (nerve energy), *Pitta* (catabolic fire energy) and *Kapha* (anabolic nutritive energy). Natural herbs and minerals are used for preparing medicines. Apart from herbs, purification and detoxification, dietary changes, body massages and meditation are used to promote health and prevent and treat illness. Ayurvedic medicines are rapidly gaining acceptance all over the world as they have no side effects and is found to have cures for even rare ailments. Check out the link *Ayurveda* to know more about the system.

The Present Scenario of Ayurvedic Education in India

Ayurvedic education in India is presently monitored by the Central Council of Indian Medicine (CCIM), a statutory central government body. At present there are about 154 recognised under-graduate and 33 post-graduate Ayurvedic colleges in India. The five and half years under-graduate programmes in *Ayurveda* lead to a Bachelor of Ayurvedic Medicine and Surgery (B.A.M.S). Post-graduate programmes are structured into 16 branches leading to a Doctorate in *Ayurveda*. Nowadays *Ayurveda* has become very popular among the tourists especially foreigners. It is a part of a new movement towards a global medicine which includes the best developments from the whole world. As modern medicine with its strong synthetic chemical drugs fails to combat nature, there is rapid and progressive acceptance of this system. Patients from all over the world are coming to India for *Ayurveda* treatment. With the popularity of the system the demand for Ayurvedic doctors are on the rise.

Eligibility and Course Areas

The Ayurvedic colleges of India award the Degree of 'Ayurvedacharya' or B.A.M.S. (Bachelor of Ayurvedic Medicine and Surgery) at the bachelor level. Duration of B.A.M.S. is five and a half years to six and a half years including internship. Eligibility required to join B.A.M.S. is 10+2 preferably with Sanskrit or an examination equivalent there to or Intermediate (Ayurvedic group – physics, chemistry, biology and Sanskrit) of any recognised University/Board which confirms to the specifications approved by the Council. Minimum age of joining for B.A.M.S. course is 17 years.

Some institutions also offer certificate courses or pre-Ayurvedic courses of one to two years. Eligibility needed for such course is S.S.L.C./ matriculation preferably with Sanskrit or an examination equivalent.

Main entrance examinations for admission to a Bachelor's degree in Ayurvedic include All India Pre-Medical/Pre-Dental Entrance Examination conducted by Central Board of Secondary Examination (CBSE), Delhi on a national level to select the candidates at an all India level (except in the state of Jammu and Kashmir and Andhra Pradesh) for admission to roughly 15 per cent of the total seats in the colleges of each state, pre-medical entrance examination conducted by different states on their own for domiciled candidates. Some national level institutions where admission does not hinge on domicile status give admission on the basis of merit in the 10+2 examination or conduct their own entrance test for admission to B.A.M.S. courses.

Candidates who have passed B.A.M.S. can apply for post graduate programmes. The post graduate programmes are conducted by many recognised institutions and has a duration of three years leading to degrees of Doctor of Medicine in Ayurveda (M.D. Ayur) and Master of Surgery in Ayurveda (M.S. Ayur). Candidates who have passed MBBS course recognised by Medical Council of India and have completed one year internship training can also apply for post graduate course in *Ayurveda*.

Post graduate Programmes in Ayurvedic Medicine

Post graduate programme is structured into 16 branches leading to a Doctorate in *Ayurveda*. The 16 branches are: *Ayurvedic Sidhanta* (Fundamental Principles of *Ayurveda*), *Ayurved Samhita* (Treatise on *Ayurveda*), *Rachna Sharira* (Anatomy), *Kriya Sharira* (Physiology), *Dravya Guna Vigyan* (Materia Medica and Pharmacology), *Ras-Shatra Bhaishajya Kalpana* (Pharmaceuticals), Kumar Bharitya (Pediatrics), Parasite Tanta (Obstetrics and Gynecology), *Swasth Vrita* (Social or Preventive Medicine), *Kayachikitsa* (Internal Medicine), *Rog Nidan* (Pathology), *Shalya Tantra* (Surgery), *Shalkya Tantra* (Eye and ENT), *Mano Roga* (Psychiatry), *Panchkarma* (Detoxification of body).

Job Prospects and Career Options

An Ayurvedic practitioner can get employment as medical officer/doctor at government and private Ayurvedic hospitals. One can also start his/her own practice or open one's own retail shop of *Ayurveda* medicines. They can also find employment as supervisors in '*Panchkarma*' (Ayurvedic massage)/health centres, as tutors in Ayurvedic colleges or do research, conduct workshops, seminars and retreats. Nowadays Ayurvedic treatments are gaining much more importance. The number of pharmaceutical companies manufacturing Ayurvedic medicines is increasing and the medicines are getting popular even in other countries.

Patients from all over the world are coming to India for Ayurvedic treatment. More and more *'Panchkarma'* centres are coming up for serving the tourists especially foreigners. With the popularity of the system the demand for Ayurvedic doctors are on the rise. In some of the states in India, it has been made mandatory to appoint at least one Ayurvedic doctor in every civil hospital. So *Ayurveda* graduates have a bright scope in future.

Remuneration

In government *Ayurveda* hospitals the starting salary scale is ₹ 8,000 to 13,500 for BAMS graduates. Tutors in *Ayurveda* colleges get more than ₹ 8,000 per month. In private practice the remuneration depends totally on the effort you put in and your professional reputation. Dedicated and competent practitioners can earn more.

Courses

- Bachelor of Ayurvedic Medicine and Surgery (BAMS),
- Certificate Course in *Ayurveda Panchkarma*,
- Diploma in Ayurvedic Medicine, and
- Diploma in Ayurvedic Massage.

Institutes

- **ALL Government Ayurvedic College**
  Warrangal-506002, Andhra Pradesh.
- **Dr. BRKR Government Ayurvedic College**
  Erragada, Hyderabad-500890.
- **Government Ayurvedic College**
  Jalukbari, Guwahati-781014.
- **Ayurved Medical College and Hospital**
  Gaya-823001, Bihar.
- **Shri Dhanwantry Ayurvedic College**
  Sector-46-B, Chandigarh-160047.
- **Government Ayurvedic College**
  Raipur-492002, Chhattisgarh.
- **Ayurvedic and Unani Tibia College**
  Ajmal Khan Road, Karol Bagh
  New Delhi-110005.

- **Shri Krishna Government Ayurvedic College**
  Kurukshetra-132118.
- **Government College of Indian Medicine**
  Dhanwantri Road
  Bangalore-560009.
- **Ayurvedic Medical College**
  Gurukul Campus
  Terdal-587315.
- **Government Ayurvedic College**
  M.G. Road, Thiruvananthapuram-695001 Kerala.
- **Bharati Vidyapeeth College of Ayurved**
  Pune-411043
  Maharashtra.

12.2.2 Homeopathy

Homeopathy is a system of medicine which is practised on the principle that drug and a disease which produce similar symptoms cancel each other out in some way thereby restoring the patient to health. The principle of *'Like can cure Like'* forms the basis of Homeopathy. It is named after the Greek words *'Homeo'* meaning 'similar' and *'Pathos'* meaning 'suffering or treatment by the same'. This system of healing was founded by a German doctor, Samuel Christian Hahnemann (1755) and is recognised as an effective means of treating diseases. Though this system was developed abroad, it has become an integral part of the Indian way of life. There are many institutes imparting Homeopathy courses in India.

Eligibility

Eligibility for bachelor's course i.e., BHMS (Bachelor of Homeopathic Medicine and Surgery) is 10+2 in physics, chemistry, biology and English with minimum 45 per cent marks. The duration of the course is five and half years including internship. There is also a diploma course of four year duration. At post graduate level, there is MD in Homeopathy which is of three years duration.

Selection

Selection of BHMS is through the same All India Entrance Examination as for MBBS. The qualification required for entrance is 10+2 or equivalent with science subjects. In the case of private medical colleges entrance examinations are conducted by the institutes individually. They can find employment in government and private hospitals or clinics, charitable institutions, research institutes as researchers, medical colleges and training institutes as teachers etc. Another option is to do private practice.

Courses

- Bachelor of Homeopathic Medicine and Surgery (BHMS),
- MD Homeopathy, and
- Post Graduate Diploma in Homeopathic Medicine and Surgery.

12.2.3 Naturopathy

What is Naturopathy?

Naturopathic medicine or Naturopathy is a distinct system of health care that uses a variety of natural approaches to health and healing. Naturopathy aims at curing a person naturally using nature cure. It is a scientific system of healing and stimulating the body's inherent power to regain health with the help of five elements of nature – earth, water, air, fire and ether. In other words, naturopathy is one of the major forms of alternative medicine that focuses on an individual's natural healing capacities. Unlike modern medications, Naturopathy is commonly used as a corresponding treatment in combination with traditional medicine. It combines traditional and holistic methods to achieve optimal health and wellness. Naturopathic medicine is based on the fact that human body has an innate power to heal itself and naturopathic physicians use treatments to support the body's inherent self healing abilities. Naturopathy is built upon the dictum of Hippocrates, the father of medicine, who declared *'Nature cures, not the physician'*. The system is known by different names such as *Nature Cure, Natural Method, New Science of Healing* and *Healing from Within.*

The Function of Naturopaths

Those who practise Naturopathy are called Naturopaths or Naturopathic physicians or Naturopathic doctors or N Ds. Naturopaths recognise the reliability of the whole person and they emphasise the individual's inherent capacity for self-healing. They recognise the connection between the health of the mind and the health of the body. Naturopaths believe that illness is caused by bad living habits like eating the wrong foods, too much stress and not having enough exercise.

Naturopaths Use Therapies

Naturopathic doctors use therapies that are exclusively natural such as homeopathy, acupuncture, hydrotherapy, botanical medicine, nutrition, massage, exercises and counselling. *'Food is the best medicine'* is the basis of naturopathic medicine. Naturopaths give importance to diet; to him medicine is the last resort. He first advices you on your diet and after that only he prescribes medicine.

Difference between Naturopathic Medicine and Other Medical Systems

Naturopathic medicine differs from common medical systems mainly in its philosophy. While usually medical doctors treat and relieve a patient's symptoms, naturopathic doctors try to discover the cause of the symptoms by taking into account the physical, mental, emotional, genetic, environmental and social factors of an individual's health. Naturopathic doctors try to support the natural healing potential of the human body using techniques like good nutrition, natural hygiene, botanical medicine, homeopathy, counselling and spirituality whereas, other medical systems use drugs and do surgeries as treatment methods.

Eligibility and Course Areas

Candidates who have completed 10+2 with an aggregate of 45 per cent marks in physics, chemistry and biology are eligible for Bachelor of Naturopathy and Yogic Sciences (BNYS). Bachelor's programme is usually of five and half years duration. However, many naturopathic schools have set their own pre-requisites for entry and may require you to have a minimum of a bachelor's degree or equivalent. The first college of Naturopathy was started in Hyderabad, Andhra Pradesh by Dr B. Venkatrao which offered a Diploma in Naturopathy (ND). Now, there are about twenty colleges in India offering bachelor's as well as diploma courses.

Job Prospects and Career Options

Naturopathy is fast gaining popularity in countries, among people who prefer natural remedies than allopathic medicine due to its various side effects. There are immense opportunities to work abroad but individuals should check whether their qualification is recognised in the country they hope to work. Some states also required license to work.

Most of the naturopaths enter the field through private practice. Naturopathy professionals can work individually or in group practice with other physicians. Job opportunities are available as consultants in wellness centers, nutrition centres, hospitals, and healthcare centres. Other career opportunities include academics, community health service settings, social welfare, manufacturing and sale of natural products and health retreats. In India, naturopaths are appointed in government as well as private hospitals and health centres. Research positions are an option for those with the aptitude and interest in R&D. in universities and medical colleges they can work as faculties. They can also work as consultants or sales representatives of natural product companies.

Candidates can find employment in many luxury hotels and health resorts equipped with naturopathic treatment centers. There is also scope in the field as writer. Some write books or articles for newspapers and magazines.

Remuneration

The naturopathic doctor's salary largely depends on the location, employer, expertise and qualification and experience in the field of nature-cure. Self-employed naturopaths earn in the range of ₹ 10,000 – 20,000 per month. Once you have gained experience, you can expect a lucrative salary. In developed countries like UK and US, the salary range is much higher.

Courses

- Bachelor of Naturopathy and Yogic Sciences (BNYS),
- Doctor of Naturopathy (ND), and
- Post Graduate Diploma in Yoga and Naturopathy.

12.3 Anesthesiology

What is Anesthesia or Anesthetics?

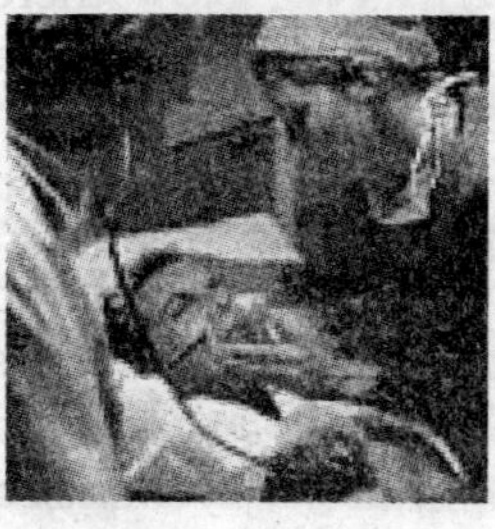

Anesthesia or anesthetics is a medication plan that causes the patient to become unconscious so that he or she feels no pain while a surgery is being performed. An anesthetist, also called an anesthesiologist is a physician who makes anesthesia related medical decisions and is responsible for the safety and well being of the patient. Anesthesiologists are trained licensed medical doctors who perform anesthesia techniques. In other words, an anesthesiologist is a medical doctor who cares for a patient before, during and immediately following a surgical or medical procedure by administering appropriate anesthesia.

Who is an Anesthesiologist and What is his/her Role?

Anesthesiologist is an important person in a surgical team. Without him, surgery would be impossible in most cases. Anesthesiologists administer drugs that reduce (or even eliminate) the pain a patient might feel during surgery or other medical procedures. Anesthesiologists are the one who put you to sleep during surgery. In addition to helping patients through surgery, anesthesiologists may also help treat patients with conditions causing chronic pain. They also involve in the care of patients with cardiac or respiratory emergencies, including the need for artificial ventilation as well as supervise post anesthesia recovery.

The anesthesiologist's role extends beyond the operating room. An anesthesiologist's first contact with a surgical patient is usually during a 'pre-operative interview'. The anesthesiologist makes pre-operative assessment of the patient, reviews the patient's medical history and medications, and discusses the upcoming surgery. Then, he decides about the best anesthetic plan for that individual based on his or her current health. The anesthesiologist is also responsible for the well being of the patient postoperatively while the person emerges from the effects of the anesthesia. Anesthesiologists calculate proper drug dosages for patients administer anesthesia and monitor patient's vital signs throughout surgical procedures. Vital signs include heart rate and rhythm, blood pressure, body temperature, breathing and brain and kidney functions.

Three Main Types of Anesthesia

There are three main types of anesthesia administered during surgery :

- General,
- Regional , and
- Local.

General anesthesia renders the patient unconscious and unable to feel pain or any other sensation. Many general anesthetics are gases or vapours administered through a mask or breathing tube, whereas others are liquid medicines introduced through the vein. Regional anesthesia numbs an entire area of the body requiring surgery. Local anesthesia is used to numb a specific part of the body (such as the foot or hand) being operated so the patient can't feel anything in that specific area. Both regional and local anesthetics are administered via injections.

The Work Schedule ofAnesthesiologists

Work hours for anesthesiologists are normally very long and irregular. They do not have fixed working hours and hence the work can be stressful. During operations, they may be required to stand for long periods of time. Many anesthesiologists are on call at all times at any hour, day or night, meaning they may have to drop everything at any given time and rush to the hospital for an emergency.

Eligibility

To pursue anesthesiology, one needs a strong background in physics, chemistry, biology and mathematics. Like any other physician, anesthesiologists, too, require a long period of medical training. After 10+2, one has to apply to medical colleges to pursue MBBS degree, admission to which is based on scores of entrance test and marks of plus-2. Next step after MBBS is one year house surgency followed by M.D. in Anesthesiology which is usually of two years duration.

Besides Anesthesiology, an anesthesiologist must also study cardiology, critical care medicine, internal medicine, pharmacology and surgery. An anesthesiologist may choose to specialise in a particular field such as neuro surgery, maxillofacial surgery and so on. They need to continuously update their knowledge and skills through professional seminars and continuing educational courses.

Job Prospects and Career Options

Career prospects for anesthesiologists are always booming since every hospital will require a team of anesthesiologists who are experienced and dedicated. One of the first and foremost duties of an anesthesiologist is to administer an anesthetic to a person undergoing a surgical treatment. This means giving the patient the necessary medicine to help them feel no pain while undergoing surgery. Anesthesiology is a lot more team oriented than any other medical specialties. These physicians work along with other doctors in order to monitor and assess a patient's body temperature, heart rate and breathing, before, during and after surgery. Anesthesiologists are often treated as the patient's advocate in the operating room, keeping the patient stable during the procedure and informing the surgeon if the patient develops problems which could influence the procedure.

Anesthesiologists also work outside the operating room such as in :

- Intensive Care Unit (ICU) where they administer pain relief to critically ill patients while helping to restore them to a stable condition.

- Pain management where they are involved in the diagnosis and treatment of patients who suffer from acute and chronic illnesses. During labor and delivery, they provide pain relief to the mother.

As long as there is a demand for surgery and relief from pain, there will be need for qualified anesthesiologists. Anesthesiologists are needed in doctor's offices, hospitals, health clinics and anywhere, where patients are in pain. Most anesthesiologists work in hospital operation theatre, while others work in outpatient surgery centers, medical offices, dental clinics etc. Some work in emergency rooms, where they handle victims of heart attacks, shock, drug overdoses, traumatic injuries and other serious health problems requiring immediate care. Other opportunities may exist in urgent care centers, academic medical centers and the military. For those who opt for a field other than medical practice can choose to work as lecturers in medical colleges. Those who are specialists in the sector may also work as visiting anesthesiologist and may charge on hourly basis. Some may move on to administrative and supervisory roles within the medical sector. Yet another group can enter into research field.

Various disciplines in the field of anesthesia: Anesthetic sub-specialties include cardiac and thoracic surgery, neurosurgery, plastic and reconstructive surgery, paediatrics, dental, maxillofacial surgery, otolaryngology, obstetrics, orthopaedic surgery and trauma and emergency surgery. Intensive care medicine and pain management are two other sub-specialty areas, both of which involve a significant amount of work outside the theatre environment.

(b) **Other careers in the field of Anesthesiology are :**

- **Anesthesiologist Assistant (AAs) :** An anesthesiologist assistant is a healthcare professional who works under the supervision of an anesthesiologist primarily assisting him while he prepares a patient for anesthesia. The job responsibilities of an anesthesiologist assistant vary according to the setting and the place. In many countries, especially in India, there is no position for anesthesiologist assistants.
- **Certified Registered Nurse Anesthetists (CRNA) :** A certified registered nurse anesthetist often works under the supervision of an anesthesiologist. They assist the anesthesiologist in medication.
- **Anesthesia Technician (AT) :** ATs are responsible for managing the anesthesia equipment and for its proper maintenance.

Remuneration

The salary ranges according to the geographic region, experience and sub-specialty. In India, an anesthesiologist may start his career with a minimum pay scale of ₹ 20,000 – 30,000 per month depending upon the medical organisation they work for. Generally, pay is much more in corporate hospitals than in government hospitals. After being established in the field, one can work on an hourly basis, too, and in this case pay is much lucrative.

Courses

- MD Anesthesiology,
- Diploma in Anesthesiology, and
- DNB Anesthesiology.

Institutes

- **Shivaji University, Kolhapur, Maharashtra**

  Course : Diploma in Anesthesia.
- **Sardar Patel University, Vidyanagar, Gujarat**

  Courses : Doctor of Medicine-Anesthesia.

  Post Graduate Diploma in Medicine: Anesthesia.
- **Rajasthan University of Health Science-Jaipur, Rajasthan**

  Course : Diploma in Anesthesia.
- **Dr. D.Y. Patil University-Pune, Maharashtra**

  Course : MD Anesthesia.
- **Indira Gandhi National Open University (IGNOU)-New Delhi**

  Course : Bachelor of Science in Anesthesia and Critical Care Management.
- **Jawaharlal Nehru Medical College-Wardha, Maharashtra**

  Course : Certificate Course in Anesthesia Technician.
- **GSL Medical College and General Hospital (GSL GH-Rajahmundry, Andhra Pradesh**

  Course : Certificate Course in Anesthesia Technician.
- **Sanjay Gandhi Postgraduate Institute of Medical Sciences-Lucknow, Uttar Pradesh**

  Courses : Post-Doctoral Certificate Course-Nero-Anesthesia,

  Post-Doctoral Certificate Courses-Cardiac-Anesthesia.

12.4 Behavioural Science

What is Behavioural Science?

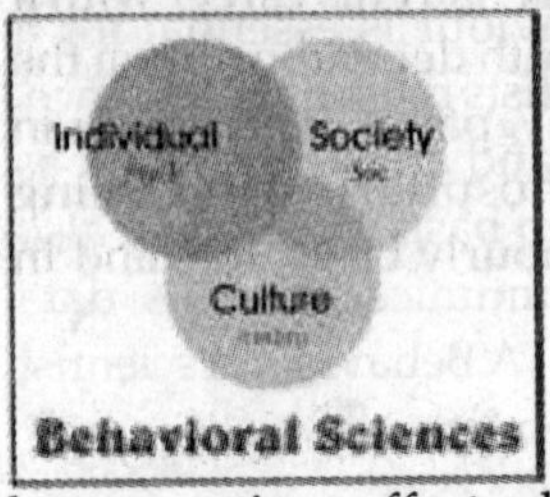

Behavioural Science is basically the study of behaviour, i.e., interactions and responses among one species or between different species within organisms in the social system. It includes both animal and human behavior, in the controlled and naturalistic world. Behavioural Science analyses how human actions affect relationships and decision making. It is the field of study that analyses and draws actionable conclusions about how specific beings think, act and react to a wide variety of internal or external situations. Behavioural scientists research human or animal behaviour and examine how they interact and communicate with each other and the processes that contribute to such specific behaviours. Behavioural science being a combination of social science and natural science absorbs some components of both fields at times overlapping with each other.

The Two Divisions of Behavioural Science

Behavioural science is subdivided into two categories, Neural Decision Science and Social Communication Science. Neural Decision Science studies the relationship between biology and decision-making. It deals with how humans make choices or decisions. The discipline in that field includes psychology, ethology, psychobiology, social neuroscience and management science. Social Communication Science focuses on communication. It is the study of how humans communicate, both verbally and non-verbally. A common discipline in this field is anthropology, other disciplines include organisational behaviour, sociology and behaviour finance.

Eligibility

To enter into a career in Behavioural Science, you need to complete either a bachelor's course in Behavioural Science or Psychology. Courses in social work, anthropology, criminology and counseling can also open doors into this field. As Behavioural science is taught in a broader sense in different courses, decide on the specific career field you want to work in, before choosing the specialised course. Taking up internships along with your degree will give you better prospects for getting a good job. Researchers in this field have a multi-disciplinary educational background.

Personal Attributes

A genuine interest in human or animal behaviour is essential for a rewarding career in the field. Behavioural scientists must have patience, strong problem-solving and mediation skills and an eye for detail as they have to study their subjects on a long term basis. They must also have critical thinking skills, interpersonal communication skills, data analysing ability and project management skills. A Behavioural scientist must be good at presenting and writing their findings.

Job Prospects and Career Options

Earlier, Behavioural scientists were limited to careers as social workers or academics. Today, situation has changed, Behavioural scientists can choose from a plethora of thriving careers. Options for them include that of anthropologist, occupational therapists, criminologist, mental health counsellors, ethologists, criminal profiler, psychologist, sociologist, corporate coach, economic analyst, market researcher, neuro-marketing and health education/public health.

- **Anthropologists :** Anthropologists study the physical, social, cultural development and behaviour of human beings.
- **Criminologists :** Criminologists study the root cause of crime by examining the factors like economics, demographics and geography, thus enabling the prevention in crime rate. Criminal profilers excel at solving challenging cases by developing clear profiles of criminals when leads are scarce.
- **Ethology :** Ethology, as part of Behavioural science instead looks at instinctual behaviour in humans. Ethologists study animal or human behaviour, specifically instinctual rather than learned behaviour.
- **Psychologists :** Psychologists study human behaviour. Sociologists look at society and social behaviour.
- **Sociology :** Sociology examines groups and organisations, different cultures and social institutions.
- **Economic analyst :** Economic analyst help understanding consumer's decision-making process thus enabling businessman to market their product and government to apply pressure on markets.
- **A market researcher :** A market researcher like economic analyst understands the customers analysing process before buying a product.

- **Neuro-marketing :** Neuro-marketing is a new field that uses neuro-science to study consumer behaviour.
- **Health education :** Role of Behavioural scientists in health education or public health department is to enable better health choice for people. This involves community-wide education initiatives on topics as diverse disease prevention, nutrition, drugs and alcohol abuse or even the quality of life for senior citizens.

  Individuals with degrees related to Behavioural science can work in law enforcement, social services, teaching, counselling and human resources. They may be employed by government agencies, private businesses or non-profit organisation.

Remuneration

Behavioural scientists work in different fields that deal with the study of human nature. Their incomes vary according to such factors as specialty, experience and location. Those employed in public sector, research institutions and departments have pay packages as per terms and conditions of the government. Those who are in international developmental agencies have even higher remuneration, perks and other benefits. For those in academic field enjoy a good pay packages.

Institutes

- **Indian Institute of Information Technology**

  Allahabad, UP.

  Doctoral Programme in Behavioural Modelling.
- **Indian Institute of Management**

  Kolkata, West Bengal.

  Fellow Programme – Behavioural Sciences.
- **Sardar Patel University**

  Vidyanagar, Gujarat.

  Master of Business Administration – Organisation,

  Behaviour and Human Resource Development.
- **International Management Institute**

  New Delhi.

  Doctor of Philosophy – Organisation Behaviours.

  Fellow Programme in Management – Organisation Behaviours.

- **Berhampur University**

  Berhampur, Orissa.

  Master Degree in Organisational Behaviours.

- **JBAS College for Women**

  Chennai, Tamil Nadu.

  Doctor of Philosophy – Organisation Behaviour.

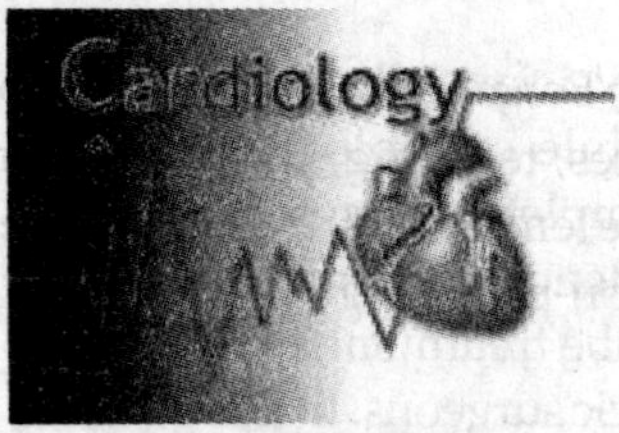

12.5 Cardiology

What is Cardiology?

Cardiology or Cardio-vascular medicine is a specialty of internal medicine. Cardiology is a division of medicine which deals with the diagnosis and treatment related to heart disorders. It is the specialisation related to one of the most important organ of our body.

Who are Cardiologists?

Medical practitioners who deal with heart disorders are generally termed as Cardiologists. Cardiologists analyse and deal with cardio-vascular or circulatory illness and disorders. This means the heart, blood vessels and many other parts of the body are a primary focus for a cardiologist. A cardiologist is a doctor of the heart, arteries and veins. Cardiologists provide diagnosis and treatment of heart failure, congenital heart defects and coronary artery disease. This includes problems caused by restricted circulation due to narrowing of the arteries, problems in the heart valves, damage to the muscle tissue and disorders of the pericardium.

Categories of Cardiologists

There are many different categories of cardiologists – some focus more on diagnosis, prevention and medications, while other cardiologists are more procedure-oriented, performing angioplasties and other life-saving operations. Cardiologists can be invasive, interventional or non-invasive.

- **Non-invasive Cardiologists** : Non-invasive cardiologists don't do procedures; they mainly perform diagnostic tests to spot early signs of heart problems. Non-invasive cardiologists perform stress tests and electrocardiograms, popularly known as EKG's to gauge the state of your heart.

- **Invasive Cardiologists :** Invasive cardiologists are trained in a diagnostic procedure called cardiac catheterisation, which is used to pinpoint blockages to the arteries.
- **Interventional Cardiologists :** Interventional cardiologist performs various surgical procedures like angioplasty and tubing.

A cardiologist is not a surgeon. The physicians who do open heart surgery are cardio-thoracic surgeons. While cardiologists take the internal medicine route, a heart surgeon completes a surgical residency programme, not internal medicine residency as cardiologists do. Cardiologists may conduct test and prescribe treatment, but in case of surgery he refers the patient to Cardio-thoracic surgeons. In this instance, a cardiologist remains the primary doctor for treatment but would work co-operatively with other specialists in the area of cardiology.

Personal Attributes

Cardiologists must have a strong background in medicine and science and must be detail-oriented and organised. They must have a desire to serve patients, have compassion towards others, be self-motivated and be able to survive the pressures and long hours of medical education and practice. Besides, one should have discipline, patience, commitment to excel and self-confidence to become a cardiologist. They must have the ability to take decisions in life-threatening situations. Cardiologists who perform surgery must have strong motor skills in order to complete delicate operations involving the heart.

Eligibility

To become a cardiologist entails several years of training beyond an MBBS degree, as well as licensure and board certification. To become a cardiologist after taking MD/MS/DNB, one has to go for a DM in Cardiology.

One who wishes to be a cardiologist must have passed 10+2 examination with biology, chemistry and physics. On completion of plus-two a student has to appear for the competitive entrance examination for MBBS. This is a five and a half years course which includes one-year internship period as well. After that one has to go for MD/MS/DNB which is of two to three years duration. Then go for specialisation in the field, i.e., DM in Cardiology. For surgical intervention one has to get M.Ch. in Cardiology. There are entrance examinations in order to get admissions to the programmes. DM and M.Ch. are of three years duration.

Job Prospects and Career Options

With the increase in heart patients and number of multi-specialist hospitals, the scope for cardiologists has widened both in government and corporate sector. A career as a cardiologist can be rewarding, career wise as well as financially. Cardiologists can find employment as doctors in hospitals in cardiology department, cardiac rehabilitation centres and clinics testing patients for heart problems. They work in hospitals on hourly, weekly and monthly basis. Most of them consider private practice and get self-employed by starting their own clinic. There are some who work in several hospitals as consultants as well as run their own clinic. They can get recruited in government health sector and defense service. Those who are willing to do research work related to heart can also do the same and become scientists in cardiology. Cardiologists who prefer teaching can opt for the position as lecturers in medical colleges.

Although cardiology is a specialised area in medical science, within this cardiology field itself several sub-specialties have developed. Nuclear cardiologists focus on the pumping functions of the heart. Electrophysiologists specialise in the electrical systems of the heart. Interventional cardiologists perform invasive procedures such as stent insertion and angioplasty. Yet another group specialises in areas such as Paediatric Cardiology. A pediatric cardiologist treats abnormalities and diseases of the heart in children who are still in utero upto adulthood.

Remuneration

A fresher who joins a government hospital can start earning from ₹ 25,000 per month; whereas in private hospitals the salary can be much more. Those who experienced in the field can earn even lakhs per month. However, there is no upper limit for those efficient cardiologists who are managing their own heart care centres. Apart from salary, cardiologists also enjoy various incentives, perks, free accommodation, as well as high positions in several medical associations.

Courses Available

- DM Cardiology,
- DNB Cardiology,
- DNB Cardio Thoracic Surgery,
- M.Sc. Cardio-vascular Technology,

- M.Ch. Cardio-vascular and Thoracic Surgery,
- Diploma in Cardio-vascular Technology, and
- Post Graduate Diploma in Preventive Cardiology.

Institutes

- **Academy of Medical Sciences (ACME)**
  Alleppey, Kerala India.
- **Armed Forces Medical College (AMFC)**
  Pune, Maharashtra.
- **B.J. Medical College and Sassoon Hospital, Pune**
  Pune, Maharashtra India.
- **Calicut Medical College (CMC)**
  Calicut, Kerala India.
- **Christian Medical College (CMC), Vellore**
  Vellore, Tamil Nadu India.
- **Christian Medical College (CMC),**
  Ludhiana, Punjab India.
- **Datta Meghe Institute of Medical Science**
  Nagpur, Maharashtra India.
- **ERA'S Lucknow Medical College and Hospital**
  Lucknow, Uttar Pradesh.
- **Guwahati Medical College (GMC)**
  Guwahati, Assam India.
- **Government Medical College and Hospital**
  Nagpur, Maharashtra India.
- **Government Medical College (GMC)**
  Kottayam, Kerala India.
- **Government Medical College and Hospital**
  Bangalore, Karnataka India.
- **Indira Gandhi Institute of Medical Sciences (IGIMS)**
  Patna, Bihar India.
- **Indira Gandhi National Open University**
  New Delhi India.

- **Institute of Post Graduate Medical Education and Research**
  Kolkata, West Bengal India.
- **Jawaharlal Nehru Medical College (JNMC)**
  Belguam, Karnataka India.
- **Kasturba Medical College**
  Manipal, Karnataka India.
- **Kerala Institute of Medical Sciences (KIMS)**
  Trivandrum, Kerala India.
- **King Edward Memorial Hospital and**
  Seth Gobardhandas Sunderdas Medical College
  Mumbai, Maharashtra India.
- **Kurnool Medical College (KMC)**
  Kurnool, Andhra Pradesh India.
- **Madras Medical College (MMC)**
  Chennai, Tamil Nadu India.
- **Osmania Medical College**
  Hyderabad, Andhra Pradesh India.
- **Post graduate Institute of Medical Education & Research (PIGIMER)**
  Chandigarh, Punjab India.

12.6 Clinical Research

What is a Clinical Research?

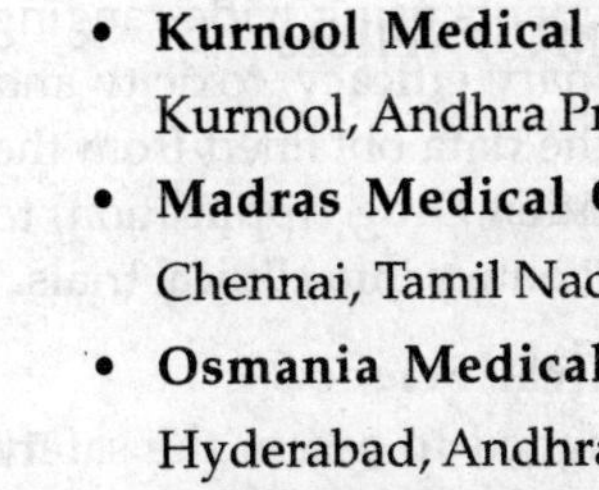

Clinical Research is an integral part of the drug discovery process to ensure the safety and efficacy of any new drug. It is the complete biography of drug from its inception in the lab to its introduction to the consumer market and beyond. Clinical research can be defined as the systematic and scientific study of effects, risks, efficacy and benefit of a new medicinal product (drug) that may be used for prevention, treatment, diagnostic or for relieving symptoms of a disease. It is the clinical research which determines the safety and effectiveness of medications, devices, diagnostic products and treatment regimens that are intended for human use.

How is Clinical Research performed?

The Clinical research of the new medicinal product is carried out through an organised Clinical Trial, prior to its release in the market. Clinical trials are used to determine whether new biomedical or Behavioural interventions are safe, efficacious and effective. These trials are conducted in four phases and each phase of the drug approval process is treated as a separate clinical trial. The drug-development process will normally proceed through all four phases over many years. If the drug successfully passes through Phase-I, II and III, it will get approved by the FDA (Food and Drug Administration) and then marketed for public use. Phase-IV are 'post-approval' studies.

Pre-clinical Study

Before pharmaceutical companies start clinical trials on a drug, they conduct an extensive pre-clinical study. These involve *in vitro* (test tube or cell culture) and *in vivo* (animal) experiments using wide-ranging doses of the study drug to obtain preliminary efficacy, toxicity and pharmacokinetic information. After this, the data obtained from the studies are submitted as an IND (Investigation Drug Application) to take permission for human studies. Then, it enters into clinical trials.

(b) The Different Phases of Clinical Trials :

- **Phase-I trials:** Phase-I trial is designed to assess the safety (Pharmacovigilance), tolerability, pharma-cokinetics and pharma-codynamics of a drug. In Phase-I trial, a new drug is administered to a small number around 20-80 healthy, informed volunteers under the close supervision of a doctor.
- **Phase-II trials:** Phase-II trial is designed to assess how well the drug work, as well as to continue Phase-I safety assessments in a larger group of volunteers and patients. In phase-II the medicine is administered to a group of approximately 100 – 300 informed patients to determine the effects and also to check for unacceptable side effects.
- **Phase-III trials:** Phase-III trial sometimes known as 'pre-marketing phase' are the most expensive, difficult and time-consuming trial which are aimed at being the definitive assessment of how effective the drug is, in comparison with current 'gold standard' treatment. In this phase the group is between 1000 – 3000, for the company to use statistics to analyse the results. If the results are favorable, data is presented to licensing authorities for a commercial license.

- **Phase-IV trials:** Phase-IV trial also known as post-marketing surveillance Trial involves the safety surveillance (pharmaco-vigilance) and ongoing technical support of a drug after it receives permission to be sold. The effects are monitored on thousands of patients to help identify any unforeseen side effects.

Clinical Research is a very sensitive field and is directly attached to human life. It is a field which demands scientific approach with quality, ethics, emotions and perfection. Future of the medical science is in the hands of clinical research professionals and a single mistake in this field can cost a lot for our upcoming generations. So, those who want to build up a career in the field of clinical research should be aware of their big responsibility.

Eligibility and Course Areas

The basic eligibility for MBA, M.Pharma and M.Sc. courses in clinical research is B.Sc. (botany, zoology, chemistry, biochemistry, biotechnology, microbiology, genetics, nursing), MBBS/BDS/BAMS/BHMS/B.V.Sc. pharmaceutics and pharmacology students have greater scope in clinical research. Several institutes in India offer M.Sc. clinical research courses. Sikkim Manipal University, Indian Institute of Clinical Research (ICRI) at Jaipur, Bangalore, Mumbai, New Delhi are some of the institutes offering post graduate clinical research courses.

For diploma and post graduate programmes in clinical research, candidates must possess graduation in any of the fields namely, life, science, pharmacy, medicine, dentistry, paramedical science, allied health sciences and biotechnology with a minimum of 50 marks in aggregate. Working professionals/practising doctors meeting the above criteria can also apply for these programmes.

Selection

Admission to the post graduate programmes and Ph. D. Programmes will be based on entrance test and interview. The selection process varies according to the institute and courses. Admission to the M.Pharms and MBA clinical research course in National Institute of Pharmaceutical Education and Research (NIPER), Hyderabad is through CGPA (Cumulative Grade Point Average).

Personal Skill

Clinical research professionals are involved in all phases of clinical trials. Clinical research is a responsible job which requires integrity, thoroughness, determination, innovation and analytical thinking. A clinical research professional should possess good knowledge of English language, reading comprehension skills, active listening skills, writing skills, critical thinking, coordination and communicating skills. They should have the knowledge of the information and techniques needed to diagnose and treat human injuries, diseases and deformities. Concern for others, flexibility, social orientation, co-operation, reliability, ability to work as a team is the other attributes needed for this professional.

Job Prospects and Career Options

Clinical research is an attractive industry which foresees tremendous growth and job opportunities not only for trained medical, pharmaceutical and paramedical professionals but also for regulatory authorities, government and the society at large. With the inflow of multinational players in research, the industry is poised to growth exponentially and opens up new vistas of employment for a large number of people.

Career Fields

Candidates can make their career in the fields of:

- Contract Research Organisation (CRO)s,
- Pharmaceutical Industries,
- Biotechnology Companies,
- Medical Device Company,
- Patient Recruitment Organisation (PRO),
- Clinical Data Management,
- Regulatory Affairs,
- Pharmaco-vigilance,
- Medical Writing,
- Central Lab,
- Logistics and Courier Services,
- Research Sites, and
- Auditing of Clinical Trials.

Basically, Clinical Research is conducted by the pharmaceuticals, biotech and medical device companies. They outsource their work to Contract Research Organisations (CRO Company). The CRO perform the clinical trial on behalf of the company in collaboration with the Site/Hospital or SMO (Site Management Organisation). Before conducting clinical trials, approval is required from regulatory authorities of that country where the trial has to be conducted. This approval process is done by the Regulatory Affair Company or by CRO itself if they have their own regulatory affair department. Data is generated during clinical trial in the form of CRF (Case Report Form) which is designed and managed by the Clinical Data Management Company. Sample collected during the trial is sent to the central lab through a logistics and courier services company and is analysed and reported by the central lab. After completing the trial, publication is done with the help of medical writing company.

Every clinical study is led by a principal investigator. These investigators can be researchers, professors, medical practitioners and scientists / medical specialists. Besides them, clinical studies may also have a research team that may include nurses, social workers and other healthcare professionals.

Varied options are available in the field of clinical research organisations. Clinical research associate, clinical research investigator, clinical research managers, clinical research coordinator, clinical data manager, clinical research auditor, biostatisticians, pharmacovigilance manager, quality assurance etc. are some of the designations in the field of clinical research. Their work areas include :

- **Clinical Research Associate :** The most common entry level position in the field of clinical research is that of a Clinical Research Associate (CRA). Clinical research associate has the responsibility to design, implement and monitor clinical trials. The administration and progress of a clinical trial is examined or monitored by him/her. They assist in preparation of presentations and manuscripts of scientific meetings and technical journals, and attend scientific/professional meetings and training courses.
- **Clinical Research Managers (CRM) :** Clinical Research Manager has the responsibility to supervise the design and writing of protocols, case report forms and informed consent forms for clinical trials. It is the CRM's who ensure that case report forms are evaluated within a reasonable time and submitted to the data management group.
- **Biostatistician :** Biostatisticians are responsible for new drug applications and biological Licence application submissions. Their duties involve planning, coordinating and providing statistical analyses, summaries and reports of studies for clinical trial projects.
- **Clinical Research Investigator/Physician :** Clinical Investigator will be generally a physician possessing licence to practise anywhere in the country. They are responsible for recruitment and treatment of patients.

- **Clinical Research Co-ordinator :** Clinical Research Co-ordinator has to co-ordinate the clinical trials using good clinical practice under the direction of the chief investigator.
- **Pharmaco-vigilance Manager :** They ensure that the individual reports are accurate and perform other related duties as assigned or requested by the senior director.
- **Quality Assurance (QA) :** Quality Assurance department supremely deals with validation of all aspects of the clinical trial process which includes proper vigilance of safety, efficacy, purity and stability of end products.
- **Project Manager and Marketing Executives :** It is the duty of these professionals to make sure that a particular drug is not only safe and effective but is also cost-effective for efficient disease management.
- **Account Directors :** This includes a number of other designations like business development analyst, clinical project director and clinical programme manager. A degree in life sciences and interest in medical writing and pharmaceutical marketing is a must.
- **Clinical Auditors :** This includes GCP specialist and QA auditors. A graduate level qualification in life sciences with strong knowledge about GCP, GMP, and GLP auditing processes is the requirement.
- **Contract Managers :** This includes Contract Associates, Senior Proposal and Contract Managers and Senior Project Managers. One must possess a bachelor's degree in life sciences with work experience in proposal writing and thorough understanding of complete clinical development process.
- **Drug Safety Scientist :** This includes Drug Safety Monitor, Drug Safety Officer and Drug Safety Associate. A master's degree in life sciences/pharmacology with good experience in medical writing, computers, regulatory requirements, drug information and other clinical processes.
- **Regulatory Affairs Manager :** This includes Senior Regulatory Associates, Manager (Regulatory Affairs) etc. A graduate degree in life sciences, clinical research experience and knowledge of FDA requirement is a must.

Career opportunities in clinical research are based on the academic qualification of the individuals.

- **Doctors :** Doctors are appointed in clinical trials as principal Investigator, Co-Investigator, Medical Advisor, Drug Developers, Regulatory Affairs Manager, and Clinical Research Physician.
- **Pharmacists, Life Science Graduates, Science Post-Graduates in Bio-chemistry :** They are appointed as Site Co-ordinators, Clinical Research Associate, Medical Writers, Clinical Research Manager and Drug Development Associate, Bio-statistician, Quality assurance.
- **Management Graduates (MBA) :** MBA graduates can choose the areas of Business Development, Clinical Project Management, Clinical Research Management, and Regulatory Affair Management.
- **IT Professionals, Bio-statistician, Engineers, Post-Graduates in Maths, Applied Maths, Operational Research, Statistics :** These professionals can find openings as Clinical Data Manager, Drug Development Associate.

Specialisation in branches of pharmacy, life sciences, bio-chemistry is useful. Studying further will also help one in bettering their current job profile. For instance, doing masters will enhance the job prospects of a CRA to become a Project Manager. Similarly, a Ph.D. in related discipline is needed to become a Medical Director.

Remuneration

There is high demand for trained professionals in the field of clinical research. But getting a job in this field as a fresher is very difficult, if they don't have the proper training and references. Most of the clinical research industry prefers individuals with prior work experience of tow – three years. The remuneration depends on the status of the industry and experience, qualifications and ability of the employee. Fresher can expect an impressive salary range from ₹ 35,000 – 50,000 per month. At the initial stage of their career, those with master's degree can earn between ₹ 5 lakh – 6 lakh per annum. Longer you are in this field, higher the salary you can expect, as clinical research is a field where experience counts.

Courses Available

- Advanced Diploma in Clinical Research,
- Advanced Post Graduate Diploma in Clinical Research,
- Advanced Post Graduate Diploma in Clinical Research and Data Management,
- Advanced Post Graduate Diploma in Clinical Research and Regulatory Affairs (APGDCR RA),

- Advanced Post Graduate Diploma in Clinical Research Management (APGDCRM),
- Advanced Post Graduate Programme in Clinical Research and Pharmaco-vigilance,
- Certificate Programme in Clinical Research (CPCR),
- Certificate Programme in Clinical Research Management,
- Integrated Post Graduate Diploma in Clinical Research and Pharmaco-vigilance,
- M. Pharma-Clinical Research,
- M. Sc. Clinical Research,
- MBA-Clinical Research Management,
- Post Graduate Certificate in Clinical Research for Nurses,
- Post Graduate Diploma in Clinical Research and Clinical Data Management (CRCDM), and
- Post Graduate Diploma in Clinical Research and Regulatory Affairs (APGDCRRA).

12.7 Criminology

What is Criminology?

Criminology is a scientific study of social crimes, criminals and criminal behaviour, crime regulations and crime prevention methodology. The field of study known as 'Criminology' involves the studying of crime as a phenomenon on an individual as well as at a social level. Approaching from a socio-scientific point of view, Criminology involves the study of various forms of crime, the reasons working behind an incidence of crime and its consequences. In other words, it examines society's response to crime and prevention of crime. It is the scientific investigation of crime through analysis of evidence. Criminology includes the examination of evidence, hereditary and psychological causes of crime, various modes of investigation and conviction and the efficiencies of differing styles of punishment, rehabilitation and corrections. Criminology involves studying all these aspects associated with crime in general. Criminology is the study of actors of criminality. In other sense, it is evaluating the circumstances that provoked to do the crime and preventing/regulating future chances to do such crime. Criminology being an inter-disciplinary subject, it derives its theory from the fields of sociology, psychology and law. Causes of crime and methods of preventing crime are the two most important aspects of the study of criminology. Other areas of interest in this field of study are – crime statistics, criminal behaviour, penology, evaluation of criminal justice agencies, sociology of law, criminal careers and desistance.

Who is a Criminologist?

A person professionally qualified in the subject of criminology is called a criminologist. The primary task of criminologists is to determine the reasons why people get into committing illegal activities. With the increasing numbers of crime and rapid diversification in the nature of it, criminology is gaining importance in today's society. So, if you are interested in the study of criminology or criminal justice, then you can become a criminologist. Criminologists often focus on specific types of crimes. Some work with murders, some with armed robbery, others with vandalism, some with rape and others with serial crimes of different sorts. They study as many cases as possible and use the results to formulate theories which can in turn be useful in preventing crimes in the future. Professionals may alternatively specialise in crime prevention, crime scene investigation, criminal litigation, corrections, rehabilitation or the privatisation of prisons.

Eligibility

There are a number of institutes and universities offering courses at graduate (B.A./B.Sc.) and post graduate level (M.A./M.Sc.) in India as well as abroad. If you are planning for a bachelor's degree in Criminology, then you must have completed your higher secondary schooling in Arts or Science. The eligibility norm for a master's programme is a graduate degree in Arts or Science with 50 per cent marks aggregate.

Personal Attributes

A criminologist like a psychologist must be interested in human nature and behaviour. One who is interested in this career must have creativity, analytical thinking capacity, problem solving ability, public speaking skill and ability to convince people. A criminologist must be able to express ideas and concepts clearly both in writing and speaking. A criminologist may need to address large groups of people and demonstrate good public speaking skills as well. Criminologist working in prisons, law firms and the like must be able to read the mind of the people and counsel them. Strong research and analysis skills are vital as so much of the job involves data collection and interpretation. Such a professional must be computer literate and proficient in computer and internet use especially research related to criminology. This professional must be dedicated to the profession of criminology and its goals of improving the criminal rehabilitation system and preventing crime.

Job Prospects

After pursuing Criminology course, one can apply for a variety of jobs in India as well as abroad. One should be willing to go through tough moments as a criminologist since one has to deal with all kinds of people including criminals with deviant mindset. A qualified criminologist can take up the jobs of teaching, counselling and rehabilitation of criminals. Teaching is one of the main professions that post graduates can pursue. Universities and government agencies employ professional criminologists for advanced teaching, research and policy assessment. Further more, public and private sector companies along with social welfare organisations require the services of a qualified criminologist in India. Corporations or financial institutions, major department stores and law firms employ security officers, private investigators or social workers. They can also find employment in drug enforcement agencies. Federal Bureau of Investigation, NGOs, research organisations, private security and detective agencies also recruit criminology professionals.

The job prospectus for people well versed in the field of criminology is even brighter outside India. A criminologist can be hired in foreign police departments as well as state medical examiners. Other typical jobs include law reform researcher, regional crime prevention co-ordinator, consumer advocate and environment protection analyst.

Criminologists may work in variety of settings including class-rooms, crime scenes, medical examiner offices, court houses, prisons, police stations or private offices. Criminologists may use their education and training to move onto other jobs either in psychological study or law enforcement.

Career Options

The various career options in this field are:

- Corrections ,
- Diversion Programming,
- Counselling,
- Criminal Investigation,
- Financial Fraud Investigation and Prevention,
- Forensics,
- Insurance Fraud Investigation and Prevention,
- Intervention Programming,

- Judicial/Courts,
- Law Enforcement,
- Medical Investigation,
- Rehabilitation,
- Research and Policy Studies,
- Private Investigation,
- Psychology-Psychopathology Specialist,
- Retail Investigation,
- Special Agencies, and
- Teaching.

Remuneration

The criminologist's salary differs a lot depending on the position of employment. The criminologist salary depends on many other factors such as city of employment, service criteria of private employers etc. For a fresher the monthly salary varies from ₹ 4,000 to 9,000 which gradually increases in the course of time. In case of experienced candidates remuneration is quite high and varies from ₹ 8,000 to ₹ 15,000. Pay scale for job abroad is also quite bright. An expected average annual salary of a criminologist with a bachelor degree is $30,000, whereas that of a criminologist with a master's degree is $55,000. The top paying state for criminologists is New Jersey at $105,750 a year. Other top paying states include District of Columbia, Virginia, Illinois and New York.

Courses

- Diploma in Criminology,
- M.A. Criminology,
- M.A. Criminology and Criminal Justice Administration,
- M.Sc. Criminology,
- PG Diploma in Criminology and Police Science,
- PG Diploma in Criminology and Penology,
- Ph.D. Criminology and Criminal Justice Administration, and
- Post Graduate Diploma in Criminology and Forensic Science.

Institutes

Some of the Top Criminology Colleges in India are :

- **Karnataka University, Hubli-Dharwad, Karnataka**

  Course : Master of Arts-Criminology and Forensic Science, Master of Law.

- **Symbiosis University, Pune, Maharashtra**

  Course : Diploma in Criminology and Penalogy, Master of Laws (Regular).

- **Guru Gobind Singh Indraprastha University, New Delhi**

  Course : Master of Arts Criminology.

- **Mohanlal Sukhadia University, Udaipur, Rajasthan**

  Course : Post Graduate Diploma in Criminology and Socio-economic Crimes.

- **Symbiosis Law School, Pune, Maharashtra**

  Course : Diploma in Criminology and Penalogy.

- **Jammu University, Jammu, Jammu & Kashmir**

  Course : Post Graduate Diploma in Criminology and Police Science.

- **Madurai Kamaraj University, Madurai, Tamil Nadu**

  Course : Post Graduate Diploma in Criminology and Police Administration.

  Master of Arts-Criminology and Police Administration.

- **University of Sagar, Sagar, Madhya Pradesh**

  Course : Post Graduate Diploma in Criminology and Police Administration,

  Doctor of Philosophy – Forensic Science and Criminology.

12.8 Dentistry

What is Dentistry?

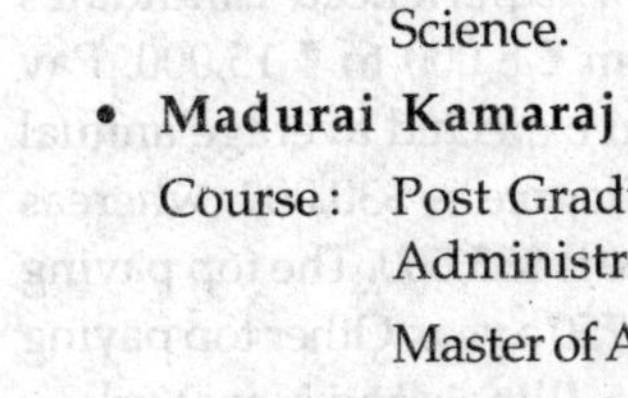

Dentistry is a medical specialisation that is concerned with all health problems afflicting the mouth, teeth, gums and other hard and soft tissues of the oral cavity. It is a professional field which includes dental care and correction. Dentists help people maintain their health and appearance. Dentistry is changing rapidly, creating many opportunities and challenges. To an extent, it includes cosmetology where corrective treatment is involved. Dentists improve patients' appearance by using a wide variety of cosmetic dental procedures. With the increasing awareness of the importance of oral health and the introduction of new fields like periodontics (care of gums and the diseases that might afflict them), oral pathology (diagnosis for diseases that affect the mouth) and orthodontics (straightening and aligning of teeth and jaws) have all enhanced the scope of this field.

Who is a Dentist?

A Dentist or a dental surgeon is one who provides surgical, medical and other forms of treatment for oral and dental disorders and diseases by examining teeth and mouth of the patients. He treats a diverse group of patients in a variety of settings using a variety of techniques and procedures such as computers and magnetic resonance imaging. This may include filling, crowning and scaling of teeth, extracting teeth, treating gum diseases and fitting artificial replacements where necessary and surgically handling injuries or other irregularities of the teeth and jaw. Problems dealing with the jaw or any invasive oral procedure are usually undertaken by an oral surgeon. Dentists perform trauma surgery, implants, tissue grafts and laser surgery to correct them. The core function of a dentist is prevention and treatment of diseases related to the oral cavity including the floor of the oral cavity, the 'roof' of the mouth, teeth, gums, tongue etc. Their job includes educating patients about oral hygiene and ways to preserve a healthy mouth and prevent dental problems.

Eligibility

Candidates who have passed 10+2 with physics, chemistry and biology with at least 50 per cent marks are eligible for admission in the Bachelor of Dental Science (BDS) course.

Selection

Admission to graduate course in dentistry is through a general, nation-wide competitive examination. The All India Pre-Medical/Pre-Dental Entrance Examination conducted by the CBSE is common for both the MBBS and the Bachelor of Dental Sciences (BDS). The allocation of institutions is based on merit. Other than the centrally run medical institutions there is at least one dental college in most states where admission is governed by domiciliary status. A merit waiting list up to a number of 1 to 2,000 is made on the basis of marks obtained in the Examination. The candidates are assigned their merit list and choice. There are also private colleges which under the management quota admit students on an all India basis. But to be eligible for practice, one must ensure that the course chosen is approved by the Dental Council of India.

Useful Contact Address :

Dental Council of India
Aiwan-E-Galib Marg
Kotla Road, Temple Lane
New Delhi – 110002.
Website: http://www.dciindia.org./

Duration

The BDS (Bachelor of Dental Science) degree programme is a four years course divided into four parts, each consisting of one year duration, followed by one year of rotating internship. Subjects such as basic anatomy, physiology, bio-chemistry, pharmacology and micro-biology are covered in the first two years. Specialisation in dentistry and hands on training are provided in the last two semesters. Those who have completed the BDS should be registered to practice dentistry by the Dental Council of India. An MDS (Master in Dental Science) requires two years of additional training. The annual fees may range from one lakh to three lakhs and the private institutions under management quota may charge five to ten lakhs as capitation fee.

Personal Skills

Dentist must have an artistic sense besides scientific knowledge. He is the scientist dedicated to the highest standards of health through the prevention, diagnosis and treatment of all oral diseases and conditions. He must have an artist's aesthetic sense as well to realign an entire jaw or to brighten one tooth, to help patients look their best. It is a very hard working profession that requires craftsmanship and skill as much as theoretical knowledge. The foremost attribute require for a good dentist is patience, stamina to work hard for long periods, good health, power of concentration, manual dexterity and accuracy. Besides these they must have a keen eye for detail, ability to memorise and recall scientific facts, comprehensive medical understanding, cool temperament and strong inter-personal skills. The best dentists are skillful communicators and their analytical and logical reasoning should be above average.

Course Areas

To practise as a dentist, one must need at least a Bachelor's degree in Dental Science (BDS). There is no specialisation at the bachelor's level. If you want your career to grow, then you will have to be specialist with a master's (MDS) degree. The main specialisation areas of Dentistry are :

- **Orthodontics :** Orthodontics which deals with straightening and aligning of teeth and jaws.
- **Periodontics :** It deals with the care of gums and the diseases that might affect them.
- **Operative Dentistry or Endodontic :** This is for root canal jobs, filling and cosmetic surgery.
- **Prosthodontics :** It deals with the making of artificial teeth.
- **Oral and Maxillofacial Surgery :** It deals specifically with operations on the mouth and jaw.
- **Pediatric Dentistry :** This is meant for treating children.
- **Oral Pathology :** This provides the diagnosis for diseases that affect the mouth.

Job Prospects

The main work of a dentist involves treatment of diseased mouths and gums, extraction of teeth that cannot be saved or might spread an infection to the rest of the mouth, fillings in the treatment of cavities, surgery of the mouth and jaw, replacement of extracted teeth through surgery or other processes, cleaning of the patient's mouth and teeth, corrective work to align or straighten teeth, dentures, i.e., the making and fitting of false teeth and preventive work which involves routine check-ups for both adults and children. Dental Assistants and Hygienists in addition to assisting the dentist during a variety of procedures such as clean and scale teeth, place temporary fillings, does other specific tasks including taking and developing dental radiographs (X-rays), sterilising instruments and equipment and making impressions of patients' teeth etc.

Career Options

Excellent employment opportunities are available for dentist in dental departments in hospitals, nursing homes, dental clinics and health departments as well as teaching departments in dental colleges. Apart from this, dentists could also work in the Research and Advisory functions of a pharmaceutical and other companies producing oral care products and medicines like toothpaste, mouth wash and gum care products. Self-employment is also a promising avenue.

With gaining experience, one can start his/her own individual practice. Many dentists prefer to be in private practice, as it provides the best financial prospects as well as greater independence. Private practitioners work either alone, often setting up a clinic on their own premises or in partnership with colleagues, sharing resources and overheads. Besides these, in dentistry one can also take up work as a Dental hygienist, Dental assistant or as a Dental consultant to models and film artists which could fetch a lot of money.

Remuneration

In government hospitals, freshly trained dentists could begin around ₹ 8,000 a month (including allowances), while in private hospitals it could be from ₹ 5,500 to 7,000. Post Graduate degree holders can expect to start on ₹ 9,000 upwards.

Dental surgeons can earn good money through their own practice. The consultation charges could be ₹ 500 upward for cosmetic filling and can be as high as ₹ 40,000 to 50,000 depending upon the nature of dental problem the patient is undergoing. A well established dentist can make around ₹ 20,000 – 1, 00,000 or more per month.

Courses

- Bachelor of Dental Surgery (BDS),
- Certificate Course in Dental Hygiene,
- Certificate Course in Dental Mechanic,
- Certificate Course in Dental Endodontics,
- Diploma in Dental Assistance,
- Ph.D. in Dentistry, and
- Master of Dental Surgery (MDS).

Top Institutes Offering Dental Sciences in India are :

- College of Dental Sciences, Manipal.
- Maulana Azad Institute, Delhi.
- Government Dental College and Hospital, Mumbai.
- Nair Hospital Dental College, Mumbai.
- Dr. R. Ahmed Dental College, Kolkata.
- Bapuji Dental College and Hospital, Dawangere.
- College of Dental Sciences, Dawangere.
- Faculty of Dental Sciences, Lucknow.
- Meenakshi Ammal Dental College, Chennai.
- Government Dental College, Bangalore.
- Sweetha Dental College, Chennai.
- AB Shetty Memorial Institute of Dental Sciences, Mangalore.

- SRM Dental College, Chennai.
- Amrita Institute of Medical Sciences, Kochi.
- Government Dental College, Thiruvananthapuram.

12.9 Dermatology

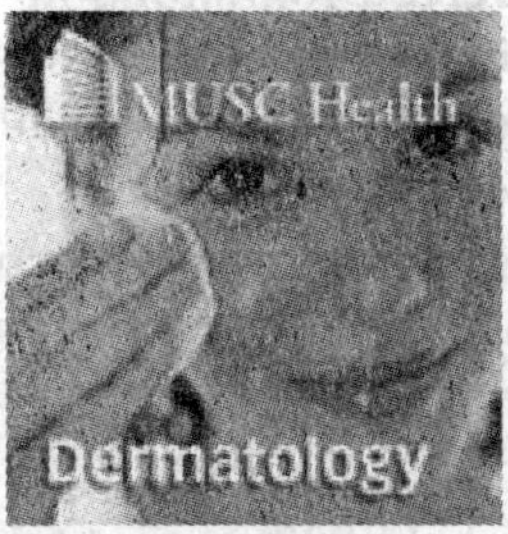

What is Dermatology?

Dermatology is one of the branches of medical sciences related to physiology and pathology of the skin, hair and nails. The field involves the diagnosis and treatment of conditions and diseases of the skin and appendages. The skin is part of the integumentary system which is the largest organ system of the human body. The word 'integumentary' comes from the Latin word *'tegere'* which means 'to cover'. In humans, this system accounts for about 16 per cent of total body weight and covers 1.5–2.2 of surface area. Accessory structures of the skin are the hair and nails, sweat glands and oil glands. The skin and accessories are prone to various acute and chronic problems from acne, rashes, warts, hair and nail problems to skin cancer, psoriasis, eczema, vitiligo and so on. Hair related problems like hair loss, dandruff, etc., are common. These diseases and beauty consciousness among people have made dermatology which treats diseases as well as cosmetic problems related to skin and scalp, a career of the present age.

Who is a Dermatologist?

A physician trained to treat diseases and conditions of skin is called dermatologist. Dermatologists manage acute and chronic disorders of the skin, i.e., they take care of diseases in the widest sense and some cosmetic problems of the skin, scalp, hair and nails. Dermatologists also study the structure and function of the skin and the relationship between skin pathologies and malfunctions of other organs of the body. They assess the affected area and take skin scrapings, tissue samples or blood samples for further testing and examination. They often examine samples using a microscope or through biological and chemical testing. Once diagnosis has been made, dermatologist creates a treatment plan. Dermatology often overlaps the practices of other medical specialties, e.g., neurology and internal medicine.

Eligibility

As dermatologist is a physician, he/she is required to complete the bachelor's degree in medicine (MBBS) and then get specialised by taking a master's degree in Dermatology. An aspiring candidate wanting to make a career as dermatologist needs to opt for science stream with physics, chemistry and biology as subjects at 10+2 level. After plus-two they have to go through the entrance examination and get a seat for MBBS. After MBBS, one can do a master's degree programme in Dermatology or a Doctorate in medical science in the related field of Dermatology. One can also opt for a post graduate diploma or diploma course in the respective field after bachelor's in Medicine.

Job Prospects and Career Options

Dermatologists could work in hospitals or clinics or take up private practice. They could even take up positions as professors, teaching faculty, supervisors or research heads in their specialised fields in medical colleges and institutes/universities. After gaining considerable experience in India, dermatologists can pursue lucrative careers abroad as the demand is increasing tremendously.

Private practitioners may opt for specialised dermatology courses in paediatric and cosmetic dermatology. The specialisations in dermatology can be done in the fields like immuno-dermatology, dermo-pathology, paediatric dermatology and cosmetic dermatology.

Areas of Specialisation

- **Cosmetic Dermatology :** Cosmetic Dermatology is a scientific super-specialty of Dematology which aims to bring science to the concept of Beauty. Dermatologists after completing a MS in the field of surgical dermatology are trained to use laser surgery, botox and fillers. Further, the cosmetic procedures include chemical peels, dermabrasion, derma roller, phepharoplasty, facelifts and liposuction. They treat scars, acne, hair fall, wrinkles, black spots, pigmentation, etc., using different procedures depending upon the type of the skin.
- **Dermatopathology :** A dermato-pathologist is a pathologist or dermatologist who specialises in the pathology of the skin. This field which is shared by pathologists and dermatologists who complete one year of derma-pathology fellowship (which includes six months training in general pathology and six months in derma-pathology). Derma-pathologist diagnoses and monitors diseases of the skin including infectious, immunological, degenerative and neoplastic diseases.
- **Immuno-dermatology :** This field specialises in the treatment of immune-mediated skin diseases such as pemphigus valgaris,

bullous pemphigoid, lupus erythema and so on. These individuals work in immuno-pathology labs.

- **Mohs-surgery :** It is a sub-specialty that focuses on the management of skin cancer using a tissue-sparing technique. Physicians trained in this technique receive exhaustive training in pathology as well as surgery.
- **Paediatric Dermatology :** Physicians qualify for paediatric Dermatology after completing a pediatric as well as dermatology residency. Some opt for a post-residency fellowship. Paediatric dermatology includes complex diseases of the neonates, hereditary skin ailments or geno-dermatoses. Paediatric dermatologist treats specific skin disease categories with emphasis on those diseases which pre-dominate in infants, children and adolescents.
- **Tele-dermatology :** It is the sub-section, wherein, telecommunication technologies are utilised to exchange medical information via media, invariably done by non-dermatologist to evaluate off-site by the dermatologists. This subspecialty deals with options to view skin conditions over a large distance to provide knowledge exchange, to establish second-opinion services for experts or to use this for follow-up of individuals with chronic skin conditions.

Remuneration

As a beginner, one can earn between ₹ 1, 40,000 and 2, 40,000 per annum in the field of dermatology. Once they have gained experience dermatologists may earn a salary package ranging between ₹ 300, 000 – 400, 000 per annum.

Courses

- MD Dermatology,
- Post Graduate Diploma in Dermatology and Venerology,
- Diploma in Dermatology, Venerology and Leprosy, and
- Courses in Cosmetic Dermatology and Cosmetology.

Top Institutes for Studying Dermatology in India are :

- **University of Delhi, New Delhi**

  Courses : Post Graduate Diploma in Dermatology,
  Doctor of Medicine in Dermatology.

- **Mahatma Gandhi Medical College and Research Institute, Pondicherry**

Courses :

Post-Graduate Diploma in Dermatology, Venerology and Leprosy,

Doctor of Medicine – Dermatology/Venerology/ Leprology.

- **Kasturba Medical College, Mangalore, Karnataka**

  Courses : Post Graduate Diploma in Dermatology,

  Doctor of Medicine in Dermatology.

- **Kasturba Medical College, Manipal, Karnataka**

  Courses : Post Graduate Diploma in Dermatology,

  Doctor of Medicine in Dermatology.

- **Smt. N.H.L Municipal Medical College, Ahmedabad, Gujarat**

  Courses : Diploma in Dermatology,

  Doctor of Medicine in Dermatology.

- **Pondicherry Institute of Medical Sciences, Kalapet, Pondicherry**

  Course : Post Graduate in Dermatology.

- **Mamata Medical College, Khammam, Andhra Pradesh**

  Course : Diploma in Dermatology, Venerology and Leprosy.

- **Father Muller Medical College, Mangalore, Karnataka**

  Courses : Post Graduate Diploma in Dermatology, Venerology and Leprology,

  Doctor of Medicine – Dermatology/Venerology/ Leprology.

12.10 Forensic Science

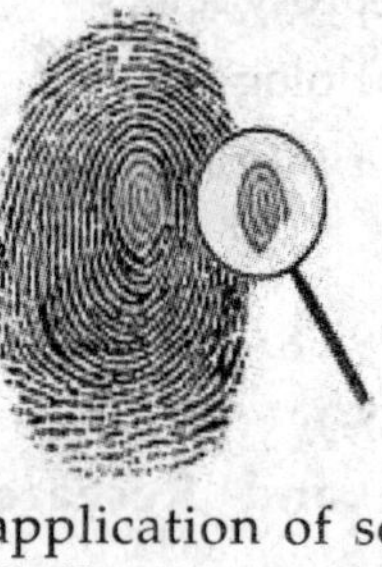

What is Forensic Science?

Forensic Science is primarily concerned with the application of scientific principles for the investigation of crime. Using the very latest in technology, forensic scientists convert the clues collected from a crime scene into evidence admissible in a court of law. It is the use or application of science in courts or legal proceedings. This is a challenging and interesting field for those who are inquisitive and loves adventure.

Forensic science is essentially a crime laboratory-based profession; the course qualifies students to apply their knowledge of science to the investigation of crime. But the expertise of a forensic professional is also used in civil cases for issues like proving the validity of a signature on a will, to a claim of the products liability, to find out whether an industry is complying with environmental rules.

The Work of Forensic Scientists

Forensic scientists analyse all physical evidence found on a victim on the scene of a crime and compare it to evidence found on a suspect andprovide expert testimony in a court of law. The evidences might include traces of blood, saliva, other body fluids, hair, fingerprints, footwear and type impressions, explosives, specimens of tissue for poisons, blood and urine for alcohol etc. Their expertise lies in the determination of facts using these evidences. They have to prepare a report of their investigation and appear in the court to give evidence. They work closely with the police to provide scientific evidence that is admissible in the court.

Different Areas of Forensic Science

Forensic Science can be broadly grouped into three: Medical, Laboratory and Field Science.

- **Forensic Medicine** : Forensic medicine is a broad medical subject which includes forensic pathology, psychiatry, psychology, forensic medicine and odontology (dentistry).
- **Laboratory Sciences** : This includes chemistry, biology, toxicology, ballistics, fingerprints, questioned documents and marks and impressions.
- **Field Sciences** : It includes crime scene investigation which incorporates areas such as fire and explosion scenes and clandestine drug laboratories.
- **Forensic Speech Science** : It is a latest addition to forensic science. Forensic speech science deals with recording, analysing voice samples using spectrogram – a machine used to identify the speaker. Voice recordings are used as evidence in the court of law in anti-corruption and other criminal offences.

In India, there are no exclusive labs for voice analysis but in European countries this analysis is widely used for detecting criminal cases. Telephone calls and text messages are considered as evidences for voice analysis. All India Institute of Speech and Hearing (AIISH), Mysore conducts course on Forensic Speech Sciences.

Eligibility and Course Areas

Candidates with a background in science subjects can pursue a career in forensic science. One can do graduation in forensic science (i.e., B.Sc. Forensic Science) after 10+2. After graduation, they can take up diploma courses in forensic science and criminology which is of one year duration. To take up a master's course in forensic science one needs to be a graduate preferably with a first division in physics, chemistry, zoology, botany, bio-chemistry, microbiology, B. Pharma, BDS or applied science.

To become a specialist who conducts post-mortems on dead bodies to find out the cause of death, you must first secure an MBBS degree and then go for an MD in forensic science. All Indian universities that offer MBBS courses also offer an MD in forensic science.

Eligibility for Research

Indian nationals below 30 years and who have obtained 1st class marks in master's degree in any one of the subjects: physics, chemistry, biochemistry, anthropology, zoology, molecular biology, mathematics (with physics as one of the subjects at the bachelor degree level), biotechnology, micro-biology, computer science, computer engineering, forensic psychology or M.Phil. in the same subjects whichever is the essential qualification for the award of Ph. D. degree of a recognised Indian university.

Job Prospects

They can find employment with law enforcement agencies, police, legal system and in the investigative services of the government and also private agencies. They can also work as teachers in institutes that conduct courses in this subject. Opportunities for forensic scientists exist in government organisations such as the Intelligence Bureau (IB), the Central Bureau of Investigation (CBI) and as investigative officers in the crime cells of state police forces. Forensic experts essentially work in forensic labs and sometimes even in large private detective agencies to establish the link between the criminal and the crime.

Career Options

There are varieties of options for forensic professionals. They can specialise in subjects as varied as medicine, engineering, finger-printing, insect study, languages and geology.

- **Crime Scene Investigation :** Scene investigation involves issues such as security, prevention of contamination, locating and collecting relevant items of evidence, interpretation of evidence and possible reconstruction of the event. Scenes can range from a relatively simple house break to a fire in a multi-storey building or a city bombing.

Qualification required : Diploma in Forensic Investigation or Degree in Forensic Investigation or Degree in Analytical Chemistry.

- **Forensic Pathology/Medicine :** Forensic pathologists determine the time and cause of death in cases of suspected murder or suicide. This involves post-mortem examinations of deaths reported to determine the cause and the manner of death (i.e., sudden and unexpected deaths or deaths due to accident or injury, suicide or homicide).

  Qualification required : Medical degree (MBBS) with M.D. or appropriate post graduate qualifications in Forensic Science.

- **Forensic Anthropology:** Forensic anthropologists use their knowledge of human skeletal anatomy to assist in the identification of skeletal remains. They are called to identify individuals murdered or killed in disasters such as plane crashes, explosions, fires and other tragedies resulting in the loss of life and mutilation of bodies. They may also be able to discover the age, sex, ancestry, stature and unique features of the deceased.

  Qualification required : A Ph.D. in anthropology with an emphasis on the study of human osteology and anatomy or a medical degree (MBBS) with appropriate post graduate qualifications.

- **Forensic Psychology and Psychiatry:** Psychiatry and psychology are concerned with whether a mental state may be a mitigating circumstance in the commission of an alleged crime, whether a person is mentally fit to stand trial and treating those convicted of crimes that are mentally ill. A forensic psychologist is any psychologist who by virtue of training or experience may assist a court or other finder in arriving at a just or correct decision. Forensic psychologists or psychiatrists may be called on to evaluate a murder scene to suggest a possible psychological profile of the killer.

  Qualification required: Medical degree (MBBS) with appropriate post graduate qualifications.

- **Forensic Dentistry (Odontology):** It is a branch of dentistry which deals with the collection, evaluation and proper handling of dental evidence in order to assist law enforcement officers and in civil and criminal proceedings. The role of the odontologist is to identify bodies and skeletal remains from dental records, reconstruct faces from skulls and where possible, interpret bite marks.

Qualification required: Degree in Dentistry, Post Graduate Diploma of Forensic Odontology.

- **Clinical Forensic Medicine:** Those involved in clinical forensic medicine amongst other things, examine victims of crime and suspects who may have sustained an injury while allegedly committing a crime. They give interpretations of their findings such as the possible causes and timing of the injuries.

  Qualification required: Medical degree (MBBS) with appropriate post graduate qualifications.

- **Forensic Entomology:** Forensic entomology is the application of the study of insects and other anthropods to legal issues. The time of death, for example, can be determined using insect evidence gathered from and around a corpse.
- **Forensic Serology:** Forensic serology is the study of blood groups, blood and other bodily fluids for identification purposes following a crime. Forensic serologists also carry out DNA fingerprinting which offers the possibility of positive identification of an individual from samples of blood or semen.
- **Forensic Chemist:** Areas of work includes the detection and identification of illicit drugs, accelerants used in arson cases, explosive and gunshot residues, trace evidence, including paint, glass, polymers and fibers.

  Qualification required: Science degree with a major in analytical, applied or forensic chemistry.

- **Dactyloscopy:** It is the scientific study of finger-prints. Finger-prints is perhaps the most well known of the forensic sciences. It also involves the identification of finger-prints and their ability to categorically link suspects to or exclude suspects from a crime scene.
- **Forensic Linguists:** Forensic linguists analyse the content of written or oral communication to identify who is speaking and indicate the speaker's intent and can determine whether two communications are from the same person. This is obviously important in cases of kidnapping.
- **Ballistics :** It is the study of the flight paths of projectiles but modern ballistics now includes the study of everything to do

with firearms. It also involves the determination of the angle and distance a gun was fired from to hit a specific target.

Qualification required: Science degree with a major in a relevant discipline, diploma in forensic investigation, degree in forensic investigation.

- **Toxicology:** It involves the detection and identification of illicit and pharmaceutical drugs and poisons, interpreting toxicity levels and the effects on the functions of the body.

  Qualification required: Science degree with a major in chemistry or bio-chemistry.

- **Forensic Engineer:** He deals with traffic accidents, fire investigations and a variety of wrongful injury cases. Engineers are involved in failure analysis, accident reconstruction, causes and origins of fires or explosions, quality evaluation of construction or manufacturing.

  Qualification required: An engineering degree with post graduate qualifications in Forensic Engineering.

- **Photography:** A crime scene must be photographed from every angle clearly to show detail with the emphasis on accurately recording the size and distance of objects.
- **Forensic artists and sculptors:** Forensic artists can draw a likeness of a person based solely on eye-witness accounts. Modern techniques of computer animation are now starting to be used to show evidence or expert testimony to courts. Forensic sculptors can reconstruct faces, usually in modeling clay or on a computer from skulls or other fragments. The expertise may enable the police to find out who a person was when no other clues are available.
- **Cytology:** Bullet cytology is a new subject which makes it possible to determine which part of the body a bullet went through by the tissue which is left on the bullet.
- **Geology:** Forensic geologists can determine such things as where the suspect or victim walked by examining soil samples taken from their shoes or feet.

Remuneration

The salary varies for state forensics departments as per government pay scales. Those doing private practice initially start by earning ₹ 6,000 – 8,000 per month. With experience, professionals earn ₹ 50,000 to 60,000 a month depending on the case. Private forensic laboratories offer lucrative pay packages to scientists with a few years of experience behind them. A freelancer in the field can charge according to requirements of the individual case.

Courses

- B.Sc. Forensic Science,
- Certificate Course in Forensic Accounting and Fraud Detection,
- M.Sc. Cyber Forensics and Information Security,
- M.Sc. Forensic Science,
- Post Graduate Diploma in Forensic Accounting,
- Post Graduate Diploma in Criminology and Forensic Science,
- Post Graduate Diploma in Forensic Science and Related Laws, and
- Post Graduate Diploma in Forensic Speech Science and Technology.

Top Institutes

- **Institute of Criminology and Forensic Science, Delhi.**
- **Anna University, Chennai**

  Course : BE Diploma in Forensic Engineering
- **University of Delhi, Delhi**

  Courses : PG Diploma in Criminology,

  Certificate in Forensic Science (three months)
- **Central Forensic Laboratory, Hyderabad.**
- **Central Forensic Laboratory, Chandigarh.**
- **Central Forensic Laboratory, Kolkata.**
- **Bundelkhand University Jhansi,**

  Course : PG Diploma in Forensic Science
- **Dr. Ambedkar University Agra,**

  Course : M.Sc. Forensic Science
- **Dr. Hari Singh Gour Vishwavidyalay, Sagar**

  Course : M.Sc. Criminology, M.A. Criminal and Forensic Science.
- **Karnataka University, Dharwad**

  Course : M.A. Criminology and Forensic Science

- **Lucknow University, Lucknow**
  Course : PG Diploma in Forensic Anthropology.
- **University of Madras, Chennai**
  Course : M.A. Criminology and M.Sc. Forensic Science.
- **Osmania University, Hyderabad**
  Course : M.Sc. Forensic Science in collaboration with AP State Forensic Science Laboratory.
- **Punjab University, Chandigarh**
  Course : PG Diploma in Forensic Science and Criminal Science.
- **Amity University, Noida**
  Course : B.Sc. and M.Sc. Forensic Science.

12.11 Gastroenterology

What is Gastroenterology?

Gastroenterology is a specialty of internal medicine. The specialty involves the diagnosis and management of patients with diseases of the intestines, liver and biliary tree and pancreas. It is a branch of medicine that deals with the digestive system. Diseases that affect the gastrointestinal tract as well as the related organs are focused on, in this branch.

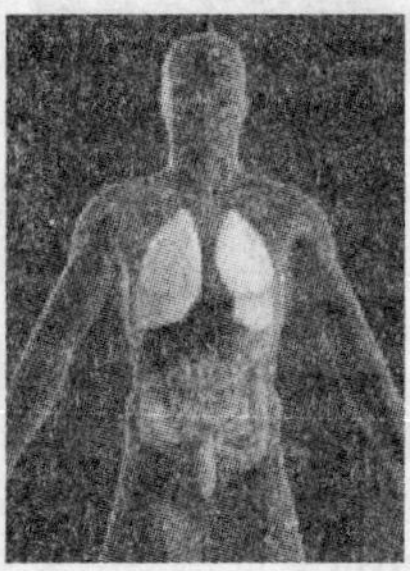

The Work of a Gastroenterologist

A gastroenterologist or GI doctors are specialists in digestive systems. Gastroenterologist specialises in the diagnosis and treatment of patients affected by problems related to gastrointestinal organs (also known as digestive system) like small intestine, gallbladder, colon, bile duct, pancreas, stomach and other related parts. So, if you have any problems of the digestive system, a gastroenterologist is the one you should consult. Two of the most common diseases which gastroenterologists need to treat are hepatitis, inflammation of the liver caused by viral infections or medication and liver cirrhosis which is usually related to alcoholism.

Eligibility

To become a gastroenterologist entails several years of training beyond an MBBS degree, as well as board certification. To become a gastroenterologist after taking MD/MS/DNB, one has to go for a DM in Gastroenterology. One who wishes to be a gatroenterologist must have passed 10+2 examination with biology, chemistry and physics. On completion of Plus two students have to appear for the competitive entrance examination for MBBS. This is a five and half years course which includes one-year internship period or house surgency as well. After that one has to go for MD/MS/DNB which is of two to three years duration. Then go for specialisation in the field, i.e., DM in Gastroenterology. For surgical intervention one has to get a M.Ch. in Gastroenterology. DM and M.Ch. are of three years duration. Admission to this doctorate level course is provided both on the basis of performance in the qualifying examination (i.e., MD) as well as on the basis of performance in the entrance test, varying from institution to institution.

Job Prospects and Career Options

Gastroenterology is considered as one of the top-paying careers in the medical field. Gastroenterologist's job includes evaluation, diagnosis, management and treatment of the diseases related to digestive system. They assess a patient's symptoms and perform a variety of diagnostic tests such as colonoscopy and endoscopy. This specialty is broadly divided into two aspects: medical and surgical. Medical gastroenterology largely involves the diagnosis and management of patients using medicine and minimally invasive interventions. Surgical gastroenterology is split into three specialties: the upper gastrointestinal tract, the lower GI tract and the liver, bile ducts and pancreas. Paediatric gastroenterology is a specialisation that can be pursued by paediatricians or gastroenterologists to become an expert in treating gastrointestinal issues of children.

Gastroenterologists have ample opportunities in private as well as government hospitals, group medical practice or healthcare network. Due to the large influx of patients with gastroenterological issues, multispecialty healthcare centres are trying to have gastroenterologists on their rolls either as full-time or visiting physician consultants. They are employed in medical research institutes and medical colleges/ schools as faculty members. More over enterprising gastroenterologists can also open their own Gastro Clinic.

Remuneration

Gastroenterology is one of the highly paying branches of medicine that treats some of the most complex illnesses of the digestive tract. Income varies according to the number of years a doctor has been in practice, geographic region, number of hours worked, skill, personality and professional reputation. Similarly, salary varies for those in private practice and in government service.

A fresher who joins a government hospital can start earning from ₹ 30,000 per month, whereas in private hospitals the salary can be ₹ 60,000 to 80,000 per month. Those who are experienced in the field can earn even lakhs per month. For gastroenterologists with their own clinic income is not a constraint once they gain reputation.

Courses

- DNB Gastroenterology,
- DM Gastroenterology, and
- M.Ch. Gastroenterology.

Institutes

- Bangalore Medical College and Research Institute (BMCRI), Bangalore, Karnataka.
- Calicut Medical College (CMC), Calicut, Kerala.
- Christian Medical College (CMC), Vellore, Tamil Nadu.
- NTR University of Health Sciences, Vijayawada, Andhra Pradesh.
- Institute of Post Graduate Medical Education and Research, Kolkata.
- King Edward Memorial Hospital and Seth Gordhandas Sunderdas Medical College, Mumbai, Maharashtra.
- Kurnool Medical College (KMC), Kurnool, Andhra Pradesh.
- Madras Medical College, Chennai, Tamil Nadu.
- Maulana Azad Medical College, New Delhi.
- Narayana Medical College and Hospital, Nellore, Andhra Pradesh.
- Osmania Medical College, Hyderabad, Andhra Pradesh.
- Postgraduate Institute of Medical Education and Research (PGIMER), Chandigarh, Punjab.
- PSG Institute of Medical Sciences and Research (PSGIMSR), Coimbatore, Tamil Nadu.
- SMS Medical College, Jaipur, Rajasthan.
- Smt. N.H.L. Municipal Medical College, Ahmedabad, Gujarat.
- St. John's Medical College, Bangalore, Karnataka.
- Topiwala National Medical College (TNMC), Mumbai, Maharashtra.
- University of Pune, Pune, Maharashtra.

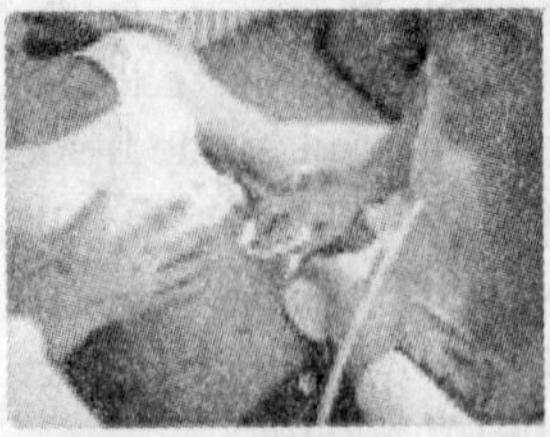

12.12 Gynaecology

What is Gynaecology?

Gynaecology is also known as the science of women is a career serving the health of women of all ages. Gynaecologists specialise in the branch of medical science concerned with the health related issues of female organs and reproductive system. As professionals, gynaecologists focus on women's health, serve as primary physicians. They are trained to diagnose and treat diseases and disorders in the reproductive system. Gynaecologists play a vital role in pregnancy, sexual health and the treatment of serious reproductive problems such as infertility or reproductive cancers. They also deal with many different conditions such as cancer, amenorrhea, urine incontinence and prolapsed of pelvic organs. Gynaecologists also provide a variety of procedures such as pap smears, biopsies, hysterectomies, tubal ligations and oophorectomy.

The Work of Gynaecologists

The work of gynaecologists is to identify the disease and issues related to female genital, urinary and rectal organs, converse with the patient and provide correct medical aid, hygiene regime or surgery if required, in order to correct the disorder or remove the diseased organ. They diagnose illnesses and infections, conduct annual/periodical examinations, prescribe medications, counsel patients on fertility options and birth control methods and treat hormonal and reproductive issues. The field requires lots of dedication, devotion, detailed and accurate medical knowledge along with years of experience.

Gynaecology and Obstetrics

Although both are related fields of study, they are different streams. Obstetricians are physicians who specialise in caring for the pregnant women all through the process of childbirth. Gynaecologists on the other hand, are the physicians who mainly treat the disorders related to female reproductive system which consists of organs like vagina, uterus and ovaries. Many physicians specialise in both and so, these two profiles are often clubbed together to say many gynaecologists are also obstetricians. Obstetrician/gynaecologists are commonly referred to as OB/GYN.

Eligibility and Course Areas

In order to become a gynaecologist, candidates have to pursue post graduate courses such as MD (Doctor of Medicine)/MS (Master of

Surgery)/DNB (Diploma of Medicine) or a Diploma course in Gynaecology (DGO).

Aspirants who have completed the four and a half years MBBS programme and the one-year internship subsequently can pursue post-graduate programmes in Gynaecology. Post graduate programmes (MD/MS/DNB) is usually in Gynaecology (DGO) course is of two years duration. The MD/MS degrees are offered by the universities affiliated to the Medical Council of India and the DNB degree is awarded by the National Board of Examination, an independent autonomous body under the Ministry of Health, India.

Selection

Selection for post graduate programme is through entrance examination. In the case of private medical colleges entrance examinations are conducted by the institutes individually.

Higher Courses

Those with post graduation (MD or MS or DNB) can further opt for super/sub-specialisation in their area of interest by opting for courses called DM or DNB (Doctorate of Medicine) or M.Ch. or DNB (Master of Chirurgery/Surgery) again of three years duration. Sub-specialties in Gynaecology include gynaecologic oncology, urogynecology, maternal and fetal medicine, reproductive endocrinology and infertility. In India, there is no M.Ch. course in Gynaecology.

Job Prospects and Career Options

Gynaecologists can get jobs in government as well as private hospitals, clinics, pharmaceutical companies, hospitals run by defence etc. Those who have interest in teaching can work as Gynaecology lecturers in medical schools or institutes. In this case, candidates with Diploma (DGO) may have to put in another two years for getting their MD or MS or DNB to take up the teaching option as colleges/institutes does not prefer to hire DGOs. One can opt for self-employment and start a clinic. One can also pursue research after completing post graduate degree in any specialised branch of gynaecology. At the same time, the field is gratifying in the sense that you assist in bringing a new life into the world.

Challenges in the Field

There are immense challenges in this field. The working time can be very hectic; they must be on call even at mid night in case of emergencies and may require working for long hours. A gynaecologist needs to be very careful during the treatment procedures, especially when dealing with pregnant women. He/She deals with two lives.

Remuneration

For a fresher at entry level salary ranges from ₹ 15,000 to 30,000 per month. After acquiring an experience of four-five years he/she can earn a salary ranging from ₹ 40,000 to 80,000 per month. At senior level salary can range in between ₹ 1, 00,000 to 2, 00,000 per month which depends on their experience.

Obstetricians/gynaecologists who work in hospitals make more money than those working in outpatient care centers and colleges, universities and professional schools. Obstetricians/gynaecologists who work in their own private practice make significantly more than all others in this field. They charge on the basis of per visit and according to the complexity of the cases.

Courses

- Diploma in Obstetrics and Gynaecology (DGO),
- DNB in Obstetrics and Gynaecology,
- MD Obstetrics and Gynaecology, and
- MS Obstetrics and Gynaecology.

Useful Contacts

- **The Federation of Obstetric and Gynaecological Societies of India (FOGSI)**

  Secretary General

  Modern Residency, 605

  Bapurao Jagtap Marg

  Jacob Circle, Mahalaxmi East

  Mumbai-400 011.

  Phone: 91 22 32954564/23021648/23021648/23021654.

  Fax: 91 22 23021383.

  Website: www.fogsi.org/

- **Medical Council of India**

  Pocket – 14, Sector – 8

  Dwarka Phase–1

  New Delhi – 110077.

  Phone: +91 11 25367033/25367035/25367036.

  Fax: General +91 11 25367024/25367028.

  Website: www.mciindia.org.

- **National Board of Examinations**

  Medical Enclave, Ansari Nagar

  Ring Road, New Delhi-110 029.

  Phone: 011 4605 4605.

  Fax: 011 45593009/45593031/45593014.

  Website: www.natboard.edu.in.

Institutes

- A.J. Institute of Medical Sciences, Mangalore, Karnataka Mangalore, Karnataka.
- Adichunchanagiri Institute of Medical Sciences, Bellur, Karnataka.
- Al-Ameen Medical College, Bijapur, Karnataka.
- All India Institute of Medical Sciences, New Delhi.
- Alluri Sitaram Raju Academy of Medical Sciences (ASRAM), Eluru, Andhra Pradesh.
- Amrita School of Medicine, Kochi, Kerala.
- Armed Forces Medical College (AFMC), Pune, Maharashtra.
- Assam Medical College, Dibrugarh, Assam.
- B.J. Medical College (BJMC), Ahmedabad, Gujarat.
- B.J. Medical College and Sassoon Hospital, Pune, Maharashtra.
- Bangalore Medical College and Research Institute, Bangalore, Karnataka.
- B.S. Medical College (BSMC), Bankura, West Bengal.
- Bharath University, Chennai, Tamil Nadu.
- Bharati Vidyapeeth Deemed University, Pune, Maharashtra.
- Burdwan Medical College & Hospital, Burdwan, West Bengal.
- Calicut Medical College, Calicut, Kerala.
- Christian Medical College, Vellore, Tamil Nadu.
- Christian Medical College (CMC), Ludhiana, Punjab.
- Datta Meghe Institute of Medical Science, Nagpur, Maharashtra.
- Deccan College of Medical Sciences, Hyderabad, Andhra Pradesh.
- Dr Ambedkar Medical College, Bangalore, Karnataka.
- Dr NTR University of Health Sciences, Vijayawada, Andhra Pradesh.

- Dr Rajendra Prasad Government Medical College (RPGMC), Tanda, Himachal Pradesh.

12.13 Hospital Management

Hospital Management

According to the recent US survey, Hospital Management is one among the top ten millennium professions which provides a direct link between healthcare facilities and those supplying the services they need. A career in Hospital Management involves ensuring effective utilisation of physical and financial resources of the hospital as well as creating an organisational climate beneficial to the growth and development of the personnel.

Hospital Administrators/Managers

Professional services of trained manpower namely, Hospital administrators/managers have now become essential to manage hospitals and medical facilities. It is the hospital administrators/managers who manage hospitals, out-patient clinics, hospices, drug-abuse treatment centers and so on. They would be responsible for overall patient care, education, research and community healthcare associated with the organisation and make sure that they conform to the rules of the hospital. These people with the help of a team of assistants look after the administrative affairs, i.e., plan, co-ordinate and direct the delivery of health services within a hospital.

Qualified people in this field can work as deans and directors of medical colleges, hospital superintendents, deputy superintendents, medical directors, nursing directors, heads of departments and as Administrators with substantial managerial responsibilities. Hospital Manager will be responsible for the overall organisation and management of the hospital to ensure its smooth functioning with the objective of ensuring complete satisfaction.

Eligibility and Course Areas

An individual from a medical or a non-medical background can pursue a career in Hospital Administration/Management. The pre-requisite is a graduation (medical/non-medical) or a degree/diploma in Hospital Administration. The main professional courses available in this field are bachelor of Hospital Management/Administration, master of Hospital Administration, MBA in Hospital Administration and M.D./M.Phil. in Hospital Administration. Apart from these programmes, there are about 70 accredited programmes in healthcare administration.

Eligibility for bachelor's degree in Hospital Management/ Administration (BHA) is 10+2 with biology attaining minimum 50 per cent marks. One can do post graduate degree/diploma courses and MBA in Hospital Administration, after graduation in any subject. But the eligibility criteria for post graduate courses may vary according to the course and the institute concerned. For institutes like All India Institute of Medical Sciences (AIIMS), Armed Forces Medical College, Devi Ahilya Vishwavidyalaya, Symbiosis Centre of Healthcare (SCHC) etc., the minimum qualification for PG courses is MBBS. MHA is required for doing M.Phil. in Hospital Administration.

Selection

Selection to the bachelor of Hospital Administration (BHA) courses is generally made on the basis of the marks obtained in plus-two and through general entrance test, followed by a group discussion and/or personal interview. In the Institute of Health Management Research (IHMR) Bangalore, the candidates are selected for admission to PGPHM/PGPPHM only on the basis of personal interviews conducted by the Faculty of the Institute at Bangalore and other cities of Delhi, Mumbai, Chennai and Hyderabad. The selection criterion will also take into account the candidates command over English language, skill in communicating, computer handling and overall managerial ability.

Duration

BBM/Bachelor of Hospital Administration (BHA) is of three years. Diploma/MBA/Master in Hospital Administration (MHA)/ Management is of two years (four semesters). Post-graduate professional programme in Hospital Management (PGPHM) is for 11 months. EMBA, PGDHM and ADHM are of one year (two semesters) duration.

Personal Skills

Tact, diplomacy, flexibility, communication and organising skills are the most essential qualities needed for hospital managers, because they spend much of their time in interacting with others. An outgoing, friendly personality, ability to handle deadlines, excellent leadership skills is necessary to be effective hospital managers. He or she should have quick decision-making capability based on up-to-date management principles and techniques, analytical and logical reasoning skill, patience, excellent verbal and written communication skills to maintain functional relationships with the hospital staff, physicians and the community. As they are responsible for the overall organisation and management of the hospital, they should possess good health, energy and stamina for working long and irregular hours.

The Work of Hospital Manager

The work of hospital manager involves administration, managing and maintaining equipment, management of the medical staff and day-to-day medical activities, financial planning and operations of the hospital. They try to bring about economy in the use of supplies, facilities and human resources of the hospital.

The Role of Hospital Manager

The hospital manager's role differs according to the size of the organisation. In a smaller, medical or health care centre, they have to handle day-to-day administrative work, which may involve billing, maintenance, equipment supply and also work closely with doctors, in group practice and decision-making. But large scale organisations may require the services of a manager in key aspects as well. Hospital administrators have to co-ordinate between the various departments of the hospital and have to ensure that all equipments are functional. They are responsible for hiring non-medical staff, maintenance of hospital services, security, building the hospital brand, marketing, accounts, financial operations, planning and control for continuous supply of materials, management of the research and clinical work.

Job Prospects and Career Options

Most job opportunities in the field of hospital management are in hospitals but one can also find openings in health agencies, laboratories and other health and allied services. Government hospitals as well as private hospitals employ hospital administrators/managers. Hospital management positions vary from Head of the department to chief executive officer at numerous organisational levels. A fresh graduate with master's degree in health services or hospital administration may start their professional career as assistant hospital administrators or as managers of various departments like front office, public relations, finance, quality control and so on. Experienced and senior hospital administrators can eventually reach the position of Chief Executive Officer (CEO). It is these people who are supposed to report to the board of directors or the governing body of the hospital.

Degree/diploma holders in hospital management can find employment in large corporate/public/private sector hospitals, clinics, international and national healthcare organisations and health insurance companies, college and universities, healthcare centres, nursing homes, mental health organisations, public health departments, rehabilitation centres, pharmaceuticals and hospital supply firms, medical software companies and hospital consulting firms. Those having a master's degree in hospital management with four-five years of experience can get employment as a lecturer. With several years of experience in the field, one could even set up their own nursing home or hospital.

Remuneration

In India, a Junior hospital manager can earn a starting pay in the range of ₹ 8,000 – 12,000 per month. An experienced and qualified hospital manager can earn more than ₹ 40,000 per month. Large corporate organisations pay a lucrative amount as salary. Lecturers in hospital Management can expect over ₹ 15,000 per month. The demand for skilled and experienced hospital managers in foreign countries is reasonably high. The salary offered by hospitals abroad may be number of times more than that of the salary offered in India.

Courses

- Bachelor of Hospital Management,
- Diploma in Hospital Administration,
- Diploma in Hospital Records Management,
- M.D. Hospital Administration,
- M.Phil. Hospital Administration,
- M.Sc. Hospital Administration,
- Master of Hospital Administration/ Management,
- Post Graduate Certificate in Hospital Management,
- Post Graduate Diploma in Hospital Administration,
- Post Graduate Diploma in Hospital and Healthcare Management,
- Post Graduate Diploma in Hospital Management, and
- Post Graduate Programme in Hospital Management.

Institutes

Some of the most reputed institutes in India are like:

- All India Institute of Medical Sciences (AIIMS), New Delhi.

- Armed Forces Medical College, Pune, Maharashtra.
- Devi Ahilya Vishwavidyalaya.
- Symbiosis Centre of Healthcare (SCHC)

12.14 Neurology

What is Neurology?

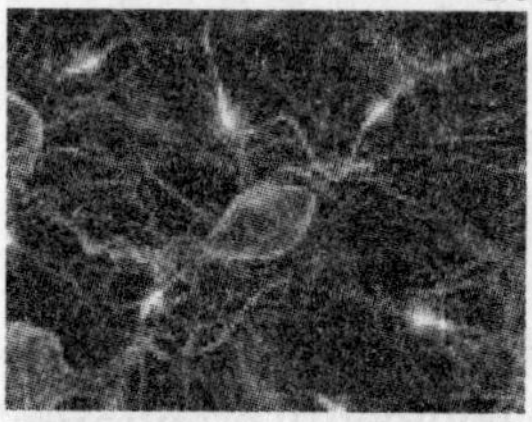

The term 'Neurology' is derived from the Greek words *'neuron'* meaning 'nerve' and *'logia'* meaning 'study of. Hence, Neurology is a specialised branch of medicine which studies the ailments of the nervous system. To be more specific, Neurology is a specialised branch of medicine which studies the ailments of the nervous system such as the brain, spinal cord, central nervous system as well as related tissues and muscles of a human body.

Who is a Neurologist?

Medical practitioner who specialises in this field is generally known as Neurologist. Neurologists are physicians who are trained for diagnosing, treating and managing the ongoing care of patients suffering from disorders of the nervous system. They treat disorders such as brain trauma, stroke, multiple sclerosis, epilepsy, Parkinson's disease, Alzheimer's disease and the like. Neurologists who deal with surgical procedures are known as Neuro-surgeons.

The Three Main Forms of Neurology

- **Clinical Neuro-physiology** – This deals with diagnosis and treatment of neurological disorder of autonomic, central and peripheral nervous system.
- **Child or Paediatric Neurology** – This deals with diagnosis and treatment of the brain and nervous system disorder in children and adolescents.
- **Pain Medicine** – It focuses on relieving serious illnesses and chronic pains caused by neurological disorders.

Apart from these main three, there are also many other specialisations. Each form of neurology deals with neural dysfunction in some form.

Difference between Neurology and Neuro-science

The terms Neurology and Neuro-science are not the same. Neurology is the branch of medicine which relates to ailments of nervous system; whereas, Neuro-science is a division of science which deals with the study of nervous system in all its aspects. There is an overlap between the field of neurology and psychiatry, as many of the diseases of the nervous systems have a psychological component or often a psychological after-effect.

Eligibility

Neurology is considered as one of the most complex branch of medicine. It requires several years of study. To become a neurologist you must first become a medical doctor.

Aspiring Neurologists after completing their 10+2 with biology, chemistry and physics must appear for the competitive entrance examination for MBBS. This is a five and half years course which includes a one-year internship period as well. Then go for MD or MS or DNB in general medicine. After that to go for specialisation in the field, i.e., for PG programmes in Neurology one should attend another entrance examination in order to get admissions to the PG programme.

Course Areas

DM in Neurology

- **MBBS :** The duration of the course will be for a period of five years.
- **MD/DNB in Internal (General) Medicine or Paediatrics :** The duration of the course will be for a period of three years.

M.Ch. in Neurology

- **MBBS :** The duration of the course will be for a period of five years.
- **MS/DNB in General Surgery :** The duration of the course will be for a period of three years.

Duration of D.M/M.Ch. courses: three years (except Neuro-surgery which is six years course directly after MBBS).

Job Prospects and Career Options

Neurologist works in one of the most complex and fascinating areas of medicine, involving the brain and nervous system. They can work in general neurology or they can choose to specialise in one of several different neurology sub-specialties. In most cases they treat patients referred by another doctor or physician. The most common diagnostic tests performed by a neurologist include the CAT scan, MRI, spinal taps, electro-encephalography and electro-myography.

Neurologists have great opportunities in private as well as government hospitals, group medical practice or healthcare network. They may be involved in clinical research, clinical trials as well as basic research and translational research. Neurologists can also publish research articles or write for medical journals. Neurologists are employed in medical research institutes and medical colleges/schools as faculty members. Self-employment is also an option available once they have a good experience in hand.

Remuneration

Medical practitioners who enter this field can expect a high salary and opportunities for advancement within a public or private setting. Pay scale of Neurologists depends on the educational qualification, years of experience in the field and the university from where the education has been acquired. At entry level one can expect ₹ 25,000 – 30,000 per month.

Courses

- DM Neurology,
- M.Ch. Neurosurgery, and
- Diploma in Neurotechnology.

Best Neurology Colleges in India

- **West Bengal University of Health Sciences, Salt Lake, West Bengal**

  Course : Doctor of Medicine (Super Specialty) – Neurology.
- **Tamil Nadu Dr M.G.R. Medical University, Chennai, Tamil Nadu**

  Course : Doctor of Medicine – Neurology (Super-Specialty).
- **Sri Ramachandra University, Chennai, Tamil Nadu**

  Course : Doctor of Medicine – Neurology (Super-Specialty).
- **Rajasthan University of Health Sciences, Jaipur, Rajasthan**

  Course : Doctor of Medicine (Super-Specialty) – Neurology.
- **University of Delhi, New Delhi**

  Course : Doctor of Medicine (Super-Specialty) in Neurology.
- **K.L.E Society Institute of Physiotherapy (KIPT), Belgaum, Karnataka**

Course : Master of Physiotherapy in Neurology.

- **Jawaharlal Nehru Medical College, Belgaum, Karnataka**
  Course : Doctor of Medicine– Neurology.
- **Kurnool Medical College, Kurnool, Andhra Pradesh**
  Course : Doctor of Medicine– Neurology.

12.15 Nursing

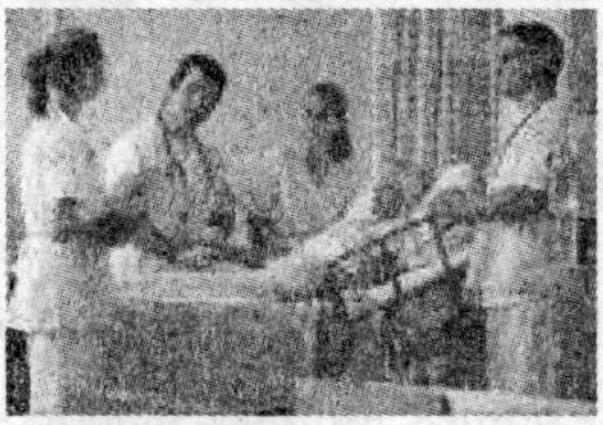

What is Nursing?

Nursing, a profession that recalls the name of Florence Nightingale is indeed one of the noblest professions in the world. It is the art of caring the sick with the science of healthcare. It is a very vital component of any form of medical care.

The Duties of Nurses

The duties of nurses are manifold and cover a wide range of functions and responsibilities that are dependent on the level of qualification and the working environment. At the initial level, nurses are required for the bedside care of patients, while at senior level they are required to manage special group of people like psychiatric, paediatric, intensive care patients, etc., which require specialised skills. They are also involved in dispensing medication, keeping records of the patients' progress, setting up and operating medical equipment, administration and several other routine chores.

Eligibility and Course Areas

- **B. Sc. Nursing**
  Eligibility : 10+2 with Biology, Physics and Chemistry.
  Duration : 3 – 4 years.
- **General Nursing & Midwifery (GNM)**
  Eligibility : 10+2 with Biology, Physics and Chemistry.
  Duration : 3–4 years.
  GNM programme is to prepare general nurses who function as members of the health team, to hold first level positions in both the hospitals and other such places.
- **Auxiliary Nurse Midwife/Health Worker (ANM)**
  Eligibility : 10th passed.
  Duration : 18 months.

ANM course provides training as to how to take care of health related needs of the people living in rural areas especially children, mothers and old persons.

Personal Attributes

The nursing profession calls for tremendous patience, responsibility and dedication. The job requires alertness of mind, team spirit, tact and compassion. One should also be physically fit and in peak health for the job involves a lot of hard work. They should have the instinct to help and serve the patient without getting sentimentally attached. Apart from all these, one must have a pleasant smiling face whatever be the situation.

Job Prospects

Nurses can find employment in hospitals, nursing homes, clinics and health departments, orphanages and old age homes, military, schools, industrial houses and factories, railways and public sector medical departments and training institutes as educators.

Career Options

- **Hospital Nursing :** Hospital nurses form the largest group of nurses. Hospital nurses are usually assigned to any special area of work such as surgery, maternity, intensive care, paediatric, obstetric, rehabilitative etc.
- **Military Nursing :** Provide healthcare services to armed forces.
- **Educators :** This field combines nursing with the teaching of students of nursing and administration of educational programmes.
- **Industrial Nursing/Occupational Health Nursing :** They work under the direction of the industrial physicians and assist in taking preventive safety measures. They provide emergency care at the time of accidents taking place inside the industrial premises.
- **Psychiatric Nursing :** This nursing involves working with patients suffering from emotional and psychological distress. Nursing these patients requires devotion and patience. They generally work in coordination with the psychiatrists, doctors and other specialists.
- **Paediatric Nursing :** It is concerned with the care of sick babies and children.
- **Orthopaedic Nursing :** This requires knowledge of physiotherapy and rehabilitation.

Remuneration

Remuneration of nurses depends on the level of seniority reached. Nurses employed by government hospitals receive a monthly salary of ₹ 15,000 – 30,000. Those working for private hospitals or the military receive a slightly higher remuneration. Private nurses have a fixed daily fee. Midwives receive above 5,000 per month approximately, plus a fixed amount per birth registered. Health workers receive between ₹ 3,000 – 5,000 per month.

Top Nursing Colleges in India

- CMC, Vellore: College of Nursing.
- RAK College of Nursing, Delhi.
- All India Institute of Medical Sciences: Department of Nursing.
- Manipal University: Manipal College of Nursing.
- B.M. Birla College of Nursing, Kolkata.
- Government College of Nursing, Kozhikode.
- Father Muller College of Nursing, Mangalore.
- Sri Ramachandra Medical University, Chennai: College of Nursing.
- SNDT Faculty of Nursing, Mumbai.
- Government College of Nursing, Trissur.
- National Institute of Mental Health and Neurosciences, Bangalore: Department of Nursing.
- Government College of Nursing, Kottayam.
- Government College of Nursing, Alappuzha.
- Government College of Nursing, Thiruvananthapuram.
- Apollo College of Nursing, Chennai.
- Tata Memorial Hospital, Mumbai: Nursing.
- St John's College of Nursing, Bangalore.
- SRM University: College of Nursing, Chennai.
- Amrita University: College of Nursing, Cochin.
- MIMS College of Nursing, Calicut, Kerala.
- Madras Medical College: College of Nursing.
- Kokilaben Dhirubhai Ambani Nursing College.
- CMC Ludiana: College of Nursing.
- Government College of Nursing, SSKM Hospital, Kolkata.
- Madras Medical Mission, College of Nursing, Chennai.

12.16 Optometry

What is Ophthalmic Optics?

Ophthalmic Optics is a science which deals with the structure, function and working of the human eye. It is popularly known as Optometry.

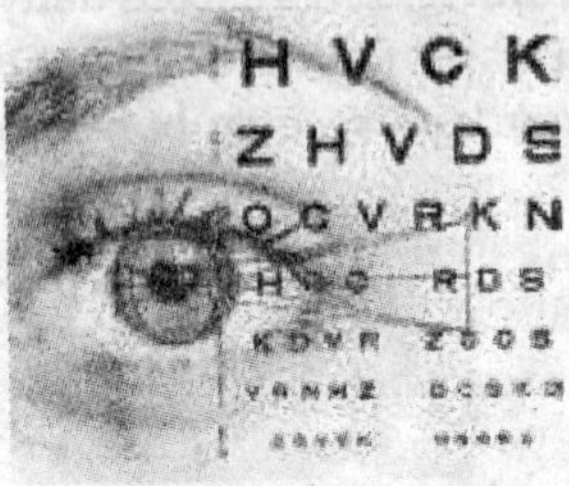

This profession is concerned with examination, diagnosis and treatment of eyes especially related to visual, optical symptoms, refractive errors and their correction using lenses and other optical aids.

Who are Optometrists?

Optometrists or optometric physicians are primary eye care and health professionals concerned with vision care. They are experts in determining one's refractive error and prescribing appropriate correction. They deal with vision screening (eye testing), diagnosis of visual problems, orthotics and vision training, optometric counselling of patients with partial sight, colour blindness and hereditary vision defects and designing and fitting of spectacles, contact lens and low vision aids. They also prescribe vision therapy eye exercises to patients complaining of visual symptoms such as squint etc.

Optometry and Ophthalmology

Though Optometry goes hand in hand with Ophthalmology in treatment of visual disorders, optometrists should not be confused with ophthalmologists or dispensing opticians. An optometrist performs all the tasks of an ophthalmologist, sort of surgery. Ophthalmologists (Eyes MDs) are trained physicians specialised in eye and vision care who perform eye surgery as well as diagnose and treat eye diseases and injuries.

Eligibility

Students who wish to do degree or diploma courses in ophthalmic technology should clear 10+2 or equivalent examination with a minimum of 50 per cent marks in physics, chemistry and biology. To practise as an optometrist, it is essential to have a bachelor's degree in Optometry (Bachelor of Clinical Optometry) or (B.Optom). Eligibility for B.Optom. course is higher secondary examination (10+2 course) or its equivalent with minimum 50 per cent marks in physics, chemistry and biology or mathematics and English, from a recognised board and the age limit is 17 years as on 31st December. Candidates satisfying the eligibility requirement for the B.Optom. course have to appear for the

EYECET examination. The EYECET examination is the centralised, combined entrance test for entry into optometry courses which is universally recognised all over the country.

For direct admission to third year B.Optom. course, candidates who have completed their 10+2 must have a two years diploma course in Optometry, Ophthalmic Techniques, Refraction, Orthotics and Ophthalmic Assistance with 40 per cent marks from an institute recognised by Indian Optometric Association and Bharati Vidyapeeth Deemed University. Candidates with secondary school certificate (Std. X) must have a three year diploma course in ophthalmic techniques and should have worked in an ophthalmic clinic or optical establishment for a minimum period of one year after completion of the course. The candidates have to submit their work experience certificate from the ophthalmic clinic or optical establishment during the time of admission. Age limit for direct admission to 3rd year B. Optom. course is 19 years. In addition, they have to appear for the EYECET test.

Course Areas

B. Optom. course is of four year duration. The first three years teaching is followed by one year of internship for clinical and trade experience. The optometry course covers a wide variety of subjects including physical optics, knowledge of optical instruments, general anatomy, physiology, abnormal and pathological conditions of the eye and the methods to measure refractive errors and their correction. Courses in pharmacology, optics, vision science, bio-chemistry and systemic disease are included in the curriculum. There will be practical training in basic science, dispensing optics and clinical subjects. The fourth and final year is internship where the students are posted at various hospitals and specialty eye clinics and optical establishments for clinical training and hands-on practice.

Job Prospects and Career Options

An Optometrist, after having completed has a lot of career options. They can establish an independent practice by starting their own eye clinic, optical shop, lens manufacturing unit etc. They can work with optician showrooms, eye doctors, contact lens and ophthalmic lens industry, hospital, eye departments etc. Optometrists can also seek employment with any multi-national organisation dealing with eyecare products as profession services executives or take up teaching as a career.

They can pursue higher education or can go for further research in the field of optometry. Optometrists could also take up the work of occupational health specialists in the vision care of industrial workers.

Remuneration

Optometry is one of the top ten income-earning professions in the country today. The initial salary of an optometrist in a government firm is ₹ 8,000 or above plus other allowance. Salaried optometrists tend to earn more initially than optometrists who set up their own practices. However, ultimately those in private practice once established usually earn more.

Courses

- B.Sc. Ophthalmic Techniques (Hons.),
- B. Sc. Optometry
- Bachelor of Optometry and Vision Science (BOPTM),
- Bachelor's Degree in Optometry,
- Diploma in Opthalmic Assistant,
- Diploma in Opthalmology,
- Diploma in Optometrical Science (DOS),
- Diploma in Optometry,
- M.Ch. Opthalmology Certification Programme,
- Master of Optometry, and
- Optician and Refractionist Course.

Useful Contacts

The Indian Optometric Association is a registered body under the Tamil Nadu Societies Registration Act, 1978 and is registered with World Council of Optometry.

- **Indian Optometric Association**

  Several Opticians

  No. 7 Rosy Tower

  Nungambakkam High Road

  Chennai – 600034.

Top Ten Optometry Institutes in India

- **College of Optometry, Pune, Maharashtra**

  Courses : Bachelor in Clinical Optometry,
  Master of Optometry.
- **Yashwantrao Chavan Maharashtra Open University, Nashik, Maharashtra**

  Course : Bachelor of Science (Optometry).

- **Vinayaka Mission University, Salem, Tamil Nadu**
  Courses : Bachelor of Optometry,
  Diploma in Optometry.
- **Sri Ramachandra University, Chennai, Tamil Nadu**
  Course : Bachelor of Science-Optometry.
- **Manipal University, Manipal, Karnataka**
  Course : Bachelor in Clinical Optometry.
- **Elite School of Optometry, Chennai, Tamil Nadu**
  Courses : Bachelor of Science-Optometry,
  Master of Philosophy (Optometry).
- **Lotus College of Optometry, Mumbai, Maharashtra**
  Courses : Bachelor of Science-Optometry,
  Master of Science-Optometry.
- **Mother Teresa Para Medical College, Saharanpur, Uttar Pradesh**
  Course : Diploma in Optometry.

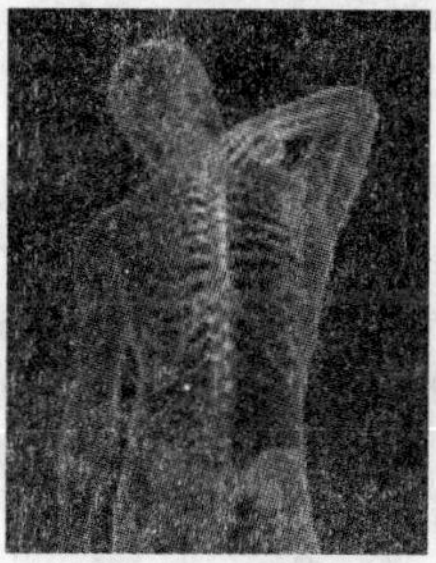

12.17 Orthopaedics

Meaning of the Word 'Orthopaedics'

The word 'orthopaedic' is a fusion of two Greek words namely *'orthos'* meaning 'straight or correct' and *'paideia'* meaning 'raising of children'. The French physician Nicolas Andry combined the terms to form the French *'orthopedique'*, which was later translated into English. Given the original Greek roots, the term means 'to straighten the child' and refers to the orthopaedist's specialisation in correcting crooked or broken bones. Jean-Andre Venel established the first orthopedic institute in 1780, which was the first hospital dedicated to the treatment of children's skeletal deformities. He is considered to be the father of orthopaedics.

What is Orthopaedics?

Orthopaedics is a medical specialty that focuses on the diagnosis, care and treatment of patients with disorders of the bones, joints, muscles, ligaments, tendons, nerves and skin. This includes, for example, broken bones, torn ligaments, some spinal injuries etc. The specialty which deals with musculo-skeletal system, gives animals and human beings the ability to move, by using the muscle and skeletal system. Those who specialise in this medical field are called Orthopaedist or Orthopaedic surgeons. Orthopaedic surgeons use a variety of surgical techniques such as lasers to remove torn cartilage and arthroscopic surgery for treating damaged joints.

Eligibility

To pursue a course in this field the candidate is required to complete MBBS course from any recognised university in India or equivalent. After the completion of MBBS course there is an all India level test for post graduation, qualifying which, the candidate becomes eligible for pursuing the course. Separate tests are conducted by some of the highly rated medical institutions like AIIMS, PGIMER and AFMC, Pune.

The courses in this specific field are MS in Orthopedics which is of three years duration, Diploma in Orthopaedics (D.Ortho.) of two years duration. Candidates with MBBS degree, who have registered permanently with Medical Council of India or any other State Medical Councils, are eligible to apply for these courses. One can further take up DNB, M.Ch. in super-specialties such as foot and ankle orthopaedics, orthopaedic sports and medicine, pediatricorthopedics, adult reconstructive orthopaedics, musculoskeletal oncology, orthopedic spine surgery, hand surgery and orthopaedic trauma.

Job Prospects and Career Options

The field of orthopaedics offers great career opportunities and the career development path for the orthopaedic surgeons is very bright. An Orthopaedist can start working with an established hospital either in public or private sector as per his choice. The other lucrative option is to open their own clinic and provide services to the patients. Many orthopaedic doctors opt to teach in universities and colleges or enter into research. Not only will doctors spend time in class rooms but they may have to attend seminars, conference and meetings. It's important for orthopaedic doctors to spend time reading medical journals and other periodicals to keep up to date on the latest technology and advancements in medicine.

They can also appear for Combined Medical Services Examination conducted by the Union Public Service Commission, Government of India for entry into central services such as railways, ordnance factories health service, central health service and municipal corporation of Delhi and the state provincial services examination conducted by the respective state provincial service commissions for entry into state services. The candidate can also join army or naval forces.

Orthopaedist can get jobs in reputed government hospitals like AIIMS and PGIMER, corporate hospitals like Fortis, Apollo and so on. They can also get jobs in rehabilitation centers established by sports and defence organisations.

Remuneration

Orthopaedics is one of the highest paying medical specialties. The salary depends on his/her reputation as well as the place where one is working. If we consider the income of orthopsedic surgeon with his own clinic, we can say that there is no upper limit to his remuneration. For those working in government hospitals, pay is much less than in private firms.

An orthopaedic surgeon in the initial stage gets a handsome salary of ₹ 20,000 – 25,000 per month. However, those at the senior level may get salary package around ₹ 15 lakh – 20 lakh per annum. Those working with hospitals and other government and private sectors may get lucrative benefits like incentives paid holidays, free insurance etc. Surgeons who specialise in spine surgery deserve the high salary range they receive as the street levels associated with their job is high.

Courses

- MS Orthopaedics
- Diploma in Orthopaedics (D. Ortho.), and
- DNB Orthopedics.

Best Orthopaedic Colleges in India

- **Saveetha University, Chennai, Tamil Nadu**

  Course: Master of Physiotherapy-Orthopaedics and Traumatology.

- **Thai Moogambigai Dental College and Hospital, Chennai, Tamil Nadu**

  Course: Master of Physiotherapy-Orthopaedics.

- **SRM University, Kanchipuram, Tamil Nadu**

  Courses: Master of Physiotherapy in Orthopaedics

  Master of Occupational Therapy in Orthopaedics

- **West Bengal University of Health Sciences, Salt Lake, West Bengal**

  Course: Diploma in Orthopaedics

- **Rajasthan University of Health Science, Jaipur, Rajasthan**

  Course : Master of Surgery-Orthopaedics.
- **RVS College of Physiotherapy, Coimbatore, Tamil Nadu**

  Course : Master of Physio-therapy (Advanced Physio-therapy in Orthopaedics).
- **PSG College of Physio-therapy, Chennai, Tamil Nadu**

  Course : Master of Physiotherapy in Orthopaedics.
- **MNR College of Physio-therapy, Hyderabad, Andhra Pradesh**

  Course : Master of Physio-therapy in Orthopaedics and Sports Physio-therapy.

12.18 Paediatrics

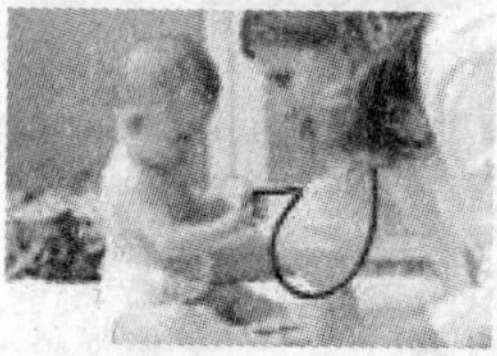

What is Paediatrics?

Pediatrics is a branch of medical science which deals with the health care of newborns, children and adolescents. In other words, it is a specialised area in medicine that focuses on diagnosis and treatment of children's diseases. Those who specialise in this medical field are called Paediatricians.

Division of the Field of Paediatrics

Paediatrics can be divided into two main fields :

- General paediatrics, and
- Paediatric sub-specialties.

A general paediatrician generally treats common illness and other diseases common to infants and children, whereas specialists identify interests in other areas as well. They can also super specialise in any of the following fields like endocrinology, gastroenterology, immunology and infectious diseases, oncology, clinical pharmacology, respiratory medicine, rheumatology and the like.

Eligibility

To become a Paediatrician, you have to first complete your 10+2 with science and then you have to appear the entrance examination to get admission for MBBS course into a medical college. After completing MBBS degree from any of the recognised medical colleges or universities, you must pursue MD (Doctor of Medicine) in Paediatrics. Then, you can start your career as a Paediatrician in India. You can further go for further specialisation in paediatric fields like endocrinology, gastroenterology, immunology and infectious diseases, oncology, clinical pharmacology, respiratory medicine and rheumatology. There is always a need for ongoing education for paediatricians as they must keep up with the trends and procedures within the field.

Job Prospects

Paediatrics has emerged as one of the most prominent career options in India. If you have a passion for children and patience to analyse their problems then a healthcare in paediatrics is suited for you. The demand for talented and proficient paediatricians is growing day by day as the number of hospitals is mushrooming and child birth is an ongoing process.

Career Options

Paediatricians or child specialists have many career paths that can be taken. They can work both in private and government hospitals as paediatricians on a regular basis. Another career path for paediatricians is working in clinics, medical centers and research laboratories. They can work as independent practitioners as well. They can enter into military service, railways and various other public sector medical departments. They can opt for teaching in medical colleges or training institutes.

Remuneration

There are many things that a paediatrician salary is dependent upon. This is based on years of experience, education, place and skills. There is also a salary discrepancy in different sectors like in non-governmental organisations and the private sector. In the government sector, per month pay package is around ₹ 50,000 for beginning level practitioners. In private sector, the equivalent packages are ₹ 60,000 – 70,000. In private practice, a doctor's earnings depend mainly upon his reputation. At the senior level, paediatricians get the income packages around ₹ 20,00,000 – 35, 00,000 per annum.

Indian Academy of Paediatrics

Kailas Darshan
Kennedy Bridge
Mumbai
Maharastra-400 007.
Phone: 022-23889565, 23887922, 23887906.
Website: www.iapindia.org/

Top Medical Colleges offering Paediatrics in India

- **Tamil Nadu Dr M.G.R Medical University, Chennai, Tamil Nadu**
  Courses : Master of Chirurgic – Paediatric Surgery,
  Doctor of Medicine-Paediatrics.
- **Medical College, Pune, Maharashtra**
  Courses : Diploma in Paediatrics,
  Doctor of Medicine-Paediatrics.
- **Kasturba Medical College, Manipal, Karnataka**
  Courses : Master of Chirurgical – Paediatric Surgery,
  Doctor of Medicine-Paediatrics.
- **Smt. N.H.L Municipal Medical College, Ahmedabad, Gujarat**
  Courses : Master of Chirurgical – Paediatric Surgery,
  Doctor of Medicine – Paediatrics.
- **Dr D.Y. Patel Medical College, Mumbai, Maharashtra**
  Courses : Diploma in Child Health (Paediatrics),
  Doctor of Medicine – Paediatrics.
- **MGM School of Health Management Studies, Mumbai, Maharashtra**
  Course : Diploma in Paediatrics.
- **Jawaharlal Nehru Medical College, Belgaum, Karnataka**
  Courses : Diploma in Paediatrics,
  Doctor of Medicine – Paediatrics.
- **Pravara Institute of Medical Sciences, Ahmednagar, Maharashtra**
  Course : Diploma in Paediatrics.

12.19 Pharmacology

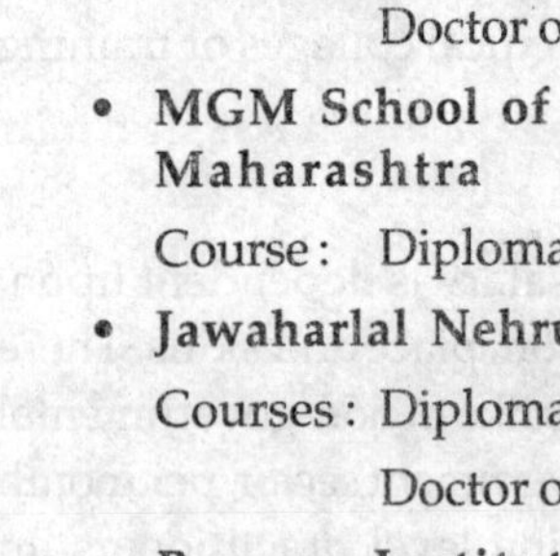

What is Pharmacology?

Pharmacy or Pharmacology is one of the main disciplines of biomedical science and the pharmaceutical industry. It is a profession responsible for the preparation, dispensing and appropriate use of medication and which provides services to achieve optimal therapeutic outcomes. A pharmacist's job is to prepare, mix, compound or dispense drugs and medicines, ointments, powder, pills, tablets and injections on the prescription of a medical practitioner, dentist or veterinarian.

Concerns of Pharmacology

Pharmacology is concerned with production of pharmaceutical products, development of the methods or processes of production and quality control. Those in research concern themselves with synthesis of new drugs (what is commonly referred to as molecules), new processes, clinical testing of the effects of such drugs on animals and humans and obtaining the required licence from the drug control authorities. A pharmacist is required to explain the mode and precautions regarding the use of medicines dispensed in hospital pharmacy prepare special formulations normally not available in the market, assist the physician in rendering necessary information about various drugs, their contra-indications, incompatibility etc.

Course Areas

The main courses in Pharmacy are the 2 years Diploma in Pharmacy (D.Pharm.), four years Bachelor of Pharmacy (B.Pharm.), two years Master of Pharmacy (M. Pharm.) and Ph. D. Programme. Admission to the Diploma in Pharmacy (D.Pharma) requires a pass in 10+2 or equivalent examination with physics, chemistry, mathematics or biology. Candidates who posses 10+2 with physics, chemistry, mathematics (PCM) or physics, chemistry, biology (PCB) or physics, chemistry, mathematics and biology are admitted to the four-years bachelors programme level (Bachelor of Pharmacy or B. Pharma). At bachelor level there is no specialisation.

At the master's level (M.Pharm.) specialisation is available in pharmaceutics, pharmacognosy, pharmaceutical chemistry and pharmaceutical engineering. And after M. Pharma candidates can go for Ph.D. programme in pharmaceutics, pharmacology, pharmaceutical chemistry, pharmaceutical marketing and management.

After obtaining a diploma or degree in pharmacy and registering with the state pharmacy council, it is possible to set up your own pharmacy or chemists and druggist shop to stock and sell medicines and dispense them according to doctors' prescription.

Job Prospects

India has a vast and growing pharmaceutical industry. Increasing number of hospitals, nursing homes and pharmaceutical companies all over the country is a clear indication of the growing scope in this area. Pharmacy offers reasonably good career opportunities both by way of jobs as well as in terms of starting your own business.

Career Options

The job avenues for a pharmacist are with pharmaceutical industry, government departments, universities, teaching hospitals, investigation and research institute etc. Within the pharmaceutical industry you might be involved in activities relating to the development, formulation, production or marketing of new drugs for clinical use. Drug control administration and armed forces also offer a wide range of opportunities to pharmacists. Appointments are also available in sale promotion work as medical representatives. As a Medical Representative, he keeps the medical practitioner informed about the new drugs and treatments developed by various pharmaceutical companies and thus indirectly promote their sales.

M. Pharma or Ph.D. holders are normally absorbed in research work, to develop new useful drugs, in laboratories and in production work in pharmaceutical industry and analysing them for purity and strength. Pharmacists can also take up teaching profession as professors and lecturers of pharmacy in colleges and universities.

Pharmacists are hired within the central and state government departments – the health protection branch of the department of Health and Welfare, the pest control division of Agriculture, the Department of National Defence, Provincial Research Councils and the Provincial Departments of agriculture or the environment. There is also an employment opportunity within the food and cosmetic industries or within any other industry that requires the assurance that new products are as safe and effective as possible. In government departments, a pharmacist maintains proper records according to various government acts governing the profession of pharmacy.

As a drug inspector or government analyst he is to make sure that drugs manufactured and sold are of standard quality.

A diploma or degree holder in pharmacy after registering with the state pharmacy council, can set up and run their own pharmacy or chemists and druggists shop to stock and sell medicines and dispense them according to doctor's prescriptions. In a retail pharmacy he has varied duties, including buying and selling of related items demanded by the public.

Remuneration

Pharmacy is a highly reputed job. In this field, monthly salary is according to the jobs, the pharmacist has taken up. The average starting salary for a pharmacist is around ₹ 4,000. Research scientists get

₹ 10,000 – 40,000 per month. Medical Representatives get ₹ 5,000 – 10,000 per month plus incentives, manufacturing pharmacists get ₹ 5,000 upwards, hospital pharmacists get ₹ 3,000 – 5,000 per month, government jobs ₹ 2,500–3,500 per month (basic) along with contributory provident fund, D.A., insurance, medical reimbursement and other allowances and benefits as per government rules.

Courses

- B.Sc. Pharmaceutical Technology,
- Bachelor of Pharmacy (B.Pharma),
- Diploma in Ayurvedic Pharmacy (DAP),
- Diploma in Pharmacy (D. Pharma),
- Diploma in Veterinary Pharmacy (DVP),
- Drug Store Management Course,
- Integrated Post Graduate Diploma in Clinical Research and Pharmaco-vigilance,
- M.Sc. Pharmaceutical Chemistry,
- Management Programme in Pharmacy,
- Master of Pharmacy (M. Pharma), and
- Post Graduate Diploma in Clinical Trial Management.

Top Institutes that offer courses in Pharmacy

In India we have about 200 degree colleges training more than 10-12 thousand students for B.Pharmacy degree and diploma. Here is a list of top and best B. Pharmacy and M. Pharmacy colleges in India.

- University Institute of Pharmaceutical Sciences, Punjab University.
- Manipal College of Pharmaceutical Sciences, Manipal.
- Bombay College of Pharmacy, Kalina, Mumbai.
- JSS College of Pharmacy, Ooty.
- University College of Pharmaceutical Science, Kakatiya University, Warrangal.
- L.M. College of Pharmacy, Ahmedabad.
- Department of Pharmaceutical Science, Dr H.S. Gour University, Sagar, MP.
- Institute of Chemical Technology (ICT), Mumbai (erstwhile UDCT).
- Pharmacy Group, BITS, Pilani.

12.20 Psychology

What is Psychology?

Psychology is the study of human mind and behavior. It is a systematic approach towards understanding a human person. As a profession, it enables students to apply the principles and theories of human behavior in solving real life problems. The study includes experiments, theories, personality tests, methods and techniques of identification of human problems, guidance and counselling and the like. To pursue the career of a psychologist, one should have a genuine desire to help other human beings. With increasing issues like stressful workplaces, increasing crime, global issues and many real life complexities, the field of psychology is gaining more attention.

The Work of a Psychologist

Psychologists study the processes, motives, reactions, feelings and nature of the human mind. Their treatment is based on changing the Behavioural patterns of the patients without medication. They do counselling and help people by bringing about changes in their thought process, thus improving their quality of life. Psychologists need not have a medical degree. But they have to study several years to specialise in various aspects of psychology. One can pursue psychology at the plus two level, graduate, post graduate and doctorate level. There are specialisations in any fields of psychology such as social psychology, child psychology, occupational psychology, clinical psychology, educational psychology and experimental psychology.

Psychologists teach, practise and do research or work in one of the many branches of applied psychology. They apply their knowledge and techniques to a wide range of endeavours including human services, management, education and law and sports.

Eligibility

- For bachelor's programme in psychology: 10+2.
- Post graduate courses in psychology: Bachelor's degree in psychology.
- For Ph. D./M.Phil.: PG or Diploma in psychology.

Duration

- Graduation in psychology is a three year programme.
- Post graduation courses in psychology are of two years duration

and during the course, specialisation in a special branch of psychology is possible.

- M. Phil. or Ph.D. is of two year duration.

Course Areas

Study of psychology includes a diverse range of activities such as the processes of thinking, learning and perceiving, remembering, forgetting, physiology of the nervous system, development of children, social relationships and their effect on personality development, mental disorders, applications of psychology to the study of psychology and some overlapping occurs between the different specialised branches. Good at science, mathematics critical reading and writing.

Job Prospects

Psychologists work in a variety of different settings including universities and colleges, primary and secondary schools, government agencies, private industry, hospitals, clinics, and private practices. They are also employed in social welfare organisations, research establishments, rehabilitation centers and prisons, child/youth guidance centres, advertising industry and in a variety of other set-ups.

Career Options

Career prospects in psychology depend on the area of specialisation. There is a variety of options for psychologists. They can specialise in various areas such as :

- **Clinical Psychologists :** Clinical psychologists work in counselingcenters, independent or group practices, hospitals, community health centres or clinics. They help mentally and emotionally disturbed clients adjust to life and may help medical and surgical patients deal with illnesses or injuries. Areas of specialisation within clinical psychology include health psychology, neuro psychology, and gyro-psychology.
- **Counselling Psychologists :** Counselling is the skill of helping normal people through discussion, to decide how best to cope in specific situations. Counselling psychologists deals with people who have serious emotional and personal problems. They use various techniques, including interviewing and testing, to advise people on how to deal with problems of everyday living.
- **Social Psychologists :** Social psychologists work with social organisations and institutions in research, systems design or other applied psychology fields. They seek to understand the nature and causes of individual behaviour with others and with the social environment.

- **Educational Psychologists :** They work in schools and colleges with teachers, students, parents and administrators to resolve learning and Behavioural problems. They may evaluate the effectiveness of academic programme, behaviour management procedures and other services provided in the school setting.
- **Industrial Psychologists :** Industrial psychologists work for business, industry or government. They apply psychological principles and research methods of the workplace to improve the working conditions and productivity of employees. They also advise companies on ways of getting consumers interested in products and services.
- **Research Psychologists :** As researchers, psychologists proceed like scientists. They investigate the physical, cognitive, emotional or social aspects of human behaviour. They use laboratory experiments and various kinds of tests, interviews, questionnaires and surveys. Prominent areas of study in experimental research include motivation, thought, attention, learning and memory, sensory and perceptual processes, effects of substance abuse and genetic and neurological factors affecting behaviour.
- **Development Psychologists :** The physiological, cognitive and social development takes place throughout life. Some specialise in behaviour during infancy, childhood and adolescence or changes that occur during maturity or old age.

Remuneration

The work of a professional psychologist is challenging and highly remunerative. Earnings depend on qualification, area of specialisation and experience. The highest-paying position is for psychologists having M.Phil. and Ph.D. degree. Remunerations in the corporate sector are the highest, though salaries vary according to the level of involvement and the job profile. At the entry level the remuneration varies approximately from ₹ 8,000 – 15,000. Established consultants in any of the fields of specialisation can earn at an average between ₹ 15,000 – 50,000 or even more. Those who are in private practice have much more earnings.

- B.A. Psychology (Hons.),
- B.A. Psychology,
- Certificate Course in Child Psychology,
- Integrated M.Phil. Ph.D. in Psychology,
- M.A. Psychology,

- M. Phil. Psychology,
- M. Phil. Rehabilitation Psychology,
- M. Sc. Applied Psychology,
- M. Sc. Holistic Psychology,
- M. Sc. Psychology,
- Ph.D. Clinical Psychology,
- Ph.D. Psychology,
- Post Doctorate in Psychology,
- Post Graduate Diploma in CAH Psychology,
- Post Graduate Diploma in Child Psychology Care and Management,
- Post Graduate Diploma in Clinical and Community Psychology (CCP),
- Post Graduate Diploma in Counseling Psychology, and
- Post Graduate Diploma in Human Resource Development (HRD) Psychology.

Top Ten Psychology Institutes in India

- **Amity Institute of Psychology and Allied Sciences, Noida, Uttar Pradesh**

  Courses : B.A. (Hons.) Applied Psychology,

  M.A. Applied Psychology, Counselling psychology,

  Post Graduate Diploma in Counselling Psychology, Family and Child Psychology, and

  Master of Philosophy-Psychology (Child and Adolescent Psychology).

- **Government College of Educational Psychology and Guidance, Jabalpur**

  Courses : M.A. Applied Psychology,

  Post Graduate Diploma in Guidance and Counselling.

- **University of Delhi, Delhi**

  Courses : B.A. (Hons.) Psychology, Applied Psychology,

  M.A. Psychology, Applied Psychology, and

  Certificate Course in Counselling and Guidance.

- **Deen Dayal Upadhaya Gorakhpur University, Uttar Pradesh**

  Courses : M.A. Psychology, and M.Phil. Psychology,

- **University of Madras**

  Courses : M.Phil. Psychology, and

  Post Graduate Diploma in Parent Counselling Psychology.

- **University of Calcutta**

  Courses : M.A./M.Sc. Psychology,

  P.G. Diploma in Cognitive and Behavioural Existential Counselling,

  M.Phil. Clinical Psychology, and

  Ph.D. Psychology/Applied Psychology.

- **Benaras Hindu College**

  Courses : B.A./B.Sc. Psychology, and

  Post Graduate Diploma in Counselling and Psychotherapy.

- **Lady Shri Ram College for Women**

  Courses : B.A. (Hons.) Applied Psychology, and

  Post Graduate Diploma in Conflict Transformation and Peace Building.

- **S.N.D.T. Women's University, Mumbai**

  Courses : M.A. Psychology.

- **Padmashree Dr. D.Y. Patil Arts, Commerce and Science College**

  Courses : B.A. Psychology, and

  M.A. Psychology (Clinical).

12.21 Physiotherapy

What is Physiotherapy?

Physiotherapy may be defined as a science that seeks to improve movement dysfunction, promote optimal health and functions of the human body. Physiotherapy helps in optimal functioning of the body. It involves the assessment, maintenance, restoration of the physical function and performance of the body and isstrongly recommended for people with degenerative disorders, the

physically challenged, sports people and those suffering from arthritis and neurological disorders. This preventive and remedial procedure is very often used as a supplement with oral medicines. It could also include heat radiation, water therapy, massages, diathermy, traction and other procedures.

The Work of Physiotherapists

Physiotherapists are as essential as doctors in helping recover and rehabilitate a patient from a state of incapacity due to genetic defect or the result of an accident or an illness. They must have a thorough knowledge of the human anatomy and the way the bones, muscles and nerves move. Physiotherapists treat a wide range of ailments and so specialisation is possible in areas such as paediatrics, geriatrics, orthopaedics, sports physical therapy, neurology, clinical electro-physiological and cardio-pulmonary therapy.

Techniques employed by Physiotherapists

Physiotherapists use various therapeutic intervention techniques to treat a patient. Some of them are manual therapy, TENS (Transcutaneous Electrical Nerve Stimulation used to control pain), ultrasound technique, electrical muscle stimulation, manipulation, acupuncture, etc. Although the work of a physiotherapist may tend to be physically very strenuous as it involves physically lifting and supporting patients, their profession brings with it much satisfaction, since it involves relieving patients of pain and helping them recover from specific physical ailments.

Eligibility and Course Areas

The basic eligibility for courses in Physiotherapy is 10+2 passed or equivalent examination with physics, chemistry, biology and English. At least 50 per cent of marks should be secured in each of these subjects. Age limit for the candidates is 17 years.

Selection

The admission to institutes is through entrance examination. There is a Common Entrance Test (CET) for the course in Bachelor of Physiotherapy (BPT). Admission is based mainly on CET scores.

Duration

There are both degrees level and short-term courses available in physiotherapy but all of them may not be recognised by the government. Degree level courses in physiotherapy generally range from three to four years. For a degree level course, the last six months involve an internship period at a hospital.

The courses are designed to give the students a basic understanding of the human body based on medical sciences, training in understanding the procedures for therapy and the related skill training. The course contents include anatomy, physiology, pathology, pharmacology, psychology, medical and surgical conditions, bio-mechanics, kinesiology, disability prevention, rehabilitation and other subjects. A major part of the course is practical in nature including an internship period where students work under the supervision of professionals at various hospitals and institutions.

Job Prospects and Career Options

Employment opportunities for physiotherapists are tremendous as it is a career where the demand exceeds supply. A physiotherapist could be employed in the rehabilitation departments, municipal corporations and private bodies. Their demand in medical institutions is increasing since physiotherapy plays an important role in the treatment of patients with muscular and cerebral problems. Like all other medical and paramedical professionals, physiotherapists can work in hospitals, orthopaedic departments, rehabilitation centres for the differently abled, schools for the mentally retarded and physically disabled children, health institutions and defence medical establishments. Physiotherapists can also opt for teaching, while those with adequate capital can establish private clinics of their own.

The demand for physiotherapists in the country as well as abroad is immense. They are in great demand in USA, Canada and Australia.

Remuneration

The initial remuneration of physiotherapists in government hospitals varies between ₹ 5000 – 7000. But the private hospitals offer a relatively better package. Most well run private hospitals offer a starting pay around ₹ 9,500 which could go up to ₹ 12,000 per month. The remuneration for established private practitioners can be almost ₹ 20,000 – 40,000 per month.

Courses

- B.Sc. Physiotherapy,
- Bachelor of Physiotherapy (BPT),
- Diploma in Physiotherapy (DPT),
- Master of Physiotherapy (MPT),
- Master of Physiotherapy in Hand Conditions,
- Master of Physiotherapy in Neurology,

- Master of Physiotherapy in Orthopaedics,
- Master of Sports Physiotherapy (MSPT), and
- Post Graduate Diploma in Physiotherapy and Nutrition.

Top Physiotherapy Colleges in India

- Dolphin (PG) Institute of Bio-medical and Natural Sciences, Dehradun.
- Amar Jyoti Institute of Physiotherapy, Karkardooma.
  Vikas Marg, Delhi-110092.
- Amity School of Physiotherapy, Yasho Bhavan, Okhla Centre.
  Opposite Don Bosco Technical Institute, Okhla Road, New Delhi-110025.
- Acharya Institute of Health Sciences, Cholanagar
  RT Nagar Post, Bangalore 560032.
- Al-Ameen College of Physiotherapy, Houser Road
  Near Lalbagh Main Gate, Bangalore-560027.
- Bangalore Medical College, Fort, Bangalore-560002.
- Banarasidas Chandiwala Institute of Physiotherapy
  Chandiwala Estate, Maa Anandmai
  Ashram Marg, Kalkaji, New Delhi-110019.
- College of Healthcare and Pharmacology, B-II/100, MCIE
  Mathura, New Delhi-44.
- Padmashree College of Physiotherapy, Nagarbhavi Circle
  Circle, Nagarbhavi, Bangalore-560072.
- Shekar College of Physiotherapy and Rehabilitation,
  81, Bull Temple Road, Bangalore-560019.
- St. Joan's College of Vocational Studies, School of Physiotherapy
  B-85, Defence Colony, New Delhi-110024.
- Pandit Deendayal Upadhyaya Institute for the Physically Handicapped, Delhi.
- Dr B.R. Ambedkar Medical College, Bangalore.
- Florence College of Physiotherapy Bangalore, Karnataka.
- Oxford College of Physiotherapy Bangalore, Karnataka.

12.22 Prosthetics and Orthotics

What is Prosthetics and Orthotics?

Prosthetics and Orthotics is a medical and engineering based healthcare

profession which deals with rehabilitation of physically handicapped individuals who suffer from limb malfunctions or abnormalities or absence or loss of limbs or other body parts. The loss of body parts may have been the result of an accident or mishap or amputation owing to medical conditions like diabetes or gangrene or cancer or in some cases the defect may be congenital, i.e., people are born with this handicap where a limb/a body part may be missing. Such a condition prevents a person from leading a normal life. There may be also cases where people suffering from conditions like polio or muscular degeneration need an external support for movement and strength to go about their day to day activities.

Who are Prosthetists and Orthotists?

Prosthetists and Orthotists are professionals who help people suffering from neuromotor and musculo-skeletal disorders such as the ones mentioned above, to return to a normal life by using their skills and advanced medical technology. In a nutshell, though the fields of prosthetics and orthotics appear to be autonomous, the professionals usually work as part of multi-skilled teams. Their clientele ranges from small children to adults and elderly population suffering from age-related injuries and illnesses.

What is Prosthesis?

A Prosthesis of what is commonly known as an artificial limb is an extension or replacement of a missing or damaged body part. It can be an artificial leg, an entire hand or just the palm of hands or feet etc. Those professionals who deal with prosthesis are called Prosthetists.

What is Orthosis?

An Orthosis is a device which can give support to weak limbs or help to correct a deformity. It is derived from the Greek word *'ortho'* meaning *'to straighten'*. Such devices include braces, splints and special footwear which assist movement and tend to lessen the amount of discomfort. Orthotists are professionals concerned with manufacture and fitting of Orthosis.

Eligibility and Course Areas

The minimum educational requirement to become a prosthetist and orthotist is a four and half years degree in prosthetics and orthotics from a recognised university. After graduation, in order to practise as prosthetist and orthotist in India candidates must register with Rehabilitation Council of India.

For admission to four and a half years bachelor's degree course in prosthetics and orthotics the candidates must have cleared 10+2 with physics, chemistry, mathematics and biology. While, candidates aspiring for a master's degree in prosthetics and orthotics should have a bachelor's degree in prosthetics and orthotics. Candidates with diploma qualifications are employed as technicians.

The diploma courses are usually of two years duration. The eligibility requirement for a diploma course is that the candidates should have passed 10+2 with science subjects (physics, chemistry, mathematics, biology) or they should have passed in 10+2 in the vocational stream in the trade of machinist or 10+2 and ITI certificate in the trade of fitter/turner/machinist/tool or die maker. Candidates with a pass in the final diploma examinations conducted by the Board of Technical Education of the state government in mechanical/electrical/ or electronics engineering are also eligible.

For most of the courses the age criteria is that the candidate should have completed 17 years of age in the year of admission. The maximum age is usually 23 years, however, it may vary according to reservation stipulations as formulated by the government or according to the rules of individual institutions.

Selection

The selection of the candidates is made on the basis of merit. Those candidates who satisfy the eligibility criteria as regards age and educational qualifications are usually required to take an entrance test for the various courses. The tests usually consist of objective type questions based on subjects – biology, physics, chemistry, mathematics, english and general Knowledge. The questions are based on senior secondary school certificate (10+2) curriculum.

Course Areas

The course is both engineering and medical based. The syllabi include classes in basic life sciences, basic engineering, prosthetics and orthotics workshop technology, orthopaedics, computer studies, physical medicine and rehabilitation, mobility aid, upper and lower limb prosthetics and orthotics, spinal orthotics. Besides theory classes, candidates are given extensive clinical practice and lab work so as to make them competent and well-qualified in this field.

Internship : After successful completion of final year examinations, students have to undergo a six month internship which comprises of clinical practice, case presentation and fabrication of different kinds of orthoses and prostheses.

Job Prospects and Career Options

The nature of work of a prosthetist and orthotist involves various stages. To start with a prosthetist and orthotist professional works as part of a clinical team which comprises of orthopedics, psychiatrists, nurses and related medical professionals. They have to study records and reports of a patient regarding the suitable orthotic/prosthetic aid required and then have to communicate appropriate information regarding this to the patients and their families.

They then have to take measurements and casts required for the proper fabrication and fitting of prosthetics and orthotics. They have to formulate designs and select materials and components. For making the aids, all these require detailed studies as the orthotic and prosthetic requirements of patients vary with the nature of disability, their body type, their working and living conditions etc. In short, the prosthesis and orthosis have to be custom made.

They then have to fit these aids and also teach their patients and their families, the use of these orthotic and prosthetic aids. They have to ensure that the fitting and alignment of the aids are proper and do not cause discomfort to the patients. Their work does not end here. They have to follow-up procedures, maintenance and replacement of the orthotic and prosthetic aids. Those involve in training and education has to supervise and conduct education and training of prosthetics and orthotics students up to undergraduate level. They have to update their skills from time to time.

Prosthetist and orthotist professional can work in hospitals, clinics, laboratories, work room and fitting rooms, device manufacturing companies, rehabilitation departments of hospitals and government agencies, ambulatory care services and special treatment facilities like arthritis centres. Teaching and research and development are other options available to them.

Prosthetist and orthotist professionals can be employed as technologists, consultants, prosthetists and orthotists and in the supervisory level as technicians or assistants. With upgrading of skills and considerable amount of job experience they may become Head of the Department. Those in the teaching field can become Instructors and lecturers. Yet others can join R&D cells of government organisations and MNCs as researchers. Trained professionals can also start their own manufacturing units.

Remuneration

Orthotists and prosthetists usually get a basic pay in the range of ₹ 8,000 – 15,000 initially plus other allowances. Those with experience and better qualification can earn upwards of ₹ 15,000. Orthotic and prosthetic technicians have a pay range of ₹ 8,000 – 10,000 per month. Those in teaching field have salaries according to UGC norms.

Courses

- B. Sc. Prosthetics and Orthotics,
- Bachelor in Prosthetics and Orthotics,
- Certificate Course in Prosthetics and Orthotics,
- Diploma in Prosthetics and Orthotics Engineering (DPOE), and
- Master in Prosthetics and Orthotics.

Useful Contacts

- **All India Institute of Physical Medicine and Rehabilitation (AIIPMR)**

  Haji Ali, K. Khadye Marg, Mahalaxmi,
  Mumbai, Maharashtra-400004.

  Phone: 91-22-4964331/32, 4964340/41.

  Website: www.aiipmr.gov.in.

- **Chakradhara Institute of Rehabilitation Sciences**

  F 10, B.J.B. Nagar, Bhubaneshwar, Orissa.

  Phone: 0674-2433677, 9437014577.

  Website: www.rehabsciences.org.

- **Indian Association of Prosthetists and Orthotists**

  A-4/436, Paschim Vihar, New Delhi-110063.

  Website: www.iapo.co.in.

- **Institute of Rehabilitation Medicine**

  KK Nagar, Chennai-600 083.

  Phone: 24891687, 24891668.

- **National Institute of Orthopedically Handicapped**

  (Under Ministry of Social Justice and Empowerment, Govt. of India)

  B.T Road, Bon-Hooghly, Calcutta-700090.

  Website: www.india-future,com/nioh/courses.html.

- **Rehabilitation Council of India**

  B-22, Qutab Institutional Area

  New Delhi-110 016.

  Phone: 91-11-26532816, 26534287.

  Fax: 91-11-26534291.

  Website: www.rehabcouncil.nic.in.

12.23 Psychiatry

What is Psychiatry?

Psychiatry is an important branch of medical profession concerned with the study and treatment of mental illness. It deals with mental,

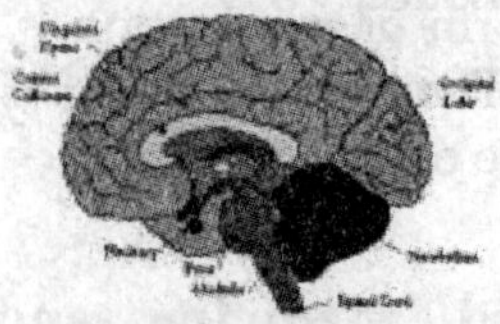

emotional and Behavioural disorders in a person. In psychiatry, medical therapies are applied to attack the organic source of the disease. After the physical and Behavioural symptoms are diagnosed, drugs and other means are used for treatment.

Who is a Psychiatrist?

A psychiatrist is a physician who specialises in the diagnosis and treatment of mental health problems, illness and emotional disorders. They look after patients with mental problems such as depression and schizophrenia. Treatment approaches may be more biologically based. The demand for psychiatrists is increasing with the increasing mental tension and stress arising from modern lifestyles. To become a psychiatrist, one should attend the medical school and receive an M.D. degree after MBBS. One could also do a Diploma in Psychiatric Medicine (DPM) from a recognised educational institute to become a qualified psychiatrist.

Eligibility

Doctors who have successfully completed the entire MBBS programme are eligible for specialisation in psychiatry. They may either do a postgraduate course (MD) in psychiatry or a diploma in psychiatric medicine (DPM). Besides MD and DPM, The National Board of Examinations conducts a programme called Diploma of National Board Exam (DNB). The DNB is considered to be equivalent to MD degree.

Duration

The Doctorate (MD) course in psychiatry is of three years duration. The person doing MD has to write a thesis on a particular topic under the guidance of a supervisor. The DPM is of two years duration. Thesis does not have to be written in DPM.

Course Areas

The subjects taught in the MD programme include psychology, anatomy, physiology and bio-chemistry of the brain, neurology and neuro-surgery. The course includes practical training at mental hospitals. Special aspects of psychology such as child psychiatry, community psychiatry, social psychiatry, forensic psychiatry and preventive psychiatry also form a part of the curriculum.

Job Prospects

Psychiatry offers a wide range of job opportunities within its subspecialties. The career of a psychiatrist is becoming important because of arising mental problems in the society. The profession of the psychiatrists begins with the diagnosis of the patient's problems, followed by treatment which could take the form of medication, counseling, psychotherapy or electrotherapy. They make use of techniques such as hypnosis and abreaction for the treatment of their patients.

Psychiatrists always work with occupational therapists and social workers for the rehabilitation of their patients, helping them to resume their normal activities.

Career Options

Psychiatrists can seek employment in regular hospitals as well as in mental hospitals. They are free to set up their own private clinics. They can work as counselors in large-scale industries, rehabilitation centres dealing with drug addiction, alcoholism and mental problems. Apart from these, psychiatrists also often work as counsellors in institutions including schools, colleges and hospitals and health centres.

Many private nursing homes and polyclinics employ psychiatrists to attend to the psychological problems arising from various medical, surgical, cardiac and gynecological cases. Psychiatrists specialised in children's problems and deal with juvenile delinquents and they can work in children's rehabilitation centres. Psychiatrists are often required to work in the courts and prisons where they are required to deal with person's suing for divorce and other such matters.

Remuneration

In the government sector, remuneration is fixed for various scales and the initial level is approximately in the range of ₹ 8,000 – 15,000 per month plus allowances. With a few years of experience, one can earn between ₹ 2,20,598 to 11,74,457 and without more years of experience the salary continues to soar higher and higher. Private practitioners can earn a lot of money. On one sitting, they charge ₹ 1,000 or more per hour for counselilng.

Top Colleges Offering MD Psychiatry in India

- **West Bengal University of Health Sciences, Salt Lake, West Bengal**

  Courses : Doctor of Medicine-Psychiatry,
  Diploma in Psychiatry.

- **Tamil Nadu Dr M.G.R. Medical University, Chennai, Tamil Nadu**

  Course : Doctor of Medicine Psychiatry.

- **Sri Ramachandra University, Chennai, Tamil Nadu**

  Courses : Doctor of Medicine Psychiatry.
  Doctor of Philosophy (Clinical Medicine) Psychiatry.

- **Rajasthan University of Health Science-Jaipur, Rajasthan**

  Course : Doctor of Medicine Psychiatry.

- **Dr. D.Y. Patil University, Pune, Maharashtra**

  Course : Doctor of Medicine Psychiatry.

- **Central Institute of Psychiatry, Ranchi, Jharkhand**

  Courses : Master of Doctor Psychiatry.
  Master of Philosophy Psychiatric Social Work.

- **Dayanand Medical College and Hospital, Ludhiana, Punjab**

  Course : Doctor of Medicine Psychiatry.

- **MGM School of Health Management Studies, Mumbai, Maharashtra**

  Course : Doctor of Medicine Psychiatry.

- **Ranchi Institute of Neuro-Psychiatry and Allied Sciences (RINPAS), Ranchi, Jharkhand.**

12.24 Radiography

What is Radiography?

Correct diagnosis is important for providing exact treatment for a disease. For some ailments it is not possible to find out the diseases by the symptoms alone. Radiography is used to diagnose the ailment and diseases of the internal and hidden parts of the body using X-ray,

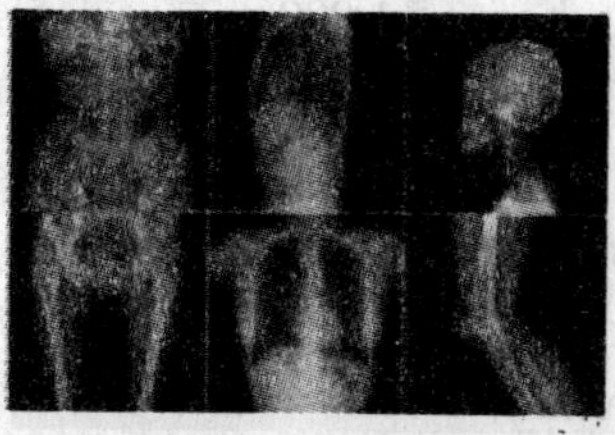

fluoroscopy, ultrasound (sonography), CT Scan (Computer Tomography), MRI (Magnetic Resonance Imaging), angiography, PET (Positron Emission Tomography) etc. PET is a nuclear medicine medical imaging, a branch of medicine and medical imaging that uses unsealed radioactive substances in diagnosis and therapy, which produces a three dimensional image of the functional processes in the body.

Radiography is concerned with operating radio imaging machines such as X-ray and interpreting results. It also involves treatment of cancers and tumors with radiation.

Who is a Radiographer?

Radiographer also known as Radiologic technologist is an important part of a medical team. Radiographer's starts states when some kind of doubt falls in doctor's mind, or when he wants to make his observation hundred per cent sure. Then he falls on the technology that the radiographer is apt to deal with. Correct diagnosis is important for providing exact treatment for a disease as it is not possible for some ailments to diagnose the diseases by the symptoms alone.

Two types of Radiography

The two types of Radiography are Diagnostic Radiography and Therapeutic Radiography. The responsibility of a diagnostic radiographer is to explain the procedure to the patients, prepare them for the tests and operate the machine and do the maintenance of equipment and records. They also assist physicians in performing procedures such as myelograms (an examination to detect injuries, cysts or tumors in the spinal cord) and surgeons in the operating room with portable X-ray machines or flouroscopic machines.

Therapeutic radiography or radiotherapy is now being used in the treatment and diagnosis of a large number of disease including cancer, tumors and ulcers. A therapy radiographer use radiation in highly controlled conditions in the treatment of tumor. Exact amount of radiation will shrink the tumor.

The Need for Radiographer Professionals

The Importance of radiographer professionals in the field of radiography is increasing. A radiographer (also called Radiologic technologist) have to handle the equipments and upgrade their skills now and then as technology advances. More sophisticated newer machines are coming up and experts in this career are less, there is an increase in the need for radiographers.

Eligibility and Course Areas

Those aspiring to make a career in this field should have a real interest in the science subjects such as biology, physiology and anatomy. The courses for radiography start at the graduate level. There are also one year certificate courses available. There are some institutes which conduct diploma in diagnostic radiography and radiotherapy of two years duration.

There are degree courses such as B.Sc. in Radiography, B.Sc. (Hons.) in Medical Technology in Radiography. The duration for the graduate programme is three years. Candidates who have passed their 10+2 or equivalent with 50 per cent marks in mathematics, physics, and chemistry are eligible for entry into the course.

Job Prospects and Career Options

Radiographers are required in large numbers in nursing homes, hospitals, diagnostic centres and super specialty hospitals. The job of a radiographer also covers areas like medicine, research and teaching. The field of nuclear medicine and photography are also open to X-ray technicians and radiographers. Radiographers have to make high quality images which in turn will help to diagnose disease and injury. They are employed in the X-ray and ultrasound departments of medical institutions and clinics.

Radiographers have to work in diagnostic imaging department, intensive care unit, operation theatre along with doctors and other hospital staff. In short they have to work as a team.

The Job Profiles under Radiography are :

- **Radio Diagnosis:** It is the method of diagnosing the patient's illness with the help of X-ray, ultrasound or other such equipment.
- **Radio Therapy:** A therapy radiographer treats patients with tumor, using radiation in highly controlled conditions.
- **Radiation Protection:** Specialists in this area monitor the levels of radiation exposure and thereby ensure that no one is over-exposed to these radiations, which could prove to be extremely harmful.

Remuneration

Radiographer gets reasonable salary in government and private hospitals, clinics and diagnostic centres and so on. In the government establishments, medical technologists get a starting salary of approximately ₹ 6,000 per month. X-ray technicians get a starting salary of ₹ 5,000 – 15,000 per month. Junior occupational therapists may initially draw salaries ranging between ₹ 4,000 and 8,000 per month. Remuneration increases with the rank and experience. In the private sector, salaries are a lot higher.

Courses

- B.Sc. Medical Technology in Radiology (Hons.),
- B.Sc. Radiography,
- Bachelor of Medical Radio Diagnosis and Imaging Technology (BMRIT),
- Bachelor of Medical Radiotherapy Technology (BMRT),
- Certificate Course in Radiography,
- Certificate Course in Radiography Diagnostic,
- Certificate Course in Radiological Assistant,
- Diploma in Radio diagnostic Technology,
- Diploma in Radiography and Radiotherapy,
- Post Graduate Diploma in Radio Diagnosis and Imaging Sciences,
- Post Graduate Diploma in Radio Therapy Technology,
- Post Graduate Diploma in X-ray Radiography and Ultrasonography.

Top Medical Colleges in India for Radiology

- **Moti Lal Nehru Medical College, Allahabad, Uttar Pradesh**

  Courses : Diploma in Medical Radiology and Electrology,
  Doctor of Medicine-Radiology.

- **Postgraduate Institute of Medical Education and Research, Chandigarh, Punjab**

  Courses : Master of Science Medical Technology (Radiology),
  Bachelor of Science Medical Technology (X-ray).

- **Tamil Nadu Dr M.G.R. Medical University, Chennai, Tamil Nadu**

  Courses : Master of Dental Surgery Oral Medicine and Radiology,
  Master of Science Medical Sociology.

- **B.J. Medical College, Ahmedabad, Gujarat**

  Courses : Diploma in Radiology Technician,
  Doctor of Medicine in General Medicine.

- **Gandhi Medical College, Hyderabad, Andhra Pradesh**

  Courses : Doctor of Medicine Radiology,
  Bachelor of Medicine and Bachelor of Surgery.

- **Shri Bhausaheb Hire Government Medical College, Dhule, Maharashtra**

  Course : Diploma in Medical Radiology and Electrology.

- **Al-Bijapur, Karnataka**

  Course : Diploma in Medical Radiology.

- **Gajara Raja Medical College (GRMC), Gwalior, Madhya Pradesh**

  Course : Doctor of Medicine in Radiology.

12.25 Speech Pathology and Audiology

What are Speech Pathology and Audiology?

Speech pathology and audiology are allied health careers where professionals are qualified by special training, education, skills and experience to provide health care service and treatment. While the field is an allied health field, the practitioners are not physicians but rather known specifically as speech pathologists and audiologists. Speech language pathology and audiology are distinct disciplines, but are so interrelated that to be fully competent in either, one should be familiar with both. Both deal with speech, language and hearing impairments that disrupt the ability of the sufferer to communicate and interact in various social situations.

The Role of Speech Pathologists and Audiologists

Speech Pathologists and Audiologists are concerned with the prevention, identification and rehabilitation of children and adults with communication disorders and hearing impairment. Audiologists examine people of all ages and identify symptoms of hearing loss, auditory, balance and related sensory and neural problems. They use specialised equipments like audiometers, computers and other testing devices to evaluate and estimate the impact of auditory and balance problems on the client's daily life. Audiologists then use the results from these tests to prepare a diagnosis and design a course of treatment by using remedial measure and rehabilitation strategies depending on what the situation demands.

Eligibility

To practise audiology, professionals need to have bachelor's/master's degree in Audiology and be registered with Indian Speech and Hearing Association (ISHA) or Rehabilitation Council of Indian (RCI). For under-graduate courses the applicants should have passed the pre-university course or 10+2 course or they may conduct specific entrance tests to gauge the merit and aptitude of the aspirants. Admission to the two year post-graduate courses requires a graduation in speech language pathology and audiology. Besides, the under-graduate/post-graduate courses, several institutes offer diploma courses of varying durations.

Course Areas

University courses in speech language pathology and audiology include acoustics, anatomy, assessment, counseling, hearing disorders, hearing aids, language development and disorders, linguistics, neurology and neuro-physiology, non-vocal communication, parent training, psychology, phonetics, speech disorders, statistics, stuttering, voice disorders and a variety of specific areas (*e.g.* Autism). The courses and clinical practice cover the development, disorders and the training or retraining of human communication in all its aspects.

Job Prospects and Career Options

Audiologic treatment may include examining and cleaning the ear canal, fitting and dispensing hearing aids and fitting and programming cochlear implants. It also includes counselling on adjusting to hearing loss, training on the use of hearing instruments and teaching communication strategies for use in a variety of environments.

The job of speech therapist includes diagnosing communication disorders like planning and implementing treatment in language, speech and voice and swallowing disorders. It also includes educating and counseling individuals, families, co-workers, educators etc. Certified speech language pathology professionals can find employment in hospitals, rehabilitation centres, nursing care facilities, industry, home health agencies, long-term care facilities, research labs, centers for persons with developmental disabilities, public or private schools, private practice, community clinics, college/university clinics, health department, state or government agencies, adult day care facilities and business.

Remuneration

The gross emoluments may sum up to ₹ 15,000 – 25,000 per month. Those in the teaching field may earn between ₹ 9,000 – 20,000 per month. For lecturers the pay scale lies between ₹ 14,000 – 40,000 per month.

Courses

- B. Sc. Hearing, Language and Speech,
- B. Sc. Speech and Hearing,
- B. Sc. Audiology and Speech Language pathology (B.A.S.L.P),
- Bachelor of Speech Pathology and Audiology,
- Diploma in Hearing, Language and Speech (DHLS),
- M.Sc. Speech and Hearing,
- Master in Audiology and Speech Language Pathology (MASLP).

Useful Contacts

- **Rehabilitation Council of India**

  B-22, Qutab Institutional Area, New Delhi-110 016.

  Phone: 91-11-26532816.

  Website: www.rehabcouncil.nic.in.
- **Indian Speech and Hearing Association**

  C/o AIISH, Manasangangothri, Mysore-570 006, Karnataka.

  Phone: 0821-2514449. Website: www.ishaindia.org.
- **Ali Yavar Jung National Institute for the Hearing Handicapped**

  K.C. Marg, Bandra Reclamation, Bandra (W), Mumbai-400050.

  Phone: 022-2640 0215/0228.

  Website: www.ayjnihh.nic.in.

Best Colleges for Studying Speech Pathology and Audiology

- **Sri Ramachandra University, Chennai, Tamil Nadu**

  Courses: Bachelor of Science – Audiology and Speech-Language Pathology.

  Master of Science – Audiology and Speech-Language Pathology.
- **College of Audiology and Speech Language Pathology, Pune, Maharashtra**

  Courses: Bachelor of Audiology and Speech-Language Pathology,

Masters in Audiology and Speech-Language Pathology.

- **Osmania University, Hyderabad, Andhra Pradesh**

  Courses : Bachelor of Science – Audio, Speech and Language Pathology.

  Master of Science – Audio, Speech and Language Pathology.

- **National Institute of Speech and Hearing, Thiruvananthapuram, Kerala**

  Courses : Bachelor of Audiology and Speech-Language Pathology,

  Masters in Audiology and Speech-Language Pathology.

- **West Bengal University of Health Sciences, Salt Lake, West Bengal**

  Courses : Bachelor of Audiology and Speech-Language Pathology,

  Doctor of Medicine – Pathology.

- **Father Muller Medical College, Mangalore, Karnataka**

  Course : Bachelor of Science – Audiology and Speech-Language Pathology.

- **Holy Cross College, Tiruchirapalli, Tamil Nadu**

  Course : Bachelor of Science – Audiology, Speech and Language Pathology.

- **J.M. Institute of Speech and Hearing, Patna, Bihar**

  Courses : Bachelor of Science – Audiology and Speech-Language Pathology (BASLP),

  Bachelor of Special Education (Mental Retardation) through distance mode (B.Ed.SE-DE).

12.26 Toxicology

What is Toxicology?

Toxicology is the science which deals with toxic properties of substances that involves the study of the effects that toxins or chemicals have on humans, animals, plants and other living organisms. Toxicologist is

one who explores the effects of chemicals on living organisms. The field studies the harmful effects of drugs, environmental contaminants and naturally occurring substances. Toxicology covers two main areas – one deals with the effects that toxic materials have on humans and the other deals with their impact on the environment.

Eligibility

To become a toxicologist one must take science stream for plus-two. After that one can opt for a bachelor's degree in botany, chemistry, zoology, bio-chemistry, medicine, veterinary science, pharmacy, bio-chemistry, bio-technology, micro-biology, environmental biology or some other life science based discipline.

For students interested in entering the field of toxicology, a bachelor of science degree in Toxicology is the minimum requirement. After bachelor's one can go for master of science in Toxicology (M.Sc. Toxicology). There are various specialisations in Toxicology and each one requires a specific background in some or the other subject. Jamia Hamdard, Delhi, Department of Toxicology is one of the few universities in India to offer a master's degree in general Toxicology.

Job Prospects and Career Options

Many industries employ toxicologists to assist in evaluating the safety of their products. Toxicologists work as consultants in companies which deal with food, chemical or cosmetic products. Numerous career avenues for toxicologists exists in chemical, food, pharmaceutical and environment related industries; in teaching and research and in government organisations dealing with regulation of chemical usage. Bio-technology and pharmaceutical industries are the largest employers of toxicologists. Pharmacovigilance (monitoring and preventing harmful effects of medicines) which is gaining prominence in India is expected to absorb more toxicologists. Toxicologists can work for epidemiological surveys done by health authorities.

Depending on the area of work Toxicologists can be divided into eight distinct groups :

- **Industrial Toxicologist :** He plays a crucial role in developing a wide range of effective and safe products including petrochemicals, medicines, pesticides, cosmetics, food and drink and household products.
- **Pharmaceutical Toxicologist:** He determines the efficiency

mechanism of actions and the potential adverse health effects of the active pharmaceutical ingredients being produced.

- **Clinical Toxicologist :** He studies the harmful effects of chemicals, drugs, pesticides and other substances on humans through clinical diagnosis of symptoms and detection and diagnosis of biological poisoning.
- **Forensic Toxicologist :** He investigates causes of death and study crime scenes with law enforcement personnel. He specialises in the study of alcohol, legal and illicit drugs and poisons, including their chemical composition, preparations and identifications.
- **Occupational Toxicologist:** He studies the effect of chemicals that may be encountered by workers during the course of their work environment.
- **Regulatory Toxicologist:** He has the primary role of ensuring public health and safety from the use of chemicals, drugs and pesticides by identifying potential health risks posed by exposure to such substances.
- **Academic Toxicologist:** He works at non-profit organisations and universities. These toxicologists concentrate on research projects and teach toxicology to students.
- **Environmental toxicologist or eco-toxicologist :** He studies the effects of chemicals on the environment. They research on the field and in laboratories to learn how pollution affects ecosystems, air and water quality, species survival and public health. Environmental toxicologist continually monitors and measures the level of toxins in the environment. They play important role in safeguarding public health.

Remuneration

As there is shortage of toxicologists, qualified and experienced ones get good emoluments. The salary range is dependent on various factors like the geographical location, organisation size and work experience. Industry positions generally pay higher than academic, non-profit or government positions in this field. Starting salary for a M.Sc. holder in this field can range between ₹ 25,000 – 40,000. Those with experience and specialisation can even earn up to a lakh per month. For example, a toxicologist with a veterinary or medical degree and a post graduate qualification can draw above 50,000 a month.

Courses

- M. Phil. Environmental Toxicology,
- M. Sc. Environmental Toxicology,
- M. Sc. Toxicology,
- Ph. D. Toxicology.

Top Ten Colleges for Studying Toxicology in India

- **Bombay College of Pharmacy, Mumbai, Maharashtra**

  Course: Doctor of Philosophy in Pharmacology and Toxicology.

- **Indian Institute of Toxicology Research, Lucknow, Uttar Pradesh**

  Courses: Doctor of Philosophy Regulatory Toxicology,

  Doctor of Philosophy Nanomaterial Toxicology.

- **Veer Narmad South Gujarat University, Surat, Gujarat**

  Course: Master of Philosophy Fish Cytogenetics Pollution and Toxicology.

- **National Institute of Pharmaceutical Education and Research, Mohali, Punjab**

  Courses: Master of Science (Pharmacy) Pharmacology and Toxicology.

  Doctor of Philosophy Pharmacology and Toxicology (Pharmacy)

- **Centre for Cellular and Molecular Biology, Hyderabad, Andhra Pradesh**

  Course: Doctor of Philosophy Genetics and Evolution.

- **Assam Agricultural University, Guwahati, Assam**

  Course: Master of Veterinary Science Veterinary Pharmacology and Toxicology.

- **G.B. Pant University of Agriculture and Technology, Pantnagar, Uttaranchal**

  Courses: Master of Veterinary Science Veterinary Pharmacology and Toxicology.

  Doctor of Philosophy Veterinary Pharmacology and Toxicology.

- **Maharashtra Animal and Fishery Sciences University, Parbhani, Maharashtra**

  Courses : Master of Veterinary Science Veterinary Pharmacology and Toxicology

  Doctor of Philosophy Veterinary Pharmacology and Toxicology.

12.27 Veterinary science

What is Veterinary Science?

Veterinary Science is the science of diagnosing, treating and curing the diverse types of diseases in birds and animals. The subject broadly covers the study of animal physiology, treatment and prevention of diseases among animals. The basic principles of this specialised branch of study are quite similar to that of human medical sciences. It involves not only taking care of animal health but also includes scientific breeding and handling of livestock.

The Role of Veterinary Doctor or Vet

Besides giving treatment, Vets perform surgery, prevent spreading of diseases transmitted through animals by administering timely vaccination and medicines and give advice on care of pets and farm animals. The activities of a vet may also include animal husbandry – animal breed improvement by 'selection breeding' and artificial insemination, animal research in order to control spreads of diseases transmitted through animals, wildlife thus protecting the public from exposure to diseases carried by animals, wildlife conservation, poultry management and healthcare, livestock and domestic animal wealth.

A Promising Scope

The scope for veterinarians in the future is bright. As keeping pets is becoming a fad nowadays, the demand for private veterinary clinics is on the rise in metropolitan cities. Similarly, there has been an unprecedented growth in the poultry sector and animal products' technology sector, resulting in an increased demand for veterinarians in different sectors of livestock and poultry.

Eligibility and Course Areas

To practise as a veterinarian it is essential to have a bachelor's degree in Veterinary Science (B.v.Sc.). To be eligible for the bachelor's in Veterinary Science and Animal Husbandry (B.v.Sc. and AH) course, a candidate should have passed class 12th examination with science subjects such as physics, chemistry and biology.

Selection

Admission to most veterinary colleges is on the basis of results obtained in the entrance examination conducted by the concerned universities. veterinary Council of India conducts 'All India Common Entrance Examination' (AICEE) for admission to first year Bachelor of Veterinary Science (B.v.Sc.) and Animal Husbandry (AH) degree course for filling up 15 per cent of the total number of seats of each veterinary college of all states; about 36 colleges where *Indian Veterinary Council Act*, 1984 extends. This entrance examination is usually held in the month of May each year. For admission to master's degree programme, an all India entrance examination is conducted by the Indian Council for Agricultural Research (ICAR).

Duration

The duration of the B.v.Sc. and AH varies from four and a half years to five years including the period of internship. The first four years of training programme are devoted to imparting skills through theoretical and practical training in various disciplines like anatomy, physiology, bio-chemistry, nutrition, livestock management and production, production technology, pathology, micro-biology, pharmacology, genetics and breeding, gynaecology, surgery, medicine and animal husbandry extension, among others and the fifth year is devoted to hands-on training of six months is through internship. The internship includes three months training at the Teaching Veterinary Clinical Service Complex (CTCSC) under the supervision of a senior clinician and in field veterinary hospitals on a rotation basis. Veterinary students undergo a one-month practical training in livestock production and management at animal farms, then one-month training in poultry production and management and one-month training in livestock products' technology and other services. Apart from learning to treat animals, training is also provided in dairying and poultry sciences. Generally, after doing B.v.Sc, most candidates go on to do a post graduation namely, a Master in Veterinary Science. The postgraduate course in Veterinary Science (M.v.Sc.) is a two years course and the candidate has the option to specialise in areas like medicine, surgery, anatomy, bacteriology, bio-chemistry, cardiology, dermatology, micro-biology, molecular biology, anesthesia, gynaecology, pathology, toxicology, virology pharmacology, etc. For jobs in the research and teaching area, a post graduate degree in veterinary science and animal husbandry is a minimum qualification, while a Ph.D. is preferred.

Job Prospects and Career Options

Veterinary science offers a large number of avenues of work and the demand for Veterinary doctors has increased tremendously. Veterinarian can choose to work with the government animal husbandry departments, poultry farms, dairy farms, sheep and rabbit farms, race clubs, stud farms, private and government veterinary hospitals and clinics. Wildlife sanctuaries and zoological parks as well as aviaries need veterinarians.

The Army and Border Security Forces also employ veterinarians for the care and treatment of their mounted regiments which have horses, the experienced professionals are recruited in various institutions to train the new entrants to the field. Besides regular practice, vets can also take up research work, either on their own or in association with the government such as ICAR. Pharmaceutical industries appoint veterinary scientists in their research and development divisions for the research and development of drugs, chemicals and bio-products particularly anti-biotics and vaccines both for human and animals. They can also work in technical sales, agribusiness, and marketing, pet food manufacturing industries and in management of industries dealing with animal feed, animal products, milk and meat products processing industries.

Remuneration

The amount of remuneration of a veterinarian depends upon the kind of practice and the animals that are treated. An average vet can earn between ₹ 10,000 – 50,000 per month. A private practitioner may get lucrative monetary returns depending on his popularity and the number of years of experience. He may be able to earn ₹ 500 – 2,000 per treatment, depending on the type of medical treatment the animal needs. As an Assistant Professor, a vet can earn a salary of over ₹ 30,000. The government also has job openings in this field.

Courses

- Animal Husbandry Diploma Programme (AHDP),
- Bachelor of Veterinary Science and Animal Husbandry,
- Master of Veterinary Science,
- Ph. D. Veterinary Science.

Institutes

- **Guru Angad Dev Veterinary and Animal Sciences University (GADVASU)**

  Ludhiana (Punjab).

- **Navsari Agricultural Univesity, Navsari (Gujarat)**
  Eru char Rasta, Dandi Road, Navsari-396450.
- **Chandra Shekar Azad University of Agriculture and Technology, Kanpur (UP)**
  Kanpur-208002.
- **Dr Panjabrao Deskmukh Krishi Vidyapeeth, Akola (Maharashtra)**
  PO Krishnagar, Akola-444104.
- **Orissa University of Agriculture and Technology**
  College of Agricultural Engineering and Technology
  Bhubaneshwar-751003.
- **Assam Agricultural University, Jorhat (Assam)**
  Faculty of Agriculture, Jorhat-785013.
- **Bihar Veterinary College, Patna (Bihar)**
  Patna-800014.
- **Bombay Veterinary Science College, Mumbai (Maharashtra)**
  Parel, Mumbai-400012.
- **College of Veterinary and Animal Science, Bikaner (Rajasthan)**
  Bikaner-334001.
- **College of Veterinary and Animal Science, Udgir (Maharashtra)**
  Udgir-413517.

12.28 New Areas of Super-specialisation in Medicine

The healthcare industry is attracting a lot of big names like Wockhardt and Max Healthcare, Apollo from USA, Dubai and Prexus partners, Parkway Group and so on. These organised hospitals due to enough finances are able to provide super-specialties centers. Some of the promising areas of super-specialisation are stem cells, which will have multiple applications. The diseases which do not have any medication, the field of stem cells will give light of new hope. Also the other very important areas are cardiology which brings multiple sciences to play; transplant surgery which involves huge team effort and require great stamina; infertility which offers a science of hope; plastic surgery which offers hope to those who have deformity.

12.28.1 Transplant Surgery

The Transplant Surgery has taken the shape of colossal medical as well as ethical challenge. A career in transplant surgery offers many intellectual and technical challenges. It is life saving surgery that has the potential to offer a high level of job satisfaction. As a discipline, it is advancing in step with technological and pharmacological developments which have led to unique opportunities to pursue numerous avenues for clinical and laboratory research. The various areas of Transplant Surgery are :

- ***Renal Transplantation :*** Demand for renal transplant surgeons is high. Renal transplants are done in about 100 centres around the country which perform about 3,000-4,000 transplants every year which is only three-five per cent of total annual demand. Efforts are being made to close the ever widening gap between supply and demand and there are several exciting areas of development, including xenotransplantation (the use of animal organs). And living related donation (a kidney from a relative, friend or spouse).

  The use of the so called marginal organs is also picking up. A marginal organ is one that in the past would have been considered of unsuitable quality for transplantation. Examples of these are organs from older donors, from people with limited chronic disease such as diabetes, the use of kidneys from donors who are hepatitis positive for recipients who are hepatitis positive and organs from non-heart beating donors.

  Laparoscopic surgery has given an impetus to renal transplants making it more promising because donor can get back to work in the span of a few days.

- ***Pancreas Transplantation :*** Pancreas Transplantation can be offered to patients with severe diabetes mellitus and is often performed at the same time as renal transplantation for patients whose kidneys have failed because of their diabetes. Many of the complications of diabetes are stabilised in such patients.

  A refinement to the technique of the whole pancreas transplantation has been transplantation of only the insulin producing B-cells contained within the islets of langerhans. These islet cells may be isolated from donor pancreata by digestion using a collagenase enzyme and mechanical maceration. Once the islet cells have been purified they are transplanted into the recipient by infusion into a branch of the portal vein using radiographic guidance.

- ***Liver Transplantation :*** Liver transplantation is considered for patients with end stage liver disease who have a prognosis of less than two years. Indications for referral include poor synthetic function, disordered metabolism, portal hypertension, poor quality of life and hepatocellular carcinoma or less than five cms diameter. Additionally, those with acute liver failure from a variety of viral and drug induced causes are considered as potential recipients. In Delhi alone, two centres of liver transplants have been set up.

Livers may be used fully intact or can be split and can be used for more than one recipient. A further refinement of these techniques has allowed living related transplantation, whether the left lateral segment or left lobe is used from a healthy donor.

- ***Cardiothoracic Transplantation :*** This discipline comprises heart, single and double lung and heart and lung transplantation. The former is performed for congenital or acquired heart disease and involves explanation of the diseased organ, leaving the atria intact. The donor heart is anastamosed to the recipient atria, aorta and pulmonary artery.

  Single and double lung transplants are performed for a variety of pulmonary diseases and heart and lung transplantation for cardiac disease means that the recipient becomes a lung donor, so called domino-donation.

12.28.2 Plastic Surgery

Plastic surgery procedures include both cosmetic enhancements as well as functionally reconstructive operations. Path breaking research and

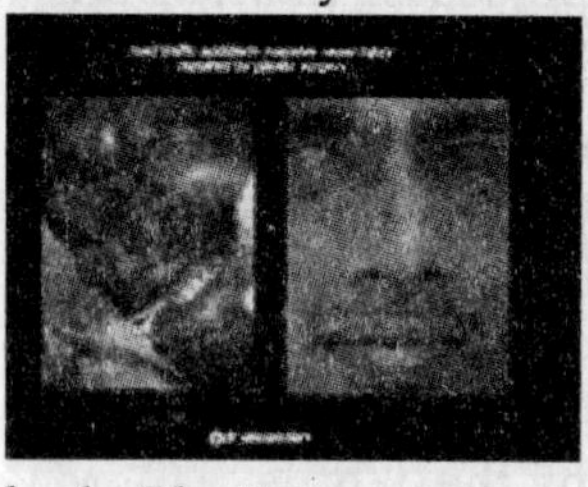

swift acceptance by the public have made both aesthetic and reconstructive two of the most dynamic and lucrative surgical fields.

Plastic surgery is a medical specialty that uses a number of surgical and non-surgical techniques to change the appearance and function of a person's body. Plastic surgery procedures include both cosmetic enhancements as well as functionally reconstructive operations. In the former case, where aesthetics are considered more of the concern than changing the functionality, plastic surgery is also referred to as 'cosmetic surgery'. Most procedures involve both aesthetic and functional elements.

Techniques and Procedures

Common techniques used in plastic surgery are :

- Incision,
- Excision,
- Micro-surgery,

- Chemo-surgery,
- Electro-surgery,
- Laser-surgery,
- Dermabrasion,
- Liposuction.

In plastic surgery, the transfer of skin tissue (skin grafting) is one of the most common procedures. In traditional surgery 'graft' is a piece of living tissue, organ, etc., that is transplanted.

Autografts : Skin grafts taken from the recipient. If absent or deficient of natural tissue, alternatives can be :

- Cultured Sheets of epithelial cells in vitro.
- Synthetic compounds (e.g., Integra-a two layered dermal substitute consisting superficially of silicone and deeply bovine tendon collagen with glycosaminoglycans).
- **Allografts :** Skin grafts taken from a donor of the same species.
- **Xenografts :** Skin grafts taken from a donor of a different species. Usually, good results are expected from plastic surgery that emphasises.
- Careful planning of incisions so that they fall in the line of natural skin folds or lines.
- Appropriate choice of wound closure.
- Use of best available suture materials.
- Early removal of exposed sutures so that the wound is held closed by buried sutures.

Reconstructive Plastic Surgery

Reconstructive Plastic Surgery is performed to correct functional impairments caused by :

- Burns,
- Traumatic injuries such as facial bone fractures,
- Congenital abnormalities such as cleft lip or cleft palate,
- Developmental abnormalities,
- Infection or disease,
- Removal of cancers or tumors such as a mastectomy.

Reconstructive Plastic Surgery is usually performed to improve function but it may be done to approximate a normal appearance. It is generally touched by insurance coverage but this may change according to the procedure required.

Common reconstructive surgical procedures are :

- Breast reconstruction for women who have had a mastectomy,
- Cleft lip and palate surgery,
- Contracture surgery for burn survivors (one of the complications of severe burns),
- Creating a new outer ear when one is congenitally absent,
- Closing skin,
- Mucosa defects after removal of tumors in the head and neck region.

Plastic surgeons developed the use of micro-surgery to transfer tissue for coverage of a defect when no local tissue is available. Tissue flaps comprised skin, muscle, bone, fat or a combination, may be removed from the body, moved to another site on the body and reconnected to a blood supply by suturing arteries and veins as small as 1-2 mm in diameter.

Cosmetic Surgery

Cosmetic surgery is a very popular form of plastic surgery. The most prevalent aesthetic/cosmetic procedures are listed below. Most of these types of surgery are more commonly known by their common names. These are also listed when pertinent.

- **Abdominoplasty (or "tummy tuck") :** Reshaping and firming of the abdomen.
- **Blepharoplasty (or 'eyelid surgery') :** Reshaping of the eyelids or the application of permanent eyeliner including Asian Blepharoplasty.
- **Mammoplasty**
- **Breast augmentation (or 'breast enlargement' or 'boob job') :** Augmentation for the breasts. This can involve either saline or silicone gel prosthetics.
- **Breast reduction :** Removal of skin and glandular tissue. Indicated to reduce back and shoulder pain or for psychological benefit in women with macrosmatia.
- **Buttock Augmentation (or 'butt augmentation' or 'butt implants') :** Enhancement of the buttocks. This procedure can be performed by using silicone implants or fat grafting and transfer from other areas of the body.
- **Chemical Peel :** Minimising the appearance of acne, pock and other scars as well as wrinkles (depending on concentration

and type of agent used, except for deep furrows), solar lentigines (age spots, freckles) and photodamagein general. Chemical peels commonly involve carbonic (Phenol), trichloroacetic acid (TCA), glycolic acid (AHA) or salicyclic acid (BHA) – as the active agent.

- **Mastopexy (or 'breast lift'):** Raising or reshaping of breasts. Involves removal of breast skin as opposed to glandular tissue.
- **Labiaplasty :** surgical reduction and reshaping of the labia.
- **Rhinoplasty (or 'nose job'):** Reshaping of the nose.
- **Otoplasty (or ear surgery):** Reshaping of the ear.
- **Rhytidectomy (or 'facelift'):** Removal of wrinkles and signs of aging from the face.
- **Suction-Assisted Lipectomy (or liposuction) :** Removal of fat from the body.
- **Chin Augmentation :** Augmentation of the chin with an implant (e.g. silicone) or sliding genioplasty of the jawbone.
- **Cheek Augmentation.**
- **Collagen, fat and other tissue filler injections (e.g. hyaluronic acid).**
- **Laser skin resurfacing.**
- **Injection of dermal fillers (collagen, hyaluronic acid, fat and others).**

Plastic Surgery Sub-specialties

Plastic surgery is a broad field, and may be subdivided further.

- Craniofacial surgery mostly revolves around the treatment of pediatric congenital anomalies such as cleft lip and palate, craniosynostosis and other disturbances in facial growth and development. This field is also practiced by oral and maxillofacial surgeons. Because these children have multiple issues, the best approach to providing care to them is an interdisciplinary approach which also includes otolaryngologists and geneticists.
- Hand surgery is a field that is also practised by general surgeons and orthopaedic surgeons. Plastic surgeons receive training in hand surgery, with some trainees deciding even to do an additional full-year hand fellowship afterwards (this fellowship can also be pursued by general surgeons and orthopaedic surgeons). In particular, plastic surgeons receive training in micro

vascular surgery, which is needed to replant an amputated hand or digit. Many hand operations (such as reconstruction of injuries, replantations, rheumatoid surgery and surgery of congenital defects) are performed by plastic surgeons.

- Micro-surgery.
- Burn surgery.
- Aesthetic or cosmetic surgery is a growing component of general plastic surgeons. However, a select few promising graduates are chosen for an extra year of advanced fellowship training in aesthetic surgery.
- Paediatric plastic surgery: Children often face medical tissues unique from the experiences of an adult patient. Many birth defects or syndromes present at birth are best treated in childhood and paediatric plastic surgeons specialise in treating these conditions in children. Many have additional training in paediatric care, including doing residencies in some of the nation's top paediatric plastic surgery programmes. Conditions commonly treated by paediatric plastic surgeons include craniofacial anomalies, cleft lip and palate and congenital and deformities. Some of the nation's top paediatric hospitals have well-established departments of Paediatric Plastic Surgery.

12.28.3 Nuclear Medicine

Nuclear medicine is the branch of imaging that uses radio-isotopes to study the physiology and metabolism of the body (rather than the anatomy shown by X-rays, Computed Tomography (CT), ultrasound and Magnetic Resonance Imaging (MRI). Nuclear medicine today is the exciting development of the early twentieth century pioneering work among others. It also helps in computer literacy. There have been many recent advances in nuclear medicine but without doubt the most exciting is the development of Positron Emission Tomography (PET) imaging and in particular PET/CT. This has revolutionised oncological imaging and ideally no major cancer centre should be without PET.

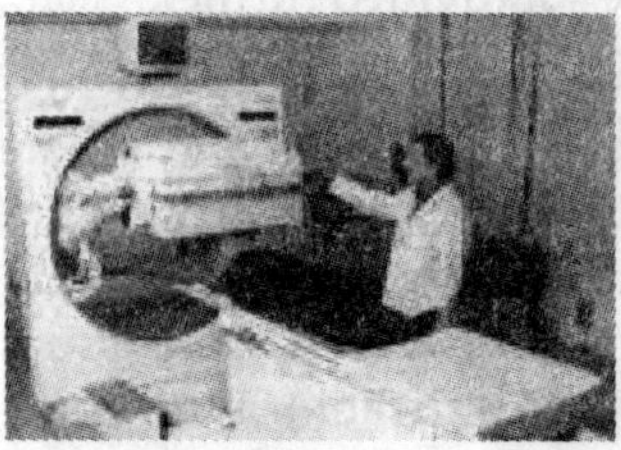

Nuclear medicine, being essentially physiological, correlates well with all other forms of imaging which are mainly anatomical. It is a vital tool for the clinician. There is, therefore, a huge interaction with the rest of imaging, the clinicians and the oncologists.

Nuclear Medicine Treatment

One can be involved in the therapeutic aspects of nuclear medicine both curative and palliative as in the administration of strontium or samarium to alleviate pain from bone metastases. In many centers, treatment of thyrotoxicosis with radio-iodine is the preferred option and has excellent results. Nuclear medicine treatment offers the possibility to target neuroendocine tumors such as carcinoid, selectively and research is continuing to label specific monoclonal antibodies to various tumors both for diagnosis and treatment.

Educational Path

To become a nuclear medicine expert after completing MBBS, you may opt for a Diploma in Nuclear Medicine (DRM) or MD in Nuclear Medicine. One is required to get licensing clearance from Bhabha Atomic Research Centre (BARC) or the Atomic Regulatory Board, Mumbai to practise Nuclear Medicine.

Career Prospects

There are two main types of consultants in nuclear medicine. If you are a physician trained consultant, you will mainly work in larger centres either purely in nuclear medicine or also with some general medical responsibility. Without doubt, the future in CT/PET, as cancer and oncology enjoy a high priority. Nuclear medicine can and does have a vital role in both diagnosis and therapy and you can be part of both diagnosis and therapy and you can be part of it. You can get a starting monthly salary of ₹ 25,000.

12.27.4 Oncology

The word 'Oncology' comes from two Greek words *'onkos'* meaning 'bulk', 'mass' or 'tumor' and *'logos'* meaning 'study of'. It is a branch of medicine that deals with cancer. It is concern with :

- The diagnosis of any cancer in a person.
- Therapy (e.g. surgery, chemotherapy, radiotherapy and other modalities).
- Follow up of cancer patients after successful treatment.
- Palliative care of patients with terminal malignancies.
- Ethical questions surrounding cancer care.
- Screening efforts :

- of populations, or
- of the relatives of patients (in types of cancer that are thought to have hereditary basis such as breast cancer).

Who is a Medical Oncologist?

A medical oncologist is a consultant physician specialising in the investigation, diagnosis and management of people with malignant diseases. This work includes preventive and palliative medicine. Medical oncology offers a diverse range of career options including clinical care, cancer research, counselling and management regarding genetic cancer risk, teaching and ethics.

What is the Work of a Medical Oncologist?

Most medical oncologists combine both clinical and research activities. Clinical work covers the diagnosis and management of people with cancer. Major therapeutic interventions include chemo-therapy, hormonal therapies and many emerging 'targeted' biological therapies. Some medical oncologists specialise in treating people with specific types of cancer, e.g., breast or bowel cancer, whilst others treat people with any one of a variety of cancers. Medical oncologists tend to work in multi-disciplinary to provide optimal treatment, supportive and palliative care for patients.

Radiation Oncologist

Oncology is the study of tumors and cancers. A radiation oncologist is a physician who specialises in treating cancer through radiation therapies and methods. Radiation oncologists investigate the use of X-rays, electrons and gamma rays to destroy cancer. Radiation therapy is used on most types of cancers including breast cancer, lung cancer, prostate cancer, skin cancer, brain tumors and others.

Radiation therapy involves various kinds of radiation treatment techniques. The most common types of radiation therapy are 3-D treatment planning, external beam radiation, IMRT, stereotactic radiosurgery, prostate seed implants, brachy-therapy and concurrent chemo-therapy and radiation therapy. The oncologist selects the most effective radiation technique for each particular patient to destroy abnormal (cancer) cells while sparing the normal surrounding tissue. The process of these treatments is not painful as patients cannot see, smell, taste, hear or feel the radiation treatment.

Roughly, half of all cancer patients need radio-therapy at some time during their illness. For those with incurable cancers, the treatment helps patients deal with their symptoms. For example, if they have pain in their bones, radio-therapy can be a very useful treatment. Radical treatment is a method used to tryand cure patients. Thus, radiation oncologists use a mixture of very aggressive treatment for people who have a good chance of being cured and very simple treatments for people who have incurable cancer but still need treatment and help. In many cases, radiation therapy is combined with surgery and chemo-therapy to achieve the best outcome.

Educational Paths

Radiation oncologists complete MBBS and then take up MD in Radio-therapy or MS-General Surgery, M.Ch. (Surgical Oncology) or MD (General Medicine) or DM (Medical Oncology). For this, you may study at Tata Memorial, Mumbai, AIIMS, New Delhi or go abroad to do higher degree after MBBS.

Remuneration

The average starting salary is ₹ 6-10 lakh per year in a government hospital. On the other hand, if you join a private hospital, you may get ₹ 75,000–1, 00,000 per month. There is a year of internship before entering residency graduate education, which usually takes about four years. During this residency programme, students will specialise in both radiation oncology and clinical oncology.

12.28.5 Endocrinology

Endocrinology comes from the Greek words '*endo*' meaning 'within', '*krino*' meaning 'to separate' and '*logos*' meaning 'study of'. It is a branch of biology and medicine dealing with the endocrine system, its diseases and its specific secretions called hormones, the integration of developmental events proliferation, growth and differentiation (including histogenesis and organogenesis), and the co-ordination of metabolism, respiration, excretion, movement, reproduction and sensory perception depend on chemical cues, substances, synthesised and secreted by specialised cells.

Endocrinology is the study of endocrine glands – a group of glands in the body which secrete hormones, evoking specific responses in other cells of the body and control basic bodily functions such as metabolism, growth and sexual development. These hormones travel to their target organs and cells and then bind to receptors either on cell surfaces or inside the cell. This results in a change in the activity of those cells. Endocrine responses are relatively slow, taking from seconds to days to occur.

The amount of hormones produced by each gland is carefully balanced. Too much or too little of a certain hormone can have effects throughout the body and cause various endocrine disorders. For example, in Type-1 diabetes, the pancreas does not produce insulin, thereby requiring the diabetic to inject the insulin hormone into their body in order to regulate and maintain balance in the endocrine system.

Who are Endocrinologists?

Endocrinologists are trained to recognise problems with hormones and restore the natural balance of hormones in a patient's system. In addition, endocrinologists conduct research on the basic and clinical aspects of endocrine glands and disorders. They also provide treatment for a wide range of functions and disorders of the endocrine system including metabolism, hormonal imbalances, menopause, osteoporosis and cholesterol disorders. Endocrinologists also develop new drugs and treatments for hormonal disorders.

Diseases Caused by Endocrine Disorders

The most common illnesses associated with endocrine disorders are diabetes and hypothyroidism which can cause hormonal imbalances such as obesity, immune problems, kidney failure, fertility problems and even heart disease and cancer. Endocrinologists help many of their patients treat their disorders and diseases with medication and proper diet. They also educate people and recommend exercise and other lifestyle health choices.

The average pay package in private hospitals for endocrinologist is about ₹ 2.5 lakh per month.

Educational Paths

Becoming an endocrinologist requires a long educational road, so be prepared for a lifelong learning experience. To become an endocrinologist, you have to first complete MBBS degree. Then, you can go for MD in general medicine or can do DM in endocrinology.

12.28.6 Infertility

Fetal Medicine is one of the most prospective upcoming areas in fertility. There is ample opportunity for doctors to set up state-of-the-art clinics particularly in smaller towns.

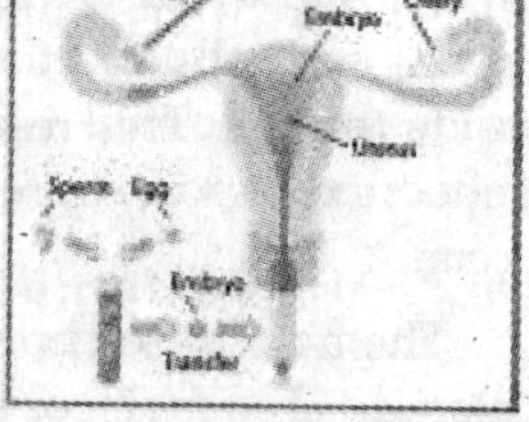

What is Infertility?

Infertility is a disease or condition of the reproductive system often diagnosed after a couple has one year of unprotected, well-timed intercourse or if the woman suffers from multiple miscarriages. Infertility can be male or female-related.

There are a few or no courses in the country that impart the requisite instruction on the problems of infertility. Most of the Indian embryologists are self-trained. The National Board now conducts a diploma programme, which is equivalent to MD/MS for reproductive medicine after completing their MBBS, MD-Gynaecology and then a diploma in Embryology. For IVF, one has to get trained in an IVF centre after MBBS. But overseas, MBBS-MD students can look to acquire a specialisation in fetal medicine, assisted reproductive technology, gynaecology and gynoecia urology. DNA on demand and *invitro* babies has become very popular recently. This field offers a science of hope.

Treatment Options

- **Fertility Medications :** There are a variety of medications used to treat infertility. It is important to understand the medications and what their purpose is and to speak with your physician about the medications that will be used in your specific treatment plan.
- **Surgery :** Surgery is a treatment option for both male and female infertility. Generally, surgery is used to correct a structural problem. Surgery often results in the return of normal fertility function.
- **IUI (Intrauterine Insemination) :** This is most commonly referred to as artificial insemination. This is a procedure where the woman is injected with carefully prepared sperm from the husband or a donor. IUI is often performed in conjunction with ovulation stimulating medications. IUI is used to treat unexplained infertility minimal male factor infertility for women with cervical mucus problems.
- **ART (Assisted Reproductive Technology) :** It is defined by the CDC as a procedure in which a woman's ovaries are stimulated, her eggs surgically removed, combined with sperm and returned to a woman's body. IVF is the most widely used of the ART procedures.
- **Micromanipulation Techniques :** Micromanipulation techniques are used to achieve or improve fertilisation and

implantation rates. These techniques may also be used to remove a cell from a developing embryo for assessment of the DNA.

- ***Third Party: Donor Egg, Donor Sperm, Surrogacy, Embryo Donation***

  Many choices exist today for couples who are facing infertility and one or both partners is/are unable to have a genetically related child. These choices are widely used, and present another option for building a family.

13
HOME SCIENCE

13.1 Food Flavourist or Flavour Chemist

What is Flavour?

Flavour is the sensory impression of food or other substance and is determined mainly by the chemical senses of taste and smell. Flavourant is defined as a substance that gives another substance flavour, altering the characteristics of the solute, causing it to become sweet, sour, tangy etc. There are two categories of flavours – Natural and Artificial flavours. The flavour of food can be altered with flvourants which affect the senses. Those who add flavour to the products are referred by the term Food Flavourist or Flavour Chemists. Flavourists are chemists who create flavours for food and other products.

The Work of Food Flavourists

The job of food flavourists involves not just mixing various ingredients to create artificial and natural flavours but requires an in-depth knowledge of aroma chemicals, essential oils, plant extracts and the likes. Professionals in this field, create unique flavor combinations in a laboratory setting known as test kitchens. Laboratories are frequently equipped with standard kitchen equipment such as micro-waves, stoves, blenders etc. In the flavour creation, food flavourists have to meet the standards prescribed by the Indian government so that it is safe and fit for human consumption.

As the career is closely related to chemistry, those with a degree in chemistry can opt for this career. Today, the vast majority of everything we eat includes natural flavours or artificial flavours developed by these professionals. As such, in products from potato-chips to toothpaste to ice cream, food flavourists have a role to play.

Eligibility

To enter the field of flavors, one must have at least a B.Sc. or M.Sc. in chemistry or bio-chemistry with some experience in the industry. A basic knowledge of food technology will be an added advantage. A student could take an under graduate degree in either chemistry or biology and then go on to receive their masters in a food science programme. A Ph.D. is usually required for independent research, teaching at a university and for executive positions in a company. In India, flavour or perfumery schools are rare; hence emphasis is given to specialisation in chemistry.

Central Food Technological Research Institute, Mysore offers various short term courses as well as research opportunities in the field of food flavouring. The department of plantation products, spices and flavor technology engages in research and development activities in the areas of spices, coffee, tea, natural food colours and flavours.

Job Prospects

Food processing companies have a great demand for food flavourists. In India, most of the flavouring companies are concentrated in North India. Hence, the scope for this career is much more in northern states of India than in any other state. Candidates with chemistry foundation are given in house training by companies to gain specified knowledge in the field.

Food flavourists are employed mainly by industries, in food-processing and ingredient supply. Some flavourists work for food production companies; another option includes working in flavour houses – companies that create flavors in a lab for numerous purposes. These flavour houses often sell the finished flavour extracts to food manufacturers and can also provide consulting services to a company to help produce specific flavours for its products. SN Kelkar, Mumbai is one of the largest flavours and fragrance houses in India.

Remuneration

Salary in this field is based mainly on experience and the ability to blend flavours. A fresher in the industry can expect around ₹ 10,000 – 20,000 per month. However, one with experience and a reputation in the field can earn even lakhs through this profession.

Courses

- B.Sc. Chemistry,
- M.Sc. Chemistry,
- M.Sc. Bio-chemistry,

- Food Technology,
- Food Science.

13.2 Food Technology

What is Food Technology?

Food Technology is a branch of science in which food science is applied in the manufacturing and preservation of food products. It is the application of science and technology to the treatment, processing, preservation and distribution of food. The term 'Food Technology' has a wide meaning, it deals with developing new methods and systems for keeping food products safe, resistant to the threat of natural problems like bacteria.

This field is so old that research has been going on for decades, on record from the time that Louis Pasteur developed the process of pasteurisation – the process of heating milk and milk products to prevent food spoilage and destroy disease producing organisms.

Important Role of Food Technologists

Nowadays, there is an ever increasing demand for packaged, processed and ready-to-eat foods. This requires continuous research and innovation of methods to preserve food stuff for long periods without losing its nutritious value. Food technologists are involved in a wide variety of activities associated with providing nutritious food. They study the chemical, physical and micro-biological make up of the food. The food is processed, preserved, packaged and stored according to the specifications by industries and the government.

Importance of Food Technology

Training in food technology gives adequate knowledge regarding the quality, analysis of raw materials, packaging standards and methodology, health and hygiene parameters, processing techniques, storage and food value, methodologies for extracting useful by-products from industrial and domestic waste. Thus, the future of the production of good food items, on the global scale is in the hands of Food technologists.

Eligibility

The general criterion for admission to a graduate course is 10+2 science. A post graduate course will require the student to complete his graduation in food technology or other related fields.

Course Areas

The course covers the various aspects like food science, food bio-technology, food analysis, micro-biology, food preservation techniques, genetics and food packaging, marketing and advertising, food logistics management, operations management etc.

Job Prospects and Career Options

Food being essential for survival, food technology has a wide scope in different government and private sectors dealings with food products. One can get jobs in food processing industries, research laboratories, hotels, soft drinks factories, rice mills, hospitality industry, packaging industries, manufacturing industries and distilleries. Those with masters and Ph.D. degree can work as assistant professors in colleges/ universities.

Food processing companies need food technology personnel to work for them in different sections like production, quality assurance and R&D (Research and Development). One can work as Product Development Manager to devise food products according to the needs of the consumers and effectively put the products in service in an innovative way. You can work as a Sensory scientist or Quality controller to monitor organic properties like aroma, flavour, quality, hygiene and more. Food technologists work in research laboratories or R&D sectors to develop new products, test current ones and control the overall food quality.

Career Options in Private and Public Sectors

There are private as well as public sectors which provide lucrative job opportunities to food technologists. In the public sector, one can find jobs in companies like the Food Corporation of India which handles the purchase, storage, transport and distribution of food grains and other food items, Modern Food Corporation which markets bread, fruit juices, edible oils, soft drink concentrates, and North-Eastern Agricultural Marketing Corporation which markets and process fruits and vegetables. Major job providers in private sector include Amul, Cadbury, Britannia, Metro Diary, Hindustan Lever, Kellogs, Nestle and such others. The food firms in foreign countries like the United States as well as Australia give special preferences to Indian candidates.

Different Post Available for Food Technologists

There are many lucrative positions open to food technologists like quality assurance manager, laboratory supervisor, production manager and food packaging manager.

- **Production Managers/Supervisors :** They are responsible for the entire processes in the manufacturing of a product, right from the purchase of raw materials to the production of the final product.
- **Quality Assurance Managers/Supervisors :** They are responsible for ensuring the quality of food throughout the whole production process. This includes the quality of raw materials, equipment, finished goods, packaging, processing and storage procedures.
- **Laboratory Supervisors/Technicians :** They carry out or supervise quality tests such as micro-biological and chemical analyses before any product is released.
- **Food Packaging Managers/Technologists :** They are responsible for the research and development of new food packaging systems and filling equipment.
- **Research Scientists :** They are responsible for the continuing research and development programme within the industry. Research scientists are employed in a wide variety of projects with government, food research institutes and food companies.
- **Product Development Managers/Technologists :** They are responsible for the improvement of the existing food products as well as for the development of new products.
- **Assistant Professors and Advisors :** They work in a range of posts in the government sector and in colleges and universities as assistant professors or in advisory and inspection jobs.

Remuneration

Food technologists having professional qualifications are easily absorbed by food processing companies, food research laboratories, hotels, restaurants and catering establishments. Earnings vary by industry, skill, geographic region and educational level. Entry level pay and perks tend to be around ₹ 10,000 – 20,000 per month. However, with experience as one specialises in a particular area of food technology, pay packages keep soaring.

Courses

- B. E. Food Technology,
- B. Sc. Food Technology,
- B. Sc. Food Science and Quality Control,
- B. Sc. Food Science, Nutrition and Food Quality Control,

- B. Tech. Food Technology,
- M. E. Food Technology,
- M. Sc. Food Technology,
- M. Tech. Food Technology,
- Ph. D. Food Technology.

Institutes

Central Food Technology and Research Institute, Mysore is a premier institute for food technology courses. Apart from this, there are several other institutes, too.

13.3 Home Science

What is Home Science?

Home Science is both a science as well as an art related field of study which draws upon many disciplines such as chemistry, physics, physiology, biology, hygiene, economics, rural development, child development, sociology and family relations, community living, art, food, nutrition, clothing, textiles and home management. The study of home science deals with the most vital aspects of modern housekeeping. Home science or the science of home in simple words includes all the things that concern yourself, your home, your family members and your resources. The science is aimed at achieving and maintaining the welfare and well-being of home and family life in an ever changing society. It includes not only nutritional needs of the family members but also planning expenditure and budgeting resources available to the family as well. The application of economic principles in relation to income, expenses and consumption comes under the purview of Home Economics. Home science aims at developing an individual to become a well-adjusted member of the family.

Different Streams of Home Science

A person can specialise in any of the five streams of Home Science:

- Food and Nutrition,
- Resource Management,
- Human Development,
- Fabric and Apparel Science,
- Communication and Extension.

Eligibility and Course Areas

One can opt for a career in the field of Home Science after 10+2 science stream. For bachelor's programme in Home Science, minimum qualification required is 10+2. For post graduate degree/diploma programme, one needs to have a graduation degree in any field. Preference is given to candidates with a bachelor's degree in Home Science.

Job Prospects and Career Options

Those qualified in the subject of Home Science can find job opportunities in the production industry, tourism industry, service industry or are suitable for teaching jobs. Self-employment is also an apt career option. One can work independently as research analyst or nutrition consultant. The opportunities for Home Science graduates lie mainly in non-governmental organisations.

- **Production Industry :** This covers food preservation, dress-making, specialised cooking, textile designing and dress manufacturing or work in production units of the food industry and hotels. In the food manufacturing industry, options are available in food processing units and food preservation departments as food analysts, quality controllers and quality managers. Major job profile of Home Science graduates in textiles industry is as apparel and textile designers.
- **Tourism and Service Industry :** They can find jobs in hotel and hospitality management services. They can be employed as dieticians in hospitals, maternity homes, slimming centers and even boarding schools. Home Science graduates are in great demand in the service industry, to look after housekeeping and food catering departments of hotels, tourist resorts, restaurants etc.
- **Research and Teaching Jobs :** Major careers available are as food scientists, research associates, teachers and professors. Candidates with master's degree can opt for teaching positions or research positions. Home Science post graduates can take up teaching assignments in senior secondary schools and home science colleges.
- **Sales :** Sales promotion jobs of food products, baby foods, ready to cook food-stuff and garments are open to Home Science graduates.
- **Technical :** There are a number of technical jobs comprising food analysts, food scientists, research assistants, demonstrators and so on.

Remuneration

A person who desires to pursue a career in this field can expect a salary of about ₹ 10,000 per month in the beginning. With experience, one can earn more income. Research work, teaching, catering jobs, etc., are generally well paid.

Courses

- B.Ed. Home Science,
- B.Sc. Home Science,
- B.Sc. Home Science (Hons),
- B.Sc. Child Development and Family Relations,
- M.Sc. Home Science,
- M.Sc. Home Science Education and Extension,
- M.Sc. Human Development and Family Studies,
- M.Sc. Resource Management and Consumer Service,
- Ph. D. Home Science,
- Ph. D. Child Development,
- Ph. D. Human Development and Family Studies.

Institutes

- Andhra University, Waltair-530003, Andhra Pradesh.
- Andhra Pradesh Agricultural University, Bapatala-522101.
- Assam Agricultural University, Jorhat-785013, Assam.
- Guwahati University, PO Gopinath, Bordoli Nagar, Guwahati-781014, Assam.
- Dibrugarh University, Dibrugarh-786004, Assam.
- Punjab University, Sector-14, Chandigarh-160014.
- University of Delhi, Delhi-110007.
- Bangalore University, Jnana Bharathi, Bangalore-560056, Karnataka.
- University of Mysore, Karya Soudha, Crawford Hall, Mysore-570005, Karnataka.
- University of Calcutta, Senate House, 87, College Street, Kolkata-700073, West Bengal.
- University of Mumbai, MG Road Fort, Mumbai-400032, Maharashtra.
- Goa University, PO Santa Cruz, Talergao Plateau, Goa -403002.

14

INDIAN CIVIL SERVICES

14.1 Indian Civil Services

What is Civil Service?

Civil Service is the backbone of the Indian government machinery which constitutes all the non-military departments of the government machinery which manage the state administration. It is a very highly competitive and challenging area which involves a variety of jobs in different departments. Compared to private sector jobs, this profession has job security. The prestige and power that comes along with these top-notch jobs is a definite reason for many students to opt for this profession. The salary, allowances and facilities, etc., also make it a lucrative profession.

The present day civil service is a legacy of the British ICS (International Civil Service) officers during the British *Raj* who were endowed with immense administrative powers and their main tasks were preservation of law and order, dispensation of justice and collection of taxes. However, today's civil servants operate within the framework of a democratic welfare state, with focus on development and progress. Therefore, unlike many other occupations, civil service is more of a vocation rather than a job. It is more of a service rather than a position of pride and prestige.

Entry into Civil Services

Entry into the IAS, IPS and the Central Services is through the All India Combined Competitive Examination for the Civil Services conducted by the Union Public Service Commission (UPSC) in different centres spread all over the country. Entry into the state civil service is through a competitive examination conducted by every state public service commission. Anyone thinking of taking up civil service should have an idea of how difficult it is to get in as lakhs of candidates apply for the 500 to 600 vacancies that may arise. So once you decide to appear in civil service examination, one should be prepared to slog endlessly.

The civil services examination conducted by the Union public Service Commission (UPSC) selects candidates for various central services including for the most coveted cadres of the Indian Administrative Service (1AS), Indian Police Service (IPS) and Indian Foreign Service (IFS). IAS and IPS are all India services created under Article 312 of the Constitution. Candidates selected for these two services are appointed to different state cadres and as and when required they also move to Central Government departments on deputation. The remaining services are categorised into two central services namely, Group-A and Group-B.

Posts under Civil Service

Services/posts to which recruitment is to be made through the examination are :

- Indian Administrative Service,
- Indian Police Service,
- Indian Foreign Service.

GROUP-A

- Indian P and T Accounts and Finance Service, Group 'A',
- Indian Audit and Accounts Service, Group 'A',
- Indian Revenue Service (Customs and Central Excise) Group 'A',
- Indian Defence Accounts Service, Group 'A',
- Indian Ordinance Factories Service, Group 'A' (Assistant Works Manager, Administration),
- Indian Postal Service, Group 'A',
- Indian Civil Accounts Service, Group 'A',
- Indian Railway Traffic Service, Group 'A',
- Indian Railway Accounts Service, Group 'A',
- Indian Railway Personnel Service, Group 'A',
- Post of Assistant Security Officer, Group 'A' in Railway Protection Force,
- Indian Defence Estates Service, Group 'A',
- Indian Information Service (Junior Grade), Group 'A',
- Indian Trade Service, Group 'A' (Grade-III),
- Indian Corporate Law Service, Group 'A'.

GROUP-B

- Central Secretariat Service (Section Officer's Grade),
- Railway Board Secretariat Service (Section Officer's Grade),
- Arms Forces Headquarters Civil Service, Group 'B' (Section Officer's Grade),
- Armed Forces Headquarters Civil Service, Group 'B' (Assistant Civilian Staff Officer Grade),
- Customs Appraisers' Service, Group 'B',
- The Delhi, Andaman and Nicobar Islands, Lakshadweep, Daman and Diu and Dadra and Nagar Haveli Civil Service Group 'B'.
- Pondicherry Civil Service, Group 'B'.

Reservation will be made for candidates belonging to Scheduled Castes, Scheduled Tribes, Other Backward Classes and differently-abled categories in respect of vacancies as may be fixed by the government.

Eligibility

The candidates applying for the examination should ensure that they fulfill all eligibility condition for admission to examination. The Commission takes up verification of eligibility conditions with reference to original documents only after the candidate has qualified for interview/personality test.

Educational Qualifications

Graduation in any discipline from a recognised university. Candidates having professional and technical qualifications recognised by the government are also eligible.

- Candidates, who have appeared at an examination the passing of which would render them educationally qualified for the Commission's examination but have not been informed of the results, as also the candidates who intend to appear such a qualifying examination, will also be eligible for admission to the preliminary examination. All candidates who are declared qualified by the Commission for taking the Civil Services (Main) examination will be required to produce proof of passing the requisite examination with their application for the main examination, failing which such candidates will not be admitted to the main examination.
- In exceptional cases the Union Public Service Commission may treat a candidate who has not any of the foregoing qualifications as a qualified candidate provided that he has passed examination conducted by the other institutions, the standard of which in the

opinion of the Commission justifies his admission to the examination.

- Candidates who have passed the final professional M.B.B.S. or any other medical examination but have not completed their internship by the time of submission of their applications for the Civil Services (Main) examination, will be provisionally admitted to the Examination provided they submit along with their application a copy of certificate from the concerned authority of the university/institution that they had passed the requisite final professional medical examination. In such cases, the candidates will be required to produce at the time of their interview original degree or a certificate from the concerned competent authority of the university/institution that they had completed all requirements (including completion of internship) for the award of the degree.

Nationality

- For the Indian Administrative Service and the Indian Police Service, a candidate must be a citizen of India.
- For other services, a candidate must be either :
  (i) A citizen of India, or
  (ii) A subject of Nepal, or
  (iii) A subject of Bhutan, or
  (iv) A Tibetan refugee who came over to India with the intention of permanently settling in India, or
  (v) A person of Indian origin who has migrated from Pakistan, Burma, Sri Lanka, East African countries of Kenya, Uganda, the United Republic of Tanzania, Zambia, Malawi, Zaire, Ethiopia and Vietnam with the intention of permanently settling in India

Provided that a candidate belonging to categories (ii), (iii), (iv) and (*v*) shall be a person in whose favor a certificate of eligibility has been issued by the Government of India.

Provided further that candidates belonging to categories (ii), (iii) and (iv) above will not be eligible for appointment to the Indian Foreign Service.

A candidate in whose case a certificate of eligibility is necessary may be admitted to the examination but the offer of appointment may be given only after the necessary eligibility certificate has been issued to him by the Government of India.

Age Limits

(i) Candidate must have attained the age of 21 years of age less than 31 years of are on the 1st August of the year in which examination is being held.

(ii) The upper age limit prescribed above will be relaxable :

(a) Up to a maximum of five years if a candidate belongs to a Scheduled Caste or a Scheduled Tribe.

(b) Up to a maximum of three years in the case of candidates belonging to Other Backward Classes who are eligible to avail of reservation applicable to such candidates.

(c) Up to a maximum of five years if a candidate had ordinarily been domiciled in the state of Jammu and Kashmir during a particular period.

(d) Up to a maximum of three years in the case of Defence Service personnel disabled in operations during hostilities with any foreign country or in a disturbed area and released as a consequence thereof.

(e) Up to a maximum of five years in the case of ex-servicemen including Commissioned Officers and ECOs/SSCOs who have rendered at least five years Military Service as on the 1st August of the year in which examination is being held and have been released

- on completion of assignment (including those whose assignment is due to be completed within one year from the 1st August of the year in which examination is being held) otherwise than by way of dismissal or discharge on account of misconduct or insufficiency, or
- on account of physical disability attributable to Military Service, or
- On invalidment.

(f) Up to a maximum of five years in the case of ECOs/SSCOs who have completed an initial period of assignment of five years Military Service as on the 1st August of the year in which examination is being held and whose assignment has been extended beyond five years and in whose case the Ministry of Defence issues a certificate that they can apply for civil employment and that they will be released on three months' notice on selection from the date of receipt of offer of appointment.

(g) Up to a maximum of 10 years in the case of blind, deaf-mute and orthopaedically handicapped persons.

Personal Attributes

The aspiring candidates are expected to have keen interest in the general studies and are supposed to have a good amount of interest in current affairs. Regular and detailed reading of a good national newspaper, a standard competition magazine and a basic book on general knowledge is the essential pre-requisite. Another important point is efficient time planning.

Physical Standards

Candidates must be physically fit according to physical standards for admission to Civil Services examination. Reservation wili be made for candidates belonging to Scheduled Castes, Scheduled Tribes, Other Backward Classes and differently-abled categories in respect of vacancies as may be fixed by the government.

Number of Attempts

Every candidate appearing at the Civil Services examination, who is otherwise eligible, shall be permitted four attempts at the examination.

Provided that this restriction on the number of attempts will not apply in the case of Scheduled Caste and Scheduled Tribe candidates who are otherwise eligible.

Provided further that the number of attempts permissible to candidates belonging to Other Backward Classes, who are otherwise eligible, shall be seven. This relaxation will be available to the candidates who are eligible to avail of reservation applicable to such candidates.

Provided further that a physically handicapped will get as many attempts as are available to other non-physically handicapped candidates of his or her community, subject to the General Category shall be eligible for seven attempts. The relaxation will be available to the physically handicapped candidates who are eligible to avail of reservation applicable to such candidates.

Recently, the Union Public Service Commission has approved two additional attempts to all categories of candidates with effect from Civil Services examination 2014 with consequential relaxation of minimum age for all categories of candidates.

Note :

- An attempt at a preliminary examination shall be deemed to be an attempt at the examination.
- If a candidate actually appears in any one paper in the Preliminary examination, he/she shall be deemed to have made an attempt at the examination.
- Notwithstanding the disqualification/cancellation of candidature, the fact of appearance of the candidate at the examination will count as an attempt.

Restrictions on Applying for the Examination

A candidate who is appointed to the Indian Administrative Service or the Indian Foreign Service on the results of an earlier examination and continues to be a member of that service will not be eligible to compete at this examination.

In case such a candidate is appointed to the IAS/IFS after the Preliminary examination of Civil Services examination and he/she continues to be a member of that service, he/she shall not be eligible to appear in the Civil Services (Main) examination notwithstanding his/her having qualified in the preliminary examination.

Also provided that if such a candidate is appointed to IAS/IFS after the commencement of the Civil Services (Main) examination but before the result thereof and continues to be a member of that service, he/she shall not be considered for appointment to any service/post on the basis of the result of this examination viz., Civil Services examination.

Career Options

- **Indian Administrative Service (IAS) :** The IAS officers handle affairs of the government. At the central level, this involves the framing and implementation of policy. They also represent the government in other countries and in International forums. They are even authorised to sign agreements on behalf of the government. At the district level, it is concerned with district affairs, including development functions. At the divisional level, the IAS officers look after law and order, general administration and development work. In IAS cadre you can be sub-magistrate, joint secretary, deputy secretary etc.
- **Indian Police Service (IPS) :** The IPS (Indian Police Service) is responsible for public safety and security. The IPS mainly takes care of law and order, which, at the district level, is a responsibility shared with the IAS; crime prevention and

detection, traffic control and accident prevention and management. On completion of probation, an IPS officer begins his career as an Assistant Superintendent of Police of a sub-division. The Police service is divided into various departments like Crime Branch, Criminal Investigation Department (CID), Home Guards and Traffic Bureau. They also offer their services to central policing agencies like the Intelligence Bureau (IB), Central Bureau of Investigation (CBI), Cabinet Secretariat Security, the Border Security Force (BSF) and the Central Reserve Police Force (CRPF).

- **Indian Foreign Service (IFS) :** The Indian Foreign Service deals with the country's external affairs including diplomacy, trade and cultural relations. It is responsible for the administration and activities of Indian missions abroad and for the framing and implementation of the government's foreign policy. Probationers at first work at the External Affairs Ministry, then, they are posted to the Indian Diplomatic Mission of a particular country as third secretaries.
- **Indian Railway Service :** It is essentially responsible for the running of India's vast railway network. There are four non-technical and technical or engineering cadres in the railways. Entry for non-technical services include – the Indian Railway Traffic Service (IRTS) which is responsible for freight, passengers and movement of trains, the Indian Railway Personnel Service (IRPS) responsible for providing security to railway properties such as railway tracks, personnel, equipment etc. is through the Civil Services examination. However, the engineering services (IRSE) have a different recruitment procedure.
- **Indian Postal Service :** The Indian Postal Service is responsible for the efficient functioning of the postal and telegraph services, officers after training with field officers are appointed as Senior Superintendent of Post Offices, Assistant Post Master General throughout the country and also in the ministry at the centre.
- **Indian Customs and Central Excise Service :** The Indian Customs and Central Excise Service (IC and CES) is basically concerned with two main aspects mainly Customs and Excise. While Customs is concerned with the checking and levy of duty on taxable goods brought into the country, the Excise department is involved with the taxation of goods manufactured within the country.

- **Audit and Account Service :** Indian Audit and Account Service come under the Controller and Auditor General of India (CAG) which is responsible for the maintenance and audit of accounts in the states as well as union and state governments. These officers work in the audit offices under CAG and in central ministries and state governments:
  - (i) **Indian Defence Accounts Service** (IDAS) is responsible for maintaining and auditing of accounts of the defence services.
  - (ii) **Indian Civil Accounts Service** (ICAS) under the control of Secretary (Expenditure), Ministry of Finance maintains accounts of the State, Central Governments and public sector enterprises.
  - (iii) **Indian Information Service** (IIS) under the Ministry of Information and Broadcasting is responsible for running government owned broadcasting and advertising agencies like All India Radio, Doordarshan and DAVP. The service is also responsible for handling press and public relations for the various central ministries, public sector enterprises and defence forces at home as well as abroad.
- **Indian Revenue Service (IRS) :** The IRS is responsible for fixing, assessment and collection of income tax. The service also has specialised branches dealing with the investigation of tax evasion, statistics and so on.

Examination and Selection

Examination details

All India Combined Competitive Examination for the Civil Services conducted by the Union Public Service Commission (UPSC) comprises two successive stages followed by an interview or personality test :

- Civil Services (Preliminary) examinations (objective type) for the selection of candidates for main examination and
- Civil Services (Main) examination (written and interview) for the selection of candidates for the various services and posts.

The preliminary examination is held in May/June and the main examination in October/November. One must begin preparations of the main examination along with preliminary examination. This is because there is little time for the main examination if one waits for the results of the preliminaries. A candidate is permitted four attempts at the examination. If a person appears in the preliminary examination or even appears in one paper, it is counted as an attempt.

Preliminary Examination

Preliminary examination will consist of two papers of objective type (multiple choice questions) carrying a maximum of 450 marks. Paper-I is of general studies (150 marks) and Paper-II called 'optional' is based on the subject chosen by the candidate and carries 300 marks. The question papers are set in Hindi as well as in English. Each paper is of two hours duration. Blind candidates are allowed an extra time of 20 minutes for each paper. Preliminary examination is meant to serve as a screening test only; the marks obtained by the candidates who are declared qualified for admission to the main examination will not be counted for determining their final order of merit. Only those candidates who are declared by the Commission to have qualified in the preliminary examination in a year will be eligible to the main examination of that year, provided they are otherwise eligible for admission to the main examination. The success rate of preliminary examination is less than 10 per cent.

The Motive behind Preliminary Examination

Preliminary examination is intended to assess the overall intellectual traits and depth of understanding of candidates rather than merely the range of their information and memory. It will consist of a written examination and an interview test. The written examination will consist of nine papers of conventional essay type in the selected subjects for main examination. Each paper is of three hours duration. Blind candidates will, however, be allowed an extra time of 30 minutes at each paper.

Candidates will have the portion to answer all the question papers, except the language papers viz., Papers I and II above in any one of the languages included in the Eighth Schedule to the Constitution or in English. Candidates exercising the option to answer papers III to IX in any one of the languages included in the Eighth Schedule of the Constitution may, if they so desire, give English version within brackets of only the description of the technical terms, if any, in addition to the version in the language opted by them. The question papers other than language papers will be set both in Hindi and English.

Papers for Main Examination

Paper-I:	One of the Indian languages to be selected by the candidate from the 18 languages included in the Eighth Schedule to the Constitution (qualifying paper), 300 marks.
Paper-II:	English (qualifying paper) 300 marks
Paper-III:	Essay 250 marks
Paper-IV and -V:	General English (300 marks for each paper), 600 marks.

Paper-VI, VII, VIII and IX: Any two subjects to be selected from the optional subjects. Each subject will have two papers (300 marks for each paper), 1200 marks.

Total marks for written examination : 2000 marks

Interview or personality test : 300 marks

Grand Total : 2300 marks.

Optional Subjects for Main Examination

Optional subjects for the main examination can be chosen from 25 subjects and the literature of one of the 30 specified languages. The subjects include :

Agriculture, Animal Husbandry and Veterinary Science, Anthropology, Botany, Chemistry, Civil Engineering, Commerce and Accountancy, Economics, Electrical Engineering, Geography, Geology, History, Law, Management, Mathematics, Mechanical Engineering, Medical Science, Philosophy, Physics, Political Science and International Relations, Psychology, Public Administration, Sociology, Statistics, and Zoology.

Literature of one of the following languages:

Arabic, Assamese, Bodo, Bengali, Dogri, Chinese, English, French, German, Gujarati, Hindi, Kannada, Kashmiri, Konkani, Maithili, Malayalam, Manipuri, Marathi, Nepali, Oriya, Pali, Persian, Punjabi, Russian, Sanskrit, Santali, Sindhi, Tamil, Telegu and Urdu.

Candidates will not be allowed to offer the following combinations of subjects :

- Political Science and International Relations and Public Administration,
- Commerce and Accountancy and Management,
- Anthropology and Sociology,
- Mathematics and Statistics,
- Agriculture and Animal Husbandry and Veterinary Science,
- Management and Public Administration,
- Of the Engineering subjects namely, Civil Engineering, Electrical Engineering and Mechanical Engineering – not more than one subject,
- Animal Husbandry and Veterinary Science and Medical Science.

Note :

1. The papers on Indian languages and English will be of matriculation or equivalent standard and will be of qualifying nature; the marks obtained in these papers will not be counted for ranking.
2. Evaluation of the papers, namely, 'Essay, General Studies' and 'Optional subjects' of all the candidates would be done simultaneously along with evaluation of their qualifying papers on 'Indian Languages' and 'English', but the papers on 'Essay', 'General Studies' and 'Optional Subjects' of only such candidates will be taken cognizance of as attain such minimum standard as may be fixed by the Commission at their discretion for the qualifying papers on 'Indian Language' and 'English', and therefore, the marks in 'Essay', 'General Studies' and 'Optional Subjects' will not be disclosed to those candidates who fail to obtain such minimum qualifying standard in 'Indian Language' and 'English'.
3. The paper-I on Indian languages will not, however, be compulsory for candidates hailing from the North-Eastern States of Arunachal Pradesh, Manipur, Meghalaya, Mizoram, Nagaland and Laos for candidates hailing from the State of Sikkim.
4. For the Language papers, the script to be used by the candidates will be as: Assamese (Assamese), Bengali (Bengali), Bodo (Devanagari), Kannada (Kannada), Kashmiri (Persian), Konkani (Devanagari), Maithili (Devanagari), Nalayalam (Malayalam), Manipuri (Bengali), Marathi (Devanagari), Nepali (Devanagari), Oriya (Oriya), Punjabi (Gurmukhi), Sanskrit (Devanagari), Santhali (Devanagari or Olchiki), Sindhi (Devanagari or Arabic), Tamil (Tamil), Telegu (Telegu), and Urdu (Persian).

For Santhali language, question paper will be printed in Devanagari script but candidates will be free to answer either in Devanagari script or in Olchiki.

Interview Test : Carries 300 marks with no minimum qualifying marks Candidates who obtain minimum qualifying marks in the written part of the main examination shall be summoned for an interview. It is usually conducted in the month of April/May every year. The candidate will be interviewed by a Board who will have before them a record of his career. He/she will be asked questions on matters of general interest. The object of the interview is to assess the personal suitability of the candidate for a career in public service by a Board of competent and unbiased observers. The test is intended to judge the mental caliber of a candidate. In broad terms, this is really an assessment of not only his intellectual qualities but also social traits and his interest in current affairs. Some of the qualities to be judged are mental alertness, critical powers of assimilation, clear and logical exposition, balance of judgment, variety and depth of interest, ability for social cohesion and leadership, intellectual and moral integrity.

Marks thus obtained by the candidates in the main examination (written part as well as interview) would determine their final ranking. Candidates will be allotted to the various services keeping in view their ranks in the examination and the preferences expressed by them for the various services and posts.

There is also a medical test, especially rigid for IPS. Out of the final candidates selected top rankers are appointed as IAS officers. Once appointed, all probationary officers of the all India and central services undergo compulsory foundation training.

Application Procedure

UPSC has developed an application form common for all their examinations which will be processed on computerised machines. The application form along with an information brochure containing general instructions for filling up the form, an acknowledgement card and an envelope for sending the application is obtainable from the designated head offices/post offices only and not from any other agency. This form can be used only once and for only one examination.

Notification along with application forms for the civil service examination will appear in all the daily newspapers and the *Rozgar Samachar/Employment News* by the end of December each year. Candidates must use only the supplied form and they should in no case use photocopy/reproduction/unauthorised printed copy of the form. Since this form is electronically scanable, due care should be taken to fill up the application form correctly.

The duty filled in application form and the acknowledgement card should be mailed in the special envelope supplied with the information brochure. The Candidates should also write the name of examination, year (*e.g.* 'Civil Services (Preliminary) Examination, 2000') on the envelope before dispatching it to: Secretary, Union Public Service Commission, Dholpur House, Shahjahan Road, New Delhi – 110 069.

All candidates, whether already in government service or in government owned industrial undertakings or other similar organisations or in private employment should submit their applications direct to the Commission. If any candidate forwards his application through his employer and it reaches the Union Public Service Commission late, the application, even if submitted to the employer before the closing date, will not be considered.

Persons already in government service, whether in a permanent or temporary capacity or as work charged employees other than casual or daily rated employees or those serving under the public enterprise are, however, required to submit an undertaking that they have informed in writing their head of office/department that they have applied for the examination.

Candidates should note that in case a communication is received from their employer by the Commission withholding permission to the candidates applying for/appearing at the examination, their applications will be liable to be rejected/candidature will be liable to be cancelled.

Note:

1. While filling application form, the candidate should carefully decide about his choice for the centre and optional subject for the examination. More than one application from a Candidate giving different centres and/or optional subjects will not be accepted in any case. Even if a candidate sends more than one completed application the Commission will accept only one application at their discretion and the Commission's decision in the matter shall be final.

   If any candidate appears at a centre/optional subject other than the one indicated by the Commission in his admission certificate, the papers of such a candidate will not be valued and his candidature will be liable to cancellation.

2. Since these application forms are to be processed in a computerised system. Due care should be taken by the candidates to fill up their application form correctly. No column of the application should be left blank. Incomplete or defective applications shall be summarily rejected. No representation or correspondence regarding such rejection shall be entertained under any circumstances.

3. Candidates are not required to submit along with their applications any certificate in support of their claims regarding age, educational qualifications, scheduled castes/scheduled tribe/other backward classes and physically disabled, etc.,

which will be verified at the time of the main examination only. The candidates applying for the examination should ensure that they fulfill all the eligibility conditions for admission to the examination for which they are admitted by the Commission viz., preliminary examination, main (written) examination and interview test will be purely provisional, subject to their satisfying the prescribed eligibility conditions. If on verification at any time before or after the preliminary examination, main (written) examination and interview test, it is found that they do not fulfill any of the eligibility conditions; their candidature for the examination will be cancelled by the Commission.

Syllabus for the Examination

Civil Service Aptitude Test-C-SAT (Earlier Civil Services Preliminary Examination).

General Studies

Main examination – English and Indian languages, essay, general studies.

Optional Subjects (Literature)

Part-A– Preliminary Examination : The examination shall comprise two compulsory papers which consists of 450 marks.

Paper-I (150 marks)

- Current events of national and international importance.
- History of India and Indian National Movement.
- Indian and World Geography – physical, social, economic geography of India and the world.
- Indian polity and Governance – constitution, political system, panchayati raj, public policy, rights issues etc.
- Economic and Social Development – sustainable development, poverty, inclusion, demographics, social sector initiatives etc.
- General issues on environmental ecology, biodiversity and climate change – that do not require subject specialisation.
- General Science.

Paper-II (300 marks)

- Comprehension.
- Interpersonal skills including communicational skills.
- Logical reasoning and analytical ability.
- Decision-making and problem solving.

- General mental ability.
- Basic numeracy (numbers and their relations, orders of magnitude etc.) (class-X level), Data interpretation (charts, graphs, tables, data sufficiency etc. – class-X level).
- English language comprehension skills (class-X level).

Questions relating to English language comprehension skills of class-X level (last item in the syllabus of paper-II) will be tested through passages from English language only without providing Hindi translation thereof in the question paper. The questions will be of multiple choice, objective type.

Part-B – Main Examination

Compulsory Subjects

English and Indian Languages.

The aim of the paper is to test the candidate's ability to read and understand serious discursive prose and to express his ideas clearly and correctly in English/Indian language concerned. The pattern of questions would be broadly as follows :

- Comprehension of given passages,
- Précis Writing,
- Usage and vocabulary,
- Short essay.

Indian Languages

- Comprehension of given passages,
- Précis Writing,
- Usage and Vocabulary,
- Short essay,
- Translation from English to the Indian language and vice-versa.

Note:

1. The papers on Indian languages and English will be of matriculation or equivalent standard and will be of qualifying nature only. The marks obtained in these papers will not be counted for ranking.
2. The candidates will have to answer the English and Indian languages papers in English and the respective Indian language (except where translation is involved).

Essay

Candidates will be required to write an essay on a specific topic. The choice of subjects will be given. They will be expected to keep closely to the subject of the essay to arrange their ideas in orderly fashion and to write concisely. Credit will be given for effective and exact expression.

General Studies – Paper I and II

Optional Subjects

Optional subjects for the main examination can be chosen from 25 subjects and the literature of one of the 30 specified languages. The subjects include :

Agriculture, Animal Husbandry and Veterinary Science, Anthropology, Botany, Chemistry, Civil Engineering, Commerce and Accountancy, Economics, Electrical Engineering, Geography, Geology, History, Law, Management, Mathematics, Mechanical Engineering, Medical Science, Philosophy, Physics, Political Science and International Relations, Psychology, Public Administration, Sociology, Statistics, and Zoology.

Literature of one of the following languages : (A candidate may be required to answer some or all the questions in the language concerned. In regard to the languages included in the Eighth Schedule of constitution, the scripts will be the same. Candidates should note that the questions not required to be answered in a specific language will have to both answer in the language medium indicated by them for answering papers on essay, general studies and optional subjects).

Arabic, Assamese, Bodo, Bengali, Dogri, Chinese, English, French, German, Gujarati, Hindi, Kannada, Kashmiri, Konkani, Maithili, Malayalam, Manipuri, Marathi, Nepali, Oriya, Pali, Persian, Punjabi, Russian, Sanskrit, Santali, Sindhi, Tamil, Telegu and Urdu.

Books and periodicals recommended for General Studies

- Manorama Year Book,
- CSR Year Book,
- Hindustan Year Book,
- Yojana/planning commission reports,
- Civil Services Chronicle/Civil Service Today,
- Employment News,
- Competition Success Review,
- India Today,
- Front Line

- Business World,
- The Economic Times,
- The Hindu/The Times of India/The Hindustan Times,
- NDTV/Star News/Ajtak/CNBC 18 etc.

Important Dates to be remembered:

- Date of issuing of application form,
- Last date of receipt of Application,
- Date for Civil Service Main Examination.

Contact Details

Address : Union Public Service Commission, Dholpur House, Shahjahan Road, New Delhi. Fax: 011-23098591. Website: www.upsc.gov.in.

14.2 Indian Police Service (IPS)

The Indian Police Service

The Indian Police Service is the premier uniform service in the country.

It is one of the most coveted positions in civil administration of the Indian democratic set-up. But to reach this coveted position one has to be really diligent and toil hard to pass through a rigorous procedure involving written tests and interviews that spreads throughout a year. It requires self-discipline, patience, punctuality, commitment, self-confidence and a burning desire to be at the top ladder of an important organisation of the country. In the final stage of the exams, the candidates are grilled in the interview to test their personality and mental ability. The final list of the successful candidates is prepared and the candidates who have secured very good rank out of 400 – 450 (approx.) top ranks are admitted to the Sardar Vallabhbhai Patel National Police Academy as IPS probationers. Here, they undergo rigorous training of nearly one year in which all aspects of policing and administration are taught to them.

After completion of their training they are posted as per requirements of the central and state governments police and investigative organisation. He serves the state government in various capacities ranging from Assistant Superintendent of Police at the beginning of his career to the Director General of Police at the stage of retirement. He can also serve the central government in various organisations like the Central Reserve Police Force, Border Security Force, Central Bureau of Investigation, Intelligence Bureau, Research and Analysis Wing (RAW) etc. It is a kind of career which is ever demanding. You cannot afford to relax after getting the post; in fact, you have to work harder after getting the job than before getting it.

Being an 'All India Services', the new IPS incumbent's services are allotted to various state cadres under Cadre System. The cadre system is allotted on the basis of lottery and the top rank holder of each state may get a chance to their home state if he had applied for one.

Personal Attributes

To be an IPS officer is not a mean thing. If you enjoy power then you also have to accept the responsibility which comes along with it. To handle things effectively a lot of hard work, stamina, alertness of mind, adaptability to follow difficult time schedules, good team spirit is required as this is not a time bound job. This is a career in which you are not supposed to work alone but have to make your team work hard for the society you have vowed to serve while joining this career.

Eligibility

Educational qualification

To be eligible for becoming an IPS office, the candidate must possess a degree from an Indian university or an equivalent qualification. Those in the final year of a degree course can also appear in the preliminary examination taken every year by UPSC.

Age :

- The candidate must have attained the age of 21 years on 1st August of the year of examination and must not have attained 30 years of age on that date.
- The upper age limit will be relaxed by three years for OBC candidates and five years for SC/ST candidates.
- The upper age limit is also relaxed in favour of Defence Personnel.

The job of an IPS officer

The IPS officer is primarily concerned with maintenance of law and order, crime detection and prevention, traffic control, accident prevention and management etc. Besides these routine duties, the other duties of an IPS officer may include VIP security, border policing, railway policing, tackling corruption in public life, counter terrorism, checking smuggling, drug trafficking, economic/cyber crimes and help in disaster management. IPS officers can also be leading officers in intelligence agencies like RAW, IB and CBI etc., or paramilitary forces like BSF and ITBP and so on.

Job Prospects

An IPS being an All India Services officer works for both the central and state governments. He serves the state government in various capacities ranging from an ASP at the beginning of his career to the DGP. He can also serve the central government in various civil defence and paramilitary organisations like the Central Reserve Police Force, Central Bureau of Investigation, Intelligence Bureau, Research and Analysis Wing (RAW) etc.

Career Options

Hierarchy (in descending order from top to bottom) in the IPS line up :

- Director General of Police (Top most post),
- Inspector General of Police,
- Deputy Inspector General of Police,
- Additional Commissioner of Police (Mumbai, Pune, Nagpur, Thane),
- Superintendent of Police in selection grade with 13+ years of service,
- Additional Superintendent of Police,
- Assistant Superintendent of Police in charge of a sub-division,
- IPS Probationer.

Remuneration

At the entry level, IPS officers are paid around ₹ 40,000 per month, Middle level IPS officers get around ₹ 60,000 a month, whereas senior, level IPS officers get around ₹ 80,000 a month. Besides their pay, IPS officers are also entitled to special perks depending on where one is posted.

14.3 Indian Foreign Service (IFS)

What is the IFS?

The IFS, an acronym for the Indian Foreign Service is the premier diplomatic service of our country. It was in September 1946, on the eve of India's Independence, the Government of India decided to create the Indian Foreign Service for India's diplomatic, consular and commercial presentation overseas. The Indian Foreign Service is a service under Grade 'A' and Grade 'B' of the Central Civil Services of the executive branch of the Government of India. The Foreign Secretary of India is the administrative head of the Indian Foreign Service.

Function of the IFS

Members of the IFS, primarily represent the country in the international arena. The Indian Foreign Service deals with the country's external affairs, including diplomacy, trade and cultural relations. It is responsible for the administration and activities of Indian missions abroad. IFS frames and implements the government's foreign policy. IFS officers are attached to the Ministry of External Affairs and may be posted either in India or abroad at any of the Indian Embassies or missions approximating 160 in number. Probationers at first work at the External Affairs Ministry and then they are posted to the Indian Mission of a particular country as third secretaries.

The service offers vast exposure to the entrants as well a prime status as representatives of the country. It is a high flying job but entry to the Foreign Service is tough and average intake is only 10-15 persons annually.

Chief functions of Indian Foreign Officers

The chief functions include: Representing India in its embassy, high commissions, consulates and permanent missions to multilateral organisations like UN, protecting India's national interest in the country of his/her posting, negotiating agreements on various issues with the authorities of the receiving state and extending consular facilities to foreigners and Indian nationals abroad. At home, Ministry of External Affairs is responsible for all aspects of external relations.

Eligibility

Age : A candidate should be between 21 to 30 years of age on 1 August of the year of examination. Maximum 30 for general category, 33 for OBCs and 35 for SCs/STs.

Educational qualification : Candidates are required to have degree or equivalent qualification from a recognised institute or university.

Personal Attributes

They must be honest, extrovert, dynamic and dedicated people with high sense of morality, integrity and love for the country. Leadership qualities and communication skills are also essential to be in this field. One must also be aware of national and international affairs.

Job Prospects and Career Options

Probationers at first are attached with a desk, dealing with a particular country, at the External Affairs ministry of India. Thereafter, they are posted abroad to the Indian Mission of that country as third secretaries. Normally, he is posted in a country where his compulsory foreign language (CFL) is the native language and enrolled in a language course. The officer is expected to develop proficiency in his CFL and pass the requisite examination before he is confirmed in service. Then he/she is promoted to second secretary as soon as he is confirmed in service. They remained in the same office as second secretary for two years.

Officers can also be posted to Indian consulates abroad where hierarchy is Vice-Consul, Consul and Consul General.

During their probationary period, the probationers are posted to the Indian mission of that country as third secretaries. During their tenure within the country they work in the ministry or are posted in any of its attached office, e.g., the passport office. They are deputed to institutions like United Nations, UNESCO, World Bank, SAARC, etc.

Service Hierarchy

Designation in Field	**Designation in Headquarters**
Attached/Third Secretary	Undersecretary
Second/First Secretary	Undersecretary
First Secretary	Deputy Secretary
Director	Counselor Director
Minster/DCM Ambassador	Joint Secretary
Ambassador/High Commissioner	Additional Secretary
Ambassador/High Commissioner	Secretary

Selection

Entry to the IFS is through the combined Civil Services examination of UPSC which is conducted annually to select officers for 23 services including the IAS and the IPS. The examination comprises preliminary test, an essay type written main examination and an interview. Once the preliminary examination is cleared, UPSC will send you the application form for the main examination. In case you do not receive the main exam application form within two weeks after the preliminary examination results are declared, you have to contact the UPSC office. When you fill in the form for the main examination, you have to mention your preference for IFS service (from IAS, IPS, IRS etc.) in the application. If you get a good score in the main examination, you will be called for an interview. A merit list is made on the basis of your interview and main examination marks. Your appointment to the IFS service will be based on your preference mentioned in the application form, merit rating, vacancies available, medical checkup etc.

On selection to the Indian Foreign Service through the combined civil services examination, the new entrants undergo a multi-faceted and comprehensive training programme. The training programme is intended to give a thorough grounding in diplomatic knowledge, qualities and skills. The probationers commence their training, together with their colleagues from the other All India Services at the Lal Bahadur Shastri National Academy of Administration, Mussourie.

Training

Thereafter, the probationers join the Foreign Service Institute in New Delhi and undergo focussed training in the various disciplines that a career diplomat needs to keep himself/herself abreast with. The entire training programme is for a period of 36 months. It instills a strong sense of history, knowledge of diplomacy and international relations and an awareness of general economic and political principles. The course includes modules on international relations and foreign policy, defense and security, economic diplomacy, international law, parliamentary affairs, cultural diplomacy, protocol and consular matters, as well as modules on practical skills such as administration and accounts, communication skills, representational skills and relations with the media.

At the conclusion of the training programme the officer is assigned his/her compulsory foreign language (CFL). After a brief period of desk attachment in the Ministry of External Affairs the officer is posted to an Indian mission abroad in a country where his CFL is the native language and enrolled in a language course. The officer is expected to develop proficiency in his CFL and pass the requisite examination before he is confirmed in service.

Remuneration

The starting pay of an IFS officer is approximately ₹ 60,000.

Useful Contacts

- **Lal Bahadur Shastri National Academy of Administration (LBSNAA)**

  Mussorie-248179 (Uttarakhand).

  Phone: 0135-2222000, 2632236, 2632367 and 2632405.

Fax: 0135-2632350 and 0135-2632720.

Website: www.lbsnaa.gov.in/.

- **Foreign Service Institute**

  Ministry of External Affairs

  Baba Ganj Nath Marg

  Old JNU Campus

  New Delhi-110067.

  Phone: +91.11.26181342, 26181321, 26181327.

  Fax: 26181337.

  Website: www.fsi.mea.gov.in/.

14.4 Indian Revenue Service (IRS)

What is an Indian Revenue Service (IRS)?

Indian Revenue Service (IRS) is the service under Grade 'A' of the Central Civil Services of the executive branch of the Government of India. This service functions under the Department of Revenue in the Union Home Ministry of Finance.

The Responsibility of Indian Revenue Service (IRS)

The IRS department is India's premier financial agency, responsible for a wide variety of financial and fiscal matters. It is concerned with the collection and administration of the various direct and indirect taxes accruing to the Union Government such as central sales tax, stamp duties, gold control and foreign exchange.

An IRS officer

An IRS officer is the fourth most respected officer of Civil Services after the IAS, IPS and IFS's. IRS officers are the tax administrators of India. They are concerned with the collection, administration and policy formation of Direct (Income, Corporate, Wealth, FBT etc.) and Indirect (Central Excise, Service Tax and even Customs Duty) taxes. These officers hold the responsibility of having a check on the proper collection of revenue through taxes which is a big source of income of the government both state and central.

Eligibility

- **Officer grade :** The two sources of entry to Indian Revenue Service (IRS) are the officers directly recruited through Civil Services examination conducted by UPSC and officers promoted from Income Tax Officers (Class-II) grade.

To enter into a career as an IRS officer/officer grade directly one has to pass the Civil Service examination conducted by the UPSC. The minimum qualification required for applying for CSE is graduation from a recognised university. Candidates who have attained 21 years of age but not attained 30 years of age on August 1st of the year of examination are eligible to apply.

- **Junior grade :** For junior level entry into the revenue service, one has to pass the Combined Graduate Level Examination by the Staff Selection Commission. This is a less rigorous selection procedure as compared to the Civil Services examination. Graduates of any discipline between 18 and 27 years are eligible to apply for this exam.

Eligibility for different job positions varies. In Customs and Central Excise and Income Tax eligibility for the posts of Customs officer/Income Tax Officer, Superintendent, Preventive officers/Inspectors, Tax assistants, upper division Clerks etc. is graduation in any discipline and clearing UPSC and SSC exams respectively. Plus-2 candidates can apply for the post of lower division clerks and 7th class candidates with minimum 175.5 cms height and chest 80 cms can apply for the post of constables. Steno, typists etc. need 10th pass. For some posts the board themselves conduct examinations for direct recruitment. The vacancies from time to time will be published in the *Employment News* and leading newspapers.

Training

After being finally selected for the IRS, the new officer recruits undergo a three month foundational training at Lal Bahadur National Academy of Administration (LBSNAA), Mussourie (Uttarakhand). After this, Customs and Excise officers undergo 15 month rigorous training at National Academy of Customs Excise and Narcotics, Faridabad, while Income tax officers are trained at National Academy of Direct Taxes, Nagpur headed by the Director General of Income Tax (Training). After completion of training, the officers are designated as Assistant Commissioner (Central Board of Direct Taxes CBDT/Central Board of Excise and Customs (CBEC) and may rise up to the level of Chief Commissioner with a few fortunate ones reaching the top post of Member/Chairperson (CBDT/CBEC).

Director General of Income Tax (Training) also supervises the functioning of seven Regional Training Institute at Bangalore, Kolkata, Lucknow, Mumbai, Chennai, Chandigarh and Ahmedabad and 26 ministerial staff training units spread over the country.

Job Prospects

Selected candidates in the officer cadre begin their career as Assistant Commissioners of Income Tax and may rise to the level of Chief Commissioners of Income Tax. The salary, allowances and facilities like healthcare, housing, conveyance etc. also make it a lucrative profession. The prestige and power attached to this top-notch job is really greater than the salary one earns in the field itself. IRS candidates can be posted anywhere in the country.

Remuneration

Top income tax sleuths get a fixed pay scale of ₹ 80,000 per month on par with the secretaries in the union government and police chiefs.

Useful Contacts

- **Lal Bahadur Shastri National Academy of Administration (LBSNAA)**

  Mussoorie-248179 (Uttarakhand).

  Phone: 0135-2222000, 2632236, 2632489.

  Fax: 0135-2632350, 0135-2632720.

  Website: www.lbsnaa.gov.in/.

- **National Academy of Customs Excise and Narcotics (NACEN)**

  Sector 29, Niacin Complex, Faridabad

  Haryana-121001.

  Phone: 0129-2504617.

  Website: www.nacen.gov.in/.

- **National Academy of Direct Taxes**

  Nelson Square, Chhindwara Road

  Nagpur-440030.

  Website: www.nadt.gov.in/.

14.5 Staff Selection Commission (SSC)

What is Staff Selection Commission?

Staff Selection Commission is an Indian organisation to recruit staff for various ministries and departments of the Government of India and in subordinate offices. This office is an attached office of the Department of Personnel and Training which consists of chairman, two members and a secretary-cum-controller of examinations.

Background

The Estimates Committee of the parliament recommended the setting up of a Service Selection Commission in its 47th report (1967-68) for conducting examinations for recruitment to lower categories of posts. Later, in the Department of Personnel and Administrative Reforms, on 4th November, 1975, Government of India constituted a Commission called Subordinate Services Commission. On 26th September, 1977, Subordinate Services Commission was renamed as Staff Selection Commission.

The functions of the Staff Selection Commission were redefined by the Government of India through Ministry of Personnel, Public Grievances and Pensions on 21st May, 1999. Then the new constitution and functions of the Staff Selection Commission came into effect from 1st June, 1999.

Functions

To conduct examinations and/or interviews to make recruitment to Group 'B' and Group 'C' posts for the various ministries and departments of the Government of India.

Examinations conducted by Staff Selection Commission (SSC)

Exam	Post	Minimum qualification	Age Limit
Combined Graduate Level Examination	Assistant, Income Tax Inspector, Central Excise Inspector, Assistant Enforcement Officer, Sub Inspector (CBI), Divisional Accountant, Statistical Investigator, Auditor, Accountant/Junior Accountant, Tax Assistant, Upper Division Clerk and Compiler	Graduation Degree	18 - 27
Combined Higher Secondary (10+2) Examination	Data Entry Operator and Lower Division Clerk	12th Standard	18 - 27
Junior Engineers Examination	Civil, Mechanical, Electrical, Quantity Surveying and contract	Degree/Diploma in Civil, Electrical & Mechanical Engineering	18 - 27
Junior Translators (CSOLS) Examination	Translator, Hindi Translator, Hindi Pradhyapak	Master's Degree	20 - 30
Stenographers (Grade C & Grade D) Examination	Grade - C Grade – D	12th Standard	18 - 27
SI in CPOs & Intelligence Officer in NCB Examination	Sub Inspectors, Intelligence Officers	Graduation Degree	20 - 25
Section Officer (Commercial) Examination	Section Officer	Graduation Degree with Commerce/CA/ICWA/CS	18 - 27
Section Officer	Section Officer	Graduation Degree	18 - 27

15

LAW

Importance of Legal Profession

Legal profession is one of the most respectable and lucrative professions all over the world. In the United States, lawyers charge money on hourly basis and not surprisingly they are the richest personalities in the country. From writers to politicians to freedom fighters, lawyers had donned many hats. Mahatma Gandhi, Dr Rajendra Prasad, Franz Kafka and Abraham Lincoln – all these were lawyers. Lawyers are held in high esteem in our society and there remains the faith that even when all else fails, one can still take recourse to the legal system. In our daily life in one way or other we may come across situations where legal advice is required. In such situation, we need the advice of a legal professional who analyses and interprets law in a proper manner.

The Work of Lawyers

Lawyers counsel clients about their legal rights and suggest course of action in a particular matter. They also advice clients and draw up legal documents such as wills and contracts and conduct negotiations on legal matters and may represent clients in court and tribunal proceedings. Academic excellence is not the main feature behind the success in this profession. Professional competence acquired through experience and practice with efficient lawyers is the main yardstick of success.

Areas of Specialisation

There are various areas of specialisation in this field which one can choose from like corporation law, civil law, criminal law, international law, labour law, patent law, tax law and so on.

Before you embark on this profession, you need to make an Informed Decision.

Many individuals choose a career in law for the wrong reasons. Before embarking on the demanding, time-intensive and expensive journey to becoming a lawyer, make certain that you are making a well-informed decision. Take a stock of few common myths regarding the life of a lawyer :

- ***As a lawyer, I can eradicate injustice and affect societal change*** - While you can make a positive impact as a lawyer, litigation has little to do with virtue winning over evil and everything to do with advocating your client's position based on the facts and applicable law. Judicial decisions are not so much about the pursuit of justice or right *versus* wrong as about reaching a compromise between all the parties. Judicial policy also affects many case decisions. According to the ABA (American Bar Association) survey, two out of every three lawyers surveyed reported concern that the court system they serve is becoming too political. The same is applicable to India also.
- ***I will make myself a great lawyer because I am good at arguing*** - Although litigation is an adversarial process, legal advocacy is not about 'arguing' in the sense of engaging in a verbal battle with your opponent. Instead, it is about persuading your audience – judge, mediator or jury through a logical, well-researched, well-reasoned discussion based on the facts and the law. Thus, to succeed as a litigator, a track record of 'winning arguments' is not as important as top-notch oral advocacy and writing skills.
- ***The work of a lawyer is intellectually challenging*** - While law practice can be intellectually rigorous, much of the lawyer's work is mundane and repetitive. New lawyers, especially those in large firms are often charged with the mind-numbing tasks of document review, cite checking and routine research. Law firm lawyers must track their time in six to fifteen-minutes increments throughout the day, a painstaking but necessary task.

How can One Become a Lawyer?

To become a lawyer, you have to pass LL.B. degree from a recognised institution and then enroll with the Bar Council of India.

Eligibility

Minimum qualification to go for a course in law (LL.B.) is 10+2. You can study five years LL.B. after 10+2 with science/arts/commerce or three years LL.B. after graduation. PG programmes in law (LLM) are of two years duration and eligibility is LLB degree. In addition to LL.B. degree, many universities and institutes also offer other diploma courses in several disciplines of law, including Administrative Law, International Law, Labour Laws, Tax Laws and Corporate Laws.

The LL.B. course is regulated by the Bar Council of India which sets rules and regulations regarding legal practice in the country. Any specialisation is done at masters, M. Phill or Ph.D. stage. A higher degree helps candidates get jobs in academics.

Selection

In most of the institutes/universities, selection is on the basis of an entrance test. The entrance examination is objective type in nature. The questions invariably cover areas like reasoning, general awareness, numerical aptitude, legal aptitude and preliminary political science.

Funding and Scholarship

Not many law schools offer financial help on the basis of entrance exam. The student must talk to the authorities and find out the specific policies on scholarship from respective universities. Students can also opt to take a bank loan or apply for various scholarships that are offered from time to time.

Cost of the Study

Three years' LL.B. course usually involves lesser expenses in the range of ₹ 20,000 to 30,000 for three years. The five years BA-LL.B. comparatively costs a little more in the lieu of about ₹ 3,00,000 for five years. Hostel expenses are exclusive of the tuition fees.

Teaching Method

Teaching is not restricted to the conventional classroom methods alone, it include case studies, mock court, etc., to make the study more practical and interesting.

Personal Attributes

Law is a career which requires loads of patience and logical skills. It needs a lot of hard work and dedication to become a successful lawyer. First generation lawyers particularly face numerous problems in their profession as is true of every other profession. It becomes easier if one trains under a senior counsel in the beginning of their career. This is not to say that newbies cannot make it on their own. Anything is possible with determination and of course hard work. Therefore, one should analyse these points before opting for law as a career.

Success in this profession is not based on marks one obtains in the examination but it depends much on one's personal calibre. One must have good oral and written communication skills, logical reasoning, power of concentration, patience, good memory to relate and quote past cases to prove your point, ability to argue and discuss matters with a variety of people, self-confidence, courage to deal with threats especially in criminal cases, etc. You should have up-to-date information on any changes in the law. A good library and a fair amount of reading is also important.

Job Prospects

There is a plethora of opportunities for a law graduate. One can either practise as an advocate in a court of law or work with corporate firms. By clearing examinations conducted by Union Public Service Commission, a law graduate can become a judge. After gaining experience, a law graduate can hope to become Solicitor General, a Public Prosecutor or offer services to government departments and ministries. One can also work as a legal advisor for various organisations. Teaching in colleges, working with NGOs and working as a reporter for newspapers and television channels are other attractive options.

Demand and Supply

An acute shortage of qualified lawyers has been a major problem in India. The Bar Council of India has often expressed its concern that young lawyers do not join the Bar. There are nearly 10 lakhs lawyers in India but according to law experts only 20 per cent of them can be considered fit enough to practise law in courts. Several law schools like NLSU, NALSAR were established to increase the level of legal education and produce skilled lawyers to meet the requirement. However, India is a country with one of the highest litigation rates among its population and Sir Ivor Jennings termed the Indian Constitution 'a lawyer's paradise.' Talented lawyers will never have to worry about their income.

Different Roles of Lawyers

- **Criminal Lawyer:** Specialises in criminal laws CrPC, IPC, Evidence Act and various other penal laws.
- **Civil Litigation Lawyer:** Specialises in civil laws, e.g., taxation laws, excise laws.
- **Legal Analyst:** Works for corporate firms or law firms and analyses laws pertaining to the sphere of the company and its operation.

- **Document Drafting Lawyer:** Specialises in drafting various documents containing agreements, terms and conditions, case material etc.
- **Legal Journalist :** Covers crime beats, legal proceedings in courts, arbitration courts, international courts and arbitration events.
- **Legal Advisor :** Offers consultancy to corporate firms regarding their legal obligations, duties, legal relations with other firms.
- **Government Lawyer:** Works for the government and in close coordination with the police.
- **Judge :** Offers judgment after conducting the court proceedings and hearing at the concerned parties.

Career Options

If one wishes to become an advocate and practice law as a profession in India, he or she should enroll with the local State Bar Council. An application for admission as an advocate shall be made in the prescribed form to the State Bar Council within whose jurisdiction the applicant proposes to practise. The Bar Council of India and the State Bar Councils form a self contained code of law for legal professionals practising in India.

In the Government Services : Hundreds of lawyers are inducted into the government ministries every year through a UPSC interview. The minimum qualification is a master's degree in Law with five years of experience, preferably in research. Those looking for employment in the government sector or in the judiciary have a lot of opportunity of getting employed even at a higher age bracket. While the UPSC is recruiting agency of Law Officers in the various ministries and departments, the State Public Service Commission performs the same task in the states. These Commissions regularly employ personnel for higher and lower judiciary. Similarly, Government Pleaders are also employed. They plead cases on behalf of government and they are the regular government employees on a salary.

In the judiciary, the posts consist of the following :

- **Magistrate and Sub-Magistrate :** A candidate who qualifies in the Law Service Commission or State Public Service Commission is eligible for appointment as Magistrate and Sub-Magistrate (monists). While Magistrate presides over criminal court, munsif delivers judgment on civil cases. Promotion may take a person higher up to sub-judge, District and Sessions Courts Judge and further (depending upon seniority and vacancy) to appointments in High Courts and the Supreme Court.

- **Public Defenders:** At the state, federal and local level, public defenders serve as court-appointed attorneys for those who cannot afford an attorney.
- **Public Prosecutor:** Government pleaders represent the state in session courts and lend advice to officers in districts in all legal matters when called for.
- **Attorney General:** Attorney General appointed by the president advises the Government of India on such legal matters as may be assigned to him by the president. He has the right of audience in all courts of India and participates in the proceedings of parliament without the right to vote.
- **Solicitor General:** He advices the government on legal matters and submits statement of important cases to Attorney General of India for his opinion or appearance in the Supreme Court as necessary. A Solicitor General is the second law officer of the country, next to Attorney General and assists the latter performs his duties.
- **Advocate General:** Similar to the post of Attorney General at centre, each state has an Advocate General appointed by state Governors. These offices generally prosecute cases that have statewide significance and work with local district attorney's offices in the prosecution of cases. One of the best ways to gain trial experience quickly after graduation is to work at a state attorney's office.
- **District Attorney :** Assistant State Attorneys (also called district attorneys) are primarily responsible for criminal matters and prosecution. The District Attorney is usually an elected official. Depending upon the size of the District Attorney's office, they may have multiple units that focus upon different types of crimes such as domestic violence, homicide, appellate work or sex crimes. If you work with a smaller District Attorney's office, you may have option of handling diverse caseloads.
- **Notary, Oath Commissioner :** A notary is a legal practitioner of at least ten years experience in the profession. He is appointed on application to Central, State government to draw, verify, authenticate, certify and attest the execution of any deed. Oath commissioner is another established authority similar to the notary.
- **Legal Advisors :** Public sector undertakings and state and central government organisations employ lawyers as advisors. They

also work in legal departments of firms or for private clients. Legal advisors counsel their clients as to their legal rights and obligations and suggest the appropriate course of action in business and personal matters. They also check deeds, issue writs, collect documents.

Other fields : Lawyer can also work as legal counsel and legal advisors for firms, organisations and families. They can work as trustees of various trusts, as teachers, law reporters, company secretary and so on. Opportunities exist in the defence services, too. Additional qualification along with law degree offers scope for a wide range of employment opportunities.

- **Defence Service :** They can work in the legal branches of defence departments such as the Indian army, Navy and Air Force. They conduct courts of enquiry and court martial of offending service personnel governed by the particular legislation acts.
- **Advocate :** An advocate practises in the court of law. He represents a party (individual, group of individuals or a company) in a court of law. They present the facts of the case to the judge, cross-examine witnesses and finally sum up the reasons as to why the court should decide in their clients' favour.
- **Solicitor :** Solicitor is a kind of advisor to clients on a variety of matters that involves law. Solicitors need never appear in court directly. Solicitor's firms undertake cases related to their area of work.
- **Teacher :** Those with a good aptitude and taste for teaching can go for LL.M. and take up job in any university or institute offering law courses to students.
- **Writer :** If one has a flair for writing he may act as an author and produce journals and legal commentaries and bring our law reports. They can write articles for magazines, newspapers etc.
- **Company Secretary :** A law graduate and/or a member of the Institute of Company Secretaries can be employed as a company secretary in a firm.

Tips for getting hired

Candidates who do five years BA-LL.B. from top law schools like NLSUI Bangalore, NALSAR Hyderabad get attractive job offers from law firms and ITES firms. Many also opt to start their own practice. All law graduates who wish to practise in the courts have to register themselves in the Bar Council of India (BCI) and practise in courts under senior lawyers. Practical training in court can enhance your chances of getting hired by law firms and with senior lawyers. Though most of the law colleges impart practical legal education to final year law students, it is students who should take initiative and start visiting court proceedings in the final year to understand the day-to-day affair.

International Opportunities

Legal education in India is similar to the one in Britain. There are several universities in UK that offer legal education to Indian students. After completion of the course, Indian students quite enjoy working in the UK wherein they receive attractive salary packages. A recent trend has been that students from India who study in law colleges in the USA receive attractive jobs after completion of the course. Harvard Law School, Yale University, Australia National University etc. are some attractive options for Indian law students these days.

Remuneration

A lawyer who wishes to start practising in a court can get a stipend of ₹ 5,000 to 40,000 depending upon the advocate he is associated with. A law graduate working with a Legal Process Outsourcing can earn attractive salary in the range of ₹ 20,000 and 50,000. It is a very high paying profession but depends largely on the calibre, popularity and success of the candidate. The college you graduate from is another factor. Many a time, salary of lawyers depends on many factors. It may vary depending upon the nature of the legal case and the status of the client involved.

Start Early

A candidate can start preparing for law entrance exam conducted at the national level for five years' BA-LL.B. at various National Law Schools soon after completing the senior secondary exam. The national law entrance exam, CLAT (Combined Law Admission Test) basically tests the student's general English, legal aptitude, general awareness, logical skills, etc.

Some universities which offer the three years LL.B. conduct entrance examination which have syllabus on the same lines.

Common Law Admission Test (CLAT)

The Common Law Admission Test (CLAT) is an all India entrance examination conducted by 14 National Law Schools/Universities for admissions to their under-graduate degree programs (LL.B. & LL.M.). The 14 participating NLUs in the order of their establishment are :

- National Law School of India University, Bangalore (NLSIU).

- NALSAR University of Law, Hyderabad.
- National Law Institute University, Bhopal (NLIU).
- The West Bengal National University of Juridical Sciences, Kolkata (WBNUJS).
- National Law University, Jodhpur (NLUJ).
- Hidayatullah National Law University, Raipur (HNLU).
- Gujarat National Law University, Gandhinagar (GNLU).
- Dr Ram Manohar Lohiya National Law University, Lucknow (RMLNLU).
- Rajiv Gandhi National University of Law, Patiala (RGNUL).
- Chanakya National Law University, Patna (CNLU).
- National University of Advanced Legal Studies, Kochi (NUALS).
- National Law University, Orissa (NLUO).
- National University of Study and Research in Law, Ranchi (NUSRL).
- National Law University and Judicial Academy, Assam (NLUJA).

The first CLAT Committee (consisting of Vice-Chancellors of the participating institutes) decided that the test should be conducted by rotation in the order of their establishment.

Eligibility for Under-graduate Programmes : To be eligible to appear in CLAT, a candidate should have obtained a 10+2 or its equivalent qualification from a recognised Board with not less than 50 per cent marks in aggregate (45 per cent in case of SC/ST/OBC and PWD). Candidates who have appeared in the 10+2 examination and are awaiting results are also eligible to appear in the test. Age of the candidate should not be more than 20 years in case of General/OBC candidates (22 years in case of SC/ST and persons with Disability) as on 1st July during the year of admission. The candidate must have passed the qualifying examination at the time of his/her admission and be able to submit its proof.

Eligibility for Post graduate Programmes: To be eligible for appearing in CLAT, a candidate should have obtained a LL.B./BL Degree or an equivalent degree from a recognised University with not less than 55 per cent marks in aggregate (50 per cent in case of SC/ST/OBC and persons with Disability).

The Pattern of CLAT Examination

The pattern of CLAT Paper for Under-graduate Programme :

Total number of multiple-choice questions of one mark each :	200
Duration of examination :	2 hours

Subject areas with weightage :

English including comprehension :	40 marks
General Knowledge/Current Affairs :	50 marks
Elementary Mathematics (Numerical ability) :	20 marks
Legal Aptitude :	50 marks
Logical Reasoning :	40 marks
Total Marks :	200 marks

Pattern of CLAT for PG Programme

Pattern of CLAT for PG Programme is as follows :

Duration of examination :	2 hours
Multiple choice Questions (100 questions of 1 mark each)	pertaining to subjects areas namely, Law of Contracts, Law of Torts, Criminal Law, Constitutional Law and Legal Theory.
Short-answer questions (100 marks):	10 questions of 10 marks each.

The Non-Participating Schools

- National Law University, Delhi.
- Army Institute of Law, Mohali.
- Barada School of Legal Studies, Faculty of Law, The Maharaja Sayajirao University of Baroda, Vadodara, Gujarat.
- Symbiosis Law School, Pune.
- ILS Law College, Pune.
- Amity Law School, Delhi.
- Tamil Nadu Dr. Ambedkar Law University, Chennai.
- Rajiv Gandhi School of International Property Law, Kharagpur.
- KIIT Law School, Bhubaneshwar.
- Faculty of Law, University of Delhi, Delhi.
- Government of Law College, Mumbai.

- School of Law, University of Petroleum and Energy Studies, Dehradun.
- Faculty of Law, Benaras Hindu University, Varanasi.

What is AIBE?

The All India Bar Examination (AIBE) is intended to test an advocate's ability to practise the profession of law in India. The AIBE will assess capabilities at a basic level and is intended to set a minimum standard for admission to the practice of law; it addresses a candidate's analytical abilities and basic knowledge of law.

The notification bringing the All India Bar Examination into force was passed by the Legal Education Committee and the members of the Bar Council of India. The All India Bar Examination (AIBE), conducted on March 6, 201 for the first time, was intended to test an advocate's ability to practise the profession of law in India. The AIBE is intended to assess capabilities at a basic level and is intended to set a minimum standard for admission to the practice of law; it addresses a candidate's analytical abilities and basic knowledge of law. All students graduating from academic year 2009-10 onwards need to clear the AIBE in order to practise law in India. Candidates may apply to appear for the All India Bar Examination only after enrolling as an advocate under Section 24 of the *Advocate's Act, 1961* and will have to submit suitable proof of such enrolment along with the application form for the AIBE.

Top Law Institutes

- NALSAR University of Law, Hyderabad.
- National Law School of India University (NLSIU), Bangalore.
- Benaras Hindu University, Varanasi.
- Faculty of Law, University of Delhi, Delhi.
- Gujarat National Law University (GNLU).
- Symbiosis Society's Law College (SSLC), Pune.
- National Law University (NLIU), Bhopal.
- ILS Law College, Pune.
- Government Law College, Mumbai.
- Amity Law School, Delhi.
- Aligarh Muslim University, Aligarh.

16
MANAGEMENT

16.1 What is Management?

The word 'Management' comes from the Italian word *'maneggiare'* which means *'to handle especially tools'* which derives from the Latin word *'manus'* meaning *'hand'*. Management literally refers to the ability to handle tools. Therefore, it means the ability to handle, organise and manage resources. Management involves the manipulation of the human capital of an enterprise to contribute to the success of the enterprise. Mary Parker Follet defined management as "the art of getting things done through people".

Management in all business and organisational activities is the act of coordinating the efforts of people to accomplish desired goals and objectives using available resources efficiently and effectively. Management comprises of planning, organising, staffing, leading or directing and controlling an organisation (a group of one or more people or entities) or effort for the purpose of accomplishing a goal. Resourcing encompasses the deployment and manipulation of human resources, financial resources, technological resources and natural resources.

Course Details

Courses in management are offered generally at undergraduate and post graduate degree/diploma levels by private and government management institutes. Individuals can pursue these courses through correspondence mode also. Usually, a 10+2 pass candidate can take up undergraduate management degree programs like BBA, BBS, BBM etc. For post-graduation courses like MBA, PGDM, etc., graduation is a mandatory minimum qualification. Courses at post graduation level are offered with specialisations in the specific field. Executive MBA programs for working professionals and part-time management courses are conducted at various leading B-Schools. Management courses can be pursued in the fields of marketing management, international business management, information technology, international business management, hospitality management, event management, business management, human resource management, financial management, hospital management, sports management, operations management, media management and many more.

Almost all reputable management institutions in India admit students through entrance tests like CET, CAT, SNAP, MAT etc. A course in management enables one to understand all major and minor aspects of business administration/management. Besides, planning, organising, leading, monitoring, delegating and controlling are some other essential of a management curriculum.

Career Prospects

After completing a course in management, one can start his/her own business or aspire to work at managerial and executive levels in corporate houses and multinational companies. There is always a huge demand for management degree holders in major fields of management as :

- Operation managers
- Human Resource Managers
- Event Managers
- Hospitality Managers and others

For working professionals of various fields, part-time diploma/ certificate courses in management can enhance their skills and improve their chances of climbing the ladder of hierarchy in their profession. Above all, a management degree is not just confined to corporate houses but it also provides exciting opportunities in the government sector.

Remuneration

Remuneration in the field of management largely depends on the organisation structure and nature of work. After completing a course in management, one can expect a salary ranging from ₹ 8,000 to ₹ 12,000 in the beginning. An MBA degree holder can be offered up to ₹ 25,000 as an initial package in multinational companies. Graduates from IIMs and other prestigious B-Schools offer attractive salary packages, ranging from ₹ 8-12 lakhs per annum or even more, depending on the hiring organization and the student's caliber.

Entrance Exams for Management Studies

- **What is CAT?**

  Indian Institutes of Management Common Admission Test (IIM-CAT) is the first step in the process of seeking admission to the

2year full time Postgraduate Degree Programs in Management offered by the IIMs. Currently IIM Ahmedabad, IIM Bangalore, IIM Calcutta, IIM Indore, IIM Kozhikode, IIM Lucknow are offering such Programmes in Management. The IIMs use the results of CAT to shortlist the candidates for subsequent part of the Selection Process.

CAT Eligibility : The candidate must hold a bachelor's degree with at least 50 per cent or equivalent CGPA [45 per cent in case of the candidates belonging to Scheduled Caste (SC), Schedule Tribe (ST) and Differently Abled (DA) (It may be referred to as persons with disability (PWD) category)], awarded by any of the Universities incorporated by an act of the central or state legislature in India or other educational institutions established by an act of Parliament or declared to be deemed as a University under Section 3 of the UGC Act, 1956 or possess an equivalent qualification recognised by the Ministry of HRD, Government of India.

Admission Process : Please note that each IIM shortlists candidates for second stage of selection which may be independent of each other. The process may include Written Ability Test (WAT), Group Discussions (GD) and Personal Interviews (PI). Performance in CAT examination is an important component in the admission process. IIMs may use previous academic performance of the candidates, relevant work experience and other similar inputs in short listing and ranking of candidates at various stages of the admission process. The processes, academic cut-offs and the weights allocated to the evaluation parameters may vary across IIMs. For more information you may refer the admissions policies of IIMs from their respective websites.

Test Duration and Pattern

CAT generally has two sections :

- Quantitative Ability and Data Interpretation
- Verbal Ability and Logical Reasoning

These two sections will be implemented sequentially with separate time limits. The examination will be 140 minutes. Candidates will have 70 minutes to answer 30 questions within each section which will have an on-screen countdown timer. Within the 70 minutes provided for the section, candidates can review the answers. Once the time ends for the first section, they will move to the second section and will no longer be able to go back. A 15- minute tutorial will be provided before starting the main examination. The total duration will be two hours and thirty five minutes including the tutorial. A practice test to provide candidates with a feel of the timed sections, as well as navigation and functionality of the actual test will be made available in the coming weeks. Once again candidates are advised to go through them carefully to familiarise themselves with the screens, layout and navigation.

At the test venue, each candidate will be seated at a desk with a computer terminal and he/she will be provided with a scratch paper for calculations. After the test, candidates must leave the scratch paper at the desk. Rough work cannot be done on any other paper/sheet, as nothing will be allowed inside the testing room. No breaks will be given during the test.

- **What is XAT?**

XAT stands for Xavier Aptitude Test. To get admission to XLRI, candidates have to appear for XAT. To register for XAT, candidates have to fill the XAT form that is available online at www.xatonline.net.in. Once the candidate logs on to this site, a full set of instructions will appear. The candidate can obtain his/her ID and password by following these instructions. This ID and password are to be indicated for all the future correspondence with the XAT Office, Jamshedpur.

A candidate may apply for a maximum of three programs. Those whoapply for multiple programs may be called for multiple interviews and/or group discussions. The selection criteria for different programs may differ depending on the nature of the program. XAT written test will have multiple components and you need to maximise your performance in each of these components. In its pursuit of academic excellence, XLRI actively encourages the students from diverse backgrounds. While preparing the shortlisted candidates for the interview, in addition to XAT performance academic ability and the relevant work experience also count while preparing the final list. For candidates who cannot be present physically for the XLRI interviews due to their being out of the country, interviews would be carried out in on-line mode via internet. XAT has three sections:

- o English Language Ability and Logical Reasoning (EL)
- o Quantitative Ability (QA)
- o Decision Making (DM)

Institutions that admit students on the basis of XAT score

There are 16 core member institutes and more than 85 associate institutes located in different parts of the country.

- o Acharya School of Management, Bangalore
- o Andhra Loyola Institute of Management, Vijayawada
- o APG Shimla University, Shimla
- o Aryans Business School, Punjab
- o Asia Pacific Institute of Management, New Delhi
- o Bengal Institute of Business Studies, Kolkata
- o Bharatiya Vidya Bhavan's Usha and Lakhsmi Mittal Institute of Management, New Delhi
- o Bhavan's Centre for Communication and Management, Bhubaneshwar
- o Birla Institute of Management Technology, Greater Noida
- o BLS Institute of Management, Mohan Nagar
- o Deen Dayal Upadhyaya Institute of Management and Higher Studies, Kanpur
- o Delhi School of Professional Studies and Research, Delhi
- o Desh Bhagat Institute of Management and Computer Sciences, Amloh
- o Disha Institute of Management and Technology, Dist. Raipur
- o Driems Business School, Cuttack
- o Entrepreneurship and Management Process International, New Delhi
- o Entrepreneurship Development Institute of India (EDI), Gandhinagar
- o Faculty of Management Studies, Goa University, Goa
- o Fortune Institute of International Business, Delhi
- o Gitam Institute of Management, Visakhapatnam
- o Globsyn Business School, Kolkata
- o Goa Institute of Management, Goa
- o IBMR-Business School, Bangalore
- o IFIM Business School, Bangalore
- o IILM College of Management Studies, Greater Noida
- o IILM Graduate School of Management, Greater Noida
- o IILM Institute of Higher Education, Gurgaon
- o Indian Institute of Finance, Noida

- o Indian Business Academy, Bangalore
- o Indus World School of Business, NCR
- o Indus Business Academy, Bangalore
- o Institute for Finance Management and Research, Chennai
- o Institute for Technology and Management, Navy Mumbai
- o Institute for Business Studies and Research, Navy Mumbai
- o Institute of Management and Information Science, Bhubaneshwar
- o Institute of Science and Management, Ranchi
- o International Academy of Management and Entrepreneurship, Bangalore
- o International Institute of Business Studies, Bangalore
- o International Institute of Business and Media, Pune
- o International School of Management Excellence, Bangalore
- o Invertis Institute of Management Studies, Bareilly
- o ISBR Business School, Bangalore
- o Jagran Institute of Communication and Management, Bhopal
- o Jaipuria Institute of Management, Indore
- o Jaipuria Institute of Management, Lucknow
- o Jaipuria Institute of Management, Noida
- o Jaipuria Institute of Management, Jaipur
- o Jindal Global Business School, Sonipat
- o JK Lakhsmipat University, Jaipur
- o Kejriwal Institute of Management and Development Studies, Ranchi
- o Kirloskar Institute of Advanced Management Studies, Harihar
- o Kohinoor Business School and CMR, Khandala
- o Krupajal Business School, Bhubaneshwar
- o Lovely Professional University, Phagwara
- o Loyola College, Secunderabad
- o Loyola Institute of Business Administration, Chennai
- o Management Education and Research Institute, New Delhi
- o Mangal vedhekar Institute of Management (MIM), Solapur

- Mar Athanasios College for Advanced Studies (MACFAST), Kerala
- Marian Institute of Health Care Management, Panaji
- MATS Institute of Management and Entrepreneurship, Bangalore
- MIT School of Business, Pune
- MIT School of Telecom Management, Pune
- Mount Carmel Institute of Management, Bangalore
- MVRR Institute of Business Management, Krishna
- National School of Business, Bangalore
- New Delhi Institute of Management, New Delhi
- Praxis Business School, Kolkata
- Prin. LN Welingkar Institute of Management Development and Research, Mumbai
- Pune Institute of Business Management, Pune
- Ravenshaw Management Centre, Cuttack
- Regional College of Management Autonomous, Bhubaneshwar
- S.P Jain Institute of Management and Research, Mumbai
- School of Management Sciences, Varanasi
- School of Management, KIIT University, Bhubaneshwar
- SDM Institute for Management Development, Mysore
- Shiva Institute of Management Studies, Ghaziabad
- SIET Institute of Management, Bangalore
- Siva Shivani Institute of Management, Secunderabad
- Sri Shrada Institute of Indian Management Research, New Delhi
- Sri Sri University, Bhubaneshwar
- St. Aloysius Institute of Management and Information Technology, Mangalore
- St. Berchman's College, Kerala
- St. Francis Institute of Management and Research(SFIMAR), Mumbai
- St. Joseph's College of Business Administration, Bangalore Pune
- TA Pai Management Institute, Manipal
- Taxila Business School, Jaipur
- The National Management School, Chennai

- The School of Business, Alliance University, Bangalore
- Training and Advanced Studies in Management and Communications Ltd. TASMAC), Pune
- United World School of Business, Kolkata
- Vanguard Business School, Bangalore
- VIT University, Vellore
- WLC College India, Noida
- Xavier Institute of Development Action and Studies, M.P.
- Xavier Institute of Management, Bhubaneshwar
- Xavier Institute of Management and Entrepreneurship, Bangalore
- Xavier Institute of Management and Research, Mumbai
- Xavier Institute of Social Service, Ranchi
- Xavier Labour and Relations Institute, Jamshedpur

- **OPENMAT Exam**

Indira Gandhi National Open University (IGNOU) under its School of Management Studies (SOMS) every year holds an all-India entrance test (OPENMAT) for admission into its various distance-learning management programs. In terms of the spread and enrolment, the IGNOU Management Program is one of the leading Management Programs in the world.

Eligibility for OPENMAT Exam : OPENMAT entrance examination is conducted by School of Management Studies (SOMS) of Indira Gandhi National Open University (IGNOU). The All-India entrance test is conducted every year for admission into its various distance-learning management programs. The eligible criteria for OPENMAT Exam are :

- The candidate should have a Bachelor's degree in any field from a recognised institution with minimum 50 per cent aggregate marks. Exemption of 5 per cent is there for candidates belonging to reserved category.
- The candidate should be a graduate with at least 3 years of supervisory / managerial / professional experience.
- The candidates with a professional degree in Engineering, Technology, Medicine, Architecture, Law, Pharmacy are also eligible.
- The candidate should have Professional Qualifications in Accountancy, Cost and Works Accountancy, Company Secretary-ship.

- o The candidates who have a Master's degree in any subject from a recognized institution can also apply.
- o For Diploma in Management, apart from the aforementioned qualification, the candidates who have passed 10+2 or its equivalent examination with 6 years of supervisory/managerial/professional experience are also eligible.
- o There is no age bar for any of the courses.

- **Examination Pattern of OPENMAT**

OPENMAT Entrance Examination is held twice a year most probably in the month of February and August. The candidates, who qualify the entrance examination, are eligible to take admission into Management program in any of the two subsequent semesters. The entrance examination consists of 200 objective-type questions with multiple options. The test is divided into the following four sections :

- o Section I comprises of 30 questions on General Awareness
- o Section II includes 50 questions on English Language
- o Section III consists of 50 questions on Quantitative Aptitude
- o Section IV includes 70 questions on Reasoning

Every correct answer fetches one mark and there is no negative marking for any wrong answers. The candidates are required to mark answer in separate OMR sheet. In case they think none of the four options as correct, they have to mark '0'. Duration of the entrance examination is three hours in a single-sitting.

Syllabus : No specific syllabus has been designed for IGNOU OPENMAT. The test includes questions from the four sections :

- o General Awareness
- o English Language
- o Quantitative Aptitude
- o Reasoning

Courses : Candidates who successfully qualify the OPENMAT seek admission to the following courses :

- o MBA
- o PG Diploma (Financial Management)
- o PG Diploma (Marketing Management)
- o PG Diploma (Operations Management)
- o PG in Human Resource Management (PGDHRM)
- o PGDM

MAT Exam

MAT stands for Management Aptitude Test. This test is conducted by All India Management Association (AIMA) for admission into various management institutions in India. Centre for Management Services (CMS) is the specialised division of AIMA undertaking testing and other management services. The testing services have been in operation since 1988 facilitating academia, industry and governments to screen and select candidates for higher studies, recruitment, promotion etc. Over hundreds of AICTE approved institutions and University departments and over lakhs of MBA aspirants having availed AIMA's testing services. MAT is approved by the Ministry of HRD, GOI as a National Entrance Test.

Eligibility for MAT Exam : The minimum qualification for appearing in MAT is graduation in any discipline from any recognized University or equivalent recognised degree. A final year student in any undergraduate (e. B.A., B.Sc., B.Com., B.Tech., etc.) can also appear provisionally. Usually there is a minimum percentage requirement in graduation which is different for MIs/University. For this refer to the prospectus of the particular MIs/University. MAT is usually conducted 4 times in a year in February, May, September and December. There is no age bar.

Modes of Test : Candidates can choose any one of the two options to take the test: Paper Based Test or Computer Based Test.

How many and which MIs participate in MAT?

The number of participating MIs may vary. The number of MIs keeps on changing from test to test. Admission criteria for every institute are different. All MIs participating in MAT are either AICTE, DEC approved, University Affiliated College, University Department. For further information you may contact the MIs/Universities of your choice. The list of various MIs/Universities is available in MAT bulletin along with the admission notification. It may be worthwhile to go through the brochure of the MIs for detailed information. The Validity of MAT score is for that particular session for most MIs is one year.

Syllabus for MAT Exam : It is an objective type test with multiple-choice answers. The test is designed to measure a person's general aptitudes as the following indicates :

- o Language Comprehension (40 questions)
- o Mathematical Skills (40 questions)
- o Data Analysis and Sufficiency (40 questions)

- o Intelligence and Critical Reasoning (40 questions)
- o Indian and Global Environment (40 questions)

ATMA Exam

ATMA is a standard test to assess the aptitude of candidates for Management Education. The test is conducted by the Association of Indian Management Schools (AIMS), which is a network of over 600 management schools in the country. AIMS represents Indian Management Schools in the international forum and is also associated with many committees of the government or its agencies looking at policies relating to management education. ATMA has nothing to do with the admission process of different management schools, which accept its scores. Candidates who take ATMA do not automatically get considered for admission by the management schools that accept ATMA scores for their admission unless they apply to them directly. In other words, scores of ATMA test are accessible to those institutions which are members. However, students must fill up applications of institutes where they want to be considered.

What is the Link between the ATMA and Admission Process of Institutions?

ATMA is a test essentially assessing the aptitude of students for management education. Around 200 management institutions accept ATMA score for their admission processes. However, at specific times of the year, lists of such PIs (Participating Institutes) may go down or up. Please check on the website both lists. Such lists will also be available on ATMA ONLINE portal. It is up to individual management institutes to decide how they will use ATMA scores. Both AIMS and ATMA do not have or not intended to have any information relating to the admission processes of different institutions. This has to be clearly understood. Each student who takes ATMA can apply to any of the schools, which have announced publicly in newspapers or brochure/ website that they accept ATMA scores.

Syllabus for ATMA Exam :ATMA checks the aptitudes of the students for management education through three major elements :

- Quantitative Skills
- Analytical Reasoning
- Verbal Skills

Validity : ATMA scores are valid for one year. ATMA paper-based and ATMA Online are administered a few times during an academic year.

MAH MBA/MMS CET

Maharashtra State Directorate of Technical Education, Mumbai conducts an all-India entrance test (Maharashtra MBA/MMS Common Entrance Test) for admission of students to First Year of full-time Postgraduate programs in Management offered by government institutes, universities and unaided institutes in Maharashtra.

Eligibility for MAH MBA/MMS CET

Basic qualifications for appearing MAH MBA/MMS CET are given below:

- Candidates should have passed the Bachelor's degree of minimum 3-years duration in any discipline with minimum of 45 per cent marks in aggregate. OR
- Candidates should have passed Bachelor's degree of 3-year duration in any discipline minimum of 45 per cent marks in aggregate.
- There is 5 per cent relaxation of marks in case of backward classes of Maharashtra only.
- Candidates who are appearing final exam of Bachelor's degree may also apply on condition that they provide evidence of passing the qualifying exam at the time of admission.
- Bachelor's degree holders appearing the final exam of their PG degree also can apply on condition that they provide evidence of passing the qualifying exam at the time of admission.

Courses : On successful qualifying of MAH MBA/MMS CET two year full-time Post Graduate Degree courses in Management are offered in these following areas :

- MMS
- PGDM

Examination Pattern

- MAH MBA/MMS CET is a single stage entrance test of two and half hours duration
- The test contains multiple choice objective type questions having maximum of 200 marks.
- The test comprises sections like: Verbal Ability and Reading Comprehension, Quantitative Aptitude and Logical? Abstract Reasoning.
- There are no negative markings for wrong answer.

- Candidates scoring 30 marks or mare in MAH MBA/MMS CET or having equivalent score of 30 marks or more in CAT/XAT/MAT/JMET/ATMA are only eligible to appear Group Discussion and Personal Interview which followed the written test.

Syllabus : MAH MBA/MMS CET has a very general type of syllabus covering the areas as mentioned below :

- Verbal Ability/Reading Comprehension
- Quantitative Aptitude
- Logical/Abstract Reasoning

The Best Management Institutes in India

The Top Management Institutes in India are :

- Indian Institute of Management, Ahmedabad (IIM A)
- Indian Institute of Management, Calcutta (IIM C)
- Indian Institute of Management, Bangalore (IIM B)
- Indian Institute of Management, Lucknow (IIM L)
- XLRI – Xavier Labour Research Institute, Jamshedpur
- Indian School of Business (ISB), Hyderabad
- FMS – Faculty of Management Studies, University of Delhi
- Indian Institute of Management, Indore (IIM I)
- Indian Institute of Management, Calicut (IIM K-Kozhikode)
- Jamnalal Bajaj Institute of Management Studies, Mumbai (JBIMS)
- SP Jain Institute of Management Studies, Mumbai (SP JIMR)
- Shailesh J. Mehta School of Management, IIT Mumbai (Bombay)
- Management Development Institute, Gurgaon (MDI)
- Nasree Monjee Institute of Management Studies, Mumbai (NMIMS)
- Xavier Institute of Management, Bhubaneshwar (XIM B)
- Symbiosis Institute of Business Management, Pune (SIBM)
- Symbiosis Centre for Management and Human Resources Development, Pune (SCMHRD)
- Institute of Management and Technology, Ghaziabad (IMT)
- International Management Institute, Delhi (IMI)
- Bharathidasan Institute of Management, Trichy (BIM)
- Mudra Institute of Communications, Ahmedabad (MICA)
- Indian Institute of Foreign Trade, Delhi (IIFT)

- T.A. Pai Management Institute, Manipal (TAPMI)
- Loyola Institute of Business Administration, Chennai (LIBA)
- Institute of Management Development Research, Pune (IMDR)

16.2 Business Administration

What is Business Administration?

Business administration is one of the most sought after career and it is all about managing business functions such as finance, management, services etc. It can be defined as the process of managing and supervising the business and related operations of a company or organisation. Business Administration has become prominent with the rapid growth of industrialisation which made the industries think of a scientific approach towards business. As a result, a large number of business schools have come up rapidly all over the world, and a degree in Business Administration has become the norm. India is one of the major countries which offer good business education.

Specialised Fields in Business Administration

The specialised fields in Business Administration are like Marketing, human resource, operations, finance etc. It is an achievement-oriented profession which has opened limitless opportunity in diverse spheres with the promise of rewards in the form of good remuneration, status and scope. Personal skills such as communication, analytical ability and professional skills like time management and presentation are needed for a bright prospect in this career. Many Indian and foreign institutes are giving professional coaching in this field and the highly paying placements through campus selection is an added attraction.

Importance of Master of Business Administration (MBA)

Master of Business Administration (MBA) is considered as the basic and ideal qualification for taking up a rewarding career in the field of management. Though there are several bachelor's degree programs like BBA, BBM, etc., from where one could get the basics of Business Administration, it is only through MBA goes a long way in getting top positions in the corporate world. It is the key to the continual success of careers in sectors like manufacturing, business, education, healthcare and other service sectors.

Careful Choosing of Business Schools

It is also important to get an MBA degree from a good Business school as the competition tightens now. There are over 1500 B. Schools in the country and students must be very careful while selecting the institute.

A good Business School comprises of good study atmosphere, infrastructure, teachers as well as impressive placement records, business associations and industry interaction, etc., that will help one to be more productive in his profession. Even though many institutes are offering full time and part time MBA courses, only such courses will be valued that have an approval of All India Council for Technical Education and the institute should be affiliated to a university. One should take all these matters into account while choosing an institute.

Eligibility

There are several diplomas under graduate and post graduate programs in management. But MBA which is the post graduate degree in management is considered as the prerequisite for top management positions in the corporate world. Bachelor of Business Administration (BBA), Bachelor of Business Management (BBM), Bachelor of Business Studies (BBS) are some of the under graduate courses. One should have 10+2 or equivalent qualification for applying for Bachelor courses. Normally Bachelors programs are 3 years duration but it variesdepending on the institutes.

The basic qualification for MBA is a graduation in any discipline such as B.Com, B.A., B.Sc., B.E./B.Tech etc. However, subjects such as commerce, economics and mathematics would prepare a candidate better for pursuing business studies.

There are full time and part time post graduate programs in management, i.e., full time/part time MBA and PGDM (Post Graduate Diploma in Management/Business Administration) programs. For better career prospects, fresh graduates are required to enroll for 2 year full time programmes. Technically there is no difference between 2 full time MBA and PGDM programmes. MBA programmes are awarded only by the universities or university affiliated colleges whereas PGDM programmes are honored by independent colleges. 2 year full time PGDM programs are considered equivalent to MBA. 1 year/part time PGDM programs which are meant for working executives are not equivalent to MBA. But there are exceptions for some top B Schools where their 1 year is considered equivalent to MBA. So students must be very careful while choosing the programmes. Doctoral degrees in business administration are generally only for those who wish to pursue the academic or research sides of the field.

Selection

Reputed Business schools admit students on the basis of a 3 stage selection process that includes a written examination followed by a group discussion and personal interview. Generally, written examination are of two to two and a half hour duration with multiple choice objective questions which covers various aspects of aptitude tests like Basic mathematics (Quantitative Analysis), Reading Comprehension, Data Interpretation, logic, general knowledge etc. Getting a good score in this written test is not enough to assure the seat. There will be group discussion (GD), team-building task and personal interviews (PI). Students are admitted based on rank lists prepared on the performances in the written test, GD and PI. Some institutes consider the marks in the graduation level also. Extra-curricular activities and qualifications like work experience will be an added advantage to the candidates but are not compulsory.

Common Admission Test (CAT) conducted by Indian Institute of Management (IIM), Management Aptitude Test (MAT) by All India Management Aptitude Testing Service (AIMATS) New Delhi, Xavier Admission Test (XAT) by Xavier Labour Research Institute, Jamshedpur (XLRI), Joint Management Entrance Test (JMET) by Indian Institute of Technology (IIT), ATMA by the Association of Indian Management Schools (AIMS) are the major national level entrance examination for admission to management courses. Even though these exams are conducted by the respective institute for their admission, its scores are widely accepted by many of the Indian Business Schools. MAT exams are conducted 4 times a year while all the others are held once in a year. Certain Business schools and universities conduct their own entrance test and some of these include National Management Aptitude Test (NMAT), Symbiosis National Aptitude (SNAP) Test, Open Management Admission Test (OPENMAT) by Indira Gandhi National Open University (IGNOU), Written Admission Test (WAT), IBSAT, CEMAT etc. All these exams follow the same syllabus and students can write 2 to 3 of these, so that they can apply to multiple institutes.

Course details

The course help students to fine-tune their business analytical skills understand the corporate world and perform to the expectations of the industry. Students are given solid foundation in the principles of Business management, Economics, organisational behaviour, marketing, accounting, finance, strategy, operations management, international business, information technology management, supply chain management and project management are the subjects covered in the management courses. Theoretical aspects of and practical issues of managing business are taught in the institutes. All the students are exposed to the practical scenarios through various methods of teaching. In the 1st year of the course, they are trained in all aspects of business like marketing, finance, human resource, operation management, production, systems etc. During the 2nd year, there will be elective areas and the students can specialiae in any one of the field of management. The core subjects of specialisation in MBA include Finance, Marketing, Human Resources, Production and Systems. Besides these, there are over 20 areas of specialisations one can choose from. Retail, Hotel, Tourism and Travel, Airport and Airlines, Hospital, Finance and Services, International Business, Construction, Banking and Insurance, etc., are some of them.

Personal Skills

Motivation and certain personal skills are needed for successful career in this profession. Hectic work pressure will be there and one needs to be tactful when dealing with clients and should be patient and possess keen business expertise. Good communication skills, leadership quality, ability to motivate and work as part of a team, time management skills, ability to understand and solve problems are the needed attributes. Quick thinking and the ability to come up with new ideas are advantageous. Merely text book knowledge will not help a candidate even though it can help him easily make a way in this field. On the job, they have to ensure that they are in touch with the latest practices and their skills should be kept updated. They should be aware of the current global scenario, economics and industry trends.

Several universities abroad have tied up with many Indian business schools to offer their International MBA programs. Students can enroll in these programmes but there is a little chance for global exposure. Another option is the twinning programme. Here students can complete the 1st year of their course in India and can go outside to the university/ institute to complete their course. Or they can enroll in the abroad university for their studies. There is ample opportunity for pursuing courses in management abroad – UK universities offer MBA as a one year program. But one must always be careful about the choice of the institute.

Job Prospects

Business management is one of the most sought after careers and a wide range of opportunities are available for Business Administration graduates. It is easy to get managerial or executive jobs for those who hold business degrees especially an MBA degree. And from this executive post one has an opportunity to climb the ladder and occupy the top most positions in the company. As many MNC's are coming up and Indian companies are going for joint ventures, there are ample career options in this field.

The major job prospects in the field of management are :

- **Marketing and Sales Manager :** He is one who manages the marketing techniques such as advertising, distributing and selling of a product to the clients properly. He should understand the four Ps well that are product, price, placement or distribution, and promotion or publicity.
- **Financial Manager :** He has the responsibility of managing the capital (finance) of the company. He should be very clear about the budgeting of the company.
- **Human Resource Manager :** He is one of the most important persons of an organization as he manages the manpower of the company. Recruitment, training, induction, employee benefit administration, performance appraisal are some of the major responsibilities of a Human Resource Manager of the company.
- **Production or Operations Manager :** He is one who manages the resources, goods and service. Apart from these major areas, there are several specialised areas like Information Technology, Hospitality, Tourism and Pharma Management.

MBA graduates with B-Tech background are highly in demand than the other degree holders. Many Indian and foreign companies conduct campus placements in the business schools so that the students can straight away join any companyas soon as they complete their course. One could also choose the field of teaching as the Business schools are mushrooming rapidly. Setting up one's own business is another option for the graduate as he has sufficient knowledge about the industry through his education. A good GMAT (Graduate Management Aptitude Test) score is needed for better placement and exposure in countries outside India. It is the standardised test required for doing MBA or Ph.D in Business Management or any other graduate management programs from a business schools in US, Europe and Canada. Some of the foreign institutes prefer TOEFL and IELTS scores.

Remuneration

This glamorous profession offers one of the best pay packages in the country, particularly in the private sector. As this profession has many fields, the remuneration varies depending on the specialised area and the company one chooses to work for. Candidates from a highly reputed management institutes can earn at least ₹ 5 – 6 lakhs per annum. This could go up to ₹ 12 – 15 lakhs annually. Even those passing out of lesser-known institutes can hope to earn about ₹ 2 – 3 lakhs per annum. The earning potential of a management graduate also depends on whether or not he/she has some prior work experience and any other additional qualification.

Management professionals from India are in great demand in international market. Excellent perks are offered to these professionals which may include free accommodation, attractive conveyance allowance, leave travel concession, medical allowance, reimbursement and much more. Apart from the high package, a job in the management field also offers outstanding developmental opportunities for dynamic managers to rise to the level of Chief-executive.

Courses

- Advance Diploma in Business Administration (ADBA)
- Advance Diploma in International Hotel and Business Administration
- Bachelor of Business Administration (BBA)
- Master of Business Administration (MBA)
- Post Graduate Diploma in Business Administration (PGDBA)

Institutes

Many institutes in India as well as abroad offer Business Administration courses and India has more than 1500 Business schools. Some institutes such as National Institute of Technology, Calicut (NIT-C) offer MBA exclusively for B.Tech graduates. The MBA courses that are offered from the institutes affiliated to a university only will be valued and such courses should get the approval of All India Council for Technical Education. Few other institutes are:

- Indian Institute of Management (IIMs), Bangalore, Ahmedabad, Calcutta, Lucknow, Indore, Kozhikode, Rohtak, Raipur, Shillong, Ranchi, Trichy, Kashipur and Udaipur.
- Indian School of Business (ISB), Hyderabad
- Xavier's Labour Relations Institute (XLRI), Jamshedpur
- Faculty of Management Studies (FMS), New Delhi
- Indian Institute of Foreign Trade (IIFT), New Delhi
- Jamnalal Bajaj Institute of Management Studies, Mumbai
- Management Development Institute (MDI), Gurgaon
- GGSIP University
- Bharatiya Vidyapeeth, Pune
- Symbiosis, Pune.

16.3 Human Resource Development

What is Human Resource?

Human Resource is the manpower of a company which plays a key role in the organisation's development with their skills and creativity. Human Resource Management (HRM) was formerly known as personal management or labor welfare and industrial relations and is a very highly competitive and sought after profession in the field of management. It involves recruiting personnel and their training, salary administration and handling union management relations. Every industry, business and trade needs Human Resource Development Managers or HR managers for the successful administration and maintenance of their work force. They focus on all the activities an organisation implements and assist employees in all areas, including boosting their morale and giving training and coaching to maximise their abilities.

What is Human Resource Management?

Human Resource Management (HRM) is a profession that deals with all levels of employees in the management or organisation. Now-a-days employees are considered as valuable corporate assets as well as trained, skilled and highly motivated staff are required for the growth of an organisation/company. This has made HRM a vital administrative function in both commercial as well as non-profit making establishments. It is the duty of HR or Personal Manager to select such appropriate employees to improve the productivity of the company. The major tasks performed by a human resource professional include developing job profiles, screening and interviewing candidates, administering and coordinating tests, conducting background checks of prospective employees and their training. In fact, Human resource management is all about the management of work and people in an organisation.

Eligibility

The eligibility criteria for applying to these courses are graduation in any discipline. The master's program will be of 2 years duration and PG Diploma programs will be of 1 year duration. Basically admission to these programs will be based on aptitude test, GD and interview. The selection procedure may vary depending on the institutes. Most institutes admit students on the basis of marks scored in exams like CAT by IIMS, MAT by All India Management Association, XAT by Xavier Institute etc. Some institutes conduct their own examinations to these courses.

Course Areas

The basic qualification required for a job opportunity in the HR department of an organisation is Master's degree in Human Resource Management. The courses exclusively meant for Human Resource Management are :

- Master of Human Resource Management (MHRM)
- Master of Human Resource and Organisational Development (MHROD)
- Post Graduate Diploma in Human Resource Management (PGDHRM)
- Post Graduate Diploma in Human Resource Development (PGDHRMD)

Many MBA courses offer Human Resource Management as a specialisation to the major course. In MBA, the specialization will be offered in the 2nd year. Compared to MBA, MHRM is an exclusive 2 year programme on Human resources.

Personal Skills

Ability to communicate and interact interpersonally is the cardinal skill necessary for this profession as HRM are the mediators between employers and employees. HR jobs need complete involvement, lots of patience, flexibility and ability to get on with all types of people. Leadership quality and time management skills will be counted for this career. As an HR has to work as a team player, they should possess good organisational skills, should be able to coordinate all the individuals as a team and make them work together. Other essential skills needed for the HR professional is a flair for seeing a problem from all sides, a good memory for names and faces, lack of prejudice and respect and a persuasive and a congenial personality.

Job Prospects and Career Options

Human resource or personal management graduates have a lot of potential as every industry or organisation need these professional for maintaining their labor force. Starting from merely collecting employee details to maintaining the human resource information (HRI) systems, HR managers' job has now extended to that of a recruiter manager, compensation manager, employer relation manager, strategic manager and much more. They are placed by industries in HR departments, HR planning/recruiting, HR auditing, etc., and are involved in all aspects of people management to improve the morale of the employees.

Graduates in Human Resource management may be recruited by companies through campus interview. They will be trained by HR

Managers in the HR department and are redeployed in different locations. HR managers can seek employment in corporate houses, multinational companies, banking and financial institutions and public and private sector industries.

HR is a profession that can be learned on the field by interacting with people. One can excel in the field only with experience. So after graduation rather than looking for the perfect opportunity, try to get into an organisation and learn the ropes of the job. Initially salary shouldn't be your main criteria. One can climb the ladder of HR after gaining experience and exposure.

Major duties of HR

Some of the major duties performed by the human resource managers are recruitment, training and development, job appraisal, promotion, keeping an eye on the idleness of employees, maintaining good employer and employee relations, maintaining all personal records and implement career development programmes.

Recruitment

Recruitment is the major function of an HR of a company, as he has to find the apt person matching for their organisation's profile. HR has to screen and shortlist the qualified candidates from various sources such as recruitment agencies, advertisements published etc.

- **Training and Induction :** It is the job of HR to introduce the new employee to the organisation and vice versa, giving him the education and training about the company's policies.
- **Personal management and development :** The HR should understand an employee and his skills for the job and help him to develop those skills. For that he should be capable of evaluating employees individually.
- **Job appraisal :** It is the duty of the HR to evaluate the performance of the employee as part of their career development. Usually the salary increment, promotion etc are decided on the basis of this appraisal. It will also help to understand the training that the employee further needs for improvement in his field.
- **Payroll :** The HR should maintain the financial records of salaries and its related such as basic wages, deductions etc. They also take care of employee benefits and its records.

Remuneration

Remuneration of HR professional varies depending on the organisation, economic activity, geographic location and profitability. Experienced Human Resource Managers are offered ₹ 10,000 to 30,000 per month especially in private organisations. Candidates from good B-Schools can earn around Rupees three lakhs to five lakhs annually. The remuneration will shoot up depending on one's skill, qualification and experience. For a senior level post, an MBA graduate will be offered ₹ 50,000 to 60,000 per month. The consultancies also pay well for the HR executives and managers.

Courses

- Diploma in Human Resource Management (DHRM)
- MBA Human Resource Management
- Master of Human Resource Development (MHRD)
- Master of Human Resource Management (MHRM)
- Master of Human Resource Management and Industrial Relations (MHRM and IR)
- Post Graduate Diploma in Human Resource Development (HRD) Psychology
- Post Graduate Diploma in Human Resource Management (PGDHRM)

Institutes

- **Rajasthan College of Engineering for Women, Jaipur, Rajasthan**
- **KCC Institute of Technology and Management, Greater Noida, Delhi-NCR**

  Course : Master in Business Administration (Human Resource Management)
- **NIILM Centre for Management Studies, Greater Noida, Delhi-NCR**

  Course : Post Graduate Diploma in Human Resource Management
- **Sri Sai Ram Institute of Management Studies, Chennai, Tamil Nadu**

  Course : Master in Business Administration (Human Resource Management)

- **Maharishi Arvind Institute of Science and Management, Jaipur, Rajasthan**

  Course : Post Graduate Diploma in Management (Human Resource)
- **Sri Krishnadevaraya Institute of Management, Others, Andhra Pradesh**

  Course : Master of Human Resource Management
- **Nagaon Gopinath Dev Goswami Commerce College, Assam-Other, Assam**

  Course : Post Graduate Diploma in Human Resource Management
- **Subash Institute of Business Management, Bangalore, Karnataka**

  Course : Bachelor of Business Administration (Human Resource Management)
- **Rajiv Institute of Business Management, Pune, Maharashtra**

  Course : Post Graduate Diploma in Management (Human Resource)
- **Deen Dayal Upadhyaya Institute of Management and Higher Studies, Kanpur, Uttar Pradesh**

  Course : Post Graduate Diploma in Management (Human Resource)
- **Mar Augusthinose College, Kerala-Other, Kerala**

  Course : Master of Human Resource Management
- **College of Management, JMS Group of Institutions, Ghaziabad, Delhi-NCR**

  Course : Master of Business Administration (Human Resource Management)
- **Jaya College of Arts and Science, Chennai, Tamil Nadu**

  Course : Certificate Programme in Human Resource Management
- **MIT School of Management, Pune, Maharashtra**

  Course : Master of Personal Management
- **Faculty of Commerce and Management, Himachal Pradesh University,**

  Shimla, Himachal Pradesh

  Course : Master of Personal Management

- **Chaitanya Degree and PG College for Women,**
  Visakhapatnam/Vizag, Andhra Pradesh
  Course : Master of Human Resource Development (MHRD)
- **Institute of Marketing and Management, New Delhi, Delhi-NCR**
  Course : Post Graduate Diploma in Management (Human Resource)
- **Pune Institute of Business Management, Pune, Maharashtra**
  Course : Post Graduate Diploma in Management (Human Resource)

16.4 Gas and Oil Management

Introduction

Oil and Gas are the world's most important energy sources. They produce power for our factories and our homes, run our cars, ships, aircraft and railways and provide us with plastics and other synthetic material.

The Work

Often referred to as petroleum, Oil and Gas includes exploration, extracting, refining, transporting and marketing of these products. This sector supplies not only fuel and gas for home and commercial use but also provides raw material for chemical products including pharmaceutical, plastics, fertilisers and pesticides. In fact, the production, distribution, refining and retailing of petroleum taken as a whole represents the world's largest industry in terms of dollar value.

Those with MBA in Oil and Gas Management have appropriate management skills and knowledge to undertake a leadership role in the oil and gas industries, one of the World's fastest growing and most dynamic sectors. These managers help develop strategic business awareness in exploration to retailing of petroleum/gas products. They have sound knowledge of energy management and an understanding of its various aspects in relation to national and international strategy.

Some of the specialised fields are pipeline operations; retail and marketing; operations and management; logistic and supply chain management.

Education and Skills

MBA course in oil and gas management is designed to provide experienced practitioners in the oil and gas sector with the advanced business, management and leadership skills needed to function at a strategic level as a contemporary energy manager.

Eligibility

The eligibility is graduation for this two-year program. In the first year, the students take courses in major functional/general management areas like Human Resources, Operations, Finance and Accounting, Marketing, Information Technology and core Oil and Gas Sector areas. In the second year, they study specialised subjects like Oil and Gas Law and Policy, Petro chemical business, Supply chain and Logistic for Petroleum industry, Petroleum Financial management, IT applications in petroleum sector, Petro-economics etc.

Key Skills

- Awareness of business and management principles
- Orientation toward quality customer service and evaluation of customer satisfaction
- Enthusiasm, good attitude and a willingness to be flexible
- Problem-solving and decision-making skills
- Excellent planning and organisational ability
- Ability to communicate persuasively both verbally and in writing.

Institutes

The following are few of the institutes where you can do your study;

- International Institute of Information Technology (IIIT-P), Pune
  Website: http://www.isquareit.edu.in/
- University of Petroleum and Energy Studies (UPES), Dehradun
  Website: http://www.upes.ac.in/
- Pandit Deendayal Petroleum University, Gandhinagar
  Website: http://www.spm.pdpu.ac.in/

Job Prospects

Employment in the energy sector is growing rapidly worldwide and offers exciting career opportunities for good managers that understand its diverse issues, demands and challenges. Some of the organisations which employ these managers are: Private and Public Sector oil Companies, Technical Service Providers, Tertiary Sector (Insurance,

Information Technology, Banking, Business Advisory and Consulting), Associated Industries – Petrochemical, Paints and Dyes, Overseas (Middle East, South East Asia, China, Russia, CIS Countries.

Remuneration

After completion of the course, one can easily get into managerial level in the Petroleum industry. Students can expect to start their salary from ₹ 50, 000 to ₹ 60, 000 per month.

16.5 Marketing Management

What is Marketing?

Business is omnipresent in our day-to-day life and for a potential growth

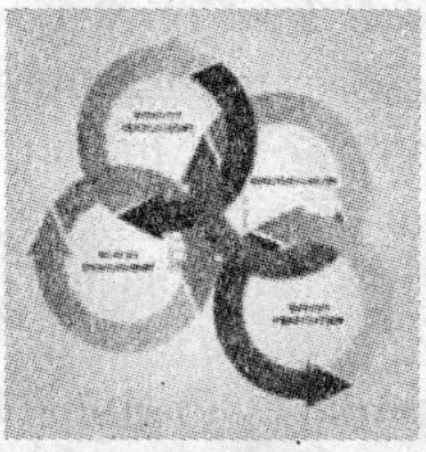

in the market; all kinds of organisations depend on the promotion of their products. For that every firm requires professionals with sales or marketing background. Marketing is a business discipline which is focused on the application of marketing techniques and administrating an organisation's marketing resources. In simple words, marketing is the method of convincing people about a product or concept using different ideas and thus help the business to grow. This field which involves advertising, distributing and selling of a product is regarded as the most important element in the growth of any company.

What is Marketing Management?

Marketing or Sales Management involves studying the marketability of the product involved and the measures to enhance sales and implementing the same. Even though the term marketing has been derived from its initial word 'market', the place where transactions between the customers and the sellers take place,a marketing process consists of four major Ps, i.e., Product, Pricing, Placement and Promotion.

Who are Marketing personnel?

Marketing personnel are professionals appointed by the company for convincing the clients and make them buy a product that the business offers. They are the people who create brands and promote their products and services. Sales and Marketing are two of the ever flourishing career sectors in the world and those having a knack for convincing people can find excellent job openings in this field. No specific qualification is required to enter the field but a managerial position in marketing requires MBA graduates preferably with marketing as the specialised area. Success in this profession depends on one's marketing skills, which include communication, tact, creativity, stress and time management.

Eligibility

The field of marketing is open to all. Though no formal educational qualification is required, most organisations prefer graduates in any discipline can apply for the two year MBA programme with specialisation in marketing. Admission is based on written examination followed by group discussion and personal interview. CAT, MAT, XAT, JMET, ATMA are some of the management entrance tests conducted by the institutes like Indian Institute of Management (IIM), All India Management Aptitude Testing Service (AIMATS), New Delhi, Xavier Labour Research Institute, Jamshedpur (XLRI), Indian Institute of Technology (IIT) and Association of Indian Management Schools (AIMS).

Even though these exams are conducted by the respective institute for their admission, its scores are widely accepted by many of the Indian Business Schools. MAT exams are conducted 4 times a year while all the others are held once in a year. Certain other Business schools and universities conduct their own entrance test and some of these include National Management Aptitude Test (NMAT), Symbiosis National Aptitude (SNAP) Test, Open Management Admission Test (OPENMAT) by Indira Gandhi National Open University (IGNOU), Written Admission Test (WAT), IBSAT, CEMAT etc. All these exams follow the same syllabus and students can attempt 2 or 3 of these tests, so that they can apply to multiple institutes. Some institutes offer executive MBA program in Sales and Marketing which require a certain years of experience.

Besides MBA programs, BBA (Bachelor in Business Administration) or BBM (Bachelor in Business Management) degree holders can also have openings in the field of marketing. The diploma course, PGDMCM (Post Graduate Diploma in Marketing Communication Management) also make the students professionally qualified in the fields of marketing research, production management, psychology are some of the subjects taught for marketing management courses.

Job Prospects and Career Options

Marketing and Sales Management is one of the most sought after careers and ample job opportunities are available in this field with the emerging number of multinational and national companies. But this field is very competitive and only skilled person could make a successful career. Marketing managers are personnel who take care of sales, marketing, product promotions, advertisement and public relation of a firm or organisation. Their major tasks involve market research, product development, promotion, pricing, sales and distribution. It is these people who develop detailed marketing strategies, analyse the demand of the company's products and services in the market, identify the competitors and potential markets and handle customer management.

They are responsible to ensure customer satisfaction and also to achieve the business goal or target of an organisation. They should always be alert, keep an eye on the changing marketing activities and makes plans accordingly and should develop new ideas and strategies for the products.

Marketing management is a profession that offers a number of opportunities in various fields. Graduates can start off their career as marketing executive and depending on their skills and experience within a couple of months or years, they could reach the post of marketing manager. From this post one has an opportunity to climb the ladder and occupy the top most positions in the company. A well-qualified MBA graduate can be offered positions such as marketing manager, brand manager, market research analyst and new product manager, sales manager, advertising manager, PR (Public Relations) director etc.

Small companies, big corporate, government and non-government organisations, consultancies, public relation agencies all offer a wide range of opportunities for marketing professionals. Advertising, sales, management, creative writing for product promotion, etc., are the areas where a lot of workis involved. They can work in department stores, computer companies, utility companies, construction firms, food producers, manufacturing firms and arts organisations regarding marketing or can start their own advertising agencies.

Remuneration

Marketing management is a well-paid profession. Apart from the salary, marketing personnel are offered high incentives for meeting their targets. A marketing executive with MBA degree from a good business school may get nothing less than 3 to 3.5 lakhs as annual income. An experienced one could take home easily an annual income of 5 lakhs. The senior most positions could get more than that depending upon the organisation and their experience. Most of the companies will also meet travel allowances for executives who do field work. Even though the basic payment in small companies may be less than that of big corporate, they offer good incentives to the employees.

Courses

- B.Com Marketing Management
- Certificate Course in Marketing and Advertising
- Diploma in Marketing Management (DMM)
- MBA Marketing
- MBA Marketing and Retail Management
- MBA Sales and Marketing
- M.Com Marketing
- Master of Marketing Management (MMM)
- Post Graduate Diploma in Advertising and Marketing Communication
- Post Graduate Diploma in Marketingand Retail Management
- Post Graduate Diploma in MarketingManagement

Institutes

There are numerous institutes in India and abroad that offer courses in Marketing Management. Marketing is an important area of specialisation in Business Administration and almost all of the business schools in India offer this specialisation in their MBA course. Always make sure to choose a good school with campus placement opportunities.

16.6 Rural Management

What is Rural Management?

Rural Management is the study of planning, organising, directing and controlling of co-operative, agribusiness and allied fields. It applies the knowledge of management studies in the rural context. India being an agricultural nation with most of its population living in rural areas, rural development has a significant impact on the economic growth of the country. Development process without inclusion of rural India would be asymmetrical and unsustainable. It is therefore, the duty of the qualified professionals in rural management to assist economically backward population in their process of development so that the whole nation could achieve progress and prosperity.

Development of Rural Areas

The Indian government is taking an active part in upgrading rural sector by investing huge amounts for the development of the people living in rural areas. All Five Year Plans were focused towards the special benefit of the rural community. Apart from the Government of India, many voluntary agencies, banks and private companies are also supporting rural development and rural management. Though the rural mass is aware of globalisation and they are ready to change themselves, management is essential for its growth as well as to be in tune with various technical and non-technical advancements in the rural sector. And here comes the importance of rural managers who can manage agricultural sector in the global arena.

The Role Rural Management Professional

The rural management professional's main work is systematic planning and execution of development schemes, thus lending a hand to develop the lives of people in the rural areas. They look at ways and methods of increasing profitability and sustainability or organisations that are involved in rural management.

Eligibility

Minimum qualification to take a course in rural management is Bachelor's degree in any stream or its equivalent qualification with a minimum of 50 per cent marks in aggregate from a recognised institute. Admission is made through entrance test conducted by the institute concerned which follows group discussion and personal interview. There are bachelor courses as well as postgraduate courses in rural management. Bachelor course is of 3 years duration and post-graduate course of 2 years duration.

Course Areas

A course in rural management includes training in agri-business, rural marketing, NGO management, micro finance, corporate social responsibility management and more. The objective of the course is to train professional managers to help create new organisations of rural people and manage them and providing training and support to practicing managers in rural areas.

Job Prospects and Career Options

Rural Management today, is one of the major areas of management studies. Most of the management schools provide direct placement assistance through campus recruitment.

Rural managers work in all functional areas of management – general management, marketing, finance, systems, project implementation, purchase, human resource development, in all segments of rural based enterprises. They work in rural enterprises as policy makers, managers, analyst and consultants advising on operational efficiency and improvements. Their work involves frequent travelling and interaction with clients.

Students who have qualified themselves may get appropriate employment opportunity in government developmental agencies and non-governmental organisations. Career opportunity in rural management includes challenging responsibilities in the rural co-operative sector, in development organisations, agri-business enterprises, areas related to micro-finance, food and agricultural marketing and management of agro products.

Co-operatives which absorb rural managers include oilseeds cooperatives, milk producers cooperatives, sugar cane producers cooperatives etc. Highly talented people can find lucrative job options in UN and its specialised agencies or programmes run by them. International NGOs are also a preferred destination for many rural managers.

They may also take up research; advisory and consultancy work with public and private organisations. Those with rural management degree can run their own NGO and thereby directly be associated with rural people. Banks, insurance companies and various other finance institutions as well as research and consultancy firms also recruit students by campus recruitment. They get offers like Tata Teleservices, Amul, Monsanto, Shriram Group, NABARD and ICICI Bank.

Remuneration

In this field, one can expect a starting pay ranging between ₹ 8,000 – 15,000 per month. As one gains more experience, one can expect a better salary package.

Courses

- Bachelor of Rural Technology and Management (Correspondence/Distance)
- MBA Rural Management
- Master of Rural Management (MRM)
- Post Graduate in Rural Management
- Post Graduate Diploma Program in Rural Development Management (Correspondence/Distance)

- Post Graduate Diploma Programme in Rural Development Management
- Post Graduate Diploma in Rural Marketing

Top institutes for studying Rural Management are

- **Indian Institute of Rural Management, Anand, Gujarat**

  Post Graduate Diploma in Rural Management

  Fellow Programme in Rural Management
- **National Institute of Rural Development, Hyderabad, Andhra Pradesh**

  Post Graduate Diploma in Rural Development Management
- **Xavier Institute of Management, Bhubaneshwar, Orissa**

  Post Graduate Diploma in Rural Management
- **Tripura University, Agartala, Tripura**

  Master in Rural Management and Development
- **Kalinga Institute of Industrial Technology, Bhubaneshwar, Orissa**

  Masters in Business Administration (Rural Management)
- **Institute of Rural Management, Jaipur, Rajasthan**

  Post Graduate Diploma in Management (Rural Management)

  Post Graduate Diploma in Business Management
- **Centurion School of Rural Enterprise Management (CSREM), Paralakhemundi, Orissa**

  Post Graduate Diploma-Rural Management

  Post Graduate Diploma-General Management and Strategic Management
- **Vaishali Institute of Business and Rural Management, Muzaffarpur, Bihar**

  Bachelor of Business Administration-Managing Rural Changes

  Master of Business Administration-Rural Management
- **Rural Development and Management Institute, Ahmedabad, Gujarat**
- **Bharati Vidyapeeths Institute of Management and Rural Development Administration, Sangli, Maharashtra**
- **PDVVP Foundations Institute of Business Management and Rural Development, Ahmednagar, Maharashtra**

16.7 Reputation Management

Reputation Management, also known as Directory Management is the process of tracking an entity's actions and other entities' opinions about those actions; reporting on those actions and opinions; and reacting to that report creating a feedback loop. All entities involved are generally people but that need not always be the case. Other examples of entities include animals, businesses or even locations exist in the international market. These software services are typically designed to connect organisations to their stakeholders, track the orchestration of stakeholder engagement and analyse measure and manage the results.

The reputation management can be separated into three different categories :

- **Building :** This type of reputation management has to do with building the reputation for a business that is just getting started. It includes building a good reputation to maintaining it for your business.
- **Maintenance :** Reputation management meant to just keep a company's good image superior in the public eye is called maintenance. This is meant for companies that are already established and have a good reputation already.
- **Recovery :** If your business has got a bad reputation for any reason, then the recovery portion of reputation management is for you. Brick Marketing works to hide the bad reputation with good marketing and self-promotion.
- **Online Reputation Management :** Online Reputation Management is a very labour intensive process. Any approach that is subtle and yet effective will take time, at least three months, before anyprogress is really seen. This includes many different strategies which include social media such as :
  - o **Blogging:** Blogs that are updated every day
  - o **Directory listings:** Listing a website in directories using optimised keywords
  - o **Direct reviews:** hiring someone to write good reviews of the company on websites
  - o **Online publicity:** Syndicated article writing, links and banners
  - o **Social networking:** Posting pages on MySpace.com and Face book.

17

MEDIA AND ENTERTAINMENT

17.1 Advertising

What is Advertising?

Advertising is a means of informing as well as influencing the general public to buy products or services through visual or oral messages. A product or service is advertised to create an awareness in the minds of potential buyers. Some of the commonly used media for advertising are T.V., radio, websites, newspapers, magazines, bill-boards, hoardings etc. As a result of economic liberalisation and the changing social trends advertising industry has shown rapid growth in the last decade.

Advertising is one of the aspects of mass communication. Advertising is actually brand-building through effective communication and is essentially a service industry. It helps to create demand, promote marketing system, and boost economic growth. Thus, advertising forms the basis of marketing.

Importance of Advertising

Advertising plays a significant role in today's highly competitive world. A career in advertisement is quite glamorous and at the same time challenging with more and more agencies opening up every day. Whether its brands, companies, personalities or even voluntary or religious organisations, all of them use some form of advertising in order to communicate with the target audience.

Today, new areas are emerging within advertising like event management, image management, internet marketing etc. Event management is wherein events are marketed and Image management is wherein a particular profile of an individual or an organisation is projected. Internet marketing has also brought about a lot of changes in advertising as Internet means that one is catering to a select group of audience rather than mass audience.

Eligibility

Most advertising agencies recruit candidates with a formal management or advertising/mass communication qualification. Preference is given for MBAs for posts in market research, client servicing and media planning departments. In the creative department, on the other hand, a general B.A. with a command of the language of communication plus knowledge of designing packages like Photoshop, Coral draw or fine arts is the requirement.

There are also specialised courses in advertising/mass communication at diploma level and post graduate level for which basic qualification is graduation. However, advertising is also offered as a subject for the graduate degree course in mass communication studies at certain institutions for which minimum qualification is 10+2. In addition there are also certificate courses for which 10+2 is enough.

Personal attributes

Basic qualities like creativity and flair for writing or ability to translate ideas into a visual format are required for making a successful career in this field. They should have insight into the interests of people from all walks of life, ability to work as part of team, mental and physical toughness to be able to withstand high pressure and criticism, must be sociable and have calm temperament. Market and media researchers should have an analytical and logical brain. Those in creative field should possess artistic abilities to make the ad appealing to the masses.

Job prospects

Career opportunities in advertising include openings in private advertising agencies; advertising department in private or public sector companies; in advertising sections of newspapers, journals, magazines, commercial section of radio or television; market research organisations etc. One can also do freelancing.

Advertising field offers a range of lucrative, interesting careers. The job in this field is categorised into two: executive and creative. Executive side includes Client Servicing, Market Research and Media Research. Creative side consists of copywriters, scriptwriters, visualisers, photographers and typographers.

The executive department understands clients' needs, finds new business and retains existing business, selects the appropriate media, analyses timing and placement of advertisement and negotiates the financial aspects of the deal. Creative department creates the advertisement copy. They verbalise the specific need of the client. As ad films are also a part of film making, career options of film are related to this field.

Executive Department

- **Client Servicing :** The Client Servicing department is linked between the client and the agency. It is an important part of any advertising firm like what the heart is to the body. This department is responsible for meeting prospective clients and getting business for the company. It involves a study of the client, the product and the market; analysis of consumer behavior and marketing; knowledge of all available media and their cost effectiveness and a strategic plan to be presented to the client. Those in client servicing must therefore interact with clients, gather information, oversee research where necessary, gauge consumer attitudes and based on this, work along with the various departments of the agency to formulate the most appropriate and effective advertising strategy within the specified budget. To be an effective client-servicing person, the candidate has to have a thorough knowledge of the client's business and also know his weak points so that, through advertising and communications, the gap can be minimised.
- **An Account Executive :** He works in the client servicing department and takes care of all the monitory dealings. He should know the most effective way to advertise clients product or service, i.e., the media and their cost effectiveness. Account executives should also have an idea about market research and target audiences.
- **Market Research :** Every good ad plans, start with research. This is the department which surveys the market and analyses and studies consumer behaviour about a product or service. They are involved with collection of data-information about the consumer, the market, existing competition and so on. The research studies provide basic information to the manufacturer for planning a new product.If you are a MBA or hold a degree in statistics/operations research, you can go for market researching jobs.
- **Media Planning/Research :** Responsibility of media planning department starts at the point when the ad is complete. Media

Department is responsible for the planning, scheduling, booing and purchase of space and time (in newspapers, magazines, radio and TV, and outdoor hoardings). The media department must therefore devise the most effective use for an advertising budget to effectively and economically transmit a campaign message to the target audience. This department consists of the following :

(i) **Media planners :** Media planners decide different media where the ads would be featured in order to get maximum viewership.

(ii) **Media buyer :** Media buyer has to negotiate to buy space in the Press or time on electronic media at the best rates for which he has to understand the buying as well as selling trends.

- **Creative Department :** This department designs and conceptualises the advertisement. This consists of copywriting department and art department. Copywriting department works on text for the ad and themes for campaign. Art department visualises the campaign.

- **Copywriters :** They evolve a theme for the campaign and provide the text for advertisements. They are responsible for making the ad look attractive and delivering the message to the point. They work out the campaign slogan, jingles, scripts and promotional literature of the product or service as well as proposals, concept notes and film treatments. They are also expected to edit all textual matter for factual, syntax and typesetting discrepancies before it goes into production. Sometimes specialists called Typographers are appointed for making the format of textual matter who gives advice on fonts, lettering etc.

  Copywriters need to have a flair for writing backed up by the knowledge of advertising and oral communication skills to become successful. They also need to have skill in analysing clients' needs and research skills for finding out about the products and services they are helping to sell. Problem-solving and time-management skills are important.

- **Visualisers :** They work on the visual concepts and decide how the ad shall eventually look. They do the overall layout of message including graphics, sketching etç. They must be artistic. A degree/diploma in commercial arts or fine arts as well as the knowledge of designing software like Photoshop, PageMaker, Corel Draw etc. is often the required qualifications.

- **Photographers :** They should have an idea about angles and lighting effects. Good technical ability and knowledge of cameras and lenses is essential.

Remuneration

Job positions and earnings in an agency vary with its size and turnover. Accredited agencies have large set up while small agencies may have just a handful of employees looking after all the various jobs. The earnings range from 7,000 for production managers to ₹ 8,000 for copywriters up to ₹ 35,000 for General Managers plus perks.

Best Advertising Colleges in India

- **National Institute of Advertising, Noida, Uttar Pradesh**

  Courses : Post Graduate Diploma in Advertising and Creative Communication

  Post Graduate Programme in Advertising and Communication Management

- **Sir Vithaldas Thakersey College of Home Science, Mumbai, Maharashtra**

  Course : Diploma in Advertising, Public Relations and Communication Management

- **Xavier Institute of Communications, Mumbai, Maharashtra**

  Courses : Diploma in Advertising and Marketing

  Diploma in Journalism and Mass Communication

- **School of Broadcasting and Communication, Mumbai, Maharashtra**

  Courses : Master of Arts in Advertising and Public Relations

  Bachelor of Journalism

- **North Orissa University, Baripada, Orissa**

  Courses : Post Graduate Diploma in Advertising and Public Relations

  Master of Arts in Journalism and Mass Communication

- **International Council for Management Studies, Chennai, Tamil Nadu**

  Course : Diploma in Advertising and Public Relations

- **Institute of Media, Mumbai, Maharashtra**

  Courses : Diploma in Advertising and Marketing

  Diploma in Public Relations

- **Netaji Subhas Open University, Kolkata, West Bengal**
  Course : Diploma in Advertising and Public Relations

17.2 Anchoring

The Career of an Anchor

The career of an anchor is one that commands immense popularity. He or she is the face seen by millions of families each day and is instantly recognised by people. To succeed in this career one must be an extrovert, be confident and should be free from inhibitions while communicating. Anchoring has immerged as a popular career option in the country with the entry of satellite channels, with several news as well as entertainment channels coming up day by day. The field is quite lucrative for successful anchors in the field.

What is an Anchoring?

Anchoring is a talent-based profession. It requires a good command over language and a sense of humor. An anchor must maintain wit and humor at all times to make up for any *lapsus langua* (slip of tongue) that they may make. The art of talking your way out of uncomfortable situations is the most important pre-requisite. Moreover, an anchor needs a cornucopia of information or must be a powerhouse of knowledge. Thorough knowledge of current affairs, politics and history are a must if you want to sustain in this profession. The popularity of the show entirely depends on an anchor's performance on stage. Being on the call always is also essential if you are passionate about the career.

Who is an Anchor?

An anchor is usually known as a presenter, host, news reader or news/ programme anchor etc. Anchors are of three types – stage anchor, news anchor and programme anchor. While stage anchor present live events, News anchor/programme anchors present news or programmes in entertainment media or news media. TV news anchors present news in different languages – national, regional and other different languages. Programme anchors focus toward entertainment programmes such as award functions, any competition shows, comedy shows, film based shows, cooking shows, reality shows, sports, crime reports or talk shows and debates etc.

Anchors are the mediators between the channel and the audience. They are not only mere presenters but are required to have updated knowledge about the world around them. Be it entertainment or sober news presentations, they must have the quality to engage the viewers throughout the programme. The task of news reading and presenting a programme is a challenging field. An anchor is responsible for not only providing information but also needs to ensure that programme is delivered in an entertaining manner.

A trusted, respected anchor reflects well on the public's general opinion of that channel. In short, people tune in that channel because of who the anchors are, their familiarity with them and the trust built over time and that's a great deal of responsibility.

Eligibility

Although academic qualification does not play a major role for news anchoring or programme anchoring, the increasing demand for good anchors has resulted in the need for specialised and professional training. The minimum eligibility criterion for most of these courses is graduation. However, for certificate courses a 10+2 will also suffice. To become a news anchor, a course in journalism will help you a lot.

Many courses have been designed to enhance the skill of aspirants. Most of the anchoring courses are of one to six month duration. The course curriculum for anchoring covers training in the change of facial expressions, voice modulation, use of proper diction and pitch according to the given script/situation etc. They are also trained in anchoring, interviewing, news reading, chat shows etc. The courses designed for anchoring also focus on other aspects like technical issues and camera handling to enhance the skills of aspirants.

Personal Attributes

Voice is the key quality to be possessed by an anchor. Anchor must have a passion towards the career and must be responsible. They must be confident and have a pleasing personality. In other words, an anchor must be presentable. Apart from these qualities he/she must have dynamism, knowledge and command over phonetics or correct pronunciation, diction and communication. Comfort before camera is also a must for this field.

Job Prospects and Career Options

Anchoring has a wide scope as a career avenue with the constant launch of various news, infotainment and entertainment channels. With the flood of reality shows, chat shows, music shows etc. demand for experienced anchors is immense. Most anchors begin their career through trial and error method – working at small broadcast stations, sometimes as reporters. Gradually, after gaining experience, move on to larger stations or television networks. Programme/news anchors specialise in news or entertainment programmes such as award functions, music and dance shows, comedy shows, reality shows and cookery shows.

The position of an anchor combines journalism and entertainment. One can work with channels as a news anchor as well as programme anchor or presenter in a reality show, games show, conduct interviews and offer commentary for various live events. Anchors are in demand not only in channels, they are wanted to introduce a product and even present a programme or event. Usually, product launches are common events which need an anchor to conduct them. Even family functions like marriages or birthdays hire anchors so that the function runs smoothly. Due to the spurt in events and festivals these days, demand for anchors is on the rise. Festivals like Christmas, New Year, Diwali are more elaborate with lots of events. There are more corporate events, celebrity nights, trade fairs, etc., all of them require anchors to present the show or event.

Anchors can find employment opportunities in TV channels, radio stations, as hosts in award functions, reality, comedy, music, dance shows etc. Most of them work on a freelance basis and are mostly occupied with anchoring live events. Employers include TV channels such as ZEE, Star Plus, Sahara news, Asianet, Sony, Sun, BBC, Surya, CNN IBN etc. if you are a good performer and dedicated employee you could also get a chance to work with international reporters and News channels.

The career is rewarding not only in monetary terms but the fame and honour one gains from this field is much more.

Remuneration

For an anchor salary is not a constraint. Salary varies according to news channel, performance and experience. Salary in local channel will be less compared to national channels. Generally anchors in local channel get a starting salary range of ₹ 8,000 – 12,000 per month. In this sector, sky is the limit you can earn as you have proven your talent. Once you gain experience in this field salary can be more than ₹ 30,000. Apart from money, good anchoring would fetch you name and fame.

Courses

The different courses available are :

- Certificate Course in Anchoring and Video Jockeying
- Certificate Course in News Reading and Anchoring (CRA)
- Certificate Course in Television News Reading, Anchoring, Presentation, Announcement Styles and Editing
- Certificate Course in TV reporting and Anchoring
- Diploma in TV Journalism, News Reading and Anchoring

- Post Graduate Diploma in TV Journalism, News Reading and Anchoring.

Institutes

Due to the increasing demand and popularity of TV anchors, a number of institutes have started conducting specialised training courses for the same. Prominent among them are Prans Media Institute, New Delhi, Center for Research in Art of Film and Television (CRAFT), New Delhi etc.

17.3 Cinematography

What is Cinematography?

The word 'Cinematography'comes from two Greek words *'kinema'* meaning 'movements' and *'graphein'* meaning 'to record'. It is the art or science of recording or capturing movements. It is the art of motion picture photography. It is the technique of movie photography including both the shooting and development of the film. It is an art form in the field of filmmaking.

Eligibility and course areas

The minimum requirement for admission into cinematography programme is 10+2. After +2 one may go for various certificate and diploma courses in cinematography to acquire knowledge in the field. Some of the prominent institutes are :

- Film and Television Institute of India (FTII), Pune
- Satyajit Ray Film and Television Institute, Kolkata
- Zee Institute of Media Arts and Whistling Woods International in Mumbai.

Course curriculum includes live shooting with digital cameras, exposure to advanced digital shooting technology and computer software for creating visual effects for individual shots, exposure to motion graphics, experience with live studios and so on.

Personal Attributes

More than educational qualification, Cinematographer must have the ability to work independently, as well as have the interpersonal skills required to work well under a director and over camera technicians. They have to be detail oriented, hard working and passionate towards the work. He should have a high sense of imagination and foresight. Good technical ability and knowledge of cameras and lenses is also essential for a Cinematographer to be successful. Expertise in computer animation and digital editing may also prove to be of great help.

Job Prospects and Career Option

A career in Cinematography is suited for artistic people with food hand-eye co-ordination, passion for photography and lots of creativity. With the increase in the number of feature, advertisement and documentary film production companies and new TV channels being launched every other day, cinematographers have immense career opportunities.

Cinematographers play an important role in film production. They work in co-ordination with the director, right from the pre-production stage of planning a shoot. Often, a cinematographer will be asked to work with the camera operators, lighting team and other production staff in a variety of roles to capture the script's scene on film. In short, Cinematographer heads a crew which is required to provide the photographic images and visual effects conceptualised by the director for advertisement, feature, television and documentary films. He is responsible for the selection of camera, lens, filter and film stock. He is the one who has to give the final image to all the imaginary efforts of the director.

Earlier Cinematographers learned on the job by working as junior cameraman. But today, highly sophisticated cameras, lighting and special effects demand trained personal with sound theoretical and practical education. Cinematographers may specialise in movie making, television programmes, documentaries, ad films etc. Most of them start their career and advance their skills through experience they gain while working with a senior Cinematographer as assistant. Once they prove their talent, they can freelance as an independent Cinematographer. But the road to fame is tough especially in films and one hás to have a lot of perseverance to succeed in the field.

Cinematographers can find employment with film production units, television or video industries, studios, etc., in India as well as overseas. Earlier, films were the only avenue available to aspiring candidates. But now, with the coming up of various channels they have immense opportunities with production houses that make short films, documentaries and television serials. One can also freelance for advertising commercials and music videos.

Remuneration

Cinematography has become a well-paid career option, since the role of a cinematographer cannot be undermined, as he plays several roles in planning and coordinating a film. The salary for cinematographer varies based on the employer type, professional experience and location of the job. Cinematographer working as an assistant can get between ₹ 15,000 to 20,000 per month. For those experienced hands sky is the limit. All this depends upon his creative skill and amount of success he gets commercially with his work.

17.4 Journalism/Mass Communication

What is Journalism?

Today, the young generation is attracted to journalism more than any other times in history. Journalism is concerned with collection and

dissemination of news through the print media as well as the electronic media. This involves various areas of works like reporting, writing, editing, photographing, broadcasting or cable casting news items.

Classification of Journalism

Journalism is classified into two on the basis of media – (i) Print Journalism and (ii) Electronic (Audio/Visual) Journalism. Print Journalism includes newspapers, magazines and journals. In print journalism one can work as editor, reporter, columnist, correspondent etc. Electronic Journalism includes working for Radio, Television and the Web; skilled people are required to maintain sites by web newspapers (which cater only to the web and do not have print editions) and popular newspapers and magazines that have their own web editions. In electronic Journalism one can be a reporter, writer, editor, researcher, correspondent and anchor.

Travel and stay expenses as well as allowances are addition with all pay packets. Freelancers are paid for each piece of work they submit.

Eligibility and Course Areas

Journalism courses are offered at graduation and post graduation level. To become a journalist one can complete a Bachelor's degree in Mass Communication/Mass Media/Journalism after 10+2. After completion in a related graduation field, one may complete a Master's degree in Journalism or Mass Communication. A graduate (who has flair for writing) from any other field can also opt for a postgraduate course in journalism.

There are some institutes which provide one year certificate courses in Journalism for which eligibility is 10+2. There are also courses in specialised areas of Journalism like sports, television, photo, press law etc.

Skills required

Inquisitive and investigative mind, alert, adaptive and tolerant of changing and difficult situations, good communication skills, command over language, confidence, enthusiasm, patience and perseverance, the ability to differentiate between fact and fiction, adhering to deadlines, team cohesiveness, sensitivity to different views and lifestyles, in-depth knowledge about various fields such as politics, culture, religion, social and current affairs. The most important fact is that people generally feel that Journalism is all about writing. It is. However, it is also about reading and most importantly, the ability to express one's thoughts on varied topics. Journalism is for people who are ready to explore various opportunities 24/7, without the constraints of cultural upbringing, gender and are also ready to go beyond geographical boundaries.

Job Prospects

They can find employment with newspapers, periodicals and magazines, central information service, press information bureau, AIR and TV channels like Doordarshan, ZEE TV, Star TV etc. At the same time they can do freelancing. One can also take up this career as a part time employment along with any other field of work.

Career Options

Journalists can work as editors, reporters, columnists, correspondents, staff or freelance writer, photojournalists, proofreaders, news analysts, etc., in print (Newspapers and magazines) and electronic (Radio, Television and Web) media.

Options in the field of Editing

- **Chief Editor/Resident Editor :** Chief Editor/Resident Editor is in charge of the over-all functions of the publication. His primary responsibility is to supervise the functions of collection, selection and presentation of news. He reads and corrects copy for publication; decide on the editorial policy and the content of publications. Resident editor is in charge of a particular edition (e.g., Chennai edition, Mumbai edition etc.).
- **Sub Editor :** Sub editor assist the chief editor in selecting and sorting the contents. Their job involves re-writing stories to fit the space assigned improve the language, insert punctuation etc. They also give headlines and help in page layout. There are a number of sub editors for each newspaper. The chief sub editor is in charge of the team of sub editors – he assigns work and coordinates and supervises them. He acts as a link between the chief editor and sub editors.

- **News/Feature Editor :** He is the right-hand man of the Chief Editor. He decides on the news to be published in the newspaper each day. He collects news, controls the network of correspondents, reporting staff and other news sources, allocate assignments and attend editorial conferences.
- **Associate Editor :** He directs the preparation of a section of a newspaper, magazine or a television or radio segment. He prepares news, feature articles and critical reviews and plans the layout of the publication, assigns reporting staff and photographers to obtain coverage of matters of news or interest related to his section.
- **Proofreader :** A proofreader compares proofs and edited copy (written, typed or printed material) to ensure that the final text is complete and accurate and that the spelling and punctuation are correct before final printing. They mark proofs for corrections, check revised proofs to ensure that the corrections have been made. They must have sound knowledge of spelling, punctuation and grammar should be able to pay particular attention to detail and retain concentration for a long period.

Options in the field of Reporting

- **Reporter :** He is the one who reports events as and when it occurs. The reporter is said to be the eyes and ears of the newspaper. Reporter attend press conferences, conduct interviews, visit sites of major occurrence and gather first hand report and present them in an unbiased manner. Their job involves a lot of travelling. A Chief Reporter is in charge of the team of reporters and assigns work to the reporters. Main newspapers employ reporters in all major cities.
- **Correspondent/Special Reporters :** They are reporters for special purposes and their task involves reporting on a particular topic like politics, foreign affairs, sports, finance etc. They often report on news covering their area of expertise from a place where the particular event is happening. Their aim is to interpret or explain news and comment on the events, trends and causes behind it. Usually one must have sufficient experience as a reporter to become a special correspondent.

Options in the field of Writing

- **Writer :** A writer chooses themes or subjects for written work, conduct research into the subject, assemble background material and obtain other necessary data. Writers may specialise in journalism, fiction writing, children's books, educational textbook writing, historical writing and transferring oral histories into written form, humor or comedy writing and so on in journalism.Writers can be feature writers, leader writers, writers for multimedia and web and so on.

- **Feature Writer :** Feature writer writes detailed stories or presents commentaries on specific news topic. They research and analyse facts and draw conclusions on a particular topic. They can cover any topic of public interest like interviews, organising data and evidence, feature story leads etc. Feature writing is more descriptive and detailed than news reporting.
- **Leader writer :** He gives ideas on news topics in the editorial columns of newspapers or magazines and discusses prospects of improvement with trainee writers.
- **Writing for Multimedia and the Web :** Writers are required in multimedia and the worldwide Web for writing news and other articles. They must have a skill for writing precise text adaptive to the environment. If you can communicate your ideas through graphics, animation, etc., it is an added advantage in this field.
- **Columnist :** They are writers who contribute regularly to a publication. Usually one column on general or a specific topic is devoted to the writer. They write a regular segment within their particular interest category, e.g., gardening, fashion, politics, films. The columnist usually projects a point of view and could either be a commentator or a critic. They review developments in special areas they write on and may contribute to a number of newspapers at the same time.
- **Critic :** A critic needs to be well read. He must have adequate knowledge and experience in his respective field. One can be a critic in various fields like film, art, drama etc. Only persons having food knowledge about a particular subject or art can authoritatively write about the subject.

Options in the field of Photography

- **Photo Journalist or News Photographer :** They are the visual reporters. Photo journalists accompany reporters on assignments to take pictures that support a news story, feature or interview. They must know what makes a good news picture; be able to write captions, work well with reporters, be quick and often work under difficult conditions. They must have good knowledge about technical aspects of photography like lighting, speed etc. to take photographs apt for the particular situation.

Others

- **Fashion Journalist :** He is overall in-charge of a fashion magazine.It is through him that the general public gets to know the latest fashion trends. He should have excellent taste for fashion and keep himself abreast with latest fashion news, consumer reaction to new collections, fashion shows, current and future trends in color, design and fabric.
- **Cartoonists and illustrators :** They make a social or political comment on public figures or events in the form of a cartoon that is funny as well as witty. A cartoon is one man's view of the world.

Other departments included in the publication of a newspaper or periodical are: production, advertising, legal affairs department, circulation and public relations.

Remuneration

The minimum salary as per government directive has to be ₹ 5,500 – 9,000 for reporters and senior reporters ₹ 5,000 – 10,500 for the chief reporters and sub-editors and ₹ 7,500 – 12,000 for editors. Actual salaries offered depend on the company one is working with and can be anything from very high to very low. Travel and stay expenses as well as allowances are additional with all pay packages. Freelancers are paid for each piece of work they submit.

Courses

- B.A. Journalism
- B.A. Mass Communication and Journalism
- Bachelor of Journalism
- Bachelor of Journalism and Mass Communication
- Certificate Course in Journalism
- Certificate Course in Mass Communication and Journalism
- Diploma in Journalism
- Diploma in Journalism and Mass Communication
- Diploma in TV Journalism and Presentation
- M.A. Journalism
- M.A. Journalism and Mass Communication
- M.Phil. Journalism
- M. Sc. Mass Communication and Journalism

- Post Graduate Diploma in Journalism
- Post Graduate Diploma in Journalism and Mass Communication

Best Institutes for Studying Mass Communication

- IIMC, New Delhi
- Xavier Institute of Communication, Mumbai
- Asian College of Journalism, Chennai
- A.J Kidwai MCRC, Jamia Millia Islamia Delhi
- Symbiosis Institute of Mass Communication, Pune
- Indian Institute of Journalism and New Media, Bangalore
- Mudra Institute of Communications, Ahmedabad
- Department of Communication and Journalism, Pune University
- Manorama School of Communication, Kottayam, Kerala
- Bhartiya Vidya Bhawan, Delhi

17.5 Photojournalism

Introduction

Journalism is a broad field with various specialisations like sports, film and television, photo, print etc. Of these, one of the leading streams today is photojournalism. It is an integral part of journalism as photographs play a vital role in depicting events. Initially, the term 'photojournalism' was restricted to still photography but its scope has now widened and photo journalist even shoots videos to come up with a good news item/ feature.

Photojournalists are visual reporters who click photographs at events that become integral part of the news. He is a photographer who is able to tell a story with pictures or contribute pictures to compliment a news story. Photojournalists may work side by side with a reporter to decide which photographs will accompany an article.

Eligibility

Photojournalism is taught in most institutes as part of curriculum of Bachelor's degree or Post-graduate degree in journalism/Mass Communication. Hence, those interested in this field need to pursue a course with specialisation in Photojournalism. There are separate courses for photo journalism offered at certificate and diploma level.

Minimum eligibility for Bachelor's degree in Journalism or Mass Media is 10+2 and for Post graduate degree courses is a Bachelor's degree in Journalism. Some institutes also provide one year certificate courses in photojournalism for which eligibility is 10+2.

Course in photojournalism covers reporting and drawing, camera operation and lighting, digital imaging, video capture, computer based image processing etc.

Personal attributes

A candidate who is interested in this field requires photography and editorial skills. Aspirants in this field also need a keen eye for aesthetic detail and a thorough knowledge of cameras and the technicalities involved in taking pictures, of light, distance and perspective. One must have interest in visuals, attentiveness to color, shape and shadow. Apart from these, candidates require creativity, good power of observation and a curious and perceptive mind.

Remuneration

Salary of a photojournalist depends on the employer and position held by him/her. Generally at the beginning of the career a photojournalist can earn around ₹ 12,000 – ₹ 15,000 per month. Experienced ones can easily earn between ₹ 25,000 – ₹ 30,000 per month. Newspapers and news agencies pay according to the assignment offered to the photojournalist. Salary increases with experience, hard work and skills. A freelancer's income could be unlimited. Those who have acquired perfection in the field are offered high pays by reputed organisations.

Prominent Institutes

- National Institute of Design (NID), Ahmedabad
- Sir JJ School of Applied Arts, Mumbai
- Shari Academy of Photography and Digital Imaging, Mumbai
- Jawaharlal Nehru Technological University, Hyderabad
- College of Art, Delhi University
- Xavier Institute of Communications, Mumbai
- Ambitions 4 Photography Academy, Chennai
- National Academy of Photography, Kolkata
- National Institute of Photography, Mumbai
- Sri Aurobindo Centre for Arts and Communication, New Delhi

- Mass Communication Research Centre, Jamia Millia Islamia, New Delhi
- Academy of Photography, Rabindra Bharati University, Kolkata
- Film and Television Institute of India, Pune
- Creative Hut, Ahmedabad
- Fergussen College, Pune
- Delhi School of Photography, New Delhi
- Satyajit Ray Film and Television Institute (SRFTI), Kolkata
- Southern Film Institute, Thiruvananthapuram

17.6 Photography

What is Photography?

Photography is a unique and creative medium of self-expression. It is an art form which entails a vibrant aesthetic sense as well as précised technical expertise. It is a pastime or hobby that can be metamorphosed into a profitable enterprise by going professional by the talented. With the explosion of the communication network, the growth of advertising and media and the fashion boom and digital photography, it has now become a profession with great commercial value. Photos are an essential part in both print and electronic media. So this is an area that offers great scope for those who have an interest and attributes needed to be a professional.

Eligibility and Course Areas

There are no specific academic requirements for full time courses in photography; however, candidates who have cleared 10+2 exam are eligible for the diploma/certificate courses in photography. There are many students who learn photography along with their college degree, doing a part-time course. Besides the Certificate and Diploma courses in the field, Photography is also offered as an optional subject for a bachelor's degree in Fine Arts. Some institutes offer full fledged B.A. courses in photography of three year duration.

Job Prospects and Career Options

One of the most exciting aspects of photography is the variety of jobs available in the field, ranging from highly specialised, technical work to jobs that require creativity and visual literacy. One can begin one's career as an assistant of a senior or professional photographer so that he or she can grasp the finger prints of photography. Photographers can specialise in different areas such as:

- **Press photographers :** They are also known as photojournalists. Press photographers supply pictures to the national and local press and must be versatile with an ability to photograph all kinds of subjects. They must have journalistic instincts, know what makes a good news picture, be able to write accurate captions, work well with reporters, be quick and often work under difficult conditions.
- **Feature photography :** It essentially involves telling a story in pictures and therefore requires knowledge of the subject. Feature photographers cover an entire theme or subject with a set of photographs. The work is varied and leads to assignments at any time and in any place – photographing people at home or life in foreign parts or schools at work, anything that makes a story. Photographers specialise in the photography of wildlife, sports travel, environment etc. They may work with news reporters or work as free-lancers and take independent assignments on environment, wildlife and so on.
- **Editorial photographers :** They work normally for magazines and periodicals nearly always as freelancers. The main task of an editorial photographer is to pictorially illustrate what is written in the article or report. Work can be varied depending on the article or report which needs illustration.
- **Commercial/Industrial photographer :** He takes pictures of merchandise, exteriors and interiors of factories and machinery both indoors and outdoors to be used for company brochures, annual reports and in advertising and selling. An industrial photographer's main emphasis is on taking pictures for a single company or firm. The main intention is to make the company's factory, machines or products look good.
- **Portrait/Wedding photographers :** They take pictures of individuals or small groups. Portrait subjects like pets, children, families, weddings, functions and activities of sports and social clubs. However, there is an increasing demand for portraits in the home, garden or workplace, especially in the case of children's portraits. Portrait photographers may work for a studio or be self-employed.
- **Advertising photographs :** They are either taken by the

photographic departments of advertising agencies by photographic studios or by freelance photographers. A large number of photographers do catalogue work, while some studios specialise in 'mail order' photography. This is the best paid and most competitive branch; success in this sphere depends entirely on ability, efficiency and the right personality.

- **Fashion photography :** This is an extremely creative and well-paid profession. Most fashion photography is done by specialist studios or freelancers who are commissioned by fashion houses or advertising agencies. They usually work under the direction of a fashion expert. They can also find employment with fashion houses, designers, fashion journals and newspapers.
- **Fine arts photographers :** They sell their photographs as fine artwork. In addition to technical proficiency, fine arts photographers need artistic talent and creativity.
- **Digital photography :** It involves the use of digital camera. The images are captured on a disk, floppy or directly on the computer. In conventional methods of photography the images were captured on films which had to be processed and then scanned with the help of a scanner onto the computer for any further changes or effects that the image may need. Digital photography is largely used in the media, as digital images can be stored easily and conveyed quickly over long distances.
- **Nature and Wildlife photography :** This involves taking photographs of animals, birds, plants and landscapes. While photos of rare species are in great demand, nature photographs are also widely used as pictures for calendars or covers.
- **Forensic photography :** A crime scene must be photographed from every angle clearly to show detail, with the emphasis on accuracy recording the size and distance of objects. They can find employment with law enforcement agencies, police, legal system and in the investigative services of the government and also private detective agencies.
- **Freelancing :** It has been the most popular career choice among photographers. Photographers who want to be self-employed need to have business management skills. They must have good communication skills, problem solving skills and be able to work independently. They can do freelancing in any of the above fields.

Remuneration

Photographers can start working as assistants to senior photographers, in which capacity they are paid around ₹ 3,500 – 6,000. Your earnings can go up to 25,000, depending upon the designation and the organisation likewise and may be more once you have established yourself as a freelancer.

Courses

- Certificate Course in Advanced Photography
- Certificate Course in Basic Photography
- Certificate Course in Digital Photography
- Certificate Course in Fashion Photography
- Certificate Course in Photojournalism
- Certificate Course in Photography
- Diploma in Motion Picture Photography
- Diploma in Photography
- Diploma in Professional Photography

Best Institutes in India that offer courses in Photography

- National Institute of Design (NID), Ahmedabad
- Sir JJ School of Applied Arts, Mumbai
- College of Art, Delhi University
- Xavier Institute of Communications, Mumbai
- Jawaharlal Nehru Technological University, Hyderabad
- Shari Academy of Photography and Digital Imaging, Mumbai
- Sri Aurobindo Centre for Arts and Communications, New Delhi
- National Institute of Photography, Mumbai
- Ambitions $ Photography Academy, Chennai
- National Academy of Photography, Kolkata

17.7 Modeling

Introduction

Modeling has become one of the most sought after career options for youngsters in India. This is one of the most thrilling as well as lucrative professions. It attracts males and females equally, though there was a time when females dominated the field. With the expansion of consumerism and media there has been a fabulous boost in the ad industry. This along with upsurge in fashion industry has made modeling an attractive career option. It has generated a large and continuing demand for fresh faces and personalities to launch and promote a variety of branded products or show a garment to its best advantage.

What is Modeling?

Modeling is a profession where educational qualifications become insignificant and physical attributes and personal qualities assume importance. Modeling is of various types. The modeling can be broadly classified into ramp modeling, television modeling and print modeling.

Modeling is undoubtedly a glamorous field which offers tremendous opportunities to travel and meet various classes of people. Moreover once established it is a highly paid job. Even with all these plus points it involves lot of hard work, dedication and perseverance to be successful in this field. It is a highly competitive and short-lived career. Further, stress factor is high and the hours are erratic. The job also requires a lot of stamina and patience.

Eligibility

There is no specific qualification or age limit to enter into this field. First step for making an entry is to prepare a portfolio. This consists of a series of photographs taken by a professional photographer. The portfolio can then be shown to an advertising agency, a model coordinating agency providing suitable models according to requirements or a fashion designer. Another way to enter into this career is to apply for the contests sponsored by magazines, cloth manufacturers, cosmetic companies etc. and participating in beauty pageants.

There are no set standards of training in this area and models are usually expected to learn on the job. A beginning for training in this field has been made by ex-models who have set up training schools; however it is restricted mainly to Delhi and Mumbai. Training programmes includes instructions on beauty care, make-up, hair styling, diet and exercise, how to walk and carry yourself elegantly and so on. These training programmes include guidance on how to make a contract and other technicalities. Guidance on making a portfolio also forms a part of such training programmes.

Personal attributes

Main attributes required to become a model is a good and healthy complexion and lustrous hair. Models should be tall, fashion industry criteria for best models are 5'7" to 6' or 6' plus. For a man, height should be 6′ or 6′ plus and he should be muscular. Being photogenic is the single most important quality to have for a model. Apart from this, good knowledge of acting, camera friendly attitude and a great amount of self confidence will reward success in this profession. They must also be open to criticism.

Job prospects

There is no dearth of jobs in modeling these days. Job prospects are available to models :

- In product advertising
- Featuring in music videos
- Doing live fashion shows
- Showroom displays or garment fairs
- Opening a school for models
- Setting up a model coordinating agency
- Acting in television programmes or films

Career Options

Modeling can be mainly classified into Television modeling, Print modeling/Still modeling, Ramp modeling/Live modeling, Show room modeling, Advertising modeling etc.

- **Television modeling :** This involves modeling before the Movie camera to be used for Television commercials, cinema, video, internet etc. Modeling for video or films often includes some acting or dance and is mostly conducted on location. To make a successful television model you need a flair for acting.
- **Print modeling/Still modeling :** Models generally pose for still photographs to be utilised in the press advertisements, brochures, magazines, catalogues, calendars etc. Models for print media have to work along with ad agencies and photographers.
- **Show room modeling :** As per the name, it takes place in the showrooms. Models work generally for the exporters, garment manufacturers and the big garment retailer to display the latest trends of fashion to the buyers.
- **Ramp or Catwalk modeling/Live modeling :** This requires models to display the garments and accessories in front of a live audience. This can be at an exhibition or a fashion show or at a showroom or point of purchase. Ramp modeling thus, requires long hours of practice. Performing in a live show before an

audience can be very stressful. It requires tremendous confidence and poise. Ramp models should have a good posture, walking style and body language.

- **Advertising modeling :** This is one where both print and electronic media has equal importance. It is in order to promote or popularise a product. Advertising models appear in press advertisement, on posters, in TV commercials and advertising films. Advertising modeling is open to models of all age groups. Basic acting skills and a photogenic face are must.

Remuneration

The amount of money paid to models depends upon how prestigious the show is and who the organisers are. Female models typically earn more than male models for similar work. An established model who is consistently on the popularity charts earns anything between ₹ 20, 000 to ₹ 50, 000 per fashion show. Low budget shows pay models somewhere around ₹ 5,000 to ₹ 10,000. Print ads pay according to the number of photographs used. Magazine spreads and billboard advertisements also pay well – reputed magazines pay around ₹ 15,000 to ₹ 25,000 per photograph.

A Few Acting/Modeling Colleges in India

- **Asian Academy of Film and Television, Noida, Delhi-NCR**

  Course : Certificate course in Acting and Presentation
- **National Institute of Film and Fine Arts, Kolkata, West Bengal**

  Course : Diploma in Acting
- **Central India Institute of Mass Communication, Nagpur, Maharashtra**

  Course : Bachelor of Acting Film and Television
- **The Media Institute, Mumbai, Maharashtra**

  Course : Course in Acting
- **Center for Research in Art of Film and Television (CRAFT), New Delhi, Delhi-NCR**

  Course : Post Graduate Diploma in Acting and Modeling
- **School of Arts and Aesthetics, Jawaharlal Nehru University, New Delhi, Delhi-NCR**

  Course : Diploma in Visual Studies
- **Digital Academy The Film School**

Course : Course in Acting

- **College of Film Technology, Mahatma Jyoti Rao Phoole University, Jaipur, Rajasthan**

  Course : Certificate course (Acting/Choreography)
- **Northeast Institute of Fashion Technology, Guwahati, Assam**

  Course : Diploma in Modeling
- **Film and Television Institute of India, Pune, Maharashtra**

  Course : Post Graduate Diploma in Acting
- **Diploma of Fine Arts and Performing Arts, Yogi Vemana University, Andhra Pradesh**

  Course : Post Graduate Diploma in Acting
- **Take One School of Mass Communication, New Delhi, Delhi-NCR**

  Course : Diploma in Acting
- **MassCoMedia, Noida, Delhi-NCR**

  Course : Diploma in Acting and Drama
- **R.K. Films and Media Academy, New Delhi, Delhi-NCR**

  Course : Diploma in Acting and Modeling
- **Andhra University, College of Arts and Commerce, Visakhapatnam/Vizag, Andhra Pradesh**

  Course : Diploma in Acting
- **Anupam Khers Actor Prepares, Mumbai, Maharashtra**

  Course : Diploma in Actor Prepares
- **Zee Institute of Media Arts, Mumbai, Maharashtra**

  Course : Course in Acting

17.8 Video editing

What is Video Editing?

Video Editing is an interesting career for creative people in the media and entertainment industry. The entire process of making art, aesthetic in the visual media ies in the technique of editing. Video editing is the process of re-arranging r modifying segments of video from one or more video tapes to form a refined and final piece of video. Video editing plays a key role in the post production process. The main task of video editor is to edit soundtracks, film and video for the motion picture, cable and broadcast visual media industries. It is the video editor's skill that determines the quality and delivery of the final product.

Classification of Video Editing

Video Editing is classified as:

- Linear Editing (Tape to tape)
- Non-linear Editing or Digital Video Editing.

Digital video editing uses computer technology to enable the editing process onscreen. Linear editing involves copying just the required portions of a film from one tape to another. Any changes or additions needed could be made only by copying the edited content onto another tape, causing undesirable degradation of images. In Non-linear editing, video and audio data are first captured to hard disks or any other digital storage device and then edited on the computer using any of the wide range of software's available for editing. Here, data can be edited and subsequent changes made without duplicating the actual film data. It is quicker, less expensive, more flexible and saves time and money when compared to the traditional way of editing. Due to all these features and the introduction of new technologies in digital video editing, it is fast replacing the traditional linear editing.

The Demand for Video Editors

Video editors are in great demand with the advent of streaming videos and movie clips in websites. As this field is becoming highly competitive, video editors can expect keen competition for job openings. The increased popularity of online video clips has also produced a large increase in video editing activity by internet users.

Eligibility and Course Areas

The field of video editing is open to all and there is no formal educational qualification required. To pursue a career in Digital video editing, one must have training in the computer systems and programmes used in digital video editing. For doing specialised courses in reputed institutes, candidates must possess the qualification prescribed by the respective institutes/colleges. Digital video editors often have a bachelor's or master's degree in animation or media arts.

A course in video editing will help the candidates to understand and learn the overall concept of editing and the way they relate to each other. The candidates are prepared through systematic training to handle the ever-changing tools used within the process of video editing. They are trained to work with professional grade linear and non-linear editing equipment. Theoretical instructions, practical exercises and the post-production work of television programmes have been designed to impart knowledge and skills in an adequate measure. The basics of video editing remain unchanged no matter which equipment is used.

Video editors usually acquire their skills through on-the-job training or formal training at various institutes. However, experience is the best training in this field. In addition, they must be able to demonstrate their skill with appropriate editing software packages.

Digital video editing uses video editing software's from every basic applications such as Windows Movie Maker to professional packages such as Final Cut Pro, ULead Media Studio, Avid's Media Composer, Xpress Pro, Adobe Premier etc. Good editing software is expensive and often requires a high-priced computer to run effectively. Editing software controls the capturing (recording) of the footage provides a way to edit the footage and allows the finished product to be output to a recording device.

Personal Skills

Video editor has to have high level of self-motivation commitment and dedication to work. Creativity is the factor for the success of a video editor. They need to have a keen eye for detail, a critical mind, the ability to listen to others and to work well as part of a team. Imagination and technical skills are essential. General computer literacy and an aptitude for working with digital equipment to achieve results are also important. They should also have a general knowledge of cameras and digital camera technology. The video editors must always be alert and updated with their skills as new and advanced technologies are invented day by day.

Job Prospects and Career Options

A college degree is not necessary for getting a job in the field of video editing. But a degree or diploma in visual arts/fine arts, multimedia/information technology, media studies etc. can increase the chances of getting a reputed job. One can enter into the field of video editing after completing the digital video editing course or a media arts degree.

Video editors work with the production personnel using advanced editing tools to analyse, evaluate, trim, arrange and join scenes according to guidelines set out by the producer or director of the project.

In fact, video editors are the ones who decide what to stay and go in terms of the content of the finished video.

Few Video Editing Colleges

- **NH School of Design**

  L-149, 6th Sector, HSR Layout, Beside Food Days Supermarket, Bangalore-560102, Karnataka.

- **Rech Computer**

  412, Ground Floor, Rajendra Nagar (Near Water Tank) C/O Ravi Electronics Lucknow-226004, Uttar Pradesh.

- **Westford School of Film Technology**

  2nd Floor Vijaya Complex, Chembumukku, Kakkanad Ernakulam-682030, Kerala.

18

SPORTS EDUCATION AND TRAINING

18.1 Sports Education

Introduction

With an enormous amount of sponsorship and prize money coming in, sports has become a lucrative profession. At the top, the earnings of professional players in some of the popular sports put them in the millionaire bracket. Even so, for every Tendulkar, Dravid and Leander in the top league, there are countless others who find it hard to eke a living out of sports. Moreover, it is not possible to earn a living from all sports. Earnings tend to be irregular and variable depending on participation fee, prize money and sponsorship. Globally, football, cricket, golf, tennis, motor racing, equestrian sports (horse riding) and boxing offer relatively more opportunities.

Professional Players

Most sportspersons show natural talent at a relatively early age. However, talent or even a passion for sports on its own is not enough. Professional players require a high order of physical and mental fitness, self confidence and extraordinary dedication to achieve success in their sport. It certainly helps to be enrolled in a sports training academy or club. Starting at the school and college level, you must also participate in the field, court or track events at a regional/state or national level.

Sports persons get preference over others in finding jobs in many government and some private companies. Special facilities are given for participating in various sports competitions like paid leave flexible hours, etc. Sponsorships and endorsements can make this a high income grosser if you are at the top. But a career at the top won't last forever – no more than a decade and often much less. When you choose any professional sport, you are going to experience a lot of ups and downs.

It definitely pays to have a good education behind you, because you always know there's something to fall back on.

Related Careers

Although several thousands of people are employed in sport and recreation, less than two-three per cent of them are professional sportspersons. The others work in a wide range of sports-related careers including teaching, coaching, sports development, sports science, sports medicine, sports administration, sports management, sports sponsorship, public relations and operation of sports facilities. Some involve in constant physical activity; while others are mainly based in the office. Some require academic qualifications; while others are opened to anyone with aptitude. However, most require good communication skills and the ability to get on with people.

Excellence in a particular discipline may be useful but in general, competence in a broad range of sporting activities (as required for teaching Physical Education for example) would be more appropriate. For some related careers. Administrative skills are more important than proficiency. The occupations listed below are directly related to sports although in some cases, further training may be required. The main professions are teaching, coaching and instructing.

- **Fitness and Health Club Instructor** : The health and fitness industry has experienced a sharp growth in the last decade. A health and fitness professional such as personal trainer or aerobics instructor will assist clients in physical education, personal training or basic aerobics. If helping others and maintaining their health interests you, then a career in the health and fitness industry may be right for you.
- **Sports Manager** : Sports Manager is mainly employed in clubs, hotels and leisure centres. He or she plans and coordinates the activities of a leisure centre that may cover a wide range of activities such as judo, archery, tennis, basketball, aerobics etc. The responsibility includes maintenance of courts and sports equipments and also administrative work such as managing accounts, planning, preparing schedules and timetables.
- **Physical Education Teacher** : Physical Education Teacher requires skills and techniques of a particular sport or a few related sports for a school, college or club. Coaches draw up training programmes for sports persons to help them develop their full potential and keep them in peak form at the time of tournament or competition.

In India, physical education is a compulsory subject up to class X : A bachelor's degree in physical education is required for jobs in schools. For teaching at the University level, you need a master's degree besides clearing the National Eligibility Test (NET) conducted by UGC.

- **Sports Coaches :** Sports coaches specialise in teaching the skills and techniques of a particular sport such as tennis, football, cricket or swimming etc. They work in sports clubs or centers and may deal with performers of all ages and varying abilities from beginners to professionals. There is tough competition for full-time posts, though opportunities are increasing. Physical training in the Armed forces is another possibility. All three services need physical training specialists although they may not always recruit specifically for the post.
- **Sports Physiotherapist :** Sports Physiotherapist is mainly concerned with the prevention and treatment of injury while participating in sports or athletics and for improving and maintaining physical performance. Cares for injured players includes using various techniques like massage, exercise therapy etc.
- **Sports Nutritionist/Dietician :** Sports dietician advises players on menus – what foods to eat to maximise their performance, build strength, energy and muscle and competitive sport. Sports nutritionists work in corporate gymnasium, fitness centers, professional sports teams, sports training camps, spas and health clubs.
- **Sports Medico :** Qualified medical professionals specialised in Sports Medicine. They work with sportspersons for prevention and rehabilitation either before or after sports injuries.
- **Sports Agent :** The main job of a sports agent is contract negotiation. However, the role of the agent as financial consultant and endorsement representative is becoming more prevalent. Depending on the type of representation offered, an agent may do everything for athletes from negotiating a contract and arranging promotional opportunities and appearances, to investing their income and filing their tax returns. Administrative affairs such as budgeting, finance and other logistics such as keeping track of client's schedules have to be undertaken by the agent. Knowledge of law is an asset for a sport agent.

- **Team Manager/Referee/Umpires/Sports Analyst :** These are other career options that require thorough knowledge and understanding about the particular sport. To be a referee / umpire one needs to be an expert in the rules and regulations of the game and has to pass an examination conducted by an authorised institute or board.
- **Sports Journalist and Photographers :** They provide the public with coverage of sports from around the globe. Familiarity with sports could be an asset for a career in sports journalism (print as well as electronic). Some ex-players become pundits giving analysis of sports writer (reporting or feature writing), sports editor, photographer, producer etc. You can also work for an online sports magazine as a content developer, graphic designer, technical developer, sports photographer etc. You will need training in the craft before you can specialise in covering sports events.
- **Sports Marketing and Sales :** Nearly, every sporting event or organisation today depends on marketing expertise to help it succeed. Opportunities on the management side are available to those who have the market knowledge and sales skill necessary to help in research, organisation and implementation of projects.
- **Sports Management and Public Relations :** People who are creative, confident, self-motivated and detail-oriented are well suited to work as an event manager or a PR manager. Event management includes executing the event, all the way to full service management, including sponsorship, ticket sales, marketing and promotional campaigns. Event managers have to oversee an event from concept to completion.
- **Risk Managers (Insurance) :** As sport continues to expand, the need for protection from accident and liability grows with it. Professionals in the sport insurance industry provide facilities with coverage in the event of accidents on or off the field. The account executive works directly with individual athletes, teams and facilities to evaluate the risk and need of each. They also write policies to cover the cost of special prize money.
- **Adventure Sports :** Adventure Sports encompasses activities such as hiking, trekking, river rafting, bungee jumping, mountaineering, kayaking, canoeing, diving and snorkeling, rock climbing, camping, ballooning etc. These activities help nurture the spirit of risk taking, teamwork and endurance in challenging situations. To pursue adventure sports as a career,

all you require is physical fitness with an adventurous bent of mind. Leadership qualities and a cool attitude is a must for aspirants. Advance planning, systematic and methodological working helps in pursuing adventure sports as a career.

Opportunities lie in travel agencies, commercial recreation camps. You can become an instructor or trainer and earn between ₹ 15,000 to 50,000 per month. A graduate with a basic or advanced level course in any adventure sport can enter this field. Proficiency in at least one foreign language proves to be beneficial as adventure tourism in India attracts many foreigners.

Courses in Physical Education

The apex body for the promotion of sports, the Sports Authority of India has institutes in a number of cities (Patiala, Kolkata, Bangalore, Gandhinagar, Gwalior and Thiruvananthapuram). It conducts various training programmes in different aspects of sports.

Career Avenues for Physical Education Graduates

Fitness and equipment manufacturers, leisure sports goods, health and fitness clubs, hotels, adventure/outdoor pursuit centers, retail firms, commercial organisations, health services, education authorities, sports governing bodies, Armed Forces etc. Mostly graduates in Physical Education proceed for special training coaches and physical education instructors. Netaji Subash National Institute of Sports (NSNIS) governed by Sports Authority of India plays an important role in imparting short term diploma courses in coaching for different games and sports.

Eligibility : Eligibility for this course is 10+2. Besides proficiency in sports, you must have at least represented the country in the concerned game. Centres for these short-term diploma courses are at Bangalore, Gandhinagar, Kolkata, Imphal and Delhi. SAI-NSNIS Patiala offers an 11 month Diploma in Physical Education (DPEd) for graduate students. Post Graduate courses MPE/MPEd are offered at over 35 universities including Aligarh Muslim University, Aligarh; Banaras Hindu University, Varanasi; Netaji Subash National Institute of Sports, Patiala; Lakhsmibai National College of Physical Education , Gwalior; Jiwaji University, Gwalior; Punjabi University, Patiala; Nagpur University, Nagpur; Bangalore University, Bangalore and Indira Gandhi Institute of Physical Education and Sports Sciences, University of Delhi.

Research Degree : While a Masters/M.Phil degree takes 2-3 years, Doctorate Degree/Ph.D. takes 3 or more years of full time study. Admission to this degree requires 55 per cent marks at the master's level in the concerned subject. Research awards are not automatic and it is often easier to obtain a seat than funds. Many bodies offer scholarship/fellowship to research students and eminent sportspersons but these are limited in number. Students must make it a point to take the NET test conducted by UGC.

Post Graduate Diploma in Sports Management

This Diploma is presently offered by only two recognised universities in India :

- Alagappa University, Karaikudi (Tamil Nadu) offers a one-year PGDSM
- Indira Gandhi Institute of Physical Education and Sports Science, New Delhi offers a one-year PGDSM.

Eligibility : 40 per cent in Bachelor's degree and Sports achievements.

New National Sports Policy

The ***National Sports Policy*** was initially formulated in 1984. In order to broad base sports and to promote excellence, Government has formulated a ***New National Sports Policy***, 2001. The salient features of the New National Sports Policy are as given below :

(i) Broad-basing of Sports and achievement of excellence,

(ii) Up-gradation and development of infrastructure,

(iii) Support to the National Sports Federations and other appropriate bodies,

(iv) Strengthening of scientific and coaching support to sports,

(v) Incentives to sports persons,

(vi) Enhanced participation of women, scheduled tribes and rural youth,

(vii) Involvement of the Corporate sector in sports promotion,

(viii) Promote sports mindedness among the public at large.

Sports Scholarship Scheme

Sports Talent Search Scholar Scheme launched in 1970-71 is now called the Sports Scholarship Scheme. It is given at National level, State level and University/College level. Besides this, there are Special Scholarships for Senior Women's Champions and for women doing Diploma in Sports coaching and for women doing M.Phil/Ph.D are sanctioned under the Scheme.

National Welfare Fund of Sports Persons

National Welfare Fund for sportspersons of yesteryears who are living in indigent circumstances, financial support is generally given in the form of a monthly pension up to ₹ 2,500. Lump sum grants are also given for medical treatment. The sports persons suffering from grievous and fatal injuries in the course of participation in sports events or during training are also helped.

Rural Sports Programme

The scheme being operated by SAI lays emphasis on arranging tournaments in rural areas and at the block, district, state and national levels. It also includes special component for the North-Eastern region, i.e., North-Eastern Sports Festival. For the organisation of State/UT level tournaments, an assistance of ₹ 30,000 per discipline is given to the State Government and ₹ 15,000 per discipline to the Union Territories. Financial assistance of ₹ 2 lakhs per discipline is made available by SAI for organizing tournaments in various states by rotation. For North-Eastern Sports Festival, up to ₹ 15 lakhs is given by SAI for holding the tournaments annually.

18.2 Fitness Trainer

What is Fitness Training?

Fitness training is one of the fastest growing careers in the health and fitness industry today. Careers in fitness industry include that of Athletic Trainer, Physical Therapist, Massage Therapist, Fitness Instructor/Trainer and so on. Fitness trainers are known by different names like Aerobics Instructor, Clinical exercise specialist, Gym instructor, Personal and Corporate trainers. Fitness trainer is a person who looks after the issues concerning the health and physical fitness of his/her clients.

Main Job of a Fitness Trainer

The main job of a fitness trainer is to train people in the various aspects of physical fitness and maintain health by staying fit. Fitness Trainer plans the exercise regimen by considering the age, lifestyle, health problems and other constraints of the person opting for the training programme. They also give them basic advice on health and nutrition. They assess the fitness level of clients and also help to set fitness goals and demonstrate the various routines and give guidance to do it the right way. Fitness trainers/instructors opt for various exercise routines such as weightlifting, aerobics, karate, kickboxing, spin cycling, yoga, Pilates etc. They can also specialise in any one of these and become a specialist trainer.

Division of Fitness Training

Fitness Training can be divided into three major sub-categories :

- **Group Fitness Instructors :** They teach any form of exercise in a group/classroom setting.
- **Exercise Specialists :** They work with people suffering from specific physical ailments. They design the appropriate exercise programme for a patient in accordance with a physician's recommendations.
- **Personal Trainers :** They are instructors who supervise the exercise and workouts on a one-to-one basis with celebrities and others who like privacy.

Today, from all walks of life – from celebrities to senior citizens are seeking personal trainers to help them learn how to exercise, lose weight, maintain all round fitness and adopt a healthier lifestyle. Hence, to be a Fitness trainer is a career with numerous opportunities.

Eligibility

The options for pursuing professional courses are many. You can opt for a certificate or diploma course in sports science/yoga/fitness/naturopathy to become a fitness instructor. One can go for professional course like the Nike Aerobics Course or Reebok Instruction Certification programme or any of the several reputed locally offered courses like those at Talwakar's in Mumbai.

Course Areas

Its basic course comprises of 80 hours out of which 30 hours are devoted to the theory portion while the rest 30 hours consist of practical training. After the completion of the course, a written and practical examination is conducted. The Nike Aerobics/Reebok Instructor Institute is located in Delhi and Mumbai besides many other Indian cities.

Diploma or Bachelor courses in Yoga and Naturopathy courses can also be taken by an instructor. The Sports Authority of India (SAI), Lakshmibai National Institute of Physical Education are prominent institutes that offer courses in Sports and Athletics Coaching.

Personal Attributes

This is not the job meant for those who love to sit and work from 10 to 5. A trainer can never sit on the bench and guide others. Those who choose this career must be energetic and have a lot of stamina. A good physique and determination is the main requirement in this field. Fitness trainer must have a good knowledge of human anatomy, diet, nutrition and other health and fitness related matters. He or she must have the motivation to be healthy and fit andencourage others to do the same. Trainers also need good communication skills, as they have to deal with all kinds of people. In addition to this patience, dedication, strong analytical skills and calm attitude are also required to excel in this field. As a fitness instructor you will also need to keep abreast with the latest developments in health science. Apart from this, a fitness trainer should ensure safety while instructing clients.

Job Prospects and Career Options

People getting more conscious about health and appearance has resulted in the mushrooming of gyms and health clubs in the recent past. As such the demand for qualified instructors is going up sharply. Fitness trainers can work as health club managers, fitness directors, aerobics instructors, corporate wellness directors, personal trainers, weight loss counselors etc.

After finishing the course one can start a career in this field by assisting a senior fitness instructor and once you gain some experience, can start your own classes or become a personal instructor. Fitness trainers are generally employed by hotels, health clubs, gyms, fitness centers, spas, tourist resorts, housing societies and large organisations.

One can specialise in any of the following – weightlifting, aerobics, karate, kickboxing, spin cycling, yoga, spinning and work as a fitness trainer. One of the best options in this field is to set up your own fitness centre. Once you have acquired a reputation, you could conduct fitness programmes or health shows on popular TV channels. Another lucrative option today is to organise workplace wellness and fitness programmes for large companies. One can become a personal fitness trainer for some celebrity. In addition to actual training, one can also earn by conducting various guest sessions for corporate houses and writing articles related to fitness in health journals/magazines.

Remuneration

Pay scale in this field is mainly based upon the reputation of the centre. As a beginner one can earn a salary ranging between ₹ 5,000 – ₹ 7,000 per month. Established trainers charge up to ₹ 1,000 – 1,500 per hour. Personal trainers are very much in demand these days. They earn a lot more than the Group Fitness Instructors and Exercise Specialists. If you are a celebrity trainer you can earn much more. They are the most highly paid category.

Institutes

Some of the prominent fitness training institutes are under :

- Sports Authority of India (SAI).
- Indira Gandhi Institute of Physical Education and Sports Sciences (New Delhi).
- Lakshmibai National College of Physical Education (Kerala).
- Netaji Subash National Institute of Sports (Punjab).
- HVPM (Amravati).
- Reebok training centers are there in almost all metros.

18.3 Sports Commentator

Introduction

If you love sports and have excellent verbal communication skills then you can choose a career as sports commentator. A job as a sports commentator falls under the broader career category of Radio and Television Announcers. A sports commentator is an expert reporting a live match on radio or television in real time. Commentary is about enhancing the viewer's pleasure by describing the scene of action pleasantly. In the radio and television field, commentating is considered as a popular form of journalism.

Who is a Sports Commentator?

A sports commentator is an expert who reports a live match on radio and television in real time. He or she is one who specialises in reporting or commentating on sporting events.

Two Kinds of Sports Commentators

The two kinds of sports commentators are :

- Play-by-play commentator,
- Color commentator.

The play-by-play commentator is actually an announcer. What he basically does is to report what is going on in the game. The other kind of sports commentator is different from a play-by-play commentator in that the former needs to be able to provide more than a report. A color commentator is expected to be able to give additional insight and analyse the goings on in the game. While play-by-play announcers provide ongoing commentary about the game, Color commentators assist the play-by-play announcers by filling up the dead air with other background information, thus making the commentary more interesting.

Eligibility

There are specific courses to become a sports commentator. A bachelor's degree in Mass Communication and Journalism is considered as an entry requirement. Also speech or voice training is beneficial to develop an appealing voice. Other personal attributes include :

- Excellent speaking manner and pleasing personality,
- Passion and dedication,
- Communication skills as well as language fluency,
- Thorough knowledge of the particular sports, its rule and regulations,
- A clear and audible voice,
- Concentration,
- Good memory to remember all the different statistics of the game, as well as the names and details of team members,
- Emotional stability and must be able to work under stress and pressure.

Job Prospects and Career Option

Sports commentators have opportunities in all major radio stations or TV stations. Apart from that, commentators have career avenues in specialised sports sites which relay play by play commentaries. Even with much scope the field of Sports commentators is extremely competitive; therefore experience in the areas is a prime factor.

Radio stations can be considered as the entry point to a career as a commentator. Later they can move on to TV or other private channels/ media. A sports commentator can be employed by newspapers, radios or by TV sports channels such as Star Sports, ESPN, Ten Sports, Zee Sports and DD Sports. Sports commentators are also employed by sports organisation and networks to cover live action, i.e., play-by-play of sporting events. Some sports commentators perform other roles in the broadcast media industry. They write a column or work as a broadcast reporter. They may go to the play ground, talk to players, and get their feedback live, in between the game. Commentators write commentaries or columns for newspapers, magazines or other publications. In majority cases, former sportsmen after retirement take up commentating as a profession. Good commentators usually build up fan bases of their own.

Remuneration

Although this can be a very rewarding career, entry is competitive and pay at many times can often be low. The pay scale for commentators varies greatly depending on the place of employment and the commentator's own quality (how good and famous he is) and presentation.

TV commentators usually earn more than radio commentators do. In India, the average salary earned by sports commentator is ₹ 5,000 to ₹ 10,000 per day that the commentator is working. A well-established commentator command a better sum from ₹ 25,000 onwards for a day.

Institutes

There are no institutes that conduct courses exclusively for sports commentators. However, those with mass communication and journalism degrees are considered.

19

TRAVEL AND TOURISM/HOTEL MANAGEMENT AND AVIATION

19.1 Air Hostess

Introduction

One of the most important essential features of air travel is concerned with making the journey of every passenger as much comfortable and safe as possible. It is in this respect the Air hostess/pursers play their role. This is a very promising career option with the vision of a smart, efficient lady in mind. Many young girls opt for the career because of the exciting experience of flying, visiting different places, interacting with different kinds of people on board and for the very attractive pay package. Liberalisation of air policies has increased the private operation of air services and this has created immense job opportunities in this field. Even though this career gives exciting experience it is not as easy as it seems. This is a highly demanding job which requires a lot of patience and involves odd duty hours. To be more specific behind this career lies a strong conviction, commitment and hard work for learning the technical aspects of aircraft operation and skills to tackle difficult situation.

The air hostess is called the first person to welcome a passenger; her welcoming smile and greeting acknowledge every passenger. Inside the aircraft, she seems to be here, there and everywhere, greeting every passenger, guiding each to his or her seat, helping a passenger get settled, co-ordination security personnel giving directions as and when required and doing a myriad things. Basically, she's on constant call all the time.

Eligibility

Eligibility for an air hostess training programme is plus two or a graduate degree with a diploma/degree in Hotel Management or Tourism Management. The aspirant must be eligible to hold an Indian Passport and should be below twenty-five years of age with a minimum height of 157.5 centimeters. The weight should be in proportion to height. Further, one must be unmarried, with normal eyesight of 6/6 uncorrected vision in each eye. Fluency in English, Hindi and knowledge of an international language is an added advantage.

A flight purser, male counterpart of the airhostess has to be a graduate below 26 years and have a minimum height of 163 cm with proportionate weight. An applicant should be physically fit with a pleasing personality and clear complexion. After the initial screening of applicants is completed the airline company calls them for a written examination, usually of the objective type (multiple choice). Those who qualify in the written examination have to appear for a group discussion followed by a personal interview of successful candidates. If selected you will be on training for 2 to 3 months in which time you learn about service, grooming, safety and first aid, after which you are initially put on trainee flights.

Course Areas

The training covers several topics, each of which deals with technical or non-technical aspects of the aircraft. Beginning with the history of aviation, the candidates are made to learn In-flight Service, Passenger Handling, Passenger Psychology, Service of meals on the Aircraft, the art of conversation, Transactional Analysis, Emergency Evacuation System, Personal Grooming and Hygiene, First Aid, Confidence Building, Handling of visually impaired passengers, Making announcements, Emergency demonstration etc.

Personal Attributes

Common sense, sense of responsibility, initiative, friendly, outgoing personality, politeness, physical stamina and the capacity to work for long hours on one's feet, ability to react quickly in times of emergency and a presence of mind, systematic approach, unruffled appearance, a well-modulated pleasant voice and a proportionate figure with a graceful carriage.

Job Prospects

With privatisation and foreign collaboration increasing every day, the future is bright for an air hostess. Most airline offices are looking for air hostesses. They can find employment with private owned domestic and international airlines namely Sahara, Singapore Airlines, Jet Airways etc. and government air services like Air India and Indian

Airlines. Advertisement for recruitment normally appears in all major newspapers.

Career Options

An Air Hostess has every chance to be promoted to the post of Senior Flight attendant and then Head Attendant. Career as an Air Hostess would last for about 8 to 10 years, after that she could move on to the ground duties including the job of a Ground Hostess, Check Hostess, training of airhostess or work in the management level. One can also diversify into anyone of the other departments in the airline industry.

The duty of an airhostess last throughout the duration of the flight. The job of an air hostess begins along before the arrival of the passengers. It starts with safety check on the aircraft, where she has to check the safety equipment, blankets, pillows, magazines, plates, napkins and medicines etc. as well as the cleanliness.

After the passengers aboard the flight the job includes assisting passengers to settle down. Special care is needed in the case of sick travelers, VIPs, babies or children or elderly people travelling alone. Once all the passengers are seated it is the duty of the air hostess to go about ensuring that safety arrangements are in proper condition and demonstrate the use of emergency equipment. They have to provide first aid if such situation arise. Her responsibilities also include serving meals to passengers. In case of an emergency during the flight, she needs to take responsibility and determine the most appropriate step to deal with the situation. In short, she has to work continuously with presence of mind and must be on call all the time.

Remuneration

In the beginning, depending on the airlines you are getting into, your salary and other allowance may add up to ₹ 16,000 to ₹ 35,000 (approximately) or more per month. The maximum you can earn as a senior air hostess is about ₹ 75,000 per month in Air India or Indian Airlines. Domestic private airlines pay more. In foreign airlines, pay for a senior air hostess can cross ₹ 3 lakhs a month in Indian currency.

Courses available

- Advance Diploma in Airline Cabin Crew and Hospitality,
- Air hostess/Flight Steward Training,
- Cabin Crew Training,
- Cabin Crew Training,
- Diploma in Air hostess and ground handling,
- Diploma in Airline Cabin Crew,
- Certified Professional in Cabin Crew Services.

Institutes

The following is the list of Top 10 Air Hostess Training Institutes in India. These Top Air Hostess Training Institutes in India train students to be part of world class airlines as cabin crew or ground staff. Placement interviews are also arranged by the best air hostess training institutes.

- Air Hostess Academy (AHA), Bangalore.
- Air Hostess Academy (AHA), Chandigarh.
- Air Hostess Academy (AHA), Delhi/NCR.
- Air Hostess Academy (AHA), Mumbai.
- Air Hostess Academy (AHA), Pune.
- Frankfinn Institute of Air Hostess Training, Mumbai.
- Frankfinn Institute of Air Hostess Training, Delhi/NCR.
- Kingfisher Training Academy (KTA), Mumbai.
- Rajiv Gandhi Memorial College of Aeronautics, Jaipur.
- Universal Aviation Academy (UAA), Chennai.

Aviation is a booming industry in India today.

19.2 Air Traffic Controller

Who is an Air Traffic Controller (ATC)?

Air traffic controllers are well-trained professionals who are responsible for the management of safe, orderly and expeditious air traffic on the ground as well as in the air. As traffic policemen handle the follow of traffic on our city roads, ATCs design the sequencing of air traffic in the air space and along pre-determined routes of arrival and departure to and from airports around the world. They are also responsible for providing advice and information useful for the safe and efficient conduct of any flight and for alerting appropriate organisations with regard to aircraft in need of assistance, search and rescue.

Every pilot has to depend heavily on the Air Traffic Controller (ATC) as the limited field of view from the cockpit restricts the pilot's ability to view any other air traffic around the aircraft during the course directing him in his flight and on the ground for all maneuvers right till the end of his journey. The ATC tell the pilot when to start, where to taxi, when to take off and in what speed to fly and what height to maintain to ensure adequate separation between aeroplanes. The controller is at constant communication with pilots and his job is of paramount importance in preventing collisions and ensuring an organised flow of air traffic. He also tells him when to descend, how fast to descend, weather at the destination,, clearing the pilot to land and telling him how to taxi his aeroplane to the parking slot so that his passengers can disembark safely at the end of the journey.

Basic Educational Qualifications (degree) Needed to Apply for the Civil ATC Entrance Examination

To become an Air Traffic Controller you must complete Engineering Degree (B.E/B.Tech) in Electronics/Telecommunication/RadioEngg. /Electrical with specialisation in Electronics with 1st class (60 per cent) OR M.Sc degree or its equivalent with Wireless Communication, Electronics, Radio Physics or Radio Engg. as a special Subject or Equivalent with 1st Class.

Age Limit : Lower age limit is 21 years, while the upper age limit is 27 years.

Selection : The selection is made on the basis of :

- Written Test,
- 50 per cent questions on subjects relating to educational qualifications prescribed,
- 50 per cent on General Knowledge, General Intelligence, General Aptitude, English, etc.
- Voice test,
- Personal Interview,
- Medical fitness examination.

Standard reservation policy applies for SC/ST/OBC/Ex-servicemen. No reservation for differently-abled candidates.

Negative and positive aspects of this profession

- **Negative :** High stress, shift duties, extra work load, non-availability of leaves, lack of social life due to strange shift pattern and no standard festivals' leaves, very high professional risk.
- **Positive :** Challenging environment, split second decision making, independent decisions, work is not to be carried home.

Various Ranks that an ATC can climb through

- Junior Executive,

- Assistant Manager,
- Manager,
- Senior Manager,
- Assistant General Manager,
- Deputy General Manager,
- Joint General Manager,
- Executive Director (ATM),
- Member (ATM) in AAI Board.

19.3 Chef

Who is a Chef?

The word 'chef' has its origin from the French phrase *chef de cuisine* which means the chief or head of a kitchen. A chef, in the contemporary sense of the term is an artist who is equipped with specialised training to master the craft of cookery. The profession of a chef is one of the most demanding and backbreaking one, which demands a lot of hard work. Numerous well paying catering jobs are there in the hospitality industry for those who have a flair and talent for preparing mouth watering delicacies.

As it is commonly believed, the job of a chef is not just cooking a recipe. The chef has to know all aspects of food and beverages including the art of vegetable and fruit sculptures and its presentation. He should have the knowledge of making wide variety of foods that include appetisers, salads, soups, main dishes, side orders and desserts. The chef has to be up to date with the managerial and administrative aspects of running the kitchen – from shopping, menu preparation and planning to nutrition analysis and inventory management.

Responsibility of a Chef

The primary and major role responsibility of the chef is to create recipes and prepare meals. As the chef moves higher up the ladder they have to play varied roles like organising the kitchen, planning the meals to be served, directing staff, supervising kitchen operations and so on. The work will keep you on your toes, a chef can be busy all day, may have to keep late hours regularly, work on weekends and even holidays. But the job of a Chef will never get bored, if you have a passion for cooking along the innovation and dedication. Everyday there will be new excitement in your job, like preparing birthday delicacies, cooking for marriage parties, planning menu for special guests and so on. Apart from these, most chefs will have the opportunity to travel to a lot of places and meet all kinds of people.

Though the culinary profession is suitable for both male and female, this field especially in the hotel and hospitality industry is considered a male dominated one. The reason for this may be that, the profession of a chef usually starts at the lower side of the spectrum and involves a lot of hard work and needs tremendous physical fitness and toughness to survive. Sanjeev Kapoor, Tarla, Atul Kochchar, Madhur Jaffrey, Rakesh Sethi are some of the celebrity chefs renowned not only in India but across the world for bringing Indian cooking and Indian cuisine to the top.

Difference between Chef and Cook

The terms chef and cook are often thought of as the same. A Chef is trained to master culinary forms as well as provide creative innovation in menu, preparation and presentation. Whereas a cook is trained to master forms of food preparation, he usually takes close direction from a chef. Usually chefs have further training and higher skills than cooks.

Eligibility

No formal education is needed in this field, but for securing a good job with a well established organisation, professional training from a reputed culinary academy is essential. Renowned restaurants prefer recruiting staff with formal training in fundamentals of cooking.

Varied courses are offered by different institutions in the field of food preparation and processing, catering technology and other relevant areas of catering field. To avoid being conned it is better to go for institutes registered under National Council of Hotel Management and Catering Technology (NCHMCT).

- **Educational qualification :** 10+2 or its equivalent is the minimum educational qualification needed for joining any course in the culinary profession. The field offers many certificate, diploma and graduate programmes. Bachelor of Hotel Management and Catering Technology which is of four year duration and three year Diploma course in Hotel Management are the major graduation courses offered in most of the reputed culinary academy/institutions.

- **Admission :** Admission to these courses is through an entrance examination conducted by the National Council of Hotel

Management and Catering Technology (NCHMCT). The entrance test comprises of subjects like English, Reasoning, General Science and General Knowledge which is followed by group discussion and an interview.

There are certain private hotel management institutes who have foreign affiliations and approvals from the All India Council for Technical Education (AICTE). Besides, several Food craft Institutes in the country also provide training in catering and food processing. One can join these food craft institutes after their 10th or 12th board examination. The duration of the courses in these institutes varies between 6 – 18 months.

- **Course Areas :** Apprenticeship courses are offered by several professional culinary training institutes in Chef training. Specialisation in the areas such as cold kitchen, hot kitchen and Bakery and Confectionery are also offered in the catering field. One can also obtain admission in a renowned institute abroad for their culinary training.

Job Prospects

Endless opportunities are available in the culinary sector for those interested in establishing a career in this field. With the upsurge in the hotel and hospitality sector, trained and experienced Chefs are in good demand to run food and beverages departments of industries ranging from restaurants, hotels, corporate catering, food processing companies, resorts, airlines, cruise liners etc. Day by day, specialty and multi cuisine restaurants are springing up in every nook and corner of major cities. The success of these restaurants depends on their unique dishes and its preparation and presentation by Chefs.

Career Options

After completing hotel management course, one can start his career as an apprentice in any restaurant or hotel. From there he can climb up a slow ladder to the position of Sous Chef, Executive Sous Chef and finally Executive Chef. Executive Chef is the top most designation in this field and to obtain this title it may take anywhere from 10 – 12 years.

Media exposure : Chefs can host television shows as TV channels are hot places for running cookery shows. Chefs can write cookery books and can also become food Journalists by writing in newspapers and magazines. Those with a post graduate degree in catering and food processing can join as a faculty member government or private institutes offering hotel management courses. One can become an entrepreneur by setting up their own restaurant or catering business and can also find job openings abroad as Indian chefs.

Catering service departments : Besides these, career avenues are opened for chefs in the catering service departments of defense and railways. 10+2 candidates with diploma/certificate course (1 or more years) in Hotel Management and Catering Technology which is recognised by AICTE can find openings in the catering department of Indian defense service. The recruitment for the post of Junior Commissioned Officer (Catering) is carried out round the year through an open rally system. The recruitment programme is published in local newspapers, two weeks prior to the conduct of the rally by the concerned ZROs (Zonal Recruiting Officers) and concerned BROs (Branch Recruitment Offices).

Categories of chefs : While planning to become a chef you need to know about different types of chefs who work in various positions in a restaurant. Generally three categories of staff are involved in food service establishments or hotels namely the Chefs, the cooks and the food preparation workers. Chefs and head cooks are in charge of directing other workers in the kitchen, estimating food necessities and ordering materials. Their major responsibilities are creating recipes and preparing meals. The food preparation workers peel and cut vegetables, trim meat, prepare poultry and ensure cleanliness.

The job titles in the food service establishments can be classified as :

- ***Executive Chef/Head Chef :*** Also known as the *Chef de cuisine*, an executive chef is in charge of all the food service operations of a restaurant or hotel kitchen. Executive chef is in control of everything inside the kitchen and their responsibilities include planning menu, determining serving sizes, ordering supplies for food, management of kitchen staff and supervising kitchen operations to make sure that the food quality and presentation is consistent. Head chef/cook is often referred to as someone with the same duties as an executive chef, but there is usually someone in charge of them, possibly making the larger executive decisions such as direction of menu, final authority in staff management decisions etc. Executive Chef/Head Chef has the overall responsibility for the food that comes out of the kitchen.
- ***Sous Chef :*** Sous Chef also known as sub chef is the assistant of Executive Chef. They are responsible for the safe running of kitchen in the absence of executive chef. They are in charge of inventory, cleanliness of the kitchen, organisation and constant training of all employees. The Sous Chef also does some actual cooking for instance, stepping in to replace one of the line cooks if necessary.

- ***Station Chef/Chef de Partie*** **:** Also known by various names, these people are in charge of a particular area of the kitchen like Chinese, French, Italian, Continental, Banquet, Pastry etc. They work at an assigned station which is supplied with the ingredients and equipment needed for grilling, cooking vegetables, making sauces etc. In small restaurants, station chef is the only worker in that department. But in large establishment, there will be several station chefs and each station chef might have several cooks or assistants.
- ***Line Cooks (Commis)*** **:** Comis/Line cooks is the entry level position in larger kitchen who works under Station Chef or *Chef de Partie* to learn the station's responsibilities and operation. A person who has recently completed formal culinary training or undergoing training can join as a *Commis.* They are assigned specific duties inside the kitchen and are further classified as :
  - **Pastry Chef/Pastissier :** They oversee the production of baked goods like pastries, breads, cakes, chocolates, biscuits, desserts etc.
  - **Pantry Chef/Grade Manger :** These cooks are responsible for cold food preparation such as salads, cold appetisers and other dishes
  - **Sauté Chef/Saucier :** These cooks are responsible for a sautéed items and their sauce.
  - **Fish Chef/Poissonier :** They prepare varieties of fish dishes and their sauces.
  - **Roast Chef/Rotisseur :** They are incharge of preparing roasted and braised meats and their appropriate sauce.
  - **Grill Chef/Grillardin :** Prepares all types of grilled foods
  - **Fry Chef/Friturier :** Prepares all types of fried foods.
  - **Vegetable Chef/Entremetier :** They are in charge of all types of hot appetisers like soups and starches such as pastas and potatoes and other vegetable items.
- ***Expediter*** **:** Expediter, the bridge between the kitchen and the wait staff, is the person in charge of organising orders by table. They should be familiar with the menu and know what the dishes should look like before being served to guests.

Remuneration

After completing a diploma or bachelor's degree, graduates are usually absorbed as trainees. After successful completion of training, they may be absorbed in positions with salaries ranging between ₹ 7,000 to ₹ 10,000 per month. Moving higher up the ladder, one can get salary between ₹ 15,000 to ₹ 30,000 as a Station Chef / *Chef de Partie*. Depending on the firm, after gaining 5-7 years of experience, one can expect higher pay packages ranging from ₹ 50,000 – 60,000 per month as a Sous Chef and ₹ 70,000 – 1, 00,000 as an Executive Chef.

Institutes

There are several culinary schools everywhere but different countries have different systems. The courses may range anywhere from 2 to 3 years. While the course may acquaint you with the basic skills to become a chef, the training truly begins after schooling. The Culinary Academy of India located at Hyderabad is the India's first professional training school for culinary arts. Varied courses are being offered by different institutions in the field of food processing, catering technology and other relevant areas of catering field. To avoid being conned it is better to go for institutes registered under National Council of Hotel Management.

Courses

- Preparatory Course as Costa Cruise Chef,
- Professional Cookery,
- Bachelor of Hotel Management and Catering Technology (BHMCT),
- Bachelor of Catering Technology and Culinary Arts,
- B.Sc. Hotel Management and Catering Technology,
- Advance Diploma in Culinary Arts and Patisserie Studies
- Advance Diploma in Food Beverage Management and Catering Operations,
- B.Sc. Hotel Operations and Catering Services,
- B.Sc. Nutrition, Food Service Management, Dietetics,
- Certificate Course in Bakery and Confectionery,
- Certificate Course in Food and Beverages,
- Certificate Course in Food Craft Management,
- Certificate Course in Food Production,
- Certificate Course in Food Production and Patisserie,
- Certificate Course in Hotel Catering Management,

- Certificate Course in Restaurant and Counter Service,
- Certificate Course in Restaurant Operations,
- Certificate Course in Bakery and Confectionery (CCBC),
- Craft Course in Food Production (CCFP),
- CTH Diploma,
- Diploma in Bakery and Confectionery (DBC),
- Diploma in Catering Science and Hotel Management,
- Diploma in Catering Technology,
- Diploma in Cookery,
- Diploma in Culinary Arts and Patisserie,
- Diploma in Food and Beverage Service,
- Diploma in Food Production (DFP),
- Diploma in Hotel Management and Ship Catering,
- Diploma in Hotel Management, Catering and Food Science,
- Diploma in Hotel Operation, Catering and Applied Nutrition
- Integrated Diploma in Hotel Management and Catering Technology,
- M.Sc. Hotel Management and Catering Technology,
- Post Graduate Diploma in Bakery Science and Management,
- Post Graduate Diploma in Culinary Arts,
- Post Graduate Diploma in Food and Beverage Division Management,
- Post Graduate Diploma in Hotel Management and Catering Technology.

Institutes

Courses in Hotel Management and Food Processing are offered by several institutes in India. The most important among them are :

- Institute of Hotel Management, Catering Technology and Applied Nutrition at New Delhi, Ahmedabad and Goa.
- Indian Institute of Hotel Management, Aurangabad
- The Welcome Group Graduate School of Hotel Administration, Manipal.
- The Oberoi Center of Learning and Development, New Delhi.
- Government Institute of Hotel Management and Catering at Dehradun and Almora.

- The Oriental School of Hotel Management at Mumbai, Delhi.
- Delhi Institute of Hotel Management and Catering Technology, Thuvakkudi.
- Amity School of Hospitality, Noida.
- Lakshay Bharthi International Institute of Hotel Management, New Delhi.

19.4 Civil Aviation

What is an Aviation?

Aviation refers to all activities involving the operation of Aircraft. Aviation courses in India deal with Flying Operation (jobs performed by Pilots), Aircrew (such as Air Hostesses), Aircraft, Air Traffic Management, Technical aspects of Flight, Aviation safety, Regulatory Policies and economics of airport. Civil Aviation courses (as opposed to the Indian Air Force, i.e., the air wing of the Indian armed forces) are necessary for those wishing to work in government or regulatory bodies of aviation or those planning to work as aviation consultants. All aviation courses in India are supposed to comply with the rules laid down by the Directorate General of Civil Aviation (DGCA). Career in the aviation industry are much sought after as they are very lucrative. But not too many people go in for career in aviation as the courses are very expensive. However, those who can manage the courses with education loans, etc., can get into high paying jobs soon after finishing the course.

The Role of Directorate General of Civil Aviation (DGCA),

In India, the Directorate General of Civil Aviation (DGCA) is the apex body under the Ministry of Civil Aviation. It controls and monitors the airports and facilities for the operations of aircraft.

International Airport Authority of India (IAAI)

International Airport Authority of India (IAAI) is responsible for the security and fire prevention systems at the five international airports in the country. It is also in charge of the actual construction of these buildings and their maintenance. Besides security officers, fire-fighting personnel and architects, IAAI employs executive professionals in various capacities such as Vigilance Officers, Personnel Managers, Managers (Cargo) etc. As the IAAI does not own any aircraft, positions are available only for work on the ground.

National Airport Authority of India (NAAI)

National Airport Authority of India (NAAI) is responsible for all the domestic aerodromes and civil enclaves at defense aerodromes. The planning, construction and maintenance of all airports, together with providing communication and security systems, is NAAI's responsibility. It also provides air traffic control services. The various levels of Ground Personnel are detailed below :

- **Aircraft Engineer :** They maintain the aircraft's engines, its ground equipment and ensure safety of the aircraft and the passengers. An engineering degree with a specialisation in Aeronautical, Mechanical or Electrical engineering is the minimum requirement for starting a career as an aircraft engineer.
- **Air Officer :** Checks the airworthiness of an aircraft and also certifies the flight schedules. Qualifications for entry include a bachelor's degree with Mathematics or Physics as the main subject and three years' experience in aircraft maintenance or a degree in Mechanical/Electrical/Electronic engineering with one year's experience in airframe, aircraft structure systems or engines/ power plants/avionics in a reputed manufacturing/ overhauling/maintenance establishment or a degree in Aeronautical Engineering or equivalent. The upper age limit is 30 years.The selection is made through UPSC examination. Future promotion prospects include promotions to the post of Senior Air Worthiness Officer and further to that of Deputy Director and Director. Air Traffic Controllers have a very specific role in the crowded skies. They have to, through various control mechanisms, control a flight's movement and make its landing safe. This is quite a technical job and entails a lot of professional experience and logical thinking. Qualifications for these jobs require a basic degree in the discipline of relevance to the function and experience.
- **Commercial Activities :** These include various functions like ticketing and reservation, marketing and allied activities. In order to join this sector, it is imperative to have a degree/diploma in Business Management. Moreover, for the ticketing staff, airlines prefer to keep good-looking women to deal with passengers. As far as educational qualification is concerned, a degree in any discipline or diploma in travel and tourism is essential. Knowledge of a foreign language is essential.

Eligibility

The educational qualification for an Air Hostess/Flight Steward training programme is 10+2 or with a diploma/degree in Hotel Management or Tourism Management. The aspirant should possess an Indian Passport and should be below 25 years of age with proportionate weight and height. Fluency in English, Hindi and knowledge of an international language is an added advantage.

Selection Procedure

The applicant should be physically fit with a pleasing personality and clear complexion. After the initial screening of applicants is completed, the air-line company calls them for a written examination, usually of the Objective-type (Multiple choice). Those who qualify in the written examination have to appear for a group discussion followed by a personal interview of successful candidates. If selected, the applicant will be on training for two to three months in which one can learn about service, grooming, safety and first aid after which one is initially put on trainee flights.

Work Structure

The work structure can be categorised into two main categories, namely the Ground Staff and the Flight Staff. The ground staff usually repairs the planes on the ground and commands the various traffic controls and the flight staff usually fly with the airlines as pilots, crew members and flight attendants.

What are Jobs available in the Aviation Industry?

The jobs available in the aviation industry are as follows :

- Aero Engineer,
- Aerodynamics,
- Air Traffic Control,
- Aircraft Interiors,
- Aircraft Mechanics,
- Airline Customer Service,
- Airline Management,
- Airline Office,
- Airport Baggage,
- Airport
- Airworthiness Engineer,
- Apprentice,

- Aviation Design,
- Aviation Material,
- Aviation Planning,
- Aviation Welding,
- Avionics Electronics,
- Cabin Crew,
- Communication,
- Composites,
- Electrician.

Educational Qualifications/Training Required Toenter into Civil Aviation Industry?

Some of the qualifications / training required to join civil aviation are :

- Flight Attendant Courses
- Commercial Pilot Training
- Aircraft Maintenance
- Flight Crew Management and other in-flights Services
- Air Hostess Courses
- Aviation Safety
- Air Traffic Control and Management
- Operations and Research
- Cargo Management Avionics

Civil Aviation courses offer technical, theoretical and practical knowledge about aircraft components and their maintenance. Training is given to students with real time controllable devices that are used in Aircraft to utilise their knowledge in a more practical way.

The Jobs available in the Government Sector in Civil Aviation Industry

Some of the jobs in Government sector of civil aviation are :

- Assistant Gliding Instructor,
- Assistant Pilot Instructor,
- Pilot Instructor Incharge,
- Chief Flying Instructor,
- Helicopter Pilot,
- Science Lecturer,

- Mechanical Lecturer,
- Chief Lecturer,
- Principal Lecturer,
- Aircraft Maintenance Engineers,
- Airport Service Staff,
- Chefs,
- Cargo pilot,
- Flight engineer,
- Flight operations support personnel.

Some of the Public Sector Companies that work in Civil Aviation Sector in India

- Airport Economic Regulatory Authority.
- Indira Gandhi Ashtray Uran Akademi.
- Pawan Hans Helicopters Limited.
- Airports Authority of India.
- National Aviation Company of India Limited and its following subsidiaries.
- IAL Airport Services Limited.
- Vyaudoot Limited.
- Airlines Allied Services Limited.
- Air India.
- Air India Engineering Services Limited.
- Air India Air Transport Services Limited.
- Air India Charters Limited.
- Hotel Corporation of India Limited.

19.5 Pilot

Who is a Pilot?

The most important person on the aircraft is the pilot or an aviator.

Pilots are highly trained professionals who fly airplanes and helicopters carrying passengers or cargo. This is a highly specialised job which requires knowledge of air navigation, interpretation of meteorological reports, operations of sophisticated electronic and mechanical controls, leading the aircraft under adverse circumstances and being a leader to the flight crew and passengers under climatic and other emergency situations.

The first recorded use of the term *'aviateur'* in French was in 1887, as a variation of 'aviation' from the Latin ***avis*** meaning bird, coined in 1863 by G. de la Landelle in Aviation Ou Navigation Aerienne (Aviation or Air Navigation). The term ***'aviatrix'*** (*aviatrice* in French), now archaic was formerly used for a female aviator. The term aviator is often applied simply to pilots but can be extended to include aviation navigators, bombardiers, Weapons Systems Officers, Electronic Warfare Officers.

What are the Duties of a Pilot?

Pilots fly Aircraft on long and short flights. One hour before take-off, pilots check pre-flights plans. These include the route to be taken and height maintained and also includes meteorological information. Pilots have to do complex calculations of take-off and landing and they have to work out the fuel needed for distance to be travelled and height and weight to be maintained. They check equipments and instruments and do briefing to the flight crew. On-flight pilots have to interpret the data on instrument and control. The most difficult part for a pilot's job is Landing and Take-off. Pilots maintain contact with air traffic controls and cabin crew throughout the flight. They also speak at intervals to passengers, giving them information over the public address system on speed and height, details of ground areas they are flying over. Duties are shared usually with one co-pilot. After landing the aircraft is taxied to its final position and engines are shut down by pilots, later they prepare a flight report, noting any problems or instrument difficulties. Pilot is a profession of discipline, patience, responsibility, punctuality, commitment and dedication. The job requires a lot of hard work, stamina, alertness of mind, adaptability to follow difficult times schedules, ability to think in crisis, good team spirit etc. Apart from possessing these qualities, the persons willing to take up this as profession should be calm, pleasant, compassionate, understanding and technically sound.

How can one become a Pilot in India?

To become a pilot first you have to obtain a Student's Pilot License (SPL). Visit the website of Directorate General of Civil Aviation (DGCA) and find aflying club approved by them convenient for you.

- **Student's Pilot License :** To get the SPL those with 10+2 with Science (with Physics and Mathematics with at least 50 per cent marks) and aged at least 18 years should register at a flying club which is recognised by Directorate General of Civil Aviation (DGCA), Government of India. Registration requires a medical certificate, security clearance and a bank guarantee. An oral examination in subjects such as Air Regulations, Aviation Meteorology, Air Navigation, Engine (technical and specific) follows the registration. Successful completion of the examination entitles you for an SPL certificate. The SPL examination is held all over India by the flying clubs. 23 flying clubs in India issue SPL.

- **Private Pilot License (PPL) :** To become a commercial pilot in India, one has to first possess a Student's Pilot License (SPL). The second step is the Private Pilot License (PPL). PPL training includes sixty hours of flying of which about fifteen hours are dual flights, that is accompanied by the flight instructor and at least 30 hours of solo flights apart from five hours of cross-country flying. This makes one eligible for the PPL exam, which consists of Air Regulation, Aviation Meteorology, Air Navigation, Aircraft Engines and Seamanship. The prescribed age for appearing for this exam is 17 years and an educational qualification issued by the Armed Forces Central Medical Establishment (AFCME).
- **Commercial Pilot License (CPL) :** A Commercial Pilot License may be obtained only after a PPL has been acquired. To obtain a Commercial Pilots License (CPL) 250 hours of flying (including 60 hours for the PPL) is necessary. Besides that you have to undergo a Medical Fitness Test which is held at New Delhi and an examination which consists of Air Regulations, Aviation Meteorology, Air Navigation, Technical, Planning and communications in the form of Radio and Wireless Transmission. With the CPL, a pilot can take up any professional assignment.

Course Fee : The Pilot Training course duration is about 2 years and fees vary from ₹ 12 – 18 lakhs depending on the training institute.

How to become a Helicopter Pilot?

Helicopter pilots need to have Commercial Helicopter Pilot License (CHPL). This license can be acquired by two stages. The Private Helicopter License (PHPL) is granted after 40 hours of flying training (15 hours should be solo) and on clearing the written exams of aviation subjects. 60 hours of flying training has to be completed and a written exam has to be clear. Helicopter pilots find employment with the commercial organisations, Public sector organisation and other security/protective agencies.

Personal Attributes

This is a field of discipline, patience, responsibility, punctuality, commitment and self-confidence. The job requires a lot of hard work, stamina, alertness of mind, adaptability to follow difficult time schedules, good team spirit etc. He must be mentally very alert in every situation. Emotional stability in crisis situations is another characteristic that the pilots should have. Apart from these qualities, the persons willing to take up this as profession should be calm, peasant, compassionate, adventurous, understanding and technically sound.

Job Prospects

With the privatisation, lots of avenues have opened for CPL holders. They can find employment opportunities in both government (Indian Airlines, Air India) as well as private domestic and international (Jet Airways, Sahara etc.) airlines. Even large corporate houses with their own aircraft require the services of pilots.

Career Options

In this field, after getting CPL one starts as a trainee pilot. After being a trainee, one becomes a pilot or first officer on board based on one's seniority. Seniority is determined by hours of flying experience and successful completion of various programmes. Then one becomes a Commander or Captain and thereafter a Senior Commander. From pre-take off to actual landing and signing off, pilot must be highly responsible. Before take-off pilots check pre-flight plans. This includes the route to be taken and height maintained, meteorological readings, conditions of all equipments, air pressure and temperature inside the aircraft etc. They have to do complex calculations of take-off and landing and have to check fuel needed for the particular distance to be traveled and height and weight to be maintained. During the flight too pilot must be constantly alert, ensuring there are no mechanical snags, maintaining contact with air traffic controls and cabin crew throughout the flight. He also has to keep a record of flight details.

Remuneration

Trainee Pilot : ₹ 15,000 – 22,000. Pilots are also entitled to a range of benefits and allowances in addition to housing, medical and out-station allowances as well as free/concessional air passage for their immediate family and dependents.

Pilot or Co-Pilot : The expansion in the aviation industry has resulted in a huge demand for trained commercial pilots. Salaries have been pushed up; a trainee pilot can earn ₹ 20,000 per month, which is a good amount for beginners. Pilots earn ₹ 65,000 – 85,000 per month;

foreign airlines pay much more, going up to ₹ 1.5 lakh per month and even higher.

A commercial pilot's license costs upwards of ₹ 5 lakhs. Private flying schools may charge ₹ 15 lakhs or above. The career is certainly not for you if you cannot spare that kind of money; no scholarships are available.

Cabin Crew : The Cabin Crew can get up to ₹ 40,000 per month for domestic flights and up to ₹ 1,25,000 for international flights on wide-bodied aircraft.

Air-Hostesses and Flight Pursers : They start on salaries between ₹ 20,000 – 22,000 per month plus benefits. In the private sector, the range is over ₹ 15,000 per month.

Courses

- Advanced Diploma in Aviation Management,
- Air Transport Pilot's License (ATPL),
- BTEC (HNC) in Aviation, Hospitality and Travel Management,
- Certificate Course in Aviation Studies,
- Commercial Pilots License (CPL),
- Diploma in Aviation and Hospitality Management,
- Diploma in Aviation Management,
- Diploma in Aviation, Hospitality and Travel Management,
- Diploma in Fast Track Aviation and Hospitality Management,
- Diploma in Global Aviation and Hospitality Management,
- International Aviation Management.

Important Institutes

There are a number of institutes under the recognition of the Directorate General of Civil Aviation which conducts training in this field. Most prominent among them is Indira Gandhi Ashtray Academy at Rae Bareli (Uttar Pradesh). The top ten flying institutes in India are :

- Government Aviation Training Institute, Bhubaneshwar.
- Coimbatore Flying Club, Coimbatore.
- Indian Aviation Academy, Mumbai.
- Jamshedpur Co-operative Flying Club Ltd, Jamshedpur.
- All India Institute of Aeronautics (AIIA), Dehradun.
- Rajiv Gandhi Aviation Academy, Secunderabad.

- Ahmedabad Aviation and Aeronautics, Ahmedabad.
- Government Flying Training School, Bangalore.
- Indira Gandhi Rashtriya Uran Akademi, Bareli.
- West Bengal Flying Training Institute, Kolkata.

19.6 Hotel Management

Importance of Hotels

Hotels are one of the most tangible and important aspects of a country's infrastructure. Hotel industry is closely linked to tourism industry. A number of factors like promotion of tourism and rapid industrial progress have given boost to hoteliering. The recent liberalisation of trade and opening up of economy will further lead to revolutionary growth in this sector.

Hotel industry involves combination of various skills like management, food and beverages service, housekeeping, front office operation, sales and marketing and accounting. Today, the rise in corporate activity (leading to greater number of business trips) as well as the wish to travel on holiday has made the hotel industry a very competitive one.

Eligibility

One can enter this field directly or through hotel management institutes. For direct entry the vacancies are generally advertised in the newspapers and the minimum prescribed qualification is graduation with 50 per cent marks. They are trained by the hotels themselves. But qualified personnel are always given a higher preference.

Minimum qualification required to go for a course in hotel management is 10+2. For certificate, diploma and bachelors courses 10+2 is sufficient. Duration of certificate courses is six months to one year. Bachelor and diploma courses are of one and half to three year's duration. Those with graduation can go for postgraduate diploma courses which are of one year duration.

Selection

Selection to most government recognised institutes is based on common entrance test. Test consists of English, Reasoning, General Science and General Knowledge. The test is of two hour duration and is held around April every year. The test is followed by a group discussion and interview, in which a person's personality and confidence is revealed.

Private institutes also conduct tests of their own, the pattern of which is almost the same.

Course Areas

Course areas include food processing, food and beverages service, accommodation operation or front office, hotel accountancy, business communication, French language, hotel engineering, computer, nutrition and food service, Hotel laws, Principles of management, sales and marketing management, Human resource management.

Personal Attributes

They should have a good organisational skills, excellent communication and interpersonal skills, strong commitment and self-discipline. One must be an extrovert, co-operative, polite and respectful to the guests, have patience to deal guests' criticism even when you know you are right, willing to work hard at odd hours and yet be cheerful.

Job Prospects

Hotel management graduates have a very interesting and lucrative field to work :

- Hotel and Restaurant management,
- Airline Catering and Cabin Services,
- Club management,
- Cruise Ship Hotel Management,
- Hospital administration and catering,
- Hotel and Tourism Associations,
- Forest Lodges,
- Guests Houses,
- Institutional Management (supervising canteens in college, schools, in factories, company guest houses etc.),
- Catering departments of railways, banks, armed forces, shipping companies etc.,
- Hotel and catering institutes,
- Self-employment.

Career Options

Hotel chief departments consist of the following :

- **General Operations :** General Manager who is the main in-charge is the coordinator and administrator, responsible for staff management, financial control, provision of services, quality control and customer care. Depending on the size of the hotel, general managers could have assistant managers to supplement their work.

- **Front Office :** It is the centre of all activities. Important functions of receiving the guests, making room reservations, handling correspondence and preparing bills and keeping accounts of the guests' services are handled at the front office. The department is headed by Front Office Manager or Executive House-keeper who supervises and co-ordinates the work. Then, there is Assistant Manager, Lobby executive, front office supervisor, information assistant, receptionist, bell captain, bell boy, and doorman, etc., to perform their assigned roles.
- **House Keeping :** The work of keeping the hotel, the rooms, the bars, the restaurants etc. clean and making it presentable to the guests and ensuring facilities and comfort to them is handled by this department. Those handling this department are Chief executive house keeper, floor supervisor, room attendants, linen supervisors, Maids etc.
- **Food and Beverages Department :** This department is the hub of the hotel industry and is responsible for all the food that is prepared and served in the hotel. The main functions performed by the department are – presentation, preparation and service of food and beverages involving kitchen, bar and baker. Overall in charge of kitchen is known as *Chef de Cuisine*, the one in charge of section is called *Chef de Parties* and the one who supervises and coordinates the work of Chef de Parties is known as *Sous-Chef*. One who cooks food is known as Cook, the person in overall charge of dining hall is called *Maitre de hotel*, Captain In charge of part of dining hall is known as *Chef de Range*, one who serves food is *Demy Chef de Range* or *Steward*. Then, there is the restaurant hostess who makes the guests comfortable and deal with any complains by the guests. Those serving drinks are called *bartenders*.
- **Accounting Department :** This department deals with both cash and credit transactions, i.e., all the financial transactions like purchase of materials, offering of services to the guests etc. This department also complies information required for budgeting, pricing of food and services and so on. Professionals like cash, cost and works accountants are given higher positions in the department. Chief cashier, cash clerk/bill clerk are the positions handled in this department.

- **Sales and Marketing :** This department keeps in touch with travel agents and tour operators as well as other potential corporate clients in order to sell hotel facilities. Advertising and Public Relations is also normally handled by this department.
- **Engineering/Maintenance Department :** Qualified engineers are appointed for the maintenance of the building and various machines involved in the premises. They are assisted by necessary staff in the electrical and mechanical departments. Mechanical Engineers, Electrical Engineers, Plumbers, carpenters, etc., are employed by this department.

Then, there is the Security department which provides security to the guests and their belongings and employs security Officers/guards for this purpose. Retired Army personnel are preferred by this department.

Remuneration

After completing the diploma or the bachelor's degree, a graduate is usually taken as a trainee. After successful completion of training, they may be absorbed in positions with salaries range between ₹ 4,000 to ₹ 7,500 per month.

Courses

- Apprenticeship in Hotel Management,
- Advance Diploma in Hotel Management,
- B.B.A. Hotel Management,
- B.B.A. Tourism and Hotel Management,
- B.Sc. Hotel Management,
- B.Sc. Hotel Management and Catering Technology,
- Bachelor in Hotel Management (BHM),
- Bachelor in Hotel Management and Catering Technology,
- Diploma in Catering Science and Hotel Management,
- Diploma in Hotel Management,
- Diploma in Hotel Management and Catering Technology,
- Diploma in Hotel Management and Ship Catering,
- Diploma in Hotel Management, Catering and Food Science,
- Dual Diploma in International Hotel Management (DIHM),

- Integrated Diploma in Hotel Management and Catering Technology,
- International Diploma in Hotel Management (IDHM),
- MBA Tourism and Hotel Management,
- M.Sc. Hotel Management,
- M.Sc. Hotel Management and Catering Technology,
- Master of Hotel Management,
- Post Graduate Diploma in Hotel Management (PGDHM),
- Post Graduate Diploma in Hotel Management and Catering Technology.

Best Colleges to study Hotel Management

- Institute of Hotel Management, Delhi.

  Governed by National Council of Hotel Management and Catering Technology.
- Indian Institute of Hotel Management, Kolkata (Autonomous institution).
- Guru Nanak Institute of Hotel Management, Kolkata(Affiliated to the National Council of Hotel Management and Catering Technology and approved by AICTE).
- Welcome group Graduate School of Hotel Administration, Manipal.
- Institute of Hotel Management, Catering Technology and Applied Nutrition, Mumbai.
- PCTE Institute of Hotel Management, Ludhiana.
- M.A. Rangoonwala Institute of Hotel Management and Research, Pune.
- Subhas Bose Institute of Hotel Management, Kolkata.
- A-IHM Institute of Hotel Management, Agra.
- International Institute of Hotel Management, Kolkata.
- Oberoi Centre , 7 Sham Nath Marg, Delhi-110054.
- Institute of Hotel Management, Veer Sawarkar Marg, Dadar (WR), Mumbai-400028.
- Indian Institute of Hotel Management (Taj Group), Aurangabad-431001, Maharashtra.

19.7 Travel and Tourism

Introduction

Travel and Tourism one of the world's largest foreign exchange earners among industries provides employment directly to millions of people worldwide and indirectly through many associated service industries. It is a very wide industry which includes Government departments, Immigration and customs services, travel agencies, airlines, tour operators, hotels etc. and many associated service industries such as airline catering or laundry services, Guides, Interpreters, Tourism promotion and sales etc.

The Work in Travel and Tourism Industry

The work in Travel and Tourism industry is essentially concerned with providing services for people who are away from home, on business or holiday. Travel can be leisure travel involving package tours, pilgrim travel, adventure travel etc. or purely business. Work at every functional level in the industry involves dealing directly with people. Travel agents assess the needs of tourists and businessmen and help them make the best possible travel arrangements from the many travel options available. Many major cruise lines, resorts and specialty travel groups use travel agents to promote travel packages to the millions of people who travel every year.

Eligibility and Course Areas

There are graduate level, postgraduate level, diploma and certification courses available to pursue in the industry. The postgraduate degree awarded is Master of Tourism Administration (MTA) which is a two year full time programme approved by the Ministry of Tourism, Government of India. The Indian Institution of Tourism and Travel Management and some universities offer MTA degree in Tourism. A postgraduate degree can be helpful in getting into managerial and administrative positions in the industry. International Air Transport Association (IATA), a World Organisation which provides recognised standard in training to travel, tourism and cargo industry offers certification courses. Several large travel agencies also offer short-term training programmes and tend to absorb most of the candidates.

The eligibility for admission to Travel and Tourism courses at the undergraduate level is, higher secondary examination pass. At postgraduate level, eligibility is graduation in any field along with a pass in the entrance test followed by group discussions and interview conducted by the institute. Proficiency in at least one foreign language is preferred. A diploma in public relations or advertising is helpful from the career point of view. It is also possible to gain these qualifications through correspondence courses. Eligibility for certification is 10+2.

Officers in the Directorate and Departments of Tourism are recruited from the candidates who have done civil service, drawn from the Civil/ administrative services of the State and Central governments. A degree in travel and tourism is required for operational jobs in government organisations. Information assistants at the office of the Tourism departments are selected through competitive examinations held by the Staff Selection Commission. The eligibility is graduation with knowledge of Indian history, art and architecture, besides proficiency in English. These vacancies are advertised through employment news.

Job Prospects

Career opportunities exist in both public and private sector. In the public sector, there are opportunities in the Directorates and Departments of Tourism of the centre and the state as Officers, information assistants, Tourist guides etc. Another good prospect for qualified tourism professionals are in the private sector with travel agencies, tour operators, airlines, hotels, transport and cargo companies etc.

Career Options

- **Tourism Department :** The jobs available in the Tourism Department are like Reservation staff, Sales and marketing staff, Tours Planners and Tour guides. Officers in the Directorate and Departments of Tourism are recruited from among the candidates who have done civil service from the Civil/administrative service of the State and Central governments. A degree in travel and tourism is required for operational jobs in government organisations. Information assistants at the office of the Tourism departments are selected through competitive examinations held by the Staff Selection Commission. The eligibility is graduation with knowledge of Indian history, art and architecture besides proficiency in English. Information assistants give out information regarding tourist spots and services available and help to plan the itinerary of the tourists. The Ministry of Tourism recognises three types of guides – regional, state and local. Guides give detailed information on the various monuments and artifacts and about the countries traditions and heritage.
- **Airlines :** In the airlines, one can work as Traffic Assistance, Reservation and Counter Staff, Air hostess and flight pursers, Sales and Marketing staff and customer services. A course in

travel and tourism or a qualification on Hotel management helps to get in.

- **Tour Operators :** Tour operators organise conducted tours to the various tourist spots and manage the travel and stay of the tourists. There are many companies operating tours for the domestic as well as the international tourist. Tour operators need people for selling the concept and then to accompany the groups to the destinations.
- **Travel Agencies :** Travel agents assess the needs of tourists and businessmen and help them make the best possible travel arrangements from the many travel options available. Many resorts, travel groups use travel agents to promote their tour packages to travelers. They deal with almost everything connected with travel including the shortest route to the destination, travel mode, the important documents that will be required (visa, passport, vaccination certificates etc.), suitable places to stay, current exchanges rates, tourist attractions to visit, climate and they will plan the trip keeping in mind the client's preferences, budgets and special needs.
- **Hotels :** The hotel industry is basically a service industry providing food and accommodation to the Visitors. It is one which requires a large number of manpower with a wide variety of skills. Hotel offers career opportunities in its various departments such as Operations, Front office, Housekeeping, Food and Beverages, Accounting, Engineering/Maintenance, Sales, Public relations and Security.
- **Transport :** Travel facilities include rail services, coach operators, car hire companies etc. Whatever that takes Tourists from one place to another – by air, road, railway, sea etc. comes under Travel and Tourism.

Remuneration

Jobs in the travel and tourism industry offer good remuneration and perquisites which include free travel for employees and their families. Salaries may vary within the industry and are higher in foreign airlines and agencies. Basic pay scales at different levels are approximately:

- Counter Clerk ₹ 1,500 – 2,000
- Assistant ₹ 2,000 – 2,500
- Junior Executive ₹ 3,000 – 3,500
- Regional Manager ₹ 3,800 – 4,500

- Air Hostess ₹ 6,000 basic salary for domestic to ₹ 40,000 in international airlines
- Regional guides: Their charges may range from ₹ 400 and above for an eight hour day. They may earn between ₹ 30,000 – 40,000 or more in the three to four months of the tourist peak season.

Courses

- Advanced Diploma in Travel and Tourism Management,
- B.Com Travel and Tourism,
- Diploma in Travel and Tourism Management,
- Foundation Course in Travel and Tourism,
- Integrated Diploma in Travel and Tourism Management,
- MBA Travel and Tourism,
- Master of Travel and Tourism Management,
- Post Graduate Diploma in Travel and Tourism Management,
- Travel and Tourism Management Courses.

Institutes

International Air Transport Association (IATA) is a World Organisation which provides recognised standard in training to travel, tourism and cargo industry. Courses conducted by IATA are IATA/UFTAA Standard (Entry Level), Advanced and Travel Agents Marketing Courses, IATA/FIATA Cargo Agents Introductory, International Air Cargo Rating, Dangerous Goods Refresher courses.

A few of these training centres in India are :

- **Akbar Academy, Kottayam (Kerala)**
  Alankar Building, Chavakad, Kottayam - 671315.
- **Akbar Academy, Mumbai (Maharashtra)**
  14 National Library Road (Nandi Cinema Lane), Near Bandra Station, Mumbai - 400050.
- **Akbar Academy of Travel and Tourism Management Studies**
  142 Continental Chambers, 1st Floor Nungambakkam High Road, Chennai - 600034.
- **Aircraft Aviation Training and Management Institute (ATMI)**
  H.O. 201, 4th Floor Adharshila Complex, South Gandhi Maidan Patna - 800001.
- **Bird Academy (Bird Education Society for Travel and Tourism-BESTT)**
  SCO 55-56, Sector-17C, Chandigarh - 160017.

20

RAILWAY SERVICES

Indian Railways

Indian railways known as the 'Lifeline of our Nation' is the World's fourth largest network, spanning more than sixty four thousand kilometers of track. This major mode of transportation for both freight and passengers were first introduced to India in 16th April 1853, when the train with 14 railway carriages and 400 guests was flagged off from Mumbai to Thane.

Division of Indian Railways

Administered by the Railway Board, Indian railway has a financial commissioner, five members and a chairman. It is divided into seventeen zones headed by a General Manager (GM) who reports directly to the Railway Board. Each of these zones is further sub-divided into certain number of divisions – under the control of Divisional Railway Managers (DRM), each having a divisional headquarter. Every division has certain number of technical and non-technical departments, which form the base structure on which the railways function. Technical departments comprise of civil, technical and mechanical engineering, signaling and telecom and several others dealing with similar discipline. The non-technical departments include general services such as accounts, personnel management, Railway Protection Force (RPF) or security and traffic services. Further down are the Station Masters who control individual stations and the train movement through the track territory under their station administration.

Eligibility and Selection

Those who want to make a career in Indian railways need to pass the Combined Civil Services Examination conducted by UPSC or an allied examination by the Railways Recruitment Boards (RRBs). These examinations are held from time to time to select a wide variety of personnel.

Technical and Non-technical Divisions : The broadly divided zones of Indian railways and its divisions have technical and non-technical service departments, categorised under the groups namely A, B, C and D.Group A and Group B posts are gazette posts which fall under the officer cadres. Selection to the posts in the Group A services are made through Civil Services Examinations/Engineering Services Examination/Combined Medical Examination conducted by the UPSC, New Delhi. The minimum eligibility required for the Group A services is graduation in any discipline or an equivalent qualification (for civil service), Degree in Engineering or M.Sc Degree or its equivalent (for engineering service), Degree in medicine – MBBS (for medical service) from any recognised University. Besides Engineering Service Examination, a Special Class Railway Apprenticeship Examination (SCRA) is also held for the selection of mechanical engineers. HSC or equivalent with PCM is the minimum qualification for SCRA exam.

No special examinations are held for Group B officers. They are directly promoted from Group C staff. Railway Recruitment Boards (RRBs) make appointments to Group B services posts. Group C and Group D are non-gazette subordinate posts. Group C comprises of the clerical staff, supervisors and skilled labour while unskilled and semi-skilled labour falls under the Group D class. Group C and D employees are recruited through 19 Railway Recruitment Boards, located at different parts of the country, which are controlled by the Railway Recruitment Control Board (RRCB). Some of the posts and its qualifications are given below :

- Enquiry-cum-Reservation Clerk (Qualification: Degree)
- Account Clerk (Qualification: Matriculation)
- Jr. Accounts Asst Railway Station (Qualification: Degree/ Diploma in Traffic and Management preferred)
- Trainee Asst. (Qualification: Matriculation and Driver (Elect/ Diesel) Certi. from ITI)
- Apprentice (Qualification: Mechanic Dip. in Elect. Engg. (DH/ Elect.))
- Apprentice (Qualification: Mechanic Dip. in Mecha. Engg. (DH/ Mecha.))
- Apprentice Signal Inspector (Gr. I) (Qualification: B.E. (Elect/ Electro/Telecom) or B. Sc. (Physics))

- Apprentice Signal Inspector (Gr. III) (Qualification: Dip. (Mecha/ Elect/Electro/Telecom) or B. Sc. (Physics))
- Skilled Artisan (Qualification: Matriculation and ITI Cert.)
- Stenographer (Eng.) (Qualification: Matriculation and proficiency in Eng. Stenography 80 w.p.m. Eng. Typing 40 w.p.m)
- Trainee Elect (Qualification: B.E. (Mech/Elect/Foreman Electro))
- Apprentice Inspector Apparent. Permanent way Inspector (Gr. III) (Qualification: Dip. (Civil/Mech/Electro))
- Apprentice Train Examiner (Qualification: Degree)
- Guard (Qualification: Degree in Law)
- Statistical Asst. (Qualification: MA/M. Sc with Eco/Stats/Maths)
- RRBs also recruit teachers, physical instructors, doctors in various departments, nurses and paramedical personnel through countrywide written tests.

Job Prospects and Career Options

With more than 2 million employees and with a wide and diverse range of operations, Indian railway system is one of the world's largest commercial employers. Vacancies in Indian railways are advertised by the Railways Recruitment Boards through the Employment News/ Rozgar Samachar as well as in prominent national dailies.

Some of the Group A services available within the department of Indian Railways are :

- **Indian Railway Traffic Service (IRTS) – Group A**

  Divided into two divisions namely commercial and operations divisions, IRTS controls the transportation and commercial matters related to transportation. Ticket checking, catering, administration and management of stations, reservation, announcements on the platforms etc. are handled in the commercial division. Whereas, operations division deals with controlling movement of trains detachment or attachment of wagons etc.

- **Indian Railways Accounts Service (IRAS) – Group A**

  IRAS are mainly responsible for the accounting and finance operations of the Indian Railways. Since this branch deals mainly with the financial transactions, an account service officer should have a thorough knowledge of accounting procedures and related practices.

- **Indian Railway Personnel Service (IRPS) – Group A**

  Officers of IRPS are the responsible personal dealings with the matters related to the personal sections like selection, promotions, training, welfare activities, transfers, increments etc.

- **Railway Engineering Services – Group A**

  This technical side of Indian railway, allied with the activities like construction and planning of railway tracks, bridges and buildings is further sub-divided into branches namely,

  - ***Indian Railway Service of (Civil) Engineers (IRSE) :*** Employees of this branch are responsible for managing the civil engineering organisation of the Indian railways. Their duties involve planning the track routes, constructing railway station, bridges, tunnels and so on.
  - ***Indian Railway Service of Electrical Engineers (IRSEE) :*** IRSEEs are responsible to maintain the assets of the electrical department in Indian railways. Their major responsibilities include power distribution networks, power generation, electrical distribution systems, monitoring continuity of supply etc.
  - ***Indian Railway Service of Mechanical Engineers (IRSME) :*** IRSMEs are responsible for the maintenance of the locomotives, wagons, carriages etc are carried out by the mechanical engineers branch.
  - ***Indian Railway Service of Signal Engineers (IRSSE) :*** The vast signaling and telecommunication infrastructure of the Indian railways is controlled by the IRSSE branch.

Selection to the posts in the Railway Engineering services is made through Engineering Services Examination of the railways.

- **Indian Railway Stores Service (IRSS) – Group A**

  The IRSS cadre is responsible for forecasting, planning, procurement logistic support and management, warehousing of very expensive and sophisticated assets meant for the national lifeline, i.e., Indian Railways. It is also responsible for giving material support to production of coaches, locomotives and other rolling stock. This service is also responsible for mopping up scrap scattered all over Indian railways, and to sell it through tender/public auction. the important function of vendor approval/development and registration of firms is also one of the main functions of IRSS.

- **Indian Railway Medical Service (IRMS) – Group A**

  Railways have full-fledged hospitals at the divisional level and at zonal headquarters. Selection to the posts in the Railway Medical Services is made through Combined Medical Examination conducted by the UPSC.

- **Railway Protection Service/Force (RPF)**

  RPF is the branch entrusted with the task of maintenance and security of law and order in the Indian Railways. The ranks in the RPF vary from Constable to Director General.Other Services in the railways includes station masters, assistant station masters, engine drivers, yardmaster, motormen, guards, signal and mechanical inspectors etc. which falls under Group C. One can also join in Indian Railways as ticket collectors, clerks, stenographers, depot store keeper, rail maintenance workers etc.

Remuneration

Candidates with qualifications ranging from 10th standard to engineering graduates can find job openings in the varied operations of the Indian railways. They can earn a monthly pay according to the pay scale of Government of India. The pay scale follows the pattern of all other civil services and it will be revised from time to time. In addition to the basic salary and perks, railway employees also get a lot of benefits like free railway passes to travel all over the country, housing facilities, health care facilities for the whole family, educational facilities for their children, provision for staying in the railway guest houses and many more. After retirement, each individual will get monthly pension-according to the post and position held.

Institutes

For imparting training for all the selected cadres, Indian railways run several training centers. There are about 170 training centers for training non-gazette staff and the training of officer cadres are conducted at six centralised training institutes (CTIs).

Some of the training institutes including the six centralised training institutes (CTIs) are :

- **Indian Railway Institute of Transportation Management (IRITM), Lucknow** (for officers of the Traffic department)

  Hardoi By-pass Road, PO Manak Nagar, Lucknow – 226 011, UP

  Phone: 0522-2458754

  Fax: 0522-2465828

  Website: www.iritm.indianrailways.gov.in

- **Indian Railway Institute of Civil Engineering (IRICEN), Pune** (for civil engineers)

  Website: www.iricen.gov.in/IRICEN 1/cmsma desimple/ index.php

- **Indian Railway Institute of Signal and Telecommunications Engineering (IRISET), Secunderabad** (for engineers of S and T department

  Tarnaka Road, Secunderabad – 500 017

  Phone: +91-40-27820315

  Fax: +91-40-27823922

  Website: www.iriset.indianrailways.gov.in

- **Indian Railways Institute of Mechanical and Electrical Engineering (IRIMEE), Jamalpur** (for mechanical engineers)

  Jamalpur-811 214, Bihar,

  Fax: +91-(0) 6344-243293

  Website: www.irimee.indianrailways.gov.in

- **Indian Railways Institute of Electrical Engineering (IRIEEN), Nasik** (for Electrical Engineers)

  Post Box 233, Nasik Road-422 101, Maharashtra

  Phone: +91-253-2462545

  Fax: +91-253-2462548

  Website: www.irieen.indianrailways.gov.in

- **RPF Academy, Lucknow** (for officers of the Railway Protection Force)

  Jagjivan Ram Railway Protection Force Academy

  Talkatora Road, Alambagh, P.O. Manak Nagar, Lucknow – 226011

  Phone: 0522-2450341

  Website: www.jrrpfacademy.org

- **Railway Staff College, Vadodara** which functions as the apex training institute for the officers of all departments in general and Accounts, Personnel, Stores and Medical departments.

  Lalbaug, Vadodara-390 004, Gujarat

  Phone: +91-265-2652987

  Fax: +91-265-2638267

  Website: www.rscbrc.indianrailways.gov.in

A Few Useful Contacts

- **Railway Recruitment Board, Allahabad**

  Opposite to G.M./NCR Building, Near Subedarganj Railway Hospital, Subedarganj, Allahabad-211 033

  Phone: 0532-2222541

  Website: www.rrbald.nic.in

- **Railway Recruitment Board, Bangalore**

  18 Millers Road, Bangalore-560046

  Phone: 080-23330378

  Fax: 0755-2746398

  Website: www.rrbbpl.nic.in

- **Railway Recruitment Board, Guwahati**

  Station Road, Guwahati-781 001

  Phone: 0361-2540813

  Website: www.rrbguwahati.gov.in

- **Railway Recruitment Board, Kolkata**

  Metro Railway A.V. Complex, Chitpur, Opposite to R.G. Kara Medical College and Hospital,

  R.G. Kar Road, Kolkata-700 037

  Website: www.rrbkolkata.org

- **Railway Recruitment Board, Patna**

  Mehendrughat, Patna-800 004

  Phone: 0612-2677680

  Website: www.rrbpatna.gov.in

- **Railway Recruitment Board, Bhubaneshwar**

  D-79/80, Vihar, B.D.A. Rental Colony, Chandrasekharpur, Bhubaneshwar-751023

  Phone: 0674-2303015

  Website: www.rrbbs.gov.in

21

TEACHER TRAINING AND EDUCATION

The Profession of Teaching

Teaching is the noblest of all professions in the world. This is because teaching is the only one profession that gives birth to all other professions–doctor, engineer, scientist, artist, soldier, lawyer, etc. All have to pass through the bosom of a teacher at least some times in one's life. There is no escape from the life of a teacher. Remove a teacher from the society and you have nothing.

Teachers are always a boon to society. Through their intelligence, patience and wisdom, they attempt to not only hone the learner's intellect and aptitude but also mould a well-rounded and wholesome personality. Teaching has an influence in developing one's mind and character and also gives the satisfaction of having sparked the light of knowledge and dispelled the clouds of ignorance.

Different areas of Specialisations

As this field is so vast having areas of specialisations, different skills and types of training are required for different levels. Areas of specialisation include teaching at nursery schools, middle schools, high schools, colleges, universities, institutes, special schools etc. Each level calls for a different expertise. Arousing students from their apathy and watching their curiosity grow is one of the biggest rewards of teaching.

Eligibility and Course Areas

From primary school all the way up to college, to arts and sports, training the handicapped, languages and so on, there is no limit to the various subjects and fields that a teacher-to-be can specialise in.

- **Nursery schools :** Nursery Teachers Training. Minimum qualification: 10+2.

- **Middle schools :** Teachers Training Certificate (TTC) or its equivalent. Minimum qualification: 10+2.
- **High schools :** Bachelor of Education (B.Ed). Minimum qualification: Graduation.
- **Colleges/Universities :** Post Graduate degree, preferably with Doctoral Degree. Now it is mandatory to qualify the National Eligibility Test (NET) conducted by University Grants Commission (UGC).
- **Special schools :** Diploma in special Education. Minimum qualification: 10+2.

Personal Attributes

A person who has a flair for teaching must have a blend of mind, patience, confidence, liking for an understanding of children which is a must. You must have organising capacity, amicable and helpful nature to enter into this field. Teacher should have the ability to articulate ideas well, to create a liking in young minds even in the case of most boring subjects. He or she should have a deep passion for the subject one handles. Must encourage in students the ability to analyse and think. A teacher must always remember that apart from teaching, it is he or she who shapes a child's character. Teacher has to be a friend, philosopher and guide to his wards.

Job Prospects

They can find employment in:

- Nursery schools,
- Primary/elementary schools,
- Secondary schools,
- Colleges,
- Universities,
- Educational research institutes,
- Special schools,
- Self-employment by starting institutes/tutorials.
- **Nursery/Primary Schools :** Nursery and primary school teachers have a huge responsibility in the sense that, it is what children learn and experience during their early years that shape their views and affect success or failures later in their lives. Thus, teachers play a vital role in the social and intellectual development of children. They introduce children to numbers,

language, science, social studies as well as social interactions. Here, games, music, artwork, computers and other tools are used to teach basic skills. While kindergarten teachers deal with children of 3 to 5 years, primary school teachers deal with those of 6 to 12 years.

- **Secondary Schools :** The secondary school teachers instruct students from 8th to 12th standard. Usually they deal with one particular subject in which they specialise. Good base in the subject is a must.
- **Colleges/Universities :** In the universities or colleges there are lecturers and professors who specialise in a particular field. They give lectures, guidance and help the students in their academic and research work. Those who have organising skills ability have a further scope to become a principal, vice principal, vice-chancellor in the management level.
- **Special Schools :** (for students with specific needs, e.g., differently abled ones). A challenging area in the field of teaching is that of dealing with children having physical and mental handicap and learning disabilities. The work is emotionally and physically demanding which needs a lot of patience. They have to work in close association with parents and medical professionals like speech therapist etc. It is different from the normal teaching norms as each child needs special care depending on his or her ability.

Remuneration

Primary School Teachers

- Grade III : ₹ 6500 – 10,500 (Grade Pay: ₹ 4,200)
- Grade II : ₹ 7,450 – 11,500 (Grade Pay: ₹ 4,600)
- Grade I : ₹ 7,500 – 12,000 (Grade Pay: ₹ 4,800)

Trained Graduate Teachers

- Grade III : ₹ 7,000 – 11,500 (Grade Pay: ₹ 4,600)
- Grade II : ₹ 7,500 – 12,000 (Grade Pay: ₹ 4,800)
- Grade I : ₹ 8,000 – 13,000 (Grade Pay: ₹ 5,400)

Post Graduate Teachers

- Grade III : ₹ 7,500 – 12,000 (Grade Pay: ₹ 4,800)
- Grade II : ₹ 8,000 – 13,500 (Grade Pay: ₹ 5,400)
- Grade I : ₹ 10,000 – 15,200 (Grade Pay: ₹ 6,600)

Vice Principal

- Grade II : ₹ 8,000 – 13,500 (Grade Pay: ₹ 5,400)
- Grade I : ₹ 10,000 – 15,200 (Grade Pay: ₹ 6,600)

Principal : Grade II: ₹ 12,000 – 16,500 (Grade Pay: ₹ 7,600)

Lecturers : ₹ 15,600 – 39,100 (Grade Pay: ₹ 7,000)

Readers : ₹ 37,400 – 67,000 (Grade Pay: ₹ 9,000)

Associate Professors : ₹ 37,400 – 67,000 (Grade Pay: ₹ 10,000)

Professors : ₹ 37,400 – 67,000 (Grade Pay: ₹ 12,000)

Courses

- Bachelor of Education (B. Ed)
- Diploma in Child Care and Education
- Diploma in Early Childhood Education
- Diploma in Education (D.ED)
- Diploma in Nursery Teacher Training
- Diploma in Pre-Primary Teacher Training Education (DPPTE)
- Diploma in Teacher Education (DTE)
- Elementary Teacher Education
- Junior Basic Training (JBT)
- Junior Teacher Training Certificate (JTTC)
- Licentiate in Teaching (LT)
- M. Phil Education
- Master of Education (M. Ed)
- Ph. D Education
- Nursery Teacher Training (NTT)
- Pre-Primary Teacher Certificate
- Pre-Primary Teaching Training Course (PPTTC)
- Primary Teachers Certificate (PTC)
- Primary Teachers Training (PTT)
- Senior Teaching Certificate (STC)

Best Institutes for B.Ed/M.Ed Course in India

- Jankidevi Bajaj Institute of Management Studies, Mumbai
- Mahatma Jyotiba Phule Rohilkhand University, Bareilly

- **Central Institute of Education Chatra Marg,**
  University of Delhi, Delhi-110007
  Website: www.du.ac.in
- **Loyola College, Chennai**
  Website: www.loyolacollege.edu.
- **University of Rajasthan JNL Marg,**
  Jaipur-302004, Rajasthan
  Website: www.uniraj.ernet.in.
- **Jamia Millia University, Jamia Nagar**
  New Delhi-110025
  Website: www.jmi.nic.in
- **University of Mumbai, M.G. Road**
  Fort, Mumbai-Maharashtra-400032
  Website: www.mu.ac.in
- **University of Calcutta, Senate House**
  87/1 College Street, Kolkata-700 073
  West Bengal
- **Guru Gobind Singh Indraprastha University (GGSIPU)**
  Kashmiri Gate, Delhi-110006
- **Amity University Campus**
  Sector-125, Noida (NCR)
  Website: www.amity.edu
- **Maharshi Dayanand University, Rohtak**
  A.G. Teachers College, Ahmedabad,
  Navrangpura, Ahmedabad Dist.-380009
- **Andhra University: College of Arts and Commerce**
  Visakhapatnam Andhra University,
  Waltair, Visakhapatnam-530003
- **D.M. College of Teacher Education, Imphal**
  Imphal-795 001, Manipur
- **Himachal Pradesh University, Summer Hill**
  Shimla (Shimla Dist.)-171005, Himachal Pradesh

- **St. Xavier's College of Education**
  PO-Dighagat, Patna (Patna Dist.)-800011 (Bihar)
- **University of Mumbai: Department of Education**
  Vidyanagari, Kalina, Mumbai-400098, Maharashtra
- Jaipur National University, Jaipur
- University of Pune, Pune
- Lucknow University, Lucknow
- Mahatma Gandhi Colleges of Education
- Shekhawati M. Ed College, Rajasthan
- Jain Vishva Bharati University, Rajasthan
- Bharati Vidyapeeth University, Pune
- Jawaharlal Nehru College of Education, Rajasthan
- Mother Teresa's Women University, Tamil Nadu
- Maulana Azad National Urdu University, Andhra Pradesh

Top B. Ed. Colleges in Delhi

- Lady Irwin College, Delhi.
- Indira Gandhi National Open University (IGNOU).
- Army Institute of Education (AIE).
- Guru Govind Singh Indraprastha University.
- Siddi Vinayak College of Science and Hr. Education.
- Excel Institute of Management and Technology.
- Lingaya's Lalita Devi Institute of Management and Sciences (LLDIMS).
- Kalka Institute For Research and Advance Studies (KIRAS).

22

A FEW CAREER QUERIES AND ANSWERS

Q. I am student studying in Class XII and after completing my 10+2, I want to go the United States of America (USA) for further studies. What are the tests, I have to take and how should I apply? Please help me in detail.

To be eligible for admission to a US university, you must meet certain minimum entry requirements. These include a secondary school diploma or examination results, English language ability and in many cases a score from one of the US university admission tests.

Application Procedure

As a part of the application process, most American colleges and universities require scores from one of the US standardised admission tests. However, some colleges and universities do not require international applicants to take admission test and some schools do not ask for admission test scores from any applicant. To find specific admission test requirements, refer US university directories such as the *International Student Handbook of US Colleges* (The College Board, New York) and *Applying to Colleges and Universities in the United States: A Handbook for International Students* (Peterson's, Princeton, NJ). Also note that community colleges do not usually require applicants to take standardised admission tests.

US standardised admissions tests are primarily multiple-choice aptitude tests that are intended to measure the skills necessary for undergraduate study. American colleges and universities use admission tests as a means of assessing all applicants (from the United States and other countries) against the same standard. Keep in mind that secondary school diplomas and examinations are not an equivalent to admission tests. And those tests are only one part of the application – good test scores do not guarantee admission to the schools of your choice.

The Three Main Undergraduate Admissions Tests

The three main undergraduate admissions tests are :

- Scholastic Assessment Test (SAT-I),
- SAT-II Subject Tests,
- American College Testing (ACT) Assessment.

Some universities may have their own in-house examinations or additional tests that applicants are required to take. For further information, make a list of the colleges you want to apply to, and then use general college directories or the colleges' own catalogs and Websites to find out each institution's specific test requirements.

Scholastic Assessment Test (SAT I) : Both SAT I and SAT II are conducted several times throughout the year at locations worldwide. Preregistration is required and deadlines are usually six weeks prior to the exam. More specific information about dates, test centers, fees and registration procedures is available in the SAT registration bulletin or on the SAT test administrators' website at http: / /www. collegeboard. org/. You can get copies of the registration bulletin from the College Board in the United States or from your nearest US educational information or advising centre. You may be asked to pay postage costs for these bulletins. US centers also usually have sample questions and other test preparation materials for the SAT tests available for reference use, loan or purchase.

- **Content :** The SAT I is primarily a multiple-choice test that measures verbal and Mathematical reasoning abilities. The test is divided into seven half-hour sections: three verbal; three mathematical; and one additional section, the equating section, which either verbal or mathematical. This last portion is used to ensure the same level of difficulty from year to year and does not count toward your score.
- The SAT II Subject Tests are also primarily multiple-choice, but are only one hour long. They measure knowledge in specific subject areas. The subjects currently offered are :
  - o American History and Social Studies,
  - o Biology,
  - o Chemistry,
  - o Chinese,
  - o English Language Proficiency,
  - o French,
  - o German,
  - o Italian,

- o Japanese,
- o Korean,
- o Latin,
- o Literature,
- o Mathematics,
- o Modern Hebrew,
- o Physics,
- o Spanish,
- o World History,
- o Writing.

Many US colleges and universities, especially those that have more competitive admission criteria either require or recommend one or more SAT-II test scores for admission and / or placement purposes. Be sure to check each institution's requirements before registering for any SAT-II test. While some colleges specify which subject tests you must take, others leave the option up to you. In this case, it is advisable to take exams in your strongest areas of study.

Scores : The mathematical and verbal sections of the SAT-I are each scored on a 200 to 800 scale. Therefore, the highest possible combined score on the SAT-I would be 1,600. Scores are reported separately to colleges for the mathematical and verbal sections. Most college directories and catalogs quote average scaled scores for each institution to give some guidance on relative selectively. The SAT-II Subject Tests are also scored on a 200 to 800 scale.

The American College Testing Assessment (ACT) : The ACT is administered by the American College Testing Programme and is given up to five times annually at testing locations around the world. Unlike the SAT, the number of times the test is offered varies from one test centre to another. As an international student, you may not need to take the ACT. If it is required, however, plan ahead to make sure you do not miss the test date(s) at your nearest centre. Preregistration is required and deadlines are two to three weeks prior to the examination. Since the ACT is not as widely accepted as the SAT, check to see if the universities where you are applying will accept ACT scores in place of the SAT exam. More specific information about dates and test centers is available in the registration bulletin, which can be obtained from the test administrators and from many US information and advising centers. Note that the centers may ask you to pay postage costs.

Content : The ACT Assessment is a multiple-choice test that measures English, Mathematics, Reading and Science reasoning.

Scores : For each of the four subject areas, you receive a raw score which is the total number of correct responses. The score is then converted into a scaled score from 1 to 36. A composite score is then calculated by adding together the scaled scores and dividing the sum by four. The highest possible composite score is 36 and the lowest is 1. Scores take several weeks to reach universities.

Below is the recommended timetable for applying to universities in the United States. It is sometimes possible to complete the process more quickly, but you may have a much more limited choice of schools. Planning well ahead gives you sufficient time to make successful applications to the colleges of your choice.

12 to 18 months prior to the academic year, in which you hope to enroll, begin to consider research and do the following :

- What are your reasons for wanting to study in the United States?
- Which universities will meet your needs?
- Will you need financial assistance?
- Find out application and financial aid deadlines. This will affect when you take the standardised tests required for admission since test results must reach admissions offices no later than these deadlines. The tests should be taken in advance of submitting university application forms.
- Register to take standardised tests if required by the universities to which you are applying.
- Begin narrowing down your choices of schools to approximately 10 to 20 institutions.

12 months prior to enrollment complete the following (months indicated are estimates, based on fall enrollment)

- **August**
  - o Contact universities for application and financial aid forms and catalogs.
  - o Obtain test registration forms to take the TOEFL and SAT-I and SAT-II, if necessary.
- **September**
  - o Request an official transcript from your school.
  - o Request letters of recommendation from your teachers.

- o Submit completed application forms (for admission as well as financial aid).
- o Double check that transcripts and references have been sent.
- o Take the necessary admission tests

- **January– April**
  - o University application deadlines must be met; note that these are for regular admission – early admission deadlines will be sooner.
- **April – June**
  - o Letters of acceptance or rejection arrive. Decide which university to attend, notify the admissions office of your decision, complete and return any forms they require.
  - o Send letters of regret to those universities you turn down.
  - o Organise finances: arrange to transfer funds to a US bank; make sure you have funds for travel and expenses on arrival.
  - o Finalise arrangements for housing and medical insurance with your university.
- **June – August**
  - o Apply to your nearest US embassy or consulate for a visa upon receipt of your 1-20 form and well in advance of your departure date.
  - o Make travel arrangements.
  - o Contact the International Student Office at your university with details of your arrival plans and confirm details of any orientation for new students held by the university.

You should now have a shortlist of colleges that match your needs, interests and abilities. You should also feel confident that you have the minimum entrance requirements for studying in the United States and that you can meet the costs of a US undergraduate education. Now it's time to start putting together your applications. This chapter gives practical information and advice to help you make successful applications to the colleges of your choice.

The entire application process, from obtaining initial information to applying for your student visa, should begin 12 to 18 months in advance of when you want to go to the United States. It is possible to complete the process in less than 12 months but late applicants usually find they have a much more limited choice of colleges.

English Proficiency

To determine you level of English language proficiency, arrange to take the Test of English as a Foreign Language (TOEFL) as early as possible– at least a year before you plan to enroll. Some institutions accept English language examinations other than TOEFL; check the information you receive from institutions to see which examinations they accept.

Even if you have a good basic level of English proficiency and have met the minimum TOEFL requirements for a university, some schools may require you to take courses to improve your mastery of American English, academic or research usage and study skills. If you studied English under the British system, you may find that US vocabulary and usage are quite different.

TOEFL Waivers : If you are a non-US citizen and nonnative speaker of English who has been educated in English for most of your school life, your TOEFL requirement may be waived. Allow time in the application process to correspond with US universities about this issue. American universities are unlikely to accept secondary school English language examination results as proof of your language ability.

For detail write to TOEFL or visit their website :

TOEFL
CN 6152
Princeton, NJ 08541-6152
USA

Website: /www.toefl.org/

Q. I want to be an astronaut like Kalpana Chawla. Kindly let me know in detail how I can fulfill my dream.

After the success story of Kalpana Chawla, many of our youngsters are now interested to become astronaut. If you are looking for a career that combines cool technology, interesting science and great adventure, you could hardly make a better choice than becoming an astronaut. And there is potential for growth in the field. With the construction of the International Space Station, there will be a permanent human presence in outer space and a need for astronauts. But becoming an astronaut in the US space programme is not easy and the process can take several years.

There are three types of astronauts in the US Space Programme :

- Commander/pilot,

- Mission specialist,
- Payload specialist.

The commander is responsible for the mission, the crew and the vehicle. The pilot assists the commander in operating the vehicle and deploying satellites. The mission specialist works with the commander and pilots in shuttle operations, performs space walks and conducts experiments. The payload specialist performs specialised duties as the mission requires. Payload specialists are people other than NASA personnel and some are foreign nationals.

- **Astronaut Pilots :** Pilot astronauts serve as both space commanders and pilots. During flight, the commander has on board responsibility for the vehicle, crew, mission success and safety of flight. The pilot assists the commander in controlling and operating the vehicle and may assist in the deployment and retrieval of satellites using the Remote Manipulator System (RMS), referred to as the robot arm or mechanical arm.
- **Astronaut Mission Specialist :** Mission specialist astronauts work with the commander and the pilot and have overall responsibility for coordinating operations in the following areas: systems, crew activity planning, consumables usage and experiment/payload operations. Mission specialists are trained in the details of the on-board systems, as well as the operational characteristics, mission requirements/objectives and supporting equipment/systems for each of the experiments conducted on their assigned missions. Mission specialists perform extravehicular activities (EVAs), or space walks, operate the remote manipulator system and are responsible for payloads and specific experiment operations.
- **Payload specialists :** Payload specialists are persons other than NASA astronauts (including foreign nationals) who have specialised on board duties; they may be added to shuttle crews if activities that have unique requirements are involved and more than the minimum crew size of five is needed.

  First consideration for additional crew members is given to qualified NASA mission specialists. When payload specialists are required they are nominated by NASA, the foreign sponsor or the designated payload sponsor. In case of NASA or NASA-related payloads, the nominations are based on the recommendations of the appropriate Investigator Working Group (IWG).

Although payload specialists are not part of the Astronaut Candidate Programme, they must have the appropriate education and training related to the payload or experiment. All applicants must meet certain physical requirements and must pass NASA space physical examinations with varying standards depending on :

The basic qualifications for becoming an astronaut are :

- o US citizenship (for pilots and mission specialists)
- o Bachelor's degree (engineering, biological sciences, physical sciences, mathematics) from an accredited college or university.
- o Three years of related experience after obtaining the bachelor's degree – A master's degree equals one year of experience and a doctorate equals three years.
- o Passing a NASA space physical examination – Pilots need to pass a Class I physical; mission/payload specialists must pass Class-II. Both are similar to civilian and military flight examinations.
- o More than 1,000 hours experience as pilot-in-command of a jet aircraft (pilots only).

- Height of 64 to 76 inches (162.5 cm to 193cm) for pilots, 58.5 to 76 inches (148.5 cm to 193 cm) for mission/payload specialists.

To apply for an astronaut position, you fill the appropriate forms and submit them to NASA, which accepts applications continuously. NASA then screens the applications and you may be asked to go for a weeklong session where you will participate in personal interviews, medical tests and orientations. Your screening performance will be evaluated and if you are lucky, you may be accepted as an astronaut candidate. NASA announces candidates every two years, selecting about a hundred men and women out of thousands of applicants.

If you are selected, you will report to NASA's Johnson Space Centre in Houston, Texas for training and evaluations which lasts two years. During the training period, you will take classes in basic science (mathematics, astronomy, physics, geology, meteorology, oceanography), technology (navigation, orbital mechanics, material processing) and space shuttle systems. You will also be trained in land and sea survival techniques, SCUVA, micro gravity, high and low-pressure environments and spacesuits. You must pass a swimming test (swim three lengths of a 25-metre pool in flight suit and tennis shoes and tread water for 10 minutes). If you are pilot, you will be train in NASA's T-38 jet aircraft and shuttle training aircraft at least 15 hours each month. Mission specialists fly four hours each month.

At the end of the two year training period, you may be selected to become an astronaut. As an astronaut, you will continue classroom training on the various aspects of space shuttle operations that you started as an astronaut candidate. You will begin training on each individual system in the shuttle with the help of an instructor. After that, you will train in stimulators for pre-launch, launch, orbit, entry and landing. Depending upon whether you are a pilot or mission specialist, you will learn how to use the shuttle's robotic arm to manipulate cargo. You will continue generic training until you are selected for a flight.

Once you are selected for a flight, you will receive specific training for the mission at least 10 months prior to the flight. This includes training in flight stimulators, full scale mockups of the shuttle and space station and underwater training for space walks. The stimulations will prepare you for every type of emergency or contingency imaginable.

After your training, you will prepare or your flight with training in the shuttle itself (pilots), meetings and more stimulations. After your flight, you will have several days of medical tests and discussions; these are called debriefings.

Astronauts are expected to stay with NASA for at least five years after their selection. They are federal civil service employees (GS-11 to GS-14 grade) with equivalent pay based on experience. They are eligible for vacation, medical and life insurance and retirement benefits.

So, you can see that you will need education, hard work and steadfast dedication to become an astronaut. However, the future and career is tremendous.

Q. I am currently in Standard XII. I am interested in doing B.Sc. in Nursing after I complete Standard XII. Therefore, what are the courses or options available in nursing?

Admission to B.Sc. Nursing is on the basis of performance in the entrance examination conducted by various colleges. Some of these are: All India Level Entrance Examination conducted by individual institutes like Bharati Vidyapeeth, Pune and AIIMS, New Delhi; MHT-CET, conducted by Directorate of Medical Education and Research, Mumbai for the admission to many institutes of Maharashtra (www.dmer.org); Asso-CET conducted by AMUPMDC, Mumbai for the admission to various courses in Unaided Private Medical and Dental Colleges of Maharashtra (www.amupmdc.org).

After B.Sc (Nursing) you may go for specialised nursing course in India or abroad. A master's degree in Nursing prepares you for leadership, management and more independent roles such as clinical nurse specialist, nurse practitioner, educator and researcher.

Q. I am in Standard XII. I want to be an Indian Air Force pilot. When am I supposed to apply? How and where?

There are two entry points for the flying branch of the Indian Air Force, through NDA or CDSE. But you must have Physics and Mathematics at 10+2 level.

Selection to National Defense Academy (NDA) is through an entrance test. After selection candidates go through a rigorous three-year training regimen followed by specialised training at one of the Air Force training establishments. On successful completion, they are commissioned as Permanent Commission Officers and posted as pilots of any of the Air Force Stations.

Otherwise, after completing your graduation (B.Sc. or B.E.), you can appear in the Combined Defense Services Examination (CDSE) and join Air Force Academy. For further details visit http:/careerairforce.nic.in.

Q. I am in Standard XII. I'm a PCM student. I am interested in automobile engineering. I love cars and bikes. What should I do after 12th to be a good automobile engineer?

Automobile Engineering deals with the design, planning and manufacture as well as repair, maintenance and up-gradation of all moving vehicles.

After 12th you should go for B. Tech in Automobile Engineering. Admission is usually through entrance test. Some of the colleges offering this course are PSG College of Technology, Coimbatore (www.psgtech.edu); SRM University, Chennai (www.srmuniv.ac.in); Manav Rachna International University (MRIU), Faridabad-Delhi/NCR (www.mriu.edu.in).

Q. I am in Standard IX. I want to be an architect. What subjects should I take in Standard XI – Science or Commerce?

To become an architect you need to go for a Bachelor's of Architecture (B. Arch.), a 5-year course. Eligibility for this course is 10+2 with Physics and Mathematics.

B. Arch. is available at many universities all over India. Almost everywhere, selection is through written examination. In addition to this, it is mandatory to have a valid score of the National Aptitude Test in Architecture (NATA) (www.nata.in) conducted by the Council of Architecture.

An aptitude test is held to judge the applicant's visual and spatial perception, creative ability, imagination, aesthetic sensitivity etc. Apart from having an aptitude for mathematics and science it is an asset if a person is able to do freehand sketching.

Q. I want to be astronomer. What subjects should I chose in Standard XI and which colleges in India offer this course?

Astronomers use the principles of physics and mathematics to answer questions about the fundamental nature of the universe, including the sun, moon, planets, stars and galaxies. The minimum eligibility criterion for becoming an astronaut is a doctorate degree (Ph.D) since most of the work is related to Research and Development.

First step is to take Mathematics and Physics in 10+2. There is no university in India which offers an undergraduate programme in Astronomy, so you should go for B.Sc. (Honors) in Physics and then for post-graduation in Physics/Astrophysics/Astronomy.

Specialised institutes for such research work include: Indian Institute of Astrophysics (IIA), Bangalore; Institute of Physics (IOP) Bhubhaneshwar; Inter-university Center for Astrophysics (IUCAA), Pune; Tata Institute of Fundamental Research, Bangalore; Indian Institute of Science, Bangalore; National Centre for Radio Astrophysics, Pune.

Q. I am a student of Standard XII. I have a keen interest in writing poems and prose and reading books, especially newspapers. I am a bright student and want to study literature. What are the courses available in this field? And the Colleges which offer them? What should I do if I want to be a newspaper editor?

Newspaper editors have a fast paced job that is constantly changing with latest edition. They plan the contents of the publication and supervise its preparation.

To pursue a career in this field, you should have a degree in Journalism or Mass Communication. Even students of M.A. Literature are suitable for this. Specialised courses in selected fields like page composition, layout designing and photo journalism are also helpful. Apart from professional degrees, other skills required are good command over the language, good general knowledge and the ability to collect information and report events quickly.

Many universities all over India offer both programmes in Journalism. Basic eligibility is 10+2 in any stream. some of the institutes are Indian Institute of Mass Communication, New Delhi; AJK Mass Communication Research Centre (MCRC), Jamia Millia Islamia, New

Delhi; Asian College of Journalism, Chennai; Bharatiya Vidhya Bhavans at various places, Times of India School of Journalism, Mumbai, The Manorama School of Communication, Kottayam, St. Xavier's Institute of Communication, Mumbai (www.xaviercomm.org).

Q. I am in Standard X and I want to be a film director. What subject should I choose in Standard XI and what further training should I take up?

The entertainment business isn't like any other business in terms of moving up the ranks. You can go from zero to the top in one step if you have talent or remarkable luck. The position of Feature Film Director is one of the few in the industry that doesn't have a distinct career path. Working as an actor, screen writer, film editor or photographer can teach you valuable skills that you will need as a director. But remember, not all aspiring directors find success in the industry.

Although not required, you can benefit from formal training in film, communications or other related areas. These courses typically explore additional areas of filmmaking, such as editing, cinematography, production and acting. Many programmes emphasise hands-on learning by having students practice techniques with equipment similar to what they'll be using in the industry. You can take any subjects in 10+2, as these courses are open to all.

Q. I am in Standard X at present and want to be a gynecologist. What subjects do I have to take?

OR

Q. I have recently given my Standard X Board exams. I want to be a heart surgeon. What courses do I need to take? Please give me some more information on this field.

First, you need an MBBS degree. Take Biology, Physics and Chemistry in 10+2. Then apply to various medical colleges and appear in entrance tests. MBBS is a five and half year degree course. After completing MBBS, go for 2 years PG diploma or 3 years M.D. (Doctor of Medicine) in Gynecology or 3 years M.S. (Master of Surgery). To become a heart surgeon, you should complete another three year M.Ch. in Cardiology.

Q. I am in Standard IX. I love Mathematics and I wish to choose a profession in the field of Mathematics only. Please guide me.

If Mathematics is your passion, become an actuary. Study of Actuarial Science requires a high aptitude in Mathematics. Eligibility is 10+2 with at least 85% in Mathematics/Statistics or Graduation/

Post-Graduation with Mathematics subjects like Mathematics, Statistics or Computer Science etc. Actuaries use statistics and probability to plan future risk. First they analyse the financial consequences of uncertain future events like property damage and loss, vehicular damage, fire, theft and individuals becoming sick, disabled or even dying. Then they pore over statistics to develop insurance policies and the rates customers should pay. They are also responsible for evolving new types of attractive policies ensuring greater business. Actuaries typically specialise in either life and health insurance or property and casualty insurance. To enter, one has to clear through self study, a series of examinations conducted by the Actuarial Society of India (ASI), Mumbai (http:/ www.actuariesindia.org). While Actuarial Science can be pursued at various universities, the ADSI alone confers the Fellowship in India. The Actuarial profession commands one of the best salary packages around the world. With 5-6 years of experience, you can easily touch a 7-figure salary.

Q. I love Physics and Mathematics and I want to become a pilot. What subjects should I take after Standard XII?

To become a pilot you should have Commercial pilot License (CPL). Procedure to get a CPL is as follows. After 10+2 with Mathematics and Physics, appear for a written test and get a Student Pilot License (SPL). You must be in good health and have good vision and no physical handicaps. On getting SPL, you are eligible for practical training in flying. After obtaining a minimum 40 hours of flight time, you can apply for Private Pilot License (PPL). After getting SPL and PPL proceed for CPL, an 18-month course that offers an in-depth study of theory subjects as well as practical training. The training is expensive and costs around ₹ 2 lakhs for a PPL and anywhere between ₹ 25-30 lakhs for a CPL, depending on whether you are trained in India or abroad. A number of banks offer educational loans.

Q. I am a Standard X student and I am interested in the Indian Foreign Service. What subject should I choose in plus 2? OR I want to know about the Indian Foreign Service and the qualifications required.

The Indian Foreign Service (IFS) is a Central Service and the premier diplomatic service of our country. Entry to the IFS is through the combined Civil Services Examination conducted by UPSC (www.upsc.gov.in). All graduates are eligible to appear at the examination, so you can take any subject in 10+2.

Q. I am studying in Standard XI (Science) and have taken biology. I want to be biotechnologist. Many people have told me that there is no scope in India, but there are colleges in Melbourne like Monash University. What are the formalities involved?

Biotechnology is one of the most revolutionary and beneficial scientific advances of the last generation. A biotechnologist may find jobs in the following fields: drug and pharmaceutical research, public-funded laboratories, chemicals, environment control, waste management, energy, food processing and bio-processing industries. You can find the admission requirements at Monash University at the following site: www.monash.edu/study/coursefinder/course/3527/internationalrequirements.html.

Q. I have completed Standard X and I have decided to take commerce with I.P. in 12th. What are the career options/courses for me since I am interested in business administration?

There are two ways to do a course in management: After 10+2, you can go for Bachelor in Business Studies/Business Administration/Business Management (BBS/BBA/BBM) a 3-year graduate course. These courses provide basic knowledge in all operational areas of management. Master in Business Administration (MBA) can be done after graduation. It spreads over two years covering foundation courses in economics, statistics, mathematics and data processing and advanced courses in finance, marketing or any chosen line of specialisation. Graduates with any stream are eligible for this course.

Q. I am a student of Standard X. I am unable to decide what to take in +1. I am really good in Mathematics and Science but I want to become a corporate lawyer. I would like to know about the stresses and luxuries involved in this career.

A corporate lawyer understands and ensures the legality of the business of an organisation. He or she is required by every organisation no matter what its size is. One can either pursue a three-year law course (LLB) after graduation in any discipline or a five-year course after Standard XII examinations, leading to a B.A. L.L.B. (Hons). To specialise in corporate law, it may be a good idea to pursue a post-graduate law degree or diploma courses in corporate or business-related law. Compared to other industries the legal profession in India is very financially rewarding. But working in this field requires continuous study for this complex and ever-changing field of law. The laws don't always change but situation will. A lot of paper work, hours of writing and proofreading, drafting and re-drafting documents is necessary in this field.

REFERENCES

BOOKS

1. Agarwal, Arun and Agarwal, Mamta, (2000), *Careers in Hotel Management*, New Delhi:Vision Books.
2. Anand, Aruna, *Careers in Beauty Care*, New Delhi: Vision Books.
3. Atkins, Peter; de Paula, Julio (2009), *Elements of Physical Chemistry* (5th ed.) New York: Oxford University Press.
4. Bhuyan, Devajit, *A Complete Guide to Career Planning*, New Delhi: V&S Publishers 2013.
5. Bright, Singh Pritam Editor et al, *Careers after 10+2 and Beyond*, New Delhi: Bright Publications.
6. Chang, Raymond (1998), *Chemistry 6th Ed.*, New York: McGraw Hill.
7. Chaudhary, Amit, *Careers in Television and Broadcasting*, New Delhi: Vision Books.
8. Crumbley, D. Larry; Heitger, Lester E.; Smith, G. Stevenson (2005-08-05), *Forensic and Investigative Accounting*, CCH Group. ISBN 0-8080-1365-3.
9. Dwivedi, Sapna, *Careers in Civil Services*, New Delhi: Vision Books.
10. Gupta, Anjani A., edit et al., *Career and Opportunities after 10+2*, New Delhi, Ramesh Publishing House 2012.
11. Hancock, James F. (2004), *Plant Revolution and the Origin of Crop Species*, Cambridge, MA: CABI Publishing
12. Harris, Marvin (1997) Culture, *People, Nature: An Introduction to General Anthropology* (7th Edition), Boston: Allyn and Bacon.
13. Isaac, Daniela; Charles Reiss (2013), *I-Language: An Introduction to Linguistics as Cognitive Science*, 2 nd edition, Oxford University Press.
14. Jamkhedkar, Shilpa, *Careers in Social Work*, New Delhi: Vision Books.
15. Kapadia, G.P. (1973), *History of the Accountancy Profession in India*, ISBN 978-0-439-41111-0.
16. Khanna, Meera, *Careers in Chartered Accountancy*, New Delhi: Vision Books.
17. Kwok, Benny K.B. (2008), *Forensic Accountancy*, LexisNexis, ISBN 978-962-8972-76-0.
18. Man, Singh Gurbir, *Careers in Armed Forces*, New Delhi: Vision Books.

19. Martinet, Andre (1960), *Elements of General Linguistics.* Tr. Elisabeth Palmer (Studies in General Linguistics, Vol. I), London: Faber.
20. Mauseth, James D. (2012), *Botany: An Introduction to Plant Biology* (5th ed.), Sadbury, MA: Jones and Barlett Learning.
21. Ovasdi, J.M, *Careers in Railways,* New Delhi: Vision Books.
22. Pandit, Geetanjli, *Careers in Law,* New Delhi:Vision Books.
23. Pandit, Geetanjli, *Careers in Management,* New Delhi: Vision Books.
24. Richard, Meyers (2003), *The Basics of Chemistry,* Greenwood Publishing Group.
25. Salzmann, Zdenek, (1993) *Language, Culture and Society: An Introduction to Linguistic Anthropology,* Boulder, CO: Westview Press.
26. Zaheer, Rima, *Careers in Computers,* New Delhi:Vision Books.
27. Zaheer, Rima, *Careers in Foreign Languages,* New Delhi: Vision Books.
28. Ziegler, Gunter M. (2011), "What is Mathematics?" *An Invitation to Mathematics: From Competitions to Research,* Springer.

MAGAZINES

1. B. Mahesh Sharma, Editor, *Careers 360,* New Delhi.
2. Satyanarayan Prasad, Editor in chief, *Renu General Knowledge World Vision,* Delhi.
3. Pritam Singh Bright, Chief editor, *Competition Refresher,* New Delhi.
4. Vishwa Bandhu Gupta, *North East Sun,* New Delhi.

ELECTRONIC MEDIA SOURCES

1. A Guide to several online economics textbooks.
2. Committee on Forestry Research, National Research Council (1990), *Forestry Research: A Mandate for Change.*
3. Economics at About.com
4. Economics textbooks on Wikibooks.
5. Introduction to Economics: Short Creative commons-licensed introduction to basic economics.
6. "Mission of ICAI" Member details, South Asian Federation of Accountants, 9 February 2011.
7. ICAI Board of Studies Announcement of the new scheme of education, 2008.
8. "Meaning of Agriculture", State of Maine. 2013-05-06.
9. "The Development of Agriculture". National Geographic. 2013-04-22.
10. "What is Chemistry?" Chemweb.icc